Public Relations

SECOND EDITION

Tom Kelleher
University of Florida

New York Oxford
OXFORD UNIVERSITY PRESS

Oxford University Press is a department of the University of Oxford.
It furthers the University's objective of excellence in research, scholarship,
and education by publishing worldwide. Oxford is a registered trade mark of
Oxford University Press in the UK and certain other countries.

Published in the United States of America by Oxford University Press
198 Madison Avenue, New York, NY 10016, United States of America.

For titles covered by Section 112 of the US Higher Education
Opportunity Act, please visit www.oup.com/us/he for the latest
information about pricing and alternate formats.

Library of Congress Cataloging-in-Publication Data

Names: Kelleher, Tom (Tom A.), author.
Title: Public relations / Tom Kelleher, University of Florida.
Description: Second edition. | New York : Oxford University Press, [2021] |
    Includes bibliographical references and index.
Identifiers: LCCN 2019034697 (print) | LCCN 2019034698 (ebook) | ISBN
    9780190925093 (paperback) | ISBN 9780190925109 (epub)
Subjects: LCSH: Public relations.
Classification: LCC HD59 .K45 2021 (print) | LCC HD59 (ebook) | DDC
    659.2—dc23
LC record available at https://lccn.loc.gov/2019034697
LC ebook record available at https://lccn.loc.gov/2019034698

9 8 7 6 5 4 3 2 1
Printed in Mexico by Quad/Mexico

To my parents, Fred and Imogene

And for my wife Robin and our sons

Miles and Henry

Brief Contents

PREFACE XIII
ABOUT THE AUTHOR XXI

SECTION I   FOUNDATIONS

CHAPTER 1 Principled Public Relations 1
CHAPTER 2 Public Relations Models Through the Ages 27
CHAPTER 3 Convergence and Integrated Communication 55
CHAPTER 4 Relationship Management 86

SECTION II   STRATEGY

CHAPTER 5 Research 117
CHAPTER 6 Planning 148
CHAPTER 7 Implementation 177
CHAPTER 8 Evaluation 200

SECTION III   TACTICS

CHAPTER 9 Writing 225
CHAPTER 10 Social Media and Mobile 256

SECTION IV   CONTEXTS

CHAPTER 11 Legal 288
CHAPTER 12 Issues and Crises 319
CHAPTER 13 Global 349
CHAPTER 14 Careers 374

APPENDIX A: UNIVERSAL ACCREDITATION BOARD COMPETENCIES 398
NOTES 402
GLOSSARY 421
CREDITS 429
NAME INDEX 430
SUBJECT INDEX 431

Preface xiii

About the Author xxi

Contents

SECTION I FOUNDATIONS

CHAPTER 1 Principled Public Relations 1

Defining public relations 2
  Textbook definitions 3
  ▌CASE STUDY: HOLD THE FIASCO, PLEASE. 4
  Crowdsourcing a definition 6

Principled public relations management 7
  Tell the truth 8
  Prove it with action 9
  Listen to the customer 10
  Manage for tomorrow 10
  Conduct public relations as if the whole company depends on it 11
  Remain calm, patient and good-humored 12
  ▌CASE STUDY: HOW CROCK-POT FOUGHT FIRE BY KEEPING ITS COOL 12
  Realize the company's true character is expressed by its people 15

Why ethics matter 15
  Reasons for studying ethics 16
  Competing duties 17

A guide for ethical decision-making 18
  ▌CASE STUDY: "TWEETING UNDER FALSE CIRCUMSTANCES" 18
  ▌VOICES FROM THE FIELD: KATHY FITZPATRICK 22

Codes of ethics 23
  Criticisms of codes 23
  Advantages of codes 23
  Professional associations 24
  ▌IN CASE YOU MISSED IT 25

Summary 25

Discussion questions 26

CHAPTER 2 Public Relations Models Through the Ages 27

Public relations models in history 28
  Press agentry/publicity 28
  ▌CASE STUDY: A TALL ORDER: GAINING ATTENTION AND PUBLICITY IN THE MARKETPLACE OF IDEAS 30
  Public information 32
  ▌CASE STUDY: EDWARD BERNAYS' "TORCHES OF FREEDOM" 35
  Two-way asymmetrical communication 37
  Two-way symmetrical communication 38

A broader social history of public relations 41
  Religion 42
  Education 42
  Politics and government 43

Major motivations for public relations 44
  Recruitment 44
  Legitimacy 45
  Agitation 46
  Advocacy 48
  Profit 48
  ▌VOICES FROM THE FIELD: KAREN MILLER RUSSELL 50

Ethics: transparency, objectivity and advocacy 51
  ▌IN CASE YOU MISSED IT 52

Summary 53

Discussion questions 54

Contents

CHAPTER 3 Convergence and Integrated Communication 55

Convergence 56
  Technological convergence 56
  Cultural convergence 58
  Economic convergence 59
  Professional convergence 61

Divergence 62
  Advertising 63
  Marketing 65

Integration 70
  Integrated marketing communication 70
  Hybrid functions 73
▌ CASE STUDY: RED BULL'S CONTENT MARKETING
  STRATEGY 75

How public relations is different at
its core 77
  Organization (beyond offerings) 77
  Publics (beyond audiences) 77
  Relationships (beyond sales) 78
▌ VOICES FROM THE FIELD: BILL IMADA 79

Ethics: free flow of information
and data protection 80
▌ IN CASE YOU MISSED IT 83

Summary 84

Discussion questions 84

CHAPTER 4 Relationship Management 86

Managing relationships 87
  Taking care of relationships 88
  Key outcomes of relationships 89

News-driven relationships 92
  Media relations 92
  Pitching 93

Commerce-driven relationships 97
  B2C 97
  B2B 98
  Employee relations 100
▌ CASE STUDY: PUTTING MONEY WHERE THEIR MISSION IS:
  MEDTRONIC REBUILDS AFTER HURRICANE MARIA 102
  Investor relations 103

Issues-driven relationships 104
  Nonprofit organizations 105
  When publics are organizations and
  organizations are publics 106
▌ VOICES FROM THE FIELD: ROB CLARK 110

Ethics: corporate social responsibility
and loyalty 111
▌ CASE STUDY: COCA-COLA AND CORPORATE SOCIAL
  RESPONSIBILITY 111
▌ IN CASE YOU MISSED IT 114

Summary 115

Discussion questions 115

SECTION II STRATEGY

CHAPTER 5 Research 117

Research in the RPIE cycle 118
Formative research 118
Summative research 119

Situation analysis 120
Situation research 120
Organization research 123
Publics research 125
▎CASE STUDY: APPLYING THE SITUATIONAL THEORY OF PUBLICS: NET NEUTRALITY 128

Quantitative research 133
Surveys 134
Experiments 134
Content analysis 134

Qualitative research 136

Interviews 136
Focus groups 136
Direct observation 137

Secondary and primary research 138

Formal and informal research 138
Reliability and validity 139
Trade-offs in research design 141
▎VOICES FROM THE FIELD: MEGAN KINDELAN 142

Ethics: doing the greatest good for the greatest number of people 143
▎IN CASE YOU MISSED IT 145

Summary 146

Discussion questions 147

CHAPTER 6 Planning 148

A hierarchy of outcomes 150
Tuning in 151
Attending 151
Liking 151
Comprehending 152
Learning 152
Agreeing 153
Remembering 153
Acting 153
Proselytizing 153
Using McGuire's hierarchy of effects for planning 154

Strategic planning 155
▎CASE STUDY: GLOBAL HANDWASHING DAY: GOALS, OBJECTIVES AND OUTCOMES 158

Timelines 161
Formative research 161
Client/management meetings 162
Action and communication tactics 163
Production of media and communication materials 163

Events 163
Evaluation 164

Budgets 165
Personnel 165
Administrative costs and supplies 168
Media and communication expenses 169
▎VOICES FROM THE FIELD: NATALIE ASOREY 170

Ethics: beware of zombies; enhance the profession 172
Define the specific issue/conflict 173
Identify internal/external factors 173
Identify key values 173
Identify the parties involved 173
Select ethical principles 174
Make a decision and justify it 174
▎IN CASE YOU MISSED IT 175

Summary 175

Discussion questions 176

CHAPTER 7 Implementation 177

Taking action 178
▌ CASE STUDY: PULLED PORK: CHIPOTLE'S CHALLENGE TO ACT ON ITS PRINCIPLES 179

Choosing channels 181

Controlled and uncontrolled media 182

Owned, paid, shared and earned media 184
Owned media 184
Paid media 186
Shared media 187
Earned media 189
Mixed media 191

▌ CASE STUDY: PUPPIES AS PUBLICS? BARKBOX MARKS ITS TERRITORY ACROSS OWNED, PAID, SHARED AND EARNED MEDIA 191

▌ VOICES FROM THE FIELD: ROSANNA M. FISKE 193

Ethics: loyalty and diversity in communication and action 195
▌ CASE STUDY: DOING GOOD BY DOING WELL: KIMBERLY-CLARK'S EFFORTS TO PROMOTE DIVERSITY 196

▌ IN CASE YOU MISSED IT 197

Summary 198

Discussion questions 199

CHAPTER 8 Evaluation 200

Message testing 202
Focus groups 202
Readability tests 203
Experiments 203

Media monitoring services 204

Metrics, analytics and data 206
Tracking visitor behavior 208
Segmenting referring sources 208
Parsing big data 208

Barcelona principles 209
Principle 1: goal setting and measurement are fundamental 210
Principle 2: measuring communication outcomes is recommended 210
Principle 3: the effect on organizational performance should be measured 213
Principle 4: measurement and evaluation require both qualitative and quantitative methods 213

▌ CASE STUDY: GILLETTE'S "WE BELIEVE" CAMPAIGN GAUGED BY MORE THAN JUST NUMBERS 214
Principle 5: advertising value equivalencies are not the value of communications 216
Principle 6: social media should be measured consistently with other media channels 217
Principle 7: measurement and evaluation should be transparent, consistent and valid 217

Measuring the right outcomes 218
▌ VOICES FROM THE FIELD: TINA MCCORKINDALE 219

Ethics: independence 220
▌ IN CASE YOU MISSED IT 222

Summary 222

Discussion questions 223

SECTION III TACTICS

CHAPTER 9 Writing 225

Five reasons to write well in public relations 226
    Relationships 227
    Influence and persuasion 227
    Goals and objectives 227
    Reputation management 228
    Impression management 228

Storytelling 229
❚ CASE STUDY: A VIRTUOUS (BI)CYCLE: HOW THE WORLD BICYCLE RELIEF ORGANIZATION TELLS STORIES WITH PURPOSE 229
    Features 231
❚ CASE STUDY: THE GOAT'S SURF RANCH: HOW A FEATURE STORY HELPED BUILD A WAVE OF INTEREST IN A NEW BUSINESS VENTURE 231
    News 236

Writing for intermediaries 238
    Writing for news media 238
    Writing for social media 243
    Writing for search engines 246

Business writing 249
❚ VOICES FROM THE FIELD: CORNELIUS FOOTE 249

Ethics: expertise and writing for mutual understanding 251
❚ CASE STUDY: WORDS MATTER: A STRANGE CHOICE FOR AN AGENCY NAME 251
❚ IN CASE YOU MISSED IT 253

Summary 253

Discussion questions 254

CHAPTER 10 Social Media and Mobile 256

Mobile first 258
    Ubiquitous 258
    Social 258
    Personal 259
    Local 260
❚ CASE STUDY: BURGER KING USES MOBILE APP TO TROLL COMPETITORS 260

Uses and gratifications of media 262

Social and visual listening 263
    What is social listening? 263
    What is visual listening? 264
    What are the benefits of social and visual listening? 264
    How do you conduct a social listening search? 267

Creating engaging content 267
    Text 269
    Images 271
    Video 273
    Curated content 275

Building relationships and community 276
    Community management 277
    Influencer and advocate engagement 279
❚ CASE STUDY: MILLIONS SHARE THEIR MICKEY MOUSE EARS FOR CHARITY 281
❚ VOICES FROM THE FIELD: SHANE SANTIAGO 282

Ethics: privacy and safeguarding confidences 283
❚ IN CASE YOU MISSED IT 285

Summary 286

Discussion questions 286

Contents

SECTION IV   CONTEXTS

CHAPTER 11   Legal 288

International legal contexts 289

The first amendment 291
▌ CASE STUDY: *AMAZON V. NYT*: A CASE IN THE COURT OF PUBLIC OPINION 292

Defamation 294

Intellectual property 295
Copyright, trademarks and patents 296
Plagiarism 296
Fair use 298
Intellectual property issues 301

Public information and the Freedom of Information Act 304

Protecting publics 305
Safety and accuracy 305

Financial information 306
▌ CASE STUDY: TESLA CEO AND FEDERAL REGULATORS GET INTO A TIFF OVER FREE SPEECH 307

Privacy 310
Intrusion into seclusion 310
Appropriation of likeness or identity 311
Public disclosure of private facts 312
Portrayal in a false light 312
▌ VOICES FROM THE FIELD: CAYCE MYERS 313

Ethics: safeguarding confidences—who owns your social networks? 314
▌ IN CASE YOU MISSED IT 316

Summary 316

Discussion questions 318

CHAPTER 12   Issues and Crises 319

Managing conflict 320
▌ CASE STUDY: IS THE CUSTOMER ALWAYS RIGHT? . . . A BIG WIN FOR LITTLE ITALY 323

Managing issues 324
▌ CASE STUDY: THE ISSUE LIFE CYCLE OF VOLKSWAGEN'S "DIESELGATE" 325

Proactive issues management 328
1. Monitoring 328
2. Identification 329
3. Prioritization 330
4. Analysis 330
5. Strategic planning 331
6. Implementation 331
7. Evaluation 332

Crisis types 333
Victim crises 333

Accident crises 335
Preventable crises 335

Crisis response strategies 335
Deny strategies 336
Diminish strategies 337
Rebuild strategies 337
Reinforce strategies 339
▌ CASE STUDY: MR. ZUCKERBERG GOES TO WASHINGTON 339

Social media and crises 341
▌ VOICES FROM THE FIELD: BARRY FINKELSTEIN 343

Ethics: conflicts of interest 344
▌ IN CASE YOU MISSED IT 346

Summary 346

Discussion questions 348

Contents

CHAPTER 13 Global 349

Public relations and culture 350
  Low-context versus high-context
  communication 352
  Cultural dimensions 354
▌ CASE STUDY: VICKS REDEFINES "CARE" DESPITE
  CULTURAL PREJUDICE 356
  Cultural intelligence 357

International public relations 359
  Environmental variables 360

▌ CASE STUDY: MASTERCARD'S WORLD CUP CAMPAIGN
  GETS A RED CARD 365

Public diplomacy 367
▌ VOICES FROM THE FIELD: PATRICK FORD 368

Ethics: dialogic ethics 370
▌ IN CASE YOU MISSED IT 371

Summary 372

Discussion questions 373

CHAPTER 14 Careers 374

Personal branding 375
  Strategic 375
  Positive 376
  Promising 377
  Person-centric 377
  Artifactual 378
  Internships and projects 380

Employers 381
  Agencies 381
  Corporations 382
  Nonprofits and NGOs 383
  Government 384
  Self-employment and small business 385

Areas of specialization 386
  Health 386

Sports and entertainment 387
Political and public affairs 388
Financial and entrepreneurial 388
Consumer 388
International 389

Education and continued learning 389
▌ CASE STUDY: CEO VERSUS NEW HIRE: WHO WINS? 392
▌ VOICES FROM THE FIELD: KRISLYN HASHIMOTO 393

Ethics: competition, loyalty and job
changes 394
▌ IN CASE YOU MISSED IT 396

Summary 396

Discussion questions 397

Appendix A: Universal Accreditation Board
Competencies 398

Notes 402

Glossary 421

Credits 429

Name index 430

Subject index 431

Contents

Preface

Writing the first edition of *Public Relations* and then developing the second edition to keep up with the times has kept me mindful of the pace of change in public relations. New technologies, new news, new cases, new faces— I've continued to try to keep the content fresh while retaining the lasting concepts that are still sound so that the lessons gleaned from each chapter can be applied to the next big app, meme, crisis, or event to fill our ceaseless newsfeeds. In addition, I have added videos to provide context for many of the case studies and examples included throughout the book and assessments to ensure students understand and can apply the concepts discussed.

The passage of time during the relatively slow cycle of writing, editing, revision and publication forces us to check how our *understanding* of the concepts and the lessons from yesterday's cases and examples can be *applied* in the present, and how we can use that knowledge to *analyze* unfolding trends and news. Unlike a status update, snap, tweet or post, the content of this text has to be *evaluated* on the knowledge it delivers more than on the momentary trends it taps.

Look at the citations and links in the references. There are hundreds of referrals that lead to countless additional resources—almost all of it freely available online. My goal for this book continues to be to offer a structure to work with so students can climb the pyramid of Bloom's taxonomy from recall to understanding to application to analysis to evaluation. For the most part, I've left the top of the taxonomy—*creation*—to students and their professors. Courses in public relations writing, multimedia production or campaigns will focus more on that part, and students will turn to other texts, trainings and online resources as they delve deeper into creating public relations tactics and programs on their own.

In any case, I am grateful for the time I've had to tweak the material and test its resilience across two editions. In a way, each of the case studies and examples is a little test. Does the moral of the story still resonate? Does the key point still hold? My highest hope for the second edition of *Public Relations* is still that it offers a cohesive enough foundation that teachers, students, and professionals can explore the changing world of public relations with mutual understanding and a common vocabulary.

NEW PERSPECTIVES

Scores of reviewers have taken time to offer feedback on countless drafts of both the first and second edition of *Public Relations*, and all of what you will read in the chapters that follow. Every single reviewer has helped improve the book in some way. Each one of them brings specific knowledge of different areas of public relations, as well as different life experiences that have informed their feedback.

One of the specific challenges of writing the second edition was to include and acknowledge all these diverse perspectives and voices while retaining my own. Sometimes the shift is subtle—the choice of a geographical reference or current event. Other times the voices are represented much more directly with specific quotes or interviews via the "Voices from the Field" included with each chapter.

As a field of communication, public relations is dynamic and conversational. And conversational communication requires authenticity. My job as *author* isn't so much to be the *authority* but to be *authentic* in presenting the field in an engaging way.

Speaking of dynamic and authentic voices, I would be remiss in discussing the revisions made for the second edition of this text without a huge acknowledgement and thank you to Natalie Asorey. It was a tremendous stroke of good fortune for me when the University of Florida was able to hire Natalie as a lecturer here at about the same time as I began working on the second edition. Looking at her bio in the "Voices from the Field" for Chapter 6, you'll see why. Natalie brings to her students a wealth of public relations wisdom and experience in cross-cultural communication and social media. She most recently was in charge of social media at BODEN in Miami, where she managed the McDonald's USA account and led Escucha, the agency's social listening practice. Natalie contributed greatly to the insights and perspectives reflected in the extensive revisions to Chapter 10 ("Social Media and Mobile") and Chapter 13 ("Global"), all while maintaining the narrative flow that has become a hallmark of this book.

NEW TO THE SECOND EDITION

Trying to maintain the mantle of "the most contemporary introduction to public relations" has proved to be one of the greatest challenges in writing a second edition. Of course, social media and current events provided a bountiful supply of fresh stories and illustrations, but reviewer recommendations were key in making sure that the pursuit of shiny new examples did not come at the expense of important student learning outcomes. Sometimes the revisions meant filling gaps pointed out by reviewers. Other times new trends were taken into account to update the setting for contemporary cases and stories, such as direct-to-consumer (or DTC) communication and branding strategies (Chapter 7), social and visual listening (Chapter 10) and the gig economy (Chapter 14).

In addition to updating and replacing examples and illustrations throughout, the second edition features the following key revisions:

- **MOBILE & SOCIAL MEDIA:** Chapter 10, "Social Media and Mobile," more clearly highlights the tactical skills needed by public relations practitioners today and how practitioners can use social media to listen to, engage with and build relationships with their publics.

- **GLOBAL PERSPECTIVES:** Chapter 13, "Global," heeds the advice of the 2017 report from the Commission on Public Relations Education, which recommends that students in introductory courses learn how the practice differs throughout the world, by integrating more examples and perspectives from outside the United States.

- **CAREER STRATEGIES:** Chapter 14, "Careers," covers personal branding as a career strategy with tips that guide students in building skill sets to bring to the dynamic public relations job market, including internships and jobs in agencies, corporations, nonprofits and NGOs.

- **NEW CASE STUDIES:** Fourteen new case studies highlight examples of public relations successes and failures. These include Papa John's, Crock Pot, IHOP, Medtronic, Bark Box, Gillette, World Bicycle Relief, Kelly Slater Wave Company, Burger King, Disney/Make-A-Wish, Tesla, Facebook, Vick's and MasterCard.

- **NEW INTERVIEWS:** Five new *Voices from the Field* interviews feature new practitioners giving practical advice on the skills students need to be successful in the industry: Rob Clark, VP of Global Communications and Corporate Marketing for Medtronic; Megan Kindelan, Director of Public Affairs for the U.S. Bureau of Labor Statistics; Natalie Asorey, University of Florida Lecturer and former head of social media at BODEN; Tina McCorkindale, President and CEO of the Institute for Public Relations; and Patrick Ford, professional-in-residence at UF and former Burson-Marstellar worldwide vice chair and chief client officer.

- **NEW DISCUSSION QUESTIONS:** Discussion questions and hands-on activities at the end of each chapter provide a jumping-off point for productive classroom discussions of every major subsection, learning outcome and case study.

- **NEW INTERACTIVE E-BOOK:** The enhanced interactive e-book includes integrated videos tied to several extended examples and case studies as well as additional assessments (multiple choice questions) tied to the main learning objective sections and end-of-chapter self-assessments.

Beyond these core content changes, the second edition features a refreshed design and art program that better signposts key examples, vivid images, and extensive social media and ethics coverage that continue to be hallmarks of the book.

ORGANIZATION

The second edition of *Public Relations* has four sections: (I) *Foundations,* (II) *Strategy,* (III) *Tactics,* and (IV) *Contexts.*

The *Foundations* section starts with Chapter 1, "Principled Public Relations," which presents classic definitions of public relations alongside the crowdsourced PRSA definition. Arthur Page's principles of public relations management provide a framework for introducing ethical practice. Professional organizations and codes of ethics are also introduced. The rest of the *Foundations* section identifies concepts that have always been core to good public relations. Chapter 2, "Public Relations Models through the Ages," covers public relations history with Grunig and Hunt's models and Lamme and Russell's taxonomy of public relations goals. The next two chapters apply scholarship on "Convergence and Integrated Communication" (Chapter 3) and "Relationship Management" (Chapter 4) to the contemporary practice of public relations.

The *Strategy* section includes all of the elements of the traditional four-step, R-P-I-E process. The section starts with "Research" (Chapter 5) and includes a discussion of formative and summative research to highlight the cyclical nature of strategy. Next is "Planning" (Chapter 6), followed by "Implementation" (Chapter 7), which covers action and communication in strategic programs and campaigns. The last chapter in the *Strategy* section, "Evaluation" (Chapter 8), returns to the importance of research with a focus on measurement and metrics for success in digital communication.

The *Tactics* section includes three major skill and technology areas: "Writing" (Chapter 9) and "Social Media and Mobile" (Chapter 10).

The *Contexts* section (Chapters 11–14) addresses the forces influencing the practice of public relations as emerging sociotechnical trends challenge public relations people to confirm, rethink or in some cases abandon past practices and ideas. Chapter 11, "Legal," discusses law and policy. Chapter 12, "Issues and Crises," covers the issues lifecycle and cases of conflict and crisis management. Chapter 13, "Global," covers global and cultural contexts that are broadening today's practice of public relations. Finally, Chapter 14, "Careers," delves into public relations careers with advice on personal branding and coverage of different areas of specialization and different types of employers.

POSITIONING STUDENTS FOR SUCCESS

Consistent with the high standard set in the first edition, the second edition of *Public Relations* showcases an outstanding set of features and pedagogy to help students understand and learn the concepts. These include learning outcomes aligned with key UAB competencies, case studies, ethics topics representing key provisions of the PRSA Code of Ethics, "In Case You Missed It" (ICYMI) practical tips, Q&A's with professionals and scholars, bulleted summaries, discussion questions and activities and defined key terms. In addition, the interactive e-book includes videos associated with examples and case studies as well as a number of multiple self-assessment questions tied to the learning outcomes.

Learning outcomes

In addition to learning outcomes specific to contemporary public relations practice, each chapter opens with public relations learning outcomes aligned with the Universal Accreditation Board (UAB) groupings of competencies (as outlined at http://www.praccreditation.org/resources/documents/2016-apr-KSAs-Tested.pdf). This ensures *Public Relations* continues to be professionally relevant.

Case Studies

Every chapter includes at least one extended run-in case study embedded in the text, and some chapters contain two or even three. These cases provide relevant, real-world examples to illustrate the important concepts introduced in the book.

Ethics Topics Mapped to the PRSA Code of Ethics

Ethics are integral to the first chapter and discussed in every chapter thereafter. Each of the six provisions for conduct in the PRSA Code of Ethics is covered to ensure students have a firm grasp of the code that governs and sets guidelines for the public relations industry.

In Case You Missed It (ICYMI)

End-of-chapter boxes summarize some of the most useful tips covered in the chapter, so students remember the most practical points.

Voices from the Field Q&As with Professionals and Scholars

Each chapter includes a Q&A with a practitioner or scholar offering additional from-the-field perspectives and insights into the success stories and cases presented in the chapters. These interviews give students a chance to see how the theories and concepts introduced in the book work in practice and also to gain some insights into ways they may enhance their chances for future success in public relations.

Captions

Queries included at the end of photo and figure captions prompt students to think more critically about the highlighted examples.

Bulleted Summaries

Summaries organized around the learning outcomes identified at the start of each chapter reinforce the key takeaways, so that students have a firmer understanding of the concepts they should have learned.

Discussion Questions and Activities

Questions and activities at the end of each chapter encourage students to demonstrate learning outcomes by discussing personal and professional experiences or by analyzing and evaluating online resources. Instructors can easily deploy these in face-to-face or online teaching as writing assignments or discussion starters that connect student learning outcomes with current events and technologies.

Glossary

Key terms are defined in the margins of the print text and hyperlinked to the bolded key terms in the interactive e-book, to reinforce key concepts. Flashcards (in the interactive e-book) also help students to review key terms in preparation for exams.

Videos (Interactive e-Book)

Between two and four videos appear in every chapter of the e-book. These videos provide context and expand on many of the examples and case studies included in each chapter.

Multiple-Choice Questions Tied to Learning Outcomes (Interactive e-Book)

Multiple-choice questions tied to the learning outcomes of the book and included at the end of every major heading and at the end of each chapter in the e-book provide students with opportunities for low-stakes assessment to make sure they understand the key terms, ideas, and concepts as they proceed through the reading.

Digital Study Guide

A robust Digital Study Guide available at www.oup.com/he/kelleher2e includes flashcards, videos and self-study quizzes. Additional materials, including summary videos, video quizzes, discussion and case study questions, and additional assignable quizzes, are available via an instructor LMS course package when students redeem the access code that comes free with every new print book and ebook.

- **FLASHCARDS:** Flashcards help students to review key terms and prepare for exams.

- **VIDEOS:** Videos related to many examples and case studies in the book help to further contextualize and reinforce ideas and concepts. In addition to being embedded in the interactive e-book, each of these videos is also available with multiple-choice questions in the interoperable cartridge to be assigned to students by the instructor.

- **MULTIPLE-CHOICE ASSESSMENT QUESTIONS:** Multiple-choice questions related to the learning outcomes of the book appear at the end of every major heading and also at the end of each chapter to test students' understanding of the material and help them prepare for exams.

- **DISCUSSION QUESTIONS AND ACTIVITIES:** Discussion questions and activities from the end of each chapter are available in the interoperable cartridge to be assigned to students by the instructor. These questions and activities require students to engage in higher order thinking and apply what they have learned in each chapter.

- **SUMMARY VIDEOS:** Videos for each chapter provide context and insights into the importance of the chapter content and relevance to students for their future in public relations.

ACKNOWLEDGMENTS

Thanks to God for blessing me with wonderful parents, family, teachers and friends. Thanks to my wife Robin and sons Henry and Miles. Revising a book sounded at first like it would be much less taxing on family time than writing the original, but they were remarkably patient and supportive on many days when that didn't feel like the case.

Thank you to UF College of Journalism and Mass Communications Dean Diane McFarlin, Executive Associate Dean Spiro Kiousis and all of my colleagues past and present. Thanks again to my colleague Natalie Asorey for her fresh perspective on the field.

Thanks to everyone at Oxford University Press, especially Senior Development Editor Lisa Sussman, who has reviewed, edited and made better every single paragraph of this book through both editions. Thanks to Acquisitions Editor Toni Magyar and her successor Keith Chasse for their continued faith in the value of this whole project. Thanks to Assistant Editor Alyssa Quinones, who commissioned reviews, helped prepare the book for production and hired supplements authors. Thanks to Senior Production Editor Keith Faivre, Senior Media Editor Michael O. Quilligan and Marketing Manager Sheryl Adams.

I also am grateful to Natalie Asorey for developing the end-of-section and end-of-chapter eBook self-tests, as well as Cayce Meyers of Virginia Tech for writing the instructor's manual, Amy Shanler of Boston University for the test bank, Katherine Fleck of Ohio Northern University for the eBook pre- and post-tests, Jamie Ward of Eastern Michigan University for the PowerPoint presentations, Melanie Formentin of Towson University for the video summaries of each chapter and to Katy Robinson here at the University of Florida for the video quizzes.

Many thanks to all of the following reviewers for their useful comments:

Liron Anderson-Bell	*Temple University*
Anastacia Baird	*University of La Verne*
P. Anne Baker	*Oakland University*
Vincent Benigni	*College of Charleston*
Kati Berg	*Marquette University*
Brigitta Brunner	*Auburn University*
Julie A. Cajigas	*The University of Akron*
Christopher Caldiero	*Fairleigh Dickinson University*
Michelle Carpenter	*Old Dominion University*
Shirley S. Carter	*University of South Carolina*
Jennifer Chin	*University of North Carolina–Wilmington*
Lolita Cummings	*Carson Eastern Michigan University*
Rochelle R. Daniel	*Bowie State University*
Veronica R. Dawson	*California State University*
Jocelyn DeAngelis	*Western New England University*
John DiMarco	*St. John's University*

Jeff Duclos	*California State University–Northridge*
Tasha Dunn	*University of Nebraska at Kearney*
James Everett	*Coastal Carolina University*
Michele E. Ewing	*Kent State University*
Patricia Fairfield-Artman	*University of North Carolina at Greensboro*
Barry Finkelstein	*Luquire George Andrews*
Robert French	*Auburn University*
Tamara Gillis	*Elizabethtown College*
Mark Grabowski	*Adelphi University*
Chris Groff	*Rutgers University*
Karen L. Hartman	*Idaho State University*
Christine R. Helsel	*Austin Peay State University*
Amy Hennessey	*Ulupono Initiative*
Corey A. Hickerson	*James Madison University*
Randy Hines	*Susquehanna University*
Sallyanne Holtz	*University of Texas at San Antonio*
Brad Horn	*National Baseball Hall of Fame and Museum*
Nathan Kam	*Anthology Marketing Group*
Katherine Keib	*Oglethorpe University*
Natalie Kompa	*Ohio Dominican University*
Thomas A. Lamonica	*Illinois State University*
Keith Lindenburg	*Brodeur Partners*
Lisa Lundy	*University of Florida*
Sufyan Mohammed	*University of Scranton*
Aaron Moore	*Rider University*
Lisa H. Newman	*University of Cincinnati*
Dana Alexander Nolfe	*Bryant University*
Susan Pahlau	*Colorado Christian University*
Veronika Papyrina	*San Francisco State University*
Heather Radi-Bermudez	*Florida International University*
Kyle F. Reinson	*St. John Fisher College*
Nazmul Rony	*Slippery Rock University*
Risë J. Samra	*Barry University*
Jean K. Sandlin	*California Lutheran University*
Kathleen Stansberry	*Cleveland State University*
Marlane C. Steinwart	*Valparaiso University*
Robin Street	*University of Mississippi*
Dustin W. Supa	*Boston University*
Kaye D. Sweetser	*San Diego State University*
Philip Tate	*Luquire George Andrews*
Richard Waters	*University of San Francisco*
Susan E. Waters	*Auburn University*
Cynthia Wellington	*Webster University*
Brenda Wilson	*Tennessee Tech University*
Quan Xie	*Bradley University*
Alissa Zito	*Loyola Marymount University*

About the Author

TOM KELLEHER, Ph.D., is Associate Dean for Graduate Studies and Research in the College of Journalism and Communications at the University of Florida.

Kelleher joined the UF faculty in 2014 after 13 years on the faculty at the University of Hawaii, where he anchored the public relations track. From 2010 to 2013, he served as Chairman of the School of Communications at the University of Hawaii, which offers two B.A. degrees (communication and journalism), an M.A. in communication, and a Ph.D. as part of an interdisciplinary program in communication and information science. He also served in the public relations department of the School of Journalism and Mass Communication at the University of North Carolina at Chapel Hill from 2004 to 2006. He earned his B.A. from Flagler College and his M.A. and Ph.D. from the University of Florida.

Kelleher has designed and taught 22 different courses at three flagship state universities (Florida, North Carolina, and Hawaii) and has published in numerous journals including *Journal of Public Relations Research*, *Public Relations Review*, *Journal of Communication*, *Journal of Computer-Mediated Communication* and *Journal of Mass Media Ethics*.

In addition to the first edition of *Public Relations*, Kelleher also wrote *Public Relations Online: Lasting Concepts for Changing Media*, which was the first scholarly textbook in public relations to focus on the implications of social media and "Web 2.0" technologies for theory and practice. He served on the editorial board for *Journal of Public Relations Research* for nearly two decades, regularly reviews papers for the AEJMC public relations division, and for 12 years served as faculty advisor to his school's chapter of PRSSA. He has been a member of AEJMC since 1996, PRSA since 1999, and ICA since 2000.

Kelleher has worked in university relations at the University of Florida; science communication at NASA in Huntsville, Alabama; and agency public relations at Ketchum in Atlanta.

CHAPTER 1

Principled Public Relations

This simple kitchen appliance became the villain in one of America's most viewed TV series. How did Crock Pot use humor to simmer down the public outrage?

KEY LEARNING OUTCOMES

1.1 Define public relations in terms of organizations, publics and the relationships between them.

1.2 Explain how public relations can serve a management function through key principles and values for ethical conduct.

1.3 Understand the importance of ethics in public relations.

1.4 Apply systematic ethical decision-making for public relations.

1.5 Identify international professional associations and become familiar with codes of ethics.

RELATED UNIVERSAL ACCREDITATION BOARD COMPETENCY AREAS

2.1 INTEGRITY • **2.2** ETHICAL BEHAVIOR • **3.3** COUNSEL TO MANAGEMENT
4.3 KNOWLEDGE OF THE FIELD • **5.5** LEADERSHIP SKILLS

Among Publix's publics are frequent shoppers, fans and coupon clippers, including the mother of two who developed the "I Heart Publix" website at http://www.iheartpublix.com/.

Are you part of a public for Publix?

Engagement. Conversation. Influence. Transparency. Trust. These concepts pepper workshops, seminars, articles and online discussions of what social and digital communication technologies mean for public relations. While essential for professional practice today, they have been at the heart of good public relations since long before Facebook, Twitter and LinkedIn.

This chapter introduces classic definitions of public relations as well as a modern description crowdsourced by the Public Relations Society of America (PRSA). By and large the crowdsourced, social-media-era definition matches the classics that have been used in the teaching and practice of public relations for decades. While keywords like *publics, organizations, communication* and *relationships* may not be buzzworthy, these concepts have stood the test of time as key components in any sound definition of public relations.

Defining Public Relations

Publics—it's not a term you hear every day outside of classrooms and strategy meetings. I still recall vividly the first day in my very first public relations course. The professor started right in discussing the importance of relationships between organizations and publics. For a moment, I was confused about why we would spend so much time talking about relationships between organizations and *Publix*, the prominent southern U.S. supermarket chain ("Where shopping is a pleasure!"). Of course, he was talking about the plural of the term *public*, which did turn out to be important to our first lesson in public relations. In public relations, **publics** are groups of people with shared interests related to organizations.

General public—now here's a term, referring to everyone in the world, you probably do hear every day. How is the general public responding to today's news events? What's the best way to get our message out to the general public? Can we engage the general public on this issue? The first two questions are nearly impossible to answer, and the answer to the third question is probably "no." That is the problem with the general public. For all practical purposes the general public doesn't help us with strategy, and it doesn't help us identify any real people with whom we want to communicate.

Engaging in public relations means communicating with people who are part of specific groups with specific interests. Some of these publics are groups that have an effect on the **organizations** for which we work. These include large corporations, small businesses, nonprofits, schools, government agencies, **nongovernmental organizations (NGOs)** organized at the local, national, or international level, and even clubs and student groups—pretty much any group of people organized to pursue a mission. Others are people who are affected by our organizations. Most publics fit both criteria in that the influence is mutual.

Charity: Water (organization) appeals to Amazon shoppers (public) to raise money to bring clean drinking water to more than 37,000 people around the world (another public). That's public relations. Representatives of a Public Relations Student Society of America (PRSSA) chapter (organization) make an announcement in an introductory communications class to recruit new members (public). That's public relations. The Japan National Tourism Organization (organization) posts photos and videos to its "Visit Japan" Facebook page and interacts with commenters (public) on the page. That's public relations. Hewlett-Packard Co. (organization) posts a news release announcing that quarterly profits have slipped and hosts a live audio conference call for media contacts (public) and investors (another public) in order to satisfy Securities and Exchange Commission (SEC—yet another public) regulations. That's public relations too. Notice that in none of these cases has the organization set out to engage the general public. Instead, Amazon shoppers, new communication majors, Facebook commenters, media contacts, investors and the SEC are identified as specific publics.

charity: water ✓
@charitywater

More than 37,000 people around the world are getting clean water because of your @AmazonSmile purchases! This #PrimeDay, choose @charitywater before you shop on @Amazon, and help change even more lives: smile.amazon.com/ch/22-3936753

Charity: Water partnered with Amazon to raise money on Amazon Prime Day. **Who were the key publics?**

The labels for publics and organizations are sometimes interchangeable. If executives from Hawaiian Electric Co. (organization) visit homes of community leaders in the neighborhood of proposed new power lines (public) to discuss options for meeting increased energy demand, that's public relations. And if neighbors in the community organize a coalition (organization) to oppose the electric company (public) at government hearings, that's still public relations.

Completing a full definition of **public relations** requires more than just identifying organizations and publics. We still have to understand the second part of the term *public relations*—the relations.

To define public relations, consider organizations, publics and the relations between them.

Public relations
Management of communication between an organization and its publics, or the strategic communication process that builds mutually beneficial relationships between organizations and their publics.

Textbook Definitions

Perhaps the most commonly cited definition of public relations is the one written by James Grunig and Todd Hunt in their classic 1984 public relations text *Managing Public Relations*: "the management of communication between an organization and its publics."[1] There's a lot to this business of managing communication, which is why so many other definitions of public relations abound. Another classic definition from another classic public relations text, *Cutlip and Center's Effective Public Relations*, defines public relations as "the management function that establishes and maintains mutually beneficial relationships between an organization and the publics on whom its success or failure depends."[2]

Naturally, people are wary, or even skeptical, of textbook definitions. Ask people outside of the field of public relations what public relations is and you'll get very different answers. In introductory communication courses, I often ask students to name the first thing that comes to mind when I say "public relations." "Damage control" and "spin" are almost always mentioned.

Case Study

Hold the Fiasco, Please.

Often when we hear about public relations in the news or on social media, it's not pretty. In fact, generally, it's a "PR nightmare," "disaster" or "fiasco" that makes headlines. These were the words used by various media outlets to describe an incident involving Papa John's founder and Chairman John Schnatter when *Forbes.com* revealed that Schnatter had used the N-word on a conference call with a marketing agency.

Ironically, the conference call was intended "as a role-playing exercise for Schnatter in an effort to prevent future public-relations snafus," according to *Forbes'* Noah Kirsch, who broke the story.[3] A few months earlier, Schnatter had publicly entered a debate about National Football League players protesting the national anthem. Schnatter had blamed slow pizza sales, in part, on the NFL's issues. Papa John's then hired a public relations agency to help recover from the fallout with the NFL. However, no one from the public relations agency was on the conference call with the marketing agency a few months later. After the story broke, both agencies terminated their contracts with Papa John's.

On the day that news of the conference call broke, Papa John's stock prices dropped nearly 5 percent. That same night, Schnatter apologized and resigned. On the very next day, Papa John's stocks jumped 11 percent. And get this—as a 30 percent stockholder, Schnatter increased his net worth by an estimated $50 million in one day as a result![4]

Inasmuch as Schnatter was the namesake, spokesperson, and even the guy whose image was on the pizza boxes, his personal actions were inextricably tied in with the Papa John's organization and its relationships with key publics. Therefore, it would be difficult to deny that this incident illustrates public relations—and also, unfortunately, what people commonly think of when they think of PR. However, the case made by Papa John's CEO Steve Ritchie the following week more closely resembles preferred definitions of public relations.

In an open letter sent via email to customers and posted on the company's web page, Ritchie attempted to speak for the whole organization in managing Papa John's relationships with its publics. Before outlining a specific plan of action to "rebuild trust from the inside-out" by "engaging a broad set of stakeholders," Ritchie set the context:

> *Papa John's is not an individual. Papa John's is a pizza company with 120,000 corporate and franchise team members around the world. Our employees represent all walks of life, and we are committed to fostering an inclusive and equitable workplace for all. Racism and any insensitive language, no matter what the context[,] simply cannot—and will not—be tolerated at any level of our company.*[5]

Schnatter, however, did not go silently. Although he stepped down as chairman after the conference call controversy, he remained the largest single shareholder in the company. Schnatter filed a lawsuit against the company and started his own website, https://savepapajohns.com, where he too attempted to appeal to multiple publics: "I built Papa John's from the ground up and remain its largest shareholder. I love my Company, its employees, franchisees and customers."[6] On the website, he made very public his criticisms of the company's leadership and included direct challenges to Ritchie, who also faced criticism for poor leadership and creating a toxic work environment.[7] The real "fiasco," it turned out, likely resulted as much from a culture of inappropriate leadership as it did from the actions of any one individual. And the real challenge for public relations professionals was to rebuild trust and relationships from the very top of the organization all the way down.

So what do we make of this disconnect between public relations as professors and professionals want to define it and public relations as so many others see it? It is tempting to just ditch the name and call it something else. Many organizations have done that, or they have never called the function public relations in the first place. Instead, they have departments of public affairs, corporate communications, community relations and so on. Some organizations have exercised great creativity in naming these roles. Dane Cobain of South Africa's Memeburn website highlighted 21 ridiculous job titles.[8] Among them are social activationist, community data guerrilla, senior social media capability architect and the dreaded social media guru.

It was labeled a PR disaster when former Papa John's chairman and CEO John Schnatter used a racial slur on a conference call with a marketing agency and later resigned.

How does this incident, and its coverage by the media, shape perceptions of public relations?

Crowdsourcing a Definition

The negative connotations and confusion over job titles have not been lost on those in the profession. In late 2011 and early 2012, PRSA set out to tackle the definition of public relations.

"Public Relations Defined" is an initiative to modernize the definition of public relations. Through an open and collaborative effort, PRSA and its industry partners are providing a platform for public relations, market-ing and communications professionals to add their voice to a new defini-tion of public relations.[9]

The effort included consultation with 12 allied organizations including the Canadian Public Relations Society, PRSSA, the National Black Public Relations Association, the Hispanic Public Relations Association and the Word of Mouth Marketing Association. The advent of social media was cer-tainly a factor, as reported by Stuart Elliot in *The New York Times:*

Perhaps the most significant changes have occurred most recently, as the Internet and social media like blogs, Facebook and Twitter have trans-formed the relationship between the members of the public and those communicating with them. A process that for decades went one way— from the top down, usually as a monologue—now goes two ways, and is typically a conversation.[10]

Given the circumstances, PRSA's use of a blog and its comments from readers (http://prdefinition.prsa.org), Twitter (#PRDefined) and an online form for submitting candidate definitions seemed appropriate. It was an exercise in crowdsourcing. Oxford Dictionaries defines the verb **crowd-source** as "obtain (information or input into a particular task or project) by enlisting the services of a number of people, either paid or unpaid, typically via the internet."[11] And that's exactly what PRSA did. In this case the help was unpaid. By day 12 of the open submission period, the top 20 words submitted as part of suggested definitions for public rela-tions were:

organization (mentioned in 388
   submissions)
public (373)
communication (280)
relationship(s) (260)
stakeholders (172)
create (170)
mutual (158)
understand (153)
build (152)
audiences (147)

inform (144)
management (124)
brand (119)
company (116)
business (112)
people (100)
engages (94)
client (92)
awareness (88)
maintain (81)[12]

The task force soon had narrowed the field of definitions down to three finalists, opened a public comment period online, hosted a second "Definition of Public Relations Summit" with partner organizations, revised the three definitions, and held a public vote to select the new definition. And the winner was . . . "Public relations is a strategic communication process that builds mutually beneficial relationships between organizations and their publics." You may have noticed that the crowdsourced and modernized definition of public relations isn't all that different from the classic definitions.

Principled Public Relations Management

Regardless of how you define it, good public relations requires excellent management. When an organization's communication is focused more on image and less on what the organization is actually doing, negative connotations like **spin** and damage control become unfortunately accurate descriptions.

The problem with communication strategies based on image and fluff, however, is that publics can see right through them. Sometimes they will play along for the fun of it. This is common in sports and entertainment. Sensationalism, snafus, ballyhoo and bombast are all part of what keep people interested in Kylie Jenner's cosmetics or LaVar Ball's business ventures well beyond their families' talents in entertainment and athletics.

This isn't to say that celebrity and social media influence doesn't have a place in legitimate public relations. **Social media influencers** who have earned credibility in specific market segments and with specific publics can be instrumental in strategic communication programs. The keys to successful social media influence are reach and authenticity, and the key to authenticity is matching influencers to organizations and their causes. For example, Serena Williams is one of the world's best tennis players, but she's also a powerful social media influencer with more than 10 million Twitter followers and more than 10 million Instagram followers. As such, she promotes Nike, Beats by Dr. Dre and the Allstate Foundation's Purple Purse, which helps domestic violence survivors by supporting financial empowerment.

Of course, publics have been discussing businesses and their **authenticity** since long before the internet, and managing relationships between organizations and publics is about a lot more than finding the right social media influencer. Arthur Page, longtime vice president of AT&T Inc., worked at the company from the 1920s through the '30s and '40s and into the '50s. Page was one of the first public relations people to reach that level of management in an organization of that magnitude. He articulated and practiced principles of public relations management that apply as well now as they did in the mid-20th century.

1. Tell the truth.
2. Prove it with action.

Spin
Disingenuous strategic communication involving skewed interpretation or presentation of information.

Social media influencer
Social media user who has earned credibility with specific publics and who can be instrumental in strategic communication programs because of his or her reach and engagement.

Authenticity
The degree to which one communicates reliably, accurately and true to his or her own character and the character of the organization that he or she represents.

Arthur W. Page was an early proponent of authenticity and transparency in American public relations.

Do Page's principles apply any more or less in the digital age?

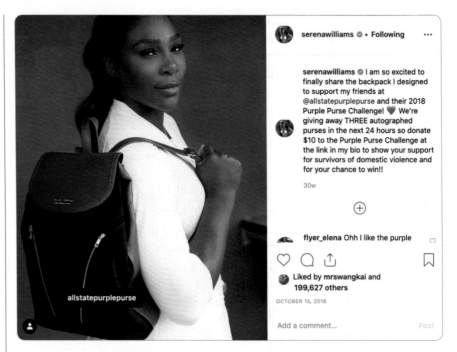

serenawilliams ● • Following

serenawilliams ● I am so excited to finally share the backpack I designed to support my friends at @allstatepurplepurse and their 2018 Purple Purse Challenge! 💜 We're giving away THREE autographed purses in the next 24 hours so donate $10 to the Purple Purse Challenge at the link in my bio to show your support for survivors of domestic violence and for your chance to win!!

30w

flyer_elena Ohh I like the purple

Liked by mrswangkai and 199,627 others

OCTOBER 15, 2018

Add a comment...   Post

Serena Williams is a powerful social media influencer who partners with Nike, Beats by Dr. Dre and the Allstate Foundation Purple Purse.

Why do these partnerships work?

3. Listen to the customer.
4. Manage for tomorrow.
5. Conduct public relations as if the whole company depends on it.
6. Remain calm, patient and good-humored.
7. Realize the company's true character is expressed by its people.

Tell the Truth

It's one thing to not lie; it's another to proactively tell the truth. This principle can be equated with the idea of **transparency**.[13] Public relations researcher and ethicist Brad Rawlins has defined it as the opposite of secrecy:

> *Transparency is the deliberate attempt to make available all legally reasonable information—whether positive or negative in nature—in a manner that is accurate, timely, balanced, and unequivocal, for the purpose of enhancing the reasoning ability of publics and holding organizations accountable for their actions, policies, and practices.*[14]

Arthur Page realized that large organizations like AT&T were particularly susceptible to public mistrust and suspicion when they overzealously protected secrecy. Governments, schools, churches, NGOs and nonprofits are all in danger of breeding fear, apprehension, dislike and distrust when they shirk

Transparency
Deliberate attempt to make available all legally reasonable information for the purpose of enhancing the reasoning ability of publics.

transparency. Of course, there are times when secrecy makes sense to publics, such as in times of national security crises or when businesses want to protect proprietary information to compete in markets, but even in those cases, organizations can still "tell the truth" about what they are keeping secret and why.

Prove It with Action

You might call it the 90-10 rule. Page said that 90 percent of good public relations should be determined by what an organization does, and about 10 percent by what they say. Publicity is important, but only if it follows action. Disneyland is the happiest place on earth. Ajax is stronger than dirt. 3M is innovation. Levi's quality never goes out of style. These are among the 50 most powerful slogans for brands, according to the Advergize website,[15] but think about how much work goes into making the slogans resonate. The slogans are hollow if the organization isn't managed in such a way as to make the words ring true.

You won't see BP's "Beyond Petroleum" slogan on the list. In 2000, BP introduced a new logo as part of a major re-branding campaign by its agency, Ogilvy & Mather. The bright, new—and of course green—sunburst logo was a textbook example of branding. Literally. In Pavlik and McIntosh's *Converging Media* textbook, the authors defined branding as "the process of creating in the consumer's mind a clear identity for a particular company's product, logo, or trademark." To illustrate the concept in the second edition of that text, the logo was captioned "British Petroleum has successfully rebranded its company with a new logo and a public image as being environmentally friendly."[16] (And I'm the first to admit I used it as an example in my own classes!)

But according to contributors on the PR Watch website, "BP's investment in extractive oil operations dwarfed its investment in renewable energy."[17] Critics immediately began to question the campaign. Then in the summer of 2010, when BP's Deepwater Horizon rig exploded, leading to one of the worst manmade environmental disasters in history, BP was just hammered on social media. Online contests were introduced to see who could design the best logo mocking BP's green sunburst. A YouTube video portraying clumsy BP executives botching an attempt to clean up spilled coffee went viral, getting 10 times more views than BP's official YouTube channel headliner following the accident. More than 160,000 Twitter users followed a fake BP Twitter account spoofing the company.

Later, BP did make some commendable efforts as part of its continuing road to recovery. They used Twitter to send important information out as quickly as possible when media inquiries were overwhelming their media relations staff. But in terms of action, BP soon became seen as "A Textbook Example of How Not to Handle PR," at least according to an NPR story title. After interviewing experts, journalist Elizabeth Shogren concluded that BP had "failed to communicate the three key messages the public needed to hear: That BP was accountable for the disaster, was deeply concerned about the harm it caused and had a plan for what to do."[18] Not only were they not able to communicate well, they also weren't ready to prove it with action.

Good public relations is based much more on what an organization does than on what it says.

BP's sunburst logo was designed to highlight the company's commitment to the environment.

What comes to your mind when you see the BP logo?

Following the BP oil spill, web users competed to design the best mock logo for the company.

Why do you think it was so easy to mock BP after the oil spill?

Listening
Deliberately paying attention to and processing what others are communicating. In public relations and organizational communication, this means processing feedback.

Two-way communication
When both parties send and receive information in an exchange, as opposed to the one-way dissemination of information from an organization to its publics.

Feedback
Information returned from the environment in response to an organization's action or communication that can be used for continuous adjustment and improvement of the organization.

Proactive
A management style that is anticipatory, change-oriented and self-initiated to improve the organization's environment and its future.

Reactive
A management style that mainly responds to problems as they arise rather than anticipating them and averting them.

To effectively listen in public relations, participate in and monitor online communities, in addition to using traditional research.

Listen to the Customer

Listening, or paying attention to and processing what others are communicating, is at the heart of **two-way communication**. For organizations with large publics, listening requires an investment in systematic research. It also requires management to be responsive to what the media and employees have to say. The press may pick up on public sentiment, and employees often have a very good sense of what people outside the organization think. In both technical terms and everyday language, listening is more than just hearing. While those managing an organization may hear what's being said about the organization in the news, at the water cooler, online or out on the street, real listening means considering what the **feedback** means for the organization and what can be done about it. Page saw listening as an important part of public relations, and he saw the public relations person's role as one of keeping upper-level management and others inside an organization informed about public sentiment.

Counting headlines, Facebook likes, Twitter followers, phone calls, YouTube views or keyword mentions gives some indication of what people are thinking and talking about, but good listening requires more careful and deliberate attention to what is being said and what that means for your organization and how it is managed. You can't manage a business on buzz alone.

Manage for Tomorrow

Be **proactive**. That's easy enough to say, but harder to do. After a crisis hits, it is much harder to engage in thoughtful dialogue with publics about what an organization can and should be doing. When public relations people are called in after a major screw-up to clean up the mess, their role is mostly **reactive**, limited to damage control, at best, or spin, at worst, unless they can report that the organization is taking real action to correct whatever problems have occurred. While even the very best-managed of organizations are susceptible to surprise crises, some organizations simply miss opportunities to stave off disasters because they are not listening well to what is going on in their environment and considering the ethical implications. This kind of listening today requires traditional research as well as participation in and monitoring of online communities and forums.

Page's proactive public relations—managing for tomorrow—means building goodwill, avoiding business practices that will lead to unfavorable business conditions, and anticipating how publics will respond to business decisions that will have negative consequences. This concept of proactive public relations is based on two big assumptions. First, public relations people have a role in managing the operations and policies of an organization. Second, public relations people are in a position to sense when major opportunities arise or when trouble is brewing.

Page acknowledged that the purpose of public relations isn't to try to answer every little complaint, "because you can't run around and put salve on every sore that appears in the world." This is good news for those monitoring online product reviews! Rather, proactive public relations is tied to a broader strategy. University of Florida Professor Emeritus Robert Kendall (the one who taught me about publics in my very first public relations course) defined proactive public relations as a "philosophy of public relations that takes the initiative in planning the nature of the relationships desired with publics and executes programs, campaigns, or activities designed to achieve the desired ends."[19] Strategic public relations is proactive.

Conduct Public Relations as if the Whole Company Depends on It

Page saw public relations as a **management function**, but he also realized that top managers were not the only ones responsible for public relations. In discussing leadership, he described how the role of a company president is "first to have the company intend to do the right thing by the public" and then to "get everyone in the company to do his part in carrying out the policy, effectively, reasonably and politely."

Employees have always been spokespeople for organizations, whether that was in their job titles or not. If we want to know what is going on with the big manufacturing plant in our community, we may read about it in the news, but we also won't be afraid to ask our neighbors who work there. Airline ticket agents and flight attendants may be our windows into the workings of the larger airline. The mail carrier may be our source on the postal service. Public relations depends on all of these people, and all of these people depend on public relations.

No one wants to be part of an organization that is dreaded in his or her own neighborhood. We want to go to schools, volunteer for nonprofits and join civic and religious organizations that are respected in our communities. We want to work for organizations that are managed well and are proactive in public relations, and of course we want them to stay solvent and avoid crises too. To the degree that public relations supports these goals, we all depend on it even if we aren't officially working in public relations.

Management function
Part of an organization involved in its overall leadership and decision-making, guiding how the organization operates in its environment, rather than merely following the instructions of others.

All members of an organization play a role in maintaining integrity and ethics.

How does that affect the job of a public relations manager?

Remain Calm, Patient and Good-Humored

I love this one. Page reminds us not to forget the importance of being good-natured, even in dealing with stressful day-to-day situations and larger organizational crises. Publics resent organizations with rude people representing them and, all else being equal, are more forgiving of those that are pleasant. It's human nature.

Throughout the ages, good public relations people have known how important it is to maintain good relationships with reporters. "Never pick a fight with someone who buys ink by the barrel," the old saying goes. The same idea applies in this era of digital publishing and consumer-generated media (CGM). Review sites like Yelp, Google Places, Angie's List and TripAdvisor give all sorts of consumers a voice. No barrels of ink required.

Case Study

How Crock-Pot Fought Fire by Keeping Its Cool

In 2018, Newell Brands, which owns Crock-Pot, found its signature slow-cooker product under fire from an unlikely public—viewers of NBC's number one hit drama *This Is Us*. In an unusual plot twist, it was revealed that one of the show's most beloved characters, Jack Pearson, had died in a raging house fire caused by a Crock-Pot that had been switched *off* after a Super Bowl party.

The plot line was fictional, but the potential damage to Crock-Pot's reputation was real. Twitter users raged with raw emotion. "Just watched the episode of This Is Us where Jack dies. I'm f***ing bawling 😭 😫 f*** that crockpot!!"[20] wrote one. "Just finished the last episode of 'This is Us', and promptly checked the smoke alarm and threw out the crockpot. #mywifeisstillcrying," posted another.[21] In response to media inquiries, Crock-Pot's public relations team at first took a rather technical approach, remarking on the internal testing protocols, safety standards, third-party testing, and wattage specifications, and so on before pleading with NBC to "help us in spreading factual information regarding our product's safety."[22] The company also reportedly considered suing NBC.[23]

Ultimately, however, Crock-Pot's public relations agency, Edelman, chose a different tack. They opted instead to remain calm, patient and good-humored. Crock-Pot representatives responded directly to commenters on their Facebook page. For example, in response to one Facebook user's concerns, they wrote, "We're heartbroken over last night's episode too! Ruthie, we're innocent until proven guilty. . . ." These and many other responses invited users to "DM us with any questions, and we'd be happy to tell you more about our safety standards!"[24]

Then Crock-Pot won the internet when NBC released a pre-Super Bowl promotional message and hashtag (#CrockPotIsInnocent) across all its online platforms. The one-minute video, titled "A Special Message from *This Is Us*," featured the actor Milo Ventimiglia, who plays Jack Pearson, making his way to the kitchen on set. Ventimiglia ruminates on what it means to gather with friends and family on a Super Bowl weekend.

> But in 2018 gathering with friends and family is—well it's not as easy as what it used to be, you know, the country's divided and sometimes that can make it tough to find common ground.

He moves toward the counter.

> This year, this year I think we should all take a deep breath, find the ability to forgive and remind ourselves there is no difference so great that we can't overcome it.

The camera pans down to a shiny new Crock-Pot on the counter as Ventimiglia ladles out a cup of chili. The screen fades to black, and then the Crock-Pot logo and #CrockPotIsInnocent hashtag appear.

The spot won Edelman a Silver Lion award in the public relations category at the Cannes Lions International Festival of Creativity. More importantly, the overall strategy won back Crock-Pot consumers. "Sales actually rebounded," said Edelman's global chair of brand practice Mark Renshaw, who reported that sales increased more than $300,000 that February. "Not only did we restore the brand and restore the reputation and trust, but we got, actually, a sales lift out of it."[25]

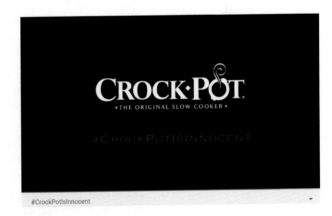

Newell Brands and its public relations firm Edelman opted to use humor in responding to the Crock-Pot backlash following an episode of *This Is Us*.

Why did humor work in this case?

Conversational voice
An authentic, engaging and natural style of communication that publics perceive to be personable.

Flaming
Hostile communication among internet users.

Academic research bears out Page's principle as well. In surveys and experiments, my colleagues and I have found that a variable called **conversational voice** is important in maintaining good relationships with publics online. This "voice" is gauged by asking people how much they agree with statements about how an organization communicates. Organizations with communicators who are perceived as making communication enjoyable, using a sense of humor, admitting mistakes and even providing links to competitors rank higher on the conversational-voice scale. And that conversational voice correlates with public relations outcomes such as satisfaction and commitment, as well as trust.[26]

PCWorld's Robert Strohmeyer offered sound advice in writing about how to deal with Yelp disasters:

> *I like to think that most people are generally sensible, but the Internet has an uncanny knack for transforming rational adults into raving, infantile morons. Yelp, doubly so. Once you accept this basic tenet, you can begin to view your online critics as the reasonable minds they probably are, rather than the juvenile half-wits they appear to be.*

He discourages hostile communication or **flaming** of critics or trying to sue them. Instead, he recommends working within the Yelp toolset by signing up for a business account, which lets you claim your business's Yelp page. Once you've done that you can both encourage positive reviews (but don't insist on them!) and respond constructively and politely to critics, the same way you would if they were at your service counter or reception desk. Moreover, says Strohmeyer, "Have fun with it."[27]

Respond constructively and politely to critics online, the same way you would if they were at your service counter or reception desk.

Sometimes the best way to handle tense situations is to stay engaged with the community and keep a sense of humor.

Would you be inclined to dine at this restaurant?

Realize the Company's True Character Is Expressed by Its People

Effective integrated communication means that publics form their beliefs and attitudes about organizations based on all their points of contact with an organization. Organizations are made up of people, and these people themselves are the most powerful points of contact that others have with the organization. "I am quite certain that the general body of our employees can be trained to represent the company effectively even on complicated subjects," said Page.[28] As Harold Burson, founding partner of Burson-Marsteller, put it, "The thinking goes like this: public relations should permeate every corporate transaction—literally involving almost every employee—from the receptionist to the person at the check-out counter, those who sell the product and those who service it." In other words, "Public relations is now everybody's job."[29]

Managing relationships between organizations and publics means managing organizations in ways that encourage constructive relationships to arise from the countless interpersonal interactions online and offline between all the people who represent the organization and all those with whom they communicate in that role. While the idea of managing for effective **integrated communication** that is consistent across organizational functions goes way back to before the internet, social media have changed the game with new management challenges in an era in which people "like me" are more influential, and mainstream media are struggling for credibility. Particularly in online contexts, this requires managing **distributed public relations**, in which public relations responsibilities are shared among a broad cross section of an organization's members or employees. People look for authenticity in online communication. They still read and view news stories told by journalists about organizations, but publics communicate directly with all sorts of people from organizations online. When that happens, there is an opportunity for the organization to communicate its true character.

Why Ethics Matter

Page's principles of public relations make sense on a practical level. It is not hard to understand why he had such a long and successful career. But these principles also show the importance of moral philosophy and ethics in public relations. Truth, action, empathy and character give meaning to the day-to-day work of public relations. Put bluntly, damage control and spin are #fails. Who wants to do that for a living? There are many good reasons to put ethics at the center of your thinking about good public relations. You are probably already familiar with a number of classic ethical concepts such as the golden rule (do unto others as you would have them do unto you) and utilitarianism (try to do the greatest good for the greatest number of people). And you may also strive for key values such as honesty, loyalty, transparency and social responsibility in your own life. Every chapter in this book includes ethical

Integrated communication
Communicating with publics consistently across organizational functions including public relations, advertising, marketing and customer service.

Distributed public relations
Intentional practice of sharing public relations responsibilities among a broad cross section of an organization's members or employees, particularly in an online context.

Learning about professional values and ethics is an important part of learning public relations.

What do you see as the major benefits of studying ethics before starting your career?

Ethics
Moral principles that govern a person's or group's behavior.

discussions and their application to public relations careers to help you differentiate *good* proactive public relations from reactive damage control and deceptive spin.

Reasons for Studying Ethics

You'll feel better about yourself. **Ethics** are moral principles that govern behavior and are deeply personal. You'll wake up in a much better mood every morning if you know you are going to work for an organization with values congruent to your own. Strategic public relations means that the public relations tactics you perform are derived from solid goals and objectives, and that those goals and objectives serve the broader mission of your organization. This doesn't mean that you have to agree with every single action the organization takes. In fact, the very nature of ethics is dealing with competing values and gray areas. You may agree wholeheartedly with the mission of a nonprofit that employs you, but that doesn't mean you agree with the way they go about pursuing that mission. Sometimes you have to take a stand in your own organization to make your case when you disagree, and you should feel empowered to do so. The important thing is that you can practice public relations in a way that feels right to you and in a place where you don't feel like you are selling your soul to get the job done every day. In a field like public relations, which year after year is listed among the most stressful career options you can choose, your sanity may well depend on how you and those you work with handle ethical dilemmas and gray areas.

Of course, ethics aren't all about gut feelings. Good people make bad decisions all the time. Resolving ethical problems is a matter of the heart, but it is also an intellectual activity. As public relations practitioners move up in their careers, and as they earn more and more respect in management, the importance of their ethical decision-making becomes more important to the organizations they represent, and, ideally, they get better at ethics. This is why it is essential to study principles and systems for ethical reasoning now and to continue to brush up on your ethics throughout your career, which leads to the next point.

You'll be better at your job. Many ethical dilemmas arise out of interactions with reporters, clients, colleagues and members of various publics. Solid relationships with reporters are built on trust, consistency and mutual understanding of professional roles and responsibilities. Retaining clients and attracting new ones requires a reputation for fairness and integrity. Loyalty and expertise are among the keys to positive and productive relationships with colleagues. And transparency is essential in dealing with online communities when strategic communication is the essence of your job. Developing a solid ethical framework that you can explain to others will help you in all of those relationships, and those relationships are the stuff of which successful, fulfilling careers are made.

You'll be more important at work. As Shannon Bowen puts it, communication professionals must pay attention to ethics before they desperately need to. "Once a crisis of conflicting ethics or high media interest befalls the organization it is too late to begin searching for ethical guidance."[30] Bowen is a professor, ethicist and member of the Arthur W. Page Society. In her research she has found that spotting ethical dilemmas is key to resolving issues before they become crises. Beyond just identifying ethical dilemmas, public relations people must be able to discuss the issues with members of their organizations' dominant coalitions. **Dominant coalition** is a term used to describe the group of people with the greatest influence in how an organization operates, including CEOs, presidents, board members, top managers, vice presidents and so on. The dominant coalition may or may not include public relations executives. However, these are the people who steer the organization at the highest levels, and a public relations person who is well versed in rational, defensible, ethical decision-making will be in the best position to inform this group in handling public relations issues before they become crises.

Competing Duties

Working in public relations means serving many masters. In their book *Public Relations Ethics*, Philip Seib and Kathy Fitzpatrick highlight the source of many ethical dilemmas as individual practitioners face them.[31] That source is competing duties. If you work in public relations, you have a duty to: (1) yourself, (2) your client, (3) your employer, (4) the profession, (5) the media and (6) society. I'm willing to bet that there are vegetarians who work in public relations agencies that represent steakhouses. I'm sure there are people who are deeply annoyed by cable news channels, but who still work hard to accommodate their TV producers prior to interviews. I even know a certain textbook author and professor who criticizes Walt Disney Co.'s massive media empire and then happily takes his kids to Walt Disney World. None of these folks is necessarily a sellout. The vegetarian may welcome the restaurant to his community to boost the economy while providing jobs, not to mention the business for his own agency, which supports his own financial stability. The public relations practitioner arranging the cable news interview may weigh the importance of free speech and vigorous debate as much more important in society than her opinion of the particular station's host and format. And your textbook author doesn't think a personal boycott of a major media conglomerate is a requisite for educating others about issues of media consolidation in society. On the other hand, there are times when public

Dominant coalition
Group of people with the greatest influence in determining how an organization operates and pursues its mission.

relations practitioners must say no to reporters. There are times when agencies should decline clients. There are times when a potential paycheck is not worth the dissonance it creates.

A Guide for Ethical Decision-Making

Addressing these apparent dilemmas ethically requires careful thinking. Fitzpatrick offers the following guide for public relations practitioners:

1. Define the specific ethical issue/conflict.
2. Identify internal/external factors (e.g., legal, political, social, economic) that may influence the decision.
3. Identify key values.
4. Identify the parties who will be affected by the decision and define the public relations professional's obligation to each.
5. Select ethical principles to guide the decision-making process.
6. Make a decision and justify it.[32]

In many ways, social media make ethical communication easier. We get to speak in our own voices in forums in which direct, informal communication is valued. Social media give us means for discussing and resolving our professional issues with easy access to others' opinions and views. We get to experiment in mixing our personal and professional identities. This can lead to a heightened sense of awareness of our consistencies and inconsistencies. At the same time, however, this breaking down of clear divisions between our personal and professional communication raises dilemmas, and digital media technologies sometimes make deception a little too easy.

Case Study

"Tweeting Under False Circumstances"

Many executives use social media like Twitter to share their personal voices in support of their organizations, but public relations counselor Todd Defren found himself facing an interesting problem when asked to serve as someone else's voice. Defren ran SHIFT Communications, a firm that specializes in digital and social media that has served clients including McDonald's, Salesforce.com, TechCrunch, H&R Block and Tyson Foods. Defren also had earned a reputation as a pioneering and highly influential blogger with a large number of readers of his *PR Squared* blog. He used that blog as a platform for working through new types of dilemmas unique to social media.

Let's walk through one of Defren's cases, "Tweeting Under False Circumstances," using Fitzpatrick's process.[33] (Quoted material is from Defren's blog post.)

Define The Specific Ethical Issue/Conflict

A client asked Defren and his associates to tweet for him at a trade show from the client's Twitter account. The client was adept at Twitter and prominent in his field. He had a significant number of loyal followers on his account who were used to hearing directly from him via that channel.

> He posts regularly, sometimes several times a day. He "gets" Twitter; he finds value in the dialogue and his followers appreciate that a well-placed exec from a Big Company is engaged with them online.
>
> Now, a big industry tradeshow is coming up. He'll be very active there, as a speaker and organizer. The executive wants his tweetstream to reflect his activity at the show, and to highlight other happenings at the conference, as well. He's very concerned that he won't be able to support this many to-do's.

Identify Internal/External Factors

A big part of the appeal of Twitter as a form of social media is that followers have access to interesting and influential people with whom they otherwise would not be able to interact. The culture of social media is an external factor that must be considered, and the executive's commitment to authenticity in this environment is an internal factor.

> You can see how this request comes from a "good place." This executive's commitment to online engagement is so fierce, he doesn't want to abandon it even for an important event. He knows his followers would understand his absences, but he thinks there is going to be real value in tracking what's happening at the conference, and in responding to folks online throughout.

Identify Key Values

Loyalty, transparency, expertise and independence are among the key values in this case. Not only did Defren have to weigh his loyalty to the client, but he also had to consider the loyalty and trust that the client's Twitter followers may have had in the executive. This loyalty brings transparency to the forefront because if those followers expected the executive to write all his own tweets and if he was planning on changing that without telling them, they may have been deceived. The behind-the-scenes change would have meant a lack of transparency. The client meant no harm—his request came from a good place, as Defren said—but part of what he was paying Defren and his firm for was expertise in knowing the lay of the land in social media and counseling on exactly this type of situation.

> While it's true he is asking us to misrepresent ourselves, he feels that it would still be authentic because of his trust in us.

Identify The Parties Who Will Be Affected

This is where those competing duties to various people come into play. This case appears to be a doozy because Defren had a duty to pretty much everyone in Seib and Fitzpatrick's list: (1) himself, (2) his client, (3) the profession, (4) the media and (5) society.

- **Duty to Self:** As was pretty clear from his blog, which included detailed analysis of ethical dilemmas like this one, Defren invested his own intellect, hard work and time in his strategic communication practice. If he botched this, it could have damaged his reputation and led to personal disappointment. There also would have been financial consequences for him personally.

- **Duty to Client:** Defren's firm was hired to do a job. Yes, a big part of that job was to communicate for the client, but he also owed the client solid independent counseling based on his expertise and knowledge of social media.

- **Duty to the Profession:** Botching this job with poor ethical decision-making would have not only discredited Defren, it also would have reflected poorly on the whole field of public relations. Unfortunately, examples of misrepresentation and deception in public relations are not hard to find, as these cases tend to get called out and told and re-told online. Mentioning public relations and ethics together in the same sentence will lead to rolled eyes and snarky responses in many circles. The only way to combat this is with performance.

- **Duty to the Media:** The media in this case are mostly social media, Twitter users in particular. Just as relationships with reporters, editors and producers are critical to effective communication via magazines, newspapers, radio and television, relationships with Twitter users are the essence of effective tweeting. If Defren disappointed his client's followers, he would have not only undermined his client's credibility and effectiveness, but he would also have taken something away from the utility of the medium as a whole as an option for effective public relations.

- **Duty to Society:** Social media have the potential to facilitate meaningful democratic dialogue and healthy economies by affording publics the opportunity to engage organizations in the honest exchange of ideas, currency, products, services and social capital. Social media also can provide a haven for misinformation, deceit, mistrust, cynicism and generally shattered expectations. Defren wanted to contribute to the former and not the latter.

Select Ethical Principles To Guide The Decision-Making Process

At this stage of the analysis it becomes fairly clear that openness, honesty, trust, transparency and authenticity are at stake. **Deontological ethics** are systems of decision-making that focus on duties or rules. To the degree that the principle of duty is central to the decision on how to act in this case based on moral obligations to each of the parties, you could say that it guides our thinking. Of course, other principles apply too, and we will look at some of those in cases in the chapters that follow.

Make A Decision And Justify It

So what did Defren do?

> *So we suggested a compromise. . . . Yes, we would tweet from his account, but with the following conditions:*
>
> *Prior to the event, he must tweet, "During the show some of my tweeting will be supplemented by our extended team."*
>
> *A reminder to that effect would go out, regularly, throughout the conference, i.e., every 10th tweet would remind followers that someone besides the executive might be "at the controls" of his Twitter account.*
>
> *When character spaces permitted, we'd add a #team hashtag to denote that the tweet was not published by the exec—but honestly, this attribution fell away more often than not; we largely relied on the "every 10th tweet" approach to cover our ethical backsides.*

In the end, the solution seemed easy, but this was largely due to Defren's expertise and careful ethical thinking. He was able to serve the client well with a compromise that didn't require compromising his ethics or causing harm to his business, his profession or society. Defren and his client experienced no "pushback" from the tweets. Interestingly, Defren still had some ethical concerns and questions (about whether some people would still be duped despite the every-10th-tweet approach), and was courageous enough to post the whole case as well as his follow-up concerns in a very public blog entry inviting feedback. His post drew more than 150 comments, and the vast majority of them were constructive and supportive. The very act of airing his case and concerns for open discussion honored the early spirit of social media while also reinforcing Defren's commitment to ethical practice—in the sense of the word *practice* that means that we are all always working to improve in this area.

Deontological ethics
System of decision-making that focuses on the moral principles of duty and rules.

Voices from the Field

Kathy Fitzpatrick

KATHY FITZPATRICK is a professor in the School of Communication at American University. She is a member of the Arthur W. Page Society, whose members are corporate, agency and academic leaders in the field of public relations. She served as head of the Educators Academy of PRSA, is a former president of the Dallas Chapter of PRSA, and was a member of the task force that developed the current PRSA Code of Ethics.

In general, do you think public relations is moving toward higher ethical standards?

Yes, I believe that higher ethical standards in public relations are more commonplace, partly due to the globalization of society and changes in technology that require a higher level of openness and transparency in organizational communications. Also, there is increased emphasis on ethical standards among industry groups. With its new code of ethics in 2000, PRSA took a big step toward becoming the ethics standard-bearer in the United States. I believe the code—and promotion of the code—has heightened awareness of ethical standards in the field. Many public relations firms also have developed extensive codes of ethics and operating standards for staff members. Globally, the International Public Relations Association, the Global Alliance for Public Relations and Communication Management and other leading associations stress ethical principles and practices as well.

What kinds of ethical issues are entry-level public relations people likely to face?

Deceptive practices are a big issue. For example, a situation might occur in which a boss (whether in a corporation, nonprofit or firm) asks an entry-level practitioner not to disclose certain information that the practitioner believes should be revealed. Activities such as greenwashing—to make a company look more socially responsible than it really is—come to mind here as well.

In addition, conflicts may surface when a practitioner's own values and beliefs are incongruent with the culture of an organization. For example, a philosophy of doing "anything to win" creates a tense operating environment for professionals who want to uphold ethical standards. Also, if an organization is promoting a cause or idea with which a practitioner disagrees, this creates internal dissonance that can result in a lot of stress. Thus, new practitioners must decide what types of organizations they are willing to represent and what they will do for them.

What kinds of ethical dilemmas come up with social media?

Issues related to honesty and transparency top the list here. For example, it's easy to be deceptive online. If you work for a hotel and your boss asks you to post a positive review of your accommodations on travel websites, what do you do? If you are tweeting about a new product or service offered by your company, do you identify yourself as an employee of the company?

In what ways have new media contexts reinforced or challenged classic principles?

The fundamentals of ethical public relations practice have not changed. They simply must be applied in new contexts and platforms.

How much can ethics be taught and learned in public relations, and how much does it just depend on the person's individual values?

At the end of the day, ethical decision-making is a personal matter with individual accountability. Whether you raise your hand at work to question a particular issue you see as unethical depends to a great extent on your personal and professional courage to do the right thing. Having said that, ethics education can have a tremendous impact in helping students and practitioners recognize ethical issues and dilemmas, better understand the implications of unethical practices and develop guidelines and processes for resolving them. Graduates of public relations programs must be equipped with the special expertise and skills required for successful practice in public relations, but they also need an understanding of the professional standards and social obligations of public relations professionals.

What is the most important guide that a public relations practitioner might use in trying to make ethical decisions?
Public relations professionals should always consider whether they are contributing to—or interfering

with—informed decision-making on the part of publics affected by an organization's decisions or actions. This really is the bottom line when practicing public relations ethically in a democratic marketplace of ideas.

Codes of Ethics

Most organizations of communication professionals offer codes of ethics to articulate their values and to guide their members. While it is debatable whether or not public relations is technically a profession, codes of ethics certainly encourage professionalism. One major factor keeping public relations from being recognized as a profession like law or medicine or architecture is licensure. You do not need a license to practice public relations. Any quack can call himself or herself a PR person. This is unfortunate, but the alternative, according to those opposed to professional licensing, would be a violation of our right to free speech. Imagine if you were not allowed to speak on matters of public concern in an official capacity because you did not have a license.

Criticisms of Codes

Lack of enforceability is one criticism against codes of ethics. If a member acts within the law, but outside of the code of ethics, revocation of the person's membership is the most the association can do in response. The good news is that it doesn't happen very often (in fact, it never happened in five decades of PRSA's original code[34]).

However, this leads to a second criticism of codes of ethics, which is that they simply are not effective or even necessary as means of policing behavior. Most members of these professional organizations practice public relations with good intention, and those few who do run blatantly afoul of the codes can probably take advantage of the subjective nature of interpretation and the relatively weak mechanisms of enforcement to evade any institutional consequences.

A third criticism is that codes of ethics can be vague and lack internal consistency. By definition, ethical dilemmas involve competing choices. Loyalty may run up against independence. Confidentiality may come at the expense of transparency. When codes of ethics call for all of the above, the member may be put in a pickle. PRSA updated its code in 2000, and one big change from the prior code was that its emphasis on enforcement was eliminated, which leads to some of the positives of codes of ethics.

Advantages of Codes

First, codes of ethics help communicate the professional standards of an association's membership to both internal and external parties. Many of you reading this book may not pursue public relations as a career. You may go into advertising, marketing or journalism. Or you may become a dentist, deep-sea diver or deputy sheriff. But if you read the codes of ethics or discuss them with anyone who knows them, you will come away with a much better idea of what members of these organizations do and what values they embrace. For better or worse, everyone is exposed to public relations in democracies like ours, and the more people understand what makes for good, ethical public relations the better.

Second, codes offer carefully articulated and professionally agreed-upon guidelines for decision-making and action. For example, the PRSA Code of Ethics is designed "to be a useful guide for PRSA members as they carry out their ethical responsibilities" and "to anticipate and accommodate, by precedent, ethical challenges that may arise."[35] The PRSA values form a foundation for ethical conduct (see https://www.prsa.org/about/ethics/prsa-code-of-ethics). The PRSA Code of Ethics also outlines six provisions of conduct. In Chapters 2–14 of this book, each of these provisions will be discussed in the context of at least one case of ethics.

Third, there are practical and reputational advantages to knowing and working with established codes of ethics. Professional communication associations such as the Universal Accreditation Board (UAB) and the International Association of Business Communicators (IABC) offer voluntary accreditation, which allows practitioners to distinguish themselves among others in the field with a professional designation. UAB grants the designation of **"Accredited in Public Relations" (APR)**, and the professional credential for IABC is **"Accredited Business Communicator" (ABC)**. Criteria include demonstrated professional experience, and evidence of knowledge, skills and abilities, including ethics. For APR, ethics and law make up 13 percent of the exam.

Professional Associations

The UAB includes several affiliates including PRSA, the Agricultural Relations Council, Asociación de Relacionistas Profesionales de Puerto Rico, Florida Public Relations Association, National School Public Relations Association, Religion Communicators Council and the Maine Public Relations Association. Dozens of established organizations with codes of ethics serve members all over the world, including the African Public Relations Association, the Public Relations Consultants' Association of Malaysia (PRCA Malaysia), the Public Relations Institute of Ireland (PRII) and the Mexican Association of Public Relations Professionals/Asociación Mexicana de Profesionales de Relaciones Públicas (PRORP). Membership (even without seeking accreditation) usually requires formally acknowledging and agreeing to abide by the standards set forth in such codes. Interestingly, the main values identified in the codes share more commonalities than differences across cultures, including common moral principles such as fairness and honesty.

For comparison to the PRSA Code of Ethics, the International Public Relations Association (IPRA) Code of Conduct (https://www.ipra.org/member-services/code-of-conduct/) represents a consolidation of three prior international codes (the 1961 Code of Venice, the 1965 Code of Athens and the 2007 Code of Brussels). You'll notice many consistencies between the IPRA code and the PRSA code, but it is also interesting to note the IPRA focus

Accredited in public relations (APR)
Credential awarded by PRSA and other UAB affiliates to those who have demonstrated competency in the knowledge, skills and abilities required to practice public relations effectively.

Accredited business communicator (ABC)
Credential awarded by IABC to recognize communicators who have reached a globally accepted standard of knowledge and proficiency in their chosen field.

on human rights and dignity. The IPRA code also includes some language specific to online media and issues of trust, credibility and privacy.

Regardless of whether you call it a field, a practice or a profession, *public relations* can be defined best by both words and actions. While there is no denying the existence of poor public relations and shady practice, professional organizations stand to help bring our body of knowledge together with ethical and effective practice for the benefit of students, practitioners and society.

In Case You Missed It

If you tell people you're studying public relations, they may not know what you mean. Here are a few tips from the chapter to help you think about what public relations people do, just in case anyone asks!

- To define public relations, consider organizations, publics and the relations between them.

- Good public relations is based much more on what an organization does than on what it says.

- To effectively listen in public relations, participate in and monitor online communities in addition to using traditional research.

- Respond constructively and politely to critics online, the same way you would if they were at your service counter or reception desk.

- Review and discuss organizations' codes of ethics to better understand the values that members embrace.

SUMMARY

1.1 Define public relations in terms of organizations, publics and the relationships between them.

According to a PRSA task force, "Public relations is a strategic communication process that builds mutually beneficial relationships between organizations and their publics."

When public relations is practiced as a management function, practitioners proactively communicate with an organization's publics, carefully consider what feedback means for the organization, develop strategy and work with the organization's leadership to implement and evaluate both actions and communication.

1.2 Explain how public relations can serve a management function through key principles and values for ethical conduct.

Arthur Page's principles for public relations management (e.g., tell the truth; prove it with action) are as relevant today as they were in his time. Practicing public relations with authenticity means managing communication and promotion in ways that are consistent with how your whole organization is managed.

1.3 Understand the importance of ethics in public relations.

Ethical public relations practitioners can work with a clearer conscience, but they also can work with a clearer sense of how to handle difficult situations with reporters, clients, colleagues and various publics. In turn, ethical public relations practitioners are more valuable to the organizations that depend on them. Value to organizations results in greater job opportunities.

1.4 Apply systematic ethical decision-making for public relations.

Step-by-step guides such as Fitzpatrick's "Ethical Decision-Making Guide," cases like Defren's client tweeting example, and codes of ethics all offer good guidance for practicing ethical decision-making offline and online.

1.5 Identify international professional associations and become familiar with codes of ethics.

PRSA and IPRA are two major professional organizations offering codes of ethics. Codes of ethics articulate common values that have been vetted by professionals. See online resources for many more codes of ethics offered by other professional organizations.

DISCUSSION QUESTIONS

1. **CASE STUDY** Ask two or three people outside of your classes and outside of public relations to name the first thing that comes to mind when you say "public relations." Ask them what they remember about the Papa John's case (or another case if a better one comes to mind). Do their answers align more with dramatic high-profile actions of people like John Schnatter or more with the "textbook" definitions discussed in this chapter?

2. Name an organization that you have worked for or had direct experience with that does some form of public relations. Would you say that public relations is part of that organization's management function? Why or why not?

3. **CASE STUDY** Crock-Pot's response to the episode of *This Is Us* in which they were featured was effective in large part because the company remained good-humored. But humor in public relations is risky. Research the Crock-Pot case online to find the case study as Edelman presented it, the actual promo video, social media comments, and how media covered the case. Why didn't humor backfire in this case?

4. Some people describe public relations as the conscience of an organization. Do you think that is a good way to define public relations? Why or why not?

5. **CASE STUDY** Todd Defren didn't actually name the CEO in his case, but you probably weren't surprised to read that ghost tweeting happens. Identify a specific CEO or celebrity on social media who you suspect does not write all of his or her own posts. Do you think this is ethical or unethical? What's the moral reasoning for your answer?

6. Search online for another communication-related code of ethics such as one for journalism, filmmaking, blogging or marketing. How are the values expressed in that code different from the values expressed in the PRSA code?

KEY TERMS

Accredited business communicator (ABC) 24
Accredited in public relations (APR) 24
Authenticity 7
Conversational voice 14
Crowdsource 6
Deontological ethics 21
Distributed public relations 15
Dominant coalition 17

Ethics 16
Feedback 10
Flaming 14
General public 2
Integrated communication 15
Listening 10
Management function 11
Nongovernmental organization (NGO) 2
Organization 2

Proactive 10
Public relations 3
Publics 2
Reactive 10
Social media influencer 7
Spin 7
Transparency 8
Two-way communication 10

CHAPTER 2
Public Relations Models Through the Ages

Promoting burgers on the menu of a restaurant
chain famous for its pancakes is a tall order.
How did IHOP's publicity stack up?

KEY LEARNING OUTCOMES

2.1 Analyze public relations models on one-way/two-way and asymmetrical/symmetrical dimensions using examples and key figures from history.

2.2 Integrate knowledge of social history with knowledge of public relations.

2.3 Identify common motivations for strategic communication in history.

2.4 Discuss the ethics of transparency, objectivity and advocacy.

RELATED UNIVERSAL ACCREDITATION BOARD COMPETENCY AREAS
2.2 ETHICAL BEHAVIOR • **4.1** COMMUNICATION/PUBLIC RELATIONS MODELS AND THEORIES
4.3 KNOWLEDGE OF THE FIELD • **6.1** RELATIONSHIP BUILDING • **6.2** REPUTATION MANAGEMENT

In the opening pages of *Managing Public Relations*, right before defining public relations as the management of communication between an organization and its publics, Grunig and Hunt reflect on the problems of the times (early 1980s). They describe public relations as a "young profession" with "roots in press agentry and propaganda, activities that society generally holds in low esteem."[1] They then chart a historical progression of public relations to frame the maturation of the profession by outlining four models of public relations in history: (1) press agentry/publicity, (2) public information, (3) two-way asymmetrical and (4) two-way symmetrical.

While the formal treatment of public relations as a field of study and practice may have been a 20th-century development, historians have traced elements of public relations back through recorded history. Modern communication historians make the case that public relations activities are as old as religion, education, business and politics.

Public Relations Models in History

Generations of public relations students have learned about the field's development through the lens of Grunig and Hunt's four models of public relations. However, these models also have been criticized for oversimplifying public relations and its history. What public relations people do doesn't fit neatly into four boxes, some say. This is exactly why Grunig and Hunt used the term *models*:

> We've chosen the term "models" to describe the four types of public relations that we believe have evolved through history, in order to emphasize that they are abstractions. In scientific usage, a model is a representation of reality . . . if we construct models of public relations behavior by observing the most important components of that behavior, then we can make some sense out of the many diverse communication activities we call public relations.[2]

In the first two models, press agentry/publicity and public information, the communication is primarily one-way. In the second two models, two-way asymmetrical and two-way symmetrical, the communication is two-way (Figure 2.1).

Press Agentry/Publicity

Born in Madagascar in 1674, Joice Heth arrived in America in her youth and was a slave to one Augustine Washington, father of George Washington. Heth was the first one to put clothes on the future father of America, and she basically raised the boy. In 1836, Heth was 161 years old and retained astonishingly good health, singing hymns, laughing heartily and telling stories of the boy Washington. Or so potential patrons were told in the billing of an

Model	Direction of Communication	Definition	Historic Examples	Modern Examples
Publicity/press agentry	organization → publics	Communication is mostly one-way, initiated by an organization with little concern for accuracy or completeness	P. T. Barnum's exploitation of Joice Heth for controversy and attention	Publicity stunts like IHOP's "IHOb" name change stunt
Public information	organization → publics	Communication is mostly one-way, initiated by an organization to inform publics with truthful and accurate information	Ivy Lee's work for railroads	Work of government public information officers for organizations like FEMA
Two-way asymmetrical	organization ⇄ publics	Communication is two-way but unbalanced, with the organization using research/feedback in an effort to persuade publics to change attitudes or behaviors	Bernays' "Torches of Freedom" and bacon-and-eggs "study"	Analytics-driven, personalized persuasion campaigns
Two-way symmetrical	organization ⇄ publics	Communication is mostly balanced, with the organization as likely to change attitudes or behavior as its publics	Earl Newsom counseling Ford on auto safety	Public utilities' community-based problem solving

Figure 2.1 Four models of public relations.

attraction that began the press agentry career of showman extraordinaire P. T. Barnum.[3]

That not everyone bought the story about Joice Heth did not bother Barnum. On the contrary, he relished the attention that controversy brought.

> *At the outset of my career, I saw that everything depended on getting the people to think, and talk, and become curious and excited over and about the "rare spectacle." Accordingly, posters, transparencies, advertisements, newspaper paragraphs—all calculated to extort attention—were employed, regardless of expense. My exhibition rooms in New York, Boston, Philadelphia, Albany, and in other large and small cities, were continually thronged and much money was made.[4]*

Case Study

A Tall Order: Gaining Attention and Publicity in the Marketplace of Ideas

With an average of 500 million tweets[5] and more than 50 million Facebook status updates[6] posted every day, social media make standing out among the competition a taller order than a double stack of pancakes. But on June 4, 2018, IHOP, the International House of Pancakes, served this short note that hit the spot: "For 60 pancakin' years, we've been IHOP. Now, we're flippin' our name to IHOb. Find out what it could b on 6.11.18. #IHOb."[7] The speculation began immediately. What did the "b" stand for?

"It's gotta be bacon. Nothing is better than pancakes . . . Except BACON!" replied one Twitter user.[8]

"It's international house of breakfast isn't it?" asked another.

IHOP/IHOb kept it close to the vest for the next week, aside from a steady stream of puns playing on the flipped letter (e.g., "The bossibilities are endless, Katie"; "Not so fast, Marissa! It could b anything."). Mainstream media took notice too. News outlets from *NBC Nightly News* to *USA Today* to *Yahoo News* picked up the story, drawing even more people into the discussion. *CNN Money*'s Paul La Monica wondered, "Is this just a short-term marketing gimmick? . . . It's also hard to imagine why the company would want to mess with a name that's so well-known and beloved."

Then a week later, on June 11, the company issued a **news release** with the headline "IHOP® CHANGES NAME TO IHOb℠ AND REVEALS THE "B" IS FOR BURGERS."[9]

As it played out, the tens of thousands of people who engaged with IHOP in the name-change guessing game were just the beginning of the story. Next came the social media outrage, word-of-mouth attention, and even some shade thrown by corporate competitors. *Washington Post* food reporter Becky Krystal mused that "IHOP's name change is what happens when brands exploit the Internet outrage cycle."[10] Others saw an opportunity for humor. When one Twitter user poked at Wendy's, "so @Wendys u just gonna let @IHOb sell burgers on your block? thought you were the og?," @Wendy's rebuffed, "Not really afraid of the burgers from a place that decided pancakes were too hard."[11]

For more than a month, IHOP took advantage of the attention to promote its new burgers across all channels. In mid-July, IHOP's president, Darren Rebelez, sat for an interview with CNN's La Monica and confirmed that IHOP never really changed its name.

We knew that if we were really going to get into the burger business in a meaningful way, then we were going to have to do something bold

News release
A statement of news produced and distributed on behalf of an organization to make information public. Traditionally news releases (aka press releases) have been issued to news media with the intent of publicizing the information to the news organization's readers, listeners or viewers.

and something creative. We came up with the idea of flipping the p to a b and it really grabbed everyone's attention. . . . We did get some blowback, but then when we told people, 'look, this is really more tongue-in-cheek, we're really just trying to launch this new lineup of ultimate steakburgers,' they took a deep breath and said, 'wow that's really brilliant.'[12]

As with P. T. Barnum's antics more than 180 years prior, the question of whether the whole controversy was really a gimmick only added to the attention. Did they really mean to do that? Or was this just their way of backing out of a bad decision to change the name?

It was no accident. To borrow words from P. T. Barnum, IHOP's tactics were "calculated to extort attention." Rebelez said that IHOP had tested the concept with a sample of IHOP customers before launching the campaign, and that "the reaction that we saw play out on social media is exactly what we saw in those focus groups." People first reacted emotionally, rejecting the idea, but then thought it was brilliant when they figured it out.[13] Moreover, Rebelez reported that the stunt generated some 20,000 news articles and at one point ranked second on Twitter as a trending topic, trailing only Donald Trump's summit with North Korea's Kim Jong Un. Rebelez didn't comment on whether burger sales had actually increased, but IHOP's parent company, Dine Brands, reported earnings that quarter that surpassed estimates by more than 9 percent.[14]

IHOP ✓
@IHOP

Follow ⌄

For 60 pancakin' years, we've been IHOP. Now, we're flippin' our name to IHOb. Find out what it could b on 6.11.18. #IHOb

0:03 7.48M views

10:00 AM - 4 Jun 2018

12,639 Retweets 32,564 Likes

When IHOP announced it was going to change its name to IHOb, the gimmick created a lot of buzz.

What are the risks and rewards of this type of stunt?

Barnum will forever be associated with the **press agentry/publicity model**.

Departing from Grunig and Hunt's four models, University of Amsterdam Professor Emeritus Betteke van Ruler studied communication management internationally and identified several typologies. Typologies help us classify things into general categories based on their common characteristics. Archaeologists use typologies to classify artifacts. Van Ruler developed typologies to classify types of public relations practitioners. One of those typologies is the town crier. Like the press agent/publicist, van Ruler's town crier is mostly seeking to be heard in the marketplace with little concern for listening to others outside of his organization. There's nothing wrong with working to gain attention in a crowded marketplace, but there

Press agentry/publicity model
Model of public relations in which communication is mostly one-way, initiated by an organization with little concern for accuracy or completeness in order to gain the attention of publics.

GREAT ATTRACTION
At the Masonic Hall!
UNPARALLELED LONGEVITY.
FOR TWO DAYS ONLY.
JOICE HETH,
NURSE TO
Gen. George Washington,

(The father of our country,) who has arrived at the astonishing age of **161** years! will be seen in the large room at the Masonic Hall, opposite the Franklin House, for TWO DAYS ONLY, as she is on her way to Boston, where she must be early next week.

JOICE HETH is unquestionably the most astonishing and interesting curiosity in the World! She was the slave of Augustine Washington, (the father of Gen. Washington,) and was the first person who put clothes on the unconscious infant who in after days led our heroic fathers on to glory, to victory, and to freedom. To use her own language when speaking of the illustrious Father of his country, "she raised him." JOICE HETH was born in the Island of Madagascar, on the Coast of Africa, in the year 1674 and has consequently now arrived at the astonishing

Age of 161 Years!

She weighs but forty-six pounds, and yet is very cheerful and interesting. She retains her faculties in an unparrelleled degree, converses freely, sings numerous hymns, relates many interesting anecdotes of Gen. Washington, the red coats, &c. and often laughs heartily at her own remarks, or those of the spectators. Her health is perfectly good, and her appearance very neat. She was baptized in the Potomac river and received into the Baptist Church 116 years ago, and takes great pleasure in conversing with Ministers and religious persons. The appearance of this marvellous relic of antiquity strikes the beholder with amazement, and convinces him that his eyes are resting on the oldest specimen of mortality they ever before beheld. Original, authentic and indisputable documents prove that however astonishing the fact may appear, JOICE HETH is in every respect the person she is represented.

The most eminent physicians and intelligent men both in New York and Philadelphia, have examined this *living skeleton* and the documents accompanying her, and all *invariably* pronounce her to be as represented 161 *years of age!* Indeed it is impossible for any person, however incredulous, to visit her without astonishment and the most perfect satisfaction that she is as old as represented.

☞ A female is in continual attendance, and will give every attention to the ladies who visit this relic of by gone ages.

She was visited at Niblo's Garden, New York, by *ten thousand persons* in two weeks.———Hours of exhibition from 9 A. M. to 1 P. M. and from 4 to 10 P. M.—Admittance 25 cents—Children 12½ cents.

Broadsides and posters were a key part of 19th-century publicity tactics.

What ethical issues does the Joice Heth case raise?

is a point of diminishing returns in simply turning up the volume without stopping to listen to others. Propaganda, attention getting and less-than-accurate information (if not downright lies) are hallmarks of the press agentry model, which is as alive in this millennium as it was then.

Public Information

Long before Bill Gates and Mark Zuckerberg dropped out of Harvard, Ivy Ledbetter Lee left graduate school at Harvard in the late 19th century, largely for financial reasons. Whereas Gates and Zuckerberg eventually changed the nature of personal media as we know them with Microsoft and Facebook, Lee started the nation's third public relations agency and went on to become the man many refer to today as the founder of public relations.

Before his stint at Harvard, Lee had graduated cum laude from Princeton in 1898 and had worked as a stringer for the Associated Press, the Philadelphia Press and the Chicago Record.[15] And prior to starting the public relations agency Parker & Lee in late 1904 with George Parker,[16] he worked for *The New York Journal, The New York Times* and *New York World*.[17] Parker & Lee's credo heralded a journalistic background: "Accuracy, Authenticity, and Interest,"[18] and it very much distinguished Lee's brand of public relations from Barnum's press agentry.

While the Parker & Lee agency only lasted a few years, Ivy Lee went on to represent some of the biggest names of the day in corporate America, including the Pennsylvania Railroad and the Rockefellers. While Lee's legacy is complex—he also counseled I. G. Farben, the German dye trust, on how to improve relations with Americans after the Nazis took control of the trust—his name is deeply associated with the **public information model** of public relations in which communication is mostly one-way, initiated by an organization to inform publics with truthful and accurate information. When he sent materials to the press, Ivy Lee was known to include his "Declaration of Principles," which stated:

> *This is not a secret press bureau. All our work is done in the open. We aim to supply news. . . . Our matter is accurate. Further details on any subject treated will be supplied promptly, and any editor will be assisted most cheerfully in verifying directly any statement of fact. . . . In brief, our plan*

Public information model
Model of public relations in which communication is mostly one-way, initiated by an organization to inform publics with truthful and accurate information.

is frankly, and openly, on behalf of business concerns and public institutions, to supply the press and public of the United States prompt and accurate information concerning subjects which it is of value and interest to the public to know about.[19]

Transparency is a value we hear much of in the age of social media. Although it is debatable to what degree Lee was walking the walk, he was talking the talk of transparency a good century before the internet. As Clive Thompson of Wired put it, "Transparency is a judo move. Your customers are going to poke around in your business anyway, and your workers are going to blab about internal info—so why not make it work for you by turning everyone into a partner in the process and inviting them to do so?"[20]

In the early 1900s, railroad accidents were not uncommon, and railroad companies would generally do what they could to keep the bad news under wraps. But when the Pennsylvania Railroad had a wreck near Gap, Pennsylvania, Ivy Lee did a little informational judo:

> *Instinctively the railroad management put its news suppression machinery into motion. Just as quickly, Lee reversed it. Reporters were invited to travel to the scene of the accident at the railroad's expense. Lee promptly set up facilities for reporters and photographers.*[21]

The resulting coverage was better than usual, and the Pennsylvania Railroad was later compared favorably to railroads that refused to adopt such an open-access policy.

Today, most public relations departments within organizations spend at least part of their time serving the public information function. Even when organizations are not seeking to gain extra attention, they still often need to get messages out accurately and reliably. In many cases, public communication is actually required by law. For example, publicly held corporations, which are organizations that have offered shares for trading in stock exchanges or other public markets, are obligated to file certain reports and to make public certain information that may affect investors' decisions. The regulatory agency governing such activity in the United States is the Securities and Exchange Commission (SEC), and the information that could affect investors' decisions is called **material information**, which we cover in more detail in Chapter 11 dealing with legal issues. Annual reports and quarterly profit/loss statements are examples of material information that must be released in a timely, accurate and fair manner. So if Papa John's or Dine Brands have a bad quarter and fail to meet their earnings goals, they still have to report that information in a way that ensures that anyone interested in buying or selling shares is properly informed as a result.

Public information is also a common practice in government work. In fact, the job title of **public information officer (PIO)** is most commonly

Ivy Lee began his career as a journalist, and he carried journalistic values into his work for corporate clients.

How was Lee's work in public relations different from journalism?

Organizations must get messages out accurately and reliably, even when they are not seeking to gain extra attention.

Material information
Any information that could affect investment decisions related to a particular security such as stock in a publicly traded company.

Public information officer (PIO)
A public relations person, commonly working in a government position, whose job focuses on the dissemination of information to appropriate publics in an accurate and timely manner.

Rather than working to obstruct reporters, Ivy Lee encouraged them to cover accidents.

Why would a public relations practitioner want to communicate openly about an organization's crises?

associated with government jobs. The Federal Emergency Management Agency (FEMA), which is part of the U.S. Department of Homeland Security, offers a public information office awareness course as part of its Emergency Management Institute. The first module in the web-based course describes the role of their public information officers:

> *They tell the public about services and programs that can affect their lives, like information about staying healthy, fire safety, and changes in community college tuition. They also tell people how they can prepare for a disaster, and protect themselves when disaster strikes. PIOs get their message out by communicating directly with the public, working through the traditional news media and through new media.*[22]

Notice that the role focuses on one-way communication: PIOs "tell the public about," "tell people how" and "get their message out." Public information and publicity/press agentry are both one-way models of communication, but the essence of the public information is quite different in character from press agentry in that the goal is much more focused on providing accurate information than attention-getting. Public affairs officer (PAO) is a more common title in military jobs. Military PAOs can be uniformed or civilian.

Edward Bernays' "Torches of Freedom"

Picture this. On the crowded streets of one of the world's busiest cities, a group of influential young people does something carefully planned but also unexpected by the crowds around them. Behind-the-scenes organizers have worked social networks and even mainstream media to maximize coverage, and the perfectly choreographed event draws the attention of onlookers. Some are shocked. Some are delighted.

No, this isn't a reference to "Worldwide Pillowfight Day" **flash mobs** organized annually for fun and entertainment in dozens of cities around the world. Nor is it part of the One Billion Rising movement, which started on February 14, 2012, as a call to stop violence against women and children and is held every Valentine's Day across international locations.

Instead, the event described was the "Torches of Freedom" march; the influencers were New York debutantes; and the site was an Easter parade on Fifth Avenue in New York. The date, however, was 1930 and the man behind the scenes was Edward Bernays. Bernays competes with Ivy Lee for the legacy of being known as the father of public relations. Oh, and about those "torches of freedom," they were cigarettes marketed to women.

Long before carefully orchestrated events like this one from the One Billion Rising movement in the Philippines of February 14, 2018, were termed "flash mobs," Edward Bernays organized the Torches of Freedom event as part of a sophisticated persuasive campaign.

Flash mob
When a group of people plans and executes a surprise public event or performance that is usually organized via electronic media and often unanticipated by those who are not participants.

Bernays coordinated the Torches of Freedom event on behalf of his client George Washington Hill, president of the American Tobacco Company. Here is how Bernays recalls the project in his memoir, *Biography of an Idea*:

> Hill called me in. *"How can we get women to smoke on the street? They're smoking indoors. But, damn it, if they spend half the time outdoors and we can get 'em to smoke outdoors, we'll damn near double our female market. Do something. Act!"*
>
> *"There's a taboo against such smoking," I said. "Let me consult an expert, Dr. A. A. Brill, the psychoanalyst. He might give me the psychological basis for a woman's desire to smoke, and maybe this will help me."*
>
> *"What will it cost?"*
>
> *"I suppose just a consultation fee."*
>
> *"Shoot," said Hill.*
>
> *[Bernays was no stranger to psychoanalysis. His uncle was Sigmund Freud.]*
>
> *Brill explained to me: "Some women regard cigarettes as symbols of freedom," he told me. "Smoking is a sublimation of oral eroticism; holding a cigarette in the mouth excites the oral zone. It is perfectly normal for women to want to smoke cigarettes. . . . But today the emancipation of women has suppressed many of their feminine desires. . . . Feminine traits are masked. Cigarettes, which are equated with men, become torches of freedom."*
>
> *In this last statement I found a way to help break the taboo against women smoking in public. Why not a parade of women lighting torches of freedom—smoking cigarettes?*[23]

Bernays called friends at *Vogue* magazine to get a list of debutantes. Then he had his secretary, Bertha Hunt, sign and send a personalized telegram to each one. Think direct-messaging, 1930s style:

> *In the interests of equality of the sexes and to fight another sex taboo I and other young women will light another torch of freedom by smoking cigarettes while strolling on Fifth Avenue Easter Sunday. We are doing this to combat the silly prejudice that the cigarette is suitable for the home, the restaurant, the taxicab, the theater lobby, but never no never for the sidewalk. Women smokers and their escorts will stroll from Forty-Eighth Street to Fifty-Fourth Street on Fifth Avenue between Eleven-Thirty and One O'Clock.*[24]

It worked. Bernays reported that the event made front-page news in both photos and text and opened editorial debates in the weeks that followed in publications from coast to coast. As evidence of his success he cited newspaper reports in Massachusetts, Michigan, California and West Virginia that women were smoking on the streets.* "Age-old customs, I learned, could be broken down by a dramatic appeal, disseminated by the network of media."[25] While Bernays' strategy was mostly intuitive and his reasoning was mostly theoretical, the case illustrates the power of public relations tactics as powerful tools for persuasion.

---

*Bernays' claims about the impact of national publicity resulting from the Torches of Freedom event were later called into question by historians.[26]

Two-Way Asymmetrical Communication

Bernays is also credited (or blamed, depending on your perspective) with getting Americans to consume more bacon for breakfast. Bernays researched breakfast diets of his fellow Americans in the early 20th century and found that for the most part Americans ate light breakfasts of "coffee, maybe a roll, and orange juice."[27] So he consulted with his doctor about the benefits of a heavier breakfast and, lo and behold, he found that "a heavy breakfast was sounder from the standpoint of health than a light breakfast because the body loses energy during the night and needs it during the day." He then asked that doctor to write to thousands of other doctors to confirm the benefits of a hearty breakfast. When about 4,500 of the 5,000 doctors to whom they wrote concurred with the conclusion, Bernays publicized the finding nationally.

Interestingly, the resulting news coverage not only headlined the benefits of a hearty breakfast as broadly endorsed by thousands of doctors, but also "many of [the newspapers] stated that bacon and eggs should be embodied with the breakfast, and as a result sales of bacon went up." How did Bernays know that bacon sales went up? Bartlett Arkell, founder and president of the Beech-Nut Packing Company, wrote to him and told him as much. Arkell would know because bacon was one of Beech-Nut's primary products. And Beech-Nut was one of Bernays' clients.

What distinguishes Bernays' work from other publicity stunts is the use of research to understand publics, develop strategy and even to evaluate the results. Bernays applied the social science of the times. He saw the role of the public relations counselor as interpreting publics to clients as well as interpreting clients to publics. He saw public relations as a two-way street.

Today's public relations professionals have access to more scientific research and ridiculous amounts of online data to help them understand publics and to gauge the success of their efforts. Surveys, email responses, Twitter comments, usability studies and focus groups are examples of ways organizations get to know their publics these days, as are less obtrusive sources of data that you as a consumer/internet user may provide without even knowing it. Just check your web browser's cookies.

The torches-of-freedom stunt and bacon-and-eggs "study" had all the trappings of press agentry and publicity, but behind the scenes was evidence of a clever two-way model of communication designed to sell more cigarettes and bacon by leveraging an understanding of desires, diets and deference to authority. The communication may have been two-way in that sense, but it was also clearly not balanced. As Grunig and Hunt put it,

Professionals today have access to more scientific research and online data to help them understand publics and to gauge the success of public relations efforts.

Edward Bernays used research and persuasive tactics to sell bacon.

Was this any more or less ethical than his use of research and persuasion to sell cigarettes?

Doris Fleischman and Edward Bernays worked together for 58 years from the time they were married until her death.

How might this sort of relationship have influenced their work?

Asymmetrical model
Model of public relations in which communication is two-way but unbalanced, with the organization using research/feedback in an effort to persuade publics to change attitudes or behaviors.

Symmetrical model
Model of public relations in which two-way communication is mostly balanced, with the organization as likely to change attitudes or behavior as its publics.

both Bernays and Lee "stressed the importance of communicating the public's point of view to management," but in actual practice, "both did much more to explain management's view to the public."[28] This two-way **asymmetrical model** of communication describes much of the work that modern public relations professionals practice as they advocate and work to persuade publics on behalf of organizations. Bernays may be criticized for promoting tobacco as liberating and bacon as healthy, but his idea of using two-way communication and research to persuade publics can be (and is just as likely to be) applied by organizations with quite different perspectives, such as the American Cancer Society or the American Heart Association.

Bernays later regretted promoting tobacco, a sentiment he expressed plainly in his memoirs, claiming that the dangers of tobacco were not understood at the time. Historians, and Bernays himself, also made it clear that his work was produced in partnership with his wife Doris Fleischman, who retained her last name throughout her career. They worked together for 58 years from their marriage in 1922 until her death in 1980. Bernays lived until 1995 when he died at the age of 103.

Bernays is associated with the unbalanced two-way asymmetrical model in the same way that Ivy Lee has been associated with the public information model and P. T. Barnum has been associated with the publicity/ press agentry model. Each has been painted with broad strokes here mostly for the purposes of providing colorful illustrations of models of public relations. It's worth noting that Edward Bernays himself is largely responsible for framing the history of public relations as a mostly 20th-century progression from press agentry to a sophisticated two-way management function that helps corporations understand public interests. Among the benefits of Bernays' longevity in life and career was that he had decades to write and promote his take on the history of the field he helped define in his earlier years.

Two-Way Symmetrical Communication

Symmetry is balance. In a two-way **symmetrical model** of communication, organizations are just as likely to change as their publics. Historical examples are out there, but are not as easy to come by as splashy stories of press agentry and persuasion. In the epilogue to his nearly 800-page authoritative volume on the history of public relations, *The Unseen Power: Public Relations, A History*, Scott Cutlip suggests that Earl Newsom's work on behalf of Ford Motor Company may fit the bill for an example of two-way symmetrical communication.[29] As principal of his own firm, Earl Newsom and Company, Newsom counseled some of America's largest and most powerful corporations of the mid-20th century such as Standard Oil, Merrill Lynch, Trans-World Airlines, CBS and Ford Motor Company. According to Cutlip, Newsom did not consider himself an "agent" for clients, responsible for publicity and promotion. Rather, Newsom saw himself as a counselor first and foremost, advising clients on management issues of public interest.

In the mid-1950s, Ford Motor Company, along with the rest of America's auto industry, was taking heat for automobile safety, or lack thereof. Newsom counseled Ford to launch a safety campaign. The campaign, however, was much more than a publicity stunt or sales drive. It included a Ford-sponsored national safety forum attended by safety researchers, auto industry engineers and law enforcement officials. Henry Ford II announced a $200,000 grant to Cornell University for the specific purpose of researching highway safety and injury prevention. The campaign also included short movies illustrating the research and development of dashboard crash padding, safety door latches and more safely designed steering wheels. While much of Ford's reputation for safety unraveled in the decades that followed, the effort to use research and two-way communication between an organization (Ford) and its key publics (researchers, safety experts, engineers and ultimately automobile owners) to the mutual benefit of both the organization and its publics illustrated the idea of two-way symmetrical communication. To the extent that Ford changed its operations and vehicle design in the interest of its publics, the relationship was more symmetrical than if they had just kept their research and development closed to outside influence and feedback and used the campaign only to promote later sales.

Arthur Page, whose principles for ethical management of public relations are outlined in Chapter 1, is also seen as an example of an upstanding practitioner with a symmetrical worldview. He saw winning public approval, confidence and trust as essential to successful management. In his words, "All business begins with the public permission and exists by public approval."[30]

Yet, if there is a name associated with the two-way symmetrical model of public relations, it is not a public relations man but a theorist, or actually two theorists. James and Larissa Grunig are emeritus professors at the University of Maryland. Together with many colleagues, the Grunigs developed and executed a decades-long program of research on excellence in public relations. Among the main ideas to emerge from these studies was that "using the two-way symmetrical or a combination of the two-way symmetrical and two-way asymmetrical model (called the mixed-motive model) almost always could increase the contribution of public relations to organizational effectiveness."[31] This line of research and theory, which started in the 1970s and 1980s, continues today.

Although we may not find any one contemporary organization or practitioner to serve as a model of pure and continuous symmetry in public relations, we do see plenty of examples of engaging public relations in which the

Cornell Aeronautical Labs, Liberty Mutual Insurance and Ford Motor Company partnered to develop the 1957 Cornell-Liberty Safety Car as one of the first auto concepts developed from crash testing.

Would you characterize the relationship between Ford and its publics as symmetrical?

engagement is fueled by moments of good, balanced communication between two or more interested parties. Many of these examples come from nonprofits and public utilities.

Public utilities have unique relationships with their publics. Whereas consumers may exercise some power in dealing with many corporations by way of their purchasing decisions, competition for market share is less of a factor than governmental regulation and community responsiveness in how public utilities are managed.

As a consumer you don't get to choose your electric company or water treatment facility the way you choose your brand of light bulb or kitchen water filter. Sure, you may feel rather powerless when you get your electric bill and find out that your rates are going up, but before those rates go up, they must be approved by some sort of regulatory agency or board. And if your electric company proposes a new power plant in your community, you and your neighbors may be quite motivated to find out how that regulation works and voice your position on the issue.

There are many different models for regulating utilities depending on the location, government structure and nature of the service being provided, but the basic idea is that in exchange for getting to operate without normal market competition, public utilities should be able to show that they are serving public interests in good faith. This situation sets the stage for public utilities to come to the table of two-way symmetrical communication with their publics fairly often.

Robbie Alm served for more than a decade as a vice president of Hawaii's largest public utility, Hawaiian Electric Co. (HECO), first as vice president of public affairs and later as executive vice president. In those roles he directly counseled the president and CEO on controversial matters such as the construction of new transmission stations, power plants, wind farms and a generating station on Oahu that was billed as the world's largest combustion turbine fueled by 100 percent biodiesel.[32]

Alm practiced what he calls community-based problem-solving, and it wasn't all rainbows and trade winds. Proposing giant windmills on the serene, small-town island of Lanai to generate power for neighboring Oahu, running power lines across scenic mountain ridges, or building massive power plants anywhere will lead to some major controversy. "I think we're terrible listeners as a society," he said, speaking from experience with so many hotly contested issues. "You can have a

The upper Wa'ahila ridge of Manoa Valley is still mostly free of power lines after key publics in the community voiced opposition to the idea.

Why are utility companies often inclined to practice two-way symmetrical communication?

desired outcome, and that can be taken into account, but you have to let the community guide the process in order to see it through."

Public approval shouldn't be a foregone conclusion. That would be all asymmetrical. In fact, those power lines across the Wa'ahila ridge behind the University of Hawaii at Manoa never were built, and the hillsides of Lanai are still without windmills. Other projects, however, have proceeded with public consent, and Alm earned respect in Hawaii for the symmetry and humility in his style. "If you really try to hold on to your positions no matter what, they're almost guaranteed to slip away," he says, "but if you're really doing the right things, people feel that and they'll work with you."[33] While still working at HECO, Alm joined an independent, nonprofit-funded program called Collaborative Leaders Network (CLN), where he is pursuing his philosophy in working with political, corporate, nonprofit and community leaders in Hawaii on strategies to solve problems of mutual concern.

A Broader Social History of Public Relations

Practitioners of color were under-represented in many 20th-century accounts of public relations history.

What made Joseph V. Baker (1908–1993) a public relations pioneer?

Historical portraits of Barnum, Bernays and even Lee are colored with a tint of infamy. But Barnum served as a mayor of Bridgeport, Connecticut, and founded Bridgeport Hospital. Bernays applied his expertise to promote the NAACP, Thomas Edison's invention of electric lighting, and the field of public relations itself. Ivy Lee worked for the American Red Cross. Indeed, a different sample of cases and clients sets a different tone for the history of public relations. The tactics that each man helped develop can, like any other instrument of communication, be used for good or evil.

Moreover, these men clearly were not the only ones innovating in public relations. Stories of women and people of color may be harder to find in public relations history books and articles of the 20th century, but public relations pioneers like Joseph V. Baker broke through many professional barriers. Baker was the first African American public relations professional to gain national prominence for winning blue chip accounts with national clients like DuPont, U.S. Steel, Chrysler, Gillette, and Procter & Gamble. He also was the first president of the Philadelphia chapter of PRSA and the first African American to earn accreditation from PRSA.[34]

Like Ivy Lee, Baker moved into railroad public relations from journalism. But Baker's career went well beyond the public information model. Public relations scholar Marilyn Kern-Foxworth noted that national corporations and politicians hired his firm for the "comprehensive research on the black consumer market that it provided." [35] When interviewed for a story in *The New York Times* in 1966 titled "Racial Image Challenges Big Business," Baker said, "The higher you go in these corporations, the less knowledge you find. So public relations men have to be knowledgeable and they have to have the guts to transmit cold facts to their clients."[36] Two-way models of public relations require public relations practitioners to interpret

Effective public relations was around long before the rise of 20th-century business in America.

organizations to publics *and* to interpret publics to organizations. Baker epitomized that practice.

Indeed, historians have debunked the "Big Bang Barnum" narrative as a comprehensive accounting of the birth of public relations.[37] And a broader, more inclusive, social history of public relations reveals that effective public relations was around long before the rise of 20th-century business in America.

Historians Margot Opdyke Lamme at the University of Alabama and Karen Miller Russell at the University of Georgia culled through decades of literature on the history of public relations and found more than 70 articles, chapters and books that focused on history prior to the 20th century.[38] Besides business, they found public relations to have a rich heritage in three "deep veins" of history: religion; education, nonprofit and reform; and politics and government.

Religion

Lamme and Russell highlighted evidence of public relations as early as the first century. Although I wouldn't go so far as to say that St. Paul was a PR guy, at least one public relations historian identifies Paul as "one of the most influential communicators in history." "In the contemporary language of public relations, he played all its roles: writer-technician, liaison, manager and strategist," wrote Robert E. Brown of Salem State University with an admitted sense of anachronism in making the case.[39] In addition to authoring much of the New Testament, St. Paul deftly segmented his publics (Jews and early Christians), tailored his rhetoric for his audiences, visited churches, and was effective enough in spreading his message to change the course of religion and world history.

Religious leaders and organizations remain adept at both traditional and emerging public relations tactics. The Religion Communicators Council (RCC), which was chartered in 1929 and promotes "faith perspectives in public discourse," claims to be the oldest public relations professional organization in the United States.[40] Current RCC members include public relations practitioners representing Bahá'í, Christian, Hindu, Jewish and Muslim faiths.

Examples of religions using social media are everywhere. Rabbi Josh Yuter was celebrated by the National Jewish Outreach Program as a top-ten Jewish influencer for his use of social media: "Yuter is not only a pulpit rabbi. He's a popular blogger, tweeter, and podcaster (his Jewish-themed podcasts were downloaded more than 20,000 times last year.)"[41] Even the pope has a Twitter page: @Pontifex.

Education

College commencements are a time of great pomp and circumstance. Graduation ceremonies are also annual fundraising campaign kickoffs. As university foundation officials stand at podiums across the globe in caps and gowns each year and plead with new graduates to remember their alma maters as they move on and start earning larger paychecks, these school officials hope

St. Paul has been referred to as one of the most influential communicators in history.

Was St. Paul practicing public relations?

that commencement acts as the start of a beautiful friendship. While we may not know exactly when this practice started, Harvard College is known to have begun fundraising campaigns as early as 1641 when college representatives were sent to England to emphasize how the college was educating American Indians as part of a pitch for donations.[42] In the 1700s Princeton and Columbia (at the time named King's College) both used news releases to publicize their commencement ceremonies.[43] Modern Princeton students also earn publicity, though the channels and tone have changed.

When Codey Babineaux of Lafayette, La., opened his digital acceptance notice from Princeton University, he recorded it and posted it on Twitter, and it was celebrated millions of times over—with more than 4.68 million views.[44]

Interviewed by *The New York Times* for a story about how universities are shifting communication strategies to connect with new generations of students, Babineaux said he appreciated the video orientation that Princeton staff and students produced for his incoming class of 2022—a "Princetified" cover of Taylor Swift's "22"—because it was "hilarious" and "didn't try too hard."[45] He said he also had watched older videos, including commencement ceremonies, and thought "that will be on my Instagram page in four years."

Politics and Government

Lamme and Russell found examples of public-relations-type activity dating back to Alexander the Great in the fourth century B.C. Tutored by Aristotle (speaking of rhetoric) as a boy, Alexander went on to become not only a great warrior but also a great war reporter, or at least he saw to it that others sent stories of his exploits in battle back to Macedonian courts. Early American history is also chock-full of classic public relations strategies and tactics such as sloganeering ("Give me liberty or give me death!"), **pseudo-events** organized primarily for media coverage (Boston Tea Party), and opinion-editorial writing (The Federalist Papers).[46]

Of course, the arena for American politics is almost as raucous in the digital era. Democratic presidential candidate Howard Dean, known for his enthusiastic stump-speech screaming in the 2004 election, also has been called the godfather of

Religious organizations remain among the most spirited in public relations.

Why do you think that is?

Colleges and universities have been practicing public relations for hundreds of years.

How does your school communicate with you, and how might that change in years to come?

Pseudo-events are organized primarily for media coverage.

Was the Boston Tea Party a public relations stunt?

Pseudo-event
An event organized primarily for the purpose of generating media coverage.

modern social media campaigning. Dean's campaign used the internet to raise money like no one had ever done before at that level of politics, racking up loads of small online donations that added up to compete with the numbers generated by more traditional large donations.[47] Dean didn't win the election, but he reset the stage for political campaign financing. Many analysts see this shift in strategy as a major factor in Barack Obama's two subsequent election victories in 2008 and 2012.

Then, in 2016, Donald Trump's political rallies, both during and after his election, drew historic amounts of media attention as he and his events made headlines at unprecedented rates. The Trump campaign's success in making so much news can largely be attributed to Trump's ability to garner "earned media," a topic discussed in more detail in Chapter 7. As observed by *The New York Times'* Nicholas Confessore and Karen Yourish:

> *Like all candidates, he benefits from what is known as earned media: news and commentary about his campaign on television, in newspapers and magazines, and on social media. Earned media typically dwarfs paid media in a campaign. The big difference between Mr. Trump and other candidates is that he is far better than any other candidate—maybe than any candidate ever—at earning media.*

Major Motivations for Public Relations

Lamme and Russell's broader view of public relations history reveals several major motivations for public relations throughout the ages. These include recruitment, legitimacy, agitation and advocacy, in addition to profit.

Recruitment
St. Paul recruited for the Christian Church. The Sons of Liberty recruited fellow colonists for their revolutionary activities like the Boston Tea Party. Today, public relations practitioners are involved in the recruitment of volunteers for nonprofits, new members for political organizations, new hires for corporations, and, of course, new students for colleges and universities.

While the timeless tactics of face-to-face visits, meetings and events are still the backbone of many recruiting efforts, today's recruiters are just as likely to use social networking sites and other forms of social media to carry out their work. In partnership with research firm Future Workplace, human resources (HR) technology company Career Arc surveyed 616 HR professionals and 438 job seekers in 2017 and found that 91 percent of employers in the sample reported using social media in recruiting. On the other side of the job market, Career Arc found that job seekers also pay close attention to online review sites in deciding where to apply. A majority (55 percent) of job seekers who had reported reading a negative review of an employer responded that they decided not to apply at that company.[48]

In a study of university officials, San Diego State University Professor Kaye Sweetser and I found that those communicators working in admissions and recruiting were among the most enthusiastic adopters of social media for public relations work. As one participant in the study put it, there's a "competitive advantage" in using social media "to attract and maintain a younger demographic, which is adept and attuned to social media." Another said, "If [students] are there and that is where they naturally are, then you have to go to [that] market. . . . We need to be there."[49]

Legitimacy

Öffentlichkeitsarbeit means "work for the public sphere" in German.[50] Scholars have found Öffentlichkeitsarbeit to date back as far as the 10th century when Austrian monarchs and statesmen disseminated coins, pictures and pamphlets to legitimize their positions.[51] Lamme and Russell also highlighted studies showing how early Christian churches sought legitimacy, and later how members of the church were used to enhance the legitimacy of others' efforts.

In the 18th century when James Oglethorpe, who founded the American colony of Georgia, was looking to promote the settlement of Savannah, he leveraged the endorsement of the Archbishop of Canterbury. "Oglethorpe and his associates were well aware of the value of the staged event to attract public attention—the pseudo-event is sine qua non of today's promotion," wrote Scott Cutlip in one such historical recounting. Oglethorpe traveled to England to "rally for support" and brought an Indian chief and some of his warriors with him. To boost legitimacy, Oglethorpe's itinerary included a staged meeting with the Archbishop of Canterbury. The visit of Oglethorpe and the Indians generated lots of publicity, and Oglethorpe's travel party upon his return to Georgia included two shiploads of new colonists.

In the 20th century, communication researchers identified a function of mass media that they called **status conferral**. Paul Lazarsfeld and Robert Merton wrote in 1948 that "the mass media bestow prestige and enhance the authority of individuals and groups by legitimizing their status."[52] For this reason, many public relations practitioners would consider it a crowning achievement to get their client or organization (or themselves) featured on the Today show, in *Time* magazine or on the front page of their major metropolitan newspaper. That type of coverage, provided it's positive, means instant legitimacy.

> *Today's recruiters are just as likely to use social networking sites and other forms of social media to carry out their work as they are more traditional tactics.*

Status conferral
When media pay attention to individuals and groups and therefore enhance their authority or bestow prestige on them.

Google confers status.

Why do you think Google recognition matters so much?

Major news and search sites confer legitimacy by way of algorithms that take into account what users are searching for and linking to.

Organic search results
Search engine results that are generated because of their relevance to the search terms entered by users and not resulting directly from paid placement as advertising.

Search engine optimization (SEO)
Process of improving the position of a specific website in the organic search results of search engines.

Today, Google, Yahoo, Bing and other major news and search sites confer legitimacy by way of algorithms that take into account what users are searching for and linking to. In a sense, they crowdsource search results. Rather than a small group of editors acting as gatekeepers for what gets covered, decisions about what gets the top billing in organic search results depend on automated calculations. **Organic search results** are those that are not paid for as advertising or sponsored links. An entire field of practice known as **search engine optimization (SEO)** has sprouted, and public relations practitioners are among the most interested in sharpening their skills. The goal of SEO is to make your links rank as highly as possible in the results when someone does a keyword search for your client's name, products or services. Having a client show up on the first page of Google results for their business's keywords is, for many, as much of a professional win as making the cover of a magazine or newspaper.

Internet power players have come to confer legitimacy in other ways too. In November 2012, over the objections of Israel and the United States, the United Nations General Assembly voted to recognize the state of Palestine, upgrading its U.N. membership from "observer entity" to "nonmember observer state." Legitimacy was implied. But that legitimacy was bolstered significantly five months later in May 2013 when Google changed the name on www.google.ps from "Palestinian territories" to simply "Palestine." As noted in a follow-up story by NPR's Emily Harris, "Google didn't announce the name change, but it didn't have to. In a place where small gestures can carry great symbolism, Palestinians noticed right away."[53] This also symbolized the rise to global power of Google itself.

In 2019, Statista.com reported that Facebook had 2.38 billion active monthly users, which is a billion more than the entire population of China.[54] In 2018, researchers estimated that Google processed more than 3.5 billion searches a day, almost half as many searches as the estimated world population of 7.6 billion people at that time. As legitimate world entities in their own right, global internet companies influence status conferral and legitimization like no media before them.

Agitation

Getting people fired up has long been a motivation of strategic communicators. For example, scholars have studied how Napoleon used the press to cultivate hatred of England and how the Female Moral Reform Society in America in the 19th century went as far as to purchase a newspaper and build its circulation as part of the organization's organized efforts to eradicate sexually transmitted diseases and prostitution.[55]

Organized agitation has evolved into new forms with the rise of the internet. In October 2017, *The New York Times* and *The New Yorker* published reports exposing allegations from dozens of women who accused high-powered Hollywood film producer Harvey Weinstein of rape, sexual assault and sexual abuse over a period of more than three decades. Those mass media reports drew a tremendous amount of attention to issues of sexual assault and harassment, particularly in the United States film and entertainment industries. But the agitation quickly elevated to the level of a full-blown worldwide social movement after one of the accusers, actor Alyssa Milano, posted a simple tweet: "If all the women who have been sexually harassed or assaulted wrote 'Me too' as a status, we might give people a sense of the magnitude of the problem." Tens of thousands of people replied directly to Milano's tweet, including celebrities and everyday Twitter users with disturbing accounts of abuse in their own lives.

Alyssa Milano's tweet echoed around the world.

What factors made #MeToo such a huge movement?

Within days, the MeToo hashtag was being used by millions across Twitter, Instagram and Facebook. Facebook reported to media that within 24 hours, 4.7 million users had engaged in the #MeToo conversation, with more than 12 million posts, comments and reactions.[56] Milano is recognized for starting the MeToo hashtag, but the actual social movement was originated by Tarana Burke, founder of Just Be Inc., "a youth organization focused on the health, well being and wholeness of young women of color."[57] While that mission is nothing but positive, Burke wrote that the movement started "in the deepest, darkest place in my soul." Burke recalled working primarily with children of color and hearing heartbreaking stories of abuse and neglect when she met a girl named Heaven, who confided her horrible experiences:

> *I could not find the strength to say out loud the words that were ringing in my head over and over again as she tried to tell me what she had endured. . . . I watched her walk away from me as she tried to recapture her secrets and tuck them back into their hiding place. I watched her put her mask back on and go back into the world like she was all alone and I couldn't even bring myself to whisper . . . me too.*[58]

Promoting a cause also means supporting a mission, which requires strategy beyond mere awareness.

From that very private moment to Burke's work to start the movement, to Milano's tweet, to the many women (and men) who first shared their #MeToo's online, to the millions who helped spread the message, the movement gained momentum well beyond any publicity stunt or marketing ploy. Why? Because the movement resonated on a deep, human level—a level where agitation has its most profound effects. With the help of many committed campaigners, #MeToo still echoes as a rallying cry against sexual abuse and harassment and has emboldened many victims to stand up to some of the most powerful men in their lives—and in some cases the world.

Advocacy

On the flip side of agitation is **advocacy**, which is the very first professional value listed in the PRSA Code of Ethics. Whereas agitation has been used in history in opposition efforts, advocacy in the history of public relations has meant promoting persons, organizations and nations. As an example of one of the longest-running promotional campaigns in history, Lamme and Russell highlight the Catholic Church's "1,000-year public relations campaign." Featuring St. James as a patron saint to Spain, it promoted both the church and Spanish nationalism in the 9th and 10th centuries.[59] The very term **propaganda** derives from the work of the Catholic Church to propagate faith. Prior to the world wars of the 20th century, the word did not carry the negative connotation it has today.

Advocacy and promotion are easy to spot. Colored ribbons are prime examples. Pink ribbons for breast cancer awareness, yellow ribbons to support troops, red to support the fight against AIDS and HIV, even periwinkle to support research on stomach and esophageal cancers. Each ribbon is a symbol of a cause with organizations working on behalf of the cause. Of course, mere awareness is only part of the process of advocacy. Promoting a cause also means supporting a mission, which requires strategy beyond mere awareness. Successful propagation of the faith may be evidenced in church membership numbers, attendance and institutional partnerships. Fighting cancer requires money for research, physician involvement, preventive behavior and early detection of treatable conditions.

Profit

Of course, generating revenue has been a major motivator for public relations throughout the ages, and not just for big corporations. Even "nonprofits" such as churches, governments, foundations, schools, nongovernmental organizations and foundations have sought to raise money as seen in the examples discussed in this chapter. That said, one of the largest roles for public relations has been and always will be working in conjunction with advertising and marketing to promote the sale of products, services and ideas. Chapter 3 will cover the differences and, perhaps more important, the integration of public relations with related functions such as marketing and advertising.

Cancer Awareness Ribbon Colors

All Cancers	Lavender
Appendix Cancer	Amber
Bladder Cancer	Marigold/Blue/Purple
Brain Cancer	Grey
Breast Cancer	Pink
Carcinoid Cancer	Zebra Stripe
Cervical Cancer	Teal/White
Childhood Cancer	Gold
Colon Cancer	Dark Blue
Esophageal Cancer	Periwinkle
Gallbladder/Bile Duct Cancer	Kelly Green
Head & Neck Cancer	Burgundy/Ivory
Hodgkin's Lymphoma	Violet
Kidney Cancer	Orange
Leiomyosarcoma	Purple
Leukemia	Orange
Liver Cancer	Emerald Green
Lung Cancer	White
Lymphoma	Lime
Melanoma	Black
Multiple Myeloma	Burgundy
Ovarian Cancer	Teal
Pancreatic Cancer	Purple
Prostate Cancer	Light Blue
Sarcoma/Bone Cancer	Yellow
Stomach Cancer	Periwinkle
Testicular Cancer	Orchid
Thyroid Cancer	Teal/Pink/Blue
Uterine Cancer	Peach
Honors Caregivers	Plum

CHOOSE HOPE® 888-348-HOPE · www.choosehope.com
SERVING THE CANCER COMMUNITY. SUPPORTING CANCER RESEARCH.

Colored ribbons are prime examples of advocacy and promotion.

How many of these colors would you recognize? What are the benefits of this type of awareness?

Voices from the Field

Karen Miller Russell

University of Georgia Professor Karen Miller Russell studies and teaches media history with an emphasis on public relations. Dr. Russell served as editor of the *Journal of Public Relations Research* from 2010 to 2015 and is author of *The Voice of Business: Hill and Knowlton and Postwar Public Relations* as well as numerous articles for communication and public relations journals. A former public relations writer for the Wisconsin Department of Transportation, public relations specialist for the American Camping Association and former photography and publicity assistant for Common Wealth Development, Dr. Russell is also interested in social media, globalization and corporate social responsibility initiatives.

Many textbooks have presented well-known historical events like the Boston Tea Party as examples of early public relations, even though no one at the time would have thought to call it PR. Do you have concerns about that as a historian?

The Boston Tea Party and other pre-20th-century events may not have been "public relations" as we know it today, but they definitely belong in PR history. Many scholars have assumed that PR started in the United States around the turn of the 20th century, but I'd argue that it started long before that in politics, religion and reform movements. These groups developed the strategies and tactics that eventually became institutionalized in corporate public relations practice, and that's a legitimate subject for study.

The UAB and other accrediting bodies include knowledge of history as part of their criteria for accreditation. How does that kind of knowledge benefit practitioners beyond helping them get the credential?

There are three good reasons for studying PR history. First, we can always learn from seeing what worked and didn't work in the past, especially if you can pinpoint the reasons behind success or failure. Second, although times have changed, basic principles of public relations remain the same. You may be communicating on a different platform, but you're still trying to share information, manage a reputation, advocate and build relationships, just as people have been doing over the ages. Third, studying history provides context for understanding what's happening today. For example, I studied business responses to the 1950s Civil Rights Movement with co-author Margot Opdycke Lamme, and we learned that although U.S. corporate executives often sincerely wanted to help bring about social change, their commitment to it slackened when public pressure died down. Seeing how that happened and what it meant to both organizations and activists can help us understand what's happening in race relations today.

How has America's history shaped differences between U.S. public relations and public relations in other countries? How has the U.S. "imported" or "exported" public relations as a practice?

Natalia Salcedo, a Spanish historian, argues that the development of public relations varies in different countries because of the history and culture of each nation. It makes sense that public relations in Eastern European countries that were behind the Iron Curtain during the Cold War would be quite different from public relations in North America and Western Europe, to take just one example. But there has also been a great deal of cross-pollination within companies operating multinationally or among politicians and diplomats watching what their counterparts are doing in other countries. The United States certainly exported some aspects of PR practices after World War II, but no doubt American executives also learned from working in Asia, Europe and South America during the same time period.

Ethics: Transparency, Objectivity and Advocacy

Disclosure and dissemination of information is a cornerstone of public relations ethics. Media ethicist Patrick Lee Plaisance argues that transparency is ethical not because of its strategic outcomes (e.g., reputation for doing the right thing), but because it is essential to human dignity.[60] He cites philosopher Immanuel Kant in building a case that the best reason to be transparent is respect for other people. By making available all relevant information, we respect others' autonomy in informed decision-making. Grunig and Hunt painted Ivy Lee as an exemplar of the public information model of public relations: "Lee viewed the public as made up of rational human beings who, if they are given complete and accurate information, would make the right decisions."[61]

As a former journalist, like many of today's public relations practitioners, Lee embraced the general idea of **objectivity**. I say "general idea" here because objectivity is a philosophically elusive concept. Oxford Dictionaries define the adjective "objective" as "not influenced by personal feelings or opinions in considering and representing facts."[62] But journalists, or any other human beings for that matter, struggle with total removal of feelings and opinions in selecting, interpreting and reporting facts. You won't find objectivity specifically stated in the Society of Professional Journalists (SPJ) Code of Ethics, but that doesn't mean they have abandoned the idea of pursuing truth. "Journalism does not pursue truth in an absolute or philosophical sense, but it can—and must—pursue it in a practical sense," according to the Pew Research Center's principles of journalism.[63]

Whereas Lee identified with journalists (and many journalists identified with Lee), Edward Bernays made it a point to define public relations as much more than a journalistic function. Bernays embraced advocacy, and in doing so unabashedly distinguished public relations from journalism. Today, there is little debate about advocacy's place in public relations as opposed to journalism.

Advocacy is a value in the PRSA Code of Ethics: "We serve the public interest by acting as responsible advocates for those we represent. We

Objectivity
State of being free from the influence of personal feelings or opinions in considering and representing facts.

provide a voice in the marketplace of ideas, facts, and viewpoints to aid informed public debate."[64]

Advocacy is a no-no in the SPJ Code of Ethics, where journalists are advised to "distinguish between advocacy and news reporting." "Analysis and commentary should be labeled and not misrepresent fact or context. Distinguish news from advertising and shun hybrids that blur the lines between the two."[65]

The case has even been made that Edward Bernays did more to advance the ethical evolution of public relations than Ivy Lee because Bernays embraced advocacy and encouraged writing it into a code of ethics rather than trying to act as a journalist while on the payroll of a non-news organization. Genevieve McBride wrote in the Journal of Mass Media Ethics in 1989 that public relations' struggle toward professionalism would benefit from a view of history that embraces Bernays' "disassociation from the journalistic perspective" rather than Lee's "dysfunctional standard of objectivity."[66]

Whether you practice public information with a journalistic set of values or advocacy with a penchant for persuasion, the principle of transparency is critical. In a democracy, it is OK to advocate, as long as you are transparent about what you're doing, meaning that you respect others' autonomy in informed decision-making.

Transparency also offers a useful lens for studying public relations history. In what ways was Bernays' work for Beech-Nut ethical? Unethical? How about Ivy Lee's work with Nazis in Germany? Should Lee be let off the hook because he was transparent? Lee could (and did) argue that his work in counseling Germans in the late 1930s was consistent with his respect for rational human decision-making. He said he was working to improve mutual understanding between Americans and Germans. In a congressional hearing in 1934, Lee testified that he counseled German propaganda minister Joseph Goebbels and other German leaders that "they would never in the world get the American people reconciled to their treatment of the Jews."[67] The same hearing revealed that Lee was receiving $25,000 a year from the German dye trust for his public relations counsel. Assuming Lee was upfront about his business arrangement, was his work ethical?

> *The principle of transparency is critical whether you practice public information with a journalistic set of values or with advocacy.*

In Case You Missed It

While public relations tactics have been around since the dawn of civilization, our body of knowledge about the field has come a long way in the past few decades. Here are some time-tested truths, along with a slightly new perspective:

- Organizations must get messages out accurately and reliably, even when they are not seeking to gain extra attention.

- Professionals today have access to more scientific research and online data to help them understand publics and to gauge the success of public relations efforts.

- Effective public relations was around long before the rise of 20th-century business in America.

- Today's recruiters are just as likely to use social networking sites and other forms of social media to carry out their work as they are to use more traditional tactics.

- Major news and search sites confer legitimacy by way of algorithms that take into account what users are searching for and linking to.

- Promoting a cause also means supporting a mission, which requires strategy beyond mere awareness.

- The principle of transparency is critical whether you practice public information with a journalistic set of values or with advocacy.

SUMMARY

2.1 Analyze public relations models on one-way/two-way and asymmetrical/symmetrical dimensions using examples and key figures from history.

One-way models of public relations are all about getting information out and, in the case of press agentry, getting attention. The public information model is one-way too, but it is more concerned with accuracy. Two-way models range from asymmetrical, in which organizations use research and feedback to persuade publics, to symmetrical, in which organizations and publics exhibit more mutual communication and change. Barnum, Lee and Bernays are often associated with press agentry, public information and scientific persuasion, respectively. But a fuller history recognizes the contributions of many other innovative communicators and strategists. Twentieth-century public relations also owes its development to figures like Doris Fleischman, Arthur Page and Earl Newsom.

2.2 Integrate knowledge of social history with knowledge of public relations.

Business, religion, education, politics and government are intertwined with public relations throughout history inasmuch as organizations and publics have communicated, persuaded and adapted to each other over time. From St. Paul promoting the New Testament to modern bloggers posting Islamic infographics, and from Alexander the Great's self-reporting war exploits to Donald Trump's political rallies, all of our major institutions have been and continue to be influenced by public relations.

2.3 Identify common motivations for strategic communication in history.

While the term *public relations* may not have existed in common use prior to the 20th century, its functions and tactics have been applied in pursuit of recruitment, legitimacy, agitation, advocacy and profit throughout human history.

2.4 Discuss the ethics of transparency, objectivity and advocacy.

Edward Bernays and Ivy Lee can be compared. Lee pursued journalistic integrity, but he still worked on the payroll of specific organizations to which he was loyal. Bernays embraced advocacy. While both public relations and journalism value transparency as a value, public relations values advocacy more and journalism values objectivity more.

DISCUSSION QUESTIONS

1. How would P. T. Barnum use social media? Provide some specific examples.

2. **CASE STUDY** There's no doubt that IHOP generated a lot of buzz with their name-change stunt. Aside from attention, what kind of benefits do you think resulted? (Feel free to research the case online.) What were the limitations? What were the risks?

3. Both Ivy Lee and Edward Bernays have been called the "father of public relations." Does either one of them deserve that title? Why or why not?

4. **CASE STUDY** In what ways is the Torches of Freedom case a "good example" of public relations? In what ways is it a "bad example"?

5. Some say that real-life public relations is better described with a mixed-motive model in which one-way and asymmetrical communication are used by the same organizations that are also practicing symmetrical communication. Describe a relationship that you have as an individual that could be seen as mixed-motive.

6. Find an example of a blogger or social media influencer doing journalism, and describe how that is different from public relations.

7. Asymmetrical public relations is much more common in everyday practice than symmetrical. Does that mean most of the field is inherently unethical? Why or why not?

KEY TERMS

Advocacy 48
Asymmetrical model 38
Flash mob 35
Material information 33
News release 31

Objectivity 51
Organic search results 46
Press agentry/publicity model 30
Propaganda 48
Pseudo-event 42

Public information model 32
Public information officer (PIO) 33
Search engine optimization (SEO) 46
Status conferral 45
Symmetrical model 38

CHAPTER 3

Convergence and Integrated Communication

Red Bull's media content serves public relations functions by promoting more than just energy drink products. Is Red Bull an energy drink company that produces media content, or a media company that produces energy drinks?

KEY LEARNING OUTCOMES

3.1 Analyze how different forms of convergence affect public relations.

3.2 Define advertising and marketing, and discuss how those functions may diverge from public relations.

3.3 Discuss how functions of advertising and marketing may be integrated with public relations.

3.4 Explain how public relations adds value to

organizations and publics beyond advertising and marketing.

3.5 Discuss the role of public relations in the free flow of information in society.

RELATED UNIVERSAL ACCREDITATION BOARD COMPETENCY AREAS

1.6 AUDIENCE IDENTIFICATION • **2.2** ETHICAL BEHAVIOR • **4.3** KNOWLEDGE OF THE FIELD

5.6 ORGANIZATIONAL SKILLS • **6.5** NETWORKS

Black box fallacy
False notion that predicts that most human communication needs will eventually be satisfied with a single device.

Admit it. One of the very first things you do in the morning is check your media device. If not, then you are a better person than I. I watch the apps update. I check my social network sites to see what clever memes my friends are propagating. I check media-business news and see how the latest round of mergers and acquisitions affects the products and services I use. Whether I realize it or not through the blur of my just-opened eyes, the world delivered to me by my bundled talk, text and data plan has continued to converge and re-converge as I have slept. Your new smartphone can undoubtedly handle many more functions than your last smartphone. There's a good chance many of your favorite TV shows, movies, music and news sources are owned by the same big company. Your cultural interests increasingly overlap with people from all over the planet. This is the world you, your organization and your publics inhabit. And, it's ever more technologically, culturally and economically converged every time you upload, download, like, snap, submit, share or agree to yet another end-user license agreement.

Communication firms are merging and converging with one another in the global marketplace of ideas, while professional communicators continue to weigh the pros and cons of integrating public relations with advertising and marketing. Making sense of all this convergence and integration and what it means for public relations requires an understanding of the multiple dimensions of convergence, an appreciation for the workings of integrated communication, and a respect for classic principles of public relations that apply steadily as times and technologies change.

Convergence

Convergence is a concept that can be difficult to understand, in part because it has different meanings in different contexts. USC Professor Henry Jenkins recommends thinking about multiple processes of convergence.[1] Convergence can be a technological process, but convergence also describes cultural, economic and professional processes.

Technological Convergence

We may be seduced by the idea that one day all of our media needs will be met with one elegant device. Jenkins calls it the **black box fallacy**. "Sooner or later, the argument goes, all media content is going to flow through a single black box into our living rooms (or, in the mobile scenario, through black boxes we carry around with us everywhere we go),"[2] but, as he points out, it just doesn't work out that way.

For me it was the iPhone 3GS. I was one stoked customer walking out of the Apple store in the summer of 2009 with my brand new device. In my hand I held a phone, a compass, a GPS, a camera, a calculator, a news reader, a video recorder, a voice recorder, an audio player, a TV and an app store that would let me turn the thing into my own portal to Twitter, Facebook, LinkedIn or any other social network service I wanted. My mediated life was going to be simple and uncluttered. Or not. As the years go by, my family and I seem to be losing the war against technoclutter. Old tablets, phones, earbuds, cameras, charging wires, game consoles, Bluetooth devices, routers, printers, monitors and remote controls litter our home, car and office.

Make no mistake. **Technological convergence** is real. Technological convergence brings together formerly separate technical capabilities. As multiple forms of media content get digitized, opportunities for mixing and mashing them increase. "When words, images and sounds are transformed into digital information, we expand the potential relationships between them and enable them to flow across platforms," wrote Jenkins.[3] **Augmented reality (AR)** extends the reach of digital information by overlaying technology on top of live video imagery. AR converges GPS with camera and virtual reality technology. We see technological convergence everywhere—on our smartphones, car dashboards, kids'

Black box fallacy: Multipurpose devices have not simplified life as much as some have hoped.

Why do you think that is?

Augmented reality is a form of technological convergence.

What types of AR applications might be useful in public relations?

Technological convergence (aka digital convergence)
When information of various forms such as sound, text, images and data are digitized, affording communication across common media.

Augmented reality
Technology that overlays digital information onto media representations of the real world.

Public relations people must understand other dimensions of convergence beyond the technological ones.

games, and even old-fashioned TV. In fact, one of the first uses of AR for mass media was the digital yellow first-down line that appeared on football fields in TV broadcasts during the late 1990s.

But human uses, needs and desires for media vary widely from person to person. There's no single solution for everyone. And there's no single media solution for any one person across every situation. This is why that magical black box doesn't exist, and it also is why public relations people must understand other dimensions of convergence beyond the technological ones.

Cultural Convergence

Just as technological convergence presents an apparent paradox (media are combining at the very same time that media technologies are proliferating), so too does **cultural convergence**. On one hand, we are witnessing vast cultural hegemony. Hegemony—now here's a term usually reserved for the most critical approaches to public relations.

Stemming from Marxism, cultural hegemony occurs when a ruling class imposes its social, political or economic ideals on subordinate groups in society at the expense of cultural diversity. Public relations people are rarely portrayed as the good guys in these scenarios. "Americanization" or "McDonaldization" are examples, with "an increasing convergence on specific forms of artistic, culinary, or musical culture—usually, but not exclusively, moving from the United States, via newly global media, to the rest of the world," writes Yale Law Professor David Singh Grewal.[4] On the other hand, clearly, "cultural borrowing" increasingly works in other directions. McDonald's restaurants in India serve chicken and fish as well as curry-infused options.

To the degree that successful public relations entails changes in human attitudes, knowledge and behavior, public relations people must work toward an enlightened understanding of their organizations' roles and their own personal roles in cultural exchanges. Jenkins describes cultural convergence as "both a top-down corporate-driven process and a bottom-up consumer-driven process."[5] Public relations people work where the two meet. They must understand and communicate from the standpoint of their organization's cultural values while understanding and interpreting their publics' cultures back to the organization as well. Participating actively and transparently in public forums—constructively

Cultural convergence works in two directions for McDonald's, which exports mainstream American culture but also adopts local tastes.

Is this a balanced exchange? What are some ramifications of this type of cultural convergence?

engaging **participatory culture**—is an important part of managing relationships, particularly in media environments characterized by cultural convergence.

Economic Convergence

Ketchum is a huge public relations agency with offices and affiliates in 70 countries.[6] Ketchum represents consumer-brand clients ranging from Wendy's to Ikea to Gillette to Doritos. Ketchum and its subsidiaries also have served government agencies like the IRS and the Department of Education in the United States and international clients including the government of Russia.

If Ketchum is huge, Omnicom is huger. Omnicom acquired Ketchum as a subsidiary in 1996.[7] Omnicom is a global advertising, marketing and communication services conglomerate that owns firms providing services in advertising, strategic media planning, digital marketing, direct marketing and, of course, public relations. Omnicom serves 5,000 clients in more than 100 countries.[8] The vastness of this network entails not just public relations, but advertising, marketing, lobbying and emerging digital and social media services as well. This is **economic convergence**.

As with technological and cultural convergence, economic convergence presents a contradiction. At the same time that agencies are diversifying services, building networks and opening global offices to serve geographically unique clients and publics in almost every corner of every continent, the overall number of major corporate players is dwindling. The Ketchum family tree is just one example that illustrates the size and scope of economic convergence in strategic communication. Omnicom, along with global conglomerates Publicis Groupe, WPP, and Interpublic, top the list of holding firms ranked by revenues from public relations operations.[9]

If you watched the Super Bowl (or rather, the Super Bowl commercials) in 2018, you might remember the award-winning Tide ad titled "It's a Tide Ad." The spot, which starred actor David Harbour, presented a weird mashup of typical Super Bowl–type ad vignettes (a bottle of beer sliding down a bar, a car racing along an open road, hipsters drinking soda on the beach, a handsome model giving himself a close shave in the mirror, etc.). All of the vignettes also showcased spotlessly clean wardrobes. In an interview with *Adweek*, Harbour described the ad as "wildly self-aware":

> *The fact that you have this character who's sort of this Rod Serling of The Twilight Zone of advertising, sort of coming in and being like, "Wow, maybe every ad is like a Tide ad," and then he pops up in all of these different ads to kind of reveal to you that what you think you're watching is not actually what you're watching. . . .*[10]

Adweek declared it the winner of Super Bowl 52. And at one point, #TideAd was the Number 2 trending topic on Twitter (behind the Super Bowl itself). The ad also became the topic for more than 640 stories in

Participatory culture
A culture in which private citizens and publics are as likely to produce and share as they are to consume; commonly applied in mediated contexts in which consumers produce and publish information online.

Economic convergence
When various media organizations and functions are merged under a single ownership structure. This form of media convergence is different from the term economists use to describe trends in world economies.

other media, and Tide's parent company Procter & Gamble (P&G) reported double digit sales growth for Tide Ultra Oxi after the game.[11] The creative composition of the ad was weirdly effective, and so was the mix of companies behind the ad.

Ad agency Saatchi & Saatchi claimed the awards, but behind the scenes P&G had assembled a joint creative team from several agencies to produce the spot. P&G pays more for household product advertising than any other company in the world and uses that leverage to push for even more convergence among its agencies. P&G's chief brand officer, Marc Pritchard, liked what he saw happen with the Tide ad. "What we found [was that], when you have a Super Bowl or Olympics deadline, you have high degrees of speed and focus and make things happen," Pritchard told *The Wall Street Journal*. "What we want to really do is institutionalize that approach."[12] To cut costs and increase efficiency, for example, P&G has formed a stand-alone agency that includes employees from several different ad agencies including Saatchi & Saatchi.

"It's a Tide Ad" scored a big win with this Super Bowl spot created and produced by a team from several different agencies working for Procter & Gamble.

How does economic convergence affect you as a consumer? How might economic convergence affect you in your career?

Economic convergence in media means big companies are building global networks that provide top-notch expertise to clients ranging from specialized and localized organizations to mainstream companies reaching the widest possible audiences and publics. At the same time, the number of voices in the marketplace, when defined by corporate interests, is shrinking. For Super Bowl advertising, much of the marketplace is for commodities like beer, automobiles and detergent. For public relations, which operates more in the marketplace of ideas than in the marketplace of commodities, the stakes may even be higher. We may not lose sleep after learning that competing brands of sodas and chips are represented by agencies owned by the same parent companies. But what if the clients are different national governments? How do you feel about a single communication firm representing both tobacco companies and healthcare organizations? How do you feel about the NFL partnering with a nonprofit organization to air anti-abuse ads during the Super Bowl? Economic convergence at the corporate level requires extra attention to public relations' role in society at large.

Professional convergence
When various functions of professional communication such as publicity, advertising, online services and marketing are combined to improve strategy.

Professional Convergence

We can add **professional convergence** to the dimensions of convergence that matter most in public relations. One of the benefits of converged, multiservice agencies is that they can integrate communication functions strategically. Publicity and advertising can be used to support the marketing of consumer products. Marketing tactics can be used to support public relations. Public affairs and government relations benefit from good public relations with an organization's stakeholders. Healthy employee relations help customer service and sales. And so on, and so on.

The architects of multibillion-dollar mergers are not the only ones who must understand how all the functions go together. Each person working for each client must also understand how the functions integrate in order to manage, communicate and counsel most effectively. From the intern to the account executive to the CEO, agencies operate best when everyone has a good sense of how their job fits into the larger mission and service to any particular client. Someone who places a hashtag in a paid TV advertisement should know what is going to happen when TV viewers jump platforms from their TVs to other screens. When the

Revlon promoted #LOVEISON with this video display in New York's Times Square.

What types of employees and media people have to collaborate to make a campaign like this work?

communication goes online, the company representatives monitoring the hashtag conversation should be in tune with the management of the organization hosting the exchange. The account executive, the media buyer, the advertising creative, the social media strategist, the online host and the executives of the organization itself all need to work in concert.

Integration raises one more apparent paradox of convergence. Successful integration of functions of communication requires an understanding of, and respect for, the unique goals and contributions of each. This doesn't just apply to the big players on the world stage. Integration is equally important for in-house communications teams and for small organizations employing only a single communication specialist. In fact, if you are working alone communicating for a small business or nonprofit, you have no choice but to think through how all your communication and management functions gel together for a common purpose. Good public relations means recognizing both the differences and commonalities of advertising, marketing and public relations.

Divergence

Using the term *paradox* to describe convergence sheds light on apparent contradictions, but philosophically it is not really that hard to reconcile ideas like professional diversity and integration. Divergence and convergence go hand in hand. The best chefs know the unique flavors of their individual ingredients well before they mix them together to serve the perfect

If you place a hashtag in a TV ad, you should know what will happen when TV viewers jump platforms from their TVs to other screens.

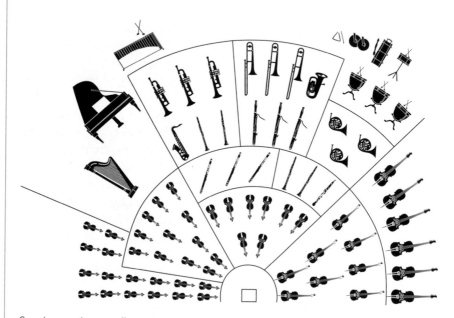

Symphony orchestras offer a metaphor for integrated communication.

How is a conductor's role different from that of a town crier?

dish. Chemists understand elements, compounds and mixtures. Music directors know how each instrument plays in their ensembles. Betteke van Ruler, whose "town crier" typology of a public relations practitioner was introduced in Chapter 2, also identified a "conductor" type of public relations person. The conductor is tasked with orchestrating different communication activities in much the same way as one leads a symphony. Before diving headfirst into integration, understand what exactly is being integrated and how public relations is fundamentally different in its goals from advertising and marketing.

Advertising

Despite the explosion of innovation and change in media industries in recent decades, most media business models still rely on advertising dollars as a primary source of revenue. In traditional mass media, **advertising** is the paid media space that sponsors use to persuade audiences. The media space in broadcast media is measured based on time—for example, a 30-second radio or TV ad. Sponsors generally pay more for prime-time and wide-audience programming events like the Super Bowl, and less for time in local programming at off-peak times with smaller audiences. In print media, the space is often sold based on column inches. If you look at a printed newspaper or magazine, you'll see that each page has space for a certain number of columns across and a certain number of inches in length up and down. If an organization wants to buy ad space that is three columns wide and six inches long, the buyers would pay for 18 column inches. Or buyers may pay for the space based on the portion of the pages used. You can look through magazines to find one-third-page ads, half-page ads, two-page spreads, and so on.

Advertisement pricing formulas include not just the amount of time or space but also the estimated audience size, the demographics and influence of that audience, contract arrangements between the organization and the media outlet and the context for placement and timing of the ad. For example, in 2018, the global circulation of the U.S. print edition of *The Wall Street Journal* was estimated at 1,099,545 copies. The standard rate for a 1/7-page (18 column inches) black-and-white ad was $39,600, while a full-page (126 column inches) color ad cost $327,103. That's about $2,596 per column inch. Meanwhile a 1/6 page local ad in *The Daily Tar Heel* student-run newspaper at the University of North Carolina at Chapel Hill, with a circulation of 10,000 copies, was priced at $250. It makes a lot more sense for the local yogurt shop to advertise in *The Daily Tar Heel*. However, for a private jet charter company, it may make more sense to advertise in *The Wall Street Journal*.

One metric for calculating advertising value is **cost per thousand (CPM)** (the *M* in CPM is the Roman numeral for 1,000). A three-column-inch ad in the student newspaper costing $42.60 to reach a circulation of 14,000 would yield a CPM of $42.60/14 = 3.04, or $3.04 per thousand readers. Public relations people sometimes use these calculations to figure

Before diving headfirst into integration, understand how public relations differs from advertising and marketing in its goals.

Advertising
Media space purchased by sponsors to persuade audiences; or the practice of planning and producing this service.

Cost per thousand (CPM)
A measure of advertising reach that represents the cost of an advertisement relative to the estimated size of the audience.

Advertising value equivalency (AVE)

A calculation of the value of news or editorial coverage based on the cost of the equivalent amount of advertising space or time.

an equivalent value for publicity when an organization is covered in the unpaid column inches of news and editorial content. This metric, known as **advertising value equivalency (AVE)**, has been widely discredited as a measure of effective public relations. Proper evaluation of public relations requires much more careful thinking about the effects of communication than simply figuring what media coverage would have cost if you had paid for it. The AVE issue will be discussed further in Chapter 8 on evaluation.

While newspapers and magazines make some money from subscriptions and single-copy sales, the majority of their revenue comes from advertising in the form of print advertising and online advertising paid for by marketers. (Some publications like student newspapers are free and depend almost entirely on advertising for their budgets.) Online advertising revenues are growing, while print advertising revenues are dropping.

For the price they pay, marketers get to choose the placement of their messages and design the message as they see fit for their purposes (within reason). Marketers hire advertising firms to strategically plan the precise words they want in the copy. The firms select fonts and colors that will work best. They choose the models and frame the pictures. In audio and video, they carefully design and produce the material to their own exact

Banner ads and pre-roll ads are criticized for being annoying and ineffective.

What kind of evidence would it take to convince you that these ads have value?

standards. In short, marketers buy not only media space, but the ability to control the content of that space.

Online, advertisers can buy **banner ads**, which display ads on a portion of web pages. Another option is **pre-roll advertising**, which is a commercial ad displayed for a few seconds as online video before the desired video is shown.

The CPM metric is commonly used with banner ads. Calculated based on the cost per thousand web page viewers, CPM is most similar to traditional advertising metrics for value. Of course, there are a lot more data that can be tracked online than with traditional mass media. **Click-through rate** is the percentage of users who view an ad and actually click on it. If a thousand people view a banner ad on a web page, and 15 of them click on the banner, the click-through rate is 1.5 percent.

Newer media enterprises rely on advertising for revenue too. Yahoo, Bing and Google sell sponsored results that appear when users search for certain keywords. So if you search for "yogurt," you'll find yogurt ads and links prominently displayed at the top of your results. **Search advertising** is a good deal for advertisers because they reach people who are searching for specific keywords related to their business, and the pricing is tied more closely to the behavioral results of the ad (e.g., clicking) than to the number of people assumed to be in the audience exposed to the ad. Even beyond clicking on the initial links, Google Analytics and similar services help track user behavior as they move from initial exposure to some target behavior such as making an online purchase or setting up an appointment to talk to a sales representative. **Analytics** is a term used to describe researching online data to identify meaningful patterns.

Media space also can be sold in the form of pop-up ads on mobile apps, promoted tweets on Twitter, banners towed behind airplanes, product placements in TV shows or movies, videos in Facebook news feeds, real billboards on the highway, virtual billboards on the highway in your video game, the hoods of NASCAR race cars, or the decks of skateboards, snowboards and surfboards.

Organizations buy advertising to reach audiences, most commonly to persuade people to buy products or services. Effective advertising sparks a desire in people. It piques interests and persuades. People who buy an organization's products and services are certainly an important public with whom to build and maintain relationships.

But beyond seeking profit, advertising can also be used to recruit employees and members, advocate and agitate for causes, and legitimize organizations and their missions. As such, advertising is an important tool for public relations. Likewise, public relations efforts can work to support advertising.

Marketing

Of course, advertising is a tool for **marketing** too. The American Marketing Association defines marketing as "the activity, set of institutions, and processes for creating, communicating, delivering, and exchanging offerings

Banner ads
Advertisements on web pages designed to encourage users to click to reach an advertiser's site.

Pre-roll advertising
A commercial ad is displayed as online video before the desired video is shown.

Click-through rate
Percentage of users who view an ad on the web and click on it to reach an advertiser's site. Analytics help track behavior as users move from initial exposure to some target behavior, such as making an online purchase.

Search advertising
Paid placement of advertising on search-engine results pages. Ads are placed to appear in response to certain keyword queries.

Analytics
Researching online data to identify meaningful patterns. In strategic communication, analytics often focus on how web traffic leads to behavioral results such as sharing information or making online purchases.

Marketing
Business of creating, promoting, delivering and selling products and services.

Three-time ASP Women's World Tour Champion Carissa Moore delivers a dynamic medium for paid sponsorship.

How many ads do you see?

that have value for customers, clients, partners, and society at large."[13] In a classic text first published in 1960, Professor E. Jerome McCarthy introduced a handy way to learn the basics of what he called the marketing mix.[14] McCarthy's four P's include *product*, *price*, *place* and *promotion*.

PRODUCT

The product is the thing to be sold. Very often it is a tangible item like a car or a serving of yogurt or an electric toothbrush. Or the "product" can be a less tangible item like downloadable computer software or a service like a mobile voice, text and data plan. Ideas and behaviors such as preventing skin cancer or registering to vote can also be marketed. Marketers are involved with the development and branding of products and product families, and they analyze product life cycles. A new product will be marketed differently from a "mature" product. Kwikset, the lock company, marketed its Bluetooth-enabled "Kevo" deadbolt—"Users can simply touch the deadbolt while the authorized smartphone remains in their purse or pocket to unlock the door"—differently from a mature product like one of their standard key-operated deadbolts. As a consumer, I found out about the new Kevo device because it was listed as a "Product of the Year" on the *Electronic House* website, which "serves discriminating consumers who enjoy the elegance, simplicity and fun afforded by integrated home technology."[15] Whether or not I can afford a $200 door lock is another issue!

PRICE

Price is obviously an important consideration, as it determines the revenue a company receives from sales, and therefore the company's profits. Pricing is sophisticated business. A product must be priced somewhere in line with customers' perceived value and affordability. If a product is priced too low, the company will not make a profit, and moreover, the product may be perceived as "cheap" in the negative sense of the word. Higher pricing may give the product some prestige, but if the product is not affordable, no one will buy it.

Understand that this is a gross oversimplification of pricing strategies. Many, many other factors come into play. For example, one pricing strategy is called **market skimming**, in which consumer products are priced higher at first when eager early adopters are willing to pay a premium for a new

Market skimming
Marketing strategy that starts with higher prices for early adopters of unique products and services and then lowers prices later to sell to a broader base of consumers when competitors enter the market.

and unique product, but then priced lower later to appeal to broader, thriftier markets once the product is more mature in its life cycle and when similar competitors have likely entered the market. If Kwikset uses this strategy, they eventually may bring down the price of a Kevo into a more affordable range, especially as more lock companies start competing for business with similar products. Understanding pricing strategy requires knowledge of psychology and economics among other social sciences. Like public relations, marketing involves research and theory to understand people and how they communicate with organizations and respond to their offerings.

PLACE

If you think of markets as places where buyers and sellers meet, you get a good sense of why distribution is such an important part of the **marketing mix**. You still can't download a pineapple or a pair of running shoes. Marketers have to figure out the best way to get products like these to their consumers. Produce has to be canned, frozen or kept fresh during harvesting, packing and shipping. Many stores and their shoppers now demand organic and locally grown foods, which means the logistics of packing and shipping interact with the appeal of the product itself. Food items are also marketed to restaurants and not just end consumers. Runners can order running shoes on Zappos.com, and they can return them for free, but many still prefer to go to an actual bricks-and-mortar store to try the shoes on and get personal advice from store staff before making a purchase.

That said, the internet has opened many new markets, and dramatically transformed others. Where do you buy music (if you buy music at all)? Probably not at a record store. At one time most music was purchased in the form of tapes and disks, and people went to record stores to buy albums. Now most music is purchased digitally. This has changed the entire economic system of the music industry, and it has changed how music is marketed too. Rather than focusing on how many CDs to burn and how to get the right number of those disks to the right stores where they will sell and to the right DJs who might play them on the radio, modern music marketers pay closer attention to online downloads, playlist apps and subscription streaming services. With digital media, the point of sale is most often online through sites like Amazon, iTunes or eBay.

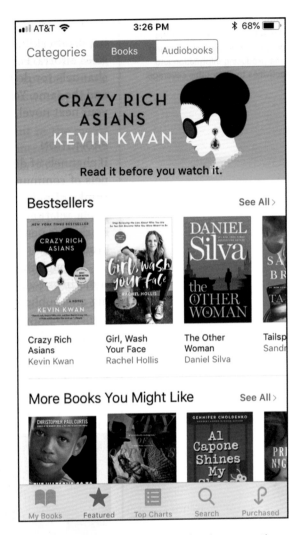

With digital media, the point of sale is often the same as the medium used to consume the media, such as music or audiobooks purchased on a smartphone.

How have digital media changed the way music, videos and books are marketed?

Marketing mix
Combination of product, price, place and promotion strategies in support of profitable exchange.

Mass production led to mass promotion via mass media during the Industrial Revolution.

How has the relationship between organizations and the consumers they market to changed?

newspaper presses or Super Bowl–sized TV audiences). Henry Ford's famous quote sums up the relationship between the mass producer and his publics: "Any customer can have a car painted any colour that he wants so long as it is black."[20]

Of course mass production and mass communication still define much of our world, but what Lauterborn and others noticed about the role of consumers changing in the 1980s and 1990s has only accelerated in this millennium.

COST

Cost to satisfy wants and needs should replace "price." Beyond just dollars and cents that people pay for goods and services are many other costs. What are they giving up to make the purchase? How much time does it take? Psychological factors come into play too. Lauterborn mentioned the costs of conscience and guilt. The dialogue of the satirical TV series *Portlandia* presents the polar opposite of Henry Ford's example in modern-era markets:

> *Waitress: If you have any questions about the menu, please let me know.*
> *Female diner: I guess I do have a question about the chicken. If you can just tell us a little more about it?*
> *Waitress: The chicken is a heritage breed, woodland-raised chicken that's been fed a diet of sheep's milk, soy and hazelnuts.*
> *Male diner: And this is local?*
> *Waitress: Yes, absolutely.*

Male diner: I'm going to ask you just one more time, and it's local?
Waitress: It is.
Female diner: Is that USDA Organic, or Oregon Organic, or Portland Organic?
Waitress: It's just all-across-the-board organic.
Male diner: The hazelnuts, these are local?
Female diner: And how big is the area where the chickens are able to roam free? . . .

The questioning continues until the waitress leaves and comes back with the chicken's papers. ("His name was Colin.")[21] The humor in this sketch comes from its kernel of truth about the increasing level of responsiveness to and understanding of consumer wants and needs required to compete in modern consumer-centered marketplaces.

CONVENIENCE

Convenience to buy should replace "place." Our concept of marketplaces has followed a similar historical cycle to media and manufacturing. The farm-to-table movement is a throwback to times before the Industrial Revolution. Back then, if you didn't raise your own chickens or grow your own vegetables, you probably interacted with the farmer who did. People bought shoes from cobblers and not mall outlets. The Industrial Revolution added convenience in some ways, but most of that convenience was driven from the supply side. Supermarkets and big-box stores stand as evidence of that. Nonetheless, there are limits to what you as a consumer can find by going to a bricks-and-mortar Walmart, Gap or Target store, and driving there to see what's available seems more and more inconvenient. "People don't have to go anyplace anymore," said Lauterborn, describing the era of catalogs, credit cards and phone orders in 1990 that would soon become the era of Zappos and Zillow, eBay and Etsy.

COMMUNICATION

Communication should replace "promotion." Perhaps this is the most profound change suggested. In *The Cluetrain Manifesto: The End of Business as Usual*, internet visionaries Doc Searls and David Weinberger painted a nostalgic picture of early markets as real places "filled with people, not abstractions or statistical aggregates" that were alive with interpersonal conversations. Those conversations, they argued, were interrupted by the industrial era. Searls and Weinberger welcomed a return to richer, less promotional, interaction between people afforded by the internet and social media, "where markets are getting more connected and more powerfully vocal every day."[22] With the growth of social media, other hybrids of journalism and marketing-related functions have arisen.

Hybrid Functions

It is no secret that one of the most common career paths for public relations people leads through a newsroom of some sort—a career track that

Content marketing
Development and sharing of media content to appeal to consumers as part of an indirect marketing strategy in which consumers are drawn primarily to media content instead of directly to the product being marketed.

Inbound marketing
Marketing strategy that focuses on tactics for attracting customers with useful, entertaining or valuable information that customers find on blogs, search results and other forms of online and social media.

dates back to Ivy Lee (Chapter 2). Some of the most skilled and influential people working in public relations have worked as journalists, and many college programs in public relations share academic space and curricula with journalism. Experience working with and training alongside journalists helps tremendously with the media-relations aspect of public relations.

You know those harsh deadlines and ridiculous penalties for factual errors in your writing assignments in school? Those really do help train you for the "real world" of public relations. If you take a news writing class or work at your college newspaper or intern at a TV news station, you are also making contacts and building working relationships with people in the media who may help you throughout your career. Learning the news business and its core values and ethics gives you a tacit sense of where the line between journalism and public relations is drawn. Yet, even if you never work in the news media—and many of the best public relations people have not—understanding newsworthiness and practicing storytelling are important for success in your job in public relations.

The most effective public relations people have always been good storytellers. Good stories, told well, make complex organizations and ideas understandable. That kind of communication helps build and maintain relationships between organizations and publics. Advertisers and marketers have always endeavored to tell stories too, but their channels have been constrained to scarce paid space, and their focus has traditionally been tied to sales and customer loyalty. The concurrent trends of integrated communication strategy and increased channels for communication have set the stage for some interesting hybrids.

In **content marketing**, organizations develop media content to attract audiences and interact with publics. The content may be narrative stories, videos, photo memes, blogs, statistics or infographics, but the idea is to make it interesting and engaging enough that people will seek it, consume it, and share it for its own information or entertainment value rather than see it as an interruption to some other media experience. People are bombarded with unrequested advertising and marketing messages all day every day, and they work hard to avoid and ignore them with DVR fast-forwarding, spam filters and ad blockers. Content marketing is a counter-tactic, but not an adversarial one. Instead of being pushier, content marketers work to draw people to them on their own accord; this is also called **inbound marketing**. According to the Content Marketing Institute, "The essence of this content strategy is the belief that if we, as businesses, deliver consistent, ongoing valuable information to buyers, they ultimately reward us with their business and loyalty."[23]

By most definitions, the goal of content marketing is still pretty much straight marketing. The "targets" are still labeled *customers*, *buyers* and *audiences*, but the fact that content marketing involves organizational storytelling and communication engagement that likely reverberates well beyond sales makes it an important point of integration in an organization's communication efforts. Red Bull is a prime example. As *Mashable* tech writer James O'Brien put it, "Red Bull is a publishing empire that also happens to sell a beverage."[24]

Case Study

Red Bull's Content Marketing Strategy

I'm trying to update a case study here, and once again Red Bull is making it really hard for me to stay focused. When I opened www.redbull.com, I soon found myself watching Polish ski-mountaineer Andrzej Bargiel make history by completing the first ever ski descent of K2, the world's second highest mountain.

I can't tell the video entertainment from the advertising from the marketing from the public relations. They've got fantastic photography, incredible videos, sharply written feature stories and inspiring blogs by extreme athletes. Not only do they have the obligatory Facebook, Twitter, Pinterest and Reddit buttons, but the content is actually something I might want to share with my friends on these networks (or in my book-writing, as with the picture of surfer Carissa Moore). From a strategy standpoint, though, the most interesting part is that there is *no mention whatsoever* of the Red Bull beverage product unless I seek it out. In the upper-right corner of the web page there's a small link to "Products." If I click on that, I'm taken to https://energydrink-us.redbull.com/, and that page includes information on the actual drinks. That's content marketing.

Red Bull's website is a prime example of content marketing strategy.

How does the website help sell their energy drink? Is that the website's main purpose?

The term **brand journalism** describes a similar strategy, but as the name indicates, the primary focus is on journalistic skills. Critics of content marketing are concerned that the practice will lead to backlash as the mad dash to provide content in support of sales will lead to poorer quality content and strategy. According to Christopher Penn of SHIFT Communications, "As content marketers struggle to keep up with the demands of creating content all the time that's high quality, increasingly they'll look to professionals who can maintain that pace without breaking a sweat—journalists."[25]

Chrysler Group LLC followed this strategy when it hired Ed Garsten, a veteran journalist with 20 years at CNN as correspondent, bureau chief, anchor and producer, and experience as a national auto writer at the Associated Press and as General Motors' beat writer for *The Detroit News*. As head of Chrysler Digital Media, Garsten led a team that handled the Chrysler media website, broadcast communications, social media and video production. "Most of us on the 8-person team have had actual television news and/or production experience giving us the background and skills to launch an in-house video operation for Chrysler Communications," blogged Garsten in describing the operation.[26] While Garsten and his team clearly brought journalistic talent to the job, the broader strategy is still one of marketing and public relations.

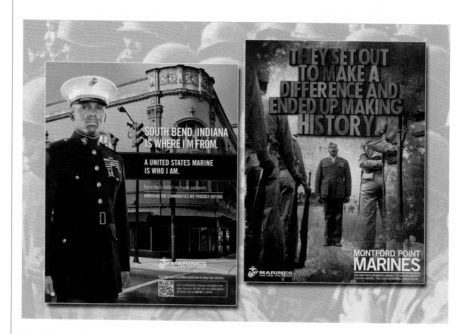

Sometimes ads are purchased to do more than sell goods or services.

How do these advertisements serve a public relations function?

How Public Relations Is Different at Its Core

In Chapter 1, we defined public relations as the management of relationships between an organization and its publics. In Chapter 2, we saw how public relations differs from journalism in that public relations people ethically advocate on behalf of their organizations, while journalists seek to report without bias favoring any one particular organization. In this chapter, we find that advertising and marketing overlap considerably with public relations. Many of the same tools and skills apply to all three endeavors, and all three work to promote an organization and its products, services and ideas. However, public relations differs from advertising and marketing in at least three ways: in its promotion of whole organizations, in its communication with all publics and in its purpose to build and maintain mutually beneficial relationships (see Table 3.1).

Organization (Beyond Offerings)

Marketing and advertising are primarily concerned with promoting an organization's offerings, and most often those offerings are products and services that the organization sells or exchanges to remain profitable. While public relations also often promotes an organization's offerings, more importantly *public relations promotes the organization as a whole*. There are exceptions to this general rule such as institutional advertising, which is paid advertising space that promotes an organization more than any of its specific products or services. However, when an ad serves an institutional goal beyond sales and marketing, it is acting as a tool for public relations.

> *When an ad serves an institutional goal beyond sales and marketing, it is acting as a tool for public relations.*

Publics (Beyond Audiences)

In this chapter's discussion of advertising and marketing, you may have noticed that the groups of people who are targeted for advertising and marketing are

TABLE 3.1	HOW PUBLIC RELATIONS DIFFERS FROM MARKETING AND ADVERTISING		
FUNCTION	**PROMOTES . . .**	**COMMUNICATES WITH . . .**	**MAIN PURPOSE**
Advertising	Brands, products and services	Target audiences	Persuasion
Marketing	Sales	Consumers, suppliers, retailers, etc.	Sales and profit
Public Relations	Whole organization	All publics	Mutually beneficial relationships

referred to as audiences and not publics. The term **target audience** implies a carefully identified group of people who are chosen in strategy development for their propensity to buy an organization's products, services or ideas. Marketers pay for advertising in the newspaper to reach readers who might buy yogurt or lease private jets. They buy ads on FM radio, Pandora or Spotify to reach listeners who may purchase software. They sell insurance to Facebook users and medicine to TV news viewers. Readers, listeners, users and viewers are all best described as audiences in this context because their primary relationship to the organization is one of financial exchange.

In advertising and marketing, organizations want to persuade audiences to buy stuff. These groups also fit the definition of publics because customers and consumers certainly have an effect on organizations, and organizations certainly have an effect on customers and consumers. However, public relations people are responsible for building and maintaining relationships with publics even when there is no exchange of goods or services. Neighbors, legislators, employees, students, volunteers, competitors, voters, taxpayers, disaster victims, veterans, beachgoers and bicyclists may all be publics for certain organizations in circumstances in which no financial exchange is involved. The term *public* implies a more balanced two-way relationship than the term *audience*—one that is not predicated on the probability of a direct profit.

Building and maintaining relationships with publics is essential, even if they never buy from or sell anything to your organization.

Relationships (Beyond Sales)

In advertising and marketing, relationships are a means to an end, and that end is usually sales. In public relations, *maintaining relationships is an end in itself* to the degree that an organization's success or failure depends on healthy working relationships with all sorts of publics beyond customers and those in the product supply chain. Media relations is a good example. Public relations people nurture relationships with journalists and editors in local, national and global media. Yes, favorable publicity is a common goal, but the scope and duration of the relationship is much greater than any one promotional strategy. Because publicity in reputable news outlets cannot be bought like advertising, public relations people have to work to understand journalists and their interests in order to understand how to provide useful information to journalists as they do their work. Public relations people also need to build trust with the media.

Publicity isn't always welcome. During crises, public relations people work under great stress to preserve their organization's interests and resolve problems, while reporters are out to report what the organization has done wrong. Their roles are at odds, yet they still rely on each other. Public relations practitioners need journalists to help them communicate with their publics. Journalists need the public relations people to help them understand what happened. The greater the amount of mutual trust, the better each party will be able to perform during tense times. As we'll see in later chapters, trust is one important dimension of relationships, and news media are just one type of public with whom public relations people must maintain relationships.

The greater the trust between public relations people and journalists, the better each party will be able to perform during tense times.

Voices from the Field

Bill Imada

BILL IMADA is founder, chairman and chief collaboration officer of the IW Group, a fully integrated marketing communications firm that specializes in the growing multicultural markets in the United States. With more than 25 years of experience in marketing, public relations, advertising and training, Imada and his company continue to represent some of the top brands, including American Airlines, The Coca-Cola Company, Godiva Chocolatiers, McDonald's USA, MetLife, Nissan North America, Pacific Gas & Electric Company, Toyota, Walmart Stores, Walt Disney Imagineering, Warner Bros. Pictures, Verizon and many others. The IW Group also represents a number of prominent governmental agencies and nonprofit organizations.

How do you feel about the merging of agencies into bigger and bigger conglomerates? Are clients being served better?

Mergers and acquisitions have occurred for decades, and we will continue to see agencies of all sizes consolidate and reposition themselves regularly. IW Group was approached more than a decade ago by all of the major communications and marketing conglomerates. I opted to go with True North, who agreed to allow me to maintain a controlling interest and to manage and operate the agency as a smaller, niche-focused firm. Not long after I sold a minority stake in IW Group, Interpublic Group purchased True North. To IPG's credit, they continue to allow me to run the agency independently.

Are clients better served by bigger and more complicated conglomerates?

Yes and no. For large, multinational companies, having one entity manage, direct and fulfill their needs in regions around the world can be more efficient and effective. Yet, many of these global firms don't always deliver on good customer service, and offices tend to run autonomously, which may discourage collaboration.

How about smaller firms or in-house communication operations? What kinds of challenges do they face in an age of convergence?

Smaller firms must deal with rising labor costs, rapidly changing digital and social media platforms, and a more demanding workforce. Although smaller firms offer greater flexibility and mobility, it has been difficult to match the salaries, benefits and extra perks a larger and better-financed firm can provide. Smaller firms also have to compete with other communications and marketing firms, in-house agencies, nimble two-person boutiques, short-term contractors and student-inspired on-campus agencies that have lower operational and overhead costs. As a result, the smaller agencies have to offer their employees an experience they cannot get at a larger firm: for example, working with a more intimate team of colleagues on different accounts covering a wider array of industries, ensuring a closer and more direct working relationship with agency clients, and offering the opportunity for co-workers to create strong emotional bonds.

Do you see public relations as fundamentally different from marketing and advertising?

No. The lines blurred years ago. In today's world, advertising agencies have PR and marketing teams and vice versa. Advertising agency leaders, who once turned their noses up whenever public relations was discussed as a legitimate profession, now realize they must have a public relations and marketing strategy folded into everything they do. And, more and more clients expect agencies to do PR, marketing and advertising. IW Group was established 25 years ago as a PR-focused agency. We realized after two years that we needed to diversify our business. Today, if we were to silo PR at our agency, it would only represent 15 percent of our business portfolio.

continues

continued

Do you see cultural convergence (when various forms of culture are exchanged, combined, converted and adapted) as a positive in global societies? What's public relations' role in cultural convergence?

Cultural convergence to me is like saying, "We need to level the playing field." The playing field will never be level; at least not in my lifetime. Every person on this planet will retain some aspect of his or her cultural heritage regardless of what happens in the world. Our agency is multicultural and includes people of different races, ethnicities, views and mindsets. Although we initially focus on life's many intersections that bring us together (e.g., food, music, entertainment, etc.), as PR and advertising professionals, we also see our individual and cultural uniqueness as one of our core value propositions. The growth of digital media hasn't changed this; rather, it has placed an accent on them. Today, it is cool to be unique.

Brand journalism and content marketing—are they anything new?

No. This has been going on for more than a decade. An example of content marketing includes "advertorials." And we have been using forms of brand journalism for years. In places such as Asia, there has always been an imaginary line between journalism and branding.

If you were invited to speak to a public relations class, what would you most want to discuss?

Diversifying diversity would be one. Diversity isn't just about race and gender; rather, it includes diversity of heart and mind, spirit, regional immersion, viewpoints, sexual orientation, socio-economic conditions and so much more. I also like to talk about "changing the conversation." We have a tendency to use idioms and sayings to guide our thinking, such as: "We shouldn't reinvent the wheel," or "We should think outside of the box." But, sayings like these tend to inhibit our ability to grow, innovate and push the boundaries that we are forced to live in at work and in many of our communities. It is critical for students and faculty to really push intellectual curiosity, including curiosity of people, places, experiences, ideologies and more.

Any specific advice for the next generation of public relations practitioners?

"Taste the street." A young woman, many years ago, asked me what I thought about the name of her new Vietnamese restaurant: "Taste of Saigon Street." Saigon, once the capital of South Vietnam and today known as Ho Chi Minh City, is very crowded, noisy and chaotic with the grit and grime of any city in the region. When I first heard this restaurant name, I thought to myself: "No American diner would ever want to eat a meal in a restaurant named after a dirty thoroughfare in a place like Saigon." When I shared this concern, the young woman said: "Mr. Imada, I grew up on the streets of Saigon. I remember fondly the smells, sounds, banter and life along the busy streets of my home country. The street represents my values and my soul. I want to bring those flavors to the people of America." There are many ways to advance PR. Clearly, one way is to get a flavor for all that is around us. Sometimes we miss that taste without even realizing it.

Ethics: Free Flow of Information and Data Protection

In April 2018, I received a note from Instagram. "Please take a moment to review some changes to our Terms and Data Policy. Let us know if you agree to them to continue using Instagram." Like millions of other users, I skimmed the note and agreed to the terms.

The next day I received an email from Twitter: "We believe you should always know what data we collect from you and how we use it. . . ." Twitter said it was part of their "ongoing commitment to transparency" and encouraged me to review the updates to their privacy policy. Then a similar notice showed up in my inbox from eBay, and then Ancestry.com. Before long I found that I couldn't open my email inbox without seeing one or more of these notices, and it was the same thing with my apps and web accounts—I was asked to accept updated terms or to review privacy settings for Facebook, Google and seemingly every other online service that I logged on to.

So why the sudden push for transparency? The short answer is GDPR, or the General Data Protection Regulation—a European Union (EU) regulation that went into effect in May of 2018 to protect individuals' privacy by giving them more control of their personal data. The regulation also requires companies to notify users and authorities in a timely manner any time there has been a data breach. For companies with users in Europe, compliance with the new regulation is a legal requirement. However, as a practical matter, the changes these global companies made affected users all over the world.

Companies are expected to obtain your consent before using your data, and GDPR requires that this consent is informed, unambiguous and freely given.[27] So before Facebook runs facial recognition technology to link photos of you to your identity, they must explain what they use this function for (letting you know when someone posts a photo of you, suggesting tags, etc.). And before collecting "location history" data, Google notifies users how this information will be used:

> If you turn this setting on, Google will create a private map of where you go with your signed-in devices, including how long and how often you visit, and how you travel between places. This map is only visible to you. This gives you improved map searches and commute routes, as well as helping you to rediscover the places you've been and the routes you've travelled.[28]

Facial recognition and geolocation technologies on Facebook and Google are excellent examples of technological convergence, but that technology can get scary when we consider the possibilities of economic

Technological and economic convergence enables companies to share user data in unique ways.

What kind of ethical issues does this raise for public relations professionals?

convergence as companies buy, sell and trade our personal data. Think about all the types of companies with which you share personal information—banks, cable and streaming media, credit card companies, genealogy services, search engines, hospitals and doctors' offices and online shopping sites. A colleague of mine searched online for specific cancer information for a relative, and shortly thereafter she was served an ad that invited her to shop for "Bile Duct Cancer at Amazon." Yikes!

Just because a company complies with laws or regulations such as GDPR doesn't mean they are acting ethically in handling user data. As a matter of law, organizations collecting data from citizens in the EU must have either a legitimate legal reason or they must obtain user consent. As a matter of ethics, organizations should be transparent with users about which data they collect and exactly what they plan to do with that data. One of the core principles of the PRSA Code of Ethics is *Free Flow of Information*: "Protecting and advancing the free flow of accurate and truthful information is essential to serving the public interest and contributing to informed decision making in a democratic society."[29]

Of course, the legal intent of GDPR was very much in line with the ethical principles of transparency and free-flowing information, but critics have pointed out a number of ways that companies have shirked the intent and even reached an end result of *less* transparency:

- *Masking the fact that they never had the right to your data in the first place.* You may have never consented to give some companies your information in the first place, but now they have your personal data and are using it to contact you to obtain permission to continue citing GDPR. Tiffany Li of Yale Law School's Information Society Project commented to *Wired*, "The companies reaching out are like a bad boyfriend: They want you to stay, but they know they did something wrong."[30]
- *Offering an all-or-nothing option for continued use of the service.* Facebook, for example, presented users in the European Union with a pop-up window when they logged in: "To continue using Facebook, you need to agree to our updated Terms. If you don't agree, you can't continue to use Facebook."
- *Taking advantage of "consent fatigue."* Realizing that users are burdened with multiple disclosures, many companies sent notices that nominally complied with GDPR knowing that in reality most users wouldn't really read them through.

"Consent fatigue" presents a public relations dilemma. How can professional communicators comply with the law to fully disclose all the burdensome details of how their organizations use people's information without violating their ethical obligation to obtain informed, unambiguous and free-willed user consent? Nitasha Tiku's *Wired* article suggests a couple of approaches:

1. *Work as hard at designing your disclosures for clear communication as your company works at perfecting its core products.* If an organization is technologically advanced and design-savvy enough to collect,

analyze and apply data to enhance users' products and experiences, public relations practitioners working there should be able to get some help designing and delivering effective disclosures. Cooperation of information technology, design and public relations professionals is a great example of professional convergence.

2. *Work with management to see to it that your company does not collect data it doesn't need.* Besides the free flow of information, GDPR also was written to discourage companies from collecting and hoarding data they have no immediate plans to use.[31] If you can't make it clear to consumers why you need the data in a way that they will agree to, your organization probably shouldn't be collecting the data in the first place.

In Case You Missed It

To fully understand public relations, you have to be able to zoom in on specific strategies and tactics and then zoom out to see the big picture of convergence and integration. Here are some snapshots from the different focal points in this chapter:

- Public relations people must understand other dimensions of convergence beyond the technological ones.

- If you place a hashtag in a TV ad, you should know what will happen when TV viewers jump platforms from their TVs to other screens.

- Before diving headfirst into integration, understand how public relations differs from advertising and marketing in its goals.

- Word-of-mouth marketing should be credible, respectful, social, measurable and repeatable.

- When an ad serves an institutional goal beyond sales and marketing, it is acting as a tool for public relations.

- Building and maintaining relationships with publics is essential, even if those publics never buy from or sell anything to your organization.

- The more trust between public relations people and journalists, the better each party will be able to perform during tense times.

SUMMARY

3.1 Analyze how different forms of convergence affect public relations.

Rather than being a single trend, convergence is better thought of as a number of processes that can be defined separately, including technological, cultural, economic and professional convergence. Technological convergence affects the communication tools and tactics public relations people use. Cultural convergence requires public relations people to understand the interaction of organizational cultures and public cultures in increasingly global contexts. As firms merge, economic convergence affects services on both a local and a global level. Professional convergence is what happens when those services (and the jobs of the people who provide them) are integrated.

3.2 Define advertising and marketing, and discuss how those functions may diverge from public relations.

Advertising is media space purchased by sponsors to persuade audiences; or the practice of planning and producing this service. Marketing is the business of creating, promoting, delivering and selling products and services. Public relations people should understand advertising and marketing as distinct communication tools with divergent goals before working to integrate these strategic communication functions with public relations.

3.3 Discuss how functions of advertising and marketing may be integrated with public relations.

When integration is done right, advertising and marketing support public relations, and vice versa. In the minds of publics, an organization's management and communication efforts should be consistent.

3.4 Explain how public relations adds value to organizations and publics beyond advertising and marketing.

Public relations is different from advertising and marketing in that it focuses on the overall relationship between the whole organization and many of its publics. Products are only part of what is promoted. Customers are only one public. Relationships are about much more than sales and profit.

3.5 Discuss the role of public relations in the free flow of information in society.

Public relations professionals have an ethical responsibility to protect and encourage the free flow of accurate and truthful information because informed citizens are essential in a democratic society. Public relations professionals also must work to keep consumers informed on matters related to their organizations so that consumers can, for example, make informed decisions about how much personal data to share with companies.

DISCUSSION QUESTIONS

1. Do you have more or fewer media devices now than you did two years ago? How has technological convergence changed your day-to-day media use?

2. Search for a familiar brand's website or social media presence as it appears in another country (for example, "McDonald's India," "McDonald's Facebook India," "Red Bull Japan" or "Greenpeace Argentina"). What evidence of cultural convergence do you see? Is the cultural sharing working in both directions?

3. Describe a paid advertisement you've recently observed that does not seem to be selling a particular product or service. Who is the ad "marketing" to and why?

4. **CASE STUDY** Why does Red Bull invest so much in content like that presented on Redbull.com? What is the return on that investment?

5. Would you rather work for a public relations agency/department or an integrated communication agency/department? Explain your preference.

6. Carefully review the terms of service for one of your social media accounts. Do they appear to be in compliance with GDPR? Have you seen any evidence of the company using/selling your data for specific purposes (example: personally targeted ads)? What's the difference between the company's legal obligations and their ethical obligations in getting your consent and handling your information?

KEY TERMS

Advertising   63

Advertising value equivalency (AVE)   64

Analytics   65

Augmented reality (AR)   57

Banner ads   65

Black box fallacy   56

Brand journalism   76

Click-through rate   65

Content marketing   74

Cost per thousand (CPM)   63

Cultural convergence   58

Economic convergence   59

Inbound marketing   74

Integrated marketing communication   71

Market skimming   66

Marketing   65

Marketing mix   67

Participatory culture   59

Pre-roll advertising   65

Professional convergence   61

Publicity   68

Search advertising   65

Target audience   78

Technological convergence (aka digital convergence)   57

Third-party credibility   69

Word-of-mouth promotion   69

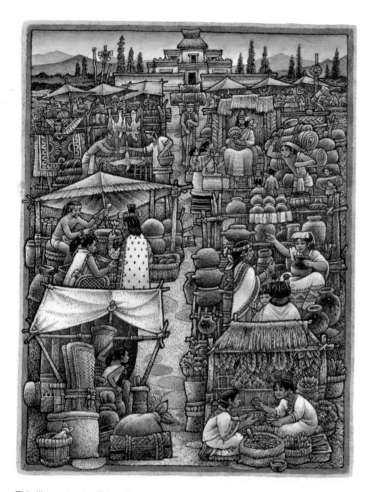

This illustration by Felipe Dávalos is of an Aztec marketplace.

How might relationships in digital marketplaces be similar to relationships in ancient marketplaces?

In the decades that followed, organization-public relationships became a more prominent topic for research and for understanding public relations in general. In 2000, Professors John Ledingham and Stephen Bruning published *Public Relations as Relationship Management*, a text that advocated turning away from the idea of public relations as mainly "a means of generating favorable publicity" and embracing "the notion that relationships ought to be at the core of public relations scholarship."[1] The ensuing shift in thinking rose concurrently with the rise of new ways for publics to communicate with organizations. Social media emerged as alternatives to mass media at the same time that we moved from seeing public relations as an overwhelmingly mass-mediated phenomenon to a more conversational, relationship-building one.

In heralding the rise of **participatory media**, social media enthusiasts welcomed a return to the more direct way of communicating that was common before industrialization and mass communication drove a wedge between organizations and their publics. They refocused on the importance of conversations in the marketplaces where organizations and publics meet.

For some insights on how to understand relationships between organizations and publics, scholars turned to interpersonal communication research. They sought to discover if what worked in relationships between spouses or between doctors and patients, for instance, might help us better understand the strategies that would succeed in organization-public relationships.

Taking Care of Relationships

Professors Dan Canary and Laura Stafford have studied interpersonal relationships for decades. In the early 1990s they cataloged a number of successful **relational maintenance strategies**, which included the following:

- *Positivity:* expressing favorable attitudes, and interacting with partners in a cheerful, uncritical manner.

- *Openness:* self-disclosure and directly discussing the nature of the relationship including its problems, and willingness to listen.

Participatory media
Media in which publics actively participate in producing and sharing content.

Relational maintenance strategies
Ways of building and sustaining mutually beneficial relationships between organizations and publics.

- *Assurances:* covertly and overtly communicating the importance of the relationship and a desire to continue with the relationship.

- *Social networking:* relying on the support of mutual friends and common affiliations.

- *Sharing tasks:* performing one's responsibilities including routine tasks and chores; in a marriage or partnership, this may include cooking, cleaning and managing finances.

In research reports for the Institute for Public Relations, Professors Linda Hon and James Grunig took these strategies and recommended a shift to focus on public, rather than interpersonal, relationships.

- *Openness* would include disclosures about the nature of the organization and information of value to its publics.

- *Assurances* would include communication that emphasized the importance of publics in the relationship.

- *Social networking* would involve an emphasis on common affiliations between the organization and publics—on social network sites, these links might take the form of shared Twitter followers, LinkedIn connections or mutual likes on Facebook.

- *Sharing tasks* would include things like asking for public support or offering support when appropriate—as when an organization voices its backing for a cause, encourages employees to volunteer or makes a donation.

Key Outcomes of Relationships

Depending on the specific goals and objectives of organization-public relationships, mutually beneficial relationships may come in many forms. The benefits may come as the result of **exchange relationships**, as when a customer buys a product or service. If the transaction goes well, the company earns sales revenue and the customer receives something of value in return. In investor relations, a publicly held corporation secures capital, and investors get a return by way of dividends or increased value of the shares they own. In contracts and legal actions, specific terms for exchanges are spelled out in detail.

Exchange relationships
Relationships in which each party gives benefits to the other with the expectation of receiving comparable benefits in return.

Small and large businesses often partner with nonprofit organizations to sponsor community events and causes like this 5K race.

What types of organization-public relationships are evident here and who benefits?

According to Hon and Grunig, **communal relationships** are equally important, if not more important, to public relations people in the long run. "In a communal relationship, both parties provide benefits to the other because they are concerned with the welfare of the other—even when they get nothing in return."[2] Hon and Grunig highlighted four key outcomes of good organization-public relationships:

- *Control mutuality*: although it may be unrealistic to expect steady and perfect symmetry, each side should have some sense of control and be comfortable with the balance of influence.

- *Trust*: Hon and Grunig identified three dimensions of trust: "*integrity*: the belief that an organization is fair and just . . . ; *dependability*: the belief that an organization will do what it says it will do . . . ; and *competence*: the belief that an organization has the ability to do what it says it will do."

- *Satisfaction*: in satisfying relationships both parties have positive expectations and feel like those expectations are being met.

- *Commitment*: is the relationship worth continuing? This question can be asked as a matter of time and effort or in terms of the emotional investment. How much does each party value the relationship relative to competing relationships?

The better the long-term relationships between your organization and publics, the more likely you are to achieve your goals.

Research has shown that these long-term relational benefits correlate with shorter-term communication effects like the achievement of specific strategic goals and objectives that may be on the table in a meeting with a CEO. That is, the better the long-term relationships you cultivate between your organization and its publics, the more likely you are to be able to achieve your daily, monthly and annual goals. Pursuing communal relationships may not on its own be enough to sustain most organizations in their missions, but when excellent public relations builds and maintains solid relationships in coordination with other organizational units doing their jobs well, the whole organization thrives. Healthy long-term relationships can save organizations money by reducing costs of strikes, boycotts, lawsuits and lost revenues from dissatisfied customers who take their business elsewhere. On the positive side, strong relationships help garner support from donors, legislators, consumers, employees, volunteers and shareholders.

There are two ways to think about interpersonal relationships and organization-public relationships. First, we can think of the interpersonal relationship as an analogy for the organization-public relationship. Relationships between organizations and publics are *like* relationships between individuals. Both require effective communication and mutual understanding. The same kinds of strategies work in both, and the outcomes sought are similar too. These relationships can be observed by asking people about their experiences with an organization as a whole.[3]

Second, we can think of interpersonal relationships *as components of* organization-public relationships. The relationship between the two groups

St. Jude ✔
@StJude

Following ⌄

This September, supporters from across the nation will join together to help end childhood cancer for kids like Keeton. Register and fundraise for the 2019 ensure that families never receive a bill from St. Jude for anything. Sign up now.
bit.ly/2IRFMbo

12:00 PM - 9 Mar 2019

41 Retweets 123 Likes

💬   🔁 41   ♡ 123   ✉

St. Jude Children's Research Hospital has some of the most loyal "followers" of any organization.

With which publics do they maintain relationships? What are some of the outcomes of these relationships?

of people is made up of all the interpersonal interactions involved when individuals in organizations communicate with individuals in publics. For example, individuals may *trust* specific people in an organization with whom they've interacted. They may be *satisfied* with the interpersonal exchanges and *committed* to continuing conversations as long as they feel a sense of *mutual control* in the relationship.

I can see you're upset. Maybe you should post more about it on Facebook. That should help eliminate any drama.

your e cards
someecards.com

Organizational-public relationships have many parallels to interpersonal relationships.

How are your relationships with organizations on social media similar to your relationships with friends on social media?

Professor Elizabeth Toth pointed out early in the relationship-management literature that interpersonal communication is the foundation for analyzing organization-public relationships. She recommended a focus on relationships between public relations people and all of an organization's constituencies within various contexts.[4] For example, the context of media relations would call for looking at relationships with journalists and editors; the context of internal communications would mean looking at relationships with employees and members; and the context of issues management might mean thinking about communication with individual advocates and activists. Three major contexts for organization-public relationships are news-driven relationships, commerce-driven relationships and issues-driven relationships.

News-Driven Relationships

Sharing news has been and always will be an important part of public relations. Whether it is editing a company newsletter, blogging about your organization's current events or working to get coverage in national or international outlets, news is very much the currency of public relations practice.

Media Relations

Media relations is literally the part of public relations that entails relationships with news media. When people speak of the *news media*, they are generally referring to the journalists, bloggers, analysts, editors and producers who report news. Relationships with these people are at the heart of media relations. Sometimes news media come to an organization for information, and other times the organization goes to the news media to get stories out. Over the course of a career in public relations, you will likely find yourself in both situations, often with the same people. The same person whom you pray will attend your organization's groundbreaking today may call you a year from now when your new building has a gas leak.

Of 900 communications professionals surveyed by *PR News* for its 2018 salary report, 42 percent ranked media relations as one of the top three "must-have" skills that public relations people need in order to get ahead. (The other two were written communication and content creation.)[5] Understanding modern media newsroom operations and the jobs of reporters,

Media relations
Management of relationships between an organization and members of the media who write, edit, produce and deliver news.

editors, bloggers and TV producers is as much a key for career advancement in public relations as it has ever been.

Pitching

Pitching is when public relations practitioners encourage the news media to cover stories involving their organizations. To keep up with industry trends, I subscribe to several email and trade publication lists for public relations. Scarcely a week goes by when one of these sources doesn't include some form of advice on pitching—"Seven Ways to Think Like a Reporter," "Five Reasons Your Pitch Stinks," "How to Pitch TV News Reporters," "Pitching a Broadcast Story? Think Visual," "How NOT to Write a Pitch Letter" and "The Dos and Don'ts of Pitching Journalists on Social Media" are just a few examples. Pitching is one of the most common and challenging tasks that public relations practitioners face. A few themes emerge from these types of advice columns.

KNOW NEWSWORTHINESS

Journalists have to make decisions every day about what qualifies as news. Depending on the size of their news organization and its audience, journalists may receive dozens if not hundreds of pitches for every one news story they actually cover. Although much of the news you see in newspapers, online and over the airwaves results from pitches made to journalists, much of it also happens without pitching. A public information officer for the National Park Service may spend a lot of time talking to reporters covering a wildfire, or a sports information director for a university may answer a sports reporter's request to interview a head football coach about a big win. A wildfire or a big win for the hometown team are both *newsworthy*.

Whether journalists find the stories themselves or become aware of them with the help of people working in public relations, **newsworthiness** is the criterion they use to determine what is worth covering as news and what is not. PBS's *Student Reporting Labs* program for aspiring journalists lists these five key elements of newsworthiness: timeliness, proximity, conflict and controversy, human interest and relevance (see Table 4.1).[6] Others include novelty, shock value, impact or magnitude and superlatives such as the first, largest, longest, oldest or most expensive of some category.

Looking at stories in the news media and identifying what makes them newsworthy is usually pretty easy. What's trickier is understanding which news from your organization is newsworthy *from the perspective of journalists and their audiences*. If your CEO adopted three new puppies, it may be timely (happened yesterday), proximal (he is bringing them into the office), controversial (some office staff are allergic to dogs), interesting (they are *soooo* cute!) and relevant (new policy—everyone can bring their pets to work one day a week). By all means, put it in your employee newsletter or tweet about it for your personal networks. But does this "news" belong on

Pitching
When a public relations person approaches a journalist or editor to suggest a story idea.

Newsworthiness
Standard used to determine what is worth covering in news media.

TABLE 4.1	**ELEMENTS OF NEWSWORTHINESS**
TIMELINESS	We care about "new" news more than "old" news.
PROXIMITY	We are interested in stories and events that happen when they are local or hit "closer to home."
CONFLICT AND CONTROVERSY	We are drawn to problems or differences within a community.
HUMAN INTEREST	We relish stories of people overcoming great challenges or rising to the occasion to achieve amazing feats. We also pay attention when cute animals, funny kids or gross facts affect our emotions.
RELEVANCE	We depend on pertinent and applicable information to help us make decisions.

tonight's local TV news or in the daily newspaper? How about national news?

The puppy story is a bit of a silly example, but look at the news releases streaming on international services like PRNewswire.com or BusinessWire .com and you'll find examples that are arguably even less newsworthy. A market research firm released a report about the demand for different kinds of molding and trim in the building construction industry.[7] A company won a teacher's choice award for best battery-powered pencil sharpener. And—I have to quote this one directly because I'm not sure what it means—"a pure-play analytics solutions provider" announced "the completion of their latest data governance engagement on the e-commerce industry." All of these news releases were pushed out over international media services in a one-hour time period on a Friday morning.

Of course context is important. If your CEO adopted the puppies as part of the launch of a major new partnership with your local Humane Society, the story may be newsworthy in your community beyond your organization. Likewise, the molding and trim report or the pencil sharpener award may be newsworthy to people who work in those industries. Newsworthiness is in the eye of the beholder. When you know a journalist and her beat, and you have newsworthy information to present in good form that is important to her readers (viewers, listeners, etc.), you will be set up for a win-win—the mutual benefit of helping the journalist with her job while benefiting your organization by getting its story out. But if you mismatch your news with the journalist, at best you will be ignored and at worst you will lose credibility and damage the relationship for the future.

Years after NFL player Colin Kaepernick first kneeled during the national anthem to protest social injustice, other players continued the practice. Miami Dolphins receivers Kenny Stills and Albert Wilson took a knee during the playing of the national anthem before a preseason game in 2018 and were featured prominently in *The Miami Herald*.

Which elements of newsworthiness lead to media attention when NFL players take a knee during the National Anthem?

EMPATHIZE WITH REPORTERS

Finding an appropriate outlet for any story means really understanding the person to whom you are sending the news, and just as important, understanding his or her audience. A famous quote from Sun Tzu's *The Art of War* says, "To know your enemy, you must become your enemy." At the risk of framing the relationship between public relations practitioners and journalists as hostile (it shouldn't be), we may apply the same general idea. To know the news media, you must become the news media.

Advice from the trade press tells us to consider journalists' deadlines, to understand their business and to answer questions such as "Why do I care?" and "Why now?" from their perspective. In other words, put yourself in their shoes. Experience working in newsrooms certainly helps. But even if you have never worked as a journalist, you can still empathize with what it's like to work on deadline and make an effort to understand the people to whom the journalist delivers the news. Read their news stories, watch their programs and follow their social media accounts; all of these things will help you to better understand their style and the type of news they cover.

Before pitching to reporters, read their news stories, watch their programs and follow their social media accounts to better understand their style and the type of news they cover.

MAKE YOURSELF USEFUL

Good journalists do a tremendous amount of research, and public relations specialists are in a unique position to help with access to an organization's people and information. If you work for a school board, you may be one of the most important sources for information for an education reporter. You may be asked for information on test scores or teacher salaries even when those are not the stories you are hoping to communicate. Knowing what information you can share, and what information you are legally obligated to share, will help you help journalists. Even when you have to decline to share information, for example because it is private personnel data or student information, being open about your constraints will help. Again, there may be no immediate benefit to you or your organization when you work with a journalist on a tough story, but building and maintaining a relationship will likely pay off in the long run with fair coverage and greater receptiveness when you do have positive news to share.

Another way to make yourself useful is to direct reporters to other people within your organization who can help as sources. Don't be offended if journalists want to skip right over you as a source. Remember: Put

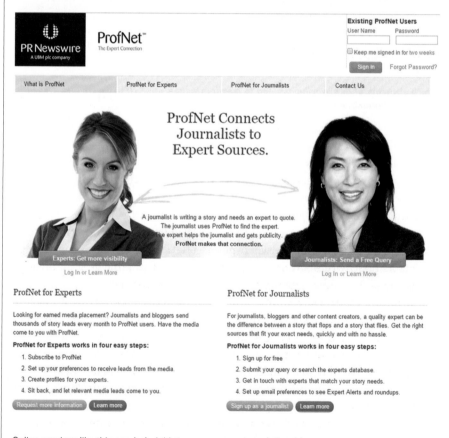

Online services like this one help initiate source-reporter relationships.

How might relationships started from "media catching" be different from relationships started with pitching?

yourself in their shoes. If you were writing a news story about school district test scores, would you rather interview a public relations representative or a school board member, principal or teacher?

Interviews and source-reporter relationships can also be initiated more proactively. Many universities maintain experts databases that catalog professors and researchers based on their areas of expertise and their willingness to work with journalists on related stories. The internet has facilitated this on a global level with services like PR Newswire's ProfNet or Vocus's HARO (Help a Reporter Out) that connect reporters with sources. This practice has been called **media catching**.[8] It reverses the traditional flow of pitching from sources to reporters. Instead of public relations people pitching stories to journalists, journalists can post queries online to which any registered user with relevant information or expertise can respond.

While relationships are key to media relations, depending on the nature of your organization or clients, many if not most of your relationships with journalists may be best characterized as exchange relationships. You exchange information or access for news coverage. Especially early in your career, you may not have longstanding relationships with many of the journalists you pitch. Nonetheless, in situations where you haven't worked with a journalist before, knowing newsworthiness, empathizing and making yourself useful will not only help your chances of **story placement**, it also may set the stage for a longer-term professional relationship.

Commerce-Driven Relationships

As we saw in Chapter 3, many of the relationships in public relations are driven by dollars. The most obvious examples are business-to-consumer relationships. Other important relationships driven primarily by commerce include business-to-business relations, employee relations and investor relations.

B2C

B2C, or **business to consumer**, can describe software, types of organizations, or the relationships between organizations and publics. B2C software usually means e-commerce platforms in which an end user can initiate and complete a transaction online. If you buy an airline ticket from an airline website, order a pair of shorts from a retail store online or purchase software to download, you are working with B2C applications. In the context of the rise of e-commerce as a major sector in world economies, B2C is used to describe companies that sell products or services directly to consumers online. Prior to the dot-com boom, people probably wouldn't have thought to refer to their local bookstore as "B2C," but when Amazon.com rose to success selling books and other products directly to consumers via the internet, the business model was seen as innovative. Amazon, along with countless other companies that have entered the direct-to-consumer market online, is referred to as a B2C company.

Media catching
When journalists post queries online inviting public relations people or others with relevant information or expertise to respond. Public relations people "catch" these opportunities rather than "pitching" story ideas to journalists.

Story placement
The outcome of a successful pitch, when a story involving a public relations practitioner's organization or client is covered in the news media.

Business to consumer (B2C)
The relationship between a business and the end users or consumers of its product or services.

Amazon's fulfillment centers cater to millions of online customers.

How is your relationship with online retailers different from your relationship with retailers when you shop in physical stores?

The term *B2C* also highlights the relationships between businesses and their customers. The four C's of integrated marketing communication (consumer, cost, convenience and communication) highlight important dimensions of those relationships. But, as any businessperson knows, financial success depends on relationships with a number of different publics in addition to customers. By definition, public relations people have an important role to play in maintaining relationships with any group of people on whom the organization's success or failure depends. In business these publics include other businesses, employees and investors.

B2B

B2B stands for **business to business**. Like B2C, B2B is often used to describe technologies such as the platforms that businesses use to perform online transactions with each other. B2B also refers to the relationships between businesspeople from different companies or organizations. For example, when a business hires another business for a service such as management consulting or accounting services, that's a B2B relationship. In the context of marketing, the supply chain from raw materials to manufacturers to wholesalers to retailers involves many B2B relationships before products ever make it to consumers. If you purchase a new smartphone, think of all the transactions that are involved before the device ever reaches the palm of your hand. Silicon is mined or extracted from sand and purchased to make microchips. Microchips are assembled with touch screens, microphones, optical devices and so on. The computer is then programmed with software including multiple apps that enable multiple services and functions. For every one smartphone that is sold, there are countless prior business transactions involving the raw materials, buying and selling of component parts, assembly, delivery, intellectual property and so on.

Besides the sheer volume of transactions involved, a major difference between B2C and B2B is the nature of the buyers. B2B buyers shop as part of their job. The individuals and committees that make decisions about where to buy raw materials for manufacturing products or which package delivery service to contract with are normally well-informed buyers. They are hired, retained and promoted for their expertise in understanding the market and for making rational, highly informed purchasing decisions based on all the data available to them. They use computers and software programs to help them, but, like journalists in media relations, they are still people who make decisions in the context of interpersonal relationships.

Public relations people play a role in B2B relationships using many of the same tactics and channels of communication used for relationships with other key publics. Next time you walk through an airport, pay attention to the display ads and billboards. You'll notice that it's not just coffee and neck pillows being promoted, but also IT systems and consulting services.

Likewise, you've probably seen ads for B2B companies on TV, online and in magazines, particularly if you pay attention to the same news and events as businesspeople. Naturally, *The Wall Street Journal* or Bloomberg .com will carry B2B news and advertising, but businesspeople also watch sports, go on vacations and attend music festivals, which is why you may notice many events (e.g., the FedEx Cup) and venues (e.g., Oracle Arena) bearing the name of B2B companies.

Consider IBM, which seeks to build and maintain B2B relationships by offering tennis fans technology products and services. IBM serves as the information technology supplier and consultant for the All England Club that hosts the Wimbledon tennis championships. In 2018, IBM demonstrated their artificial intelligence (AI) capabilities by automatically producing video highlight packages within minutes after tennis matches ended. The technology ranked the excitement of key moments by matching crowd noise, key statistics from the game, and even players' body language. The resulting highlight videos were then shared almost instantly across social media. Posts linked back to IBM, which provided more information on how the technology could be used to help businesses. Viewers who made their way to the main Wimbledon site and clicked on the IBM logo were directed to a full page of IBM products "that deliver the Wimbledon experience" and a pop-up-window invitation to "Chat now with an IBM Sales Representative who can assist you in finding the right products and services to meet your needs."[9]

Internal publics
Groups of people with shared interests within an organization.

External publics
Groups of people with shared interests outside of an organization. These groups either have an effect on or are affected by the organization.

IBM sponsors Wimbledon and uses the event as a showcase for products and services that it wants to market to other businesses.

How are B2B relationships similar to B2C relationships?

Employee Relations

Internal publics are an important part of public relations. If we're talking about businesses and commerce-driven relationships, the internal publics are employees. Perhaps nowhere else in public relations are the relational outcomes of trust, satisfaction, commitment and control mutuality so apparent. Trusting, satisfied, committed and empowered employees are sure to be more productive and more attuned to and invested in the organization's mission. Moreover, in a world where employees are often the first line of communication with **external publics**, healthy internal relations are prerequisites for healthy external ones.

Internal trust is essential to the operating climate of most businesses, and that trust works both ways. When employees trust the organization and the organization's management trusts the employees, everyone benefits. On the employees' side, most indices of "best places to work" include trust as a central component. When *Fortune* partners with the Great Place to Work Institute to pick the 100 best companies to work for, two-thirds of

Healthy relations with internal publics, such as employees, are prerequisites for healthy relations with external publics.

the score is based on the results of a trust index survey.[10] On the business side, Nan Russell writes in *Psychology Today* that organizational benefits of workplace trust include the following:

- Greater profitability

- Higher return on shareholder investment

- Decreased turnover of top performers

- Increased employee engagement

- Heightened customer service

- Expanded staff well-being

- More collaboration and teamwork

- Higher productivity

- Enhanced creativity and innovation[11]

Establishing and maintaining trust isn't always easy. In fact, it's really hard to foster a trusting workplace when the relationship isn't already positive to begin with. Many variables come into play as part of the overarching organizational culture. Some of these, such as the personalities of the people involved, are outside of the scope and control of public relations, but others, particularly communication and policy, may be areas in which public relations people can offer some help.

Professor Rita Linjuan Men surveyed more than 400 employees of U.S. companies across several industries to see which channels of internal communication were most effective. She found that email and direct face-to-face communication in traditional meetings and with direct managers facilitated information exchange, listening and conversation. Social media, including social network sites, blogs, instant messaging, wikis and streaming audio and video channels were less commonly used, but they served to improve the organizational climate by boosting employee engagement: "In other words, the more often companies use social media to connect with employees, the more engaged employees feel. When employees are engaged, they feel empowered, involved, emotionally attached and dedicated to the organization, and excited and proud about being a part of it."[12] Print media such as newsletters, brochures, reports and posters, though still important for disseminating information, had less of an effect on employee engagement in Men's study.

Because employees know their organizations from the inside out, the principle that excellent public relations requires both communication *and* action is essential to the practice of employee relations. A company's public relations office can communicate all it wants about the organization's culture, the management's commitment to employees, and unwavering pursuit of a noble mission, but for those communications to ring true internally, employees must experience the culture and commitment firsthand.

"It's easy to be someone's friend when times are good," writes evolutionary psychologist David Buss in discussing how humans have evolved to work in groups. "It's when you are really in trouble that you find out who your true friends are."[13] Organizations that support their employees when the going gets tough build stronger relationships. Medtronic is a good example.

Case Study

Putting Money Where Their Mission Is: Medtronic Rebuilds After Hurricane Maria

With a market value well above $100 billion, Medtronic is one of the largest medical technology companies in the world. They make devices like heart monitors and insulin pumps that are critical for patients' treatments and therapies. Topping their mission statement is "To contribute to human welfare by application of biomedical engineering in the research, design, manufacture, and sale of instruments or appliances that alleviate pain, restore health, and extend life." The mission also includes a commitment to product quality, fair profits, good corporate citizenship, and the recognition of the personal worth of employees.[14] That mission was challenged on September 20, 2017, as Hurricane Maria made landfall in Puerto Rico, where about 5,000 Medtronic employees live and work.

The deadly hurricane turned into the worst natural disaster on record to hit Puerto Rico, destroying entire neighborhoods, bringing down the whole island's power grid, and killing a dozen people immediately. Many Medtronic employees lost their homes completely. All four of the company's manufacturing plants were incapacitated. An entire year later, much of the island was still without power, highways and schools were still in shambles, and government reports tallied the number of deaths in the aftermath at more than 1,400.[15]

Remarkably, within only a couple of weeks after the storm hit, Medtronic had all four of its facilities running at partial production levels. And then, just six weeks after the storm hit, the facilities were again running at full capacity.[16, 17] How was this even possible? Employee relations made it happen.

Employees who returned to work in the days after the storm were greeted with a simple sign at the gate that said, "Come help us." Hundreds of workers returned right away to help with the cleanup. Medtronic provided free meals to all 5,000 of its employees, paid wages even while production was offline, brought in more than a million bottles of water and thousands of boxes of food, provided 40,000 gallons of free gasoline, and set up on-site laundromats and day care for employees, along with other services such as banking and help with FEMA applications.[18]

During Hurricane Maria, one employee of Medtronic, Rafael Rodriguez, huddled in the first floor of his home with his family as the winds tore the roof from the top floor. In the months afterward, the family's only shelter was the floor of the second story. With no drinkable running water and no electricity, Rodriguez worked on rebuilding his house in the evenings. But during the day he went to work at Medtronic. "I come to work because people around the world depend on the instruments we build," he said. "I know my family is safe. So why would I stay home when I could be helping others who have probably suffered a different tragedy."[19] On the very same day that Medtronic posted Rodriguez's story on its website, *Investor's Business Daily* reported that Medtronic expected its earnings and revenue to take a big hit.[20]

But remember, earning profits is only part of Medtronic's mission, and in the wake of Hurricane Maria, profits took a back seat to "contributing to human welfare" in real ways that employees felt firsthand. "I know the health and security of us, the employees, is a top priority for Medtronic," Rodriguez said. "I feel very proud to be a part of Medtronic right now."[21]

Investor Relations

If you use salary data as a measure of organizational importance, **investor relations** (IR) is one of the most valued functions among job titles that include the word "relations." According to a survey of employees and analysis of IR job advertisements on Indeed.com in 2018, the average salary was $72,757.[22] And according to Salary.com, U.S. IR managers in 2018 earned an average of more than $128,000.[23] Even though investor relations managers are just as likely to come from backgrounds in business management, accounting or finance as they are to come from communications or public relations, investor relations is very much a public relations function. The National Investor Relations Institute defines investor relations as "a strategic management responsibility that integrates finance, communication, marketing and securities law compliance to enable the most effective two-way communication between a company, the financial community and other constituencies, which ultimately contributes to a company's securities achieving fair valuation."[24]

Professor Alexander Laskin has researched investor relations as a subfunction of public relations. When Laskin interviewed investor relations managers, he found they overwhelmingly agreed that building relationships with investors and analysts is one of the most important things they do. Most cited the importance of good relationships in building trust that the company can do what it says. This leads to financial publics giving the company and its management the benefit of the doubt during times when they might otherwise second-guess their investments. In his panel study, Laskin developed the following statement on relationship building in investor relations, which the participants endorsed:

Investor relations
Management of relationships between an organization and publics in the financial community—for example, investors, analysts, regulators.

The logo for Rite Aid is displayed above a trading post on the floor of the New York Stock Exchange. In 2018, Rite Aid and the grocer Albertsons called off an agreement to become a single company with the deal facing shaky prospects in a shareholder vote.

What role does public relations play in this type of financial business?

> The rewards of this relationship can be significant. Value gaps tend to diminish because investors believe management can accomplish what it says. Positive events and development earn higher stock gain rewards. A flat or down quarter isn't an automatic sell signal. . . . Patience is more likely to be accorded.[25]

While financial information is tightly regulated, as discussed in Chapter 11, investor relations managers use many of the same channels of communication as any other public relations person. These include face-to-face meetings, conference calls, press conferences, news releases, brochures, periodic (e.g., quarterly or annual) reports, websites, blogs and online video.

While financial information is tightly regulated, investor relations managers use many of the same channels of communication as any other public relations person.

Issues-Driven Relationships

Social and environmental issues are big concerns for even the most profit-focused organizations. Relationships with customers, employees, investors and other businesses may be driven by money, but they are also driven by where the organization stands on issues that affect human and natural resources. Some organizations, however, exist for the very purpose of addressing social or environmental issues. They focus specifically on issues for the sake of making a difference, with a much less direct link to any commercial motive.

Nonprofit Organizations

The Nature Conservancy's mission is "to conserve the lands and waters on which all life depends." The American Heart Association exists "to build healthier lives, free of cardiovascular diseases and stroke." People for the Ethical Treatment of Animals (PETA) concentrates "on the four areas in which the largest numbers of animals suffer the most intensely for the longest periods of time: in the food industry, in the clothing trade, in laboratories, and in the entertainment industry." With mission statements like these, nonprofit organizations define themselves by a commitment to some sort of environmental or social benefit besides profit.

Of course, this doesn't mean nonprofits don't need to generate revenue. They still need money to pursue their missions, but the relationships that they maintain with their publics are centered on the issues. Among the most important publics for nonprofit organizations are volunteers and donors. Both support the missions of nonprofits. Donors donate money, and volunteers donate time.

Volunteers and donors are among the most important publics for nonprofit organizations.

VOLUNTEERS

Managing relationships with volunteers involves a mix of external and internal communications. Recruiting volunteers means reaching out into the community and other organizations to find and initiate relationships with people who are likely to help your organization by volunteering time and effort. When college public relations campaign classes take on nonprofit organizations as clients, a common initial goal for the campaigns is to recruit volunteers. Another common goal, which often emerges after students do some initial research, is *retaining* volunteers.

DONORS

Although nonprofits do make money from fees for services and goods, government grants, and other sources, they also depend on donors for revenue. Issues-driven organizations must work just as hard as—if not harder than—commerce-driven organizations to meet their financial goals. That said, those financial goals should not be confused with the greater social benefits the organizations exist to support. The money is only a means to an end. Thus, the most fruitful donor relationships are long-term and based on mutual commitment to the organization's mission. Both research and practice bear out the idea that "fundraising is less about raising money and more about building relationships."[26] PRSA

A volunteer at a Berliner Stadtmission shelter for refugees in Germany gives out clothing donated by Japanese brand Uniqlo to help refugees from Syria and Iraq.

What sustains the relationships between the charity that runs this shelter, its volunteers, its donors, and the migrants and refugees it serves?

Fellow, former fundraising executive and professor of public relations Kathleen Kelly recommends stewardship as a key practice for success in nonprofit public relations management. Four elements of stewardship have been found to influence how donors perceive their relationships with nonprofit organizations. Kelly's four R's are reciprocity, responsibility, reporting and relationship nurturing.

- *Reciprocity*: When donors support an organization, the organization should respond with appreciation. This may be as simple as a handwritten thank-you note or recognition in a member magazine. In cases where someone has made a tax-deductible contribution, the organization can reciprocate with a written thank-you and confirmation that will help the donor file for a deduction.

- *Responsibility*: If you make a donation to aid disaster victims, or to help feed local families in need, you want to be able to trust that the organization is using your donation for that specific purpose. Nonprofits have a responsibility to do what they promise to do. However, all nonprofits use at least a small part of their budgets for administrative functions, so nonprofit executives need to work hard to make sure that donations are managed properly. Public relations people can serve to make sure that donors' wishes are clearly understood, communicated and honored in the management of funds.

- *Reporting*: Digital media have made it much easier for organizations to share tax forms, financial plans, audit information and detailed information about programs and services that demonstrate social accountability as well as financial accountability.[27] The best nonprofits are readily transparent.

- *Relationship nurturing*: This final "R" echoes the idea of communal relationships in which financial exchanges take a back seat to mutual respect and recognition. One measure of relationship nurturing is how often donors hear from an organization when they are *not* being asked for money.[28] As Kelly puts it, the best way to nurture a long-term relationship is simple: "Accept the importance of previous donors and keep them at the forefront of the organization's consciousness."[29] Include donors on e-mail lists. Network with them on social networking sites. Send them copies of breaking news releases that are going to news media. Invite them to events. All of these are ways to keep them in the loop and in the organizational "consciousness."

When Publics Are Organizations and Organizations Are Publics

An **issue** is any important topic or problem that is open for debate, discussion or advocacy.[30] If products, services, stocks and money are the stuff of exchange in regular marketplaces, issues are what fuel exchange in the

Issue
An important topic or problem that is open for debate, discussion or advocacy.

marketplace of ideas. When groups of people are organized on more than one side of an issue, the terms *organization* and *public* become interchangeable.

Imagine working for one of the largest snack food companies in the world and parent company to brands like Nabisco, Oreo and Ritz. You receive a letter with a simple request. Please free the cartoon animals on your cracker box so that they do not appear to be stuck in cages. Knowing that your Barnum's Animals Cracker box is a brand packaging icon that has lasted for more than 100 years, you might be tempted to smile and discard the request. Now imagine that the letter comes from the largest animal rights organization in the world, and that the request is worded like this:

> *Given the egregious cruelty inherent in circuses that use animals and the public's swelling opposition to the exploitation of animals used for enter-tainment, we urge Nabisco to update its packaging in order to show animals who are free to roam in their natural habitats.*[31]

Nabisco's parent company, Mondelēz International, actually received this letter from PETA. With more than 6.5 million members and supporters, PETA is the largest animal rights organization in the world, and it considers the food industry one of its most important publics.[32] But is the feeling mutual? Does a food giant like Mondelēz's Nabisco consider an organization like PETA to be one if its key publics?

You bet they do.

A

B

Nabisco's parent company, Mondelēz International, redesigned its animal cracker box in response to a request from PETA.

Considering the relationship between Mondelēz and PETA in this story, which do you consider to be the "organization" and which one is the "public"? Are those labels interchangeable?

In response to PETA's request, Nabisco in 2018 rolled out redesigned packaging for its Barnum's Animals. The new box shows animals happily moving along with an open savannah in the background, freed from Barnum's caged train cars.

While corporations like Mondelēz International often find themselves in intractable conflict with activist organizations like PETA, in this case they were able to recognize each other as legitimate publics. "We're always looking at how we do things to ensure we're staying relevant for our consumers," said Kimberly Fontes, a spokeswoman for Mondelēz International in a *Washington Post* story. "It seemed like the right time for the next evolution in the brand's design."

PETA's social media manager Ashley Frohnert also was pleased that Nabisco had "joined society in taking a stand for all the animals" that are mistreated in circuses and entertainment. She reported that both organizations enjoyed social media recognition from the case as well. As *PRNews*'s Seth Arenstein quipped, "It's hard to know whether Nabisco or PETA got more of a PR boost from this story."[33]

ACTIVISTS

Larissa Grunig defines an *activist public* as "a group of two or more individuals who organize in order to influence another public or publics through action that may include education, compromise, persuasion, pressure tactics or force."[34] In issues management and crisis management, activists are often defined from the perspective of one organization, but in thinking about two-way relationships, organizations themselves may be activists. Many nonprofits and NGOs are just as organized, sophisticated and effective in their public relations strategies as the other organizations with which they interact.

Take Chicago surfers, for example. Yes, real surfers—not the kind who browse websites but the people who ride freshwater waves in Lake Michigan. For the City of Chicago and the Chicago Park District, surfers did not constitute a public to be concerned with until 2008, when a surfer was arrested for surfing in Lake Michigan. At that point, surfing in Lake Michigan became a recognized *issue*.

Then a *public* emerged. By 2009, "a group of local surfers, watermen, and assorted activists, many of whom had never met," had organized enough to get the attention of city and park district officials.[35] City officials met with this new public and communicated with them in a two-way process that resulted in the lifting of the surfing ban with some restrictions, which were outlined in a 2009 document titled "Non-Motorized Water Sports Information and Safety Awareness," published by the Chicago Park District.[36]

But instead of seeing their collective action as a one-time deal and dissolving their affiliation once the matter was temporarily settled,

SURFRIDER FOUNDATION

The Chicago chapter of Surfrider Foundation was founded partly in response to an issue in which a surfer was arrested for surfing in Lake Michigan.

When did this group become more of an organization than a public?

the group of surfers and activists started the Chicago chapter of the Surfrider Foundation. In doing so, the *public* became a bona fide *organization*. The organization remains active and engaged with city government in Chicago. In fact, in 2017 the Surfrider Foundation and the City of Chicago joined together in a lawsuit against U.S. Steel. They alleged that U.S. Steel illegally dumped nearly 300 pounds of highly toxic chromium into a small waterway adjacent to recreational beaches and surfing spots on Lake Michigan.[37]

GOVERNMENT AGENCIES

Organizations of all types practice advocacy. For example, Allstate insurance company advocates issues related to federal insurance regulation. In this case, a for-profit company is advocating a position on an issue that directly affects its business interests. For this purpose, Allstate pays for **lobbying** activity to influence legislation ($2,290,000 in 2017 according to OpenSecrets.org[38]). This type of activity might also be called **legislative relations** or **government relations** because it involves relationships between the organization and the government entities that regulate the organization's business environment.

Chapter 11 covers some key regulatory agencies with which public relations practitioners should be familiar, and Chapter 2 discusses politics and government as part of the heritage and contemporary practice of public relations. One of the primary functions of government **public affairs** is the dissemination of information *to* constituents (i.e., public information). Another key function is advocating *for* those constituents.

In this chapter, and throughout the text, we see how the idea of building and maintaining relationships applies in the public sector. A government agency may be seen as either an organization or a public depending on your perspective. In the school board example for media relations, we saw the public school board as an organization with a public relations person who was responsible for communicating with news media and other publics. With the Chicago surfer example, we saw how the case could be framed with Surfrider Foundation as the organization and the Chicago Park District as a public.

Members of the Boston Children's Hospital's government relations team attend an event at the Massachusetts State House to meet with elected officials and advocate for legislation.

Are they acting as an organization, a public, or both?

Lobbying
Working to influence the decisions of government officials on matters of legislation.

Legislative relations
Management of relationships between an organization and lawmakers, staffers and others who influence legislation.

Government relations
Management of relationships between an organization and government officials who formulate and execute public policy.

Public affairs
Management of policy-focused relationships between an organization, public officials and their constituents.

Voices from the Field

Rob Clark

ROB CLARK serves as VP of Global Communications and Corporate Marketing for Medtronic, the world's leading medical technology company. He leads corporate marketing, global public relations, employee communications, digital and social media, and philanthropy communication teams worldwide.

Medtronic's work with employees in Puerto Rico following Hurricane Maria must have cost the company millions. What's the return on that investment?

The returns come in many forms. We spent approximately $70 million to restore operations there. From a purely financial standpoint, this was a "no brainer" because we had extensive revenue tied to the products that come through Puerto Rico. From a customer and company mission perspective, also a "no brainer." These products contribute to life-saving medical procedures and therapies, and without them our healthcare customers around the world could not do their jobs. From an employee perspective, also a "no brainer." We have had operations on the island for more than 30 years. These folks are not only our employees but also our family. You would do this for your family, and we did it for ours.

When looking for information on Medtronic's involvement in aid efforts following Hurricane Maria, I had to delve deeply into the company website for details. The stories look to be mostly written for and about employees and focus on the company's impact in the local area. What was the communication strategy?

Your observation was correct. The main rationale for the creation of these stories was to tell our non–Puerto Rico employees what was happening there,

the status of our operations and what our colleagues needed. As you would expect, our non–Puerto Rico employees wanted to help and wanted information—all of which was difficult if literally not impossible to provide. We took some staff members (one who was a former TV journalist) and flew them down there on our plane the second day after the storm. We just said, produce what you can . . . tell us stories on what is happening there and what they need. So the first priority was internal communications to our own people. We quickly realized that these same stories told our customers, government officials and others what we were experiencing and what we were doing to get back up and operational. So then we just started posting them to our newsroom and social feeds. We didn't overly promote them but used them to tell everyone our story.

Which other publics besides employees and media are important in your work?

We are a regulated industry and so government officials and regulators are key audiences for us. In addition to governments being our regulators, they are also our customers—in the form of public health systems, etc. This is a key audience for us. Investors are another one.

What advice do you have for public relations students who want to pursue careers in health-related fields?

PR/comms people don't often gravitate to science and math, but you will need some form of base knowledge to be able to understand scientific and clinical data. Much of healthcare and healthcare communications is tied to this science, so take some classes in this area!

Ethics: Corporate Social Responsibility and Loyalty

Corporate social responsibility (CSR)

Companies' commitment of resources to benefit the welfare of their workforce, local communities, society at large and the environment.

Corporate social responsibility (CSR) refers to a company's commitment to allocate resources to benefit society and the environment. The contributions may come in the form of financial donations, employee time or socially beneficial business practices. While nonprofit organizations exist primarily to make a positive difference in their communities and the natural environment, for-profit businesses and corporations exist primarily to make money. If they don't make money, they eventually will not exist at all and cannot benefit anyone.

Nobel Prize–winning economist Milton Friedman took this logic to an extreme in a famous 1970 article published in *The New York Times Magazine* titled "The Social Responsibility of Business Is to Increase Its Profits." Whether you agree with Friedman or not, he raises interesting ethical questions about how for-profit companies balance their need to make money with their responsibilities as corporate citizens. At the heart of the matter are competing loyalties. Companies may have loyalties to their communities and the natural environment, but they also must be loyal to their shareholders and employees who rely on them to remain profitable. Ethically balancing loyalties in a company's relationships with publics as diverse as environmentalists, government agencies, unions, employees and stockholders is one of the toughest jobs of public relations managers.

> *Ethically balancing loyalties is one of the toughest jobs of public relations managers.*

Case Study

Coca-Cola and Corporate Social Responsibility

Coca-Cola's position atop the branding world hasn't come easily, and its future there isn't guaranteed. In 2012, Coca-Cola was the number one brand in the world, but by 2017 it had slipped to fourth place behind Apple, Google and Microsoft on Interbrand's list of best global brands.[39]

In recent years sugary drinks have been identified as culprits in the fight against obesity. Now being the number one soda brand in the world carries with it the risk of also being labeled as public enemy number one in the fight against obesity, particularly in America. How can a company that relies on sales of sugary drinks that lead to obesity, diabetes and tooth decay make a compelling case that it also cares deeply about the health of consumers?

Former Elon University student and PRSSA president Heather Harder won the Arthur W. Page Society case study competition with her analysis of how Coca-Cola has managed its precarious position. She summarized the company's strategy as one of corporate social responsibility. "By acknowledging the

Coca-Cola's brand faces threats as sugary drinks are seen as a public health problem.

How can a soda company promote its main product while simultaneously working to be socially responsible?

obesity issue and spending millions of dollars on anti-obesity efforts, Coca-Cola is demonstrating corporate social responsibility—if not in its products, then at least in its community involvement."[40]

In response to consumer health issues, Coca-Cola launched a campaign called "Coming Together" that included a theme that "all calories count." The theme emphasized logic that consumers should balance the number of calories taken in with the number of calories they burn, and that calories from Coke products are essentially the same as calories from any other source. Coca-Cola used a variety of tactics to support the theme including:

- videos aired on mainstream media (CNN, Fox, MSNBC)

- a crowdsourced effort that invited consumers to email comingtogether@coca-cola.com with personal stories

- online video via http://www.coca-colacompany.com/coming-together/

- the announcement of several "commitments to fighting obesity" including:
  - offering low- or no-calorie options in every market
  - more prominently displaying calorie information on product labels
  - funding physical activity programs worldwide
  - adopting more responsible marketing practices that avoid targeting children under the age of 12.[41]

The PRSA Code of Ethics features loyalty as a core value. "We are faithful to those we represent, while honoring our obligation to serve the public interest." In this case, those working in public relations for Coca-Cola must balance their loyalty to their employer with their loyalty to many publics with varying interests.

According to Harder, "The challenge is for Coca-Cola to find a way to be taken seriously as a player in anti-obesity efforts while simultaneously increasing sales and offering consumers the products they love." Harder's conclusion highlights the importance of relationships with several key publics in defining the success of the CSR efforts.

CRITICS AND ACTIVISTS

Coca-Cola has begun to offer more low-calorie options including Coca-Cola Life, which is made with stevia, a plant-based sugar substitute.

To which publics is Coca-Cola loyal in this marketing effort?

Perhaps the most vocal opposition in this case is the Center for Science in the Public Interest (CSPI), a nonprofit organization that seeks "to educate the public, advocate government policies that are consistent with scientific evidence on health and environmental issues, and counter industry's powerful influence on public opinion and public policies."[42] The essence of CSPI's criticism was captured in the brevity of a single tweet: "Coca-Cola is desperately trying to disassociate itself with #obesity. Too bad the core product causes it."[43]

CONSUMERS

Let's face it. People don't drink Coke for their health these days. If you work for Coca-Cola, you can be loyal to your consumers in a lot of ways with a lot of different products, but it would be a stretch to imply that your signature

CSPI
@CSPI

👤 Follow

Coca-Cola is desperately trying to disassociate itself with #obesity. Too bad the core product causes it.

The Center for Science in the Public Interest (CSPI) criticizes Coca-Cola on Twitter.

How can Coca-Cola balance loyalty to its shareholders and employees with loyalty to the consumers represented by organizations like CSPI?

cola equates to healthier food options. That said, research shows that consumers pay attention to CSR. In 2015, Nielsen surveyed more than 30,000 consumers in 60 countries. Sixty-six percent of them said they would be willing to pay more for goods and services from socially responsible companies, up from 50 percent in 2013.[44] And, in 2017, Cone Communications reported results from a similar survey in which they found that 87% of respondents said they would purchase a product because a company advocated for an issue they cared about.[45]

INVESTORS

To preserve excellent investor relations with its thousands of shareholders around the world, Coca-Cola must maintain a profitable business model. Can you imagine what it would mean to shareholders—and even entire economies—if Coca-Cola just stopped selling soda because the product was unhealthy? The **golden mean** is an ethical principle in Aristotelian, Buddhist and Confucius philosophies which holds that the most ethical course of action lies between extremes. A golden CSR strategy for Coca-Cola undoubtedly lies somewhere between shuttering its flagship product line to allay the concerns of its critics and ignoring its critics altogether with an uninhibited drive for profit. In fact, CSR may help with profitability, as is evident in research suggesting a link between charitable giving and corporate revenues.[46]

EMPLOYEES

Positive relationships with employees are an important part of the equation linking social responsibility with profitability. It is not hard to imagine how companies with satisfied, committed, trusting and empowered employees (i.e., those with excellent relational outcomes) are more likely to profit in business. CSR trends include programs that encourage employees to participate in service such as pro bono work or paid release time to volunteer in their communities.

Golden mean
Ethical doctrine holding that the best courses of action are found between extremes.

POLICYMAKERS

Legislative relations also come into play, and Coca-Cola invests strategically in its own advocacy. The company lists corporate taxation, environmental policy and product-specific policies including taxes and regulation as areas for investment. Product-specific policy was made more salient when former New York Mayor Michael Bloomberg proposed a ban on the sale of sugary drinks larger than 16 ounces. In its relationship with regulators and legislators, Coca-Cola "advocates for choice and opposes discriminatory tax policies that single out certain beverages."[47] The New York City Board of Health fought for years to impose the policy, but the New York State Court of Appeals ruled that the attempted big-soda ban exceeded the scope of the city's regulatory authority.[48]

Managing an organization requires managing relationships with all sorts of publics. Ethical issues arise when loyalty to any one public risks damage to mutually beneficial relationships with others. Those who work in public relations for Coca-Cola, like people in organizations of all sizes all over the world, face ethical challenges in remaining faithful to those they represent while honoring their obligation to serve the public interest. Corporate social responsibility can be both a strategy for and an outcome of careful relationship management in public relations.

In Case You Missed It

ICYMI

Effective public relations means managing relationships between an organization and its publics. Social skills and business skills both come into play, as highlighted in some of the key takeaways from this chapter.

- The better the long-term relationships between your organization and publics, the more likely you are to achieve your goals.

- Before pitching to reporters, read their news stories, watch their programs and follow their social media accounts to better understand their style and the type of news they cover.

- Healthy relations with internal publics, such as employees, are prerequisites for healthy relations with external publics.

- While financial information is tightly regulated, investor relations managers use many of the same channels of communication as any other public relations person.

- Volunteers and donors are among the most important publics for nonprofit organizations.

- Ethically balancing loyalties is one of the toughest jobs of public relations managers.

SUMMARY

4.1 Describe public relations management in terms of relationship maintenance strategies and relational outcomes.
Managing relationships between organizations and publics for mutual benefit is at the heart of public relations. Many o the same relationship strategies that work in personal relationships—positivity, openness, assurances, social networking and sharing tasks—also work in maintaining relationships between organizations and their publics. The outcomes are similar too: trust, satisfaction, commitment and a sense of mutual control.

4.2 Discuss how news and media attention drive many of the relationships that public relations people manage.
Public relations people build and maintain relationships with media (journalists, editors, producers, bloggers, etc.). Whether journalists find stories themselves or become aware of them with the help of people working in public relations, newsworthiness is the criterion used to determine what is covered as news and what is not. Knowing newsworthiness, empathizing with reporters and providing useful information are all ways that public relations professionals earn fair news coverage.

4.3 Discuss how business and commerce drive many of the relationships that public relations people manage.
Investor relations, marketing communication, customer relations and employee relations are mostly driven by commercial transactions. In addition to consumers, key publics in this domain include financial publics (investors, analysts, regulators, etc.), internal publics (employees, members, etc.) and an array of external publics including other businesses.

4.4 Discuss how issues and causes drive many of the relationships that public relations people manage.
Public affairs, legislative relations and issues management are mostly issues-driven. An issue is any important topic or problem that is open for debate, discussion or advocacy. Donors, volunteers, government officials, community leaders and activists, including those who oppose the organization, are all key publics for organizations as they deal with various issues in the marketplace of ideas.

4.5 Evaluate corporate social responsibility as a strategy for balancing the interests of diverse publics (stakeholder analysis).
The Coca-Cola case illustrates how one company has attempted to balance the varying interests of investors, employees, consumers, activists, lawmakers and global communities. The CSR strategy involves committing resources to benefit society and the environment while also seeking profits. The question for analysis is how effective the company is in building and maintaining simultaneous relationships with a range of stakeholders with very different interests.

DISCUSSION QUESTIONS

1. Relationships can be complicated. Discuss a love-hate relationship that you have with a particular organization. What does that organization do well in the relationship? What does that organization do that causes frustration? What is the role of public relations in that relationship?

2. Look at the ten most recent news releases on https://www.prnewswire.com or https://www.businesswire.com/. Which one is the most newsworthy as a national or international story and why? Which one is least newsworthy and why?

3. Search for an advertised public relations job in investor relations or employee relations at an organization where you'd like to work. In what ways does the job description match your expectations for a "public relations" career? In what ways is it different from what you may have expected?

4. **CASE STUDY** Pretend you are working at Medtronic after Hurricane Maria and the CEO asks you to draft a letter to shareholders for him. He wants to explain why the company spent so much money on employee relations following the storm. What key points will you emphasize?

5. Identify a case from the news in which an activist group has challenged a company. In what ways are the activists a "public" and in what ways are they an "organization"? In what ways is the company a "public"?

6. **CASE STUDY** It was a hard-hitting tweet from @CSPI: "Coca-Cola is desperately trying to disassociate itself with #obesity. Too bad the core product causes it." If you were managing Coca-Cola's social media, would you respond on Twitter? If yes, write the tweet. If no, explain why not.

KEY TERMS

Business to business (B2B)   98
Business to consumer (B2C)   97
Communal relationships   90
Corporate social responsibility
    (CSR)   111
Exchange relationships   89
External publics   100
Golden mean   113

Government relations   109
Internal publics   100
Investor relations   103
Issue   106
Legislative relations   109
Lobbying   109
Media catching   97
Media relations   92

Newsworthiness   93
Participatory media   88
Pitching   93
Public affairs   109
Relational maintenance strategies   88
Story placement   97

CHAPTER 5
Research

Are you active, aware or just meh on the issue of net neutrality?

KEY LEARNING OUTCOMES

5.1 Explain the role of formative and summative research in the RPIE cycle.

5.2 Describe the contents of a situation analysis.

5.3 Discuss applications of quantitative research.

5.4 Discuss applications of qualitative research.

5.5 Compare costs and benefits of secondary and primary research.

5.6 Differentiate between formal and informal research based on reliability and validity.

5.7 Evaluate utilitarianism as an ethical principle for public relations research.

RELATED UNIVERSAL ACCREDITATION BOARD COMPETENCY AREAS

1.1 RESEARCH CONCEPTS · **1.2** RESEARCH APPLICATIONS · **1.3** ANALYTICAL SKILLS
1.4 STRATEGIC THINKING · **2.2** ETHICAL BEHAVIOR

Figure 5.1 The RPIE Cycle campaign begins, ends, and begins again, with research.

What are some of the very first questions campaign planners should ask, and what kind of research helps answer them?

In politics, it is sometimes said that a new campaign starts the day after Election Day. Although we hope that our elected officials will focus more on getting their new job done than on getting reelected, there is quite a bit of truth here for campaign strategists. An election is like a survey of voters, and fresh election results yield all sorts of new data to kick off planning for future campaigns.

Strategic planning is a cyclical process. Whether a college student is planning one semester's budget based on the prior semester's spending, a volleyball coach is reviewing last season's performance to plan for the next season, or a campaign strategist is analyzing the results of one campaign to plan for the next one, the process is similar. Successful planning begins, ends, and begins again, with research (Figure 5.1). In between are planning (Chapter 6) and implementation (Chapter 7). This chapter explains how strategy starts with research. Public relations campaigns and programs with research-based goals and objectives lend themselves to proper evaluation (Chapter 8). Proper evaluation helps you make a case for the value of your work. Being able to demonstrate the value of your work gets you hired and promoted.

Research in the RPIE Cycle

For years, public relations students studying for exams and practitioners reviewing for accreditation interviews have referred to the four-step process of researching, planning, implementing and evaluating programs. RPIE and acronyms that start with "R" have served as trusty mnemonic devices. RACE,[1] ROPE[2] and ROSIE[3] are three common examples. RACE stands for research, action, communication and evaluation. ROPE stands for research, objectives, programming and evaluation. ROSIE includes research, objectives, strategies, implementation and evaluation. Not only do they all start with an "R," but they all end with an "E" for evaluation, which is a type of research in and of itself.

If we think of strategic public relations as a dynamic and cyclical process, it makes sense that the evaluation of one action, program or campaign feeds back into the next. In fact, evaluation can happen at any point in a strategic program, not just at the end.

Formative Research

When research comes at the beginning of the planning process, or during the implementation of a plan, it is known as **formative research**. The information acquired during formative research helps you formulate your program or campaign and its components, including goals, objectives, strategy and tactics. On one hand, formative research, or formative evaluation, can be casual

Evaluation can happen at any point in a strategic program, not just at the end.

Formative research
Research conducted at the beginning of the planning process, or during the implementation of a plan.

and unscientific. If you call a few reporters to pitch a news story idea and they all decline abruptly, you may want to step back and re-formulate your approach based on that information before you call anyone else. That's *informal* formative evaluation. However, informal trial and error on its own does not constitute strategic public relations.

On the other hand, formative research and evaluation can be carefully planned and sophisticated. Public relations professionals may begin campaigns or programs with detailed web **analytics**, carefully collected survey data on key publics or formally designed interviews. They also may continue to track those analytics, re-administer the surveys and interview people for the duration of the campaign or program, using the live feedback to make corrections to strategy.

Summative Research

Summative research is when you've reached an end or stopping point in your campaign and you want to answer the question, "Did it work?" One way to differentiate between a campaign and an ongoing program is that a campaign has a defined beginning and end. A political campaign ends with an election. A year-end fundraising campaign ends on December 31. A product-launch campaign ends when the product is fully available in the market, or at some specific date determined by the campaign's planners. In identifying an end-date for a campaign, planners make themselves accountable for specific outcomes at a specific point in time. Yes, those summative results can and should inform ongoing work and future campaigns, but as final evaluations, they answer the question of whether and to what extent the campaign achieved its goals (e.g., won the election, raised the target amount of money or met sales projections for a new product).

When the "E" is placed at the end of an acronym like RACE or ROPE, it suggests summative evaluation. Remember, however, that research and feedback are important throughout the entire process of public relations work. This chapter focuses mostly on research as part of the planning process. Chapter 8 delves into specific methods for measurement including evaluation research designed to quantify results of campaigns. One method to begin planning is to organize research into three major areas: (1) situation, (2) organization and (3) publics.

"I must say, your hindsight on this project was far more accurate than his foresight."

Evaluation of one project can serve as insight for the next one.

How does public relations research help turn hindsight into foresight?

Analytics
A field of data analysis used to describe, predict and improve how organizations communicate with publics; commonly refers to tracking of website traffic and resulting behavior.

Summative research
Research conducted at the end of a campaign or program to determine the extent that objectives and goals were met.

AT&T mounted the "It Can Wait" campaigns to curb smartphone-distracted driving.

What kind of research could they do to know if the campaign efforts worked?

Situation Analysis

Good public relations cases read like good stories, and good stories rely on an interesting setting. The setting provides the context for the problem or opportunity from which the public relations goals arise. At the very beginning, the situation may be only vaguely stated or implied (e.g., "We need to raise awareness"), but with research the situation can be analyzed more carefully to initiate strategic planning. Public relations case studies and write-ups for public relations case competitions such as PRSA's Silver Anvil awards normally include a **situation analysis** at the beginning. Table 5.1 provides some examples of situation analysis starters from PRSA Silver Anvil winners.[4]

Each of the cases described in Table 5.1 begins with a narrative presentation of the situation. The impetus for a public relations effort is either a problem, an opportunity or some combination of the two. And, getting started means doing research to first identify the problem or opportunity and then to understand it well enough to create a narrative.

An effective situation analysis leads to a clear, concise **problem or opportunity statement** on which the client or organization and the team representing them agree. In their text *Strategic Communications Planning*, Brigham Young University's Laurie Wilson and Joseph Ogden write that a core problem statement can be written in a single sentence.[5] Others recommend a paragraph or two. Because it captures the essence of the situation and determines the scope and value of your proposal, your core problem or opportunity statement may well be one of the most carefully constructed sentences or paragraphs you write in all of your work in public relations. Distilling a vague, complex and ambiguous context down to a brief statement that everyone involved can agree upon requires careful analysis.

Situation Research

One common approach for structuring the analysis is the **SWOT analysis** (Figure 5.2). SWOT stands for strengths, weaknesses, opportunities and threats.

Strengths are factors internal to your organization or client that will help you reach your goals or fulfill your mission. If your client is the faculty of a local college, some strengths might be a range of faculty projects that benefit local communities or a record of faculty involvement in community

Situation analysis
A report analyzing the internal and external environment of an organization and its publics as it relates to the start of a campaign or program.

Problem or opportunity statement
A concise written summary of the situation that explains the main reason for a public relations program or campaign.

SWOT Analysis
Description and discussion of an organization's internal strengths and weaknesses and its external opportunities and threats.

TABLE 5.1 EXAMPLES OF SITUATION ANALYSIS STARTERS: PRSA SILVER ANVIL WINNERS

CAMPAIGN	SITUATION
FLEISHMANHILLARD AND KWI'S "AFLAC: PERCEPTION PLAY IN SOCIAL RESPONSIBILITY" FOR AFLAC	"Chances are you're familiar with supplemental insurance giant Aflac and its quirky Duck. The 60-year-old company is one of Fortune's Best Places to Work and World's Most Ethical Companies, but in spite of these accolades, its successful business and brand were not translating to well-earned recognition for corporate social responsibility (CSR)—at least not beyond its Georgia HQ. That's a reputational deficit for a national consumer brand. There was no ducking this disconnect. . . ."
KETCHUM AND DIGITASLBI'S "CARE COUNTS" FOR WHIRLPOOL	"Whirlpool uncovered a surprising reason why students nationwide weren't coming to school: many kids lacked clean clothes, staying home to avoid mockery and bullying. Could we find a solution to chronic absenteeism with something as simple as a washer and dryer and rise above a world of worthy causes?. . ."
GÜD MARKETING'S "DON'T WAIT EVALUATE" FOR EARLY ON® MICHIGAN AND GENESEE INTERMEDIATE SCHOOL DISTRICT	"Health officials in Flint, Mich., are still trying to minimize the effects of lead exposure of nearly 100,000 people, which began when the city started drawing water from the Flint River as its source of drinking water. Among those most impacted by the crisis are approximately 3,600 children between ages 0 and 3 who are potentially at risk of lead-related developmental delays.. . . ."
HELVEY COMMUNICATIONS AND KD/PR VIRTUAL'S "WHEN NIGHTMARES COME TRUE: A CRISIS COMMUNICATIONS PLAN"	"When a tutoring company discovered a top employee was being investigated for the possession of child pornography and sexual relations with a minor, an effective crisis communications plan was imperative. Maintaining the confidence of its clients and partners would be a challenge in the midst of legal constraints, uncertainty of facts and quickly changing circumstances.. . ."

organizations as part of their professional service. It would take research to learn what these projects and organizations are and understand who benefits.

Weaknesses are internal factors that make it harder for your organization or client to do what it wants to do. In the college example, weaknesses may be a lack of training or professional incentive for faculty to communicate their scholarship outside of their peer groups. Or, perhaps there is a gap in communication between college faculty and the professional communicators representing the school. Again, it would take research to obtain an accurate sense of the internal communication environment.

Opportunities and threats are external variables. A relatively close-knit college town where there are few degrees of separation between citizens and

SWOT ANALYSIS

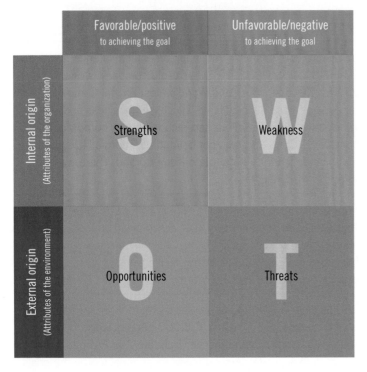

Figure 5.2 SWOT analyses help you identify key factors in planning for public relations.

How might researching factors of internal origin (strengths and weaknesses) be different from researching factors of external origin (opportunities and threats)?

Gaining a deeper understanding of a situation requires digging for information of substance beyond an internet search.

the people working in the college could be an opportunity for word-of-mouth communication. A decreasing revenue projection that will put greater scrutiny on the college's budget may be a threat.

As with strengths and weaknesses, opportunities and threats are often two sides of the same coin. Greater scrutiny of an organization's budget may be perceived as a threat. Programs could be cut or jobs could be at risk. But at the same time, close attention to an organization's budget may provide an opportunity to communicate the value of the organization's work. In addition to educating students, colleges and universities employ thousands of people, generate revenue in patents and licenses and provide launching pads for start-ups. Discovering strengths, weaknesses, opportunities and threats and listing them in a table is an appropriate start, but the actual analysis of that information requires closer examination and discussion. Prioritizing the most relevant information, deciding what *not* to focus on, and understanding how different factors relate to one another and to your organization's mission are all part of the work you do in getting ready to tell the story.

In all likelihood, situation research starts with an internet search and conversations with the clients. However, gaining a deeper, more analytic and more nuanced understanding of the situation than what the client already knows from their own quick Google search requires digging deeper for information of substance. Here are some potential resources for researching the situation:

- Summaries of relevant media coverage, including stories placed in print, broadcast or online media. The organization may already have reports on file or may subscribe to media monitoring services (see Chapter 8) that generate such reports.

- Copies of any organizational documents related to the problem that the client is willing to share, including policies, reports, archived correspondence and web or intranet material.

- Collateral material from prior campaigns and programs (brochures, web content, product information, etc.), news releases and ads.

- Any available statements, reports or information from or about the organization's competitors that is relevant to the situation.

- Calendars or schedules of related events.

- Copies of relevant laws, regulations, budgets or pending legislation that are publicly available through government web pages or upon request from government agencies.

- Any research already conducted and reported (surveys, interviews, content analyses, communication audits, message testing and usability studies, etc.).

- Web analytics reports, which track website traffic such as the number of unique visitors to a site, the number of page views, how much time people spend on a site, the percentage of people who leave after seeing only one page (bounce rate) or indicators of other objectives such as the number of registrations or downloads (see Chapter 8).

- Prior marketing, advertising and public relations plans.

As a cohesive narrative analysis of the situation comes together, and as that brief problem or opportunity statement begins to take shape, it's crucial to stay in touch with the client or organization's management to ensure you are on the right track. For example, consider the problem/opportunity statement for Ogilvy Public Relations Worldwide and DuPont's "Welcome to the Global Collaboratory" campaign:

> DuPont was challenged by its "chemical company" reputation, despite being a long-time global contributor to food production, nutrition and safety. It also confronted a landscape with a chief competitor, Monsanto, espousing a strong, public POV [point of view] that biotechnology is the primary answer to the problem. DuPont retained Ogilvy to develop a campaign to showcase to the global food influencer community its commitment to bringing together key audiences who can create solutions to ensuring global food security.[6]

An organization and its publics are embedded in the situation and must, therefore, be researched concurrently. Although practitioners may start with a general background and broad context for strategic public relations efforts, delving deeper makes apparent the need for research specifically focusing on the organization and its publics.

Organization Research

Perhaps the best place to start understanding an organization is its mission. The mission is the organization's steady, enduring purpose. For example, a college or university's mission may entail research, teaching and service. Even if you are working **in house** or are already familiar with a client, you may still find it useful to review the organization's mission or vision statement if one is available.

MISSION OR VISION STATEMENTS

A for-profit corporation's **mission statement** may be quite different from the mission statement of a nonprofit or NGO. For example, compare Chewy.com's mission statement:

In house
When public relations people are employed directly within an organization rather than working for an external agency or contracted as independent consultants.

Mission statement
A formal statement of an organization's steady, enduring purpose.

Vision statement
A declaration of an organization's
desired end-state.

We're working to become the most trusted and convenient online destination for pet parents and our partners—vets and service providers—alike. Our success is measured by the happiness of the people and pets we serve, not simply by the amount of pet supplies we deliver. That's why we continue to think of outside-the-Chewy-box ways to delight, surprise, and thank our loyal pet lovers.[7]

To the mission statement of the American Humane Society summarized in four words that pack a punch:

Celebrating Animals, Confronting Cruelty.[8]

Many organizations also develop **vision statements**, which describe a desired end-state resulting from an organization's work. For example, the University of Oregon's mission statement differs from its vision statement. Like many universities, Oregon's mission statement focuses on what it does teaching, research and service:

The University of Oregon is a comprehensive public research university committed to exceptional teaching, discovery, and service. . . .[9]

Its vision statement, however, describes its aspirations and a desired end-state:

We aspire to be a preeminent and innovative public research university encompassing the humanities and arts, the natural and social sciences, and the professions. We seek to enrich the human condition through collaboration, teaching, mentoring, scholarship, experiential learning, creative inquiry, scientific discovery, outreach, and public service.[10]

Mission statements, vision statements and other key publications give researchers a sense of the organization's values and culture. Given the amount of effort and levels of review that these major organizational statements often require before being published, they should be taken seriously as indicators of the reason the organization exists and deeper purpose of why people work there. Of course, not all organizations publish mission or vision statements, but you can still find evidence of an organization's broadest guiding principles and philosophy in key publications such as annual reports, or even the "About Us" section of a website or app.

RESOURCES FOR ORGANIZATION RESEARCH

Other written documents to seek in learning about an organization may include the following:

- Any written history.

- The organization's charter and bylaws.

- A flow chart or other description of the organizational structure.

- Product or service descriptions.

- Biographies of or interviews with key executives and board members.

- Summary budget reports, and other summary data on staffing, profits, stock values and so on.

- Social media account profiles, posts and networks including individuals and other organizations.

- Organizational communication policies and social media policies if available.

- Any prior research reports or audits of internal communication channels or programs.

Of course, researchers cannot rely on formal written material alone to understand what makes an organization tick. Reviewing a company's webpage, publications and archives is not sufficient to gain tacit knowledge of something as intangible as **organizational culture**. Designing a public relations campaign with an appreciation for organizational culture in the context of a particular situation (or a situation in the context of an organizational culture) requires astute observation not just of written evidence but of people and their behavior.

Publics Research

In conducting research on the situation and organization, you gain a good understanding of the benefits that an organization seeks from public relations campaigns and programs. Public relations professionals use that research, along with research on publics, to develop goals and objectives that serve the organization's broader mission. But remember that the best relationships are mutually beneficial. This means you have to work to understand not just the interests of your own organization, but also the interests of your publics. What are *they* going to get out of the relationship? This kind of understanding requires thinking about research as part of a larger process of two-way communication. The RPIE process is very much a cycle of interactive communication between organizations and their publics. Just as your richest interpersonal communication happens when you listen as much as you talk, organization-public relationships flourish when public relations people spend as much energy trying to understand publics as they do trying to get their messages out.

INTERNAL AND EXTERNAL

Publics can be either internal or external to the organization, and that designation may depend on the context. Employees and members are almost always thought of as **internal publics**, and as such they can be reached via internal channels such as face-to-face meetings, company email lists, hallway bulletin boards, intranets and even the organizational grapevine. To the degree that these channels are used for gaining feedback, they can be used for research and evaluation.

Organization-public relationships flourish when you spend as much energy trying to understand your publics as you do trying to get your message out.

Organizational culture
Groups of people that identify as part of an organization such as employees and members.

Internal publics
The unique character of an organization comprised of beliefs, values, symbols and behaviors.

External publics
Groups of people that exist mostly
outside of an organization and have
a relationship with the organization.

Teachers in Los Angeles participate in an organized protest.

When teachers go on strike, are they internal or external publics for their schools?

While an organizational chart may offer a relatively simple map for reference when identifying internal publics, it is important to think about the definition of a public when identifying and prioritizing internal publics. Remember, publics are groups of people with shared interests who have an effect on an organization or whom the organization affects. Most people internal to an organization will fit both these criteria, but specific situations will mean prioritizing internal publics differently. If a university is working to gain funding based on its faculty research and community service, faculty members will be a key internal public. In a campus nighttime safety campaign, university police and resident assistants may be more important. Alumni, who share an identity with the school, may be considered internal or external, depending on the situation.

External publics are outside of the organization and are generally reached via channels such as mass media, direct mail and the web. Each of these channels also can serve as a resource for feedback and research. Even though mass media such as TV, newspapers and radio are mostly one-way forms of communication, audience data from services like Nielsen TV ratings, responses to radio promotions, coupon codes from print ads or traffic data from web pages can all be useful in researching external publics.

Of course, there are limitations on how precisely publics can be segmented based on the media they use. The most massive of mass media will certainly reach internal publics. You can bet employees are as affected by a Super Bowl commercial for their company as their global customers are—hopefully in a positive manner. Favorable cable news coverage or a front-page story in the news may have a similar effect. For internal publics, a well-received, big-time mass media hit may provide a boost in morale or give employees extra confidence that people have heard of their company when they pursue a sales lead or introduce themselves at a meeting. Likewise, even the most interpersonal channels can reach external publics. This has always been the case with word-of-mouth communication, and it is more pronounced with social media.

As it becomes easier to share internal communication externally online, the lines between internal and external communication blur. Research shows that good internal communication—which includes all sorts of formal and informal communication such as CEO announcements, employee forums, and peer-to-peer social media—affects external communication because employees serve as brand advocates. Professor Rita Linjuan Men, author of *Excellence in Internal Communication Management*, maintains that employees should be seen as the highest-priority publics "because of their role as corporate ambassadors."[11, 12]

But it can go the other way too. When Amazon sent a 45-minute training video to team leaders at its Whole Foods grocery stores, it was meant to encourage employees to bring grievances to their bosses individually instead of through union representation. The video was leaked externally, however, and became the center of a story about Amazon's employee relations and adversarial relationship with employees who favor unions. *Gizmodo* quoted anonymous employees who complained of fear of retaliation for voicing opinions about management externally. For example, one Amazon worker described an internal culture of intimidation: "You're

Good internal communication affects external communication . . . because employees serve as brand advocates.

Employees are among the most important publics for organizations like Amazon and Whole Foods.

In what types of situations might the lines between internal and external communications be blurred?

Situational theory of publics
Theory that the activity of publics depends on their levels of involvement, problem recognition and constraint recognition.

Net neutrality
When data transmitted on the internet is treated equally by governments and service providers in a way that does not slow down, speed up or manipulate traffic to create a favorable business environment for some organizations or users over others.

somebody that talks and you're somebody they're gonna absolutely make the job as difficult as humanly possible for."[13] Research for a situation analysis on this case would have to include internal publics (Amazon management, Whole Foods team leaders), external publics (Gizmodo, other media and their readers, unions) and employees who are thinking about organizing and communicating externally about the situation, thereby blurring the lines between internal and external communication.

LATENT, AWARE, ACTIVE

According to Kurt Lewin, a pioneer in social and organizational psychology, "There is nothing so practical as a good theory."[14] A good example of practical theory in public relations is James Grunig's situational theory of publics. The theory applies easily to practice, in that it helps us identify and strategize about publics in the context of a situation analysis and the planning that follows. The situational theory of publics basically says that publics range from latent to aware to active based on their levels of involvement, problem recognition and constraint recognition.

Case Study

Applying the Situational Theory of Publics: Net Neutrality

The case of net neutrality offers an example of how the **situational theory of publics** can be applied. **Net neutrality** is the idea that internet service providers (ISPs) should allow all internet users equal access to content, without giving some content providers a fast lane or slowing or blocking other content providers. According to Free Press's "Save the Internet" Campaign at www.freepress.net, net neutrality "is the basic principle that prohibits internet service providers like AT&T, Comcast and Verizon from speeding up, slowing down or blocking any content, applications or websites you want to use."[15]

The Free Press organization and its supporters celebrated in February 2015 when, after much public input, the Federal Communications Commission (FCC) voted narrowly (3-2) to adopt regulations ensuring that ISPs would treat all internet content equally, including streaming video, audio and games. But not everyone was happy with the outcome. Many sided with broadband companies in arguing that the new rules were too restrictive on companies that invest in innovation and that ISPs would be put at a disadvantage by the excessive regulation.

In 2017, the composition of the FCC commission changed, and the rules in support of net neutrality were repealed. Activist organizations such as Free Press, Fight for the Future, and the Free Press Action Fund, along with companies like Netflix, Vimeo, Dropbox, Google and Facebook renewed the fight for net neutrality. But do everyday internet users really care either way? How about you? Are you part of a latent, aware or active public for the issue? The answer depends on how you would answer three questions related to your *problem recognition*, *involvement* and *constraint recognition*.

PROBLEM RECOGNITION

How often do people stop to think about the issue? If people haven't detected an issue, they won't think about it much. This doesn't mean they aren't affected or don't have a say. They may well still be part of a key public. They just don't realize it. Think of all the Netflix viewers, YouTube uploaders, and online gamers who never stop to think about net neutrality even though they could be affected by changes to the rules. These are **latent publics**, because even though they can be defined as a public, they themselves don't recognize it. Once they do recognize the issue—**problem recognition**—and start thinking about it, they become **aware publics**. Most strategic public relations efforts involve not just mere awareness, but some level of understanding of the issue, and, beyond that, behavior.

LEVEL OF INVOLVEMENT

How connected do people feel to the issue? A key factor in whether people will become **active publics** on an issue is their **level of involvement**. People who use the internet primarily for low-bandwidth activities like checking email or occasional light web browsing may have been aware of the net neutrality issue, but they just didn't see a strong enough connection between the issue and their personal situations to get active on the issue. Some people may have become active prior to 2017, but then felt less involved with the issue when they didn't notice any difference in their service after the net neutrality rules changed.

From a public relations planner's perspective, research on demographics and psychographics is useful in identifying involved publics. Research on **demographics** answers questions like how old these people are and where they live. Research on **psychographics**, on the other hand, answers questions about variables such as the personality types of heavy internet users and their preferences for online content. The psychographic profile of a potential active public in the net neutrality debate is one of a heavy data user who combines professional, personal and social use of bandwidth. Political leaning comes into play too.

CONSTRAINT RECOGNITION

What, if anything, can people do about the issue? Let's say your public now really understands net neutrality and they're good and mad about it being taken away (high problem recognition) because they feel the change is a political move that only benefits big ISPs (high level of involvement). What are they going to do about it? The answer depends on **constraint recognition**, and a smart public relations plan will have a response to that question ready for publics at this stage. Users who found the Free Press website by

Latent publics
People who are affected by a problem or issue but don't realize it.

Problem recognition
When people detect a problem or situation in their environment and begin to think about it.

Aware publics
People who recognize that they are affected by a problem or issue in their environment.

Active publics
People who behave and communicate actively in response to a problem or issue.

Level of involvement
The degree to which people feel or think that a problem or issue affects them.

Demographics
Data describing objective characteristics of a population including age, level of income or highest educational degree obtained.

Psychographics
Data describing psychological characteristics of a population including interests, attitudes and behaviors.

Constraint recognition
When people detect a problem or situation in their environment but perceive obstacles that limit their behavior to do anything about it.

Netflix tweeted this message from the website BattleFortheNet.com, which is hosted by a non-profit organization called Fight for the Future. This meme made the rounds on social media sites in 2014-2015 and again in 2017.

What types of research do you think led to this tactic?

clicking through from social media links or following hashtags such as #NetNeutrality were greeted with a call to action: "Stop the Trump administration's attack on the open internet!" and an "Act Now" button. Clicking the button opened an easy-to-use form for generating an email to Congress.

In 2015, the FCC adopted rules to protect the open internet and, in so doing, sided with millions of people who took an active stance on the issue.[16] And in 2017, when the FCC considered repealing the 2015 rules, the agency received more than 23 million comments on the issue! However, according to *USA Today*, "millions of them were fake submissions, many sent by bots, and nearly a half-million comments came from Russian email addresses."[17]

Despite the loss, many activist organizations such as Free Press, Fight for the Internet, and the Free Press Action Fund continue to fight for net neutrality by working to sustain grassroots campaigns. The success of their efforts will depend in large part on whether people feel like they can make a difference in this environment (constraint recognition) as well as if people sense that the new regulations have made any difference in their online experience (problem recognition).

Fight for the Future is a nonprofit organization that creates civic campaigns including this one advocating for net neutrality.

Do you think this is an effective tactic for moving publics from aware to active?

OTHER WAYS OF SEGMENTING PUBLICS

Depending on the context, public relations strategists may choose to segment publics in a number of other ways. For clear prioritization, publics may be labeled as primary, secondary and tertiary. Suppose you are planning a community park cleanup. You may decide that young volunteers are your **primary public**. According to the Useful Community Development website (http://www.useful-community-development.org), you could recruit local children: "At age 3 and up, they can pick up trash," and "Teenagers can be drawn in, especially if you provide a good-looking T-shirt...." In planning, you would also want to develop strategy to communicate with their teachers and parents, especially if some of your recruits are only three years old. Parents of small children also would be primary publics, but you might decide to label parents of older teenagers and teachers who might encourage participation as **secondary publics**. Additional groups, known as **tertiary publics**, could include city officials, sponsors or private waste removal companies as well as other park users who will benefit.

In cases involving competition or divisive issues, publics may be segmented into proponents, opponents and uncommitted. Campaign strategy, especially in political campaigns, often focuses on the uncommitted. While it is important to reinforce the attitudes of supporters, and occasionally those opposed to your candidate or position may be won over in an election, the greatest gains in many campaigns come from undecided or independent voters. The same logic applies outside of politics. Some people will support your efforts even without a public relations program, and others will never get involved; however, you can make progress with

Some people will support your efforts without a public relations program, and others will never get involved, but you can make progress with publics that are somewhere in between.

Primary publics
Groups of people identified as most important to the success of a public relations campaign or program.

Secondary publics
Groups of people who are important to a public relations campaign or program because of their relationship with primary publics.

Tertiary publics
Groups of people who indirectly influence or are indirectly affected by a public relations campaign or program.

Planners need to consider many publics that will be involved in various ways with an event like this neighborhood cleanup in Detroit.

Can you name some primary, secondary and tertiary publics for this event?

publics that are somewhere in between, moving them from latent to aware to active.

Sometimes it makes sense to segment publics based on their role in the communications process. For example, you may want to think about the sources for your messages such as employees or members of your organization, the intermediaries such as reporters, community leaders or social media influencers, and the target publics who will receive and respond to the message. Keep in mind that in two-way communication, senders and receivers will have interchangeable roles. For example, company representatives may be expected to send information out, but having those same people positioned to receive and respond to feedback is important too.

RESOURCES FOR RESEARCH ON PUBLICS

The following are useful resources for conducting research on publics:

- *Results of prior surveys.* These may be conducted either by the organization or by others who have sampled from populations that overlap significantly with key publics.

- *Publicly available databases, including census data.* Funded by the government, U.S. Census data are free to access, and www.census.gov allows for searching and analysis based on geography, demographics and topics such as education, economy, health and business.

- *Market research reports.* These generally cost money if you want data tailored to your specific questions about key publics, but they can be useful and fascinating if your budget permits them. For example, the Strategic Business Insights' VALS™ (values, attitudes and lifestyles) system offers demographic and psychographic profiles of consumers.

- *Media lists.* These include journalists and other opinion leaders (e.g., columnists, editors, commentators) and influencers online (e.g., bloggers and other actively engaged social media users).

- *News stories or online reports about key publics.* For example, if you search for "Sacramento park cleanup" you'd find information from the city of Sacramento about volunteer programs, a nonprofit organization called American River Parkway Foundation that coordinates cleanup activities, and news and information about "Creek Week" including its past sponsors and Facebook group ("First we clean . . . then we celebrate!"). More controversial situations will more likely have been covered in news reports including descriptive information about proponents and opponents. News stories or prior research reports may also include perspectives gained from interviews that offer richer perspective than is available from statistical reports.

- *Social media accounts of representatives of key publics.* Blogs, Twitter accounts, public Facebook groups and Instagram accounts can offer a better understanding of a public's motivations, concerns and general culture from a first-person perspective.

- *An organization's past communication records with key publics.* Look around for collections of comment cards, email folders with public feedback, archived comments or replies to social media posts, minutes from public meetings, guest lists for special events and even logs of incoming phone calls (including complaints). As a customer, I actually like it when I'm told that my call to a company "may be recorded." It gives me hope that my concern will be taken seriously (though somehow I doubt those call recordings are listened to often).

Census data are freely available at www.census.gov.

How might this type of data be useful in a public relations program?

Quantitative Research

When numbers and statistics accompany the results of research, it is considered **quantitative research**. In a blood drive, quantitative data could include demographic statistics on blood donors and non-donors in a county, the number of email accounts that are known to have received an invitation, the percentage of people who click on a link in an email invitation, the number of people who respond to a Facebook invitation, the number of retweets of a Twitter announcement, other more sophisticated analytics of the pattern of social media activities, the number of people who make an appointment to donate blood, the number of people who actually board the bloodmobile on a given day and, perhaps most important, the amount of blood actually donated. Surveys and experiments are common methods for quantitative research.

Quantitative research
Research that results in numerical or statistical data and analysis.

Treatment group

A group of subjects or people in an experiment who receive or are exposed to a treatment.

Control group

A group of subjects or people in an experiment who do not receive or are not exposed to a treatment for the purpose of comparison.

Content analysis

A systematic method for analyzing recorded information such as audio, video or text.

Surveys

Questionnaires that are administered online, on printed paper or face-to-face allow researchers to gather data from respondents that can be presented in quantitative form. Reports can include the number or percentages of people who answered questions in certain ways (yes, no, maybe, strongly agree, etc.) and more sophisticated statistics such as correlations, and tests of the significance of interactions between variables.

For example, researchers who surveyed a sample of Polish university students with questionnaires administered in lecture rooms found that 19 percent had considered blood donation and that 37.9 percent had not decided about donating blood or had never even thought about it. They also reported that religious obligation (measured with a numerical scale of agreement with the statement "My religious beliefs encourage me to help other people") correlated with another item that measured "definite consideration of blood donation."[18] A positive correlation in this case means that people who reported stronger religious beliefs were more likely to consider donating blood.

Experiments

Experiments allow researchers to test predictions based on controlled differences between groups. For example, researchers working with the Swiss Red Cross and the Zurich Blood Donation Service sent three different invitations out to people who were registered in the blood donation service's database. Recipients of the invitations were randomly assigned to one of three groups. Members of one group, a **treatment group**, were offered a lottery ticket as an incentive to donate. A second treatment group was offered a free blood screening. The third group, known as a **control group**, was offered no special incentive. Because more than 10,000 donors were part of the study and participants were assigned to groups randomly, any difference between groups could reasonably be attributed to the different invitations and incentives. The researchers found that "offering a lottery ticket increases usable donations by 5 percentage points over a baseline donation rate of 42 percent."[19]

Content Analysis

Content analysis does not involve direct interaction or questioning of people, but rather analyzing the content of people's communication. Any type of recorded communication—from newspaper articles to TV shows to YouTube comments to Instagram feeds—can be systematically analyzed.

In planning a blood drive, it may be useful to analyze the content of comments on the organization's Facebook page, news stories that mention the organization by name, letters and e-mails written to the organization or internal communication such as memos and newsletters. University of Miami Professor Emeritus Don Stacks identified four types of units of analysis that can be quantified.[20]

Social media allow countless ways for people to communicate.

What are some useful units of analysis that can be quantified in a medium like Facebook?

1. *Words or symbols.* How many times has the word *bloodmobile* been used in the local newspaper in the past year? How many times during a drive was #bloodmobile used on Instagram? How many arm selfies appeared?

2. *Characters.* These are the people involved or the roles that they play. How often do stories include *volunteers, donors, doctors* or *recipients*?

3. *Time and space.* How many minutes of news coverage does a blood drive get on TV? How much space does the announcement get in a company email newsletter?

4. *Items.* An item is the message itself. How many tweets? How many comments on a blog? Even the number of likes on Facebook could count as items.

Content analysis also can reveal themes and underlying messages in communication. Stacks calls this *latent* content. A careful analysis of blog

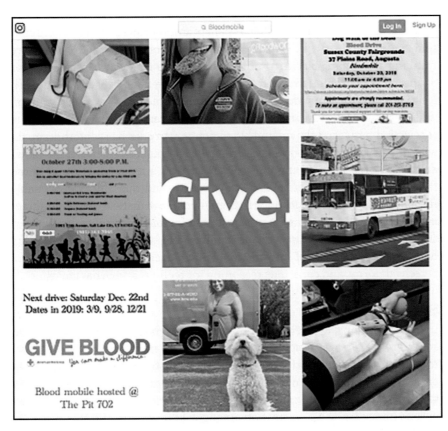

The label #Bloodmobile aggregates an interesting sample of user-generated content related to blood drives.

How might you use Instagram in the research process for planning a blood drive in your community?

entries about donating blood may, for example, reveal a theme of interpersonal influence if bloggers regularly mention key people who motivated them to donate. Convenience, guilt, safety or altruism could also show up as themes. Exploring deeper themes and meaning, however, is much more of a qualitative endeavor than quantitative. Therefore, content analysis can be quantitative or qualitative.

Qualitative Research

Qualitative research answers open-ended questions that can't be answered with numbers alone. What motivates people to donate blood? What fears, concerns or misconceptions do potential donors have? What differences have volunteers observed between one-time donors and donors who give blood repeatedly? Interviews, focus groups and direct observation give researchers and strategists a deeper understanding of human behavior.

Interviews

While it is interesting and useful to know that researchers have found a statistical correlation between religious beliefs and consideration of blood donation, much more can be learned about what potential blood donors are thinking and feeling by sitting down with them (or talking on the phone or Skype, etc.) and asking carefully considered open-ended questions. In-depth interviews allow respondents the opportunity to elaborate, sometimes revealing answers the researcher may have never even considered. Perhaps the connection between religion and blood donor attitudes has something to do with deep-seated personal values. Or maybe it's just convenience if the blood drives are organized at churches? Or perhaps it's a combination of these factors? Interviewing people is a good way to find out. Interviews enable respondents to answer questions in their own terms instead of merely agreeing or disagreeing with statements in surveys or answering questions within the constraints of short-answer questionnaire formats. Interviews can focus on facts and biographical information, beliefs, feelings, motives, behaviors, perceived norms and conscious reasoning for feelings and behavior.[21]

Focus Groups

In public relations, we are very often interested in how people think, feel and act in groups. Focus groups are essentially group interviews. Instead of sitting down with an individual, you would arrange to interview a small group of 6 to 12 people together. While each person may not have the opportunity to articulate his or her own insight at length the way he or she would in a one-on-one interview, the conversation among people in a focus group may yield results that more closely approximate the way people form and express ideas in social settings.

A well-moderated focus group will allow group members to explore points of agreement as well as areas in which members diverge in their

Focus groups were commonly used by advertising firms in the *Mad Men* era of the 1950s and 1960s to test ad concepts, and they have been widely adopted in social sciences in recent decades.

How can public relations researchers use focus groups?

attitudes, beliefs and behaviors. In his book *Focus Groups as Qualitative Research*, sociologist David Morgan wrote about how focus groups can bring to life topics that may be mundane or difficult to explore in depth with any one individual: "I once watched a marketer with a background in sociology conduct a lively demonstration focus group of professors and graduate students who discussed their use of bar soap."[22] Indeed, it would be hard to imagine sitting down with one person for an hour or so to talk about a bar of soap. Imagine what a skilled group moderator could do with the right group of people from one of your key publics discussing a topic like blood donation.

Direct Observation

Of course, what people say is not always consistent with what they do. Therefore, do not overlook direct observation as a form of research. Two types of direct observation are participant and nonparticipant observation. In **nonparticipant observation** the researcher does not interact with the people being observed. A researcher might sit unnoticed a few feet away from volunteers who are staffing a blood drive registration table or out of the way in the back of a bloodmobile and watch what people do and say. In **participant observation**, the researcher interacts with those being observed, sometimes for very long periods of time. You may have seen documentaries dealing with anthropologists who go to great lengths to become part of the cultures they wish to understand. Research in public relations planning likely will not require such an intense personal commitment. If your organization is a local blood bank, you could learn a lot by serving as a volunteer or by going through the blood donation process yourself while observing others.

Nonparticipant observation
Research method in which the researcher avoids interaction with the environment or those being observed.

Participant observation
Research method in which the researcher deliberately interacts with the environment and those being observed.

Secondary research
Collection, summary, analysis or application of previously reported research.

Primary research
Systematic design, collection, analysis and application of original data or observation.

Informal research
Research conducted without clear rules or procedures, which makes the findings difficult to replicate or compare to other research or situations.

Formal research
Research designed with clear rules and procedures for collection and analysis of information.

Primary research allows you to tailor your research to your own specific purposes.

Direct observation can also reveal important variables to measure in other types of research. For example, a blood bank may decide to do further research on factors that influence donors, such as cleanliness of facilities, the comfort of waiting areas, food and drink options and donor interaction with counselors.

Secondary and Primary Research

Many of the resources for research listed earlier would be considered **secondary research**, which is the re-use of research and data that already have been collected. When public relations strategists explore census data, read market research reports, search for blogs or news stories on the web or review research from past case studies, they are conducting secondary research. Consider how much you can learn about blood drives (situations), blood banks (organizations) and blood donors (publics) without even stepping away from your computer. In writing this chapter, every single resource on blood drives consulted was available online. But if I wanted to plan my own blood drive here in my own hometown, I would still have some specific questions that would require primary research to answer.

Primary research involves designing research and collecting your own data for communication planning. One clear benefit of primary research is that it allows you to tailor research to your own specific purposes. While I have learned that lottery tickets were an effective incentive to convince people to donate blood in Switzerland and that college students in Poland are motivated in part by religious beliefs, I may want to test other incentives with my own research.

Formal and Informal Research

As mentioned near the beginning of this chapter, research in public relations ranges from casual and unscientific to carefully planned and sophisticated. In other words, the options range from **informal research** to **formal research**. The more carefully that public relations strategists design research with clear rules and procedures for the collection and analysis of information, the more formal the research.

The U.S. Department of Health and Human Services includes an agency called the Substance Abuse and Mental Health Services Administration (SAMHSA). SAMHSA funds a national survey on drug use and health that involves interviews with a random sample of nearly 70,000 Americans aged 12 or older. The company selected to conduct the research, Research Triangle Institute, won the bid to conduct the research based on their expertise in research design, sampling and data collection, processing, analysis and reporting. This formal process has obvious advantages over less formal research. The survey is designed to "provide national and state-level estimates on the use of tobacco products, alcohol, illicit drugs (including non-medical use of prescription drugs) and mental health in the United States."[23] Goals for the research include providing accurate data on drug use and abuse, tracking national trends in the use of alcohol, tobacco and various types of drugs, studying the consequences of substance use and abuse, and identifying high-risk groups. The resulting data are of great value to SAMHSA and the organizations it serves, including state and local health departments, the U.S. Department of Education and the White House Office of National Drug Control Policy. It is easy to imagine how the research would be useful in strategic planning for anyone practicing public relations in any one of these organizations. The research yields a wealth of data on the situation and the publics with whom these organizations are most concerned.

Informal research just wouldn't provide the same value in results. The main issue with formal research, however, is that it doesn't come cheap. The SAMHSA contract award with optional surveys running from 2018 to 2022 costs U.S. taxpayers $300,514,412![24]

The Substance Abuse and Mental Health Services Administration (SAMHSA) spends millions of dollars on scientific research, including face-to-face survey administration, to attain good data on drug use and health issues in the United States.

Why is this research so expensive?

So, let's say you don't have a couple hundred million in your budget, but you still need to do some research. Informal research can be designed and conducted for practically free. If you were researching drug and alcohol issues, you could ask your friends and family about drugs and alcohol (informal interviews or focus groups), create a quick online questionnaire or Facebook poll and post it on your organization's page (informal survey), compare a few different types of brochures to see if they have different effects on people (informal experiment) or skim local newspapers for drug- and alcohol-related stories (informal content analysis).

Of course, asking some questions to a few friends and conducting a $300 million national survey represent extremes on the spectrum from informal to formal research. Deciding on research that best meets your organization's needs and budget means weighing costs and benefits. Two of the biggest factors driving decisions about research are reliability and validity.

Reliability and Validity

Reliability refers to how well a particular research technique can be applied multiple times and yield comparable data. In getting ready for a long trip, I often lift my suitcase and estimate how much it weighs because I don't want to get dinged with a $25 fee for overweight luggage if my bag weighs more than 50 pounds. I zip my bag closed and lift it a few inches off the ground. "About 40 pounds," I figure. "No problem."

Reliability
Consistency and precision of a particular research technique.

Validity is a big concern when trying to measure intangibles like attitudes toward an organization or involvement with an issue.

Two hours later, I unload my family's luggage from the car to the curb at the airport. I lean way into the back of the car to heave my bag out. "Oh no!," I think this time. "This thing has got to weigh at least 55 pounds." In reality, my bag weighs the same at the airport as it did at home, but my guestimate is not reliable.

I get to the ticket counter for the moment of truth. "Please put your bag on the scale," says the ticket agent. The digits on the display scramble and then settle in on the reading—52 pounds. "D'oh!" I take my bag off the scale, pull a jacket and a book out, and heave it back on the scale. The digits on the scale scramble again as we all wait for the new reading . . . 49 pounds. "Woohoo!" No one argues with the scale. We assume it is reliable. If you place the same bag with the same contents on the scale multiple times it should give the same reading. That's reliability. If you get a different reading on a second measure, as in my case, you assume that the weight of the suitcase actually changed, not that something is wrong with the scale. Again, the assumption is that the scale is reliable.

One of the goals of the national drug use survey is to track changes in drug and alcohol use. The formal research methods employed are designed for reliability so that if the results show a year-to-year change in drug or alcohol use among a certain population, researchers can be confident that the change in results is due more to actual changes in the population than to errors in the survey as a measurement tool. Smaller (and less expensive) research designs can be reliable too if they are designed well.

Validity refers to the accuracy of a measurement or observation in reflecting what the researcher intends to measure or observe. After the agent checks my bag at the ticket counter it rides on a conveyor belt and disappears into another part of the airport, likely to go through an X-ray machine or pass by bomb-sniffing dogs. The scale at the ticket counter may offer a reliable reading of weight in pounds, but no validity in representing the contents of the bag. From the weight scale, the agent would have no idea whether the bag contains 49 pounds of books or 49 pounds of clothes or 49 pounds of pineapples.

Validity in public relations research and social science research can be particularly tricky because we often try to measure and observe things that are much harder to define than books, clothes or pineapples. When the concepts to be measured include intangibles like attitudes toward an organization, involvement with an issue or behavior that is not easily observed in public, validity is a big concern. Even in a very reliable survey of alcohol use for example, we have to wonder about validity. Consider the following finding from a SAMHSA report.

"Nationally, 15.9 percent of all persons aged 12 to 20 were binge alcohol users in the 30 days prior to being surveyed. Estimates ranged from 9.2 percent in Shelby County, Tennessee, to 46.3 percent in the District of Columbia's Ward 2."[25]

Reading this report after reviewing the research methods, I am fairly confident in the reliability of the results. I'm confident that there is significantly more binge drinking in D.C.'s Ward 2 than in Shelby County, Tennessee. But I'm a little less confident in how well the data from a self-report drinking survey represents the complexity of alcohol use and abuse. The researchers carefully define binge drinking as having five or more drinks on the same occasion at least one time in the past 30 days, but people may reasonably disagree about what these self-reports actually indicate in terms of alcohol abuse.

Another example is campus crime safety campaigns. If you organize a campus safety campaign that emphasizes the importance of reporting suspicious activity, how would you feel about an increase in calls to police on your campus? Would you be disappointed because this indicates more suspicious activity? Or would you welcome the news that more suspicious activity was actually reported? Or would you need more information to draw a conclusion? This is a question of validity and requires a deeper understanding of the information available. You may obtain that information from further quantitative data (number of actual convictions or data on property loss) or you may obtain it from qualitative research (in-depth interviews with law enforcement, riding along with police on their beats, etc.).

Trade-Offs in Research Design

No single research method, no matter how formal, is perfect. There are always trade-offs. The strengths of a large-scale national survey with tens of thousands of participants can become limitations in understanding deeper social phenomena. Careful observation or in-depth interviewing can reveal rich information to help you understand your organization and publics and their deeper motivations, attitudes and behavior, but reliability becomes an issue with this type of research because it would be difficult to repeat with consistent results.

A research methods course will help you design and evaluate research for reliability and validity. Even if you end up performing secondary research or hiring others to conduct research, understanding the different types of research and the strengths and limitations of your options is a critical part of planning for strategic public relations and for reporting the results of your work with confidence.

> *No single research method, no matter how formal, is perfect. There are always trade-offs.*

Qualitative and quantitative research often complement each other.

What are the trade-offs of surveys and less formal questioning as research methods?

Voices from the Field

Megan Kindelan

MEGAN KINDELAN is Director of Public Affairs for the U.S. Bureau of Labor Statistics (BLS) and teaches strategic public relations in The George Washington University Graduate School of Political Management. Kindelan also served for eight years as a Public Affairs Specialist for the U.S. Census Bureau.

How do public relations people use the labor statistics your office provides?
The Bureau of Labor Statistics has millions of data points that measure the ever-changing economy. We like to say that from your very first job to retirement and everything in between, BLS has a stat for that! Public relations professionals often use our data to back up their own research on everything from how much consumers spend on certain items to which jobs are in demand. Using quantifiable data from a trusted federal statistical agency is a great way to prove (and improve!) whatever pitch you are trying to make to reporters—from showing how Americans spend their time (our *American Time Use Survey*) to exploring the spending patterns of Millennials compared to earlier generations (our *Consumer Expenditure Survey*).

You're in an interesting position because you work for a government office that conducts research and makes it available to everyone else, but you're a professional communicator yourself. How do you use research to support your own communication efforts?
Working for a statistical agency surrounded by data experts makes my job even more fun! I create a quarterly digital metrics report for all BLS staff, and I appreciate the enthusiasm my colleagues have for the data I provide. I have to be prepared to answer very in-depth and savvy questions about the statistical methods I've used in the report. This metrics report is just one example of how I'm using data to show the ROI (return on investment) of the communications work we do. I'm speaking to executives at BLS in the language they understand to show that what we are doing is having an impact.

You also teach strategic communications. What are some of the best research resources you share with your students?
My favorite (and free!) resource is Google Alerts. Budgets are tight at BLS and across the federal government, and this news alert system is better than some of the media monitoring I've paid for in the past. It's a time saver and a great way to track coverage. Excel is another (often overlooked) resource that I use for just about everything—from making my own media database to running statistics. I also go to PRSA to keep up-to-date on research trends and case studies. Their *Public Relations Journal* is fantastic.

What's the most interesting statistic or trend your office has turned up recently?
Ridden in an Uber or Lyft recently or used TaskRabbit? BLS recently did a study on this type of gig (short-term work), focusing for the first time on people who do short jobs or tasks they find through websites or mobile apps. I think I can safely say most of you reading this book have worked for or used what we call here at BLS "electronically mediated work." BLS found that about 1.6 million people do this type of work, accounting for about 1 percent of total employment.

How's the job market looking for those seeking to enter the public relations field in the next few years?
Employment of public relations specialists is projected to grow 9 percent through 2026, about as fast as average for all occupations. BLS pay data show that the median pay for public relations professionals is $59,300 per year. The typical entry-level education required? A bachelor's degree. So, keep studying!

Ethics: Doing the Greatest Good for the Greatest Number of People

Utilitarianism
Principle that the most ethical course of action is the one that maximizes good and minimizes harm for people.

Research helps us make informed decisions. Public relations practitioners use research not only to inform their own thinking and strategy, but also to inform and persuade their organizations and publics. Contributing to the marketplace of ideas in a way that informs citizens in democracies is one of the highest ideals of public relations. One of the most common ways that public relations professionals engage the marketplace of ideas is to present research data.

In democracies, ideas are often judged based on the question of which course of action will do the greatest good for the greatest number of people. In philosophy, this approach to decision-making is called **utilitarianism**. Nineteenth-century English philosopher Jeremy Bentham and one of his students, political economist and philosopher John Stuart Mill, spelled out utilitarianism as an ethic of consequences. That is, they wrote that you can decide on an ethical course of action by determining which actions will have the best consequences. Take into account all the good and bad consequences of competing actions and determine which action does the most good and the least bad, and then you are ready to act ethically.

Ethics of consequences can be applied in everyday decision-making. In deciding how to handle media interview requests when bad news breaks, which stories to include in newsletters, what photos to pin on Pinterest and even which employee tweets to retweet, public relations practitioners think through the consequences of their actions in an effort to make the right decisions every day. But when dealing with large-scale issues of public concern, research is often brought into the mix to help organizations decide on their positions and then advocate appropriately.

Research the consequences of competing actions and determine which action does the most good and the least bad. That's utilitarian ethics.

Take, for example, the issue of raising minimum wages for fast-food restaurant workers. It's an interesting and difficult political and economic issue, and we have organizations with paid professionals ready and willing to help us sort out the best course of action.

A nonprofit organization called the Employment Policies Institute published a research report by an economics professor at San Diego State University that found that raising minimum wages actually leads to reduced employment opportunities for entry-level laborers. The study of data over two decades shows that in weak labor markets "each 10 percent minimum wage increase reduces employment

Workers protest for a higher minimum wage.

In what ways could reasonable people disagree about the consequences of raising minimum wages?

for young drop-outs by over four percent."[26] John Stuart Mill would love this, right? The data show us that even though some people would benefit from raised wages, others—particularly the least skilled and least experienced employees—would suffer because there are fewer jobs. The thrust of the research posted by the Employment Policies Institute suggests that *not* raising minimum wages would do the greatest good for the greatest number of people.

Of course there is another side to this issue. The Center for Labor Research and Education at UC Berkeley published results of a study that showed "the fast-food industry costs American taxpayers nearly $7 billion annually because its jobs pay so little that 52 percent of fast-food workers are forced to enroll their families in public assistance programs."[27] If low wages hurt both the fast-food workers and taxpayers, then the utilitarian answer seems to be to raise wages. What would Mill say now?

As the minimum wage case shows, determining the most ethical answers to public-interest questions by trying to maximize positive and minimize negative outcomes can be difficult. Philosophers call it utilitarian calculus, and it has its limits. In the minimum wage case much of the confusion stems from the fact that the organizations promoting the research have very different political agendas. The data from the Berkeley study were used by a group called the National Employment Law Project, which hosts websites such as http://www.raisetheminimumwage.org and https://www.justpay.org that advocate for higher minimum wages. On the other side, the Employment Policies Institute is closely tied with a public relations firm called Berman and Company and the website http://www.minimumwage.com. According to a report in *The New York Times*, Berman and Co. bills the nonprofit Employment Policies Institute for services of its employees, and "the arrangement effectively means the nonprofit is a moneymaking venture" for Richard Berman and his associates who actively represent and advocate for the restaurant industry.

Perhaps the moral of the story for public relations is to avoid confusing the use of research for advocacy and profit with the process of utilitarian ethics. As

The website minimumwage.com uses research to argue one side to a contentious issue.

Is this an example of ethical utilitarianism?

public relations scholars Shannon Bowen and Don Stacks point out, a primary weakness of utilitarian ethics is that the person who applies them can use them "to sanction whatever he or she wants to maximize in their *personal* good outcomes, as opposed to maximizing the greatest good for the greatest interest in the public interest."[28]

The Institute for Public Relations measurement commission has adopted a statement on ethical standards in public relations research and measurement that promotes many core values beyond utilitarianism: "All research should abide by the principles of intellectual honesty, fairness, dignity, disclosure, and respect for all stakeholders involved, namely clients (both external and internal), colleagues, research participants, the public relations profession and the researchers themselves."[29]

In Case You Missed It

The very first thing most of us do when we need an answer to a new question is hit the search button. But research in public relations is about so much more than online searching and "re-searching." To develop effective strategy and achieve worthwhile outcomes, we have to ask the right questions and understand the best methods for answering them. Here are some tips to consider as you get started with your programs and campaigns, maybe even before you open Google.

- Evaluation can happen at any point in a strategic program, not just at the end.
- Gaining a deeper understanding of a situation requires digging for information of substance beyond an internet search.

- Organization-public relationships flourish when you spend as much energy trying to understand your publics as you do trying to get your message out.
- Good internal communication affects external communication . . . because employees serve as brand advocates.
- Some people will support your efforts without a public relations program and others will never get involved, but you can make progress with publics that are somewhere in between.
- Primary research allows you to tailor your research to your own specific purposes.
- Validity is a big concern when trying to measure intangibles like attitudes toward an organization or involvement with an issue.
- No single research method, no matter how formal, is perfect. There are always trade-offs.
- Research the consequences of competing actions and determine which one does the most good and the least bad. That's utilitarian ethics.

SUMMARY

5.1 Explain the role of formative and summative research in the RPIE cycle.

Formative research is conducted before and during a campaign or program to develop and fine-tune strategy. Summative research is conducted at the end to answer the question, "Did it work?" However, one campaign or program normally leads to another, so what may be considered summative for one effort may become formative for future strategy. Research and evaluation can be thought of as connected parts of a cycle rather than the beginning and end of a linear process.

5.2 Describe the contents of a situation analysis.

In writing a situation analysis, the planner researches and reports on the strengths and weaknesses of an organization along with the opportunities and threats in the organization's environment (i.e., SWOT analysis) as they relate to the motive for a public relations program or campaign. The narrative analysis leads to a concise problem or opportunity statement that clearly articulates the reason for planning a public relations program or campaign and sets the stage for campaign goals.

5.3 Discuss applications of quantitative research.

Quantitative research is when numbers and statistics are used to answer research questions. It allows for clear numerical reporting and analysis of large amounts of data. Surveys, experiments and content analyses all provide data that can be used to describe and analyze public relations situations, public relations efforts and public relations results.

5.4 Discuss applications of qualitative research.

Qualitative research is when open-ended research questions are answered with in-depth descriptions that don't rely on numbers or statistics. Interviews, focus groups and direct observation help public relations researchers understand the behavior of various publics. Qualitative research allows for rich description and deep understanding of the people or content studied before, during and after public relations efforts.

5.5 Compare costs and benefits of secondary and primary research.

Secondary research is generally cheaper and easier than primary research. However, primary research yields custom results that are directly applicable to the situation at hand.

5.6 Differentiate between formal and informal research based on reliability and validity.

Informal research is easier than formal research, but formal research is conducted with rules and procedures that allow for more confidence in the results. Reliability refers to the consistency and precision of a research technique: Does the instrument produce the same or comparable results in repeated trials? Validity refers to the accuracy of the technique: Are you measuring what you think you're measuring?

5.7 Evaluate utilitarianism as an ethical principle for public relations research.

Utilitarianism is a useful ethical principle to the extent that the person applying it makes unbiased and informed decisions based on a clear understanding of the relative harm and benefit of competing courses of action. When researchers work with a biased perspective on the data available, they tend to calculate benefit and harm in ways that support their own opinions or agendas rather than society at large.

DISCUSSION QUESTIONS

1. Recall an event or activity that you've planned and conducted in the past year. What kind of formative research, if any, did you do? How could summative evaluation of that effort help you next time you do a similar event or activity? What kind of research would you do next time?

2. **CASE STUDY** Would you say you were part of a latent, aware or active public for the issue of net neutrality before reading this chapter? Identify one organization that might want to see your status on the issue change? What types of research would a public relations person from that organization do to have a better chance of understanding people like you as part of their situation analysis?

3. Look through https://www.census.gov or another site that presents quantitative statistical data about people. What's the most interesting statistic you can find? Name an organization that would be interested in that information for public relations purposes? How would they use it?

4. How do you think the public relations insights gained from a focus group would be different from the insights gained from individual interviews with the same people?

5. Have you ever conducted a survey, focus group or other type of social research? Aside from cost, what are some advantages and disadvantages of doing primary research yourself versus using secondary research?

6. Suppose you are asked to organize a fundraising drive for a local nonprofit group or student organization. After identifying the organization, name two types of research you might do as part of your efforts—one type more informal and one type more formal. Which would be more reliable and why? Which would be more valid and why?

7. Name a decision that a politician made that you don't agree with. Make a utilitarian argument for why you would make a different decision. What kind of research supports your case (and his or hers)?

KEY TERMS

Active publics   129
Analytics   119
Aware publics   129
Constraint recognition   129
Content analysis   134
Control group   134
Demographics   129
External publics   126
Formal research   138
Formative research   118
In house   123
Informal research   138
Internal publics   125

Latent publics   129
Level of involvement   129
Mission statement   123
Net neutrality   128
Nonparticipant observation   137
Organizational culture   125
Participant observation   137
Primary publics   131
Primary research   138
Problem or opportunity statement   120
Problem recognition   129
Psychographics   129
Qualitative research   136

Quantitative research   133
Reliability   139
Secondary publics   131
Secondary research   138
Situation analysis   120
Situational theory of publics   128
Summative research   119
SWOT analysis   120
Tertiary publics   131
Treatment group   134
Utilitarianism   143
Validity   140
Vision statement   124

CHAPTER 6
Planning

Convincing people to wash their hands more is a universal challenge. How do international organizations collaborate to change behavior and measure success?

KEY LEARNING OUTCOMES

6.1 Analyze strategic communication outcomes.

6.2 Define key terms of strategic communication planning.

6.3 Develop basic timelines to organize tasks in a strategic public relations program.

6.4 Identify key categories of public relations budget items.

6.5 Apply consequentialism to make ethical decisions about setting and achieving public relations objectives while enhancing the profession.

RELATED UNIVERSAL ACCREDITATION BOARD COMPETENCY AREAS
1.4 STRATEGIC THINKING • **1.5** PLANNING • **2.2** ETHICAL BEHAVIOR
4.2 BARRIERS TO COMMUNICATION • **5.2** RESOURCE MANAGEMENT

Appear or occur suddenly and unexpectedly—that's how Oxford Dictionaries defines the term *pop up*.[1] But there is nothing sudden or unexpected about pop-ups as strategic communication tactics. A **pop-up** is a temporary storefront, event or experience designed to gain attention and generate engagement by appearing quickly in an unusual place. Effective pop-ups take planning with bigger organizational goals in mind. Melissa Gonzalez, author of *The Pop-Up Paradigm*, advises, "Step back and think of your goals before starting to plan a pop-up. Why are you doing a pop-up—besides sales—and what are you ultimately looking to achieve, learn and gain from it?"[2] These are good questions for any kind of public relations activity, from one-time tactics to long-term campaigns. **Planning** in public relations refers to the forethought about goals and objectives and the strategies and tactics for achieving them (Figure 6.1). Studying outcomes of past campaigns and programs can help us develop goals and objectives for future ones.

Think of all the planning required for the shoe company Timberland to host a weeklong series of events in New York City, including the launch of its first experiential pop-up store on Fifth Avenue. The 3,500-square-foot retail store was designed to exist for only a few months during the fall and holiday shopping season, but it featured live full-sized ficus and birch trees, giant terrariums with ferns and moss, and various weather-themed rooms including an immersive digital rain room and a "blustery, photo-ready winter scene."[3] This was all very "Instagrammable" of course. But beyond Timberland's wish "to inspire the community to embrace the outdoors in the city"[4] (as stated in a Timberland news release), what was Timberland really trying to accomplish? Or, as *Vox's* Kaitlyn Tiffany asked, "What does any of this have to do with actually buying Timberland's shoes?"[5]

To better understand and evaluate public relations tactics like Timberland's pop-ups, we have to understand how and why they were planned in the first place. According to Argu Secilmis, the company's vice president of global brand marketing, beyond product sales, one major goal was making an emotional connection to Timberland's commitment to environmental and social responsibility.

There are a number of steps that take place between someone noticing a giant boot on a city block, which was part of the pop-up park in the Flatiron District of New York City, or seeing friends' Instagram selfies from a weather experience room on Fifth Avenue, and purchasing a $200 pair of boots or rolling up their sleeves in Harlem to create a living rooftop. This chapter discusses those steps as well as the key components of plans to achieve them: goals, objectives, timelines and budgets.

Figure 6.1 In the RPIE cycle, planning is preceded by research (including evaluation of past programs and campaigns) and drives implementation.

How does research help planners write better goals and objectives?

Pop-up
Planned events or experiences that are set up quickly in a temporary location for a short time.

Planning
Forethought about goals and objectives and the strategies and tactics needed to achieve them.

For one day, this giant replica of Timberland's iconic wheat boot drew families to a pop-up park in the Flatiron District of New York City, kicking off a week-long series of events that also included the opening of a temporary 3,500-square foot Timberland store on Fifth Avenue.

What kind of planning is needed to make a pop-up event like this successful?

A Hierarchy of Outcomes

There are times when a client or organization knows they need help with public relations, but they have a hard time specifying exactly what it is that they want you to do. Your job as the public relations professional is to convert fuzzy thinking into a strategy that will lead to meaningful results for the organization.

One of the most common client requests is "Help us raise awareness." Awareness may be part of the desired results, but more often than not awareness is only an intermediate step in a larger process to reach some other goal. Awareness of a cause, a new product or an app is only part of the process in leading people to donate, purchase or download, and to continued involvement or use beyond that.

Planning for public relations means considering a number of outcomes beyond awareness. Public relations practitioners need to think strategically about communication. That is, they need to think about the specific outcomes of their action and communication. Yale social psychologist William McGuire developed a hierarchy-of-effects model that outlines key steps in public communication campaigns (Figure 6.2): tuning in, attending, liking, comprehending, learning, agreeing, remembering, acting and proselytizing.

Awareness of a cause, new product or app is only one step in leading people to donate, purchase or download.

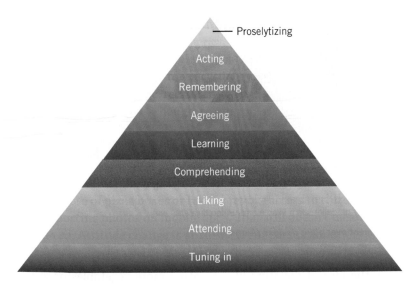

Proselytizing

Acting

Remembering

Agreeing

Learning

Comprehending

Liking

Attending

Tuning in

Figure 6.2 McGuire's hierarchy of effects.

Where does "raising awareness" fit in this hierarchy? What are the limitations of making awareness a campaign goal?

Tuning In

Before communication can have any effect at all, people must be exposed to the messages. Think of all the messages you see and hear every day: advertising, announcements, posters, fliers, email, social media posts and so on—you get the picture; even the most tuned-in media users are exposed to way more messaging than anyone can possibly pay attention to. While exposure is necessary in communication, it is only the first step in effective communication.

Attending

Attention is the next challenge. Take almost any bulletin board in any college hallway, classroom or lecture hall. Watch as people walk by the posted fliers day after day. They are all exposed to the message if they even glance at the bulletin board, but how many of them actually pay attention? Next time you listen to ads on a streaming music service like Pandora or Spotify (assuming you haven't subscribed to the ad-free version), pay attention to how you pay attention. Do you notice the first ad or two more than the ones that come on after you've been listening a while?

Liking

On Facebook, we can signal our "likes" with a thumbs-up. It's one of many emotions we can express. According to McGuire, "liking" in particular is an important step in message processing because people must maintain interest in a message in order to process it further. In public relations, our messages are often more complex than a Facebook photo, a hallway flier announcing an event, or a streaming radio ad for tacos. Our publics may

There's evidence of limited success with this hallway flier because some of the contact tabs have been taken.

When someone takes a contact tab, which steps to persuasion are complete? Which still remain?

Billable rate
Amount that an agency or firm charges clients per hour for an employee's time.

Overhead expenses
Costs of running a business that are not directly related to the product or services delivered.

out of my chair when I saw that he was getting $150 an hour for his work. I did the math and figured he must be making more than $300,000 a year! How could this be? Why wasn't he driving a Ferrari?

When agencies bill clients for their work, they often include billable hourly rates as a major part of the budget, but the amount billed is considerably larger than the amount the employee gets paid. Author, consultant and PRSA Fellow James Lukaszewski offered the following example on his website.[15] Suppose an account supervisor at a public relations agency earns a salary of $65,000 a year. Assuming the employee is paid for 40 hours a week over the course of 52 weeks, her hourly pay comes out to $31.25. However, the agency also pays for her benefits including costs such as health insurance and retirement contributions. These fringe benefits can cost the firm up to 30 percent or more of her base pay. With 30 percent fringe added, her hourly cost to the agency is $40.63 per hour. Of course, agencies wouldn't make any money if they only charged their clients their actual costs, and they have many other expenses to cover besides those payroll costs, so they bill clients at a rate of three or even four times the cost of paying the account executive. Using a multiple of three, the **billable rate** for the account supervisor would be $121.89 per hour. Using a multiple of four, the billable rate would be $162.52 per hour, even though she is earning an annual salary of $65,000 and not $338,000. Now I understand why my internship supervisor was driving a nice Toyota but not splurging on an Italian sports car.

We can see how important it is to factor in the amount of time people will spend on particular projects when developing budgets. While an agency's HR and accounting departments may handle all the specifics of salaries, fringe and billing, planners must still provide an estimate of how many people will work on which projects and for how long. Other personnel costs to consider include hiring freelance writers and editors, photographers, artists, spokespeople, social media influencers or any type of temporary workers such as event security staff for a concert or drivers to take nurses to remote communities in an international healthcare campaign.

Administrative Costs and Supplies

In agencies or established businesses, regular and ongoing administrative costs such as electricity, paper and internet services are often considered **overhead expenses**, meaning public relations planners normally wouldn't need to account for them specifically in developing a campaign strategy or program budget (though clients pay for them indirectly with marked-up prices for services). Beyond those costs, or if you are working independently, you have to think about budgeting for any stuff that you will need for your campaign that you don't plan on having donated or paying for out of your own personal funds. These costs may include anything from specialty items like coffee mugs or T-shirts, to nametags, pizza and drinks, soap for handwashing, bins for recycling, computers and tablets—you name it. If you are organizing an event as part of a larger program, you may estimate the total cost of the event in your initial program proposal rather than getting too specific with each line item. Other major non-media expense categories include travel, facility rentals, speaker fees and research costs.

Media and Communication Expenses

Advertising and promotion are important costs to consider in most public relations programs. For traditional media, price quotes can be attained to get an accurate estimate of how much to budget for advertising. As discussed in Chapter 3, newspaper ads can range from less than $20 per column inch in a student newspaper to hundreds of thousands of dollars for a full-page ad in a national or international publication. As with print media, advertis-

OK, who ordered pizza? Even smaller expenses like food and snacks for events add up when you are working independently.

Where might you find pizza in a public relations budget?

ing sales representatives from radio and TV stations can give you quotes for media space (e.g., a 30-second spot during prime time). Someone budgeting for a national branding campaign may have to choose between, say, spending $327,000 for a full-page color ad in *The Wall Street Journal*, and spending $400,000 for a 30-second TV spot during a top-rated prime-time network sitcom. Of course, many factors go into such decisions, and when the stakes are high, professional media planners are part of the process. **Media planning** entails considering factors such as strategy and audience demographics to make sure that advertising budgets are spent wisely and in line with SMART objectives. **Reach** (the percentage or number of people exposed to a message) and **frequency** (the average number of times people in an audience are exposed to a particular message in a given period) are two of the most important variables. Media planning is a career path in and of itself.

Advertising in digital and interactive media has evolved into new models of buying and selling media. **Programmatic media buying**, for example, involves automated real-time bidding (RTB) that is preprogrammed by marketers and automated to buy space when certain criteria are met. In programmatic media sales, publishers use software called supply-side platforms (SSPs) and buyers use demand-side platforms (DSPs). Former Instagram and Twitter executive Ameet Ranadive explains the process with an example:

> *Based on its knowledge about this user (e.g., the user recently searched for flights to Hawaii on a travel website), a DSP will bid on the right to serve an ad to this user. The RTB exchange will then run an auction for the ad impression generated by this user. The winning DSP will serve a creative—potentially a dynamic display ad with personalized content, perhaps including the recently browsed flight details, price, and image of the destination—to the user.[16]*

Media planning
Choosing media channels to achieve strategic communication goals and objectives. Media planning drives advertising purchases.

Reach
Percentage or number of people exposed to a message at least once via a specific communication channel during a defined period of time.

Frequency
The average number of times people in an audience are exposed to a particular message in a defined period of time.

Programmatic media buying
Automated media buying that is preprogrammed so that advertising purchases are completed when certain criteria set by buyers (marketers) and sellers (media) are met. Programmatic media buying commonly occurs via computer-run, real-time auctions.

Social media command center war rooms like this one allow for 24/7 monitoring of client mentions and trends.

Setting up social media accounts may be free at first, but what other expenses need to be considered in budgeting for continued operation?

A social media presence may be "free" of advertising costs, but it still requires personnel costs.

Programmatic media buying can be used for everything from basic ads on news websites to promoted tweets to Google search returns to sponsored posts in Facebook. Again, this type of media planning requires specialized expertise, but understanding the basics will help public relations planners work with media planners in buying space in digital and interactive media.

At this point, you may be thinking, what about "free" media? You can write your own newsletter, distribute your own fliers or set up your own Instagram account, Facebook group or Pinterest board for free, right? It's true that these communication tactics don't incur advertising costs, but you will have other costs to consider. An effective social media presence requires time and effort—in other words, personnel costs. If you are including fliers in your budget, you should include the cost of designing and printing.

For professionalism with just about any communication tactic, public relations planners must also consider the costs of production. Production costs for national TV ads can range from tens of thousands of dollars to millions of dollars. For a basic event flier, you might design it yourself or buy lunch for a talented friend to design it. Even so, you'll want to check with a local printer on printing prices if you don't have access to a good copy machine with a full supply of paper and toner. For example, to print in full color on premium paper, FedEx Office charges $29.99 for 50 copies and $149.99 for 250 copies. These numbers undoubtedly vary (and the FedEx quote probably won't apply any more by the time you read this), but it goes to show how important it is to think about production costs and to build them into your budget.

Voices from the Field

Natalie Asorey

NATALIE ASOREY is a lecturer in public relations at the University of Florida. She most recently was head of social media at BODEN, a leading cross-cultural communication agency based in Miami, where she oversaw the McDonald's USA scope of work as Hispanic agency of record. She led the account team and collaborated with McDonald's communication, marketing and digital teams to develop communication and social media strategies to reach the Hispanic consumer market. Asorey also led the agency's award-winning social listening practice, Escucha, to build brand advocacy through influencer and consumer engagement and real-time content.

You've taught and supervised many entry-level communicators and interns. How much do entry-level practitioners need to be concerned with strategic planning, and to what degree can they get by early in their careers by just being good with tactics?

The entry-level practitioners who have a strong grasp of strategic planning are the ones who will propel quickly in their careers. But even in developing tactics, you have a chance to show your strategic thinking. Consider one of the most common entry-level public relations tasks: creating a media list (a list of potential outlets and journalists to pitch a news story). Identifying the *right* journalists who will care about your organization's story requires research and strategy. Every task, no matter how small or tedious, is an opportunity to show you go above and beyond.

McDonald's has been recognized for successfully experimenting with innovative forms of social media engagement. What kinds of metrics have you used to track engagement objectives and goals?

To track objectives and goals on social media, we'd measure both quantitative and qualitative metrics. We'd analyze metrics like engagement rate, click-through rates (to websites) and conversions (how many people signed up, provided contact information, completed a transaction, etc.), among others. These allowed us to understand not just how many people were seeing the brand's content, but how they were interacting with it. We'd also analyze tweets and comments for sentiment, giving us a better sense of how people perceived the brand and helping us manage its online reputation. When analyzed together, this gave us a more holistic, accurate view of how we were tracking against our objectives.

How have budgets for public relations programs and campaigns changed with the rise of social media?

Many organizations now have dedicated budgets for social media, which can include everything from agency fees for content production to out-of-pocket expenses for influencer partnerships and social media promotion. Sometimes, though, these are part of larger public relations budgets, and it's up to the client or agency to determine how much will be allocated to social media. Regardless of how small or large the budget, the key is to manage it strategically and effectively and demonstrate how you're using the resources to meet goals and objectives.

Are there times when it makes more sense just to wing it and go with instinct?

Simply "winging it" is a recipe for disaster. Say it works once . . . great. That doesn't guarantee it will work every time, and you don't want to risk failure because you didn't take the time to plan. Sometimes you have a strong gut feeling that something will or will not work—but you can't quite pinpoint why. Always speak up when that happens, but also back up that instinct with research. Clients are more inclined to take a chance on a big idea if you have data to support it.

What's the coolest campaign outcome you've achieved?

When BODEN planned the "¡Síganme los Buenos!" campaign for McDonald's, the brand challenged the agency to not only deliver on traditional public relations outcomes (like impressions and engagement), but to also drive traffic to the restaurants and boost sales. The campaign centered on a partnership with a legendary Hispanic character, El Chapulín Colorado (like the Mickey Mouse of Latino culture), to show the brand's commitment to Hispanic consumers and launch its new dollar menu. Consumers had such a powerful cultural connection that the line wrapped around the restaurant on the day of the event. Families even dressed up as the character! It was such a rewarding experience—and the proof was in the numbers, which showed an increase in guest count and sales.

Ethics: Beware of Zombies; Enhance the Profession

When public relations strategy includes a social media platform like Instagram, a common element of SMART objectives relates to the number of followers or likes or comments the account receives. As you know if you have ever started a social media account, the first batch of friends and followers comes relatively easily.

That first batch of friends and followers may be all you need if you're keeping your account for personal reasons. Your network may grow slowly and organically from there as you discover new friends and others discover you. That's how most of us expect social media to work. So when we see that @selenagomez has more than 150 million followers on Instagram but follows only 59 others, we know a different pattern of influence is in process. The communication is one-way. However, in between small interpersonal accounts and pure mass-communication-by-Instagram, there are many ways that strategic communicators build social media influence into their plans.

One way to harness influence in social media is to work long and hard to build a large and lasting base of friends and followers. Over time, working to provide content that people enjoy and find useful enough to like and share will earn you or your organization followers and clout. Consistent and regular interaction (i.e., two-way communication and relationship building) with others online is also a big part of what it takes to be successful in building online social networks.

As noted in the budget section, social media aren't really free. Success with social media requires an investment over time in providing valuable content and building relationships. The return on that investment in public relations comes when it's time to get the word out about your recycling drive, to introduce your company's new product, or to remind voters to go to the polls in support of your cause on Election Day. From tuning in to going viral, a large and well-maintained social media network can support each and every one of the steps in McGuire's model of strategic communication.

Now, what if I were to offer you a shortcut? A site called Buzzoid offers 500 followers for $6.99 or 5,000 followers for $39.99. Another site, iDigic.net, has similar prices—500 followers for $7.95 up to 5,000 followers for $39.95. According to iDigic, when you buy followers, "you add more visibility and credibility to your Instagram account and get more engagement numbers without breaking a sweat."[17] It is widely acknowledged that these followers are not the same as the real people who would otherwise follow your account out of real interest in you or your organization. What these services offer are "zombie" followers. The companies operate thousands of fake accounts that exist for no other purpose than to follow other accounts. More sophisticated services offer packages that include automated "like" and commenting functions. One Dutch blogger who paid for a service told how real commenters called out an automated comment that said "Nice pic" when the actual post was a video. I think it's safe to say that zombie followers are not high on anyone's list of primary publics.

These services could be seen as an effective and budget-friendly tactic for eventually increasing real followers. A longer-term goal to increase communication via social media may be helped along by a shorter-term objective to get social media accounts up and running with a respectable number of followers. Is there really any harm buying followers to meet your social media objectives? A quick run through Kathy Fitzpatrick's guide for ethical decision-making (see Chapter 1) will help answer that.

It's possible to pay for fake followers on social media accounts.

What are the pitfalls of buying zombie followers?

Define the Specific Issue/Conflict

Buying followers is a quick, inexpensive, legal and effective way to boost quantitative results (followers, likes, comments, etc.) for social media objectives. However, the followers aren't real people. The benefit of buying followers is one of perception—accounts with more followers *appear* to be more credible, reliable and popular.

Identify Internal/External Factors

Major internal factors include program budget, goals and objectives. An important strategic question is whether or not purchased followers will actually contribute to the larger goals of a campaign. External factors include the perceptions of external publics who may be impressed with large numbers but feel deceived and lose trust if they were to learn that the account holder had paid for zombie followers. Could you report to a client with confidence and good faith that thousands of purchased followers would help you achieve a goal to get more people to buy a product, make a donation or volunteer time?

Identify Key Values

Authenticity, transparency and expertise are key values. A big part of what makes social media social is that people are motivated to engage other real people. Authenticity matters in any social context (not just online media). Touting fake friends or followers is not an authentic approach to self-presentation in any type of communication. Most people keep the practice hush-hush and would feel "busted" if the word were to get out that they had paid for followers. If you were to buy followers as part of a public relations strategy, would you want people to know? Probably not, and wanting to keep something a secret indicates a lack of transparency. Building a base of followers for an organization by creating engaging content and maintaining mutually beneficial relationships requires expertise. That expertise is what employers and clients pay public relations people for. Employers and clients might feel duped if they knew you "earned" your money with cheap shortcuts.

A big part of what makes social media social is that people are motivated to engage other real people.

Identify the Parties Involved

Again, one party is the employer or client. The practitioner himself or herself is another. I don't think I'd count the zombie followers as a party, but people in real publics who see the social media account and make decisions based on perceptions of that account would be another party. At the broadest level, anyone working in public relations whose reputation may be damaged by unethical practices in this area is also a party.

Select Ethical Principles

In Chapter 1, we applied deontological (duty-based) principles to decide whether ghost tweeting was ethically defensible for a public relations practitioner. In Chapter 5, we applied the principle of utilitarianism to evaluate how public relations research is presented. Utilitarianism focuses on the results of one's actions. For this case, let's consider **consequentialism**—a results-based system of ethics that holds that the best ethical decision is the one leading to the best outcomes or impacts.

What are the consequences of buying followers? A very narrow view would be that buying followers results in short-term success in meeting objectives. One might even expand this into an ethical argument by saying that buying followers is ethical if it leads to larger, more important consequences. For example, if you bought followers for an NGO account, and those followers led to more real followers, and those real followers donated money, and that money was used to produce vaccines against Ebola, preventing disease would be the result. Fighting deadly viruses would certainly be an end that one could use to justify the means of buying followers. But come on. You could drive a truck through the logic of that strategy. The following consequences are more likely:

1. Nothing happens. You spend part of your budget buying followers and no one even notices.

2. It kind of works. You buy followers and it somehow makes your account look more legit. A few real followers ensue, but they are deceived in the process because they assume you are producing content and communicating in a way that others have found worthwhile.

3. It backfires, and you get called out on it. This happens. Services like IG Audit and Socialbakers' fake followers app make it easy to check your own or others' social media accounts for fake followers. Your client may get mocked online for doing this because the lack of authenticity and transparency runs directly counter to the values listed earlier. This hurts your client's reputation and your own credibility as a professional. It also drags down the reputation of public relations as a profession in general.

Make a Decision and Justify It

Although buying followers may offer a quick and inexpensive way to meet short-term social media objectives, there are plenty of ways to justify the decision not to do so. In all likelihood, the consequences will not be positive or productive. Real expertise and professionalism in public relations means being willing and able to put in the time and effort required to build relationships. PRSA lists "Enhancing the Profession" as a key provision of conduct: "Professionals work constantly to strengthen the public's trust in the profession . . . to build respect and credibility with the public for the profession of public relations . . . to improve, adapt and expand professional practices."[18]

Professionalism in public relations means being willing and able to put in the time and effort required to build relationships.

In Case You Missed It

Public relations professionals are some of the busiest people in business, but mere *busyness* is a waste of time without planning. These tips from the chapter will help you see day-to-day activities as ways to serve the broader missions of organizations in society:

- Awareness of a cause, new product or app is only one step in leading people to donate, purchase or download.

- When campaign goals include helping publics acquire relevant skills, public relations basically becomes an act of teaching.

- Avoid setting goals at one level (e.g., liking) when what you and your client really want is effectiveness at a greater level (e.g., acting).

- A good timeline determines when to spend resources (such as time and money) on what.

- Social media analytics allow communicators to monitor real-time feedback in response to any post.

- SMART objectives make it clear when, what and how evaluation should be conducted.

- Organize budgets in a way that makes sense to the people funding them.

- A social media presence may be "free" of advertising costs, but it still requires personnel costs.

- A big part of what makes social media social is that people are motivated to engage other real people.

- Professionalism in public relations means being willing and able to put in the time and effort required to build relationships.

SUMMARY

6.1 Analyze strategic communication outcomes.

Planning for public relations means considering a number of levels of outcomes. McGuire developed a hierarchy-of-effects model that outlines key steps in public communication campaigns: tuning in, attending, liking, comprehending, learning, agreeing, remembering, acting and proselytizing. Beyond exposure and attention/awareness, strategists must think about steps leading to behavior change and proselytizing when communication goes viral. Minding these outcomes helps planners set goals, identify appropriate objectives and tactics, and be realistic about expected outcomes.

6.2 Define key terms of strategic communication planning.

Strategic decision-making means that daily action and communication *tactics* can be tied with specific *objectives*, which help achieve broader *goals*, which serve an organization's vision and *mission*. When public relations action and communication are implemented without this context, decision-making is more tactical than strategic. *Outputs* describe the tangible efforts of public relations practitioners—what people do. *Outcomes* describe the results of that work—what people accomplish. *Impacts* are the broadest and furthest-reaching results of public relations.

6.3 Develop basic timelines to organize tasks in a strategic public relations program.

Timelines foster accountability in the management of strategic programs and campaigns. Key steps to consider include formative research, client/management meetings, implementation of tactics, production of communication materials, events and evaluation.

6.4 Identify key categories of public relations budget items.

Three key resources to consider in any public relations budget are personnel, administrative costs and supplies, and media. These three categories overlap.

6.5 Apply consequentialism to make ethical decisions about setting and achieving public relations objectives while enhancing the profession.

Consequentialism entails thinking through the outcomes of one's actions in making ethical decisions. The case of whether or not to buy followers on Twitter or Instagram raises questions about consequences such as misspent budget or ineffective strategy. More important, ethical decision-making in this case means considering broader consequences such as deception of publics and damaging (rather than enhancing) the profession.

DISCUSSION QUESTIONS

1. When was the last time you changed your behavior as a result of an organization's strategic communication? Which of McGuire's steps did you go through?

2. Search for an organization that (a) has its vision or mission statement posted online, and (b) has conducted a public relations tactic that you think was effective. Describe how the tactic might help achieve an objective, which helps with a goal, which supports the vision or mission. What's the strategy?

3. **CASE STUDY** Take UNICEF's general handwashing goal and apply it to your own school or workplace: "Increase, improve and/or sustain good hand washing behaviour and form good handwashing habits." Write at least two SMART objectives, one key output, one key outcome, and one impact for a proposed campaign.

4. Set an academic or professional goal for yourself for some time in the next year. Draw or chart a timeline such as the Gantt chart in Figure 6.4 that shows how your activities will lead toward your goal over time.

5. Suppose you are the leader of a student or community organization that is given a budget of $1,000 to compete with other similar groups to recycle the largest number of plastic bottles in your community. How would you allocate your budget between personnel, administrative costs and supplies, and media?

6. Not all fake followers on social media are bought. Almost every account is susceptible to at least a small percentage of unwanted fake followers (in the same way that we get spam via email). Should public relations people be responsible for removing these fake followers for clients? Why or why not?

KEY TERMS

Benchmarking   161
Billable rate   168
Consequentialism   174
Frequency   169
Funnel   155
Goals   157
Impacts   161
Impressions   154
Media planning   169

Mission   157
Objectives   157
Outcomes   161
Outputs   160
Overhead expenses   168
Planning   149
Pop-up   149
Pro bono   165
Programmatic media buying   169

Proselytizing   153
Reach   169
Strategic decision-making   155
Strategy   157
Tactical decision-making   155
Tactics   157
Unconferences   164

CHAPTER 7

Implementation

With the right mix of owned, paid, shared and earned media, direct-to-consumer startups can take a bite out of market share from competitors. How did BarkBox implement public relations to tug business away from companies with longer pedigrees?

KEY LEARNING OUTCOMES

7.1 Explain how organizational action is the foundation for credible communication.

7.2 Decide which communication channels are appropriate for which public relations purposes.

7.3 Outline media options on a continuum from controlled to uncontrolled.

7.4 Differentiate among owned, paid, shared and earned media.

7.5 Describe the relationship between the values of loyalty and diversity.

RELATED UNIVERSAL ACCREDITATION BOARD COMPETENCY AREAS

1.6 AUDIENCE IDENTIFICATION • **1.8** IMPLEMENTATION • **2.2** ETHICAL BEHAVIOR
4.2 BARRIERS TO COMMUNICATION • **6.4** MEDIA RELATIONS

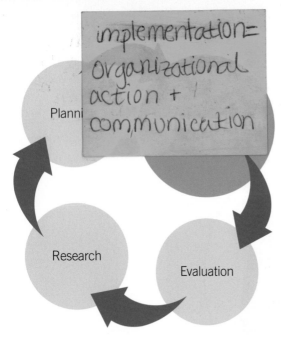

Figure 7.1 In the RPIE model, a well-planned, research-based public relations program will be implemented in a way that allows evaluation of outcomes.

How can action and communication both be part of implementation?

After research and planning, it's time to implement programs and manage the communication that goes along with them. The third step in the RPIE (research-planning-implementation-evaluation) process is implementation, which includes a combination of organizational action and communication (Figure 7.1). As important as communication is in public relations, excellence in the public relations field is based on meaningful action.

We've all heard spokespeople use buzzwords about "maximizing potential," "taking it to the next level," "providing thought leadership" or "giving 110 percent." But what do those phrases mean, especially if they can't be tied to anything specific that the organization is actually doing? "Actions speak louder than words," the old adage goes. The same logic applies in the implementation of public relations. It's one thing to say your organization values diversity and inclusion, for example. It's another to manage the organization in a way that proves it.

Excellence in the field of public relations is based on meaningful action.

Organizations must bring something beyond talk to their relationships with publics.

Taking Action

Recall from Chapter 1 that Arthur Page said principled management of public relations means you have to "prove it with action." The American Red Cross doesn't just send thoughts and prayers when disaster strikes. They send aid workers with blankets, water and first aid.

In Chapter 2, on the history of public relations, we saw how public relations matured when organizations started taking it seriously as a management function based on action. With the counsel of Earl Newsom, Ford Motor Company didn't just talk about the importance of auto safety in the 1950s, it actually funded research on safety and changed its operations and vehicle design in the interest of its publics.

In Chapter 3, on convergence and integration, we explored the link between public relations, marketing and advertising based on the shared communication function of the three fields. We also learned that promotion is just one of the four P's, along with product, place and price. Kwikset enjoyed great publicity for its technological savvy when its Kevo deadbolt (which enables you to unlock doors at home using a Bluetooth-enabled smartphone) was named product of the year. But that publicity resulted only after the company did the heavy lifting of research and development to bring the new product to market.

"What have you done for me lately?" could have been the theme for Chapter 4 on relationships. Relationships with employees, investors, media and other organizations and publics are all predicated on organizations bringing something beyond talk to the relationship.

Chapters 5 and 6 on research and planning bring us to the doorstep of action. A well-planned, research-based public relations program will be implemented in line with the organization's mission and broad goals. But living up to these ideals and "walking the walk" can be tough, as Chipotle Mexican Grill can attest.

Case Study

Pulled Pork: Chipotle's Challenge to Act on Its Principles

Chipotle Mexican Grill endured one of the toughest restaurant food-safety crises in U.S. history in 2016 when multiple locations across several states were investigated as sources of *E. coli* outbreaks. One of the main factors in Chipotle's ability to withstand the initial shock of that massive crisis was its organizational history of building and maintaining strong relationships with its publics based on both action and communication.

Chipotle's "Food with Integrity" program outlines the company's commitment to using only quality ingredients and respecting the welfare of farmers, animals and the environment. Online (chipotle.com/food-with-integrity.html), they communicate this commitment:

> We care deeply about where our ingredients come from. While industrial farming practices have evolved to maximize profits and production, we make an extra effort to partner with farmers, ranchers, and other suppliers whose practices emphasize quality and responsibility. See how we're making choices with farmers, animals, and the environment in mind.[1]

For meat in particular, Chipotle claims to work with farmers whose animals are raised in ways that meet specific criteria. "We think that animals raised outdoors or in deeply-bedded pens are happier and healthier than those raised in confinement." Chipotle takes "a firm stand" on sourcing from farmers who abide by their strict guidelines including "pasture-raised animals that have room to be animals," and no "nontherapeutic antibiotics or added hormones on the farms that produce our ingredients."[2]

Of course, maintaining these standards comes at a cost, but the business model worked for Chipotle—up to a point. The chain surged in growth between 2001 when it began implementing the policy and 2014 when Chipotle shares jumped 37 percent.[3] Chipotle was soaring in the markets and in public relations, minding investors, customers and even pigs, all at the same time.

But that beautiful balance was knocked off-kilter in 2015 when Chipotle discovered that one of its major pork suppliers was not complying with the humanitarian guidelines. So what did they do? They pulled the pork from about a third of their restaurants. This was a huge management decision for a burrito chain known for its *carnitas*.

In a way, Chipotle was a victim of its own success. Its eco-friendly business model became harder and harder to sustain as the chain grew. While farms that met Chipotle's standards still made up a relatively small percentage of food suppliers, Chipotle had grown into one of the nation's largest fast food chains. "Those two realities could eventually prove untenable, because . . . they simply don't add up," wrote *Washington Post* blogger Roberto Ferdman.[4] This was the public relations challenge for Chipotle.

Chipotle, however, stuck to its principles. "This is fundamentally an animal welfare decision and it's rooted in our unwillingness to compromise our standards where animal welfare is concerned," Chipotle Communications Director Chris Arnold told Ferdman. As the case continued, Chipotle management had to make tough decisions to balance their own interests with the interests of their publics. They resorted to rotating their restaurant menus periodically so that no one restaurant would go without carnitas for any extended period of time.

Of course, Chipotle still has its critics. The case even gave rise to the hashtag #carnitasgate, while "pork-ocalypse" trended on Twitter. Some speculated that the whole ordeal was a conspiracy to sell more of its

Yes, we have no carnitas.

How do you think pulling a major menu item affected Chipotle's reputation? How do you think it affected their sales?

meatless, tofu-filled "sofritas," which were introduced at about the same time.[5] Within a few years, Chipotle was back on track financially. The company was considered "one of the unsung heroes of the stock market" after gaining 49 percent market value in 2018.[6]

Any way you slice it, this case illustrates how much management goes into real public relations. Anyone can slap a web page up, post some tweets, or send out news releases claiming that an organization is green and sustainable, but living up to the promise while growing an organization's bottom line entails a lot of hard work (i.e., implementation).

Choosing Channels

Two-way communication and relationships are the heart of public relations. Most of what you can expect to do on a day-to-day basis in public relations is indeed communication. In between meetings, phone calls and presentations, you'll spend your time on email and social media. You'll probably chat like mad—both in person and via instant messaging. Skyping, blogging, tweeting, posting—even old-fashioned reading and writing—they're all forms of communication. In managing relationships, you have to make smart choices about when to send a text, when to "reply all" in an email, when to call someone on the phone, when to tweet, when to send a photo, and perhaps most important, when to turn off all your devices and pay attention to the people in the room with you.

A lot of these decisions are not unique to public relations. Most people working in modern organizations have to make these same decisions as

Selecting the channels for communication is a big responsibility.

What factors are most important to consider before launching social media efforts?

Make wise and informed decisions about which channels of communication to use, when and for what purpose.

they manage their professional interactions. What makes public relations different is that we also have to manage the communication that we plan and do on behalf of the organizations that we represent. In implementing public relations programs, we are expected to make wise and informed decisions on which channels of communication to use, when and for what purpose. When communicating to meet specific goals and objectives, we have to carefully analyze the pros and cons of various media for communications between organizations and publics.

Controlled and Uncontrolled Media

Traditionally, public relations practitioners have thought about media in terms of how much control they have (or how much control they give up) when using various channels and tactics for communication. Internal newsletters or television ads would be thought of as **controlled media** because communicators may write and edit, or create and produce, messages exactly how they want them. They also control where and to whom the messages are sent. If you edit your own newsletter, you choose exactly what stories you want to include, you choose the images and layout, you define the angle on the stories, and you decide whose mailboxes the newsletter lands in. If you are paying for a TV spot, you are buying control of the message. You can make creative and strategic decisions about how the message is produced (or at least you contract the people who do). You also decide where, when and how often the ad airs. Recall the concepts of reach and frequency from Chapter 6.

On the other side of the spectrum are uncontrolled media. According to the *APR Study Guide*, **uncontrolled media** include newspapers, TV and radio news, and external websites, as well as blogs and social media that are not produced internally.[7] You can spend days crafting a news release to perfectly align with your organization's goals and objectives, but the second that you send it to a journalist or blogger, you lose control. It's up to the journalist how (and if) to tell the story after that.

Of course, most communication falls somewhere in between entirely controlled or uncontrolled. Real, interactive and two-way communication doesn't allow one party or another total control. Press conferences and interviews are good examples.

Gaming press conferences combine entertainment, technology and ardent fan interest, and they are among the most elaborately planned and staged media events. But that doesn't mean they are entirely controlled channels for communication. When Electronic Arts Inc. (EA) hosted its EA Play press conference in summer 2018, the company hyped a live look into some of its biggest games of the year (e.g., Battlefield™ V, Anthem™, FIFA 19, Madden NFL 19, NBA LIVE 19 and Star Wars™ Battlefront II) as well as big reveals for new games. However, many members of the media who attended focused more on the bumpy production of the press conference itself rather than the smooth features of the games that the event was designed to promote. GamingBolt's USA Editor Pramath Parijat called it "One of the worst press conferences of all time":

> The fact that most of the show was just people awkwardly talking about games without footage or in a lot of cases, even trailers, made other things stand out even more—there was a complete lack of preparation (one of the few times we were shown gameplay footage, it seemed like the demo was not set up). . . . Developers stumbled over what they were saying, often being prompted pretty aggressively by the presenter, who ended almost any segment of the show with a fake excited "HOW COOL WAS THAT?!?"[8]

"No, EA. That was not cool," concluded Parijat. "No part of that was cool. It was so uncool it made even a goddamn Star Wars game reveal boring."

So why would any strategic communicator want to mess with uncontrolled media? Well, for starters, money is a factor. You don't pay for the space for a newspaper story that runs as the result of a news release or an interview with your CEO that airs on national TV. When press events go well, organizations receive a lot of good publicity; this means that they reach publics via mass media that otherwise would be prohibitively expensive. Some also see credibility as a big advantage for uncontrolled media. When your message is vetted by a journalist or editor and told as part of a news story it may carry more credibility.

Actress Janina Gavankar introduces Star Wars: Battlefront II at the Electronic Arts (EA) E3 press conference at the Hollywood Palladium in Hollywood, CA.

In what ways are press events like this uncontrolled, and what are the risks and benefits of hosting them?

Third-party credibility
Tendency of people to attribute greater trustworthiness or expertise to a source other than the original sender of a persuasive message.

Think about the Chipotle story. What's more compelling—a statement directly from Chipotle's communications director or a story in *USA Today*? The actual effectiveness of **third-party credibility** is the subject of academic debate and very much depends on the context.

In most situations, like the Chipotle case, public perceptions of and relationships with organizations are the result of a converged mishmash of communication and experience with those organizations. A news report consists of a mix of the reporter's story and quotes from her sources. Readers will consider that story along with everything else they have heard about the organization. Of course, they also will think about any firsthand experience they have had. In implementing public relations programs, we have to consider what our organizations are doing as it affects publics (action), what we are saying (communication) and what others are saying about us (third-party communication).

Owned, Paid, Shared and Earned Media

Another way to think about the spectrum of media options is in terms of owned, paid, shared and earned (Figure 7.2). Public relations people and their organizations have always had options for all four. But new technologies have changed the way media are owned and paid for. Social media in particular have changed how we share information. And today's public relations professionals seek to earn followers, fans, likes, search engine rankings and positive reviews, in addition to earning news coverage.

Owned Media

Owned channels include newsletters, corporate video, brochures, direct mail, voicemail messaging systems, intranets and web pages. Since organizations own the channels, they more or less control the message and its dissemination, as well as the opportunity for feedback or two-way communication. For example, while intranets allow for two-way communication on organization-owned platforms, public-facing web pages allow organizations to communicate externally.

Most early organizational web pages were designed primarily for delivering messages in a one-way fashion. Many

Pardon the low resolution and snazzy fonts, but here's the very first White House home page as it appeared in 1994.

While this is a typical Web 1.0 image, do you see any evidence of movement from one-way/controlled to two-way/uncontrolled media?

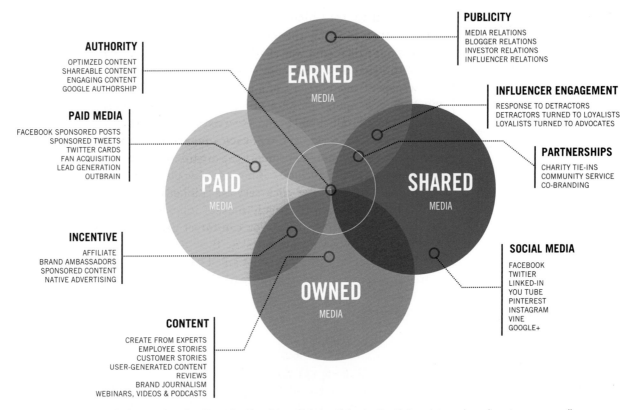

AUTHORITY
OPTIMZED CONTENT
SHAREABLE CONTENT
ENGAGING CONTENT
GOOGLE AUTHORSHIP

PAID MEDIA
FACEBOOK SPONSORED POSTS
SPONSORED TWEETS
TWITTER CARDS
FAN ACQUISITION
LEAD GENERATION
OUTBRAIN

INCENTIVE
AFFILIATE
BRAND AMBASSADORS
SPONSORED CONTENT
NATIVE ADVERTISING

CONTENT
CREATE FROM EXPERTS
EMPLOYEE STORIES
CUSTOMER STORIES
USER-GENERATED CONTENT
REVIEWS
BRAND JOURNALISM
WEBINARS, VIDEOS & PODCASTS

PUBLICITY
MEDIA RELATIONS
BLOGGER RELATIONS
INVESTOR RELATIONS
INFLUENCER RELATIONS

INFLUENCER ENGAGEMENT
RESPONSE TO DETRACTORS
DETRACTORS TURNED TO LOYALISTS
LOYALISTS TURNED TO ADVOCATES

PARTNERSHIPS
CHARITY TIE-INS
COMMUNITY SERVICE
CO-BRANDING

SOCIAL MEDIA
FACEBOOK
TWITIER
LINKED-IN
YOU TUBE
PINTEREST
INSTAGRAM
VINE
GOOGLE+

EARNED MEDIA

PAID MEDIA

SHARED MEDIA

OWNED MEDIA

Figure 7.2 In her "Spin Sucks" blog, Gini Dietrich offers this model classifying tactics that work in each media category, as well as overlaps between categories.

Can you name an organization (or organizations) using the range of tactics effectively?

websites still fit this description. Think Web 1.0. These websites are sometimes referred to as **brochureware** because they basically present the same information that can be delivered in static brochures. They enable organizations to disseminate information, potentially to worldwide audiences. *Potentially* is a key word here because—let's be realistic—people in Kazakhstan or Kenya probably won't search the web for a kickboxing club in Kansas. For websites to reach their potential they need to be part of a communication strategy that drives people to them. After all, websites don't get delivered to targeted publics in the same way that brochures, newsletters or in-house videos do. People have to actively search them out and find them.

Owned media include newer and emerging channels for communication as well. Podcasts, webinars, text messaging systems, blogs, apps and online video can all be owned. But like web pages in general, their utility to users is often enhanced when organizations give up some control and allow for feedback and sharing. This brings us to a more profound implication of the internet for public relations—the way it opened new channels for two-way communication and interaction between organizations and publics.

Organizations can enhance the utility of owned media when they give up some control and allow for feedback and sharing.

Brochureware
Web pages that present essentially the same material as printed materials such as brochures.

Paid Media

Advertising is probably the first thing that comes to your mind when you think about paid media, and rightly so. As defined in Chapter 3, advertising is the stuff that fills paid media space. That space could be column inches in a newspaper, page portions of a magazine, seconds on the radio or TV, or pixels on a computer monitor or a giant high-definition LED display at a sports arena. Product and brand advertising are designed primarily to help sell products and services. **Corporate advertising** or institutional advertising is designed more to promote the organization as a whole.

Paid media also include banner ads, Google AdWords, targeted email distribution and pay-per-click services. LinkedIn, for example, sells ads that will appear on profile pages, in users' inboxes, on search results pages and in LinkedIn group pages. You can target your ads based on job titles, location, age, gender or company size. Then you set up your account to **pay per click**—whereby the sponsor of an ad pays each time an ad is clicked—starting at $2 per click and going up to whatever maximum you set in a bid.[9]

Outdoor advertising seems to be everywhere.

Is this owned, paid, shared or earned media?

Native advertising, another paid option, refers to ads that match the format of the primary content of the medium or channel. A sponsored column or **advertorial** in a newspaper or magazine, a promoted tweet, a sponsored Facebook post or an in-feed ad—they're all paid media. And they can get expensive. When Snapchat first offered companies the opportunity to buy one day's worth of ads to appear in users' "recent updates" feeds, they reportedly charged $750,000. Apparently it was worth it to big brands like Macy's, Samsung, McDonald's and Universal Pictures, the last of which used the paid service to promote the film *Dumb and Dumber To.*[10] Within a few years, Snapchat began offering a wider array of pricing options. By 2018, Snapchat ads were available for an average of $2.95 per thousand impressions compared to more than $4 for Instagram and more than $5 for Facebook.[11] But the costs still add up. An Australian teeth-whitening product company called HiSmile budgeted approximately $10 million for their Snapchat advertising budget that year, including Snapchat's Story Ads, which are sponsored videos that display along with posts from professional media in Snapchat's "Discover" section.[12]

Whenever you see the words "Sponsored content" or "You may also like" on a web page or in an app, you're very likely looking at native advertising. A word of caution: this type of communication risks being deceptive. Stealth advertising that is designed and placed to trick people into thinking they are seeing third-party news, reviews or editorial content is a bad idea if your goal is to build and sustain trust between your organization and its publics.

Shared Media

Think about your social media use. How often do you "share" your own original content, and how often do you share stories, memes, photos, videos and other content from organizations that may consider you a member of one of their publics? Organizations invest a lot of resources in developing content that they hope will be shared. When broad sharing is a goal, the biggest successes are the posts that go viral.

Amazon.com tells me that many customers who buy this book also buy *The Associated Press Stylebook*, so many of you are among key publics for the *AP Stylebook*. If you follow @APStylebook on Twitter, you will notice that the social media team indeed has its own "style" that lends itself to sharing. A big part of @APStylebook's success is infusing humor into tweets as they share important information for students and professional writers.

A   B

When The Kansas City Star sports writer Brooke Pryor posted this tweet (A), it generated thousands of likes and retweets, including a response from @APStylebook (B) that resulted in thousands of additional retweets and likes.

What makes @APStylebook effective as shared media?

GoPro's YouTube channels have millions of subscribers.

Why is GoPro so successful in leveraging shared media?

Another key to success is how those who manage the @APStylebook account monitor news and other social media to find opportunities to engage key publics. Follow @APStylebook and you'll definitely learn some writing tips, but you also might find yourself laughing and maybe even sharing. Learning, laughing and sharing are solid public relations outcomes in my book.

Successful efforts to share (and be shared) are usually no accident. In public relations, shared media tactics are very carefully planned and implemented. GoPro's YouTube strategy is a good example. GoPro is a company that makes HD, waterproof video recording devices. With more than seven million subscribers as of this writing, a big part of the company's strategy is the way it facilitates sharing among its subscribers. "Subscribers provide velocity," writes *Econsultancy* blogger Christopher Ratcliff. "YouTube loves velocity," he continues. "They'll watch it, they'll share it and your video will end up in more places."[13]

To be sure, it doesn't hurt that the nature of GoPro's product line lends itself perfectly to a social media site that is built on the concept of amazing videos. But GoPro leverages the medium particularly well by providing a forum for users to determine which videos are the best by viewing, liking, sharing, commenting and discussing. Most of the sharing is between and among the organization's publics, and GoPro representatives are careful and strategic about how they get involved. For instance, they may feature "staff's top picks," offer a few comments on popular videos, post tutorials or occasionally answer product-related questions in the discussion section of their YouTube channels. However, the biggest act of sharing may be the way GoPro shares its platform by letting users provide some of the content and dominate the discussions. In communication strategy, sharing can refer to either the sharing of content such as a tweet or a video, or the sharing of a forum or channel such as a discussion page or YouTube channel. Either way, sharing means ceding some control.

It's just as easy to find examples of organizations that have gone viral for regrettable reasons when the shared communication about them spun out of control. When Lockheed Martin attempted to take advantage of #WorldPhotoDay by tweeting, "Do you have an amazing photo of one of our products? Tag us in your pic and we may feature it …," the response was not at all what they had hoped for. Instead of soaring jets or hi-tech helicopters,

A

B

Lockheed Martin deleted their request for Twitter followers to post pictures of their products for #WorldPhotoDay (A), but not before some users noticed and took advantage of the opportunity to criticize the company (B).

How might the company make better use of shared media?

Twitter users posted photos of bomb fragments and blood-stained children's backpacks. These responses stemmed from recent reports that a 500-pound laser-guided Lockheed Martin bomb had been used in an attack that had killed dozens of people, including children on a school bus in Yemen.[14] In the same way that public relations practitioners give up control of a news story as soon as they send a news release to journalists, they also give up control when they share information or invite engagement with publics on social media.

Earned Media

Just as advertising may be the first thing that people think of when they think of *paid* media, publicity may be the first thing that comes to mind for public relations practitioners when they think of *earned* media. The *APR Study Guide* defines publicity as "information from an outside source that is used by the media because it has news value" and "an uncontrolled method of placing messages because the source does not pay the media for placement."[15] In other words, publicity isn't bought. Publicity is earned.

A classic example is a newspaper story that is written and published as the result of a news release. If an organization has done something newsworthy, its public relations person will have a higher probability of success getting the story reported in the paper than if the news release is mostly spin and is deemed by editors to have little news value. As discussed in Chapter 4 on relationships, effective public relations people understand how journalists think. They understand news value. They know when their

Just as you give up control of a story as soon as you send a news release, you give up control of information when you share it with your publics on social media.

Media gatekeepers
People or processes that filter information by deciding which content is published, broadcasted, posted, shared or forwarded.

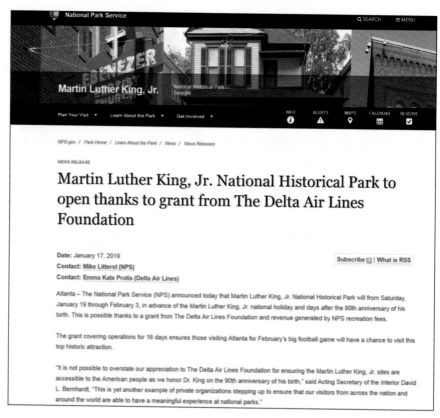

During a partial government shutdown in 2019, The Delta Airlines Foundation supported the National Park Service (NPS) with a grant to keep Martin Luther King, Jr. National Historical Park open. The two organizations issued this news release to publicize the story.

Do you think the two organizations earned further news coverage?

organizations have done something that merits media coverage. When public relations people work in a management role, they help organizations perform in the public interest, and they also help organizations tell that story by garnering media coverage. They help organizations *earn* media attention.

Of course, the concept of media attention today is much broader than making news in newspapers, magazines, television and radio. In addition to traditional editors and producers, today's **media gatekeepers** are social media influencers, everyday media consumers and even computer algorithms. Having a picture of your product pinned on a top Pinterest board, trending on Reddit, getting retweeted by a celebrity, or showing up at the top of organic search results on Google are all forms of earned media.

Wikipedians define *search engine optimization (SEO)* as "the process of affecting the online visibility of a website or a web page in a web search engine's unpaid results—often referred to as 'natural,' 'organic,' or 'earned' results."[16] While you can buy placement at the top of search results with programs like Google AdWords, effective SEO requires earning that placement by offering useful information, designing your site well and building relationships with other sites that may link to yours. On the last point, Google rewards earned links more than self-placed ones. Google treats a link from an external page as a "vote" by that page for the page to which it links. In Google's algorithms, "votes cast by pages that are themselves 'important' weigh more heavily and help to make other pages 'important.'"[17] In the same way that news operations draw a line between paid advertising and editorial content (sometimes referred to in publishing lingo as the separation of "church and state"), search engines take care to separate paid and unpaid results to protect the relevance of their search results and the credibility of their service.

Mixed Media

In the universe of owned, paid, shared and earned media, communications functions and effects mix and overlap considerably. Content from an owned channel like a company blog, Pinterest board or Twitter timeline can easily be shared with a re-post, re-pin or retweet. Paid advertising, including native advertising and paid search results, can complement earned coverage in those same channels.

Today's media gatekeepers include social media influencers, everyday media consumers and even computer algorithms.

Case Study

Puppies as Publics? BarkBox Marks Its Territory Across Owned, Paid, Shared and Earned Media

BarkBox is a subscription service that delivers boxes of themed dog treats and toys to millions of dogs and their humans each month. The Bark company designs and makes most of its products in-house and customizes each delivery based on the dog's breed, size and temperament. As a **direct-to-consumer** (DTC) brand, you might expect BarkBox to fetch most of its business from its own channels and from social media. But BarkBox and other DTC brands have learned to sniff around more in deciding the right mix of owned, paid, shared and earned media.

In the medical world, direct-to-consumer advertising has long referred to pharmaceutical companies that promote prescription products directly to patients rather than relying entirely on medical professionals to recommend prescriptions. More recently, DTC also has come to describe brands like BarkBox, Dollar Shave Club and Blue Apron that market and deliver products directly to consumers. Part of the formula for success for these companies has been cutting out the intermediary. By delivering products directly to your door, these companies don't have to split profit margins with the PetSmarts, WalMarts and Krogers of the world. So it may be tempting to assume that they would want to go direct to consumers with

Direct-to-consumer
Business model in which organizations such as home-delivery and subscription services market products and services directly to consumers and bypass traditional retail channels.

their communication strategies as well and bypass media gatekeepers in the process. However, as BarkBox has shown, optimizing the media mix means weighing the costs and benefits across all available media channels.

As consumers, social media feeds are where many of us first become exposed to and aware of the hippest new DTC brands. In fact, Facebook featured BarkBox as a prime example of how the platform's news feed, along with Facebook video ads, Facebook Marketplace, and other Facebook research and measurement tools generated conversions from views to subscriptions. "Because it signed up more subscribers by showing ads in Marketplace and News Feed," Facebook reported, "BarkBox will continue to tap Facebook's shopping destination to generate more subscriptions."[18] This is definitely *paid* media because Bark paid Facebook for BarkBox to be featured in users' news feeds and in the Facebook Marketplace.

Of course, Facebook and Instagram (owned by Facebook) also are top channels for *shared* media too. And BarkBox quickly became a darling on Instagram, where dog owners and dog lovers post funny pictures, quotes and videos of their four-legged friends tearing into their freshly delivered toys and treats. *Adweek* reported in 2017 that BarkBox had 500,000 subscribers and more than 4 million fans on Facebook and Instagram. The *Adweek* report highlighted the Bark social media team's knack for cultivating sharable content by working with comedians instead of traditional marketers to infuse humor into the content in ways that resonate with dog owners and dog lovers.[19] Stacie Grissom, Head of Content at Bark, identifies with her publics as "an iceberg of a population who's just like us, total weirdos about their dogs."

Just as Bark owns and controls much of its manufacturing and packaging, it also owns and controls many of its media channels including its website Barkbox.com ("Ready to spoil your pup with a BarkBox of their very own?"), its "Pupdates" email service (I have to admit I subscribe) and *BarkPost*, which started as a blog for BarkBox and evolved into a leading entertainment site for dog lovers.

BarkBox *earns* media too by making news with programs such as "Snacks That Give Back," a line of dog treats for which a portion of sales are used to support shelter and rescue organizations across the United States, and BARK for Good, which is an online program that gives 5 percent of BarkShop proceeds to organizations that assist animals in need. It also has sponsored events including the CMA Fest in Nashville.

Perhaps the most important part of BarkBox's implementation strategy, though, is its flexibility and responsiveness to research and evaluation in the RPIE cycle. As of this writing, the darling of DTC was moving more of its advertising budget to old-fashioned radio, TV and print media and had started selling toys in Target stores with plans to expand to other brick-and-mortar retail chains.[20] You may not be able to teach an old dog new tricks, but apparently new dogs can learn old tricks.

PER MY LAST EMAIL

barkbox ✓ • Following

barkbox DID YOU EVEN READ IT, KAREN?! #pleaseadvise #permylastemail #officepup #shibainu @jemelehill via Twitter @ohayo_kuma

Load more comments

kathsnacks @andrewdamus every day ♡

jessicap2011 @andrewdamus haha truth ♡

cbrooke.colden @pinkbleedsblue ♡

thepaintedpoochnyc Shiba's are the best! ♡

♡ 💬 ⬆️ 🔖

Liked by kristicamara and 26,701 others

NOVEMBER 1, 2018

Add a comment... ...

@jemelehill

BarkBox relies heavily on user-generated content and humor in its mix of owned, paid, shared and earned media.

What are the risks and benefits?

Voices from the Field

Rosanna M. Fiske

ROSANNA M. FISKE, APR, is a PRSA Fellow and senior vice president of corporate communications at Wells Fargo. Widely known for her cross-cultural understanding and expertise, Fiske is responsible for all aspects of corporate communications including executive advocacy, social media and internal and external communications for Wells Fargo's Florida and Southeast regions, which include 1,200+ branches and more than 30,000 team members. Fiske has a proven track record developing successful, multi-channel campaigns working with some of the world's leading brands such as Charles Schwab, American Airlines, GE, Google, Absolut Vodka and MTV Networks. Fiske was the first Latina CEO of

PRSA, received four Silver Anvils, was named a PRWeek Diversity Champion, and was honored as one of the Top 100 Influential Hispanics in America by Hispanic Business magazine.

In 2018 Wells Fargo launched the "Re-Established" campaign to win back trust after a challenging period in its history. ("Established in 1832. Re-established 2018 with a recommitment to you.") What's the role of public relations in that effort?

Our transformation is grounded in our vision of satisfying our customers' financial needs and helping them succeed financially. Our five values guide every action we take: what's right for customers, people as a competitive advantage, ethics, diversity and inclusion, and leadership. And by delivering on our goals, we want to become *the* financial services leader in: customer service and advice, team member engagement, innovation, risk management, corporate citizenship and shareholder value. Our communications effort is engrained in everything that we do and every single effort we embark on as a company. The overall takeaway we want to impart upon audiences, through our public relations efforts, is that it is a new day at Wells Fargo.

Can you tell us about how that plays out as real action within the organization?

We have made foundational changes to identify and fix problems so they do not happen again. We've made significant progress on our commitment to make things right for our customers and build a better bank. We have more work to do before we fully transform into the Wells Fargo we aspire to be—but we know what we need to do to make that aspiration a reality. We have a vision, a plan, and the drive to get there.

How do you make the business case for diversity?

People as a competitive advantage—one of our key values. Wells Fargo sees our diversity and inclusion council, and really diversity and inclusion as a whole, as a great professional development and engagement opportunity. In addition, diversity and inclusion enable us to use creativity and multiple perspectives to adapt and respond to our customers' needs faster and more effectively. To be successful as a company and as team members we must be as diverse as the customers and communities we serve.

What risks and rewards do you consider when deciding to communicate with uncontrolled channels like shared social media vs. more controlled channels like owned media?

Well, I actually think most work in public relations is uncontrolled! I worked in advertising too, and in advertising you're controlling message, frequency and placement. I see social media as an extension of public relations. You have the same pull and push philosophy on social media. You can push out a lot of messaging but wonder, "is anyone listening?" You can pull a lot of messaging, if you *do* the listening.

For Wells Fargo we have owned content in a number of ways, including Wells Fargo Stories (stories.wf.com) where we tell stories of everyday things that happen at Wells Fargo and with Wells Fargo customers. Our vision is to help customers succeed financially and you can find a lot of ways that we do that through those stories. Interestingly, if you go to one of our ATMs you'll find some of those stories—some of that owned content—showing on the screen. You may even be asked if you want the story printed so that you can take it with you, and share it with someone else.

Have you made much progress with diversity since you identified it as a core tenet for PRSA in 2011?

I was elected to the PRSA board in 2004. Right around that time we did a comprehensive member survey, and the percentage of ethnically diverse membership was in the single digits. By the time that I ended my year as CEO and chair of PRSA, we were at 13–14 percent. I was the first Latina CEO and chair, the first Latina who was national treasurer, and the second Hispanic member on the board. Since then, and looking at ethnicity as one dimension of diversity, three African American women, two Hispanic women, one African American man, one Hispanic man, and one Asian American man have served on the board. The fact that we have been able to make those changes in the last ten years at that top level of leadership definitely shows that we're making progress.

However, you can't look at diversity and inclusion separately. You can't say, "We need a few diverse people here because we're lacking that." It really needs to be built into everything that you do. A perfect example comes from back in 2011. Whenever we provided national news from PRSA that went beyond the profession, we provided it in Spanish to Spanish-language media and to diverse media. Supplying this content in different languages and to diverse media wasn't an add-on. It was *part of* the outreach and part of the strategy.

Ethics: Loyalty and Diversity in Communication and Action

Just as communication without action produces meaningless spin, diversity initiatives without loyalty amount to window dressing or a "misguided attempt to gain political correctness points," as media critic Eric Deggans puts it.[21] A key step in the process of ethical decision-making is identifying the diverse parties who will be affected by a decision and defining the organization's loyalty to each. **Loyalty** is a core value of public relations. It is listed in the *PRSA Code of Ethics* along with advocacy, honesty, expertise and independence. "We are faithful to those we represent, while honoring our obligation to serve the public interest."[22]

Interestingly, **diversity** is not mentioned directly in the PRSA Code of Ethics, but it is certainly an important issue to PRSA's leadership, as it is to professional organizations worldwide. In response to a *PRWeek* editorial titled "Agencies Must Find Answers for a Lack of Diversity,"[23] PRSA Chair and CEO Rosanna Fiske wrote that PRSA had "made increasing diversity in the profession a core tenet of our mission." Fiske noted that PRSA, along with the Arthur W. Page Society and the Council of PR Firms, among others, had identified diversity as a priority to "engender not only greater diversity within our ranks, but higher value for our services."[24] So what does diversity have to do with loyalty, and what does this ethical question have to do with implementation?

In their book *Doing Ethics in Media*, ethicists Jay Black and Chris Roberts write that we expand our empathy as we grow personally and professionally. At earlier stages of moral development we tend to be loyal to ourselves and to those who have power over us such as parents, teachers and bosses. But as we mature in life and in our professional careers, we expand our worldview and our empathy with "people who are not like us—people different in race, ethnicity, physical ability, religion, sexual orientation, age, economic class, etc."[25] In public relations—a field defined as the management of relationships with all sorts of publics—empathy and loyalty go hand in hand with diversity. The more diverse the decision-makers are within an organization, the more effective the organization will be in relating to its various publics. Diversity initiatives that are implemented as part of an organization's mission and loyalty to both internal and external publics are more than window dressing. They are the implementation of good strategy.

The more diverse decision-makers within an organization, the more effective the organization will be in relating to various publics.

Loyalty
A sense of obligation or support for someone or something, including both organizations and publics.

Diversity
Inclusion of different types of people and different types of views.

Case Study

Doing Good by Doing Well: Kimberly-Clark's Efforts to Promote Diversity

When Kimberly-Clark Corp. named Sue Dodsworth to the role of vice president and chief diversity officer, they communicated all the right things. "Diversity and inclusion is critical to the success of our business," said Chairman and CEO Thomas J. Falk in the news release.[26] With global brands like Huggies, Kotex, Kleenex, Scott and Pull-Ups, it didn't take advanced analytics to understand that many of Kimberly-Clark's most important publics are women. Data available at the time showed that 85 percent of the company's customers were female.[27] While naming Dodsworth to this post sent a message, Kimberly-Clark needed more for any lasting effect. "We must build a more diverse and inclusive global organization that looks, thinks and behaves like the people that use our products," said Falk. Dodsworth had her work cut out for her.

Research and planning came first. In sharp contrast to the demographics of its customers, only 17 percent of the Kimberly-Clark's upper-level (director level or higher) employees were women. In closer analysis of HR data, Dodsworth found two **glass-ceiling** points in women's careers at Kimberly-Clark. Many women were "stuck" in the position they attained right after their first promotion, and others were stuck just below the director level.[28]

A company like Kimberly-Clark often promotes managers from areas like manufacturing or millwork that traditionally may not include many women. Dodsworth and her team analyzed hiring and promotion data and interviewed employees. They learned that women were deterred by leadership job descriptions that mentioned years of experience in these areas as desirable qualifications. As Dodsworth explained in a *Fortune* article, "When we asked why, it was, 'Because of these 10 things that I need for the role, I've only got eight.' Whereas when I talked to the men who applied, they had five and they were going for it."

Dodsworth and her team then developed and implemented a strategy that focused on career development. Dodsworth asked hiring managers writing job postings to focus more on skills that could be transferred to new positions than on accumulated years of past experience. Other actions included global networking forums, mentoring programs, hiring policies that were more amenable to work-life balance, and the implementation of specific business plans for recruiting and developing more women leaders. As reported in a news release announcing that Kimberly-Clark had won a Catalyst Award, the results were impressive:

- The number of women who held director-level or higher leadership positions globally increased by 71 percent.

- The number of women with racially or ethnically diverse backgrounds in "director-plus" positions at Kimberly-Clark in the United States doubled.

Glass ceiling
Metaphor used to describe a present but unseen barrier to promotion for women and minorities.

- Internal promotions of women to "director-plus" jobs increased from 19 percent to 44 percent.

Catalyst is a nonprofit organization dedicated to advancing business leadership opportunities for women. The Catalyst Award "annually honors innovative organizational approaches with proven, measurable results that address the recruitment, development, and advancement of all women, including diverse women."[29]

While some may see the award and the publicity it earned as "great PR," that recognition is less important to the success of the organization than the role of public relations as part of the way the organization is managed. As Dodsworth reported in the *Forbes* article, "This started as an initiative, but now it's the way we work."

Kimberly-Clark claimed, "We're changing more than just diapers around here."

How did the company's efforts to promote diversity also promote the company's business interests?

In Case You Missed It

Communication in public relations will ring hollow without action to back it up. Here are some key points from the chapter to help you hit the right notes in implementing a successful public relations plan.

- Excellence in the field of public relations is based on meaningful action.

- Organizations must bring something beyond talk to their relationships with publics.

- Make wise and informed decisions about which channels of communication to use, when and for what purpose.

- Organizations can enhance the utility of owned media when they give up some control and allow for feedback and sharing.

- Just as you give up control of a story as soon as you send a news release, you give up control of information when you share it with your publics on social media.

- Today's media gatekeepers include social media influencers, everyday media consumers and even computer algorithms.

- The more diverse the decision-makers within an organization, the more effective the organization will be in relating to various publics.

SUMMARY

7.1 Explain how organizational action is the foundation for credible communication.

You have to walk the walk if you are going to talk the talk, and actions speak louder than words. Both of these common sayings speak to the idea that the implementation of solid public relations programs requires the management of organizational action. Communication that is not based on meaningful action is spin. Chipotle's pork issue illustrates how an organization implemented public relations with both action and communication.

7.2 Decide which communication channels are appropriate for which public relations purposes.

In managing relationships, you have to make smart choices about which channels of communication to use when and for what purpose. You must carefully analyze the pros and cons of various media for communication on behalf of the entire organization.

7.3 Outline media options on a continuum from controlled to uncontrolled.

Media like brochures, newsletters, intranets and advertising fall on the controlled end of the spectrum because the public relations practitioner can, to some extent, control the production and distribution of content. Social media and publicity are considered uncontrolled because public relations practitioners cede control to social media users, news editors and producers. The most uncontrolled media often provide better options for two-way communication, credibility and influence.

7.4 Differentiate among owned, paid, shared and earned media.

Owned media include organizational web pages, newsletters, intranets and other controlled media that organization employees own and operate. Paid options include advertising and other media services that require payment for placement and distribution of information. Shared options are more common in social media, where users share by reposting, retweeting, tagging, linking and so on. Earned media include traditional publicity as well as coverage by third parties online (i.e., influencers). These channels often overlap, and integrated strategies may use all of the media types for implementing common goals, as was illustrated in the BarkBox example.

7.5 Describe the relationship between the values of loyalty and diversity.

At more advanced stages of professional and moral development, we expand our empathy to people who are different from us, thereby expanding our loyalty to more diverse groups. Understanding an organization's obligations to and relationships with diverse publics informs ethical decision-making as well as informed management of an organization. The more that diversity of public relations staff and internal publics reflects the diversity of an organization's external publics, the better suited the organization will be for building and maintaining mutually beneficial relationships, as illustrated in the Kimberly-Clark case.

DISCUSSION QUESTIONS

1. **CASE STUDY** The Chipotle case suggested that the company's eco-friendly business model became harder to sustain as its success led to rapid expansion. In what ways is it is easier for small organizations to live up to environmental and social justice promises? What advantages do large organizations have in being able to act on their principles? Cite examples of each.

2. Name an organization that you believe lives up to high standards. What does the organization do to earn your respect, and how does the organization communicate about those actions?

3. When might it be a *bad* decision for an organization to use social media to communicate with its publics? Give an example and explain why you would choose alternate channels.

4. Provide an example of a case when an organization benefited from something going viral, and compare that to a case in which viral communication harmed an organization. To what degree did the organizations have control of the channels in each case?

5. **CASE STUDY** BARK started off as a direct-to-consumer (DTC) company. Name another DTC company that you are familiar with. What types of owned, paid, shared and earned media have you observed them using? Does the company favor social media in its communication strategy? Why or why not?

6. **CASE STUDY** Kimberly-Clark has been recognized for its efforts to promote more women in the organization. What other kinds of diversity are beneficial to organizations like Kimberly-Clark, and why is this a public relations issue?

KEY TERMS

Advertorial   187
Brochureware   185
Controlled media   182
Corporate advertising   186
Direct-to-consumer   191

Diversity   195
Glass ceiling   196
Loyalty   195
Media gatekeepers   190
Native advertising   187

Pay per click   186
Third-party credibility   184
Uncontrolled media   182

CHAPTER 8
Evaluation

PR News called it a "close shave" when Gillette's "We Believe: The Best a Man Can Be" video drew millions of viewers and a range of very strong responses. How did Gillette evaluate its controversial campaign?

KEY LEARNING OUTCOMES

8.1 Explain how evaluation research can be used in public relations program development and message testing.

8.2 Describe how media monitoring services work.

8.3 Discuss how digital technology has expanded our ability to track and analyze data in evaluating public relations programs.

8.4 Evaluate public relations research practices using industry standards for research (i.e., Barcelona Principles).

8.5 Match appropriate metrics with the various public relations outcomes they measure.

8.6 Analyze the relationship between independence as a core value of public relations and the ethical conduct of research, measurement and evaluation.

RELATED UNIVERSAL ACCREDITATION BOARD COMPETENCY AREAS
1.9 EVALUATION OF PROGRAMS · **2.2** ETHICAL BEHAVIOR · **5.1** BUSINESS LITERACY
5.2 RESOURCE MANAGEMENT · **5.4** PROBLEM SOLVING AND DECISION-MAKING

valuation is the process by which we determine the value o[f]
When we invest time, energy and budgets in both short-
term projects, we use evaluation to understand our return [invest]ment. We also use evaluation to demonstrate to employers and [clients the] value they receive when they invest in us and our programs. Fr[om deter]mining whether it's worth it to update an Instagram feed daily t[o pitching] a million-dollar campaign proposal, evaluation is how we k[now—and] show—the value of our work.

The "E" (evaluation) may come last in the four-step RPI[E model] (Figure 8.1), but as we've discussed throughout the book, evalu[ation and] research go together, and both are used continuously throughout [our] public relations programs. In the introduction to Chapter 5, we [discussed] research as a cyclical process. Evaluation of prior programs can [begin] right at the very beginning of a new campaign or program. In Cha[pter 6, on] planning, we discussed the concepts of formative research and ben[chmark]ing. In planning goals and objectives, it's important to understand the current state of your organization, situation and publics so that you can measure your progress against that baseline or starting point. Then, in Chapter 7, we looked at how implementing public relations programs with digital and social media allows us to track and analyze activity across owned, paid, shared and earned media. In this chapter, we examine what we count as successful communication and our metrics for understanding that success.

All of the major research methods described in Chapter 5—surveys, experiments, content analysis, interviews, focus groups and direct observation—are just as useful now as they have been through the history of social science. The purposes for these methods haven't changed much. For example, surveys are still conducted to gather data that describe demographics and what people think, feel and do. In addition, as a method for evaluation, the data from surveys conducted before a campaign can be used as a baseline for comparison to data collected during and after a campaign to assess changes in cognition, attitudes and behavior.

Of course, online survey tools make it much easier to collect and analyze data than it was in the days when most surveys were conducted using paper and pencil. However, online surveys still serve much the same purpose as paper surveys. In fact, for some research with some populations, you may receive a higher response rate and a more representative sample of participants with a survey sent by snail mail or handed to respondents in person. Nielsen still mails pen-and-paper surveys, along with crisp dollar bills as incentives, to collect data on household TV viewing behavior.

Figure 8.1 In the RPIE model, evaluation demonstrates the value of what was planned and implemented, but it also helps current and future planning and implementation.

How can evaluation of one program or campaign serve as formative research for the next?

[Handwritten note:] Evaluation: Process by which we determine the value of our work — Evaluation requires research, before & after a campaign

Virtual reality headsets are widely available for gamers and other digital media consumers.

How might virtual reality be evaluated as a public relations tactic?

Digital watermarking
Information embedded into digital audio and video signals that can be used to track when and where the content is delivered.

Eye tracking
Process of measuring eye movements to determine where people are focusing; often used in website testing.

Functional magnetic resonance imaging (fMRI)
Tests that use magnetic fields to generate images of brain activity, including responses to communication and media stimuli.

This isn't to say, however, that there hasn't been significant innovation in research methods. Nielsen and other research firms also have developed **digital watermarking** technology that enables audio and video to be tracked with digital information woven into the signals that carry programming content. This helps copyright owners protect their information, and it also helps companies like Nielsen track which signals reach your TV and mobile devices. This digital research technology has the advantage of providing more accurate accounting for what content is delivered, but unlike paper surveys and diaries, the watermarking technology can't tell researchers whether you are actually paying attention.

In a laboratory setting, communication researchers might use software for **eye tracking**, or even **functional magnetic resonance imaging (fMRI)**, to observe how people pay attention to and respond to messages. Virtual reality headsets are available to everyday gamers and consumers. And, with new technology for communication comes new ways to measure and evaluate the experiences. Every virtual movement can be recorded and analyzed.

Whether you use traditional or new research technology, and whether you evaluate traditional or new public relations efforts, your research decisions should be driven by the specific purpose of your evaluation. Three major areas for evaluation research are: (1) message testing, (2) media monitoring, and (3) measurement of outcomes (i.e., metrics and analytics).

Message Testing

As a way to evaluate your tactics for communication, message testing can range from informal to formal and from qualitative to quantitative. Ever type a tweet and then quickly show it to a friend before posting? That's message testing: you are doing a tiny bit of evaluation research to see how others will receive your message before you send it. Other examples of ways to test messages with more rigor include focus groups, readability tests and experiments.

Focus Groups
Focus groups have been a popular method of message testing in advertising, entertainment and public relations for decades. Focus groups can be formal. Trained moderators may lead discussions with small groups of

carefully recruited participants who must respond to campaign concepts. Organizers of a health campaign may run focus groups to see what types of messages and appeals resonate most with high school students. A startup tech company getting ready to launch a new app may invite early adopters to focus groups to discuss the design of the app's icon or various display pages.

Readability Tests

Every time an editor or reviewer reads through copy and offers feedback, they are helping with message testing. This feedback is normally qualitative in the form of editorial suggestions and comments, either written or oral. But message testing also can be quantitative. For example, if you paste the text from the previous paragraph into a readability tester window on the site www.webfx.com/tools/read-able/, the software will tell you that the paragraph has five sentences, 95 words, 14 complex words, an average of 1.58 syllables per word and 19 words per sentence. The software calculates that this all adds up to an average readability score for a grade level of 12. So if you've graduated high school, we should be OK. However, this little bit of message testing reminds me to try to keep my sentences short.

Even informal message testing can be useful as formative evaluation in public relations.

What kind of message testing have you conducted?

A/B testing can be used to quickly compare the effects of different digital content and messages.

Experiments

Experimental design also can be applied in message testing. Message testing experiments are known as **A/B testing** in the parlance of digital media (Figure 8.2). Let's say you want to test different news release headings as links on one of your organization's web pages. You could set up two versions of the web page—an "A" version with one news release heading and a "B" version with another heading. These are basically two conditions in a simple experiment. Your website can then be programmed to randomly display either A or B to a sample of visitors over a period of time. A/B testing programs allow you to compare the two conditions against each other to see, for instance, whether the A version or the B version generates more clicks through to the full text of the news release. The independent variable (the cause) is the type of headline, and the dependent variable (the effect) is click-through behavior. When software and computer programs are used to automatically test digital messages, marketing and advertising researchers call this **automated copy testing**.

A/B testing
Experiment in which one group of participants is randomly assigned to see one version of a message and another group is randomly assigned to see a second version. Results are then compared to test the effectiveness of message variations.

Automated copy testing
Using computer programs to automate the process of testing digital messages such as promotional copy.

Clipping services
Businesses that monitor print and electronic media for mentions of clients in local, national or international outlets.

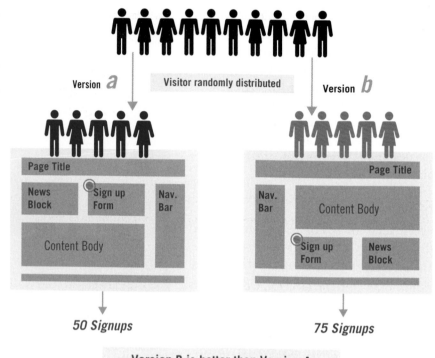

Figure 8.2 This example shows how different page layouts (independent variable) can be compared to see which delivers more signups (dependent variable).

What other independent and dependent variables can be tested with A/B testing?

Media Monitoring Services

Monitoring media is another area of evaluation that has sped up considerably in the digital age. In the days before Google (and Google alerts), interns and other entry-level employees used to get paper cuts and calluses from paging through stacks of newspapers and magazines every morning looking for mentions of a client's name or product. After finding a story, they would review it to see how relevant it was and whether it was primarily positive, negative or neutral (a very basic form of content analysis). Then they would use scissors, a glue stick and a copy machine to create pages for the clip book. The clip book was a three-ring binder that included all the print media coverage they had found and categorized.

Evaluating TV coverage was another issue. In some offices, VCRs would be programmed to tape-record the morning and evening news programs whenever the public relations person expected coverage of his or her organization. Another option was to contact TV stations directly to request copies of the coverage. The cassettes or transcripts would be saved for later analysis, reporting and presentation.

But that was for do-it-yourselfers. Bigger agencies and organizations with larger budgets subscribed to **clipping services**. Clipping services

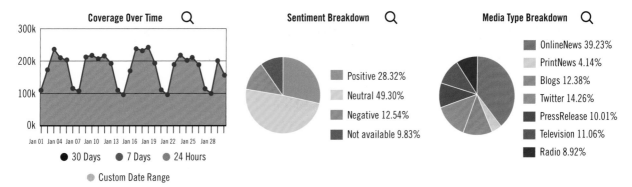

Figure 8.3 Media monitoring services offer a variety of tools for the collection, analysis and reporting of media data.

Which of these charts indicates public relations outcomes beyond just media coverage?

monitored print and electronic media for mentions of clients in local, national or international media. Their menu of services included monitoring coverage in different types of media, capturing related content, and conducting content analysis of news and editorial mentions. They would also calculate numbers like total number of impressions. In fact, they still do. Fortunately, **media monitoring services** have evolved with digital media and are among the most useful tools in digital public relations because of the way they support public relations professionals in the collection, analysis and reporting of media data for evaluation (Figure 8.3).

Aside from the obvious advantage of automating the process of scanning, "clipping," compiling and sorting media coverage, media monitoring services have also expanded the range of evaluation available. While legacy clipping services of the 20th century included opinion pieces and editorials, the content was limited to what was published or broadcasted, not how people responded to the content. Old clipping services measured earned media and not shared media. They offered little evidence of what publics were thinking, feeling or doing as a result of the coverage. Today's media monitoring services still measure publicity, but they also monitor online conversations and facilitate the sharing of information. For some examples, see Table 8.1.

As with the public relations industry in general, new media monitoring technologies and startups constantly emerge, services converge, and companies merge. Search online for demos and you'll find varying suites of related services that include targeted search, report generation, analytics and consulting.

As defined in Chapter 5 on research, content analysis is the systematic analysis of any type of recorded communication. Media monitoring services enable large-scale content analysis of both traditional and social media. That said, many of the most important goals and objectives of public relations programs—affecting what people think, feel and do offline—cannot be measured with content analysis.

Media monitoring services
Vendors that assist public relations practitioners in the collection, analysis and reporting of media data for evaluation.

Media monitoring services enable the analysis of social media content that is actively produced, discussed and shared by publics online.

TABLE 8.1 EXAMPLES OF MEDIA MONITORING FIRMS AND SERVICES

MEDIA MONITORING FIRM	DESCRIPTION	WEBSITE
Agility PR	"Monitor topics wherever you need with broad content coverage of online, print, broadcast, and social media," and "Stay up to date on coverage & track all vital content sources with our easy-to-use, self-serve monitoring tool." They also use artificial intelligence (AI) to track images.	https://www.agilitypr.com/our-solutions/media-monitoring/
Hootsuite	"Capture more conversations with a wide selection of monitoring apps, letting you do everything from reviewing site ratings to tracking the tone of voice being used for your brand."	https://hootsuite.com/platform/monitoring
Cision	"With more than 2 million stories delivered daily, Cision Communications Cloud's monitoring capabilities allow you to cut through the noise and understand the impact of your coverage across the largest collection of online, social, print and broadcast channels under one earned media cloud."	https://www.cision.com/us/products/monitoring/
BurrellesLuce	"BurrellesLuce subscribes to every major online publication and database . . . . Our PR software and human search experts sort through every possible keyword mention to ensure you receive every relevant article, and our verified service means you have access to just those stories that match your specific search instructions."	https://burrellesluce.com/what-we-do/media-monitoring/what-we-monitor/

Metrics, Analytics and Data

Metrics and analytics are essentially synonyms for measurement and evaluation. It's not unusual for people to append the words "real-time," as in "real-time analytics," to emphasize the immediacy of digital measurement. Large media organizations with high-traffic websites can run countless A/B tests in any given day to optimize their content. These simple experiments are just the tip of the analytics iceberg.

Multivariate testing allows planners to compare various combinations of factors (e.g., message selection, message placement, image selection, headline styles, color) leading to various outcomes (e.g., click-through rates, time

Multivariate testing
A method of message testing to compare how various combinations of message factors (e.g., message selection, message placement, image selection, headline styles, color) lead to various outcomes (e.g., click-through rates, time spent on page, sharing behavior).

spent on page, sharing behavior). A simple A/B test can be run with a relatively small email list or low-traffic website. Statistically significant differences in results between the effects of an "A" version of a message and a "B" version could begin to show up with as few as 30 to 40 readers (15–20 people seeing each version), if the effects are strong. For example, if 12 out of 20 people open one email version and only 3 out of 20 open the other, this would be a significant difference. Just by eyeballing those numbers you would know you were observing a real advantage of one version over the other.

However, because multivariate testing involves countless versions of messages that may change continuously over time, the amount of data required is much larger. Now imagine you want to also account for other variables besides message design, such as the readers' zip codes or their web-browsing histories. In no time, you might find yourself trying to make sense of millions of possible data points. While the term **big data** means many things to different people, this is one example of what people are talking about when they use the term. *Forbes* contributing writer Lisa Arthur defines big data as "a collection of data from traditional and digital sources inside and outside your company that represents a source for ongoing discovery and analysis."[1] You can collect this information directly from your organization's or client's publics through **cookie** or registrations. This is known as **first-party data** because you collect the information yourself—the "first party" is you. You can also buy **third-party data** from vendors who collect and aggregate data from other sources and then sell you more data about your publics than you may even know what to do with.

Big data
Large amounts of data from traditional and digital sources that can be used for ongoing discovery and analysis of media content and human behavior.

Cookie
A text file stored on a user's computer that is used to track and remember the user's activity online.

First-party data
Data on user or consumer behavior that is collected by an organization from the people who use the organization's websites or online services.

Third-party data
Data on user behavior that is collected or aggregated by one organization and sold to another organization.

© marketoonist.com

Just because data are available doesn't mean they are useful.

What are some specific uses for big data in public relations?

2 Analytics most important in PR:
1. Tracking visitor behavior
2. segmenting referring sources

...g to consider very carefully. There are so much data avail-... don't really know what to do with it all.

...eries of message-testing experiments that may have taken ... to set up a few years ago can now happen almost instantly, ... speak. The problem with running 45 A/B tests or multivari-... ne day is that anyone doing that probably hasn't put much ... ctly what they're testing and why. Testing messages with ... ments is just one type of analytics. As defined in Chapter 5, ... to any analysis used to describe, predict and improve how ... mmunicate with publics online. According to researcher ... common applications of analytics are particularly useful in ... tracking visitor behavior and segmenting referring sources.[2]

...tor Behavior

...nt use of web analytics in public relations is tracking the behavior of website visitors. When someone visits your web page, searches for a word or phrase, or clicks on an ad or other link, all that information can be recorded and analyzed. The data available from this process include number of unique visitors to a page, number of visits, number of page views, how long a user stays on a site and **bounce rate**, which is the percentage of visitors who go to your site but then leave the site instead of continuing toward other goals you may have established. Specific goals that can be tracked include downloads, registrations, completed forms, electronic petition signatures, donations and purchases.

Once you have identified your measurable goals, you can calculate a **conversion rate**, which is the number of goals reached divided by the number of unique visitors to your site. Let's say you are trying to get people to sign an online petition to make a statement to your local lawmakers. The goal is to have people sign the online petition. You track 1,000 unique visitors to your website. The data show that 700 visitors to your site leave right after seeing the first page, but 150 of them actually click through to the petition and "sign" it. Your bounce rate is 70 percent and your conversion rate is 15 percent.

Segmenting Referring Sources

A second important use of analytics is segmenting the referring sources for web visitors. Web analytics enable you to know whether people found your site online by directly typing in the URL (direct traffic) or as a result of organic search results or paid search results (e.g., Google Ad Words). You can also find out what keywords people used in those searches. Other referring sources that public relations people track include clicks from email campaigns, banner ads, native advertising, social media posts and coverage by news media. Notice how these could be classified as owned, paid, shared and earned.

Parsing Big Data

Again, the availability of data in digital research and evaluation is usually not the problem. It's figuring out what to do with the data. Researchers aren't the only ones facing this challenge. Those working on the creative

you can track include downloads, registrations, completed forms, electronic petition signatures, donations and purchases.

side of public relations also can be overwhelmed by how to develop communication strategies for large-scale campaigns when such huge amounts of data are available.

Traditionally, campaign messages have been tailored for relatively general demographic profiles. A political TV ad may be created for "soccer moms" or "blue-collar workers." But with the abundance of data available now, demographic profiles easily can be segmented into hundreds, thousands or even millions of unique profiles. Think about your own social media profile. Are you a male in a relationship who shares certain Bark-Box content, lives in New York, "likes" posts by Alexandria Ocasio-Cortez and posts about craft beer? Instagram, which is owned by Facebook, knows that. Or are you a female who lives in the Midwest who tweets about coffee, reads *National Review* and goes to a state school? Twitter probably knows that. Facebook and Twitter and all sorts of third-party companies collect, buy and sell data that can be used for deciding which media to use and which influencers to target in delivering targeted messages.

Thanks to some particularly foresighted public relations practitioners and researchers, we have guidelines for how to work with all these data. The Barcelona Principles provide useful instructions for keeping it real when it comes to metrics (i.e., measurement), analytics (i.e., analysis) and evaluation.

Barcelona Principles

By 2010, public relations had matured into a field that was global, digital and relationship-focused. Social media was blowing up, and organizations worldwide had to figure out what to do about it—how to demonstrate the value of public relations in a new era of media. It was one of those opportunity-or-threat moments for the whole field. In order to earn and keep their seats at management tables, public relations executives would have to tackle the question of how to do research that would not only drive success but also demonstrate public relations' contributions to organizational missions. That was the stage for the 2nd European Summit on Measurement in Barcelona. The group was convened by AMEC, the International Association for Measurement and Evaluation of Communication, and IPR, the Institute for Public Relations. By the end of that meeting, delegates from 33 countries had agreed to the "Barcelona Declaration of Research Principles," which was billed as the first global standard of public relations measurement.[3]

In 2015, AMEC updated the principles to "reflect the significant changes we have seen in the media landscape and the emergence of integrated communications," according to David Rockland, past chairman of AMEC, and these principles are still the standard today.[4] The Barcelona Principles include seven key items. You may notice that most of these ideas resonate with other key points we've covered in prior chapters on the RPIE process.

Cognitive
Having to do with mental processes such as thinking, knowing, perceiving, learning and understanding.

Attitudinal
Having to do with affect, emotion, favor or disfavor toward an organization, brand, product, service, idea or any other attitude object.

Behavioral
Having to do with observable human action.

Tools like this Pinterest analytics dashboard allow you to track social media activity.

Why is goal setting important in interpreting this type of data?

Principle 1: Goal Setting and Measurement Are Fundamental

You may recall from Chapter 6 that good goals are supported by SMART objectives, and that the "M" in SMART stands for "measurable." Measurable implies quantifiable. For example, you can count (i.e., quantify) the number of followers on Twitter, story views on Snapchat, people who physically attend an event, dollars donated to a cause, or downloads of applications. However, the strategic importance of those metrics depends on what they tell you about your progress toward a goal. Is 5,000 followers a good thing? It depends on your organization and its goals. For a local nonprofit that started a campaign two months ago with 25 followers, a count of 5,000 followers could be fantastic news, showing evidence of exceeding goals. For an international coffee brand or a national political candidate, a total of 5,000 followers may be a depressingly low number. It's the combination of the number and the goal that yields actual strategic value. As stated in the original Barcelona Principles,

> *Fundamentally important, goals should be as quantitative as possible and address who, what, when and how much impact is expected from a public relations campaign. Traditional and social media should be measured as well as changes in stakeholder awareness, comprehension, attitude and behavior.*[5]

Notice that the last part doesn't focus on communication tactics or media coverage, but on what people feel, think and do as a result of public relations efforts. This leads us to a second principle. . . .

Principle 2: Measuring Communication Outcomes Is Recommended

As discussed in Chapter 6, outputs are tasks that you complete, but the outcomes of public relations programs are changes in knowledge, attitudes and behavior. **Cognitive** outcomes may include understanding an organization's position, learning how to do something or comprehending a complex issue. **Attitudinal** outcomes may be related to advocacy, reputation, trust, commitment, satisfaction and feelings of control mutuality (see Chapter 4). The last four (trust, commitment, satisfaction and control mutuality) are key indicators of relational outcomes. If we define public relations as the management of relationships between organizations and publics, these four outcomes are as important as any. **Behavioral** outcomes include purchases, donations, healthy activities, volunteerism, public policy actions, financial investment and so on.

Measuring outcomes requires defining them specifically. Measurement forces you to think about what you are actually accomplishing with your efforts. Measurement is an antidote for ambiguity. Think about the term *engagement*, for example. There's no doubt that engagement is of huge importance in public relations. But the specific value of engagement depends on how you define it. And how you define it determines how you measure it.

2.0

BARCELONA PRINCIPLES

prca | amec | global alliance | ICCO | PRSA | IPR

The Barcelona Principles are the framework for effective public relations and communication measurement.

1 Goal setting and measurement are fundamental to communication and public relations

- Identify who, what, how much, and by when.
- Be holistic, integrated and aligned across all PESO channels.

S M A R T

| Specific | Measureable | Attainable | Relevant | Time Based |

4 Measurement and evaluation require both qualitative and quantitative methods

Qual helps explain Quant

2 Measuring communication outcomes is recommended versus only measuring outputs

5 AVEs are not the value of communication

OUTCOMES

Corporate Reputation	Comprehension
Investment Decisions	Public Policy	Brand Equity
		Behavior
Employee Engagement	Other shifts in stakeholders
Attitude	Awareness	Advocacy related to purchase
	Donations	

6 Social media can and should be measured consistently with other media channels

3 The effect on organizational performance can and should be measured where possible

Provide reliable input into integrated marketing and communication models, including through advanced econometrics and advanced survey analysis.

7 Measurement and evaluation should be transparent, consistent and valid

RELIABLE HONEST INTEGRITY ETHICAL CONTEXT REPLICABLE

| Profitability | Customer Retention | Revenue | Market Share | Brand Equity |

Have a question? Reach out to us!

David B. Rockland Ph.D., Partner/CEO
+1 646 935 4083 | David.Rockland@Ketchum.com

Yoo Mee Pontonnier, Senior Associate, New Business
+1 646 935 4031 | YooMee.Pontonnier@Ketchum.com

 Ketchum Global Research & Analytics

The Barcelona Principles 2.0 apply broadly to all sorts of communication, media and organizations.

How will applying these principles benefit the status of public relations as a field?

Engagement can be defined as attitudinal and based on emotions—how your publics feel about your organization and what it is doing. This kind of outcome might be observed with qualitative interviews or measured with a quantitative questionnaire that includes **Likert-type items**, which ask respondents how much they agree or disagree with statements about the organization (Figure 8.4). For example, Charlotte-Mecklenburg Schools in North Carolina includes items in their survey of employee engagement that say, "I am proud to work for CMS" and "I would feel comfortable referring a good friend to work for CMS."[6]

Engagement also can be cognitive and based on what people think, learn and know. Can people recall your hashtag? Do they understand how to register for your service? Will they remember your brand name when they do a keyword search? Cognitive engagement can be measured with questionnaires or even quizzes and tests. But cognitive engagement may also be inferred from metrics like how much time people spend reading a web page (or how far they scroll down), the number of people who watch a YouTube clip from beginning to end, or the keywords they use when searching for information.

Beyond implying cognitive activity, reading, scrolling, viewing and searching also can be considered behavioral outcomes because these activities indicate that people are doing something as a result of your public relations efforts. When you host a web page, curate information for a social media presence, send a news release or post a Vimeo video, those are outputs. When people scroll and download information from the web page,

Measurement forces you to think about what you are actually accomplishing with your efforts.

Please indicate to what extent you agree or disagree with the following statements about the relationship you have with your organization.

	Strongly disagree	Disagree	Somewhat disagree	Neither agree nor disagree	Somewhat agree	Agree	Strongly agree
Whenever my organization makes an important decision, I know it will be concerned about people like me.	○	○	○	○	○	○	○
My organization can be relied on to keep its promises.	○	○	○	○	○	○	○
I believe that my organization takes the opinions of people like me into account when making decisions.	○	○	○	○	○	○	○
My organization has the ability to accomplish what it says it will do.	○	○	○	○	○	○	○
I am happy with my organization.	○	○	○	○	○	○	○
Both my organization and people like me benefit from the relationship.	○	○	○	○	○	○	○

Figure 8.4 These Likert-type items were used in a survey of employees.

What types of public relations outcomes do they measure and not measure?

comment on and share your social media posts, write about your news or watch and recommend your videos, those behaviors are outcomes. The Barcelona Principles remind us about the importance of measuring outcomes, but we also need to remember that not all behavioral outcomes are equal when it comes to achieving our goals. This leads us to a third principle. . . .

Principle 3: The Effect on Organizational Performance Should Be Measured

Collecting data that show that 80 percent of people who open a video watch it to the end or that people spend an average of four minutes reading your story on Medium definitely indicate levels of attention and behavior as outcomes, but these metrics don't necessarily mean success in supporting your organization's goals and mission. When goals are marketing-based, the metrics should include the steps involved in the conversion funnel discussed in Chapter 6. The funnel entails traceable steps like searching for key terms, clicking on links, browsing product offerings and making purchases.

Programs like Google's Brand Lift allow marketers to run A/B testing with video ads on YouTube. As part of this service, Google randomly selects two groups of people that fit the profile of campaign target demographics. An "A" group is served a specific video ad from the campaign, and a "B" group sees unrelated ads. In other words, A is the treatment group in the experiment and B is the control group. Then Google tracks those same users later to see which exact words they use when doing searches. Any significant differences in searches between the groups can be attributed to the campaign video. After a few days, if the "A" group searches for the specific brand name or related keywords more than the "B" group, Google calls that a "lift in brand interest," and it's one of many ways the company monetizes its data by packaging it for marketers, advertisers and public relations people who use their paid services.[7]

Programs like Google Analytics and Brand Lift are designed specifically with marketers in mind, but there's clearly a role for public relations in the marketing mix, and the same measurement tactics can be applied on non-sales-driven organizational performance. "Our field is growing in its service to NGOs, charitable organizations, governments, the military; organizations that fall outside the business perimeter," said Ketchum's John Paluszek, who is a past chair of the Global Alliance for Public Relations and Communication Management. "We should be talking about 'organizational results' instead of only 'business results.'"[8]

Programs like Google Analytics and Brand Lift can help measure both sales- and non-sales-driven organizational performance.

Principle 4: Measurement and Evaluation Require Both Qualitative and Quantitative Methods

Principles 1 to 3 all emphasize the importance of developing measures in evaluation, and measurement is essentially a quantitative endeavor. But we know from Chapter 5 that qualitative research is also important in understanding public relations outcomes. Barcelona Principle 4 reminds us that we need both quantitative and qualitative understanding of public relations outcomes to evaluate our work.

Case Study

Gillette's "We Believe" Campaign Gauged by More Than Just Numbers

When razor company Gillette introduced a minute-and-48-seconds-long commercial titled "We Believe: The Best a Man Can Be" across all its social channels in 2019, it struck a chord. The first part of the short film highlights boys and men being bullies and harassing women. One particularly memorable cut of the video disturbingly frames an infinite line of white males with crossed arms standing behind barbeque grills, all watching two boys fight on a suburban lawn. In unison, the men repeat, "Boys will be boys." But then, about 40 seconds into the ad, the narrator proclaims that "something finally changed, and there will be no going back, because we, we believe in the best in men." The latter half of the ad then presents an emotional call to action against bullying and "toxic masculinity." [9]

As of this writing, the view count on YouTube is more than 31 million. The Instagram post has nearly a half-million views with 31,000 comments, and more than 246,000 Facebook users have shared the post. Those are some impressive numbers for shared media. Released three weeks before

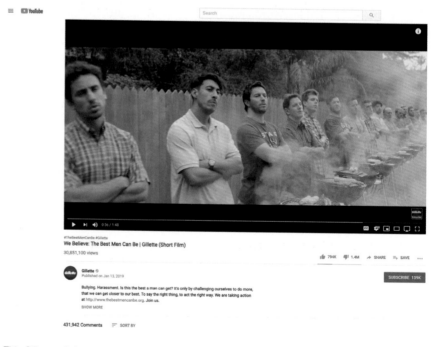

This Gillette ad drew a lot of attention.

What kinds of quantitative and qualitative methods should be used to evaluate it?

the Super Bowl, the ad gained almost as much attention as a Super Bowl ad without the company ever paying for TV airtime.

But the ad's success or failure as a public relations tactic lies as much in how you read the qualitative feedback as in the sheer numbers of clicks, views and shares. King Center CEO and Minister Bernice King tweeted, "This commercial isn't anti-male. It's pro-humanity. And it demonstrates that character can step up to change conditions."[10] Huffington Post Founder and CEO Arianna Huffington tweeted, ".@Gillette's new campaign thoughtfully and critically examines what 'The Best a Man Can Get,' the brand's iconic tagline, means today. A must watch."[11] Countless others praised the brand advocacy across social media, mass media and in everyday conversations.

But not everyone liked the ad. For every "like" on YouTube there was at least one "dislike." In fact, at last look, there were 1.4 million thumbs down compared to 794 thousand thumbs up, with many YouTube visitors to the Gillette Channel noting that their negative comments were being deleted. Top among the hundreds of thousands of comments at the time I checked:

- "I am deeply offended by your calling me a toxic masculine man. If you put it out there you should be willing to take the backlash. Don't delete anymore comments. I will NEVER use or buy another Gillette product ever again. Yours truly a MAN who Shaves."[12]

- "Hey Gillette, weren't you one of the companies that overcharged women for the same product simply because you changed the color to pink?"[13]

PRNews called it a "close shave," observing that the campaign had divided audiences on whether it was genuinely an effort for social good, a profit-driven rebranding, or both.[14] The only way for Gillette's parent company, Procter & Gamble, to evaluate the campaign is to take into account *both* qualitative and quantitative measures. And that's what they did. P&G Chief Brand Officer Marc Pritchard wrote:

> We respect different viewpoints and we're paying attention to all of them. But it's important to distinguish between actual consumer sentiment and some of the social media reaction that does not represent the majority opinion. Independent research from multiple sources indicates a far more positive response than what has been reported. Most consumers—men and women alike—support the messages, particularly younger Millennial and Gen Z consumers. The majority who've seen the film feel that Gillette shares their values and indicate they feel better about the brand and are more likely to purchase its products. If nothing else, we hope people take time to view the entire film, and even if they don't agree, they will have a constructive conversation about it.[15]

Organizations like Procter & Gamble don't take risks as big as this and double down on them unless they have done their homework, including both quantitative and qualitative evaluation.

Advertising value equivalency (AVE)
A calculation of the value of news or editorial coverage based on the cost of the equivalent amount of advertising space or time.

Multipliers
Formulas applied to circulation or other media reach numbers based on assumptions that more than one person will be exposed to each copy of a message or that being covered as part of a news story is more valuable than paid advertising in the same media space.

Principle 5: Advertising Value Equivalencies Are Not the Value of Communications

When Nathan Kam, president of one of Honolulu's largest public relations agencies, guest-lectured in Amy Hennessey's public relations strategy class at the University of Hawaii, the students apparently learned an important lesson: "AVEs must die!"

"AVE" stands for **advertising value equivalency**, which is a calculation of the value of news or editorial coverage based on the cost of an equivalent amount of advertising space or time. If a public relations person places a story in a newspaper or magazine, she can measure the column inches and total space occupied by the story and then figure out what it would have cost to buy an ad in the newspaper taking up the same amount of space. Likewise, if her organization is covered in a TV news story that lasts 30 seconds, she can look up the price of a 30-second advertisement during the program. Then, when she's ready to illustrate the value of her campaign, our public relations pro can compute a dollar value for all the publicity and—voila!—she shows success.

However, there are limits to the AVE approach of evaluating public relations programs. While Kam may have been goofing around a little in the classroom when he said that AVEs must die, he showed that he is serious about measurement and evaluation. Kam's success in running a major public relations firm depends on his ability to show clients what they are getting for their money.

The first problem with AVEs is that they falsely indicate reach based on media placement and do not measure attitudes, knowledge or behavior. Second, they use multipliers. **Multipliers** are formulas applied to circulation numbers for print media based on the assumption that more than one

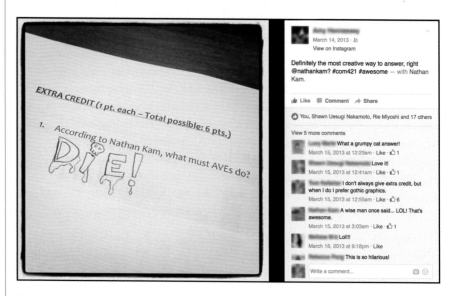

Students are being taught to avoid AVEs (advertising value equivalencies).

What was the original purpose of AVEs?

person on average will read each copy of a publication, or that being covered as part of a news story is more valuable than paid advertising in the same media space. So, for example, a public relations person might argue that for each copy of a magazine that goes into circulation, four people will have the opportunity to read it. He may also propose that editorial coverage in the magazine is worth twice as much as advertising because of third-party credibility. Such a practitioner would reason that since four people have an "opportunity to see" (OTS) each magazine article and that each of those four people is twice as affected by the editorial content than they would be by a normal advertisement, then the multiplier should be $4 \times 2 = 8$. If his organization, brand or cause is mentioned in a news magazine with a circulation of 100,000, he would apply the multiplier of 8 and calculate the AVE as the rate it costs to advertise for 800,000 impressions.

In addition to problems introduced in Chapter 6 with measuring campaign success based on mere exposure/impressions, the assumption that a mention in a print story has eight times the effect of a paid advertisement is at best not supported by science and at worst seriously delusional. The Barcelona group called multipliers flat-out silly unless they can be proven valid for a specific set of circumstances.

Principle 6: Social Media Should Be Measured Consistently with Other Media Channels

Of course, the scope of public relations is much larger than communication on social media, but digital media and media monitoring services certainly present new opportunities to use data to improve the evaluation of public relations programs. As with the measurement of most public relations outcomes, social media metrics should be tied to clearly defined goals and objectives. Compared to other more traditional and one-way media communication, social media measurement should focus more on conversations and communities and less on coverage. Chapter 10 covers social media and the process of listening in more depth. The Barcelona group also emphasized the importance of technology-assisted analysis.

Principle 7: Measurement and Evaluation Should Be Transparent, Consistent and Valid

The final Barcelona principle emphasizes the importance of maintaining integrity in the design, conduct and reporting of evaluation research. **Transparency** in research means that researchers are open and not secretive about their methods. If someone says that a campaign generated 100 million media impressions or that they achieved a 30 percent lift in brand interest, they should be open about how they calculated those figures. We might be suspicious of a campaign that boasts 100 million impressions if we learn that the researcher applied a multiplier of 8. On the other hand, if someone uses well-defined methods of analytics to show how keyword queries in a treatment group differed significantly from a control group in an A/B test, we would have more confidence in the researcher's results. This is

Evaluation of social media metrics should be clearly tied to defined goals and objectives.

Transparency
In research, openness in describing and explaining methods.

Replicability
The ability to perform a research
procedure or experiment repeatedly
to attain comparable results.

especially true if we felt like we could run the same test and achieve consistent results. **Replicability** is the ability to perform a research procedure or
experiment repeatedly to attain comparable results. While a lot of research
results in competitive business environments may be justifiably proprietary,
public relations researchers should still be able to explain their methods and
results clearly and transparently to those who are paying for their services.

Measuring the Right Outcomes

Writing about the Barcelona Principles in *The Public Relations Strategist*, Andre
Manning and David Rockland acknowledged that the wide array of tools and
services for measuring outcomes across different media may make measurement decisions harder because of all the different approaches to choose from.
"If we don't use AVEs," they asked, "then what are the right metrics?"[16]

Measurement consultant and author Katie Delahaye Payne is widely
recognized as a pioneer in social media measurement as it relates to public
relations. Her answer to the question of how we can make sense of it all can
be gleaned from her book *Measure What Matters*. In the book, she advocates
measuring what people are saying, what people are thinking and what
people are doing (Table 8.2).

In a similar approach, social change agency Fenton recommends a see-
say-feel-do model for social media metrics (Table 8.3). Fenton represents
clients ranging from National Geographic to the United Nations Foundation to the American Academy of Pediatrics to Patagonia.

TABLE 8.2 **KATIE PAYNE'S "MEASURE WHAT MATTERS"**		
OUTCOME TO BE EVALUATED	**DESCRIPTION**	**MEASUREMENT**
WHAT YOUR MARKETPLACE IS *SAYING.*	What people are saying about your organization in print, broadcast or online in social networks, blogs or communities.	Media content analysis including analysis of visibility, tone, messages, sources and conversation type.
WHAT YOUR MARKETPLACE IS *THINKING.*	People's opinions, awareness, preference, perceptions of relationship with your organization or engagement.	Facebook likes and shares, retweets, email forwards, claps on Medium.
WHAT YOUR MARKETPLACE IS *DOING.*	Whether the behavior of your publics has changed as a result of your efforts.	Careful study of specific programs conducted by your team and systematic analysis of changes in awareness, web traffic and sales; analytics.

SOURCE: Adapted from Katie Delahaye Payne, *Measure What Matters: Online Tools for Understanding Customers,
Social Media, Engagement, and Key Relationships* (Hoboken, NJ: John Wiley & Sons, 2011).

TABLE 8.3 **FENTON'S "SOCIAL MEDIA METRICS THAT MATTER"**

OUTCOME TO BE EVALUATED	DESCRIPTION	MEASUREMENT
SEE	Exposure to brand and messaging.	Page views and likes on Facebook, followers on Twitter, website traffic, email signups, RSS subscriptions, advertising impressions, Medium views and reads, and YouTube views.
SAY	Sharing information within and across social networks.	Facebook likes and shares, retweets, email forwards, claps on Medium.
FEEL	When people "engage with your messages or content, internalize your messages, and add their two cents."	Facebook comments or shares with comments, retweets with personalized messages, blog comments and YouTube comments.
DO	The conversion goal: "the thing you want people to DO."	Donations, advocacy actions, event attendance, membership, volunteerism and sales.

SOURCE: Adapted from "Social Media Metrics Guide," Fenton, accessed June 14, 2019, https://www.sreb.org/sites/main/files/file-attachments/fentonseesayfeeldo.pdf

These approaches are not too dissimilar from the basic psychology of attitudes, cognition and behavior applied earlier in this chapter and the discussion of engagement. The outcomes also align loosely with McGuire's steps in the persuasion process covered in Chapter 6.

Voices from the Field

Tina McCorkindale

TINA MCCORKINDALE, Ph.D., APR, is the President and CEO of the Institute for Public Relations, a nonprofit research foundation that creates, curates and promotes research and initiatives in the public relations industry. She taught as a professor for 15 years and has more than 10 years of experience working in corporate communication and analytics. She is a member of the Arthur W. Page Society, The Seminar, the Commission for Public Relations Education Steering Committee, the PRSA Foundation Board, and the AMEC Academic Advisory Board.

continues

continued

How are "big data" changing the way practitioners do evaluation research?

Big data are having a significant impact on the profession and how we do research throughout the whole cyclical campaign process—from inception to the evaluation. Because of the technology and ease with which we can collect vast amounts of information about our stakeholders, we can make stronger predictions for future campaigns. Evaluation should not be limited to just looking at what was done but also how we can help our organizations grow in the future. With patterns in the data, we can build algorithms that can help people make more accurate predictions. And with better technology, smart learning machines can adapt and help further refine our decision-making.

What advice do you have for college students about preparing for public relations careers that will involve digital measurement?

Measurement is just one component. Being successful in this field requires a combination of skills but also smarts. Students should take not only research methods, but go outside communication departments to take research and statistics classes in other areas, such as business, sociology and psychology. In addition to having a solid understanding of the skills, classes that are more theory-based that allow students to apply critical thinking (and higher cognitive) skills and to interpret the data to move to

insights and impact would be extremely beneficial. If students can't find a class, they can watch YouTube videos or take advantage of online learning classes from LinkedIn and Lynda.com.

What isn't changing in public relations evaluation as a result of new technology?

You should always operate from your overall goals and strategy. You should always think about what question you want to answer and then use the technology to help answer it, rather than the other way around. Sometimes, we get so caught up in the visuals that we forget about ensuring our measures are valid and purposeful.

What's the coolest research result you've seen recently?

I'm fascinated by the area of behavioral economics and science. Kahneman and Tversky posited in their seminal work on System 1 vs. System 2 decision-making that 95 percent of the decisions we make are System 1 levels of thinking—they are fast and impulsive, and sometimes without much thought.[17] However, many times in research studies we ask people to recall and explain their decision-making processes, which could be at the subconscious level. A new area of research uses MRIs and other physiological methods to study neural decoding or responses to see whether your attitudes and actions actually align with behavioral outcomes.

Ethics: Independence

"There are lies, damned lies, and statistics." This quote, often attributed to Mark Twain, was the source of sociologist Joel Best's book title *Damned Lies and Statistics: Untangling Numbers from the Media, Politicians, and Activists.*[18]

> *Statistics, then, have a bad reputation. We suspect that statistics may be wrong, that people who use statistics may be "lying"—trying to manipulate us by using numbers to somehow distort the truth. Yet, at the same time, we need statistics; we depend upon them to summarize and clarify the nature of our complex society.*[19]

Public relations can easily be lumped in with media, politicians and activists in Best's book title. In fact, one of the most critical books on public relations is subtitled *Lies, Damn Lies, and the Public Relations Industry.*[20] Yet, at the same time, we need statistics in public relations; we depend on statistics in public relations to summarize and clarify the nature of our complex society.

Advocacy is a longstanding value in the history and current practice of public relations. As stated in the PRSA Code of Ethics, "We provide a voice in the marketplace of ideas, facts, and viewpoints to aid informed public debate."[21] The ethics section at the end of Chapter 2 discussed the tension between the ideal of advocacy in ethical persuasion in public relations and the elusive ideal of objectivity in journalism. Transparency was recommended as a way to deal with this tension, particularly in media relations and communicating with external publics. But public relations people also have to avoid excessive advocacy in their roles as counselors to clients and organizational leadership. In public relations counseling, practitioners must balance advocacy and loyalty with **Independence**. As defined in the PRSA Code of Ethics, independence means "we provide objective counsel to those we represent" and "we are accountable for our actions."

Summarizing and clarifying the nature of complex society and of the data that we use to interpret human attitudes, knowledge and behavior are essential parts of the internal counseling function. Remember that two-way communication means public relations people interpret the organization to publics and interpret publics to the organization.

There are many traps that a public relations person could fall into in the interpretation and reporting of data to their clients and organizations:

- A computer program may code sarcastic comments as positive.
- **Spambots** and fake followers could inflate numbers for comments and followers.
- Some channels could be left out and others included in analyses, making public relations results look better.
- In global and cross-cultural campaigns, some languages or keywords could be left out and others included in analyses.
- News releases could be counted as media coverage.
- And, of course, AVEs and multipliers could be misused!
- As critics of public relations like to point out, unbridled advocacy and subjectivity in collecting and analyzing data can lead to lies—even damned lies—and these traps only make it harder for a loyal advocate

"That's what I want to say. See if you can find some statistics to prove it."

Ethical public relations requires balancing advocacy and loyalty with independence.

How would you respond to a request like this?

Independence
In public relations ethics, the value of autonomy and accountability in providing objective counsel.

Spambots
Computer programs that automatically send unsolicited email or post comments in online forums.

to keep numbers straight. Public relations researchers and ethicists have hashed this out carefully and recommend industry-wide standards for research to help practitioners perform "in a true counseling function rather than simply as an advocate for whichever client is paying the bill."[22]

In Case You Missed It

Digital technologies have not only expanded our options for communication, they have profoundly enhanced our ability to track and analyze social media activity. Here are a few takeaways from this chapter:

- A/B testing can be used to quickly compare the effects of different digital content and messages.

- Media monitoring services enable the analysis of social media content that is actively produced, discussed and shared by publics online.

- Specific goals that you can track include downloads, registrations, completed forms, electronic petition signatures, donations and purchases.

- Measurement forces you to think about what you are actually accomplishing with your efforts.

- Programs like Google Analytics and Brand Lift can help measure both sales- and non-sales-driven organizational performance.

- Evaluation of social media metrics should be clearly tied to defined goals and objectives.

SUMMARY

8.1 Explain how evaluation research can be used in public relations program development and message testing.
Evaluation of prior programs can be useful at the start of a new program for formative research and benchmarking to understand the current state of the organization, to assess their situation, and to set a baseline for measuring progress. Informal and formal message testing research, including focus groups, content analysis and automated copy testing, can be used for message and strategy development throughout a campaign or program.

8.2 Describe how media monitoring services work.
The process of monitoring media coverage has sped up considerably. Traditional clipping services monitored print and electronic media for mentions of clients in local, national or international media. Today's media monitoring services still measure publicity, but they also

monitor online conversations and facilitate the analysis and sharing of information all day, every day, in real time.

8.3 Discuss how digital technology has expanded our ability to track and analyze data in evaluating public relations programs.

Data analytics are particularly useful in public relations for tracking online visitor behavior and segmenting referring sources. Media monitoring services present new opportunities to use data to improve the evaluation of public relations programs with social media components. Compared to traditional media, social media measurement can focus more on conversations and communities and less on coverage.

8.4 Evaluate public relations research practices using industry standards for research (i.e., Barcelona Principles).

Seven principles for evaluating public relations research, measurement and evaluation provide a working template for understanding industry standards: (1) goal setting and measurement are fundamental to communication and public relations, (2) measuring communication outcomes is recommended versus only measuring outputs, (3) the effect on organizational performance can and should be measured where possible, (4) measurement and evaluation require both qualitative and quantitative methods, (5) AVEs are not the value of communications, (6) social media can and should be measured consistently with other media channels, and (7) measurement and evaluation should be transparent, consistent and valid.

8.5 Match appropriate metrics with the various public relations outcomes they measure.

Tools ranging from traditional surveys and direct observation to advanced technology for content analysis and behavioral tracking can be applied in the measurement of media content, attitudes, knowledge and behavior as outcomes of public relations programs.

8.6 Analyze the relationship between independence as a core value of public relations and the ethical conduct of research, measurement and evaluation.

Public relations professionals must balance advocacy and loyalty with independence. Independence in this context means providing objective counsel and being accountable for actions including proper conduct and reporting of research. Industry standards empower public relations researchers to conduct research that is both transparent and replicable. Abiding by such standards helps practitioners maintain their independence as counselors in presenting research with integrity.

DISCUSSION QUESTIONS

1. Discuss your experience with message testing. If you haven't been part of formal message testing, how have you seen it portrayed on TV or in movies, books and so on?

2. How do media monitoring services assess publicity (mentions in news media)? Review online services to identify at least one quantitative and one qualitative example. Here are some possible sites to check:

   a) https://www.agilitypr.com/our-solutions/media-monitoring/
   b) https://hootsuite.com/platform/monitoring
   c) https://www.cision.com/us/products/monitoring/
   d) https://burrellesluce.com/what-we-do/media-monitoring/

3. How do media monitoring services assess online conversations? Review services to

identify at least one quantitative and one qualitative example. (See list in question 2 for sites.)

4. Find a public relations case study online that illustrates some or all of the Barcelona Principles and describe how each of the principles is (or is not) evident in the case. Here are some possible sites to check:

   a) https://www.prnewsonline.com/category/case-studies/

   b) http://prcouncil.net/resource/pr-case-studies/

   c) https://www.prweek.com/us/the_work

5. **CASE STUDY** In the Gillette case, a P&G executive said, "It's important to distinguish between actual consumer sentiment and some of the social media reaction that does not represent the majority opinion." What are the limitations of gauging "majority opinion" from responses on social media like Twitter, Facebook and YouTube? What other types of qualitative and quantitative research would help?

6. Describe one tool or app for measuring attitudes or behavior online, and explain how it can be used in public relations.

7. Identify a case when an organization had to release "bad news" (perhaps a news story about an organizational crisis). Discuss what kind of research was involved and how you think the public relations person balanced advocacy and independence.

KEY TERMS

A/B testing   203

Advertising value equivalency (AVE)   216

Attitudinal   210

Automated copy testing   203

Behavioral   210

Big data   207

Bounce rate   208

Clipping services   204

Cognitive   210

Conversion rate   208

Cookie   207

Digital watermarking   202

Eye tracking   202

First-party data   207

Functional magnetic resonance imaging (fMRI)   202

Independence   221

Likert-type items   212

Media monitoring services   205

Multipliers   216

Multivariate testing   206

Replicability   218

Spambots   221

Third-party data   207

Transparency   217

CHAPTER 9
Writing

Writing compelling narratives is a great way to transport readers to the places where your organization makes a difference. How does World Bicycle Relief use storytelling to help farmers in Africa?

KEY LEARNING OUTCOMES

9.1 List five key purposes of good writing in public relations.

9.2 Analyze news and feature styles of storytelling.

9.3 Discuss the role of news media, social media and search engines as intermediaries between public relations writers and publics.

9.4 Compare and contrast business writing and social media writing.

9.5 Explain how expertise in public relations writing relates to public relations ethics.

RELATED UNIVERSAL ACCREDITATION BOARD COMPETENCY AREAS

1.7 DIVERSITY • **2.2** ETHICAL BEHAVIOR • **4.2** BARRIERS TO COMMUNICATION
6.2 REPUTATION MANAGEMENT • **6.4** MEDIA RELATIONS

Listicle
An online article presented in the format of a numbered or bulleted list.

Clickbait
Promotional and sensational internet content designed primarily to entice users to visit another website.

ove 'em or hate 'em, **listicles** are part of the online media landscape. The term *listicle* is a portmanteau word, combining "list" and "article." (*Spork* is another portmanteau, combining spoon and fork.) You've no doubt run across many listicles in your online browsing: for example, "10 New Year's resolutions that will make your online life a little better"[1] or "5 Creepy Things A.I. Has Started Doing On Its Own."[2]

Critics complain that listicles are lazy writing, that they simply recycle content, and that they encourage shallow reading and thinking in an age of shrinking attention spans. If you look up "listicle" on Wikipedia, you will find the definition along with a cross-reference to **clickbait**.[3] Like popsicles—another portmanteau, come to think of it—listicles can be sweet and appealing, but not very substantive and nourishing.

But elsewhere, listicles get more love. *Forbes* contributor Steph Denning writes that the rise of listicles "reflects a more profound reality that we need a way to filter and process the information being thrown at us."[4]

Taking the writer's perspective, Arika Okrent describes listicles as literary form in *The University of Chicago Magazine*: "The true essence of the list form is consecutive order, taking a mass of stuff and finding a way to break it into pieces and lay it out in a line," she writes. "That also happens to be, in a way, the essence of language."[5]

The debate over listicles draws our attention to the challenges of public relations writing in a time when so much of what people read appears in short bursts via endless social media newsfeeds. At times, we must draw attention, but we don't want to cheaply bait readers with fluff or spin. We write to communicate important and useful information with both form and substance. As representatives of complex organizations in society, we also have a responsibility to curate important information. We are charged with filtering and processing. We have to take a "mass of stuff" and make sense of it.

Public relations practitioners use a number of writing tactics to do their jobs. From features and factual news to tweets and texts, this chapter will cover some of public relations' most common writing assignments. But why not start with a list?

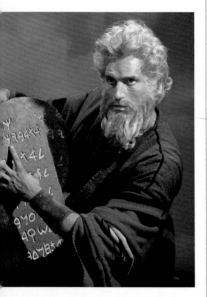

The Ten Commandments may be the greatest list of all time. Imagine Moses on BuzzFeed!

Why do listicles remain popular as a style for online writing?

Five Reasons to Write Well in Public Relations

Writing is one of the most sought-after skills that employers screen for when hiring public relations talent. Many aspects of public relations work can be taught on the job, but writing takes a lifetime of learning and improvement. You probably had to demonstrate that you could write well to be admitted to college. If you're enrolled in a public relations program, you will have to write even better to earn your degree. The bar will be set even higher after graduation. Why is writing so important in public relations? What follows are discussions of five of the most important reasons.

Relationships

In any kind of writing, but especially in professional writing, the best writers have a good sense of who their readers are. A great news release speaks to the journalist or the editor running the story as well as to the readers of their publications. A clever tweet resonates with followers who may be inclined to retweet. A persuasive PSA (public service announcement) script convinces a teenager to second-guess risky behavior. A thoughtful thank-you note plants the seed for a donor to consider a larger gift in the future.

While writing tactics like these appear to be one-way communication, two-way communication is the essence of their larger context. Each tactic requires the writer to understand readers, listeners, watchers, fans or followers. Remember that when you write for public relations, you are writing to build and maintain relationships.

Influence and Persuasion

Simply because you engage in two-way communication doesn't mean you can't use influence and persuasion. Think about your personal relationships with friends and family. From small decisions, like where to eat lunch or what to wear, to big decisions, like where to live and whom to associate with, you and your closest friends and family influence each other. At times you may be persuaded, and at other times you are the one doing the persuading. It's the overall balance of your relationships, however, that determines whether or not they are symmetrical.

The same idea applies in public relations. The most influential influentials in social media engage their publics. They don't use megaphones. Instead, they interact with their readers, which helps them write in ways that earn them respect and credibility. Good research in strategic planning, as discussed in Chapters 5 and 8, is another tool that helps writers understand their publics' thoughts, feelings and behaviors, thereby making it easier for writers to influence those publics.

Goals and Objectives

It takes clear writing to articulate your goals and objectives as part of a public relations strategy. Write crisp, clean proposals and you'll get business. Write clear reports and you'll demonstrate results. Sharp technical writing convinces readers of the value of what you plan to do, the way in which you are going to do it and the success that you will have when you're done. But you also have to do the work you propose. In order to achieve those goals and objectives and to implement that brilliant strategy, you have to pull off the tactics. In public relations, that means writing well.

OK—I know what some of you may be thinking now. "Wait, what? I'm going to do most of my work in meetings and on the phone. I'm going to shoot videos and shake hands and talk to people. Where's the writing in that?" There's some truth to that. However, those meetings will lead to reports and news stories. Those phone calls will be followed up with emails. Handshakes may turn into deals that need to be formalized in writing. And those videos

Reputation management
Acting and communicating—often in writing—to influence an organization's reputation as part of a process that includes planning, analyzing feedback and evaluating.

Impression management
Process in which people influence perceptions of themselves or their organizations by regulating and controlling information in social interactions.

may need scripts and captions and written responses to the comments they generate on YouTube. Go ahead and include that little "Excuse-my-typos-I-wrote-this-with-my-phone" disclaimer on your email signature, but there's only so far you can go in achieving the communication goals and objectives for your organization without doing some good writing.

Reputation Management

Professor Craig Carroll defines a corporate reputation as "a widely circulated, oft-repeated message . . . revealing something about the organization's nature."[6] While the practice of **reputation management** includes many activities such as planning, analyzing feedback and evaluating an organization's reputation, a major component also entails writing. Think about the reputation of big brands like Apple or Toyota. Think about the reputation of your school. And think about the reputation of smaller organizations to which you belong. No doubt a big part of those reputations is based on their actions (Chapter 7), but what people write about these organizations also is important.

Carroll says that reputation management can happen "through controllable media (advertising, marketing, public relations or sponsorships) or uncontrollable media (word of mouth, news reports, commentary or social media)." Given that search engines are primary portals for publics to learn about organizations, writing for search engine optimization is an important part of reputation management, too.

Impression Management

Social, mobile and multimedia venues provide us with new ways to communicate and extra latitude in our writing styles. Some contexts allow you to write less formally than others, and some contexts have new grammar that you'll know better than your professor or boss. That said, if your boss messages you with a lunch invitation, you may want to think twice before you respond with "Yassss!" or a clever GIF that she doesn't relate to the way you and your friends do.

Closely related to the concept of reputation management is **impression management**. Most college students don't talk to their parents the same way they talk to their friends, which is quite different from how they may speak during a class presentation or a job interview. Psychologists will tell you that this is all part of being

"Yes, a winky face is correct... But in ancient times, the semicolon was actually used to separate archaic written devices known as 'complete sentences.'"

Achieving goals and objectives in public relations still requires proper writing.

In what contexts might emojis and less formal writing be appropriate or inappropriate?

a well-adjusted adult. I can only imagine the response I would get if I spoke with my dean in the same way I talk trash with my surfing buddies or play around with my 10-year-old after school. The same goes for writing. The most effective writers understand the contextual difference between a text, a tweet, a cover letter, a news release, an annual report and so on. Successful public relations people also realize that how they present themselves in social media requires a mindful balance between being authentic and being professional.

Impression management involves presenting yourself in ways that help you achieve your goals and aspirations in social interactions. When you work in public relations, you are responsible for managing the impression of your organization as well as your own impression. In face-to-face interactions, this may come naturally, but it takes careful attention and deliberate practice in writing. People will look to you for expertise in writing across all the media that serve as channels of communication between your organization and its publics. In order to be hired and promoted, you'll need to demonstrate fluency and flexibility in how you write across all the different contexts.

When presenting yourself in social media, balance being authentic with being professional.

Storytelling

When you think of storytelling, you may think of sitting around a campfire, reading to a child or even open mic night at a coffeehouse, but storytelling is serious business for anyone who works in professional communications. Journalists tell stories for a living, as do advertisers, social justice advocates and international diplomats. In public relations we tell stories—nonfiction stories—that help us represent our organizations and build mutual understanding with publics. Brian Solis and Deirdre Breakenridge, authors of *Putting the Public Back in Public Relations*, describe the importance of storytelling. They write that excellent public relations in social media contexts has less to do with the mechanics of online publishing and "more to do with storytelling, an understanding of what you represent, why it matters to certain people, and a genuine intent for cultivating relationships."[7]

Excellence in social media requires good storytelling— understanding your organization's stories and why those stories matter to your publics.

Case Study

A Virtuous (Bi)cycle: How the World Bicycle Relief Organization Tells Stories with Purpose

"Esawo, a 59-year-old Malawian dairy farmer, carried 5 liters of milk on his head to the milk collection center every day for almost 4 years."[8]

Are you wondering what this opening sentence about a man in southeastern Africa has to do with public relations? What's the purpose? Or are you more interested in finding out what happened to Esawo? Either way, the goal is to get your attention and engage you. Telling a story is one of the best ways to do that. As writing god William Zinsser wrote, one of the best approaches to writing is to just tell a story. "It's such a simple solution, so obvious and unsophisticated, that we often forget it's available to us."[9] But success in public relations writing means telling stories with a purpose.

"*As a father of 10, Esawo depends on his cows and milk sales to take care of his family and send his children to school*," the story continues. "*He became a dairy farmer because it offered a source of stable income, regardless of the time of year*." After presenting the setting, the narrative continues with the problem, describing Esawo's hardship in trying to make a living at the risk of not delivering the milk on time before it sours. Then the solution: "*The Buffalo Bicycle changed all of that*." Buffalo Bicycles are rugged bikes manufactured in Africa for the World Bicycle Relief Organization. They are specifically designed for durability in rural African terrain. Completing the arc of the story, the author explains that Esawo has doubled the amount of milk he sells, takes his daughters to school by bicycle, and now even rides just for fun.

But this story is not designed to sell you a Buffalo Bicycle. Rather it is meant to encourage you to donate to support the World Bicycle Relief Organization. At the bottom of the page, right above a red "Give GO" button, is a call to action. "With your help, Buffalo Bicycles can give entire communities the opportunity to GO the distance and thrive."

On Writing Well author William Zinsser reminded writers of the power of "just telling a story."

Why did World Bicycle Relief tell the story of a 59-year-old dairy farmer in Malawi?

Writing compelling stories candidly and credibly is tricky in any context, but doing so as part of a deliberate communication strategy may be one of the toughest jobs in public relations. It's easy to fall back to the relative safety of a corporate voice to conservatively deliver your organization's key messages. But ironically, writing conservatively can also be a risky strategy. Writing trainer Ann Wylie advises public relations professionals to drop the corporate "'At XX, we . . .' construction." With tongue in cheek, she outlines three reasons:

Feature story
A story that explores some angle of an event, a person's life, an organization or a place.

1. It's patronizing. "At Wylie Communications, we don't believe our insurance company really understands us."

2. It's formulaic. "At Wylie Communications, we feel that this cliché might make us vomit."

3. It's off target. "At Wylie Communications, we prefer that you write about us instead of about your organization and its beliefs, understanding and knowledge."[10]

Wylie recommends focusing on the reader. She says you should write with more "you's" and fewer "we's." This is pretty solid advice for any kind of persuasive writing. Tell readers what's in it for them. In public relations, however, you inevitably will have to tell your organization's story (or side of a story) at times. When you have to do that, one option is to tell an interesting story. Human interest is what's in it for your readers.

Features

Feature stories have long been a primary tactic in public relations writing. Rather than plainly reporting facts and information, a feature story digs deeper into some angle of an event, a person's life, an organization or a place.

Among the stories I've read in the past few days are a profile on the best surfer in history in *The New Yorker*, "Kelly Slater's Shock Wave,"[11] and an AP story posted on NBA.com about the first female player drafted into the NBA 2K e-sports league.[12]

Case Study

The GOAT's Surf Ranch: How a Feature Story Helped Build a Wave of Interest in a New Business Venture

As an aging surfer who grew up trying to ride small messy waves in Florida before moving to Hawaii for most of my adult life, I have been in awe of fellow Florida native and 11-time world champion Kelly Slater for decades.

I'd argue that Slater is surfing's GOAT (Greatest Of All Time). I also have become a fan of *New Yorker* contributor and Pulitzer Prize–winning author William Finnegan, who happens to surf too. I was reading Finnegan's 10,000-word magazine article for pure enjoyment when halfway through I realized it's a fantastic example of a public relations tactic (a feature story) supporting a long-term strategy to promote Slater's wave pool business.

Slater's corporate venture, The Kelly Slater Wave Company, has innovated with technology to produce what looks to be the world's best human-made wave at a "surf ranch" wave pool. Located more than 100 miles from the Pacific Ocean in a small California farming town, access to surf the "perfect wave" is ultra-limited right now to world-class competitive surfers, super-wealthy customers who can afford undisclosed amounts of money for access, elite surf industry insiders and—as became apparent to me as I read the story—influential storytellers. But the plan is to go big and increase access with new locations. Finnegan interviewed K.S.W.C. president Nick Franklin as part of the story.

> *Franklin spent eighteen years at Disney, most of them in the theme-park division, where he was the executive vice-president for next-generation experience. "This," he said, meaning Surf Ranch, where we met, "it's like Walt created this little model of Disneyland. Do you want to replicate and expand it around the world? Uh, yeah."*

To be clear, Finnegan does not work for Slater. But the access to the surf ranch that he and photographer Ben Lowy were given that day was carefully orchestrated to help him write about the endeavor for the *New Yorker's* million-plus print and online readers. After watching an invitation-only contest with many of the world's top surfers, he observed that the wave pool was kept open for select visitors.

> *I noticed Slater helping a group of Brazilians, which included a young movie star who could surf and a television host who could not. The television host, I was told, was the "Brazilian Oprah." . . . There were cameras rolling on all sides as he wobbled to his feet, arms out wide, bent at the waist, in what is known as a poo stance. This was going to make great TV.*

Finnegan's *New Yorker* article was not the first I had heard about Slater's wave pool. Along with millions of other surfers and surf-interested YouTube and social media users, I had witnessed the slow drip of video clips and photos of the mysterious perfect wave in the years prior. I was mesmerized trying to figure out if it was even real. Where is it? How does it work? Is this some sort of trick photography? It became real to me when Slater posted to his Instagram account that he was planning a new wave park in my old hometown: "Well . . . it's official . . . we have a building permit in Palm Beach County for #SurfRanchFlorida. I'm beyond proud and stoked to see the first of our developments at @kswaveco going to my home state of #Florida."[13]

Tom Kelleher shared a post.
October 26, 2017 · 👥 ▼

Kelly Slater
October 26, 2017 · 🌐

👍 **Like Page**

Well ... it's official ... we have a building permit in Palm Beach County for #SurfRanchFlorida. I'm beyond proud and stoked to see the first of our developments at Kelly Slater Wave Co going to my home state of Florida.

Thank you to Mayor Burdick and the city commissioners for your approval and support of the project. Also thank you to Jupiter Farms for your comments and support. Looking forward to being neighbors. I keep joking about it ... but it might be true that now I can move back home and surf as much as I want!

Cannot wait to see a bunch more stoked people riding waves. This is gonna be fun.

Approvals for building permits at county commission meetings normally aren't stories that go viral on social media.

What made this one more sharable?

I checked the *Palm Beach Post* to confirm, then I posted the story to my own Facebook page. **Transmedia storytelling** is an important context for public relations writing. When shared/social media are added to the storytelling mix, stories have more of a chance of going viral because readers and users have the opportunity to become part of the storytelling process as well.

The Finnegan story, however, was the first time I really understood how it all worked. And as much as I think the wave pool is cool, I do worry about what this all means for surfing in general. Is standardization and

When readers and users have the opportunity to become part of the storytelling process, stories have a better chance of going viral.

Transmedia storytelling
Telling a story across multiple platforms like games, web pages, apps, social media and traditional media.

The New Yorker ✔
@NewYorker

Following ⌄

The best surfer in history made a machine that creates perfect conditions on demand. Will Kelly Slater's invention democratize surfing or despoil it? nyer.cm/sGAvj5l

11:11 PM - 10 Dec 2018

A ten-thousand-word *New Yorker* feature story was part of a groundswell of interest in Kelly Slater Wave Company.

Was this a deliberate public relations tactic?

commercialization good for the sport? That's a longer story that Finnegan covers too, offering Slater a chance to address the concerns proactively:

> *The next iterations of the pool might be different. "It will democratize surfing," Slater said, about the technology. . . . Surf Ranch Florida, already approved for construction in Palm Beach, will reportedly offer youth programs and lessons. . . .*

In any case, there's no way I or any other casual reader would have read 10,000 words about the business if the story wasn't interesting. By allowing a great writer access to the elite insiders of the organization (and to the pool to ride the wave itself!), the Kelly Slater Wave Company scored a major media win. I imagine the Brazilian TV show turned out pretty well too.

In *Writing PR: A Multimedia Approach*,[14] Meta Carstarphen and Richard Wells list the following as feature types that public relations writers may produce:

1. How-to features

2. Personal profiles

3. First-person accounts

4. Opinion and editorial

5. Humor or satire

6. Historical writing

7. Round-up stories with perspectives from multiple sources

8. Photo essays

9. Stories about products or services

10. Trend articles

What they all have in common as basic elements, according to Carstarphen and Wells, are human interest and timelessness. **Human interest** stories have a personal or emotional angle. By timeless, they mean that these stories maintain their relevance and value long after they have been told.[15] Of course, features can have a chronology or be tied to particular events in time, but they do not need to be timely in the same way that breaking news does.

All sorts of organizations benefit from features to help tell their stories in ways that draw interest and raise understanding on a personal level without getting too technical. Feature stories work in public relations when they are interesting and informative at the same time. People read feature stories for enjoyment but then learn something important about the subjects. That learning can be an important outcome in strategic public relations. While everyday gamers are well aware of the appeal of video games like NBA 2K, general sports fans may not understand the greater impact and significance of e-sports leagues as businesses and as cultural phenomena. That was the case for me until I ran across a story about the NBA 2K in browsing ESPN news. The story, which also was featured on the AP wire and the NBA website, started with an interesting vignette:

> *After over three hours of sitting, waiting and stressing, Chiquita Evans heard her name called. She stood, smiled and put on a Warriors cap, striding to the stage backed by the loudest applause of the night.*[16]

Notice that the "why?" of this story is missing from the first few sentences. The **delayed lead** is common in feature writing. The first sentence's job in a story like this is to make the reader want to read the second sentence. Then, according to Zinsser, every sentence should do the same, "each

Human interest
A personal or emotional storytelling angle that focuses on the human condition.

Delayed lead
A style of beginning a story in a way that entices readers to continue reading without summarizing the story's main points.

Chiquita Evans responded to media questions after being selected by the Warriors Gaming Squad at the NBA 2K League draft. Evans was the first woman selected in the e-sports league.

What role do you think public relations people played in helping tell Evans's story?

tugging the reader along until he is hooked." Well, I was tugged along far enough in this one to learn that Evans had become the first woman ever drafted in the e-sports league. She was also one of only 126 players selected and offered contracts between $33,000 and $37,000 plus team housing and other benefits.

Although the story byline in this case goes to AP sportswriter Jake Seiner, public relations people working for NBA 2K likely did much of the legwork. When you work in public relations, your role in producing feature stories often happens in the background. You may write queries to media about their interest in the story, write the supplemental materials, set up interviews and photo opportunities, or even write full drafts of the story to send to reporters to use as they wish.

The NBA 2K story ended up all over the world in all kinds of media, including national newspapers and online-only media like ESPN.com. The public relations team was likely thrilled about all the earned media even though their names were not mentioned. This isn't to say that you never get credit for writing feature stories in public relations. You are more likely to write your own stories with your own name in the byline when you write for paid, owned or shared media (Chapter 7) such as native advertising, internal newsletters or your organization's social media sites.

It's difficult to nail down an exact definition of feature story. One approach is to define it with examples (as I've tried to do with the Kelly Slater and Chiquita Evans features). Another is to distinguish features from the second major type of storytelling in public relations: straight news.

News

Whereas a feature writer may delay the most important points while appealing to human interest and emotion, straight news stories get right to the business of reporting the news with a **direct lead**. Even if readers never read past the first paragraph, they can get the gist of the content from direct leads. In the first sentence, reporters tell readers who, what, where, when and why. This news style of writing is often called the **inverted pyramid** because all of the most important information in the story is presented at the broad top of the story, and the narrower supporting details are written below as the story continues to the bottom. Figure 9.1 illustrates the structure.

Direct lead
A style of beginning a news story that summarizes the story's main points (e.g., who, what, where, when, why, how) in the first sentence or two.

Inverted pyramid
A style of newswriting in which the most important information is presented at the broad top of a story and narrower supporting details are written below.

Consider the following two-sentence lead for a news story:

LOS ANGELES (AP) — "Jeopardy!" host Alex Trebek says he has been diagnosed with advanced pancreatic cancer. In a video posted online Wednesday, the 78-year-old said he was announcing his illness directly to "Jeopardy!" fans in keeping with his long-time policy of being "open and transparent."[17]

With just 45 words, the lead answers all five key questions. The inverted pyramid has played an important role in defining an era of journalism. Although the exact history of the inverted pyramid is murky, most journalism historians seem to agree that the convention grew with the rise of technologies for mass communication. One story maintains that reporters during the U.S. Civil War learned to place all of the important information in the first line or two in case telegraph lines were cut during wire transmission. The inverted pyramid also made sense as multi-page newspapers grew in size and popularity because many readers would not turn past the front page to finish reading complete stories that continued on inside pages.

In any case, traditional mass media technology encouraged the telling of succinct, fact-based stories without a lot of fluff or extraneous information, and news readers came to expect that. Concise writing became a news virtue, and if public relations people wanted to work with journalists to get their stories out through mainstream media, they needed to understand the function of a good news lead and the type of information required to support it. The same values apply today when it comes to telling stories in direct news style. Online news feeds, blog rolls, email preview panes and search engine results all favor writers who know how to write a good lead.

As with features, sometimes the public relations person's role in telling news stories resides in the background, setting up the press conference or interview, compiling the fact sheet, or even drafting the entire news story with a direct lead and supporting details. In media relations, your job is to help others tell your organization's story (or your organization's side of the story) in their outlets. To do this, you need to understand news values and the way that journalists write and organize their stories.

At other times, you will have the opportunity to tell your organization's news stories directly to your publics. The internet has increased these opportunities to serve as a direct source for news about your organization. When Alex Trebek decided to share his news, he released a video via Twitter, YouTube and Facebook. He addressed his fans directly with a carefully

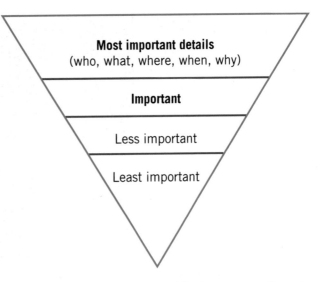

Figure 9.1 The inverted pyramid has defined a generation of journalistic style.

How has communication technology influenced the way we tell stories?

Online news feeds, blog rolls, email preview panes and search engine results favor good leads.

When "Jeopardy!" host Alex Trebek was diagnosed with Stage 4 pancreatic cancer, it made international news.

Why do you think "Jeopardy!" and Trebek himself communicated directly to publics during this difficult time?

written and heartbreakingly personal message, even though the news certainly would have spread via intermediaries due to its clear newsworthiness for *Jeopardy*'s international fan base.

Writing for Intermediaries

Public relations writers can earn attention online beyond their direct networks through three main intermediaries: (1) traditional news media gatekeepers (i.e., earned media), (2) social media (i.e., shared media) and (3) search engines. The three overlap considerably, but public relations writers must use different writing strategies and tactics for success in each.

Writing for News Media

In the gatekeeping model of media relations, publics find stories based on what editors and producers decide is newsworthy. Back when people obtained their news primarily by reading daily newspapers and watching 30-minute newscasts, publics relied on the editorial judgment of the gatekeepers in these news organizations to decide what news they should read or watch. In this model, people let others serve as the first filter of what news and information they should pay attention to.

To some extent, this gatekeeping still happens online. People still go to news websites without knowing exactly what the editors will deliver. They still count on editors to decide what's important. And that's why news releases, backgrounders and fact sheets written primarily for journalists and editors are still key public relations tactics, even as their channels for delivery have moved online. Writing for these media requires attention to traditional news values, **Associated Press (AP) style** and other conventions of news writing.

NEWS RELEASES

A **news release** is basically a news story, written in news style, by a public relations practitioner writing on behalf of an organization or client. News releases are often referred to as press releases because historically they were written for distribution to members of the press. With a news release, a public relations writer drafts and edits a news story, pitches it to reporters and editors, and hopes that various news media will retell the story. In other words, news releases are tools for seeking earned media (Chapter 7). **Video news releases (VNRs)** serve the same function for TV media, providing broadcast journalists with pre-produced news packages including audio and video material. **Social media releases** adopt the conventions of social media to include sharable online material such as useful chunks of text, quotes, photos, infographics, suggested tweets, social media handles, hashtags and embeddable multimedia elements.

Online, releases are more likely to directly reach non-media publics who find news directly from the organization. The "press" may or may not be involved as intermediaries in the distribution of an organization's news. Therefore, in today's media environment, *news release* is probably a better term than *press release*. In any case, public relations writers should keep two key characteristics in mind when they produce news releases: format and newsworthiness.

Format is important, so that the news looks like news. In pitching a straight news story to journalists or editors in news organizations, public relations writers should do the following:

- Start with a good headline and **dateline**.

- Write using the inverted pyramid style.

- Include important factual information that journalists would need to support the main points of the story.

For traditional print news releases, public relations writers follow certain conventions, such as including "For Immediate Release" with a date at the top. Many news release writers still include the word "-more-" at the bottom of the page if the release continues to another page, and "-###-" or "-30-" at the end of the story to let journalists know they've reached the last

Associated Press (AP) style
Rules of writing (including grammar, capitalization and punctuation) published by the Associated Press news agency.

News release
A news story, written in news style, by a public relations practitioner writing on behalf of an organization or client.

Video news release
A news release that provides broadcast journalists with pre-produced news packages including audio and video material.

Social media release
A news release that applies the conventions of social media and includes content designed for social media distribution and sharing.

Dateline
Text at beginning of a news story that describes when and where the story occurred (e.g., "BEIJING, June 16—").

Organizations often create templates for news releases.

What are the advantages and disadvantages of writing with templates?

Fact sheet
Short (often one-page) document that presents factual information in concise format.

page. These symbols are a bit archaic, but in the right context, they signal that you understand the news business and its traditions. Check with your client or employer for templates, or work with them and news media to develop a consistent format for your news releases.

With most traditional news media, you'll want to write with AP style. If you ever have taken a newswriting or editing course in a journalism program, you know that journalistic training includes some tough lessons on editing. In some of the best J-schools, journalism students are slapped with 50-percent-off grade penalties for fact errors and harsh point reductions for AP style errors. Students who graduate from these programs are sharp writers, but they also are sharp critics of others' sloppy newswriting. Don't let your news be discarded because you overlook simple AP style editing rules. As discussed in Chapter 4, the best way to understand the needs of journalists is to develop solid working relationships with them.

The more important factor in whether your news release gets traction with third-party media is the actual newsworthiness of the information it delivers. Newsworthiness, also covered in Chapter 4, means that a story includes elements of timeliness, proximity, conflict and controversy, human interest or relevance. But there's no direct formula for calculating news value. To understand which news from your organization is newsworthy, you need to understand the perspective of journalists and their audiences.

FACT SHEETS

Fact sheets can accompany news releases or be presented on their own. They present factual information about an organization or its events, people, products or services. They may be presented as frequently asked questions (FAQs), advice sheets, infographics or even listicles. But rather than applying a news story or feature narrative style, they focus more on the delivery of useful information. With just one or two clicks or taps, a reporter—or anyone else interested in the story—can access all sorts of related facts and background information written by people working in public relations.

BACKGROUNDERS

Imagine practicing public relations before the internet. If you sent a news release to a journalist, she may have needed additional information on your organization or its key people. Without Google, she could have gone to the

Although not a substitute for the actual AP Stylebook, the @APStylebook Twitter feed offers timely tips, such as this thread of advice leading up to Valentine's Day.

Why is AP Style important for public relations writers?

library or to her news organization's **morgue** (storage space for archived files), but chances are she wouldn't have had that background information at her fingertips unless she regularly covered your organization. So you would have provided it, or at least had it available upon request.

For bigger media events, public relations people developed (and still develop) **media kits** that include news releases, fact sheets and backgrounders, as well as photos, graphics, position papers and anything else that might be useful for a reporter researching and producing a story. As technology advanced, public relations people began producing electronic media kits on CD-ROMs that could include all of that plus audio, video and interactive components. Today, all this information is shared online, but reporters still need background information for context. Regardless of the medium, it still makes sense to package background information in an easily accessible format for whoever is writing about your organization. Three useful tools are backgrounders, bios and profiles.

Backgrounders provide the stories behind the straight news stories. They often are written as features and give depth and context to news stories by explaining the history—or background—of an organization or one of its events. Like fact sheets, backgrounders deliver information that will be useful to anyone writing a story about the organization, but backgrounders use a narrative structure that connects the factual information in a meaningful way that explains context. For example, the National Oceanic and Atmospheric Administration (NOAA) regularly issues press releases, such as one with this lead:

NOAA, working with private industry partners and the U.S. Navy, has confirmed the location and condition of the USS Independence, the lead

Regardless of the medium, you should package background information in an easily accessible format.

Morgue
Storage space for archived files of old stories, notes and media materials kept by news organizations.

Media kits
Packages of information assembled by public relations people for news media. Common contents include news releases, fact sheets, backgrounders, position papers, photos, graphics and so on.

Backgrounder
Writing tactic used to give depth and context as background information for news stories.

ship of its class of light aircraft carriers that were critical during the American naval offensive in the Pacific during World War II.[18]

That's the start to the news release. The website with the news release also included high-resolution maps and images and links to information from industry partners such as a fact sheet on Boeing's unmanned underwater vehicle called the Echo Ranger that was used in the search. But what if a reporter wasn't familiar with NOAA in the first place? An NOAA backgrounder told the story, starting with this lead:

> *October 1970. President Richard M. Nixon was on his way to the Middle East when Egyptian President Nasser died. The Pittsburgh Steelers were putting a lot of faith in their new rookie quarterback, Terry Bradshaw. The top grossing movie of the month was Tora! Tora! Tora!—and the National Oceanic and Atmospheric Administration, a new federal agency to observe, predict and protect our environment, was born.*[19]

Note that this backgrounder offered historical context for the founding of NOAA. The writer used a delayed lead to generate readers' interest and then transitioned into background on NOAA itself, which would apply to any NOAA-related story. The USS Independence news was presented specifically by NOAA's National Marine Sanctuaries. It's mission "to serve as the trustee for the nation's system of marine protected areas, to conserve, protect, and enhance their biodiversity, ecological integrity and cultural legacy" is posted on its "About" page, along with "information about our history, the steps taken in designating a marine protected area, and the legislation that helped to create our marine sanctuaries."[20] Background information on the USS Independence is also available as a resource for media.

BIOS

A biographical profile, or bio, is essentially a backgrounder for a person.

"After 64 years on the seafloor, Independence sits on the bottom as if ready to launch its planes," said James Delgado in the NOAA news release. Who's James Delgado? Delgado is identified in the release as the chief scientist on the Independence mission and maritime heritage director for the National Marine Sanctuaries, but his longer bio is also available on the NOAA website:

> *James P. Delgado, PhD, FRGS, RPA, has led or participated in shipwreck expeditions around the world. His undersea explorations include RMS Titanic, the discoveries of Carpathia, the ship that rescued Titanic's survivors, and the notorious "ghost ship" Mary Celeste, as well as surveys of USS Arizona at Pearl Harbor. . . .*[21]

The bio goes on to outline Delgado's professional career and accomplishments.

Writing for Social Media

With social media, people find organizations online via links and referrals from other people. They can then read, comment, share or create their own stories related to these organizations. They can participate, and they can interact. This is the essence of social media. Public relations writers must observe carefully before diving in. You wouldn't just walk into a room at a party and try to lead a discussion without first getting to know who was in that room, what they are talking about and how they are communicating. The same goes for online communication. You must work to understand both the social and technological contexts first. Then, you can join the conversation. "The most important lesson in social media," write Solis and Breakenridge, "is that, before engaging anyone, you must first observe and understand the cultures, behavior, and immersion necessary to genuinely participate in the communities where you don't already reside."[22]

BLOGS AND LONGER FORM

Blogs were among the first social media writing forms adopted on a wide scale by public relations practitioners. They remain primary vehicles for longer-form writing in social media. Blogs are sort of the old-timers of social media, but in 2004, they were a hot new thing. Blog was the most sought-after new word in Merriam-Webster's online dictionary that year.

Webster's 2004 Word of the Year was defined as "a Web site that contains an online personal journal with reflections, comments, and often hyperlinks provided by the writer."[23] Compared to other forms of published writing, blogs were easy to update. The reverse-chronological order of most blogs made it easy for writers to regularly add new posts and accumulate serial content. Linking enabled blogs to be more social, too. Public relations writers quickly recognized the potential utility of blogs for communicating with stakeholders and publics. However, to realize that potential would require some adaptation of traditional corporate writing. Dave Winer, who developed much of the software that enabled blogging to catch on in the 1990s, suggested that the only real requirement in identifying a blog was that the "personalities of the writers come through."[24]

Writing with personality was—and still is—a big part of blogging well. It is also still a tough challenge for many businesses and other types of organizations. Technology journalist Erica Swallow has outlined 10 tips for successful corporate blogging:[25]

1. Establish a content theme and editorial guidelines. While you can write about anything you want on your own personal blog, readers of an organization's blog should know what to expect, and the general theme should be closely related to what your organization does. Guidelines will help different writers from within the organization work together to support this theme.

2. Choose a blogging team and process. This team does not have to all come from the communications department. You want good

Before jumping into an online conversation, first you need to know how people are talking and what people are talking about.

Blog
Online post (or web log) with reflections, comments and often links provided by the writer.

THE BLOG · June 14th, 2019

TO SEE   TO READ   TO BUY   TO MEET   TO DO

· 07/17/2018

The latest on Pupils Project

We're definitely enjoying summer but after another great school year with
Pupils Project, we're looking forward to the next one. Pupils Project has
come a long way but first, to bring you up to speed:

+ MORE

The Warby Parker blog provides a forum for employees to write about new styles of glasses, but also community service projects, travel and books that employees recommend.

How do corporate blogs help "humanize" a company?

writers, but you also want authentic voices that represent different parts of your organization.

3. Humanize your company. As Dave Winer advised, let the personalities of writers come through. Let your team tell their stories (and their co-worker's stories) as they relate to the theme of the blog. Use the blog and its "Comments" section to have real conversations.

4. Avoid PR and marketing. Um, yeah, about this one, it depends on how "PR" is defined. Swallow equates PR with salesmanship. You do want to avoid that on blogs. It's a different story altogether, however, if you define public relations as building and maintaining relationships.

5. Welcome criticism. Criticism is part of human communication, and it's also a great opportunity to respond to constructive feedback.

6. Outline a comments policy. Of course, not all criticism is constructive. Guidelines for handling comments will make it transparent to both bloggers and readers which comments will be deleted and why.

7. Get social. Take advantage of social media affordances to connect your blog to your organization's other social media activities and to encourage sharing among your publics.

8. Promote your blog. Even if your blog has great content, you'll still need to drive people to it via other channels. Post new blog headlines to your other feeds with links back to the blog. Promote the URL in your email signature. Remind employees about it when you see them face-to-face.

9. Monitor mentions and feedback. Comments and feedback on your blog are not limited to the comments section of the blog. People will also comment on their own blogs and other forums. Google alerts and other search services can be set to monitor for specific terms and links, and notify you when your blogs get mentioned.

10. Track everything. In other words, use analytics. While number 9 on Swallow's list refers mainly to qualitative feedback, this last item reminds us to set up systems for tracking quantitative data. "At the minimum, make sure you're tracking site traffic, where referrals are coming from, and traffic-wise which posts are doing best," advises Swallow.

Most, if not all, of this advice applies to **microblogs** as well.

MICROBLOGS AND SHORTER FORM

Microblogging, according to Oxford Dictionaries, is simply "a social media site to which a user makes short, frequent posts." Under that definition, you can count Instagram, Facebook, Twitter, Snapchat, and China's Weibo, which had reached nearly 500 million users by the end of 2018[26], as micro-blogging platforms. But before you dive in to reach all those users, you'll want to think about your public relations strategy and the technology and culture of each.

For example, let's compare Twitter to China's Sina Weibo. Like Twitter, Weibo used to limit users to 140 characters per post but dropped that limit in 2016. Although the change allows longer messages, readers still only see the first 140 characters unless they click through to see the rest of the content. Because Chinese characters convey so much more information than Roman characters, that character limit is less of a constraint on Weibo than Twitter. And perhaps the most obvious difference between Weibo and Twitter is that most Twitter users log in from countries like the United States, Brazil and Japan,

Microblog
A shorter blog post limited by space or size constraints of the delivery platform.

The 140-character limit on Twitter and Weibo allows for very different styles of writing.

What cultural differences would you research before starting a Weibo account?

while most Weibo users are in China. But before you hire a translator to expand your social media reach into China, consider some of the cultural differences.

In comparing the two social media platforms, Edelman China's Cathy Yue noted that Weibo and Twitter present content differently, follow different business models and attract different demographics. Censorship is also a big factor. You would want to do a lot of research and work with people who really understand both the technology and the context of a platform like Weibo before representing your organization there. Yue concludes, "In order to successfully engage on Sina Weibo as a brand, it's important to keep in mind a classic Chinese saying, 'Precise knowledge of self and precise knowledge of the threat leads to victory.'"[27]

Writing for Search Engines

Sometimes, we have to write for robots.

As public relations writers, we must understand newsworthiness and the conventions for newswriting, if we plan to get our stories out via news media. We must understand the cultures and contexts of social media, if we plan to write for social media. And, if we want publics to find our organizations and stories when they do internet searches, we must understand how to write for search engines. Whereas journalists act as gatekeepers in news media, and everyday internet users serve as influencers in social media, computers are the intermediaries when we write to reach publics via search technology.

Search engine optimization (SEO) was defined in Chapter 7 as "the process of affecting the online visibility of a website or a web page in a web search engine's unpaid results—often referred to as 'natural,' 'organic,' or 'earned' results."[28] In the same way that people rely on news media to select the most newsworthy information in the day's news or friends in their social networks to provide feeds of interesting information, they count on search engines to filter for the content that is most relevant to their search queries. So what do these robots look for?

Although all search engines operate differently, with different rules (i.e., algorithms) for how search results are produced, some common elements that factor into most searches are: keywords (of course!); headlines, page titles and descriptions; meta tags and URLs; links and content.

KEYWORDS

If you want your page to be found when people search for keywords, include those words on your page. It sounds obvious, but it takes planning to integrate keywords with your writing. If your company sells beach umbrellas, your decision would be fairly straightforward. You would want to make sure you mention "beach umbrellas" on your page. On second or third references, you would want to write "beach umbrella" instead of "our product." Research on other words that people use also will help. Maybe "shade" and "sun protection" make sense as keywords too. But don't go overboard to the point of ridiculous repetition. If you mention beach umbrellas 15 times in two paragraphs, you'll come across as annoying to human readers, and the computers will figure out your trick too. There's a point of diminishing returns—search engine algorithms actually punish excessive repetition. Google calls it "keyword stuffing," and warns against filling your pages with duplicate words because it "results in a negative user experience, and can harm your site's ranking."[29]

HEADLINES, PAGE TITLES AND DESCRIPTIONS

In print media, headlines capture attention and make the difference between whether someone reads a story or not. The same applies online, except potential readers have to go through the extra step of clicking or tapping on your headline from all the other ones that are going to be really similar in search results. The headline also helps you distinguish your page from others with similar keywords but different purposes.

META TAGS AND URLS

Meta tags are the snippets of text that you use to describe a web page to search engines. When you post a web page you should enter the page title and description as meta tags. Your webmaster or IT people can help if you are not the one who actually uploads the web pages, but you will want to work with them to make sure they include the right words. For titles, avoid default tags like "Untitled" or "New Page 1." The page description and specific keywords also should be entered as meta tags. Google recommends using different titles and descriptions for each page.

Another recommendation is to include keywords in the URL. Remember that the URL also shows up in search results pages, and many people decide whether to click based on the URL structure. There's a lot of information about the broader website's content with a URL.

LINKS

Like public relations itself, linking is a two-way street. Search engines reward pages that have good relationships with other pages. When you link to other pages, avoid generic **anchor text** like "click here." Instead, choose the words carefully that you use to link to other pages (including other pages on your own website).

On the other side of the street are inbound links, or **backlinks**, which are links on others' pages that direct people to your pages. Search engines count these kinds of links as votes for your page, and the more you have, the higher your pages will rank in search results. That said, search engines are designed to sift out "unnatural links," which are "placed there specifically to make your site look more popular to search engines."[30] Earning **natural links** means nurturing relationships with other sites by offering information that the writers and designers of those sites will find valuable. This brings us back to the core of good writing: useful and

Meta tags
Text used to describe a web page to search engines.

Anchor text
Clickable text that provides a hyperlink.

Backlinks
Incoming links that direct web users to a web page from another web page.

Natural links
Hyperlinks to a web page that are provided by other people who see value in the content of the page, as opposed to links that are posted for the primary purpose of manipulating search engines.

To earn natural links, nurture relationships with other sites by offering information they will find valuable.

One of the best SEO "strategies" is also one of the simplest. Focus on good content that matters to your publics.

original information and good storytelling. Even in writing for robots, we have to think about the humans who will take interest and see value in what we write.

CONTENT

Google and other search engines change their algorithms so often it might feel like you would need to make it your full-time job just to keep up. While it is true that Google changes its algorithms thousands of times a year, and that gaming algorithms and social media strategy for SEO has become a career track in and of itself, one of the best "strategies" is also one of the simplest. Focus on good content that matters to your publics.

After Google released a "broad core algorithm update" in 2018, SEO strategists scrambled to adjust strategies. But Google recommended they keep calm and focus on content rather than trying to game the system. Via its @SearchLiaison Twitter account, Google referred concerned digital strategists back to an earlier set of tweets. "As with any update, some sites may note drops or gains," Google advised. "There's no 'fix' for pages that may perform less well other than to remain focused on building great content."[31]

Google updates its algorithms all the time, but recommends strategic communicators focus more on content than computer science.

Should organizations trust Google's advice to just focus on content?

Business Writing

While not unique to public relations, emails, memos, proposals and old-fashioned letters on letterhead are a major part of the writing you will do in public relations. Every time you write something as an employee of your organization, you are managing your own impression as well as that of your employer or client. Business writing often calls for more formal structure and style. As with any of the types of writing mentioned in this chapter, you'll want to observe the norms. Train yourself with practice, peer feedback and adaptation.

Being able to **code-switch** from the syntax of text messaging and Instagram to the formalities of an interoffice email or a client status report is a critical career skill. If you have a vacation planned that is going to delay a client project, you probably don't want to LOL about it or include #SorryNotSorry in the email to your boss or client. And u r smart 2 not get too cute w txt punctuation and emojis!!! 😊 With careful observation and practice, you may notice other, more subtle conventions that apply, depending on the context. A few examples are contractions ("we will" or "we'll"?), salutations ("Hi Tom," or "Dear Dr. Kelleher:"?), formal titles ("Ole Miss" or "University of Mississippi"?), and punctuation ("." or "!!"?). When in doubt, the *AP Stylebook* is an excellent fallback, but many organizations also publish their own style guides for consistency in organizational communication. In fact, public relations writers often are tasked with developing these style guides for in-house use.

Just because you are writing formally does not mean you have to sacrifice your voice. As Zinsser reminds us, "It's what stockholders want from their corporation, what customers want from their bank, what the widow wants from the agency handling her social security. There is a deep yearning for human contact and a resentment of bombast." Write for clarity. Be concise. Remember your reader.

We present ourselves differently in different contexts—this social media graphic was used to welcome new students both personally and professionally and features yours truly.

What are the major contexts for which you write in an average day, and how do you adjust your style for each?

Code-switching
Alternating between two or more languages or cultural styles.

Voices from the Field

Cornelius Foote

CORNELIUS FOOTE has worked at *The Miami Herald*, *The Washington Post*, *The Dallas Morning News* and the *Tom Joyner Morning Show*. In addition to being a newspaper reporter, Foote has led advertising sales teams, helped develop strategy and launch websites, and developed and managed public relations for Tom

Joyner and his media company. President of Foote Communications LLC, a Dallas media consulting firm, Foote is also chairman of the National Kidney Foundation Serving North Texas, president of the National Black Public Relations Society Inc., past chairman of the National Association of Minority Media Executives and a longstanding member of the National Association of Black Journalists.

Has public relations writing become easier with the rise of social media or harder?

Public relations writing has gotten harder. You must now learn how to tell your clients' stories in multiple ways. You've got to learn as many facets of the story to develop pitches that will resonate in print, in broadcast, on the internet and in social. You now need to think through headlines, subheads, leads and keywords to hook readers—and to cater to search engines. In addition to being a strong writer, a public relations professional today must know how to take that 600-word press release and convert it into a Facebook and Twitter campaign. Good PR professionals suggest ideas for posts, tweets and hashtags rather than relying on the social media team.

What role does writing play in social media success?

There's an expectation that any "younger person"—21 to 28 years old—already knows social media and can pick up this kind of writing on the fly. That's really not the case. Good, short writing tied to a social media campaign is not random. It requires skill. It also requires the ability to understand the analytics, measuring and tracking which posts and tweets are resonating most with the customers. Quite often, I'll get requests in my PR consulting business from clients who want my help to launch their social media efforts. Often, they want an instant viral campaign instead of a consistent, sustainable campaign that requires a well-thought-out editorial calendar tied to themes and involving various levels of engagement from the customer. While I'm always eager to gain new business, I've ended up talking clients out of pursuing this strategy when they're not ready.

Are there any forms of public relations writing that have become obsolete in recent years?

Two- to three-page press releases. I know publicly traded companies are required to have certain language and boilerplates. The problem is too many other releases are written in such a cumbersome, wordy style that is a throwback to the old days. As a former newspaper reporter, I used those kinds of press releases to generate story ideas, and then I did all my original reporting, fact gathering and interviews to gather quotes. The only benefit companies get from these traditional, lengthy press releases is coverage, because many news websites publish feeds from PR Newswire or Business Wire. But these sorts of releases don't guarantee quality stories about companies' new products or services.

How is new technology helping or hurting the quality of writing you see from new graduates and young practitioners?

What I've found is that it's hard for many students to think critically and write long articles or essays because they're so used to writing for the moment. The lack of critical thinking has stunted curiosity for many who are only thinking about what's in front of them—literally—their smartphones! In other ways, technology is enabling these new graduates and young practitioners to use their devices to help their clients—and co-workers—understand the importance of creating and producing content that's mobile-friendly.

What's your favorite new convention in public relations writing? What annoys you most?

There's no single "new convention" that's my favorite. What is exciting is that now we can tell a client's story without solely relying on a straightforward press release. What annoys me the most is when companies and agencies try to adapt to the new world order of social media by creating a series of hashtags that are too long and not relevant.

Overall, one of the most important characteristics of good public relations writing today—as it was yesterday—is the ability to tell a good story. If anything, public relations professionals must work that much harder to get their clients to realize that their story has to stand out above the rest.

Ethics: Expertise and Writing for Mutual Understanding

The most effective writers know their readers. Public relations writing, in particular, depends on expertise in fostering mutual understanding. By definition, public relations is building and maintaining mutually beneficial relationships between organizations and publics. But this expertise is not just a matter of effectiveness; it's also a matter of ethics. Along with advocacy, honesty, independence and loyalty, the PRSA Code of Ethics lists expertise as a core value of the profession:

> EXPERTISE
> We acquire and responsibly use specialized knowledge and experience. We advance the profession through continued professional development, research, and education. We build mutual understanding, credibility, and relationships among a wide array of institutions and audiences.[32]

Media ethics scholars Jay Black and Chris Roberts note that almost every major world religion, political culture and philosophical system includes some version of the ethic of reciprocity, or the **golden rule**.[33] In Christianity, "Do unto others as you would have them do to you." In Confucianism, "Do not do to others what you would not like yourself." In Islam, "Hurt no one so that no one may hurt you." In Judaism, "Love your neighbor as yourself."

We all know the golden rule, and we learn it very early in life: "How would you feel if someone did that to you?" It's an important lesson on the kindergarten playground, and just as important in the business of managing relationships between organizations and their publics. In public relations, you have an ethical responsibility to work hard to understand publics.

Case Study

Words Matter: A Strange Choice for an Agency Name

As one Texas-based public relations firm learned, reciprocity takes research and planning, and getting one important turn of phrase wrong can spell disaster, especially if you make that turn of phrase the name of your firm.

> Southern trees bear strange fruit,
> Blood on the leaves and blood at the root,

Golden rule
Ethic of reciprocity—treat others as you would like to be treated yourself.

This Twitter user mocked @StrangeFruitPR for lack of expertise in public relations.

What does expertise have to do with public relations ethics?

The @StrangeFruitPR account on Twitter was removed, as were the firm's website and Facebook page.

In what ways does removing the accounts help rectify the problem? In what ways is damage from an incident like this irreversible online?

Black bodies swinging in the southern breeze, Strange fruit hanging from the poplar trees.[34]

These haunting lyrics from a 1937 poem by Abel Meeropol about racism and lynching in the U.S. South entered the American psyche on the voice of jazz legend Billie Holiday, who recorded the song "Strange Fruit" in 1939. Throughout the century that has followed, "Strange Fruit" has served as a painfully important cultural reminder of one of the nation's ugliest memories. More than seven decades later, two public relations practitioners starting a firm in Austin, Texas, "thought the name would be perfect for a hospitality PR firm that specializes in food and drink."[35]

It's hard to imagine a scenario in which "strange fruit" would be an appropriate name for anything outside of serious racial dialogue. Of course, not everyone is familiar with the reference and history, and it would be understandable if someone used the term in everyday conversation without awareness of its deeper cultural significance. But if you are naming a new business, that is not everyday conversation. That single word or phrase should be as carefully conceived as any you ever write.

Strange Fruit Public Relations founders claimed they Googled the term when they thought of the name and found the Billie Holiday song, but figured it was not at all related to their firm and that "it wouldn't be top of mind in the public consciousness." For a period of time after they named the firm that reasoning appeared to hold up. But then @StrangeFruitPR became a thing on Twitter.[36] As Twitter user @BlackGirlDanger, put it: "You named your hospitality PR firm after a song about black people hanging from trees, @StrangeFruitPR? Really?"

The firm first tried to explain on Twitter: "Our passion is telling the stories of hospitality professionals. We chose our name bc these incredibly talented artists stand out in a crowd." They also tried to ingratiate on Twitter: "We believe in hospitality. Including all. No exclusion. The author & its famous singer hoped for a world where that would be a possibility." Ultimately, however, the company's principals shut down the @StrangeFruitPR Twitter account along with the company's website and Facebook page.

They eventually emailed a longer statement to the *Austin American-Statesman*: "We were wrong. . . . We extend our deepest and sincerest apologies for the offense caused by the name of our public relations firm. . . . We now know we were naïve to think that, and should have known better."[37]

Words matter.

In Case You Missed It

While principles of good writing apply across all media, writing for social media requires understanding both technology and culture. Here are a few takeaways from this chapter:

- When presenting yourself in social media, balance being authentic with being professional.

- Excellence in social media requires good storytelling—understanding your organization's stories and why those stories matter to your publics.

- When readers and users have the opportunity to become part of the storytelling process, stories have a better chance of going viral.

- Online news feeds, blog rolls, email preview panes and search engine results favor good leads.

- Regardless of the medium, you should package background information in an easily accessible format.

- Before jumping into an online conversation, first you need to know how people are talking and what people are talking about.

- To earn natural links, nurture relationships with other sites by offering information they will find valuable.

- One of the best SEO "strategies" is also one of the simplest. Focus on good content that matters to your publics.

SUMMARY

9.1 List five key purposes of good writing in public relations.

Five of the most important reasons to write well in public relations are: (1) to build and maintain relationships, (2) to influence and persuade, (3) to strategize (to identify and achieve goals and objectives), (4) to manage your organization's reputation and (5) to make your own impression as you build your professional identity.

9.2 Analyze news and feature styles of storytelling.

In straight news writing, writers report on the facts of a story (who, what, where, when, why, how), usually in inverted-pyramid style with the most important information in the lead and the narrower supporting details later in the story. Feature writers dig deeper into some angle of an event, a person's life, an organization or a place. Feature stories are more likely to be told with a delayed lead.

9.3 Discuss the role of news media, social media and search engines as intermediaries between public relations writers and publics.

In news media relations, publics find an organization's stories based on what editors and producers decide is newsworthy. Tactics for news media include news releases, fact sheets, backgrounders, bios and so on. In social media, people find organizations online via links and referrals from peers or others in their social networks. One way to think about tactics for social media writing is to consider longer-form blogs and shorter-form microblogs that are common on platforms like Twitter, Instagram and Snapchat. With respect to searches, publics count on search engines and algorithms to filter for the content that is most relevant to their queries. Writing for SEO requires thinking about keywords, headlines, titles, meta tags and links, as well as original content that others will find valuable.

9.4 Compare and contrast business writing and social media writing.

Although writing for social media requires understanding many conventions (hashtags, reposts, etc.), writing for social media is generally less formal than business writing. Both benefit from clarity, conciseness and authenticity.

9.5 Explain how expertise in public relations writing relates to public relations ethics.

As a core ethical value of public relations, expertise means being able to "build mutual understanding, credibility, and relationships among a wide array of institutions and audiences." Practicing moral reciprocity (i.e., the golden rule) at the level of organization-public relations requires writing for mutual understanding. Working to understand diverse publics is part of that expertise.

DISCUSSION QUESTIONS

1. How would it help or hurt your job prospects if a potential employer reviewed all your social media profiles online right now?

2. **CASE STUDY** Browse through the website and social media channels for World Bicycle Relief (https://worldbicyclerelief.org/) or one of your favorite charities. What kinds of stories do they tell, and how do those stories help advance their mission?

3. **CASE STUDY** Human interest and timelessness are said to be key elements of good feature stories. Do you think the Kelly Slater and Chiquita Evans stories still meet these criteria now that some time has passed? Find an interesting feature story that you think a public relations person had a role in writing that you would judge to be relatively "timeless." What kinds of strategy, goals and objectives does it serve?

4. Imagine you are announcing your own graduation and getting hired at your dream job. Write (a) a text to your best friend, (b) a post to one of your personal social media accounts, (c) the headline for a blog entry on LinkedIn or another job-focused site and (d) the headline for a news release to send to your hometown newspaper. How are the four similar and how are they different?

5. Do you feel like you are sacrificing authenticity when you change your voice for different

contexts (e.g., texting, blogging, business writing)? Why or why not?

6. Will AP style be important to you in your career? Will you write in inverted pyramid style? Why or why not?

7. What's the worst public relations mistake you've seen written online? (You can search for one if none comes to mind.) Was information removed from the web, and did that help?

What might the writer have done differently to avoid the mistake?

8. **CASE STUDY** Suppose you were interning for the founders of Strange Fruit Public Relations when they first proposed the agency name. And suppose they asked you to register their name for Twitter and other social media accounts. What specifically would you have done or recommended to help them?

KEY TERMS

Anchor text   247
Associated Press (AP) style   239
Backgrounder   241
Backlinks   247
Blog   243
Clickbait   226
Code-switching   249
Dateline   239
Delayed lead   235

Direct lead   236
Fact sheet   240
Feature story   231
Golden rule   251
Human interest   235
Impression management   228
Inverted pyramid   236
Listicle   226
Media kits   241

Meta tags   247
Microblog   245
Morgue   241
Natural links   247
News release   239
Reputation management   228
Social media release   239
Transmedia storytelling   233
Video news release   239

CHAPTER 10

Social Media and Mobile

One fast-food restaurant is using mobile to get ahead of the competition. Can a mobile app make you think twice about where you're grabbing lunch?

KEY LEARNING OUTCOMES

10.1 Assess the strategic value of mobile tactics.

10.2 Discuss how publics' uses and gratifications of mobile media may help drive public relations strategy.

10.3 Explain how social and visual listening can help public relations professionals better understand and communicate with their publics.

10.4 Evaluate how different forms of social media content can be created to engage publics.

10.5 Describe how public relations professionals can use social media to build community.

10.6 Apply privacy as an ethical value to consider in handling data gleaned from mobile media.

RELATED UNIVERSAL ACCREDITATION BOARD COMPETENCY AREAS

1.2 RESEARCH (APPLICATIONS) • **1.8** IMPLEMENTATION • **2.2** ETHICAL BEHAVIOR
2.4 PRIVACY ISSUES • **2.5** OTHER LEGAL ISSUES • **6.5** NETWORKS

Even in the days when most news was printed on paper, when tweets were sung by birds, when a snap meant something had broken, and when chatting was something you did with the person in front of you, your average human couldn't pay attention to all of these stimuli at the same time. The internet hasn't helped matters.

It may appear that people focus intently as they stare into their smartphones but, actually, as they swipe and tap on their devices, they must rapidly make decisions about what to pay attention to and what to ignore. They must also decide *whom* to communicate with and whom to ignore. This is **selective attention**, and every time you scroll and stop on a news feed, click on a YouTube video, or watch a story on Instagram, you select what to pay attention to in the virtual world.

So how do public relations professionals get and keep people's attention in this environment? How do we maintain relationships and engage in interactive communication without being annoying? As discussed in Chapter 9, telling a compelling story is one way. Sophisticated use of technology is another. But knowing what will make a story compelling and what will make technology sophisticated from the user's perspective hinges on understanding publics and their use of media.

No doubt you already have experience creating and communicating with mobile and social media. You've more than likely snapped Insta-worthy food photos, written your candid thoughts on Twitter, or gone on a "streak" (sending snaps back and forth for at least three consecutive days) with your friends on Snapchat. Depending on your experience, you may be a step ahead of some of your professors or more senior public relations colleagues when it comes to mobile and social media.

However, there is so much more to effective public relations than personal experience with emerging platforms and technology (see Figure 10.1). Mobile and social media are channels through which to communicate with your publics. In the bigger picture of effective public relations, the channels you select are driven by strategy, and strategy is designed to achieve goals and objectives that are developed from research (see Chapters 5 and 6). Without proper management and strategy, pumping out how-to videos, livestreams and mobile app notifications is no more indicative of effectiveness or relationship quality than emailing press releases or placing flyers on car windshields. Some of the most in-demand communicators in public relations are those who understand current and emerging communication technologies but who also have a firm grasp on writing, strategy and global issues.[1]

Selective attention
Process of filtering information by focusing on some stimuli in the environment while ignoring others.

In-demand communicators in public relations understand current and emerging technology but also grasp the importance of writing, strategy, and global issues.

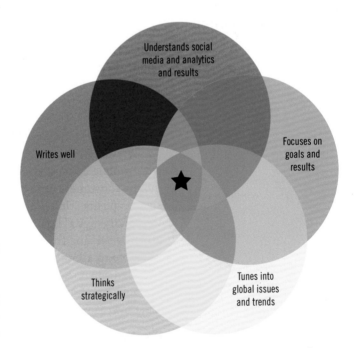

Figure 10.1 Young public relations professionals may be at an advantage in experience with emerging media and technology, but that's only part of the recipe for career success.

How can you improve in other areas?

Mobile First

In a parody of their hit song "Year 3000" on *The Late Late Show with James Corden*, the Jonas Brothers gave a hilarious and accurate portrayal of mobile use today. They sang (*cue music*), "He said I've been to the year 2019. TV has changed now it's all on your cell phone. You can filter any photo. Look I'm a dog, a sexy dog."

But there's more to this example than a funny song lyric. The parody first aired on the late-night show, which amasses approximately 1 million TV viewers each week.[2] The YouTube video of the parody garnered more than four times that many views *in less than five days*.[3] This isn't surprising; Nielsen reports that when looking solely at mobile data, YouTube reaches more adults each week during prime time than any cable network.[4]

More than 5 billion people, or 66 percent of the global population, have mobile phones. Of that 5 billion, more than half access the internet through their phones.[5] Businesses across industries, from cable networks to airlines, have shifted to accommodate the profound increase in communication via mobile devices and the rise of "mobile only" users.

Mobile provides organizations with the opportunity to be part of the daily lives of the individuals in their publics, from customers to employees and shareholders. It is ubiquitous, social, personal and local—and the most successful mobile tactics reflect most of these characteristics.

Ubiquitous

If you have a smartphone, it's probably within arm's reach as you read this chapter. Your screen is likely lighting up with notifications—an alarm, a text from a friend or a "like" on your latest Instagram photo. We keep our smartphones nearby at all times of day, no matter where we go.

This means we're consuming more digital content, too. Mobile users consume more than two times the digital minutes that desktop users consume.[6] And according to Nielsen, smartphones alone accounted for 65 percent of total digital usage in 2018.[7]

What does this mean for the organizations trying to reach and connect with mobile consumers? It means they must walk a fine line: keep their mobile consumers interested and engaged 24/7/365 but avoid being intrusive or pushy. Understanding consumers' journeys is critical. What are their daily digital habits? When are they using specific apps? What content are they seeking from organizations? Even though 63 percent of millennials agree to allow push notifications from an app, 71 percent say they get annoyed when they get too many notifications.[8] It's up to you and your organization to find the right balance to maintain that relationship and build trust over time.

Social

Mobile apps are the go-to method for accessing social networks. In 2017, social networking and instant messaging apps accounted for nearly

25 percent of time spent on mobile apps, and seventy percent of adults indicated using mobile apps to log in to their social networks. What's the number one app by far? Facebook. It even surpassed functional apps like Google Maps or Gmail.[9] Add to that the growth of mobile-first social networks, like Instagram and Snapchat, and you can see how it would be difficult to develop a mobile strategy that doesn't build on social uses of the technology.

Communication via social media means considering not just how you will reach your organization's followers, fans and subscribers but also how they will reach back to your organization and how they will share content with one another. Think about how your organization can become part of the social conversation. What content will people respond to and share, and why? How will your organization respond to what people are saying online? Social means interactive, and interactive means that individuals in your organization have the opportunity to communicate with individuals in your publics. That back-and-forth communication is very likely to happen on a mobile phone, so make sure any tactics you plan and any content you publish make sense for the devices on which the communication will happen.

Personal

Mobile media also allow for a tremendous amount of personalization. When you use your mobile device to shop for plane tickets, download an audiobook or put in a coffee order for pickup, there's a good chance that the app you use will give you options based on your prior purchases and browsing history. Marketers were among the first to mine user data—from apps, registrations and browsing histories—to reach mobile consumers with messages tailored to their individual profiles.

Public relations practitioners can work with app developers and marketers who have access to consumer data to obtain a better understanding of their publics' uses of mobile and to coordinate on communication strategy. Spotify's "Wrapped" is one example of a brand using consumer data to provide a personalized experience. Each December, Spotify listeners can look back at their year on the music-streaming platform, find their top songs and explore new music recommendations, specially tailored to their preferences.[10] In just one week in 2018, Spotify's year-in-review initiative brought in 28 million users, illustrating the power of personalization to drive behavior.[11]

We know consumer demand for personalized content is at an all-time high.[12] Yet, people are also concerned about how their data is tracked and used to deliver this personalized content. In a study of Facebook users, the Pew Research Center found that more than half of those surveyed said they were "not very comfortable" or "not at all comfortable" with Facebook tracking their activities to create a list of their interests and traits.[13] In an interview with *The Atlantic*, researcher and Professor Benjamin Johnson,

Consider how you will reach people on mobile and social media but also how they will reach back to your organization and how they will share content with one another.

Spotify Wrapped gives you more than your top artists and songs—it gives you a reason to share.

How might this type of personalization be used to support public relations goals?

Kara Page
21h ago

Bought internet y'all.. Snaps from the cruise

BAHAMAS

CHAT

Snapchat's geofilters allow users to share place-themed messages and promote events in specific geographic locations.

What kinds of organizations can benefit from the combination of social and local mobile content?

who studies how people share their music tastes to influence how others view them, explains that Spotify avoids the "creepiness factor" that may come with data collection by giving users control over if and how they share their results.[14]

Local

Localization is basically the geographic version of personalization. Unless you deliberately disable **geolocation** functions in your mobile apps, many apps you use will track your location and apply that to your communication preferences. Geolocation makes apps like Uber or Yelp much more convenient as you try to arrange a ride across town or find a local restaurant when traveling.

In developing public relations strategies, you should know *where* you plan to reach your publics and communicate with them. Mobile media offer the opportunity to engage publics almost anywhere they go, provided they opt in to communication that they feel is worthwhile. You're likely familiar with Snapchat's **geofilter**, which allows individuals and organizations to create a photo filter for users in a specific geographic location.[15] For example, if you were planning a fundraiser for a local nonprofit, you could set up a geofilter for everyone using Snapchat in that area at that time. Those who attend the fundraiser and use the geofilter would then share their photos with their friends, increasing the reach of your event. The service is free for public places such as parks and landmarks and can be purchased for businesses and brands.

Case Study

Burger King Uses Mobile App to Troll Competitors

The right message at the right time can be the difference between someone clicking a notification or swiping it off the screen. With mobile devices and localization technology (e.g., GPS), we can engage publics almost anywhere they go—even a competitor. Burger King did just that with its "WHOPPER® Detour" stunt. By relying on mobile **Geofencing**, which uses GPS-like technology to alert when a mobile device enters or leaves an area, Burger King tried to lure customers away from McDonald's and to its mobile app. The news release announced:

> Today, the BURGER KING® brand is turning more than 14,000
> McDonald's into BURGER KING® restaurants. Sort of. For a limited time,

Geofencing
The use of localization technology, like GPS, to create a virtual geographic boundary for a real-world area. Triggers can be set up to alert when a mobile device enters or leaves that area.

when you go within 600 feet of a McDonald's restaurant you can order a flame-grilled WHOPPER® sandwich for only 1¢ on the newly revamped BK® App. It's what we call a WHOPPER® Detour.[16]

Basically, when customers with the BK® App (with location settings turned on) got close to a McDonald's restaurant, they would be able to order a Whopper® from the BK® App for only 1 cent. Then, the app would redirect them to the nearest Burger King to pick up their order.

With the "WHOPPER® Detour" stunt, Burger King sought to increase downloads of its newly revamped mobile app. And it worked. According to Restaurant Brands International Inc. (Burger King's parent company) CEO José Cil, the brand "generated over 1.5 million downloads from the initiative, making the Burger King app the number one most downloaded app in the Apple store for several days in a row."[17]

Why the push for app downloads? *QSR Magazine* reports that 6 out of 10 restaurant digital orders are on mobile apps. Of those mobile app orders, the majority are coming from restaurants' apps, as opposed to third-party apps like Uber Eats or Postmates. Simply put, restaurants that want to capitalize on the growth of digital orders must have their own mobile apps.

Burger King gave customers a step-by-step guide to redeeming the "Whopper Detour" promotion—and it all started with downloading the BK® App.

What would prompt you to download one restaurant's mobile app over another?

Geolocation
Function of communication devices that identifies the specific geographic location of the device.

Geofilter
Feature of social media (particularly Snapchat) that encourages communication among users within a specified geographic area by allowing users to post images with location-specific overlays.

Rewards, convenience and savings are the top reasons people are drawn to restaurant mobile apps.[18] Burger King counted on this when it took a swipe at its next target: Starbucks. In March 2019, Burger King launched a BK® Café Coffee subscription, which lets BK App® users pay a $5 monthly fee to receive one daily coffee at participating restaurants. Its main message? "Enjoy BK® Café Coffee for a month for the price of a large cappuccino from Starbucks."[19]

Quick-service restaurants, like Burger King, are using mobile apps to meet the growing demand for convenience from millennial and GenZ consumers, who don't want to wait in long drive-thru lines. The success of initiatives like the "Whopper Detour" stunt shows that Burger King understands that it's more important than ever to intercept mobile customers at the *right* moments, not all the time. In addition, although a national initiative, the stunt was also local and personal by enabling customers to order and locate the nearest Burger King restaurant all in one app. Mobile devices are allowing organizations like this one to provide more value to their publics, but the pressure is on to innovate quickly.

Uses and Gratifications of Media

Because mobile media lets organizations be part of people's lives, it's critical to understand *what people do with media*. Do they use it for information? Entertainment? Staying in touch? When communication scientists want to understand what people do with media, they have applied an approach called **uses and gratifications**, which focuses on how people use media and the gratifications they seek from media.[20] The user-oriented approach of uses and gratifications is particularly well suited to the study of new communication technologies.

Public relations researcher Ruth Avidar and her colleagues explored how and why 21- to 31-year-old Israelis were using smartphones.[21] They found that uses and gratifications such as staying in touch with friends and family, sending personal messages, and acknowledging others were most important. In other words, *relationships* were the top reason these young Israelis used smartphones. *Information*, such as obtaining news updates, was the second-highest rated reason found in this study. This was followed by *amusement* and *diversion*, which included gaming, relaxation and passing time.

Think about your own use of mobile devices. What kinds of apps do you use for maintaining relationships, obtaining information, amusing yourself and seeking diversion? And what role do organizations practicing public relations have in those experiences? How do you communicate directly with them via mobile?

In developing strategy for mobile media, consider asking what people are doing with mobile media instead of what mobile media will do to people.

Uses and gratifications
Approach to studying communication that focuses on how people use media and the gratifications they seek from media.

While thinking about your own experiences with organizations is a good exercise to help you develop questions to drive your planning, it's not normally a good idea to think of yourself as representing your organization's publics. It takes research to understand your publics from their perspectives (see Chapter 5). As discussed earlier in the chapter, analyzing mobile data is one way to do so. Listening to what they have to say on social media is another.

It seems like anywhere people wait, mobile media are being used.

How do you use mobile media when you're waiting in line or commuting to school? What kinds of organizations attempt to communicate with you in that time?

Social and Visual Listening

Social media are much like digital focus groups that we can access all day, every day. David Shadpour, co-founder of Social Native, writes for *Forbes* that "social media users have the freedom to express their unfettered, unsolicited opinions."[22] As a result, social media provide public relations professionals with a wealth of valuable data about their brands, publics, competitors and industries. It's up to us to listen and make sense of that data.

But why spend our time and energy listening, when we can be creating #trendy content instead? The answer to this question lies in understanding what social and visual listening are, the benefits they reap and the simple ways you can get started.

What Is Social Listening?

Think about the last time you searched a hashtag on Twitter. Maybe you searched for the last show you binge-watched on Netflix or your favorite sports team. You probably wanted to know what other Twitter users thought about it, and you may have even replied to a few tweets or posted one of your own. If that sounds familiar, then you've done basic social listening.

Social listening allows you to track, analyze and respond to conversations about specific topics, such as a company or industry, online. Individuals in your publics are probably already talking about your brand or your competitors on social media. Some of them might even tag the brand. You want to know what they're saying—the good, the bad and the ugly—so you can act on your findings. Social listening lets you do this; it reveals broad trends and themes that can inform public relations strategy.

Brands like music-streaming platform Pandora use social listening to monitor conversations and engage and interact with users online. But Pandora isn't only a music-streaming platform. It's also a jewelry company

Social listening reveals broad trends and themes that can inform public relations strategy.

Social listening
The process of tracking, analyzing and responding to conversations about specific topics online.

Peek inside Dell's Social Media Listening and Command Center, complete with multiple screens to monitor real-time conversations, track customer profiles and uncover global trends.

How can Dell use social listening to tailor its public relations strategy across the globe?

and a Disney theme park hotspot. Sysomos, one of several social media monitoring and analytics tools, helps Pandora not only to distinguish mentions of its music services from mentions of other same-name brands, but also to determine sentiment and interact and engage with fans.[23]

Some companies have invested heavily in social listening, even creating in-house social media command centers to monitor and listen to conversations in real time, 24/7. Dell, Gatorade and The American Red Cross are a few examples. Karen Quintos, Chief Customer Service Officer at Dell, explained the power of social listening for the company:

Through Dell's Social Media Listening and Command Center, we aggregate and find our way through the 25,000 conversations about Dell every day (more than 6 million every year). And that's just conversations happening in English! We're monitoring conversations in 11 languages 24/7, and each one is an opportunity to reinforce our brand.[24]

What Is Visual Listening?

If you post a picture of a Starbucks drink on Instagram but don't mention Starbucks in the caption or tag it in the image, will the brand ever know you're a fan of its Nitro Cold Brew? If we listen only to mentions of a brand or topic in text—such as hashtags, captions or comments—we are seeing only a portion of the total conversation.

Visual listening uses image recognition to identify visual "mentions," such as logos or products, in images and videos. This is especially important because approximately 80 percent of images shared on social media that include brand logos do not directly mention the brand in the text.[25] In fact, a study by social media listening and analytics company Talkwalker found that Starbucks would miss more than 30,000 logo mentions each week without visual listening.[26] The only way to know if and how your brand is being "talked about" is by understanding the context of the image.

What Are the Benefits of Social and Visual Listening?

While **social monitoring** lets you track social media mentions and conversations, social and visual listening take this one step further. Listening requires that you act on your findings and use them to inform your social media or

Visual listening
The use of image recognition to track and analyze logos or products in online images.

Social monitoring
The process of tracking social media mentions and conversations.

diastudies · Follow

2,471 likes

Natural, candid photos of your product or logo on social media can be just as valuable as those that are styled and posed.

How might the composition and style of visual content help brands learn about their customers?

public relations strategy. It's part research (Chapter 5), part implementation (Chapter 7) and part evaluation (Chapter 8). The benefits abound for those who invest time and resources in doing it right.

MANAGING BRAND REPUTATION

An organization's biggest fans and biggest haters will be the loudest on social media. According to Apptentive (a company that helps organizations engage with their customers on mobile), this "vocal minority" only makes up 1 percent of the total customer base.[27] Still, this group can heavily influence **sentiment** on social media. Social listening allows organizations to track positive, negative and neutral sentiment and set benchmarks. If suddenly you notice a negative shift, you can quickly react and mitigate the effects of a brewing crisis.

Sentiment
A measure of the tone or emotion behind social media mentions or comments, typically categorized as positive, neutral or negative.

Several brands were tagged in this tweet, but only one responded: Hulu. @hulu_support is a dedicated social media account for customer service, used to reply to customer complaints and ideas.

Can you describe two ways Hulu benefited from finding this tweet?

DISCOVERING NEW PRODUCT OR SERVICE IDEAS

Your customers can be your best product developers and creative geniuses. Sometimes they'll even tell you exactly what they want. Social media teams should be ready to respond and take note. For years, Frito-Lay has used social media to crowdsource new Lay's chip flavors, asking fans to pitch their flavor ideas and vote for their favorites with the #DoUsAFlavor campaign.

JOINING RELEVANT CONVERSATIONS

Brands don't always need to be the subject of a conversation to join the conversation. **Newsjacking**, a term coined by David Meerman Scott (an online marketing expert and author), "is the art and science of injecting your ideas into a breaking news story so you and your ideas get noticed."[28] Social listening lets you monitor what's trending, so you can determine if it makes sense for your organization to participate in a trending topic. You may have seen brands do this: Panera jumped on the popularity of Netflix's "To All the Boys I've Loved Before" when it tweeted: "To All the Bread I've Loved Before." Poor attempts at newsjacking, however, can damage an organization's reputation.

Brands that have tried to capitalize on natural disasters, tragedies or days of remembrance have been met with swift backlash from social media users who've deemed them tone-deaf and insensitive. That's exactly what happened when Florida State University's football recruiting Twitter account (@FSU_Recruiting) posted an edited image of Dr. King appearing to do a tomahawk chop (the university's sports celebration) while wearing a football glove. The tweet, which included the hashtag #MLK2019, was posted on a Martin Luther King Jr. Day of Service. While it was quickly removed and an apology was issued, the blunder still made headlines on media outlets like *Sports Illustrated* and *USA Today*.

How Do You Conduct a Social Listening Search?

Social listening efforts would be futile if we listened to *everything* on *every* platform. Before you start listening, you have to know what to listen to and where to listen to be most effective. Where are people talking about your organization? Is it on Facebook, Twitter or Instagram? Or is it on YouTube? If you're not sure, start broad. Conduct social listening searches across multiple social media platforms to better understand where these conversations are happening.

To set up a basic social listening search, public relations professionals must identify relevant keywords for their organizations, such as:

- The organization's name, social media handles or branded hashtags, and those of their competitors

- Specific products or services offered

- The organization's slogan or tagline

- Names of key people in the organization, like the CEO or spokesperson

- Specific campaign names or hashtags

- Industry buzzwords or topics

To make social and visual listening easier, public relations professionals can invest in tools, like Brandwatch and Critical Mention, which provide dashboards with real-time metrics and analytics. Word clouds and colorful graphs synthesize listening data, making even the most complicated information easy to understand. There are also a few free resources, like TweetDeck and Hootsuite, for those who can't invest in more sophisticated tools right away. The downfall is that most of these free resources are limited and can only monitor mentions on Twitter.

Creating Engaging Content

The ability to combine media elements in meaningful ways is one of the most powerful aspects that drove early growth of the internet and the web.[29] Today, in societies in which mobile communication technology is widely

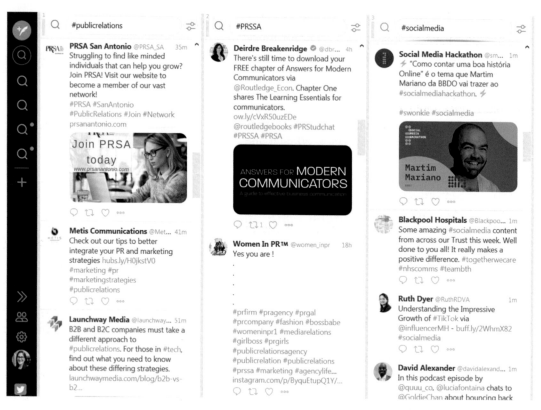

With TweetDeck you can take social listening one step further and comment, like or retweet other posts—right from your dashboard.

What hashtags or keywords could you monitor to stay up to date with the public relations industry?

Multimedia
The combination of any two or more forms of media such as text, graphics, moving images and sounds.

available, digital content is changing the very nature of interpersonal communication as well as communication between organizations and publics.

But, what *is* content? Is it a simple 280-character tweet? A 20-minute video on Facebook? A photo on your Snapchat story? Yes, yes and yes. Content has been difficult to define because it is broad and seemingly all-encompassing. Social media thought leaders vary in their definitions:

- *Derek Halpern* (Founder, Social Triggers): "Content comes in any form (audio, text, video), and it informs, entertains, enlightens, or teaches people who consume it."

- *Joe Pulizzi* (Founder, Content Marketing Institute): "[Content is] Compelling information that informs, engages or amuses."

- *Joan Damico, APR* (Communications Manager, Accenture): "Content is any communication in any medium that serves a purpose, whether it be to influence, educate, inform, warn, express one's self or spark conversation within a given context."

However, what's consistent in these definitions is that content has a form and purpose. Content can take the form of text, graphics, images, videos or audio—or a combination of these, known as **multimedia**. A meme is multimedia because it combines images and text. Regular old television is multimedia because it combines audio and video. Content also has a purpose, and how effectively content accomplishes its purpose is often measured by **engagement** (how often others interact with your content and how they do so).

Today, anyone with a smartphone can capture and consume content just about anywhere that their devices will function. You can even plan and schedule content for delivery on mobile devices using social media management tools, like Buffer and Sprout Social, which are available as apps. The key to creating content on social media is to understand the main forms—text, images and video—and how they can engage users. It's equally important to know the value of curating content to complement the original content you're creating (Figure 10.2).

Text

Text may be the last thing we think of when we think of social media content. But it's the most pervasive. Nearly every tweet, image or story we post is accompanied by text. Robert Wynne, principal of a public relations firm in Manhattan Beach, California, and regular *Forbes* contributor on public relations topics, explained the importance of words and text in multimedia:

> You are trying to convince the media, the public, your employees, your vendors, shareholders, someone, to do something—change their opinion, reinforce their attitudes, write about or film your client, vote for your issue or candidate, or purchase your service or product. Sometimes this is done in person, sometimes over the phone. But the majority of communications are done via words, whether in email, Twitter or online media. It all starts on the page or screen. With words.[30]

Sometimes you write words to explain other elements of multimedia such as an image or a video. Other times words play the leading role, like when you thread tweet after tweet to tell a story—because sometimes 280 characters simply isn't enough.

USE CAPTIONS TO COMPLEMENT YOUR IMAGE
When you post a picture on social media, the words you use to describe that image enhance the context and the meaning. As *Wall Street Journal*'s Elizabeth Holmes put it, "A picture may be worth a thousand words, but on social media you need a caption."[31] Part of the beauty of mobile photo-sharing apps like

How can you improve in other areas?

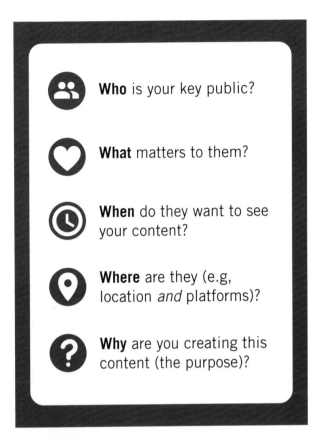

Figure 10.2 Before you start creating content, have a clear grasp of your publics and who this content is meant to reach. Start by asking yourself these 5 W's.

What other questions could you consider before you create content?

Engagement
Measure of how (likes, shares, comments, etc.) and how often others interact with your content.

Even though they're captured by users all over the globe, photos shared on @ ihavethisthingwithfloors on Instagram all have one thing in common: they're over-the-head shots of feet on really cool floors.

What organizations do you immediately recognize on social media?

Freelancers
People who work on a project-by-project basis instead of working more permanently for a single employer (e.g., freelance writers, photographers, video producers).

Public domain
Works of intellectual property for which the copyright has expired, the creator has forfeited rights, or copyright laws do not apply, making the works freely available for public use.

MAINTAIN HIGH QUALITY

Even though hastily snapped selfies have found a place in social media culture, high-quality imagery is still important, especially for organizations. Fortunately, advances in digital camera technology have made do-it-yourself photography more accessible. As Apple's #ShotoniPhone campaign set out to prove, your average smartphone camera can generate image quality that used to be reserved for only those willing to invest heavily in expensive digital cameras. Today #ShotoniPhone photos are featured not only across social media but also on billboards and TV commercials internationally.

However, just because the camera phone in your pocket *can* capture amazing images at high resolution doesn't mean you should capture all photos on your own—or that photos will be the only types of images you use. **Freelancers** can be paid by the hour or hired by the project for photography, graphic design or illustrations. Free and easy-to-use tools like Canva can also help beginners create graphic designs.

USE IMAGES WITH PERMISSION

Sometimes, the best image for your social media needs already exists, but be careful not to repost it without permission. Chapter 11 discusses common copyright issues in more detail, but the good news is that there is an abundance of great imagery available online, if you pay attention to copyright and permission requirements.

Public domain images are "free" images, including images produced by government entities (e.g., an image of a fish from the U.S. Fish and Wildlife Service), those that are so old that the copyrights have expired (e.g., the *Mona Lisa*), or those that the original creators have explicitly released for public use. Be careful, however, in making unchecked assumptions. Use of government logos or seals such as the logo for the Fish and Wildlife Service, a photograph or modified version of the *Mona Lisa* as it is presented in a copyrighted book, or certain types of **Creative Commons** licenses are restricted.

To break beauty stereotypes, Dove partnered with Getty Images and Girlgaze to launch the #ShowUs project, a library of stock photos taken by women and non-binary individuals. The library has 5,000 images featuring 179 women from 39 countries.

Why is it important for organizations to select stock images that represent diversity?

iPhone cameras can capture detail and depth, like in this iPhone photo, but photographers should also consider other important factors, like lighting, composition and angles.

When might you choose to hire a freelance photographer instead of taking your own photos?

Many images are available for sharing as long as you obtain permission, properly attribute the image to its source and, in some cases, link back to that source. Even Getty Images, one of the world's largest for-profit **stock image** providers, permits free use of its images online, as long as the images are embedded with the proper HTML code. [38]

Video

The growth of services like YouTube and Vimeo catapulted the movement to online video in the early 2000s, making it easy for users to convert, upload, share and watch video material online. By the end of the first decade of the millennium, billions of video streams were being watched by hundreds of millions of unique users each month, and the largest video service by far was YouTube. In 2019, the service claimed more than 1.9 billion monthly users.[39] In March 2019, Twitter also reported impressive numbers: more than 2 billion video views on Twitter each day, a growth of 67 percent from the previous year.[40]

Public relations professionals can create videos for social media that captivate their publics and relay their messages. Like social media, however, video creation is not one-size-fits-all.

Creative Commons
Nonprofit organization that encourages fair and legal sharing of content by helping content creators make their work available with clear terms and conditions.

Stock image
Image that is professionally produced for selling or sharing, commonly available in searchable databases.

Talk Show
#NFLBlitz

The latest news in the NFL

Several major sports leagues, like the NFL, NBA and MLB, have partnered with Twitter in the last few years to livestream key moments, games and interviews on the social media platform.

Why might an organization choose to stream content on social media?

Landscape orientation
Images or video framed so that width is greater than height, like traditional movies. The aspect ratio is 16:9.

Vertical video
Video framed in an orientation in which height is greater than width. The aspect ratio is 9:16.

Snackable content
Easy-to-consume pieces of content that are available on the go.

USE VERTICAL VIDEO WHEN POSSIBLE

The age-old advice to always shoot video in a **landscape orientation** (or horizontal) for best viewing on TV and computer screens has changed. In fact, doing so may indicate that your content was not produced for mobile and social media (a classic example is when an organization takes a 30-second TV commercial and posts it on Instagram, though the ad wasn't created for that platform or its audiences). While horizontal videos have a place when capturing b-roll or even recording a typical YouTube video, **vertical videos** have claimed their rightful spot in social media content thanks to vertically oriented smartphones, tablets and social media apps like Snapchat. To help organizations adapt to these changes, companies like Snapchat have even created how-to YouTube videos to show how to transform a horizontal video into a vertical one.[41]

THINK BEYOND BASIC RECORDED VIDEO

If you're feeling creative and are comfortable with the software, you might consider creating animations or video infographics. Even if you're a novice, tools like Vyond let you easily create animated videos for a monthly fee. Another option is live-streaming video, which allows online viewers to watch whatever you point your camera at in real time. And though it's been around since the early 2000s, mobile-friendly services like Facebook Live and Instagram Live have led to renewed interest among public relations practitioners in live video. One example is NASA, which has given social media users an insider's look at space with Facebook Live videos of spacewalks with its astronauts.[42] Other organizations have created weekly live shows, while others have used live videos to launch new products or engage in Q&A with their fans.

CAPTURE ATTENTION EARLY, WHETHER YOU GO SHORT OR LONG

Remember the days of Vine? Organizations and influencers sought to make short, **snackable content** to capture our decreasing attention spans. And while 6-second videos are highly effective,[43] it turns out that length isn't the determining factor in whether we choose to watch a video or even how long we stay glued to the screen. The not-so-secret secret is to capture the viewer's attention in the first three seconds. According to Facebook, "65% of people who watch the first three seconds of a video will watch for at least ten seconds and 45% continue watching for thirty seconds."[44]

But even videos longer than only a few minutes are engaging viewers, too. A quick scan of the trending videos on YouTube substantiates this, with most falling in the 15- to 30-minute range, which is more akin to a TV show than a commercial.

How do you know whether to use a long or short video? Jason Bercovici, Director of Creative Strategy for Exponential, recommends understanding your objectives with the video: If you want people to click and visit your website, keep it short, but if you want people to watch, then go long, with 2 to 6 minutes being ideal.[45]

Shorter videos continue to reign in Instagram and Snapchat stories. Both platforms allow users to capture continuous video, but that video is segmented into smaller "snackable" pieces that are available for 24 hours. This **ephemeral content** reminds us that we must catch viewers' attention quickly, lest they swipe away and skip the rest of the story.

CREATE A COMPELLING STORY ARC

A story arc gives your story—and its viewers—a clear path to follow. Generally, there are two types of story arcs to consider: linear and non-linear. Videos that have a **linear story arc** follow a logical sequence or chronology (think: beginning, middle and end), while videos with **non-linear story arcs** portray the story seemingly "out of order." Facebook found that video ads using non-linear story arcs were more successful than those using linear story arcs in terms of number of views and interaction rates.[46] Though videos should challenge the viewer to piece together the story, they should still be easy to digest.[47]

You may be familiar with two simple non-linear storytelling formats: boomerang videos and looping videos. **Boomerang videos**, which originated on Instagram's Boomerang app and are integrated with Instagram stories, are bursts of photos combined into very short videos that play forward and backward.[48] **Looping videos** are videos that play and repeat multiple times, similar to GIFs.

Curated Content

Social media users can experience adventure through the GoPro lens with GoPro's "Photo of the Day" on its Instagram page. And if they want a peek inside vacation homes from the perspective of the guests, they can explore Airbnb's Instagram page.

Any time an organization reposts a fan photo, retweets a relevant article or

Ephemeral content
Images or videos that are available for a limited time and then disappear, like Instagram and Snapchat stories.

Linear story arc
Storytelling that follows a logical sequence or chronology.

Non-linear story arc
Storytelling that portrays the story seemingly out of order.

Boomerang video
Bursts of photos combined into very short videos that play forward and backward.

Looping video
Videos that play and repeat multiple times, in a loop.

Tagged photos on Instagram and other social media platforms, like these from OPI (a nail care company), are a great source for user-generated content.

How else can organizations engage with tagged content?

Successful content curation relies on identifying content that is both valuable to your audience and aligned with your organization's values.

shares a trending meme, it is curating content. **Content curation**, which is the process of gathering and sharing content from reputable sources or users, should complement an organization's original content creation. General guidelines encourage a healthy mix of created and curated content: 40 percent should be created by your organization and 60 percent should be curated from other sources.[49]

Successful content curation relies on identifying content that is both valuable to your audience and aligned with your organization's values. **User-generated content** or **UGC** is content voluntarily created by online users, and it's a prime source of curated content for brands. UGC gives public relations professionals the opportunity to tell their organizations' stories from the public's point of view, and its inherent authenticity creates trust. According to an Ipsos study, millennials trusted UGC 50 percent more than other media.[50]

Some organizations proactively ask users to share their content, creating a continuous content stream. GoPro tells users to share with #GoPro. Airbnb writes in its Instagram bio, "Share your stories with @airbnb." With permission from the user, who owns the rights to the content, organizations can repost, retweet and share with their own followers.

Building Relationships and Community

Social media are uniquely positioned to allow organizations to build relationships and community with their publics. Emerging technologies scholar Jan Kietzmann and his colleagues outlined the building blocks of social media, which included relationships and groups. The relationships between social media users determine what information they exchange and how they do so.[51] People can voice their opinions about anything and everything—from their cult favorite lipstick to serious calls for public policy and reform—with their online audiences. And others, including organizations, can participate in those conversations and take action as a result. Depending on the organization's use of social media, the two-way communication (see Chapter 2) may be mostly balanced, or symmetrical, with the organization as likely to change its attitudes or behaviors as its publics are.

Social media users can also connect with each other to form communities. Kietzmann et al. identified two types of groups: those you self-create (like Twitter lists) and those that are like real-life clubs (like Facebook groups). Organizations have also turned to social media to create their own communities. Research has found that social media–based brand communities have positive effects on the members of these communities, making them feel united and even enhancing brand loyalty.[52] Community management and influencer and brand advocate engagement are two ways public relations professionals can use social media to build relationships with individuals and connect with niche groups.

Community Management

Jay Baer, author and founder of Convince & Convert, said, "We are in an era now where customer service is a spectator sport."[53] Every time someone praises an organization or complains about a product on social media, those comments are amplified for the world to see (depending on privacy settings, of course). In the same way, organizations' responses to those comments—if they respond at all—are also watched closely. Choosing not to respond to a comment sends a message, albeit a negative one, too.

Those who reply to customer complaints, praises and questions on social media are partaking in community management. **Community management** is what happens after you hit "publish" on your social media content. It requires that you listen to the individuals in your publics on social media and engage them, often responding to customer service inquiries or participating in online groups. Whereas content creation is generally focused on a **one-to-many** approach, where organizations reach multiple people with the same message, community management is generally focused on one-to-one communication.[54] Successful community management begins with thorough social and visual listening, discussed earlier in this chapter. Beyond listening, community managers must also effectively engage their communities to build relationships and moderate their social media pages.

ENGAGING YOUR COMMUNITY

If you've ever received a response from a brand on social media, you've engaged with a community manager. Community managers are the people behind the screen, and they set the example for other members of their social media communities. They start conversations, answer questions, address complaints and thank fans, and they empower others to do the same.

But it's not an easy job, especially if an organization receives a high volume of mentions on social media. Some organizations are even using **artificial intelligence** to automate responses, while others have set up **chatbots** to answer customer questions on Facebook Messenger. If the organization has global reach, then it must employ community managers who are fluent in various languages, too. Amazon has a separate @Amazon-Help Twitter account to answer customer support questions in nine languages seven days a week.[55] A quick scan of its replies shows not only personalized responses in a multitude of languages, but also an average response time of 10 minutes or less, much faster than most customers' expectations. Eighty-three percent of people expect a response within a day,[56] which can still be challenging for smaller organizations.

Community managers can also use social media—and online groups, forums and blogs—to tap into existing fandom and connect with niche groups. Video game company SEGA recognized the power and fandom behind Sonic the Hedgehog and created a Facebook page dedicated to the character to connect with its devoted fans. The page has more than 5.5 million followers,[57] three times as many followers as SEGA's own Facebook page.[58] Fitbit took a slightly different approach, opting for Facebook groups to bring fitness

Community managers must know when and how people are talking about their organizations on social media to find opportunities to join conversations, answer questions and empower their publics.

Community management
The process of listening to, engaging and moderating online communities and those who make up those communities.

One-to-many content (1:many)
Content from one sender that is designed to reach mass audiences with the same message.

Artificial intelligence (AI)
A machine's ability to mimic human behavior and intelligence, like learning or solving problems.

Chatbots
Artificial intelligence programs designed to mimic human conversation. Chatbots receive and automatically respond to messages.

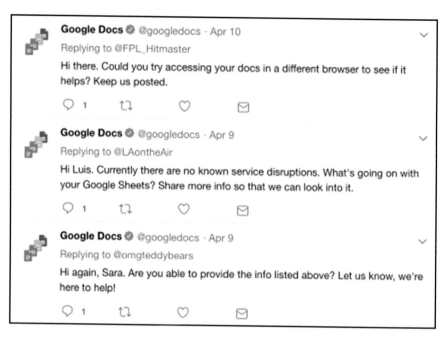

@GoogleDocs replies to tweets about customer issues and new ideas with personalized, detailed and timely responses.

Why would an organization want to personalize a response with the user's name?

enthusiasts together in their local communities. Fitbit's groups are tailored to people in U.S. cities, like Miami, San Diego and Washington, D.C., giving them an opportunity to share workout events, tips and motivation with each other.[59] These tight-knit groups, sometimes with just a few thousand followers, help organizations engage their publics in highly relevant and relatable ways.

Public relations professionals often have the responsibility of deciding what is and isn't allowed on their organizations' social media pages.

MODERATING YOUR PAGES

Imagine that someone decides to use your social media page to spew hate and racist rhetoric. Do you allow it? Public relations professionals often have the responsibility of deciding what is and isn't allowed on their organizations' social media pages. Moderation features and filters on the social media platforms allow users to hide and block specific words or users, and many organizations even outline their community guidelines on social media. But organizations must be careful what and who they choose to hide. Blocking users simply because they have posted a negative comment may raise concerns of censorship and deception.

Generally, organizations will hide spam or overly offensive comments and users who repeatedly post this kind of content. In 2019, YouTube found itself in the middle of a child exploitation scandal when YouTuber Matt Watson posted a video on how to find soft pedophilia rings. Pedophiles who were leaving inappropriate comments and timestamps on videos of children were being served even more videos of young children by YouTube's recommendation algorithm, exacerbating the crisis. In response, YouTube deleted hundreds of accounts, disabled comments on millions of videos and reported illegal comments to law enforcement.[60] This example raises the question: Whose responsibility is it to moderate offensive, fake or illegal comments or content on social media? Does that responsibility fall solely on the social media platforms or also on the individuals and organizations that use them?

Influencer and Advocate Engagement

The word "influencer" has earned a bad rap recently. **Influencers** are trusted individuals who can influence the opinions of their established social media audiences. Some organizations have had to cut ties with influencers because of controversy. Others have opted to work with trendy influencers with high follower counts, only to be "called out" by the same people they were trying to reach. And some organizations have wrongfully used influencer content without permission.

But if done right, with permissions and agreements in place, engaging influencers can help organizations build trust and relatability with their key publics. Influencers don't need millions of followers to be influential. Some of the most influential people may be the **brand advocates** or employees who champion a brand. Public relations professionals must carefully vet and select the influencers who can authentically connect with their audiences and who genuinely love the organizations they will represent.

There are different types of influencers, from high-profile celebrities to brand advocates. Here are some of the most commonly used terms to categorize influencers:

- *Celebrities:* Celebrities and the Kim Kardashians of the world have massive reach but generally low engagement. That means a whole lot of people will see the content, but few of them will do anything about it. Partnering with a celebrity is also going to cost your organization big bucks. One #sponsored Instagram photo from Kylie Jenner can cost more than $1,000,000.[61]

- *"Top-Tier" Influencers:* This is what most people think of when they hear the word *influencer*. Top-tier influencers are those social media person-

Comment Controls

Controls

Block Comments From   0 People >

Any new comments from people you block won't be visible to anyone but them.

Filters

Hide Offensive Comments

Automatically hide comments that may be offensive from your posts.

Manual Filter

Hide comments that contain specific words or phrases from your posts.

Individuals and businesses can manually block specific users or words from their Instagram pages, or they can opt to automatically hide potentially offensive comments.

What words might you want to block from appearing on your social media pages?

Carefully vet and select the influencers who can authentically connect with their audiences and who genuinely love the organizations they will represent.

Influencer
Trusted individual who can influence the opinions of established social media audiences.

Brand advocate
A person who is loyal to your brand and speaks favorably about your brand to others.

alities who've amassed large followings, usually in the hundreds of thousands or millions of followers. Video game streamer Tyler "Ninja" Blevins, whose popularity skyrocketed in 2018, is one example.

- *Opinion Elites:* Opinion elites are subject matter experts, or SMEs, and professionals who also have large, dedicated followings. Their credibility lends itself to mutually beneficial partnerships. Opinion elites may be world-renowned doctors, lawyers and thought leaders.

- *Micro-Influencers:* Micro-influencers are becoming increasingly popular because, despite their low follower counts (often in the lower thousands),

Brands like T-Mobile and Honda have partnered with Hispanic social media influencer LeJuan James to reach and connect with Hispanic consumers in the United States.

Why else might brands choose to partner with diverse influencers?

their audiences tend to be more dedicated and engaged. Working with micro-influencers can be up to seven times more effective than working with top-tier influencers.[62]

- *Brand Advocates:* Brand advocates are the everyday people who love a brand. They can be fiercely loyal customers or even employees. Southwest Airlines spotlighted these loyal customers with its "Behind Every Seat Is a Story" campaign, which featured the individual stories of 175 passengers (also the number of seats on its Boeing aircraft).[63] The result? Even *more* people shared their experiences with #175Stories on social media.

Sure, the possibility of reaching millions of followers with a message is alluring—but what if those followers don't care about the message? What if they think the influencer is "selling out" by partnering with an organization? Instead of looking solely at reach, public relations professionals must also consider how audiences engage with the influencers they follow. This is especially important because some "influencers" may have bought fake followers to boost their numbers and grow their communities quickly (see Chapter 6). A smaller but dedicated and engaged audience base is more valuable than a large audience that's disengaged. It's important to ask how the influencer or advocate aligns with the organization's values, too. Someone who hunts deer may not be the right influencer for PETA, but he or she may be the perfect fit for the Mule Deer Foundation. To maintain the trust of publics, influencers must follow Federal Trade Commission guidelines and disclose their partnerships with organizations clearly and conspicuously, using a hashtag like #ad or #sponsored at the beginning of a post or superimposed on a story.

Case Study

Millions Share Their Mickey Mouse Ears for Charity

Disney-related wishes are the number one most requested wishes by Make-A-Wish® Foundation children.[64] Since 1980, Disney and the Make-A-Wish® Foundation together have granted more than 130,000 wishes for children with critical illnesses.[65] And in 2016, Disney Parks invited its fans to join this spirit of giving with a simple social media call to action: #ShareYourEars.

The classic Mickey Mouse ears became a means for social good with three easy steps: snap, share and smile. Disney Parks around the globe asked fans to snap a photo of themselves wearing a pair of Mickey Mouse ears—or with their own creative "ears"—and share the photo with the hashtag #ShareYourEars on Facebook, Twitter or Instagram. In its first year, Disney pledged to donate $5 for each photo shared publicly, up to $1 million.

Fans were already sharing photos of their Mickey Mouse ears on social media; but the question was "how do you get fans to share with the hashtag?"

#shareyourears

Disney fans shared their photos of support for Make-A-Wish® and the #ShareYourEars campaign, encouraging others to participate.

Have you supported a cause by posting social media content with a particular hashtag?

To encourage participation, Disney used its size and scale to strategically seed the message globally across multiple channels, including but certainly not limited to social media. Disney's various social media accounts—@Disney, @WaltDisneyWorld, @DisneyParks, etc.—shared the call to action with photos of guests and celebrities sporting their Mickey Mouse ears. The brand also partnered with celebrity influencers, like Neil Patrick Harris and Gwen Stefani, to share photos donning their own Mickey Mouse ears and encouraging fans to do the same. It tapped TV and radio shows on Disney Channel, ABC and ESPN to encourage viewers and listeners to snap and share photos, too. Even reporters rocked their ears on the evening newscasts. (Disney Television Studios owns ABC Studios and ESPN, making it easier for these crossovers to happen.) In its theme parks and cruises across the globe, Disney set up #ShareYourEars photo walls and booths, prompting engagement from guests. It even created a #ShareYourEars cheeseburger. Disney's 360-degree approach accounted for the many ways consumers interact with the brand in their daily lives, both online and offline, and made sharing easy and fun.

And the response was overwhelming. In the first year alone, more than 1.77 million photos were shared on social media with #ShareYourEars in a three-week span. This was eight times more than the 200,000 photos needed to reach the initial $1 million donation, prompting Disney to double its donation that year to $2 million. Make-A-Wish® also saw an increase in audience size, jumping 15 percent and 13 percent on Facebook and Instagram, respectively.[66] The campaign has continued driving photo shares and community engagement since then.

Jon Stettner, president and CEO of Make-A-Wish® International, said, "We are so grateful to Disney, and its guests and fans worldwide, for their ongoing support. Disney's continued generosity strengthens our global organization and allows us to grant life-changing wishes in more than 50 countries." Each year, Disney grants more than 10,000 wishes.[67] #ShareYourEars has given fans the opportunity to share in the magic of these thousands of wishes, too.

Voices from the Field

Shane Santiago

SHANE SANTIAGO is president and chief experience officer at Bravely. Santiago honed his craft at various agencies—including Ogilvy Interactive and GMMB, a FleishmanHillard agency—developing interactive campaigns for a wide range of clients before founding SBS Studios in 2006. SBS Studios cultivated relationships with brands such as Marriott International, Discovery, the NBA, Disney, the Ad Council, ADCOLOR, Comcast, Axe and Sony Pictures. St. John & Partners acquired SBS Studios in 2013, and after 4 years, he started Bravely, an innovation-focused creative consultancy. Santiago served as an AD-COLOR advisory board member and was named an ADCOLOR Innovator in 2012.

Are you seeing more do-it-yourself multimedia tactics in public relations now? Why would you recommend or not recommend that public relations people produce more of their own multimedia?

I think we're seeing it more in terms of a blur of traditional public relations and social channels. As such, many tactics come across as more authentic if it feels as if it's coming straight from a brand/source/advertiser. I do recommend a general knowledge base or capability for public relations practitioners to produce their own multimedia—they're already likely great writers, so creating content today should just be an extension of that. Especially with all the access afforded to technology to produce high-quality content, it's easier/more accessible than ever.

How is the technology of multimedia and mobile media helping or hurting diversity in public relations?

Diversity is an issue regardless of technology when it comes to public relations, advertising and media. I think in terms of many communities of color, access to technology is actually not an issue that hurts diversity since those communities typically index highly with mobile and social use. It's more of access to public relations as a practice in those communities as a viable career path that is the issue. If anything, technology would better prepare diverse communities if they did have more awareness of public relations as a job option.

How is mobile media changing the way practitioners develop strategy? How is it making it easier? Harder?

It makes things more accessible. Mobile puts everything at your fingertips. Research. Participants. Social channels. The list goes on. Mobile is the cost-of-entry as a tool for job performance today and it's expected of colleagues and clients for you to be accessible by a mobile device.

What advice do you have for college students about leveraging their familiarity with digital and mobile media for public relations career success?

Embrace technology. Students are digital natives, yet just because you are active on digital/mobile/social channels doesn't make you an expert. Use it as a differentiator when job seeking. Learn to code, learn how it works, learn how/why your peers are sought on these channels and use the technology to address behavioral tendencies.

Internet of Things (IoT)—cool or creepy? What does all this connectedness mean for public relations?

IoT is typically an opt-in experience, so in my opinion, it's cool. When done right, with security and privacy kept at a premium, it can empower a relationship with technology to provide experience AND utility and does so in a way that makes it relevant to an individual. Connectedness means public relations practitioners need to understand all the various use-cases and experiences in which they can reach their publics, and that goes so much deeper today than before. Truly understanding "a day in the life" of their publics and all the relevant cross sections of experience and technology is vital to success.

Ethics: Privacy and Safeguarding Confidences

It's not just our tablets and phones on which we communicate. We also communicate more than we realize on the **Internet of Things (IoT)**. Although experts haven't yet agreed on a single definition, the basic idea of IoT is that

Internet of things (IoT)
Global network of physical objects that are connected to one another in a way that enables them to communicate with one another and the internet at large.

End-user license agreements (EULA)
Legal agreement between a software provider and the person using the software.

more and more objects in our environment are connected to each other in a way that enables them to communicate via a network, and by extension the internet at large.

"The premise behind the IoT," according to eMarketer, "is that any object, whether natural or manufactured, can gain the ability to transmit data over a network."[68] Cars with built-in GPS are on the IoT. Home security systems that can be activated remotely and that report activity are on the IoT. My running watch can transmit data about my workout over the internet, and I can share that with other users including running groups and organizations that may want to advertise running-related products and services to the group and me.

As members of publics, we often communicate without even trying. When was the last time you checked your privacy settings for location services on all your apps? Do you actually read the **end-user license agreements (EULA)** you agree to when you register for new apps? Most of us skim those EULA screens and trust that the organizations won't do anything evil with our data. From a public relations standpoint this trust may indicate a healthy relationship between the end user and the organization using the data. But it also raises the stakes for the organization we entrust.

Safeguarding confidences is a key provision in the PRSA Code of Ethics. The provision is commonly read to mean keeping client information confidential, but the larger intent also applies to publics: "To protect the privacy rights of clients, organizations, and individuals by safeguarding confidential information."[69]

Media ethicists Jay Black and Chris Roberts frame privacy issues as questions of competing values. We weigh the value of privacy with the values of information, entertainment and convenience. "The bottom line," they write, "is that while a great deal of information about millions of us is conveniently and centrally available for a multitude of uses, do we want corporations and government to know this much about us?"[70] Your answer may depend on how much you trust the organizations.

Apple Computer Inc. is as big a player as any in the global arena of mobile, multimedia, big data and the Internet of Things. That company knows more about its customers than their customers know about themselves. Think of all the data it holds from people

These apps offer a lot of information, entertainment and convenience, but they require trusting organizations with private information.

Which organizations do you trust with your private data and why?

running apps, using Apple Pay, making purchases with their Apple IDs, and working on their desktops, laptops, iPads and iPhones.

In 2016, Apple came head to head with data privacy when it received an FBI order to unlock an iPhone used by a gunman in a San Bernardino, California, mass shooting. Until that point, Apple had provided data to comply with search warrants and subpoenas. But Apple refused to unlock the phone, stating that doing so would "build a backdoor" that would weaken its safeguards. In a message to its customers, Apple CEO Tim Cook wrote, "The same engineers who built strong encryption into the iPhone to protect our users would, ironically, be ordered to weaken those protections and make our users less safe."[71]

As publics, we make decisions every day about which organizations we trust with our personal information. Organizations have to earn that trust—not just with speeches, but with everyday management. When ethical public relations is part of an organization's management function, organizations must take safeguarding confidences and protecting the privacy of their publics seriously.

In Case You Missed It

The use of mobile and social media for public relations must be driven by research and strategy. These emerging and ever-changing platforms and technology are transforming communication between organizations and their publics. Here are some takeaways from this chapter:

- In-demand communicators in public relations understand current and emerging technology but also grasp the importance of writing, strategy and global issues.

- Consider how you will reach people on mobile and social media but also how they will reach back to your organization and how they will share content with one another.

- In developing strategy for mobile media, consider asking what people are doing with mobile media instead of what mobile media will do to people.

- Social listening reveals broad trends and themes that can inform public relations strategy.

- As more people view video on mobile devices with the sound off, subtitles have become crucial for helping viewers understand what they're watching.

- Successful content curation relies on identifying content that is both valuable to your audience and aligned with your organization's values.

- Community managers must know when and how people are talking about their organizations on social media to find opportunities to join conversations, answer questions and empower their publics.

- Public relations professionals often have the responsibility of deciding what is and isn't allowed on their organizations' social media pages.

- Carefully vet and select the influencers who can authentically connect with their audiences and who genuinely love the organizations they will represent.

SUMMARY

10.1 Assess the strategic value of mobile tactics.

The evaluation of mobile tactics requires examining how well the tactics achieve objectives and goals as part of strategies to advance the organization's mission and its relationships with key publics. Mobile is ubiquitous, social, personal and local—and the most successful mobile tactics reflect these characteristics.

10.2 Discuss how publics' uses and gratifications of mobile media may help drive public relations strategy.

Major uses and gratifications of mobile media include relationships, information, diversion and amusement, and participation. Mobile media also offer excellent opportunities to obtain feedback from publics. Research should be conducted to understand publics from their perspectives.

10.3 Explain how social and visual listening can help public relations professionals better understand and communicate with their publics.

How an organization is perceived on social media goes beyond the number of followers, likes or shares. Social and visual listening allows an organization to track, analyze and respond to conversations about specific topics, such as a company or industry, online.

10.4 Evaluate how different forms of social media content can be created to engage publics.

Today, anyone with a smartphone can capture content just about anywhere that their devices will function, and mobile allows us to consume content just about anywhere, too. But not all content is created equal. Public relations professionals must understand the main forms of social media content—text, images and video—and how they can be used to capture attention, tell stories and drive action.

10.5 Describe how public relations professionals can use social media to build community.

Though social media can be used to reach large audiences, the ability to reply to comments immediately and create and join groups can help organizations create a sense of community with their key publics. Engaging with influencers and brand advocates can also help organizations establish relationships and trust with these publics.

10.6 Apply privacy as an ethical value to consider in handling data gleaned from mobile media.

In exchange for information, entertainment and convenience, mobile media users entrust organizations with tremendous amounts of private information. Safeguarding confidences and protecting privacy are key ethical values that public relations professionals and their organizations must honor, if they are going to maintain public trust.

DISCUSSION QUESTIONS

1. Select one app you've downloaded on your mobile phone. What's the organization behind the app? Think about the characteristics of mobile media: ubiquitous, social, personal and local. Does the app you selected meet these characteristics? How?

2. **CASE STUDY** Burger King's "Whopper Detour" stunt led to more than a million downloads of its BK® App. What can Burger King do to keep customers engaged and retain app users? Consider the characteristics of successful mobile tactics in describing your suggestions.

3. How have you used mobile media to communicate with an organization? What were your "uses and gratifications"? What were the organization's objectives? Why was (or wasn't) their strategy effective?

4. Imagine that you want to discover what people are saying about your college or university. What keywords might you want to listen to on social media? If you had the ability to conduct visual listening, what visuals would you monitor? Explain how you could use this information to learn more about your college, its students and faculty.

5. Think about the best paper or essay you have ever written. Now suppose you were asked to share it on social media. You couldn't share the whole essay—instead, what kinds of snackable

content might you create? Explain how you would create this content and apply the recommendations shared in this chapter.

6. Identify an organization partaking in community management on Twitter or Facebook, and compare how the organization responds to positive comments versus negative comments. Take a stab at drafting your own responses to comments, too. Is the organization effective in its one-to-one communications?

7. **CASE STUDY** Disney's #ShareYourEars campaign inspired people to create and share content to support the Make-A-Wish® Foundation. Think about a nonprofit organization you support and imagine you're the organization's public relations director. How could you use social media to rally the support of others?

8. Thinking more about your experience interacting with an organization via mobile media, what specific information do they now have about you? What makes you confident (or not confident) that they will handle it properly?

KEY TERMS

Artificial intelligence 277
Boomerang video 275
Brand advocate 279
Chatbots 277
Community management 277
Content curation 276
Creative Commons 273
End-user license agreements
   (EULA) 284
Engagement 269
Ephemeral content 275
Feed proofing 271

Freelancers 272
Geofencing 260
Geofilter 260
Geolocation 260
Influencer 279
Internet of Things (IoT) 283
Landscape orientation 274
Linear story arc 275
Looping video 275
Multimedia 268
Newsjacking 266
Non-linear story arc 275

One-to-many content 277
Public domain 272
Selective attention 257
Sentiment 265
Snackable content 274
Social listening 263
Social monitoring 264
Stock image 273
User-generated content (UGC) 276
Uses and gratifications 262
Vertical video 274
Visual listening 264

CHAPTER 11

Legal

When federal regulators took Tesla CEO Elon Musk to court over Musk's tweets, a judge told them to "put your reasonableness pants on." Why is this type of legal "reasonableness" important in public relations?

KEY LEARNING OUTCOMES

11.1 Discuss the importance of understanding national laws in international contexts.

11.2 Apply principles of free speech and the First Amendment to the practice of public relations.

11.3 Describe limits to free speech, including libel and slander as forms of defamation.

11.4 Identify common types of intellectual property and how they are protected.

11.5 Summarize the role of public relations professionals in providing public information.

11.6 Identify key federal agencies responsible for regulating communication to protect publics.

11.7 Identify legal concerns related to privacy in public relations.

11.8 Discuss the ethical balance between safeguarding organizational confidences and respecting the privacy of individual social media accounts.

RELATED UNIVERSAL ACCREDITATION BOARD COMPETENCY AREAS

2.2 ETHICAL BEHAVIOR • **2.3** FIRST AMENDMENT ISSUES • **2.4** PRIVACY ISSUES
2.5 OTHER LEGAL ISSUES • **5.3** ORGANIZATIONAL STRUCTURE AND RESOURCES

Where did you get this textbook? If you're a student at a U.S. college or university, you probably purchased it from your campus bookstore or directly from the publisher. Or perhaps you borrowed it from a library or from a friend. In any case, the price of the "first sale" book printed and sold in the United States is based on the idea that written materials can be sold by those who hold the U.S. copyright. If you are studying in Thailand and purchase a textbook at a local bookstore or from the publisher's global website, you may pay considerably less than students in the United States pay for the same text, depending on a range of global economic factors.

But what if someone buys textbooks that were printed and first sold in Thailand at a much lower cost and then ships the books to a relative in the United States or sells them online to students in the United States at a higher price? When Supap Kirtsaeng moved from Thailand to the United States to study mathematics at Cornell University, he realized the textbooks he purchased were much more expensive in the United States than the same books in Thailand. So, he asked family and friends to purchase copies in Thailand. He then sold those books in the United States at a higher rate. After reimbursing his friends and family, he kept the profit. Is that legal?

According to the U.S. Supreme Court, yes, it is legal. John Wiley & Sons, Inc., the book's publisher, sued Kirtsaeng, but Supreme Court Justice Stephen Breyer wrote in *Kirtsaeng v. John Wiley & Sons, Inc.* that "the 'first sale' doctrine applies to copies of a copyrighted work lawfully made abroad."[1] The first sale doctrine holds that if you purchase a copy of a work from a copyright holder, you can do what you want with your copy, including selling it to someone else.[2]

As Justice Breyer observed in his 2015 book *The Court and the World: American Law and the New Global Realities*, the Kirtsaeng case indicates a new reality that has implications for public relations. "At a moment when ordinary citizens may engage in direct transactions internationally for services available only locally before," Breyer wrote, "it has become clear that, even in ordinary matters, judicial awareness can no longer stop at the border."[3]

International Legal Contexts

At the heart of *Kirtsaeng* is the idea of **intellectual property**—who *owns* the ideas in books, websites, videos, poems, blogs, photos, graphics, software and so on. Intellectual property is any product of the human mind that is protected by law from unauthorized use by others. Also central to the case is the question of the reach of U.S. laws in determining how this property is bought, sold, copied and shared across borders. The Wiley textbooks were hard copies of printed materials, but think of the implications for everyday public relations when all it takes for international distribution is a couple of keystrokes to copy and paste and the tap of an icon to upload digital property for global distribution.

Intellectual property
Any product of the human mind that is protected by law from unauthorized use by others.

Privacy
The right to be let alone; or, the right to control access to your personal information.

Like intellectual property, personal information also can be shared easily across borders, and that means **privacy** is another legal concept that must be considered as an international concern. In 1890, Samuel Warren and Louis Brandeis (before Brandeis became a Supreme Court Justice) famously defined privacy as "the right to be let alone,"[4] but in the context of data protection, privacy also can be defined as someone's right to control access to and use of their personal information.

As discussed in Chapter 3, the General Data Protection Regulation (GDPR), a European Union regulation to protect individuals' privacy, immediately became an issue of global impact beyond Europe when it went into effect in 2018. Organizations like Facebook, Google and the vast majority of international online service providers found it impossible to comply with GDPR regulations in Europe without changing policies for users in other parts of the world because they exchange users' personally identifiable information across borders all the time. Any enterprise with a significant number of users, employees or even computers processing data in Europe, regardless of where their headquarters are located, is required to comply with the regulations.

Intellectual property and privacy are just two of many legal concepts that communications professionals run across in day-to-day public relations. Those working in public relations also need "judicial awareness"—as Justice Breyer put it—to determine what's legal. For instance, consider the following:

It's easier than ever to buy, sell, reproduce and share intellectual property across international borders.

Why would public relations professionals be concerned with laws related to intellectual property?

- *Defamation:* Can you sue when someone from another country tweets something mean and nasty about you or someone else in your organization?

- *Sunshine laws:* If you work for the government, do you have to share the results of that survey you ran with anyone who asks?

- *Business regulations:* Can you tell your buddies that the value of your company stock options is about to double?

- *Appropriation:* Can you use that picture of Priyanka Chopra on your Facebook event page?

These questions provide just a small sample. While you will not become a legal expert as a result of reading this chapter, you will gain an awareness of some common legal issues that apply to your work in public relations. Many legal issues are based on laws written by local, state and federal governments and interpreted in court cases. Others are regulations enforced by federal agencies. If you work in public relations, you may even play a role in communicating legal information, such as when you write social media policies or handle media inquiries related to your organization's legal disputes. Even though this chapter focuses largely on law and policy in the United States, this awareness must extend across international borders.

The First Amendment

Congress shall make no law respecting an establishment of religion, or prohibiting the free exercise thereof; or abridging the freedom of speech, or of the press; or the right of the people peaceably to assemble, and to petition the Government for a redress of grievances.

Clear and present danger
Circumstance that may limit rights to free speech in the interest of preventing "substantive evils."

At its core, the practice of public relations in democratic societies is a communication function, dependent on free speech. Sometimes that speech is primarily political, as when practitioners engage publics about ideas, policy and laws that involve their organizations (e.g., public affairs, political campaigning). Other times that speech is primarily commercial, as when practitioners communicate strategically in support of their organizations' financial goals (e.g., integrated marketing communication, investor relations). Over the years, U.S. courts have ruled that the Constitution protects political speech more than commercial speech. For example, courts are more likely to uphold laws and regulations that prohibit false advertising for products and services than laws that restrict political campaigning.

As introduced in Chapter 2, the PRSA Code of Ethics identifies advocacy as one of its core values: "We serve the public interest by acting as responsible advocates for those we represent. We provide a voice in the marketplace of ideas, facts, and viewpoints to aid informed public debate."[5] The First Amendment generally guarantees the right to exercise such advocacy, but the right to free speech has its limits.

In a classic 1919 Supreme Court opinion, Justice Oliver Wendell Holmes wrote that you cannot falsely yell "Fire!" in a crowded theater and cause a panic. Some circumstances present enough of a possibility of harmful outcomes that they justify limits on First Amendment freedoms—this is sometimes called the **clear and present danger** doctrine. Let's hope you never find yourself in a situation in which your work in public relations puts you at risk of causing such danger, but you may well face situations in which you need legal counsel to understand your rights (and the limits on those rights) as a professional communicator. Working with the press and communicating on behalf of an organization requires understanding your role in the marketplace for ideas that the First Amendment serves to protect.

The First Amendment protects free speech, but courts have ruled that some forms of speech are more protected than others.

Which of these signs gets the least legal protection and why?

Case Study

Amazon v. NYT: A Case in the Court of Public Opinion

If you've ever shopped online for a book or movie or even a selfie stick or Halloween costume, you're probably well aware that Amazon is one of the world's largest marketplaces for physical goods and digital products. Its founder, Jeff Bezos, has been widely heralded as an entrepreneur extraordinaire and a visionary in marketplace innovation. The company has redefined how people buy, sell and recommend books. It has even changed how people *read* books (think Kindle).

Along with its enormity in the world's marketplace of physical and digital products, Amazon also has grown into a formidable voice in the marketplace of ideas. As such, the company invested heavily in its public relations firepower when it hired former White House press secretary Jay Carney as senior vice president for corporate affairs.

Less than six months after Carney's hire, David Streitfeld and Jodi Kantor published a lengthy *New York Times* article calling Amazon a "bruising workplace," based on dozens of anecdotes about the harsh working conditions. One of the most damning stories was a vivid vignette from an interview with former Amazon employee Bo Olson. "You walk out of a conference room and you'll see a grown man covering his face," Olson was quoted. "Nearly every person I worked with, I saw cry at their desk."[6] Several other former employees relayed tales of hostile peer evaluation systems, 85-hour workweeks and pressure to work through holidays and vacations.

At this point in the case, we can already see the First Amendment in action. As journalists, Kantor and Streitfeld exercised their right to free speech, as did many of the sources cited in their article. Though the story would certainly offend Amazon management, expose some of its executives to public criticism and possibly even hurt its recruiting and profits, the article was protected speech under the Constitution's First Amendment.

Of course, Amazon and Carney also have the right to respond. And respond they did. In a roughly 1,300-word retort posted on his page (https://medium.com/@jaycarney/) on the self-publishing platform Medium.com titled "What *The New York Times* Didn't Tell You," Carney disputed many of the claims.[7] Carney wrote that Olson's "brief tenure at Amazon ended after an investigation revealed he had attempted to defraud vendors and conceal it by falsifying business records" and that Olson had admitted this and resigned immediately after being confronted with the evidence.

Again, we see the First Amendment in action in that Carney is allowed to publish his opinions and advocate strongly on behalf of his employer.

Obtain permission (or seek legal counsel) before publicly discussing private information about any current or past employee.

The New York Times Executive Editor Dean Baquet speaks at the National First Amendment Conference in Pittsburgh in 2018.

Why would high-power communicators like Baquet and Amazon spokesman Jay Carney take to a self-publishing platform like Medium to air their differences?

Another First Amendment question emerges—what gives Carney the right to discuss the terms of a former employee's resignation? It seems likely that Carney would have cleared his Medium piece with Amazon's legal department before publishing, and this illustrates the importance of public relations people working well with attorneys.

Amazon's response was designed as much to make a case in the court of public opinion as in the court of law. As Krishnadev Calamur wrote in *The Atlantic*, Amazon's pushback "illustrates the level to which Amazon is trying to correct the narrative that depicted Amazon as a brutal place to work."[8]

The battle in the court of public opinion raged on. Later in the very same day that Carney published his piece on Medium, *New York Times* Executive Editor Dean Baquet responded with his own Medium piece defending the accuracy of the journalism. Carney responded again, criticizing the journalists' fact checking. It may never end.

Who wins in this battle? You do, concluded *Fortune*'s Matthew Ingram. He wrote that both sides in the Amazon-NYT case are guilty of some degree of spin, "but at least we can see it happening and judge for ourselves whom to believe."[9] That's what the marketplace of ideas is, and always has been, all about. Social media and platforms for self-publishing like Medium help the process. It's remarkable that some of the most privileged voices in the world are now using platforms like Medium to exercise their free speech. You can too.

Defamation
False communication that injures someone's reputation.

Slander
Oral communication that is false and injures someone's reputation.

Libel
Written or otherwise recorded false communication that injures someone's reputation.

Limitations on free speech kick in when your right to free speech infringes on others' rights. In public relations, you may run into situations in which your right to free speech infringes on someone else's reputation, intellectual property, financial interests or privacy.

Defamation

One of the ways that someone can hit the legal limits for free speech is to infringe on someone else's reputation. **Defamation** is a statement that injures someone's reputation. Slander and libel are both forms of defamation. **Slander** refers to spoken communication, while **libel** refers to written or recorded communication that can be reproduced and shared repeatedly. This means that Facebook posts, Instagram posts, and tweets are subject to libel laws. In fact, there's even an informal term for Twitter libel.

The word "twibel" rose in public consciousness after fashion designer Dawn Simorangkir sued punk rocker and actress Courtney Love Cobain for libelous Twitter statements. Following a dispute over payments for wardrobe items, and according to the libel complaint filed by Simorangkir, Love Cobain tweeted to her tens of thousands of followers that Simorangkir was a "nasty lying hosebag thief," and that police should "haul her desperate cokes [*sic*] out ass to jail" because "she has a history of dealing cocaine, lost all custody of her child, assault and burglary."[10] The parties later settled out of court for $430,000. Had Love Cobain spoken these statements in person instead of tweeting them, the defamation case would have been one of slander instead of libel.

Before you sue the first person who writes something mean and nasty about you or about someone else in your organization, however, keep in mind that courts are rather strict on what counts as defamation.[11]

1. *The statement must actually be false and hurt someone's reputation.* Truth is a fantastic defense in libel cases. And even false statements have to do more than just hurt someone's feelings. They have to actually cause damage to the person's reputation in a way that can be proven.

2. *The statement must be published or spoken to at least one other person besides the person who is the subject of the statement.* Other people must also be able to identify the subject of the statement. For example, a private text probably would not count, but a tweet mentioning someone's recognized Twitter handle would.

3. *The false statement has to be factual.* Name-calling and hyperbole can't really be proven true or false and, therefore, cannot be the basis of a defamation suit.

4. *The statement must be made with fault.* This concept of fault means that the defendant was either careless and negligent in making the statement or the defendant actually knew the statement was false and hurtful and made it anyway. If the subject (plaintiff) is just a

private citizen in the context of the case, he or she would need to show only that the defendant was negligent and acted carelessly. If the plaintiff is a public figure, he or she has to prove that the defendant knowingly made a false statement.

The fourth point is an important one for this book because public relations people often represent **public figures** in their work. Public figures may include celebrities, politicians and business leaders. Although the exact definition of who counts as a public figure depends on the legal context and decisions of courts, the general idea is summarized well in the landmark Supreme Court case of *Gertz v. Robert Welch, Inc.* in 1973. The Court held the following:

Courtney Love Cobain became the first celebrity sued for defamation on Twitter ("twibel") in 2009. In this photo, she arrives at court for an unrelated case.

Why do you think she settled out of court in the twibel case?

> Because private individuals characteristically have less effective opportunities for rebuttal than do public officials and public figures, they are more vulnerable to injury from defamation. Because they have not voluntarily exposed themselves to increased risk of injury from defamatory falsehoods, they are also more deserving of recovery. The state interest in compensating injury to the reputation of private individuals is therefore greater than for public officials and public figures.

Basically, if you work for a politician, a celebrity, a CEO or any other famous person, you may have to deal with quite a bit more flak before you can sue for libel than you would if you were representing a private citizen.[12] The courts have said that public figures just have to deal with libelous comments unless they can prove **actual malice**. According to the Supreme Court in *New York Times Co. v. Sullivan*, another landmark First Amendment case, actual malice means "that the statement was made with knowledge of its falsity or with reckless disregard of whether it was true or false."[13] If you work for a public figure, the standard for claiming libel is much higher than if you represent a private citizen.

If you work for a public figure, the standard for claiming libel is much higher than if you represent a private citizen.

Intellectual Property

When you communicate on behalf of an organization, you often must ask who owns the information being exchanged and whether you, or someone else, have the rights to the words, images, music or multimedia being exchanged. As discussed in Chapter 10 on social media and mobile, digital

Public figure
Someone "of general fame or notoriety in the community" who is subject to less protection in libel cases than a private individual.

Actual malice
When a defamatory statement is made with knowledge of its falsity and reckless disregard for the truth.

> *When you share someone else's intellectual property without permission or proper attribution, you run the risk of legal trouble.*

convergence has made it much easier to acquire, mix, mash, share and re-share content online. In many cases, re-pinning on Pinterest, sharing posts on Facebook or retweeting on Twitter are great ways to build social capital. Often, the people who created the content might even be excited that you are helping them go viral and obtain more exposure. But not always. When you share someone else's intellectual property without permission or proper attribution, you run the risk of legal trouble.

Copyright, Trademarks and Patents

Three major types of intellectual property that can be claimed are copyright, trademarks and patents. **Copyright** is a claim to authorship of an original work, including the rights to reproduce, distribute, perform, display or license the work. These "works" include literature, music, drama, choreography, pictures, graphics, sculptures, music and even architecture. Copyrighted works are often indicated with the symbol ©, but the symbol is not necessarily required for the owner to claim copyright.

Trademarks are any words, names, phrases, symbols or designs used to distinguish a product or service from others in the competitive marketplace. Registered trademarks are indicated with the symbol ®.

Patents cover inventions. With patents, the United States grants patent holders "the exclusive right to exclude others from making, using, importing, and selling the patented innovation for a limited period of time."[14]

The U.S. Patent and Trademark Office (USPTO) authorizes both trademarks and patents. Trademarks and patents are particularly important to startups as they are used to develop organizational identity (e.g., trademarking logos) and to innovate with new products and services (e.g., patenting inventions).

Plagiarism

As a student, you've learned the importance of proper attribution. If you present someone else's specific ideas or words as your own, that's **plagiarism**. Digital media have made it much easier to "borrow" someone else's words, but that same technology makes it easier to identify plagiarism. Just put quotes around a sentence or excerpt of text and run a web search for that quoted material, and if the words have been plagiarized, there's a good chance you'll uncover an earlier source. Services like Turnitin, which boasts the ability to search more than 67 billion web pages, 929 million student papers and 178 million academic articles, offer automatic checking for possible plagiarism.[15] However, building on the contributions of others is essential to good scholarship. The key to avoiding plagiarism, then, is proper attribution. When words or specific ideas are not your own, you must let your instructors and anyone else reading your work know where those words and ideas come from. Give credit where credit is due!

Plagiarism is an issue outside of the classroom too. When an executive or organizational leader uses someone else's words without attribution in public communication, plagiarism can become a public relations problem.

Copyright
Claim to intellectual property rights of an original work of authorship including rights to reproduce, distribute, perform, display, license and so on.

Trademark
Word, name, phrase, symbol or design used to distinguish a product or service from others in the competitive marketplace.

Patent
Claim to intellectual property rights of an invention.

Plagiarism
Presenting someone else's words or ideas as one's own.

You may have read about high-profile politicians or commencement speakers who have been called out for lifting major parts of their speeches from other sources without attribution. When this happens, an opportunity for public honor turns into a case of public shame.

Easy sharing and reposting of others' ideas, words, images and works of art are essential parts of what makes social media work, but that spirit of sharing and free-flowing information doesn't excuse plagiarism. Skye Grove, a rising "celebrity Instagrammer" in South Africa who had reached more than 40,000 followers on her Instagram account, was featured on national TV and successfully began selling her photography online. That all came to a stop when another Instagram user contacted the internationally popular technology news website Memeburn to report suspicions that Grove had plagiarized many of her images, including some that she sold.[16] Memeburn investigated and found evidence of several suspected instances of plagiarism.

This photo by Stephen Ball was downloaded from Flickr and published here with the express written consent of its owner.

Do you like it when people repost your content on social media? When is it OK, and when would you consider it to be plagiarism?

A week later, Grove's Instagram and Twitter accounts had disappeared, although it is unclear whether she deleted them voluntarily or whether they were removed for violating terms of service. Grove also was suspended without pay from her job as a communication manager for the NGO Cape Town Partnership.[17] Before deleting her Instagram account, Grove explained:

> *For a long time I didn't believe my work was good enough. I wanted to impress people with my photography but didn't believe I was good enough. So, from time to time, I posted photos that didn't belong to me but that I claimed as my own. The more I honed my skill, the more I became compelled to be true to myself. ...[18]*

In an email to Memeburn, Cape Town Partnership CEO Bulelwa Makalima-Ngewana explained that she had no reason to believe that Grove's mistakes were made as part of her official duties at the organization, but she also noted, "Personal and professional reputations are intertwined in the current social media climate."[19] With that hard lesson learned, Grove returned to both social media and her job later in the same year.

While attribution of words or ideas to a specific source is often enough to avoid plagiarizing, plagiarism is different from **copyright infringement**. If you want to include the full lyrics to a Maya Angelou poem on your for-profit Etsy page, use a Jack Johnson song as the soundtrack to a surf video you will distribute via paid downloads, or take an image from ESPN.com to put on T-shirts to sell at homecoming, attribution is not enough. Even if you make that

The key to avoiding plagiarism is proper attribution. Give credit where credit is due!

Copyright infringement
Use of protected works without proper permission from the copyright holder.

attribution clear on the web page or video or T-shirt, you need permission to use the copyrighted material, because that material is someone else's intellectual property. Profiting from someone else's work or taking it out of context without permission can be treated as a form of stealing. You can get in trouble for copyright infringement even if you've cleared yourself of plagiarism.

Fair Use

If you're essentially selling someone else's property for a profit, chances are they are going to want a cut. But, you may ask, doesn't the First Amendment protect our free speech? And what if we're not trying to make a profit? How can we participate in the marketplace of ideas if the only way to work with someone else's ideas is to obtain their permission and pay for the right? The concept of **fair use** helps answer some of these questions. According to the U.S. Copyright Office, the following four factors are often taken into consideration in determining whether use of copyrighted material without permission qualifies as fair use:[20]

1. *The purpose and character of the use.* Is it transformative? Have you transformed the original work in some way to give it new meaning? Or have you added something to the work that serves the public interest? Parody, exaggerating or humorously imitating the work or style of another may be considered fair use. In a way, ridiculing a work actually makes it more likely to be considered fair use. Using material with significant commentary or criticism for the purposes of education or research also may qualify as fair use.

2. *The nature of the copyrighted work.* Published works and works that primarily consist of factual material are more likely to qualify for fair use. Repeating facts and spreading knowledge serves a public benefit. But to encourage original imaginative and creative works, courts are more protective of original creative expression—for example, a screenplay or a song would be more protected than a news item in a financial report or traffic update.

3. *The amount and substantiality of the portion taken in relation to the copyrighted work as a whole.* Quoting a few lines from a 500-page book or sampling a few notes from a symphony might be more likely to be seen as fair use than quoting four lines from a six-line poem or playing the entire chorus from a pop song.

4. *Effect of the use upon the potential market for or value of the copyrighted work.* According to the copyright office, courts "consider whether the use is hurting the current market for the original work (for example, by displacing sales of the original) and/or whether the use could cause substantial harm if it were to become widespread."

The 2nd U.S. Circuit Court of Appeals applied this four-part test to decide whether a media monitoring company called TVEyes could claim that their service, which allowed subscribers to view, download and share segments from TV news shows, was protected by fair use.

Recall from Chapter 8 that media monitoring services assist public relations practitioners in the collection and reporting of media data for evaluation. For a $500 monthly fee, TVEyes recorded and tracked the content of more than 1,400 radio and TV channels, allowing subscribers to search for, download, archive and share segments of up to ten minutes in length. Besides tracking media material related to their own clients and organizations, many news and political organizations also use media monitoring services to track and criticize competitors. Many political operatives, for example, used TVEyes to search Fox News for clips they found to be disparaging and then replayed or reposted these videos. Not surprisingly, Fox didn't like competitors using their own material against them. But Fox also held that TVEyes was illegally exploiting their content for profit, and Fox sued TVEyes for copyright infringement.

In ruling on the case, the court went through the four-part test:

1. On the first factor (purpose and character of the use), the court favored TVEyes "slightly" because judges found the service "somewhat transformative" in that users could search for clips and view them in different times, places and contexts.

2. The court said the second part (nature of the copyrighted work) was not a significant factor in this case.

3. On the third factor (amount and substantiality of the portion used), the court found that TVEyes provided whole news segments

Fox sued a media monitoring company for copyright infringement and won.

Why did the company not pass the "fair use" test?

that included "virtually the entirety of the Fox programming that TVEyes users want to see and hear" and "therefore both extensive and inclusive of all that is important to the copyrighted work."

4. Finally, on the fourth part (effect of use on potential market), the court said that when TVEyes charged users for the service without payment to Fox, they were depriving Fox of revenues.

After weighing all of the factors, the court ruled that TVEyes' service did not constitute fair use.[21] TVEyes still offers its media monitoring services, but the court ruled against the part of their business model that allowed subscribers to repost entire news segments.

Sports leagues are notoriously zealous about protecting copyrights. If you watch sports on TV often, you are probably quite familiar with the disclaimers. For baseball, it's "Any rebroadcast, retransmission, or account of this game, without the express written consent of Major League Baseball, is prohibited." For football, it's "This telecast is copyrighted by the NFL for the private use of our audience. Any other use of this telecast or of any pictures, descriptions, or accounts of the game without the NFL's consent, is prohibited."

Therefore, when sports websites Deadspin and SBNation used Twitter accounts (@Deadspin and @SBNationGIF) to post short GIF clips of key plays in NFL games, the NFL did not see that as fair use. Rather than trying to take Deadspin and SBNation to court, however, the NFL and other sports organizations like the Ultimate Fighting Championship (UFC) went straight to Twitter with a takedown notice. They demanded that Twitter "immediately disable access to the individual who has uploaded the copyright infringing content" and to "terminate any and all accounts this individual has through you."[22] The UFC further demanded that Twitter take down the two accounts within 10 minutes of receiving the email!

We can't be sure how the courts would have ruled on the posting of animated GIFs of sporting plays on Twitter, because Twitter complied with the takedown notice. While both @Deadspin and @SBNationGIF went back online within a few days, and they both continue to post GIFs, they clearly had to work out legal issues with both Twitter and the original copyright holders to continue the practice. Publishing content is an important part of public relations. So is maintaining relationships with

SBNation posts animated GIFs of NFL games and other sporting events on its Twitter account.

What fair-use questions come into play here? Bonus question: How many trademarks can you identify in this picture?

other content providers. This case illustrates how legal issues may come into play in both functions.

Intellectual Property Issues

The @Deadspin and @SBNationGIF case raises another interesting point about intellectual property in the digital age. In addition to the NFL's and UFC's claims to original copyright on one side and arguments that could be made for fair use on the other side, we must also consider the role of Twitter and other social media platforms. Now—as you're thinking about legal issues—may be a good time to review the terms of service for your Instagram, Facebook, and Snapchat accounts. Take Twitter, for example. Here's what you've agreed to if you have a Twitter account:

- By tweeting anything at all to your account, you grant Twitter "a worldwide, non-exclusive, royalty-free license (with the right to sublicense) to use, copy, reproduce, process, adapt, modify, publish, transmit, display and distribute such Content in any and all media or distribution methods (now known or later developed)."

- At the same time, everything tweeted "is the sole responsibility of the person who originated such Content."[23]

So, basically you need to assume that anything you post on Twitter can be used against you or your organization if something goes wrong, but that

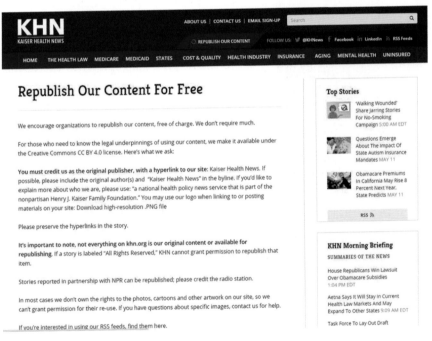

Kaiser Health News, "a national health policy news service that is part of the nonpartisan Henry J. Kaiser Family Foundation," encourages other organizations to republish its content.

How does the organization benefit from the Creative Commons license?

Balance participation with respect for intellectual property; use caution when posting anything that may be seen as offensive or illegal.

Twitter also has all the rights to anything you post when things are going well. In an age of participatory media, user-generated content and global memes, we have to balance enthusiastic participation in a culture of sharing with respect for intellectual property. Use caution when posting anything that may be seen as offensive or illegal.

CREATIVE COMMONS

Sometimes intellectual property holders want to put their content out there for everyone to use, share, mash up and redistribute. Other times they want to claim their content and protect it like a financial asset. In public relations, you (or your organization) may face these issues as the owner of intellectual property in some cases and as the party who wants to use someone else's intellectual property in other cases. The nonprofit organization **Creative Commons** serves to assist both sides.

Creative Commons offers free legal tools at http://creativecommons.org/that make it easy for content creators (i.e., licensors) to designate the permissions that they want to allow. For example, by answering a series of questions, a licensor may determine that he would like to offer an "Attribution-NonCommercial-ShareAlike" license. This license gives others permission to share and adapt the work, as long as they give appropriate credit (attribution), don't use the material to make money (noncommercial), and distribute any remix or transformation of the original with the same license as the original (ShareAlike). Once the licensor has agreed to the terms, the Creative Commons tool generates a nifty little graphic and link, which will clearly indicate the permissions that the licensor can use to post on a web page.

Kaiser Health News, a national health policy news service that is part of the nonpartisan Henry J. Kaiser Family Foundation, invites other organizations to republish their content for free. "We don't ask much," the site says about sharing its content. For attribution they only require that re-publishers include the Kaiser Health News reporter's byline, preserve hyperlinks, and maintain the tagline at the bottom of the story (e.g., " Kaiser Health News is a nonprofit news service covering health issues. It is an editorially independent program of the Kaiser Family Foundation, which is not affiliated

Boing Boing editor, blogger, journalist and science fiction writer Cory Doctorow was an early adopter of Creative Commons licenses.

What kinds of permissions are indicated in this photo? How do they benefit him as an author and benefit those who want to share his work as fans?

with Kaiser Permanente").[24] Otherwise, they make all their content available under a Creative Commons license.

LINKING

Hyperlinks are what originally distinguished the web from other media. A link makes a connection to other content. While that other content may be copyrighted, linking to content is generally not considered copyright infringement. That said, some organizations have tried out policies requiring users to obtain permission before posting **deep links**, which are links that bypass an organization's home page and take users directly to otherwise copyrighted material. In 2002, National Public Radio (NPR) tried to make users obtain permission to link to stories with a policy stating, "Linking to or framing of any material on this site without the prior written consent of NPR is prohibited." It did not go over well. Author and *Boing Boing* editor Cory Doctorow called the policy "brutally stupid" in that an organization dedicated to public discourse would obstruct users from accessing content that would otherwise be freely available.[25]

Framing refers to clickable material in a link that is actual content from the site to which it links. For example, when a web page includes a clickable photo, graphic, or chunk of text from another page, this is considered framing. At least one court has found framing to be copyright infringement when the "framed link duplicates or recasts" material from the original page.[26]

REPOSTING

Linking and framing issues are *so* Web 1.0. At least back then, in order to publish a link or frame, a user would have to consult the original source, copy the URL, and paste it as a hyperlink. Now all we have to do is click a button or two to retweet, re-blog, re-pin, or otherwise rebroadcast someone else's work. Along with technologies that facilitate commenting and conversation, the easy creation, sharing and re-sharing of information on social media are hallmarks of Web 2.0 communication. But this easy sharing and re-sharing leads to questions about who owns what content and who is responsible for inappropriate or unauthorized content.

If you post original content on Twitter, Pinterest or Facebook, you can't really be too upset if someone else shares that material. The facility for sharing is part of the deal of social media, and the rules are laid out in the terms of service you agree to when you sign up for an account. On the other hand, if you are challenged for reposting someone else's intellectual property without permission, don't count on getting much help from your social media service provider in your defense. The same idea applies if you were to repost libelous or obscene material. Remember, the terms of service are primarily written to protect the service provider. Practice common sense and conservative decision-making about attribution and permission on social media. If for some reason you think you need to push the limits, first check the terms of service you've agreed to. If you are still uncertain, consult a legal expert.

When in doubt about your ownership rights of social media content, check the provider's terms of service.

Hyperlink
A piece of text or an image online that can be clicked on to reach another resource online.

Deep link
Hyperlink that bypasses an organization's home page and takes users directly to resources deeper in an organization's website structure.

Framing
When clickable material in a link is actual content from the site to which it links.

Public Information and the Freedom of Information Act

Intellectual property laws apply to information and ideas that can be claimed as privately owned by people and organizations. However, some works have entered the public domain, meaning that copyrights have expired, been forfeited by the owner, or otherwise do not apply. If you work in public relations for a publicly funded or government organization, you may find that laws that determine what you *must* communicate are much more a part of your day-to-day work than laws about what kinds of information you can claim and protect. Although there are some exceptions, most information that the government collects and uses in the United States is treated as public information.

The **Freedom of Information Act (FOIA)** is a U.S. federal law that went into effect in 1967 to ensure that the government makes its information accessible to citizens. With a few exceptions (nine categories to be exact—ranging from national defense secrets to personnel records to information about oil and gas wells), FOIA requires government agencies to make information public. According to the U.S. Department of Justice, more than 100 agencies are subject to FOIA, and several hundred offices are tasked with responding to requests for government information. Beyond just responding to requests as they come in, government agencies are also expected (and in some cases required) to proactively make government information available in a useful form. Many of these agencies are working to develop and improve online interfaces for delivering and presenting data for public consumption. For example, www.usaspending.gov enables users to enter custom information to generate a report and graph illustrating how government money is spent.

States also have specific freedom of information laws, called **sunshine laws**, that stipulate which documents and

USAspending.gov | Data Lab
An official website of the U.S. government

USASPENDING.gov

Spending Explorer

Explore the spending landscape.

The Spending Explorer makes it easy to understand the big picture of federal spending.

Learn More

This user-friendly website allows anyone to track various types of government spending.

Why does the U.S. government invest in making this information available?

records must be open to the public and also which meetings and events must be open. These state laws echo the sentiment of Supreme Court Justice Louis Brandeis, who wrote in a 1913 *Harpers Weekly* article that government in the open serves well the public interest: "Publicity is justly commended as a remedy for social and industrial diseases. Sunlight is said to be the best of disinfectants; electric light the most efficient policeman."[27]

Protecting Publics

In addition to information that must be made available to citizens in the marketplace of ideas in democratic societies, laws and regulations also stipulate which information should be made available to consumers in the marketplace for goods and services. Depending on the area of public relations that you work in, you will need to become familiar with various government agencies that are responsible for protecting your key publics. Do you work with food and drug consumers? There's an agency for that: the Food and Drug Administration (FDA). Does your organization advertise and promote consumer goods and services in the United States? If so, you'll need to know the Federal Trade Commission (FTC). Do you work with stockholders and financial publics? There's an agency for that too: the Securities and Exchange Commission (SEC). In fact, hundreds of government agencies enforce regulations related to all sorts of organizations and their public relations efforts.

Safety and Accuracy

You've no doubt seen drug ads featuring peaceful landscapes or serene elderly couples happily arranging flowers or riding bicycles under blue skies with laughing grandkids. Have you noticed that the voiceover in those ads often shifts—almost imperceptibly—from the benefits of the drug to an unsettling list of disclaimers that tell you about possible side effects like dizziness, dry mouth, frequent urination, diarrhea, hallucinations, coma or even death?[28] That's because pharmaceutical advertising in the United States is regulated by the **Food and Drug Administration (FDA)**. The FDA requires that product claim advertisements include the following:[29]

- The name of the drug (brand and generic)

- At least one FDA-approved use for the drug

- The most significant risks of the drug

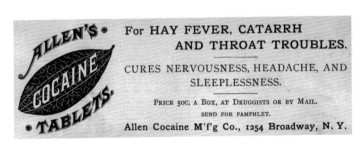

The pharmaceutical industry is regulated quite a bit more these days than it used to be.

How do regulatory agencies try to protect publics when it comes to advertising and marketing?

That said, the FDA's regulatory authority extends well beyond drug ads. At www.fda.gov, the agency includes information for a range of organizations and publics including consumers, patients, health professionals, scientists, researchers and industry. In addition to food and drugs, the agency regulates the business of (and communication related to) medical products, animal and veterinary products, cosmetics and tobacco products. If you work in public relations in any organization that deals with these types of products and services, you'll definitely need to become familiar with the FDA. The FDA's regulations are likely to affect how your organization communicates with its publics.

Of course, food and drug companies are not the only organizations regulated by government. The **Federal Trade Commission (FTC)** serves a mission to protect consumers of all types of products and services and "to enhance informed consumer choice and public understanding of the competitive process."[30] The FTC acts as a watchdog over truth in advertising and promotion. If you promote your products or services as environmentally friendly, make health claims or state that your products are "made in the USA," the FTC requires that you can back up those claims with evidence. The FTC is also concerned with how products and services are marketed to children, any type of online advertising and marketing, and the practice of telemarketing. In fact, the agency runs the National Do Not Call Registry for telemarketers. Unfortunately—if your inbox looks anything like mine—they haven't had tremendous success fighting the growth of email spam.

Financial Information

As discussed in Chapter 4, investor relations (maintaining relationships and communicating with financial publics such as current stockholders, potential investors and financial analysts) is an important sector of public relations. The **Securities and Exchange Commission (SEC)** regulates communication activities with investors, including **initial public offerings (IPOs)**. IPOs are highly choreographed financial events in which private companies first offer sale of stocks to public investors. As they would in any new corporate initiative or offering, public relations people play a role in the successful launch of IPOs. For example, before Fitbit, the company that makes fitness tracking bracelets, went public, it hired two major public relations agencies, FleishmanHillard and Burson-Marsteller, to help it gear up to sell more than 22 million shares of stock.[31] By the end of Fitbit's opening day of trading on Wall Street, shares were up to $29.68, and the company was valued at $4.1 billion.[32]

The SEC also regulates financial reports. As professional communicators, public relations professionals often write, edit and present annual reports and other financial documents (see Chapter 9). The stakes for accuracy in these required reports are extremely high, and enthusiasm and optimism must be carefully balanced with attention to accuracy.

Federal Trade Commission (FTC)
U.S. federal agency responsible for regulating all types of consumer products and services, including the promotion of these products and services.

Securities and Exchange Commission (SEC)
U.S. federal agency responsible for regulating financial activities and investing.

Initial public offering (IPO)
Financial event in which a private company offers sale of stocks to public investors for the first time.

Case Study

Tesla CEO and Federal Regulators Get into a Tiff over Free Speech

"Am considering taking Tesla private at $420. Funding secured."[33] This August 7, 2018, tweet by Tesla CEO Elon Musk sparked a legal battle over the billionaire's right to free speech. At first reading, this tweet may sound harmless enough, and it certainly doesn't seem to present a clear and present danger like yelling "Fire!" in a crowded theater. But according to the SEC, the first problem with the tweet is that it wasn't true. The SEC held that Musk hadn't actually secured funding to take the company private. When a company goes private, it means that company executives or another company buys stocks from shareholders, and the company's stock is no longer traded on stock exchanges like NASDAQ or the New York Stock Exchange.

The SEC's second big problem with Musk's tweet was that he misled investors. Tesla stock was trading at $341.99 per share before the tweet, and later that same day it went as high as $379.57.[34] In less than three hours the company's total market value soared more than $900 million, and during that brief time Musk's post was "possibly the most valuable tweet in the history of social media," according to *Observer* business reporter Sissi Cao.[35] Then the price dropped again after it became apparent he wasn't actually in a position to "go private" at $420 per share after all. Rumors began to emerge that he wrote the tweet to impress his girlfriend and that the $420 figure was a joke reference to marijuana. The number 420 is often used as a code word for pot. The SEC's co-director for enforcement said in a press conference:

> While leading Tesla's investors to believe he had a firm offer in hand, we allege that Musk had arrived at the price of $420 by assuming 20 percent premium over Tesla's then existing share price then rounding up to $420 because of the significance of that number in marijuana culture and his belief that his girlfriend would be amused by it.[36]

While we may never know Musk's true intentions or how his girlfriend responded, we can be sure the SEC was not amused. They sued Musk for misleading investors and manipulating stock prices. The case was settled with four conditions[37]:

- Tesla and Musk would pay $40 million in fines combined.

- Musk would step down as the company's chairman (though he retained the role of CEO).

- Two new independent directors would be appointed to Tesla's board.

- Tesla would "establish a new committee of independent directors and put in place additional controls and procedures to oversee Musk's communications." This last condition raised new free speech issues, and sure enough, within six months, Musk and the SEC were back in court for round two.

On February 19, 2019, Musk tweeted, "Tesla made 0 cars in 2011, but will make around 500k in 2019."[38] Once again, the tweet sounded harmless enough to those outside the investment world, and once again, Musk riled the SEC because the statement that Tesla would make 500,000 cars in 2019 wasn't quite true. Musk attempted to clarify with a second tweet a few hours later in which he wrote that he had intended to say that Tesla's *per-year* rate of production would be up to 500,000 by the end of 2019. In other words, Musk expected the rate of production to be near 10,000 cars a week by December 2019, but the company was not on track to actually produce 500,000 cars during 2019. The SEC was not in a forgiving mood, and brought Musk back to court for violating the terms of the earlier settlement. The SEC claimed that Musk was acting in contempt for not seeking preapproval of his tweet. Musk called the SEC's claim "an unconstitutional power grab" and an infringement on his First Amendment rights to free speech.[39]

This case raises both First Amendment issues and public relations issues, and it illustrates the overlap between the two. The First Amendment question centers on Musk's right to tweet freely and the government's power

Tesla CEO Elon Musk exits federal court after the SEC accused him of violating a settlement deal that required him to get pre-approval for social media posts about the electric car company.

Why is this a First Amendment issue and a public relations issue?

to control his communication. As we'll see later in this chapter, because Musk is a public figure and because his tweets influence the stock market, he enjoys less constitutional protection than he would as a private citizen. His public status as someone communicating to publics on behalf of an organization makes this a public relations issue as well. Public relations people are often involved with vetting employee tweets and setting social media policy. Managing or monitoring CEO communications is often labeled a public relations function. Can you imagine being asked to manage Elon Musk's Twitter activity? How would you balance his right to free speech with the importance of not unfairly manipulating markets or misleading publics?

You don't have to work for a billionaire CEO for these issues to be relevant. U.S. District Judge Alison Nathan, who listened to the SEC and Musk argue their cases, said the rule of law must apply whether you are "a small potato or a big fish." She also recommended that the SEC and Musk try to stay out of court if at all possible. "My call to action is for everyone to take a deep breath, put your reasonableness pants on and work this out."[40]

A key legal concept in the Tesla case is **material information**, which is defined as any information that could influence the market value of a company or its products. If you work in public relations and are involved with IPOs or the creation or dissemination of financial reports, you will undoubtedly have access to material information. As a result, public relations executives must be especially careful not to illegally take advantage of inside information for their own financial gain. Known as **insider trading**, this may include tipping off friends, family or associates so that they benefit illegally from information that has not yet been made public. The SEC carefully monitors for cases of illegal insider trading. As an example, the SEC's web page cites a case of a public relations executive charged with insider trading on information he gained while representing a transportation and logistics company:

> The SEC alleges that Robert M. Morano, a former employee of UTi Worldwide, Inc., obtained more than $38,000 in illegal profits by purchasing shares in the company before it and DSV Air & Sea Holdings A/V jointly announced UTi's acquisition. According to the SEC's complaint, Morano, who was responsible for helping the company publish press releases and other communications, learned confidential details about the planned acquisition the day before it was publicly announced and immediately bought approximately 17,500 shares of UTi in three brokerage accounts. The next day, after DSV and UTi's announcement was made public, UTi's shares increased over 50% on heavy trading, and Morano sold all of his shares.[41]

Morano was ordered to pay $75,000 as a penalty, which was almost twice the amount he profited from the alleged insider trading.[42]

Material information
Any information that could influence the market value of a company or its products.

Insider trading
When a company's employees or executives buy and sell stock in their own organization or share information with others who buy or sell before the information has been made public.

Customer relationship management (CRM)
Process of tracking and forecasting customers' interactions with an organization, often leveraging data for sales support.

Privacy

As your level of responsibility grows in an organization, so does your access to information about internal and external publics. Depending on the type of organization you work for, you may have access to employee performance evaluations, student academic records, volunteer contact information and even photos of your colleagues with their families from their Instagram accounts. In addition to the obvious legal and ethical issues that may arise if you release negative information about someone, you must be careful even when your intentions are positive. If you write a biography of an employee or student who is receiving an award, you should check with that person to make sure it is accurate and that the person consents to the information being released. Likewise, if you pull a photo of someone from a social media account, you'll want to obtain permission before using that photo on your company web page.

Externally, **customer relationship management (CRM)** describes the process of tracking and forecasting customers' interactions with an organization. Ridiculous amounts of data can be collected and analyzed to better serve customers with personalized experiences that are customized to their browsing history and preferences. These relationships—facilitated by data and technology—can be mutually beneficial. Customers gain customized experiences and convenient service. Organizations obtain lots of data to use to support their business decisions. Think about the organizations that offer you the most convenient and customized services. Maybe Google? Facebook? Amazon? Netflix? How about your online news sources or favorite retailers for shopping? Your school? Your bank? Your hospital? You as a customer (or student or patient, etc.) put an enormous amount of trust in these organizations. Public relations people have to be very careful with that trust.

In many cases, the right decisions about privacy of both internal and external publics can be made with good business sense and careful ethics, but you must also be aware of the legal rights and responsibilities of people inside and outside your organization. According to Cornell University Law School's Legal Information Institute, there are a "bundle of torts" to watch out for in privacy cases.[43] These torts (acts that can lead to lawsuits) include intrusion into seclusion, appropriation of likeness or identity, public disclosure of private facts and portrayal in a false light.

Intrusion into Seclusion

Intrusion into seclusion is what most people think of when they hear "invasion of privacy." It includes trespassing into someone's private space such as a home or car, but it also includes electronic surveillance to access online activity that someone could reasonably expect to be private. Since intrusion into seclusion must be highly "offensive to a reasonable person" and cause "mental anguish or suffering," public relations people are unlikely to encounter this type of invasion of privacy in the context of their daily professional communication.[44]

Appropriation of Likeness or Identity

Appropriation of likeness or identity applies in cases in which a person's name, picture, or other personal attribute (signature, voice, portrait, etc.) is used without permission. When the subject is a celebrity, that person can claim a right to publicity, meaning that you cannot use the person's likeness for commercial purposes.

If you look at the photo credits section at the very back of this textbook, you'll see that many of the images we use come from photo agencies such as Getty Images. We pay a fee for the right to republish high-resolution photos from Getty Images with assurance that any necessary permissions have been secured for pictures that feature people. *MIT Technology Review* also uses Getty Images. So when they published a story about the hipster effect, "the counterintuitive phenomenon in which people who oppose mainstream culture all end up looking the same,"[45] accompanied by a Getty stock photo of a generic hipster, they were surprised to receive the following threat from a reader:

> *Your lack of basic journalistic ethics in both the manner in which you "reported" this uncredited nonsense, and the slanderous, unnecessary use of my picture without permission demands a response, and I am, of course, pursuing legal action.*[46]

MIT Technology Review Editor Gideon Lichfield looked into the issue and found that Getty Images had indeed cleared permissions for the model

A Getty Images photo originally captioned, "Shot of a handsome young man in trendy winter attire against a wooden background," was used in a story about the "hipster effect."

What are the legal benefits of using reputable stock photo services?

in the photo, but that the man who had complained was not the man in the image. He was apparently just another hipster who looked the same as the generic hipster in the stock photo! Whatever the lesson is here about hipsters, this story also reminds people working in public relations of the risks of republishing images without permission from the source and anyone identifiable in the image.

Public Disclosure of Private Facts

You also can find yourself in legal trouble for publishing information that has not previously been released, if that information is personal and not deemed to be of legitimate public interest. Examples of private facts include a person's health status, sexual orientation or financial situation. In public relations, you may want to celebrate your organization's diversity, publicly congratulate an employee on expecting twins or encourage retirement savings by highlighting the financial success of one of your organization's retirees. However, even with the best intentions, you must be careful to obtain consent before publicizing anyone's private facts. Any of these situations could be seen as public disclosure of private information.

Portrayal in a False Light

Portrayal in a false light occurs when someone spreads wrong information about a person that reasonably can be considered offensive or objectionable. False light overlaps with defamation, but a key difference is that plaintiffs claiming false light can seek damages for emotional harm caused.[47] A Southwest Airlines gate agent sued a customer for social media complaints that the agent felt cast her in a false light. The customer, Natalie Grant-Herms, ranted heartily on Twitter and Facebook when not allowed to board a flight at the same time as her young children:

> Nashville. Gate A25. Flight to Denver. Her name is Jennifer. She said "get over it. Follow the rules. Or don't fly."

> She has done this to me before. She has the WORST customer service ...

Southwest's customer service staff apparently defused the situation as indicated in later tweets by Grant-Herms:

> Well, we've caused quite a stir, tweeps. @southwestair just called me. I appreciate their concern & prompt attention 2 the problem.

> I've got wifi on my flight. I'm impressed with how quickly @southwestair responded to my complaint. I'll keep u posted as to what they do.[48]

However, the gate agent, Jennifer Patterson, was not appeased, and she sued Grant-Herms. Patterson lost her case in a lower court but appealed. While the appeals court agreed with the lower court that Patterson did not

Even with the best intentions, obtain consent before publicizing anyone on social media.

have a case for defamation, it concluded that Patterson did have a case for false light invasion of privacy:

> We believe that a reasonable person could find, under the entire circumstances of the incident, that Ms. Grant-Herms' posting of selective facts placed Ms. Patterson in a false light by implying that Ms. Patterson was rude and a bad service agent, one who was more concerned with adherence to the airline rules and procedures than the welfare of the child, and that these implications caused injury to her.[49]

Voices from the Field

Cayce Myers

CAYCE MYERS is an associate professor in the Department of Communication at Virginia Tech where he teaches public relations. His research focuses on laws and regulations affecting public relations practice. Dr. Myers holds a Ph.D. in mass communication from the University of Georgia, Henry W. Grady College of Journalism and Mass Communication, an LL.M. from the University of Georgia School of Law, and a J.D. from Mercer University Walter F. George School of Law. He is also the legal research editor for the Institute for Public Relations.

Justice Stephen Breyer has written about how new "global realities" are changing the way we approach law and that our "judicial awareness" must extend beyond borders more than ever before. What does that mean for public relations?
Public relations practice is increasingly international, and large companies and PR firms usually have offices spanning the globe. Because of this, practitioners need to be aware that their work may be subject to other countries' laws. In the United States there are specific protections given to corporate speech, commercial speech, intellectual property and privacy that are not found outside the United States. Given the diversity of laws that affect public relations

it is important for practitioners to think globally when they produce content of any kind.

What's one of the most common legal mistakes new public relations practitioners tend to make?
We live in a society where social media and mobile technology are everywhere. New public relations practitioners may not realize that sharing, posting and messaging can have legal consequences. For example, using intellectual property of another for promotional purposes without permission can lead to expensive and unnecessary lawsuits. In addition, because tweets, posts and sharing can be done in a matter of seconds, there is a misperception that this content is not really important. However, words, no matter how few or seemingly unimportant, can be the basis for a lawsuit.

How about senior public relations professionals—what legal pitfalls should they watch out for?
The biggest issue for senior practitioners is keeping current on new laws affecting public relations. Well-established legal doctrines, such as defamation, copyright, trademark and trade secrets are now being applied to new media. While this does not

necessarily represent a change in core legal tenets, new applications of the law may not be obvious to seasoned practitioners. There are also major changes in agency regulations of new media. These changes represent only the beginning of what is sure to become a major recalibration of older laws and regulations to fit the contours of new media.

The rise of social media has led to a big increase in sharing others' information. It also has provided more space for public relations people to communicate less formally with publics. Will legal concerns eventually put a damper on these trends?

There is recognition that social media platforms have power, and some entities have attempted to restrict access and use. However, as recent decisions by the National Labor Relations Board show, organizations will have a difficult time restricting use of social media by employees, though content regulation has increased for promotional material. In effect, these new laws mandate greater amounts of authenticity, transparency and honesty—all of which should be embraced by PR practitioners.

In writing social media policies, can organizations really limit what employees say or require them to obtain approval before posting?

Like many things in law the answer to this depends on the circumstances. If a social media account is owned by the organization then limits can be set on what can be posted. However, regulation of private accounts of employees is very restrained. The National Labor Relations Board has struck down social media policies that require employees to get pre-approval from managers before posting about workplace grievances. However, straightforward, well-written policies can survive legal scrutiny. For instance, employers can prohibit employees from engaging in harassment, disclosure of trade secrets, or posting their intellectual property. The bottom line is organizations can regulate social media speech in limited circumstances, but employees do not forfeit their speech rights because they work for a specific organization.

Public relations people and lawyers—at times they've had a rocky relationship. How are they doing these days? Are they getting along any better (or worse) than they used to?

There will probably always be some level of disagreement between lawyers and public relations people because each profession has a different perspective. Lawyers are trained to be risk-averse and sometimes have to deny allegations or risk further legal exposure. Communication of any kind, even if it is good PR, can also become evidence that is used against an organization at trial. Conversely, public relations practitioners are communicators. They value transparency, honesty and fostering relationships with key publics. Practitioners recognize that winning in the court of public opinion can be as important, if not more important, than winning in a court of law. Because of these perspectives there is a natural tension between lawyers and PR practitioners. However, some of the best PR and legal strategy comes when practitioners and lawyers work together. The truth is that PR practitioners and lawyers need each other to best serve the needs of their clients.

Ethics: Safeguarding Confidences— Who Owns Your Social Networks?

At this point in your life, you have probably heard the saying that just because something is legal doesn't make it ethical. As a public relations professional, privacy is one area in which you may need more than a legal interpretation to make ethical decisions. Safeguarding confidences is a core principle in the PRSA Code of Ethics, which states, "Client trust requires appropriate protection of confidential and private information."[50] The

A LinkedIn network could be considered one of an organization's "trade secrets."

How can public relations professionals ethically balance personal and professional uses of social networks?

principle applies not just to clients but also to the privacy rights of other individuals internal to and external to your organization.

In business law, a **trade secret** is information that is not generally known to others and not readily available to others who could profit from its disclosure or use.[51] As much as public relations ethics focus on disclosure and public information, these values of openness must be balanced with other values including competition and privacy. Trade secrets may include recipes, business processes, research methods, or the formula for a product like WD-40 (named for its "water displacement" function discovered by the chemist who developed it on his 40th try[52]). How about your social network on Facebook or LinkedIn? Would you ever consider that a trade secret? And if so, do you think that information could be owned by anyone besides you?

According to some courts, yes, social media accounts can be considered trade secrets when those accounts contain client lists or valuable information about customers. Professor Cayce Myers serves as research editor for the Institute for Public Relations (IPR) in the area of public relations law. Myers believes that because some accounts on social media contain abundant information about clients and customers, they could conceivably be considered "trade secrets." Myers writes, "If an employee can take these connections with them to a new job or startup they have a competitive advantage to steal valuable clients from their old employer."[53] Myers advises that public relations people keep personal and professional social media accounts separate as much as possible.

So, legally, organizations can claim ownership of an employee's social media accounts in certain circumstances. But many organizations encourage employees to use their own voices and networks in opening and

Trade secret
Business information that is not generally known to the public and not readily available to others who could profit from its disclosure or use.

maintaining dialogue with publics, including clients and customers. The first chapter of this book cited Arthur Page's principles of public relations management to advocate for allowing employees to speak with their own authentic voices and to follow Page's principle that a "company's true character is expressed by its people."[54] Is it ethical for organizations to encourage employees to work their networks on social media but then to turn around and claim corporate ownership of those networks and relationships? Is it right to treat someone's social interactions as "trade secrets" in the name of safeguarding confidences?

Myers offers advice that makes sense from both a legal and ethical standpoint: Make sure to clarify expectations. If organizations offer employees reasonable social media policies including details of who owns what accounts, misunderstandings can be avoided. Employees will know which social media interactions are "private" as in personally private and which are "private" as in organizationally owned "trade secrets."

In Case You Missed It

Social media have been called the Wild West of the internet, a place where participants make up the rules as they go. While it is true that technology often advances faster than the law, these legal principles still apply.

- Obtain permission (or seek legal counsel) before publicly discussing private information about any current or past employee.

- If you work for a public figure, the standard for claiming libel is much higher than if you represent a private citizen.

- When you share someone else's intellectual property without permission or proper attribution, you run the risk of legal trouble.

- The key to avoiding plagiarism is proper attribution. Give credit where credit is due!

- Balance participation with respect for intellectual property; use caution when posting anything that may be seen as offensive or illegal.

- When in doubt about your ownership rights of social media content, check the provider's terms of service.

- Even with the best intentions, obtain consent before publicizing anyone on social media.

SUMMARY

11.1 Discuss the importance of understanding national laws in international contexts.
The internet has opened borders for online marketplaces to offer goods, services and ideas more than ever before. Trends in globalization have led to a great deal more international exchange, and this means that the laws of any one country such as the United States

must be interpreted in a more global context. As Justice Stephen Breyer put it, "Judicial awareness can no longer stop at the border."

11.2 Apply principles of free speech and the First Amendment to the practice of public relations.

Working with the press and communicating on behalf of an organization requires understanding your role in the marketplace of ideas that the First Amendment serves to protect. Key legal concepts for public relations professionals include rights to reputation, intellectual property, financial interests and privacy.

11.3 Describe limits to free speech, including libel and slander as forms of defamation.

Rights to free speech may be limited when they infringe on others' rights or someone else's reputation, intellectual property, financial interests or privacy. Slander and libel are both forms of defamation, which is any statement that injures someone's reputation. *Slander* refers to spoken communication, while *libel* refers to written or recorded communication that can be reproduced and shared repeatedly.

11.4 Identify common types of intellectual property and how they are protected.

Intellectual property includes writing, inventions, logos, images or designs, and all sorts of combinations thereof. These forms of intellectual property can be claimed and protected with copyrights, registered trademarks and patents. Creative Commons licenses allow content creators to designate the specific types of permissions they wish to allow.

11.5 Summarize the role of public relations professionals in providing public information.

Public relations people who work for publicly funded or government organizations in the United States are responsible for making information available to citizens under the Freedom of Information Act and various open-records laws (i.e., sunshine laws). Although there are some exceptions, most information that the government collects and uses in the United States is treated as public information and must either be offered when requested or proactively made available in a useful format. Interactive online technologies have facilitated the latter.

11.6 Identify key federal agencies responsible for regulating communication to protect publics.

Depending on your area of public relations, you will need to become familiar with various government agencies that are responsible for protecting your key publics. The FTC regulates all types of consumer products and services, including the promotion of these products and services. The FDA regulates food- and health-related industries. The SEC regulates financial information.

11.7 Identify legal concerns related to privacy in public relations.

Handling privacy in public relations requires awareness of the legal rights and responsibilities of people inside and outside of your organization. Legal areas to consider include intrusion into seclusion, appropriation of likeness or identity, public disclosure of private facts and portrayal in a false light.

11.8 Discuss the ethical balance between safeguarding organizational confidences and respecting the privacy of individual social media accounts.

Safeguarding confidences is a core principle in the PRSA Code of Ethics. The principle applies not just to organizations and clients but also to the privacy rights of individuals internal to and external to an organization. Competing values in privacy cases mean that public relations people have to consider both law and ethics. Clarifying expectations about what information is considered proprietary to an organization and what information is private to individuals will help avoid both ethical and legal problems.

DISCUSSION QUESTIONS

1. What types of organizations have access to your personally identifiable information? Are you comfortable knowing that these organizations may share your data across national borders? How do international laws help?

2. Search for a U.S. Supreme Court case involving a public relations practitioner (e.g., someone advocating for an issue on behalf of an organization or someone serving as a corporate spokesperson). Useful websites include https://www.freedomforuminstitute.org/first-amendment-center/supreme-court-cases/ and https://www.uscourts.gov/about-federal-courts/educational-resources/educational-activities/first-amendment-activities. Summarize what the Court's ruling means for future public relations practitioners. What limit to free speech was set or reinforced?

3. **CASE STUDY** Amazon spokesman Jay Carney responded to a *New York Times* article that was critical of Amazon's treatment of employees by disputing the claims on Medium.com. In the piece, Carney also aired "dirty laundry" about a former employee who had served as a source for the *Times* story. Why was he able to do so without getting sued? What were the risks and benefits in the court of public opinion?

4. Identify a piece of your own intellectual property that you would consider publishing online (perhaps a photo, term paper, blog entry, infographic, song or artwork). Select a specific type of Creative Commons license you would apply (see https://creativecommons.org/choose/) and explain why you chose that particular type of license.

5. Would you support a tax increase to hire more public affairs people and develop better technology to make government information more available than it currently is? Why or why not?

6. What's your dream job in public relations? Assume you get the job. Name at least one regulatory agency you would need to know more about and why. (If your answer is "none," explain why your work would not be regulated by any agency.)

7. **CASE STUDY** Whose speech is more legally regulated—yours or Elon Musk's? Why? What other powerful or influential individuals might face increased legal scrutiny for their social media tweets, and why?

8. Discuss a scenario in which a well-meaning public relations professional who intends to communicate something positive about an employee could get into legal trouble for violating that person's privacy. How could the situation be avoided?

9. Assume you've landed your dream job in public relations. But your new employer requires you to sign an agreement that any social media accounts you use for any tasks related to your job may be accessed by the company. How would you handle the situation?

KEY TERMS

Actual malice   295
Clear and present danger   291
Copyright   296
Copyright infringement   297
Creative Commons   302
Customer relationship management (CRM)   310
Deep link   303
Defamation   294
Fair use   298

Federal Trade Commission (FTC)   306
Food and Drug Administration (FDA)   305
Framing   303
Freedom of Information Act (FOIA)   304
Hyperlink   303
Initial public offering (IPO)   306
Insider trading   309
Intellectual property   289
Libel   294
Material information   309

Patent   296
Plagiarism   296
Privacy   290
Public figure   295
Securities and Exchange Commission (SEC)   306
Slander   294
Sunshine law   304
Trade secret   315
Trademark   296

CHAPTER 12
Issues and Crises

Facebook ended up in the hot seat in front of Congress.
How did they respond?

KEY LEARNING OUTCOMES

12.1 Analyze responses ranging from advocacy to accommodation in public relations conflict cases.

12.2 Identify stages in the issues life cycle.

12.3 Describe how issues management can prevent or lessen the impact of crises.

12.4 Identify public relations crisis types.

12.5 Define crisis response strategies.

12.6 Discuss how traditional media, social media and offline word of mouth interact in the spread of crisis information.

12.7 Assess competing values in ethical conflicts of interest in the context of public relations issues and crises.

RELATED UNIVERSAL ACCREDITATION BOARD COMPETENCY AREAS

2.2 ETHICAL BEHAVIOR • **3.1** ISSUES AND RISK MANAGEMENT • **3.2** CRISIS MANAGEMENT
3.3 COUNSEL TO MANAGEMENT • **5.4** PROBLEM SOLVING AND DECISION-MAKING

Much of this book so far has been about how to conduct public relations as part of a management function that helps organizations meet goals and avert crises. However, even the very best public relations professionals working for the most responsible organizations face issues and crises. Some crises, such as natural disasters, are unavoidable, while other crises are not. One of the toughest jobs in public relations is being called on to help organizations navigate crises they created themselves. Before delving into ways organizations respond to crises, this chapter covers how issues evolve and how issues may be identified and managed proactively to minimize the need for crisis management.

Managing Conflict

"My god they're throwing guitars out there!" Though not quite as legendary as Paul Revere's "The redcoats are coming!" this exclamation from a passenger in the window seat of a United Airlines airplane started a bit of a revolution. Baggage handlers at Chicago's O'Hare International Airport had picked the wrong guy's guitar to toss around. The result was a flashpoint case illustrating the power of individuals to confront large, powerful organizations on social media.

After hearing the startling observation from the back of a plane, Dave Carroll and fellow band members of *Sons of Maxwell* looked out to see that, indeed, their instruments were being heaved carelessly by United Airlines luggage handlers. Concerned about his $3,500 Taylor guitar, Carroll immediately brought the issue to the attention of a flight attendant. The flight attendant referred him to a "lead agent" in the terminal who said he needed to talk to another lead agent and dismissed his request before she disappeared into a crowd. Carroll then spoke to a third employee, who referred him to a fourth at his next airport.[1] This all-too-familiar story line of poor customer service goes on and on. Carroll's guitar was smashed, and for nine months he tried and failed to reach an acceptable resolution with the airline.

The narrative was so ridiculous it was almost funny, and so Carroll decided to tap into that sentiment with the YouTube music video "United Breaks Guitars." The video featured a catchy tune and clever lyrics describing the whole experience, and it struck a chord with millions of frustrated passengers. In fact, the video went viral. Nineteen million views later, Carroll's bio describes him not only as a singer-songwriter but also as a master storyteller, professional speaker and social media innovator.

On the other side of the story, United Airlines saw its market value drop $180 million in the four days after Carroll's video was uploaded to YouTube. While a claim that Carroll's social media attack was the main reason for the financial loss would be hard to prove, the damage to the airline's reputation was "undeniable" according to a Huffington Post business report.[2]

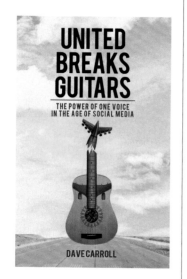

Musician Dave Carroll became famous for launching a musical protest on social media with his YouTube hit "United Breaks Guitars."

How do social media change the way organizations and customer publics interact in conflict?

Like United Airlines, New York–based fashion powerhouse DKNY also had to come to terms with the power of individual influence on social media. The DKNY case started when Brandon Stanton, a photographer known for his Humans of New York photography project, declined an offer of $50 per photo from DKNY to display his work in their stores. Then, when Stanton found out that DKNY had gone ahead and displayed his photos in a store window in Bangkok without his permission, he posted the following on his Facebook page: "I don't want any money. But please REBLOG this post if you think that DKNY should donate $100,000 on my behalf to the YMCA in Bedford-Stuyvesant, Brooklyn."[3]

Recognizing that it was facing both a legal and a public relations issue, DKNY responded with the following statement: "DKNY has always supported the arts and we deeply regret this mistake. Accordingly, we are making a charitable donation of $25,000 to the YMCA in Bedford-Stuyvesant Brooklyn in Mr. Stanton's name."

Stanton accepted the apology: "We are going to take them at their word that it was a mistake, and be happy that this one had a happy ending." Even legal issues can be raised—and settled—on social media.

Respond quickly and appropriately to challenges on social media to prevent issues from becoming crises.

DKNY displayed a New York photographer's work in this storefront window in Bangkok without his permission. The photographer called DKNY out on Facebook.

Did DKNY handle the situation well by apologizing and donating $25,000 to a charity? Why or why not?

Dave Carroll versus United Airlines, Brandon Stanton versus DKNY—both cases present conflicts that played out on social media and, therefore, played out in the public eye. Managing conflict, especially public conflict, is a major function of public relations. Public relations scholars have studied how public relations people in all sorts of organizations (not just big corporations like airlines and fashion companies) make decisions on how to communicate with publics when two-way relationships become contentious.

To help understand this decision process, University of Missouri Professor Glen Cameron and his colleagues developed a contingency theory of conflict in public relations.[4] A **contingency theory** suggests that the best course of action in any situation depends on the specifics of the situation. In conflict, the action or communication tactic that a public relations person chooses depends on factors internal and external to the organization. Internal factors may include an organization's size, structure and culture, as well as the autonomy of a public relations department within an organization and the level of practitioner experience. External factors may include the threat of litigation, business competition, political support, and the size and power of publics. Contingency theory also describes response options ranging from **pure advocacy** (firmly pleading the organization's case without compromise) on one side to **pure accommodation** (completely conceding to a public's demands) on the other side (Figure 12.1). In many cases, social media have given publics greater power relative to organizations. But that doesn't mean public relations people have to always accommodate publics, nor do they always have to go to battle and advocate hard on one side of an issue.

United Airlines and DKNY had to consider very different contingencies. If you have ever actually read all the fine print in an airline passenger contract, you'd probably *not* be surprised to learn that United Airlines did *not* have to reimburse Carroll. In contrast, DKNY faced a legitimate legal challenge based on Stanton's claim to intellectual property. United Airlines customer service agents had no reason to believe that Carroll would find an audience of millions for his complaint. DKNY likely realized that Stanton already had quite a following on Facebook and other social media.

The two organizations also offered very different levels of accommodation. United Airlines pretty much refused to accommodate Dave Carroll, while DKNY accommodated Brandon Stanton by apologizing and offering a

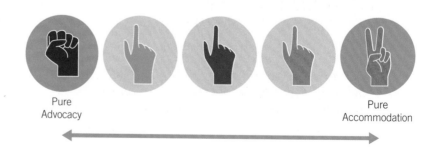

Pure
Advocacy

Pure
Accommodation

Figure 12.1 Continuum of options for managing issues and conflict, according to contingency theory.

$25,000 charity donation. Although the case had a happier ending for DKNY than it did for United Airlines, this doesn't mean that more accommodation is always better. In fact, that's the point of contingency theory. Sometimes you should advocate, and other times it makes more sense to accommodate.

Sometimes it's better to advocate than to accommodate.

Case Study

Is the Customer Always Right? ... A Big Win for Little Italy

Contingency theory reminds us that firm edicts, such as "The customer is always right," are sometimes just too simple. When an angry customer called Little Italy Restaurante in Anchorage, Alaska, to complain about a delivery driver, owner P. J. Gialopsos advocated for her employee rather than accommodating the customer.[5]

Remember, the customer may not always be right.

The driver, who has a speech impediment and autism, delivered the wrong order, leading the customer to complain irately, use foul language and accuse the driver of being on drugs. When the driver returned to the restaurant, he was visibly upset and reported that the customer had called him names and belittled him. Instead of apologizing and accommodating the customer, Gialopsos opted to "fire" the customer. She told her staff to refuse calls and to not deliver to the customer's address.

Gialopsos said later in an interview that this wasn't the first time a customer had called about the driver, but that normally when she explained the situation, customers were understanding. Acknowledging the driver's disability, she described him as a hard worker and successful university student with a good sense of humor. "So (the driver) is a little awkward socially—gee whiz—that doesn't give you a right to call him a foul name and make his day miserable," said Gialopsos. A few days after the incident, she posted about it on Facebook. The post went viral. Within two days, the post had 14,000 likes and more than 15,000 comments. Gialopsos, the driver and the driver's family were delighted with the overwhelmingly positive feedback. For example, a Facebook post from Judy Berry read:

> *So proud of Anchorage's own Little Italy Restaurante & its owner P. J. Gialopsos for standing up for her employee. How refreshing to see her stance that perhaps "the customer isn't always right" when they berate an employee with development disabilities. Thank you also to Little Italy for shining a spotlight on Autism & for hiring people whom others may not![6]*

Interestingly, Gialopsos said she did not notice any substantial increase in business immediately following the incident.[7] Was the Facebook love

Little Italy Restaurante owner P. J. Gialopsos chose to advocate for her employee instead of accommodating an unhappy customer.

What contingencies (i.e., internal and external factors) made her approach to the conflict right or wrong?

enough to consider this case a public relations "win"? Was advocacy the right strategy here given the circumstances? In deciding to advocate for her employee instead of accommodating the customer, many internal and external contingencies were at play. How do the contingencies in this case compare to what the public relations staff of large, complex organizations like United Airlines or British Airways face when they receive a customer complaint?

You will probably never see a YouTube video of an airline passenger singing about his luggage that arrived undamaged or a viral Facebook campaign celebrating a company for attaining proper permissions for artwork. Most small business owners won't get 15,000 hits and national media attention for sticking up for their employees. In fact, the vast majority of issues will not rise to the level of a major public issue or crisis. It's also important to remember that customers are only one type of public with which we maintain relationships. Perhaps the best public relations "crises" are the ones that never happen, meaning that full-blown crises are averted with effective communication and issues management—not just with customers, but with all publics.

Managing Issues

Organizations face all sorts of issues that can develop into crises, if they are not managed appropriately. **Issues management** is an area of public relations that focuses on proactive monitoring and management to prevent crises from happening.[8]

In order to manage issues, you must first be able to identify them. The earlier you uncover an issue, the more options you will likely have for dealing with a situation. Issues management scholars have outlined several stages in the issue life cycle:

Monitor social media to uncover issues sooner and give you more options for dealing with a situation.

Issues management
Systematic process whereby organizations work to identify and resolve issues before they become crises.

1. *Early/potential:* when a few people begin to become aware of possible problems
2. *Emerging:* when more people begin to notice and express concern
3. *Current/crisis:* when the negative impact on an organization becomes public and pressure on the organization builds
4. *Dormant:* when the organization has no choice but to accept the long-term consequences

The longer an issue exists without being addressed, the more entrenched publics become in their opposition and the fewer options for strategic response are available to organizations (Figure 12.2).[9]

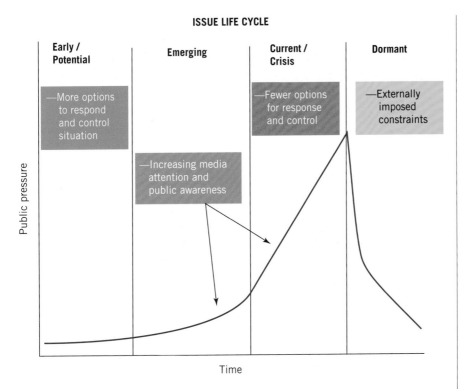

ISSUE LIFE CYCLE

| Early / Potential | Emerging | Current / Crisis | Dormant |

—More options to respond and control situation

—Increasing media attention and public awareness

—Fewer options for response and control

—Externally imposed constraints

Public pressure

Time

Figure 12.2 This illustration of the issue life cycle shows how public pressure builds over time as an issue moves from potential to emerging to current/crisis.

Case Study

The Issue Life Cycle of Volkswagen's "Dieselgate"

Volkswagen's diesel emissions scandal, dubbed "dieselgate" by some and "the diesel dupe" by others, provides an example of how an issue can grow into a full-blown crisis with major consequences.

EARLY/POTENTIAL

At the earliest stages, issues are often identified first by experts or specialists who pay close attention to small changes in the internal or external environments of organizations. When these experts or specialists perceive a potential problem and people within an organization begin planning to respond in some way, the issue has entered the *early/potential* stage.

In 2012, Arvind Thiruvengadam, an assistant professor at West Virginia University, and a few of his colleagues won a grant from the International Council on Clean Transportation (ICCT) to test the environmental friendliness and fuel efficiency of diesel cars. As part of their research, Thiruvengadam and his team ran emissions tests on a 2012 Volkswagen Jetta and a 2013 VW Passat. In the decade prior, Volkswagen's marketing message had emphasized "clean diesel."[10] Therefore, Thiruvengadam and his team expected to find that these two VW models, which were designed for sale in the United States, would run cleaner than cars sold in other countries with more lax emission standards. Instead, the researchers were surprised to find that the two VWs emitted significantly higher levels of pollutants.

In May 2014, the ICCT alerted the Environmental Protection Agency (EPA) and the California Air Resources board about the unexpected findings. At this point, Volkswagen had a *potential* issue. In fact, it was later revealed that people inside the company had known about the emission problem since 2005, so the early/potential stage for this issue lasted nearly ten years. Corporate culture likely played a big role in the case. In exploring the role of Volkswagen's management in the circumstances leading to the crisis, *The New York Times* described the company's corporate culture as "confident, cutthroat and insular."[11]

EMERGING

In the emerging stage, groups begin to form and take sides on an issue. In their book *Risk Issues and Crisis Management in Public Relations*, Michael Regester and Judy Larkin describe the emerging phase as a time when industry insiders, specialist media, professional interest groups, activist organizations or any other publics with direct interest, begin to notice and to voice concerns or opinions.[12] Media attention may be sporadic in this stage, but if public relations people are monitoring the media, including specialty media like blogs and trade publications, they still may have an opportunity to intervene and begin to formulate plans for action. As mentioned previously, the more an issue develops, the fewer available options there are for proactive management both internally and externally.

There was very little media attention for several months after the fuel efficiency researchers published their results. Volkswagen denied there was a problem and offered other explanations for why results from the road tests did not meet the expected standards.[13] Meanwhile, regulators continued to investigate. The issue was *emerging*.

CURRENT/CRISIS

In the current/crisis stage, the issue matures, and pressure builds as the impact of the issue on the organization becomes clear. Public relations people have very little control of the situation at this stage. Strategy options become mainly reactive. According to Regester and Larkin, issues become enduring and pervasive in the current stage. They increase in intensity. In September 2015, the EPA publicly accused VW of using "defeat devices" hidden in its diesel cars that manipulated the results of emissions tests. Basically, the devices were software designed to detect when cars were undergoing an emissions test and then improve performance accordingly.[14] Volkswagen had been caught cheating.

On September 21, 2015, Volkswagen Group of America's chief executive Michael Horn had to use what should have been an occasion to celebrate—the company's launch event for its 2016 Passat—to issue an apology instead. "Our company was dishonest, with the EPA and the California Air Resources board, and with all of you, and in my German words, we have totally screwed up," Horn told the Brooklyn, New York, audience. "We have to make things right, with the government, the public, our customers, our employees and also very important, our dealers." Volkswagen was in a crisis that had spun well beyond its control.

Consider for a moment how you would feel if you owned one of the approximately 10,000 affected cars in the United States sold by Volkswagen (e.g., VWs, Audis or Porsches). You've chosen to invest in what you believe to be smart, environmentally friendly technology, only to learn that your now highly devalued car emits "up to nine times the legal limit of smog-produced nitrogen oxide pollutants."[15] Is it safe to say you'd be, um, peeved?

Now think of how dealers and employees felt, not to mention the governments and regulators who were deliberately deceived. When an organization has damaged relationships like this with so many key publics, it is clearly in *crisis* mode. In Volkswagen's case, all they could do at this point was react to a series of painful consequences as they unfolded for years:

- The company admitted that 11 million of its diesel cars had been "rigged to fool emissions tests," going back to 2005 when it began focusing major marketing efforts on selling diesel cars in the United States.[16]

- Volkswagen chief executive Martin Winterkorn resigned on September 23, 2015.

- By September 25, 2015, Volkswagen stock had plummeted more than 50 percent below its 52-week high in March 2015.[17]

- The value of used VW and Audi diesels fell more than 13 percent in the month following the EPA announcement.[18]

- By late October 2015, more than 350 U.S. lawsuits against Volkswagen had been filed, and legal experts expected many of those suits to be consolidated into mass class action suits. Volkswagen reportedly had set aside $7.3 billion to prepare for the fallout from the crisis, no doubt including the millions of vehicle recalls.[19]

- At the end of 2015, Hans-Dieter Pötsch, chairman of Volkswagen's supervisory board, said in a press conference that an organizational climate of poor ethical standards was partly to blame, and "there was a tolerance for breaking the rules."[20]

"We have totally screwed up," announced Volkswagen Group of America's chief executive Michael Horn in September 2015.

If you were an owner of one of the cars affected in "diesel dupe," what could Volkswagen have done "to make things right"?

Following its diesel crisis, Volkswagen became the target of the brandalism movement (e.g., www.brandalism.org.uk) as part of a protest campaign tied to international climate change talks.

How could Volkswagen have responded (if at all)?

- By 2018, *Fortune* estimated that the total cost of the crisis had reached $25 billion in the United States, including compensation to consumers, criminal fines and legal penalties.[21]

DORMANT

According to Regester and Larkin, an issue reaches the *dormant* stage when an organization comes to terms with the consequences.[22] This does not mean, however, that the issue is over and gone. Rather, this means that the organization has had to accept, and live with, the consequences of its actions (or inaction). Even as of this writing, the consequences continue to mount for Volkswagen. In 2019, German prosecutors fined Porsche, a unit of Volkswagen, nearly $600 million (€535 million) "as punishment for lapses in supervisory duties which allowed the company to cheat diesel emissions tests"[23] and in the United States, the Securities and Exchange Commission (SEC) sued the company, claiming that "Volkswagen made false and misleading statements to investors and underwriters about vehicle quality, environmental compliance, and VW's financial standing" as it raised more than $13 billion from investors.[24,25]

Proactive Issues Management

Now that we've seen how organizations can get into trouble, let's look at how they can work to prevent issues from turning into crises. Regester and Larkin have outlined a seven-step process for proactive issues management: (1) monitoring, (2) identification, (3) prioritization, (4) analysis, (5) strategic planning, (6) implementation and (7) evaluation.[26] Notice how these seven steps run parallel to the four-step RPIE process presented earlier in this text (Table 12.1).

1. Monitoring

The first step to avoiding crises is to continuously monitor your organization's internal and external operating environments. What is being said about your organization offline, on social media and in traditional media? Listen carefully at meetings and events, systematically pay attention to internal and external communications, formally and informally analyze

TABLE 12.1 **OVERLAP BETWEEN RPIE AND PROACTIVE ISSUES MANAGEMENT**	
FOUR-STEP PROCESS FOR PUBLIC RELATIONS (RPIE)	**SEVEN-STEP PROCESS FOR PROACTIVE ISSUES MANAGEMENT**
RESEARCH	Monitoring Identification
PLANNING	Prioritization Analysis Strategic Planning
IMPLEMENTATION	Implementation
EVALUATION	Evaluation

media content (including social media) and keep lines of communication open with opinion leaders. Remember that it is just as important to listen to your organization's detractors as it is to listen to supporters. The methods for research outlined in Chapter 5—primary and secondary, quantitative and qualitative, formal and informal—are all ways to monitor the environment. Your goal is to find any early, potential or emerging issues and turn them into opportunities instead of crises.

One example of systematic monitoring is the practice of **responsible supply chain management**, which occurs when organizations carefully monitor all stages of production and distribution to ensure that working conditions are safe, wages are fair and that generally high ethical standards of social and environmental responsibility are maintained. This helps organizations avoid public relations crises of the type Nike and Gap faced in the 1990s and 2000s when news broke that their supply chains included child labor and sweatshops.[27]

2. Identification

Once you notice an issue, you'll need to be able to describe it and determine if it is something significant or just a random blip on the radar. Think about financial data. Company stock values rise and fall every day, but that does not mean that every time a company's stock value falls that the organization faces a crisis. Instead, analysts watch data over time and in a broader context to identify trends. Is the daily dip in stock prices part of a larger pattern? Are there other factors in the environment such as legal challenges, competitor activity, potential boycotts or broader political and economic changes that suggest a trend that needs further attention?

It's just as important to listen to detractors as it is to listen to supporters.

Responsible supply chain management
Careful monitoring of product production and distribution to ensure that generally high ethical standards of social and environmental responsibility are maintained.

producebunny
@producebunny

Follow

#Chipotle should pay more attention to food safety than hyping anti-GMOs. Foodborne pathogens are deadlier than GMOs

A FAREWELL TO GMOs
When it comes to our food, genetically modified ingredients don't make the cut.
CHIPOTLE.COM/GMO

4:37 PM - 10 Nov 2015

This Twitter user faulted Chipotle for not prioritizing its issues well.

How should Chipotle balance its attention to the two issues of GMOs and food-borne illnesses?

In a PRSA Open Forum online discussion about a neighborhood social networking service called Nextdoor, PRSA member Michael Grimaldi, who works for KC Water (the public water utility serving Kansas City, Mo.), described how he uses the Nextdoor app to identify issues.

If I see several comments about a specific topic—either in responses to our agency posts or in conversations I can see within my neighborhood or adjoining neighborhoods—I might put that topic on our list of topics to address in our own outreach. In my case recently, Nextdoor neighbors had issues with water meters. As a result, we published an item in our customer newsletter, inserted with all bills, about how water meters work. I figure if five or 10 people are talking about something on social media there probably are a couple hundred or even thousand other people who are not on social media but who have the same issues or questions.[28]

You have to assess the environment and look for patterns. In a student organization, you might pay close attention to meeting attendance numbers or data on new applications to identify issues with membership. A nonprofit might compare year-end or holiday donations from year to year in the context of trends in competition.

3. Prioritization

Most organizations have issues. A big part of the *management* in *issues management* is deciding which issues require resources and when. Prioritizing issues means weighing the potential scope and impact of each. When investigating an active E. coli outbreak in the United States, the Centers for Disease Control and Prevention (CDC) released a report that linked 53 illnesses in nine states with 47 people who said they had eaten at a Chipotle restaurant. Twenty people were hospitalized.[29] Chipotle was then criticized by some for paying more attention to GMO issues (see Chapter 7) than the more immediate issue of restaurant food-safety procedures.

4. Analysis

Once issues have been identified and prioritized, they need to be analyzed to determine how they might affect the organization and its publics. Chipotle expected that same-store sales would fall 8–11 percent in the quarter following the E. coli outbreak.[30] Of course, issues management, and public relations in general, is about much more than sales. Analysis should include all sorts of publics besides customers. How, specifically, will employees be affected? Will they have to work longer hours? Earn less pay? Will they face public criticism? If you work for a nonprofit organization, you may analyze an issue's impact on volunteers and donors. In a college or university, you would consider students, faculty, staff and alumni. Each public will have its own specific concerns related to the issue.

5. Strategic Planning

After research and analysis, including the identification of key publics and how the issue will affect them, you can begin developing communication and relationship management strategies for each. If your role in public relations gives you a voice in the management of the organization (let's hope so!), you can work on both the strategic action response to the issue and the messages that will be communicated in conjunction with that response. For example, on the same day that the CDC released one of its key reports about the E. coli outbreak, Chipotle announced new food-safety procedures that it had developed, including improved programs for training employees for safer food handling.[31] Strategy at this stage means considering the specific actions that should be taken as well as who should take these actions, when and with what resources. Even if the management plan is developed outside of the public relations department (Chipotle worked with an outside consulting group to develop its new safety procedures), your communication plan must be coordinated with those management operations. Such strategy involves goals, objectives, timelines and budgets, as outlined in Chapter 6 on planning.

Ensure your communication plan matches the crisis response action plan, even if the response plan was developed outside of the public relations department.

6. Implementation

Implementation includes both action and communication. This is where policies and programs are put into action, and you activate owned, paid, shared and earned media (Chapter 7). In issues management, the underlying purpose of implementation is to prevent negative outcomes and encourage beneficial ones. In response to sweatshop and child labor problems that arose in the 1990s and persisted well into the 2000s, both Nike and Gap began funneling considerable resources into preventing further supply chain issues. Nike and Gap now tout their efforts on websites that they host to draw attention to their corporate social responsibility efforts. Other companies have built their entire brands on the concept of social and environmental responsibility.

Patagonia, for example, engages in a range of what the company calls "due diligence activities" to ensure fair labor practices and environmental responsibility. These include publishing and abiding by a strict code of conduct for suppliers, affiliating with the Fair Labor Association (FLA), participating in Social and Environmental Responsibility (SER) audits, and publishing on their website a complete list of factories that make their products.[32]

Socially responsible management also can be leveraged by organizations of any size to recruit and retain top talent. According to a Cone Communications study of millennial employees (people born between the 1980s

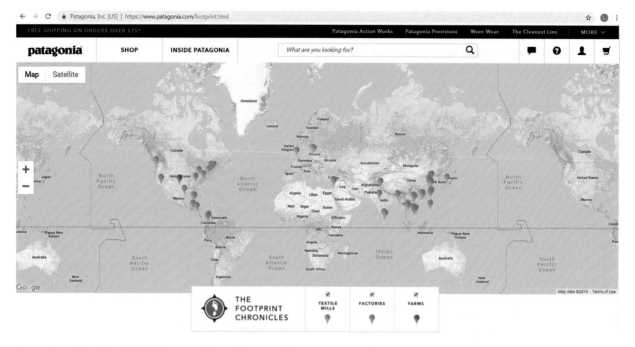

Patagonia monitors its global business practices and promotes its corporate social responsibility by reporting details on an extensive website, including the "The Footprint Chronicles," which reveals the company's supply chain.

How might such transparency help the company in issues management?

and mid-1990s), 76 percent said they would take a pay cut to work for a socially responsible employer and 64 percent would not take a job with an employer that does not have a good corporate social responsibility (CSR) policy.[33] Gen Z (people born between the mid-1990s and early 2000s) will likely follow that lead, but likely with a greater focus on the diversity and inclusion practices of employers. In a survey of more than 5,000 college students who expected to graduate between 2018 and 2021, "equality" was found to be the top cause that respondents wanted employers to support.[34] Implementation of equality as defined in the survey includes hiring women and people of color into leadership positions, challenging inappropriate behavior in the workplace, advocating for the worth and dignity of every person, and seeking and listening to diverse points of view.

7. Evaluation

In the evaluation stage, you assess the results, just as you would with any other public relations strategy (Chapter 8). If you're working with clearly articulated goals and objectives from your strategy, you will be able to measure the beneficial outcomes. However, many of the most important results of issues management stem from the crises *prevented*, or negative outcomes averted. These kinds of outcomes can be harder to measure with certainty because they are based on speculation about what might have occurred had the issue not been managed properly. Think of all the car companies that have not cheated (and been caught) on emissions tests. Think of all the restaurants that have *not* had E. coli outbreaks, or the student groups that maintained membership despite changes in leadership, or the nonprofits that rode out bad slumps in the economy, and so on. In some cases, alternate models can be used to illustrate what would have happened if a crisis occurred and had been managed poorly. And this is a happy outcome! Managers, experts and others with deep knowledge of an organization and its day-to-day and year-to-year options will appreciate knowing they avoided a boycott, illness outbreak, bankruptcy, product recall, lawsuit, embarrassing media scandal or any other potential crisis. What's more important—and this may be the result of either an issue averted or a crisis that played out all the way—is that evaluation allows you to learn lessons from experience and develop strategies for the future. Evaluation of how one issue was managed informs the first efforts of monitoring for the next one.

Evaluation of how one issue was managed informs the first efforts of monitoring for the next one.

Crisis Types

Not all crises are preventable, and how organizations respond to crises should depend on the degree to which people attribute responsibility for the crisis to the organization. Public relations scholars Tim Coombs and Sherry Holladay have developed one of the most well-researched and practical theories for crisis management called **situational crisis communication theory (SCCT)**. SCCT is a contingency theory because it suggests that how organizations should respond to crises depends on the situation. Coombs defines an **organizational crisis** as "a significant threat to organizational operations or reputations that can have negative consequences for stakeholders and/or the organization if not handled properly."[35] When people think that an organization is responsible for a crisis (e.g., Volkswagen), its reputation suffers, and the crisis leads to more anger, less purchase intent and greater likelihood of negative word of mouth about the organization. While issues management focuses on how to prevent organizational crises, crisis management deals with how to repair damage and rebuild reputation.[36]

Who's to blame? That is the question at the heart of initial crisis assessment. Researchers have identified three main groups of crisis types: (1) victim crises, (2) accident crises and (3) preventable crises.

Victim Crises

When publics see the organization as a victim, they assign minimal responsibility for the crisis to the organization. Natural disasters such as hurricanes, tsunamis and earthquakes are prime examples. People outside of an organization can cause victim crises too, such as in cases of sabotage, terrorism or product tampering.

One of the most famous examples of crisis management in the history of public relations stemmed from a victim crisis that arose because of product tampering by someone from outside an organization. In 1982, news broke that six adults and one 12-year-old girl in the Chicago area had died from

Situational crisis communication theory (SCCT)
Theory that proposes that effective crisis communication entails choosing and applying appropriate response strategies depending on how much responsibility for the crisis is attributed to the organization by key publics.

Organizational crisis
A major threat to an organization's operations or reputation.

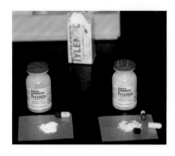

A sample of Extra-Strength Tylenol is presented side-by-side with a sample of cyanide-laced medicine in a medical examiner's office in October of 1982.

Why is this classified as a "victim crisis"? Would Tylenol's response have been different if it were an accident or preventable crisis?

cyanide poisoning after taking capsules of Extra-Strength Tylenol.[37] Since the tampered-with bottles of Tylenol capsules had come from different production facilities but were all purchased in the Chicago area, investigators ruled out sabotage or foul play at Tylenol factories. Police suspected that someone had purchased the bottles from local stores, poisoned the capsules, and then returned the products to store shelves. The murderer was never caught.

Tylenol's parent company, Johnson & Johnson, cooperated extensively with news media in expressing sympathy and sharing accurate information about both the crimes and the organization's response. At a cost of more than $100 million, Johnson & Johnson quickly pulled more than 30 million bottles of Tylenol from store shelves. They did not return the product to market until months later after developing now-standard tamper-resistant packaging.[38] The combination of quick, ethical action and communication earned the Tylenol case a place in history as an example of "how a major business ought to handle a disaster."[39]

Rumors are another category of victim crises. Social media have accelerated the pace at which false, damaging information can be spread. Just check the rumor-busting websites Snopes.com or FactCheck.org for daily

Fact-checking site Snopes.com found this story to be false, though the city government did introduce plans to reduce the purchase of processed meats consumed at city-run facilities.

Should city officials respond? Why or why not?

examples. For example, New York City did not ban hot dogs in an effort to combat climate change, U.S. Congresswomen Alexandria Ocasio-Cortez and Ilhan Omar did not praise the destruction of Notre Dame Cathedral in a 2019 fire, and President Donald Trump did not praise *Mein Kampf* or Adolf Hitler in public statements. (However, Snopes did confirm that Kim Kardashian wore mirrored glasses to a poker tournament.)

Accident Crises

Accidents happen. Industrial accidents, mechanical failures or IT crashes could all be considered accidents. In situations like these, an organization may not get a full pass as it would in a victim crisis, because publics still might question the organization's operations. In an industrial accident, were the appropriate safety procedures in place? In a mechanical failure, was the equipment maintained properly? In an information systems crash, were the data backed up in a timely manner? In any of these situations, if people label the source of a crisis as an accident, the amount of responsibility that they attribute to an organization is still relatively low compared to the next category, preventable crises.

Preventable Crises

Consider an airline crash. If investigators determine that an act of terrorism took place, the airline would likely be considered a victim. If, instead, they determine that equipment failure was to blame, this could be seen as an accident. If, however, the crash was due to inadequate pilot training, publics would see the crisis as preventable. Preventable crises caused by mismanagement, illegal activity or unethical action are the worst kind for organizations, and they may be intensified when the organization already has a reputation for breaking rules or a history of similar crises. By contrast, an airline with a strong safety record and evidence of following proper safety procedures has more latitude in its crisis response. This was the case with Ethiopian Airlines after a deadly crash of a Boeing aircraft. As we will see in the section that follows, knowing the crisis type helps determine the most appropriate crisis response strategy.

Crisis Response Strategies

In his book *The Crisis Manager: Facing Disasters, Conflicts and Failures*, crisis communication scholar and Boston University Professor Emeritus Otto Lerbinger likens effective crisis response to good medical practice. Lerbinger suggests crisis managers should take a page from the AMA *Family Medical Guide* in handling crises by following the same logic as a physician treating an illness. Track down the significance of a symptom or combination of symptoms and logically conclude what should be done about them. "To help in such diagnoses, crisis consultants list a wide assortment of crisis types from which to choose,"[40] writes Lerbinger, citing other scholars

> *In a crisis, follow the same logic as a physician treating an illness. Track down the significance of a symptom or combination of symptoms and logically conclude what should be done.*

such as Timothy Coombs. In addition to classifying the most common types of organizational crises, Coombs and Holladay offer an outline of crisis response strategies: deny, diminish, rebuild and reinforce. SCCT recommends selecting a response strategy appropriate to the situation.

Deny Strategies

Organizations applying deny strategies aim to absolve themselves of responsibility. Flat out denial was the initial strategy employed by representatives of New England Patriots owner Robert Kraft. When prosecutors announced they would charge Kraft with soliciting prostitution at a spa that was suspected of human trafficking in Jupiter, Florida, his representatives issued a statement that said: "We categorically deny that Mr. Kraft engaged in any illegal activity."[41] Kraft changed his tune a few weeks later after evidence of his involvement became more public, including documents showing that hidden-camera surveillance videos were taken of the alleged sex acts: "I am truly sorry," Kraft said in a prepared statement. "I know I have hurt and disappointed my family, my close friends, my co-workers, our fans and many others who rightfully hold me to a higher standard."[42] (Apology is a form of rebuild strategy to be discussed later in the chapter.)

Scapegoating or attacking the accuser is another form of denial that generally is not received well by publics. For example, when Chipotle co-CEO Monty Moran appeared to blame the CDC for the intensity of its E. coli crisis by saying that it was "fueled by the sort of unusual and even unorthodox way the CDC has chosen to announce cases related to the original outbreak," *Fortune* Senior Editor Geoff Colvin characterized the response as "how crisis leadership is *not* done."[43]

In other cases, deny strategies might make more sense. After Ethiopian Airlines Flight 302 crashed, killing all 157 people aboard, some news organizations, including Reuters and *The New York Times*, cited anonymous sources who said that the pilot had not been properly trained to fly the Boeing 737 MAX 8 aircraft. Ethiopian Airlines, which was recognized as one of the world's safest airlines, disputed the claims, noting that their pilots had indeed completed all training recommended by the U.S. Federal Aviation Administration and Boeing.[44] "We urge all concerned to refrain from making such uninformed, incorrect, irresponsible and misleading statements during the period of the accident investigation," posted the airline on both Facebook and Twitter.[45]

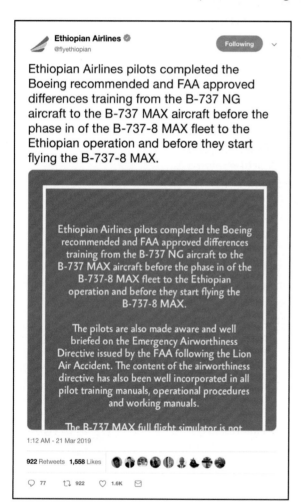

Ethiopian Airlines released this statement on Twitter and Facebook after the crash of Flight 302.

Did the deny strategy make sense in this case, or do you perceive it as scapegoating?

The investigation is still ongoing as of this writing, but the airline's denial seems more plausible and justified given that preliminary findings have shown that faulty sensor data in the Boeing equipment was likely involved in both the Ethiopian crash and a deadly Lion Air crash of another Boeing 737 Max that occurred a few months prior. With the information known to date, this could be considered more of an accident crisis with minimal responsibility attributed to Ethiopian Airlines and its pilots, while being considered more of a preventable crisis for Boeing.

Diminish Strategies

Diminish strategies acknowledge the existence of a crisis, but they minimize the organization's responsibility for the crisis or any bad intentions. The organization may also try to reframe the situation. For example, when state school systems receive media attention for low scores on national standardized tests, they may use a diminish strategy that questions the validity of the tests, claims that the school system is under-resourced compared to other states, or focuses on how hard teachers are working with so little compensation.

Rebuild Strategies

Crises test relationships. If the heart of public relations is relationship management, then there is perhaps no greater role for public relations in a crisis than rebuilding relationships. If an organization is responsible for a crisis, one of the most important communications it must issue is a public acceptance of that responsibility. If you realize you've screwed up in an interpersonal relationship and you want to repair the damage, you apologize. The same goes for organization-public relationships.

Apology, accepting responsibility and asking for forgiveness or understanding, is key to your rebuild strategy. That said, we all know that forced apologies come across as fake and insincere. One kid trips another on the playground and laughs. No remorse whatsoever. But then the teacher steps in and forces an apology. The words "I'm sorry" are muttered, but the relationship between the two kids doesn't improve. Adults have the same issues—even CEOs of major companies. When, in 2010, British Petroleum's CEO Tony Hayward stepped in front of a microphone following the largest U.S. marine oil spill ever, he appeared at first to apologize to local communities and families. "I'm sorry. We're sorry for the massive disruption it's caused their lives." But then Hayward delivered one of the most infamous lines in the history of corporate crisis

Following BP's tragic Gulf of Mexico oil spill, CEO Tony Hayward became the subject of ridicule for saying, "I'd like my life back."

Why might people have responded so negatively to his initial apology?

management. "There's no one who wants this over more than I do. I'd like my life back." Hayward later had to issue a statement that apologized for his apology![46] An apology that doesn't play well can have a **boomerang effect**, causing more damage than it repairs. Rebuilding relationships usually takes more than just words. Publics will look for evidence of sincerity.

Compensation is another classic rebuild strategy. Organizations may offer products, services or money to help make amends with publics. When Target experienced a credit card breach, they wrote to the owners of about 40 million credit and debit card accounts to explain the situation and to offer a year of free credit monitoring service.[47] Interestingly, Target did not actually apologize, but

Dear Target Guest,

As you have likely heard by now, Target experienced unauthorized access to payment card data from U.S. Target stores. We take this crime seriously. It was a crime against Target, our team members and most importantly you–our valued guest.

We understand that a situation like this creates stress and anxiety about the safety of your payment card data at Target. Our brand has been built on a 50-year foundation of trust with our guests, and we want to assure you that the cause of this issue has been addressed and you can shop with confidence at Target.

We want you to know a few important things:

- The unauthorized access took place in U.S. Target stores between Nov. 27 and Dec. 15, 2013. Canadian stores and target.com were not affected.
- Even if you shopped at Target during this time frame, it doesn't mean you are a victim of fraud. In fact, in other similar situations, there are typically low levels of actual fraud.
- There is no indication that PIN numbers have been compromised on affected bank issued PIN debit cards or Target debit cards. Someone cannot visit an ATM with a fraudulent debit card and withdraw cash.
- You will not be responsible for fraudulent charges–either your bank or Target have that responsibility.
- We're working as fast as we can to get you the information you need. Our guests are always the first priority.
- For extra assurance, we will offer free credit monitoring services for everyone impacted. We'll be in touch with you soon on how and where to access the service.

Please read the full notice below. And over the coming days and weeks we will be relying on corporate.target.com and our various social channels to answer questions and keep you up to date.

Thank you for your patience, understanding and loyalty to Target!

Gregg Steinhafel

Target sent this letter to customers after experiencing a credit and debit card data breach.

Would you categorize this as an apology?

they did offer compensation. In thanking customers for their patience, understanding and loyalty, they clearly were pursuing a rebuild strategy.

Reinforce Strategies

Another common response to crises is to reinforce relationships through either bolstering or ingratiation. **Bolstering** is reminding people of all the good things your organization has done in the past, while **ingratiation** is praising or thanking stakeholders to win their good favor. In a crisis, many of an organization's most important relationships are with the people who help to solve the crisis or aid its victims. Thanking first responders, praising volunteers and expressing appreciation to authorities who are involved in the crisis cleanup are ways organizations work to curry favor with key publics. However, as with apology strategies, ingratiation strategies risk backfiring if they are seen as insincere.

Be careful of issuing apologies or applying ingratiation strategies on social media unless they are clearly sincere and authentic.

Case Study

Mr. Zuckerberg Goes to Washington

Facebook has long faced public scrutiny over how it handles user data and protects consumer privacy. In 2018, this scrutiny culminated in congressional hearings in which U.S. lawmakers grilled CEO Mark Zuckerberg over privacy concerns. The hearings were called following a scandal in which the political consulting firm Cambridge Analytica was suspected of improperly harvesting the personal information of more than 87 million Facebook users. It all started with a personality survey.

Cambridge Analytica used online survey services from Amazon and Qualtrics to recruit hundreds of thousands of respondents who would be paid $2 to $5 per survey. There is nothing unusual or inherently unethical with this. But it became a Facebook issue and a legal and ethical issue when, at the end of the survey, respondents were asked to log in to Facebook to get the payment code to receive their compensation.

Once respondents logged into Facebook, Cambridge Analytica had access not only to the personality data from the 120-question quiz but also to all of the respondents' personal data on Facebook such as their name, location and contact details. And here's where it really blew up in scale. Cambridge Analytica also could scrape private information from all the Facebook friends of all the people who took the survey—that's how a privacy issue for 300,000 people became a major breach for more than 87 million.[48] Cambridge Analytica then weaponized massive amounts of computing power and data to target Facebook users with highly personalized political ads in the 2016 election. When all this came to light in 2018, thanks to investigative journalists and a whistleblower at Cambridge Analytica named Christopher Wylie, both Cambridge Analytica and Facebook were put into crisis response mode.

Bolstering
Attempting to offset reputational damage to an organization during a crisis by emphasizing the good work that the organization has done in the past.

Ingratiation
A type of reinforcing crisis response strategy in which stakeholders are praised or thanked to win their good favor.

Cambridge Analytica chose a *deny* strategy, and ended up collapsing within a few months. According to a company statement denying the allegations, "Despite Cambridge Analytica's unwavering confidence that its employees have acted ethically and lawfully . . . the siege of media coverage has driven away virtually all of the Company's customers and suppliers. As a result, it has been determined that it is no longer viable to continue operating the business. . . .[49]

Of course, the case also set off a wave of public concern and even outrage about Facebook. When Zuckerberg was called to testify in congressional hearings in 2018, lawmakers threatened more stringent regulation of Facebook. Both Facebook and Zuckerberg employed a number of response strategies, which included *apology* as part of a *rebuild* strategy. In his testimony to congress, Zuckerberg said,

> . . . It's clear now that we didn't do enough to prevent these tools from being used for harm as well. That goes for fake news, foreign interference in elections and hate speech, as well as developers and data privacy. We didn't take a broad enough view of our responsibility, and that was a big mistake. It was my mistake, and I'm sorry. I started Facebook, I run it, and I'm responsible for what happens here.[50]

Before the testimony, Facebook announced a number of new measures to better ensure user privacy and to increase transparency about how the organization operates. These actions also are consistent with a rebuild strategy, as evident in Zuckerberg's 2018 testimony.

All eyes (and lenses) were on Facebook CEO Mark Zuckerberg as he testified to congress following the Cambridge Analytica scandal.

What crisis response strategies were apparent in this case? Did they work?

It's not enough to just give people a voice, we have to make sure people aren't using [Facebook] to hurt people or spread misinformation. It's not enough to give people control of their information, we have to make sure developers they've given it to are protecting it too.[51]

A year later, Facebook was still wrestling with the issues raised in the Cambridge Analytica scandal, with fresh allegations about executive cover-ups still emerging. The company chose to use reinforce strategies such as *bolstering* and *ingratiation*. In a blog entry titled "A Privacy-Focused Vision for Social Networking," Zuckerberg led with some *bolstering*: "Over the last 15 years, Facebook and Instagram have helped people connect with friends, communities, and interests in the digital equivalent of a town square." He then outlined a vision for also providing more of a "living room" where privacy is more central and protected than it would be in a town square. He pointed to Facebook products Messenger and WhatsApp as more private channels. "We're focused on making both of these apps faster, simpler, more private and more secure, including with end-to-end encryption."[52]

He then closed with a hint of *ingratiation*, reinforcing a commitment "to consulting with experts, advocates, industry partners, and governments—including law enforcement and regulators—around the world to get these decisions right."

This case illustrates how Facebook applied a number of different response strategies with a number of different publics. With most of these relationships, Facebook's best status description might be "It's Complicated." Facebook's success in rebuilding damaged relationships will very much depend on the degree to which the organization is managed in ways that make its actions consistent with its communication. Time will tell if the apologies, bolstering and ingratiation are more than just words.

Social Media and Crises

One of the biggest challenges in managing crises is handling the rapid spread of information and the constant demand for that information. Prior to the rise of social media, crisis managers talked about the importance of the "golden hours"—the first few hours after a surprise crisis breaks—when an organization has its best opportunity to try to get out ahead of crisis communication with accurate information. With social media, those hours are reduced to minutes or even seconds. Social media have increased both the volume and the speed of communication in crisis situations and opened new channels for both organizations and publics to communicate. Crisis managers may see social media as a blessing (for communicating quickly and directly with publics) and a curse (for fueling the uncontrolled spread of misinformation and rumors). Recognizing the importance of

Social media crisis communication model (SMCC)
Model describing the role of social media influencers, followers and inactives in spreading information in crisis situations.

Social media creators
Influential social media users who are among the first to identify and post about crises online.

Social media followers
Social media users who receive crisis information from social media creators.

Social media inactives
People who receive crisis information indirectly from social media via traditional media and offline word of mouth.

Make yourself and your organization "influential social media creators" by setting up and maintaining crisis-specific social media accounts.

social media in particular in the ecology of crisis situations, public relations scholars Yan Jin, Brooke Fisher Liu, Julia Daisy Fraustino and their colleagues have developed a **social media crisis communication model (SMCC)** that highlights the interaction among social media, traditional media and word-of-mouth communication in crisis situations.

Think for a minute about a recent organizational crisis that you've heard about. How did you receive the information? There's a good chance that all three sources came into play. You may have heard about the crisis in a conversation with friends or family (word of mouth), seen it on TV or read about it in the newspaper (traditional media), and seen it on Twitter, Facebook and so on (social media). SMCC emphasizes that these sources are not mutually exclusive. If you learned about a crisis from a friend who used Facebook to repost and comment on a CNN.com article, this is an example of how word of mouth, traditional media and social media sources are all integrated in the crisis communication process.

The SMCC identifies three types of social media users for public relations practitioners to pay attention to during a crisis:

1. Influential **social media creators** are among the first to identify crises online and then post about them.
2. **Social media followers** receive their information from the influential creators.
3. **Social media inactives** receive information from traditional media and offline word of mouth. This does not mean that social media are not involved. Instead, what social media inactives learn offline may be informed by what their sources have learned from social media.

By understanding the relationship among these three sources, public relations professionals can think strategically about how an organization communicates during a crisis.

In most cases, it is good practice for the crisis team to centralize the flow of information. For example, a school crisis guide published by the National Education Association instructs, "The need to control information released to the media and public requires that the crisis plan clearly designate the person or persons responsible for this function."[53] Historically, these sources would operate with tactics such as periodic press conferences or conference calls that enabled the organization to communicate consistently and accurately with the news media. This is still common practice. Today, however, those news media then report breaking news via print, radio and television, as well as via social media platforms. SMCC describes one process whereby news media act as influential social media creators who share breaking news with followers on social media in addition to reaching social media inactives with traditional outlets like radio and TV.

SMCC also outlines another process for the spread of information in which the organization itself acts as a social media creator, as when companies set up new Twitter accounts for crisis-specific updates and inquiries.

While it's difficult to think of anything either controlled or "centralized" about the wildly crowd-fueled nature of how major crises break on social media, this doesn't mean public relations people can't play an important role in the process. As representatives with inside knowledge of the latest news related to the crisis, public relations people have the option of becoming influential social media creators. In that role they can work to communicate accurate and useful information directly with followers and indirectly with inactives.

Voices from the Field

Barry Finkelstein

BARRY FINKELSTEIN is senior vice president and associate director of public relations for Luquire George Andrews, a leading advertising, PR and digital marketing firm based in Charlotte, North Carolina. A frequent speaker on such topics as crisis communication, social media and integrated communications planning, Barry has served on the boards of the Georgia and South Carolina Chapters of the Public Relations Society of America. He also chaired the Client PR Committee for the American Association of Advertising Agencies (4A's).

What's the biggest crisis you've ever had to manage? What was the most important thing you learned from it, and what would you do differently if you had another chance?
The one that sticks out to me is the Atlanta school bus drivers' strike in the early '90s, because it impacted thousands of families who were depending on buses to get their kids safely to school. We spent the first few days on defense, doing press briefings a few times each day to let parents know when the buses would be running, or if they'd even be running at all. Around the third day we devised a strategy to use PR to turn the situation in our favor by inviting the news media to cover the hundreds of people who were lining up to apply for positions as replacement bus drivers. The strike literally ended the next day, and that was my big takeaway: I wish we had

been more proactive from the outset in using PR to not just manage the crisis, but to try to resolve it.

How do you go about monitoring for emerging issues for clients?
It varies by client. Some are in crisis-prone industries like utility companies or quick-service restaurants, so we have well-defined systems to alert us to internal events like robberies or fires, while also relying on traditional and social media monitoring to stay aware of any negative stories that are breaking. And for all of our clients, we stay abreast of trends and issues in their respective industries by monitoring traditional and social media for keywords tied to potential issues.

How are social media changing the way practitioners manage issues and crises? How is it easier with social media? Harder?
Social media have transformed the nature of crisis communications. News—and misinformation, in particular—now travels at the speed of light. Through social media, organizations are able to communicate with their most important publics in real time and without the editorial filter of the news media, which can be very advantageous in the event of a crisis. However, this also means organizations have a responsibility to be accurate and transparent in communications. Perhaps even more important,

organizations have an opportunity to use social media to *listen* to audiences and publics in a time of crisis, which may help an organization determine what steps and messages will resolve the matter with the least damage to the organization's reputation. But again, organizations must be careful not to squelch social media posts that may be negative toward their brand. It's OK to correct misinformation—and even to manage social media content that is offensive or intentionally misleading—but one of the keys to social media success is to allow publics to feel like their voices are being heard and valued.

What's the biggest crisis you've ever averted? And what did you do to avoid it?
Years ago I worked with a behavioral health system that was under investigation by "60 Minutes" for practices that were alleged to be a threat to patient safety. They were reluctant to participate in the story, but we knew if they did not participate, the story would be one-sided and almost certainly lead to more media and regulatory scrutiny. Ultimately, we persuaded the CEO to be interviewed after intensive media training, and the resulting story was more balanced and greatly minimized any follow-up coverage.

How does someone become a crisis communication expert?
Crisis communications is one of those areas where experience truly is the best teacher. I've been doing it for more than 20 years, and each episode teaches me something that will allow me to better counsel the next client. There are certainly some basic principles that can be picked up by reading articles and books or attending seminars. But the most important lesson in crisis communications is probably one you learned from your parents: Do unto others as you would have them do unto you. Put yourself in the shoes of the publics who will be most affected by the situation, and chances are you will instinctively know the right things to do and say.

Ethics: Conflicts of Interest

Public relations people are often faced with the challenge of balancing conflicting loyalties among various publics. If conflicts aren't managed well, they can become crises. Some of the most difficult ethical dilemmas that you may face in public relations, however, arise when *you yourself* are one of the parties in a conflict of values involving your organization.

The PRSA Code of Ethics includes the following principle: "Avoiding real, potential or perceived conflicts of interest builds the trust of clients, employers, and the publics."[54] One example of a conflict of interest provided in the code is failing to disclose that you have a major financial interest in a competitor of your organization or client. For example, if you work for Coca Cola, you wouldn't want to own stock in PepsiCo. However, sometimes conflicts of interest are unavoidable. In *Doing Ethics in Media*, Jay Black and Chris Roberts present a particularly sticky example that they developed as a hypothetical case study from real-world, firsthand experiences.[55]

In the scenario, you work as a public relations officer for a big mill operation in a small town that is facing tough economic times. The company has been good to you. They were very generous and supportive when your spouse (also a company employee) died in an accident at the plant a few years back. They've also rewarded your hard work with a series of promotions. You feel a strong sense of loyalty. But that loyalty is seriously tested when, in a meeting with upper management, you learn that the company's long-term plans include major layoffs at your plant. Thousands will lose jobs. You are upset, but the reasons for layoffs are understandable. Environmental problems and economic forces have made the plant's continued operation unsustainable. You're asked to keep the information confidential so the company will not lose its last major contract and set of work orders.

To make matters worse, you have family members who will be impacted in major ways. Your sister works in real estate and is planning to close some big deals on local homes in the area, and you now know the local real estate market is about to tank because of your company, taking those deals down with it. Your brother-in-law works at the company too, as a shift foreman. What do you do?

What makes this decision so difficult? It's the conflict of interest. On one hand you are a loyal employee and representative of the organization and you have accepted the responsibility of safeguarding confidences to lessen the impact of a crisis. On the other hand, you are very close to your sister and her husband, and your close family ties make it even more difficult to ignore the interests and values of the local community as a public with which you are deeply connected.

One tenet of crisis management that may help both the organizational and personal crisis is "Tell it all and tell it fast." Ralph Barney, a founding editor of *Journal of Mass Media Ethics*, offered this in response to an earlier version of this case when it was first published: "A principled response would be to make public the plans the company has for the plant, thereby demonstrating a willingness to serve larger society."[56] In a case like this, "larger society" includes your family and friends in the community. While you may serve as an advocate for your organization, traditional news media and social media influentials will no doubt serve to advocate for the interests of larger society. If these sources get wind of the story before your company is ready to release it (a common occurrence for organizations that try to keep a crisis secret for too long), your organization will be behind the eight ball.

Social media crisis communication theory suggests that your organization can serve as a primary source of information to publics during a crisis if you act quickly enough. Crisis communication researchers have applied the term **stealing thunder** to describe this strategy. In law, attorneys are known to "steal thunder" when they expose weaknesses in their own cases and address those weaknesses before their opponents have the opportunity to do so.[57]

Negative information spreads extremely quickly in the communication ecosystem of traditional media, social media and word of mouth. But if you work with traditional media and/or act as a social media creator for crisis-related information, it is possible to get ahead of the story and save some people from harm. One possible solution is for the public relations practitioner to apply both crisis communication theory and a deep understanding of the affected publics to make a case to upper management that "telling it all and telling it fast" is a better strategy than prolonged secrecy.

Stealing thunder
Crisis response strategy in which an organization exposes its own problems (and works to address those problems) before opponents have the opportunity to do so.

In Case You Missed It

While classic principles of conflict management, issues management and crisis management still hold, social media have increased options for detection, prevention, response and communication. Social media must be used with a clear understanding of their role in the communication process.

- Respond quickly and appropriately to challenges on social media to prevent issues from becoming crises.

- Sometimes it's better to advocate than to accommodate.

- Remember, that the customer may not always be right.

- Monitor social media to uncover issues sooner and give you more options for dealing with a situation.

- It's just as important to listen to detractors as it is to listen to supporters.

- Ensure your communication plan matches the crisis response action plan, even if the response plan was developed outside of the public relations department.

- Evaluation of how one issue was managed informs the first efforts of monitoring for the next one.

- In a crisis, follow the same logic as a physician treating an illness. Track down the significance of a symptom or combination of symptoms and logically conclude what should be done.

- Be careful of issuing apologies or applying ingratiation strategies on social media unless they are clearly sincere and authentic.

- Make yourself and your organization "influential social media creators" by setting up and maintaining crisis-specific social media accounts.

SUMMARY

12.1 Analyze responses ranging from advocacy to accommodation in public relations conflict cases.
In conflict, the action or communication tactic that you choose depends on the specifics of the situation. Contingency theory holds that response options range on a continuum from pure advocacy on one side to pure accommodation on the other.

12.2 Identify stages in the issues life cycle.
Stages in the issue life cycle include (1) early/potential, (2) emerging, (3) current/

crisis and (4) dormant. As issues grow, publics become more active and an organization's options for proactive management become more limited.

12.3 Describe how issues management can prevent or lessen the impact of crises.
The seven-step process for proactive issues management—(1) monitoring, (2) identification, (3) prioritization, (4) analysis, (5) strategic planning, (6) implementation and (7) evaluation—runs parallel to the four-step RPIE process. Actively monitoring the

environment with research increases the likelihood of identifying issues early enough to allow for proactive, strategic public relations rather than reactive, constrained damage control.

12.4 Identify public relations crisis types.
Crises can be categorized by the degree to which people attribute responsibility for the crisis to the organization. Victim crises happen when publics perceive that the organization has done nothing wrong (e.g., natural disasters, sabotage, terrorism, product tampering). Accident crises, such as those caused by mechanical failures, industrial mishaps, or computer crashes, involve some attribution of responsibility to the organization. Preventable crises caused by mismanagement, illegal activity or unethical action are the worst kind.

12.5 Define crisis response strategies.
How organizations respond to crises should depend on the crisis type. Deny strategies are used when organizations try to absolve themselves of responsibility. Diminish strategies attempt to minimize the organization's responsibility or bad intentions. Rebuild strategies involve accepting responsibility and working to rebuild relationships with publics. Reinforce strategies remind publics of all the good things the organization has done or is willing to do to reinforce relationships.

12.6 Discuss how traditional media, social media and offline word of mouth interact in the spread of crisis information.
Traditional news media are still an important source of information in crises, and—as has always been the case—offline word of mouth interacts with news media as people discuss what they learn from news media and as news media report on issues that people discuss. Social media offer greater opportunities for people to discuss and share information interpersonally (online word of mouth) and new channels for traditional media to reach publics. During a crisis, it is useful to identify (1) influential social media creators, who are among the first to identify and post about crises online, (2) social media followers, who receive their information from the influential creators, and (3) social media inactives, who receive information from traditional media and offline word of mouth. Both traditional media and offline word of mouth may be informed by social media activity.

12.7 Assess competing values in ethical conflicts of interest in the context of public relations issues and crises.
Public relations professionals face difficult ethical dilemmas when they have a deep personal connection with one of their organization's publics in a conflict or crisis situation. A classic dilemma involves a plant closing that will negatively affect the practitioner's close family and friends. One possible solution is for the practitioner to apply both crisis communication theory and deep understanding of the affected publics to make a case to upper management that "telling it all and telling it fast" is a better strategy than prolonged secrecy.

DISCUSSION QUESTIONS

1. **CASE STUDY** Was it right for Little Italy Restaurante's owner to "fire" a customer? Describe a time that you thought an organization was right to advocate instead of accommodate a key public during a publicly disputed issue. What contingencies of the situation made advocacy a better strategy than accommodation?

2. Select an organization to which you belong (could be a club, school, place of employment, etc.), and then identify one early/potential issue for the organization. What recommendations do you have for how the organization can handle the issue? Consider the seven-step process in your answer.

3. **CASE STUDY** "Dormant" issues have reached the final stage of the issue life cycle. Is the Volkswagen "dieselgate" issue dormant now? What consequences remain for the company?

4. Briefly describe one crisis of each type (victim, accident, preventable) that has occurred in the past year.

5. In the crises you identified in question #4, which crisis response strategies (deny, diminish, rebuild, reinforce) did the organizations employ? Explain whether you think the strategies were a proper match for the crisis type and whether the responses worked.

6. **CASE STUDY** Facebook applied multiple crisis response strategies when its handling of private user data came under fire. How would you categorize the crisis (victim, accident, or preventable)? What do you think Facebook's top two response strategies were? Did they work? Research Facebook privacy issues in the news to identify specific examples of consequences for Facebook that resulted from their response strategies.

7. What is the biggest organizational crisis you've directly observed in the past year? Were you a social media creator, a social media follower or a social media inactive in the case? How so? What role did the organization play in communicating to you about the crisis?

8. Suppose you find extremely biased information on the Wikipedia page for your organization. This information makes your organization look bad. Technically, anyone can edit Wikipedia entries, but why would it be a conflict of interest for you to do so? (You can find hints at https://en.wikipedia.org/wiki/Wikipedia:Conflict_of_interest and http://www.instituteforpr.org/wp-content/uploads/Beutler_WikiPrimer.pdf.)

KEY TERMS

Apology   337
Bolstering   339
Boomerang effect   338
Compensation   338
Contingency theory   322
Ingratiation   339
Issues management   324
Organizational crisis   333

Pure accommodation   322
Pure advocacy   322
Responsible supply chain
    management   329
Scapegoating   337
Situational crisis communication theory
    (SCCT)   333
Social media creators   342

Social media crisis communication
    model (SMCC)   342
Social media followers   342
Social media inactives   342
Stealing thunder   345

CHAPTER 13

Global

Understanding cultural dimensions can help us better communicate with publics around the globe. But what happens when a brand challenges traditional norms?

KEY LEARNING OUTCOMES

13.1 Apply high- and low-context communication and cultural dimensions to public relations strategy and practice.

13.2 Explain how environmental variables, such as politics, the economy and the media can affect international public relations.

13.3 Examine the role of nations, corporations and NGOs in public diplomacy.

13.4 Discuss the ethics of balanced dialogue in global public relations.

RELATED UNIVERSAL ACCREDITATION BOARD COMPETENCY AREAS

1.6 AUDIENCE IDENTIFICATION • **1.7** DIVERSITY • **2.2** ETHICAL BEHAVIOR
4.2 BARRIERS TO COMMUNICATION • **6.5** NETWORKS

Public relations strategy should be grounded in cultural insights and research from the beginning—not as an afterthought.

"This isn't a niche culture. It is the culture. This isn't a market. It's a movement. This isn't just about them. It's about all of us." This is how Condé Nast introduced its new platform, "Them.," in a social media video in 2017.[1] Them. is a digital community platform that covers topics like pop culture, politics and news from the perspective of today's LGBTQ community.[2] And while the platform's focus is the LGBTQ community, its message is all-inclusive: people and culture are more than "niches" and "markets" to reach.

In the United States, we're feeling the effects of this cultural movement all around us. Puerto Rican trap artist Bad Bunny performed at Coachella 2019, an annual music and arts festival in California that attracts thousands. *Billboard* described Bad Bunny's performance as "part of a seemingly unprecedented number of Latin acts on this year's Coachella roster."[3] That same year, BTS made history as the first K-pop (Korean pop) group to perform on *Saturday Night Live*.[4] In the box office, movies like *Black Panther* and *Coco* have gone beyond representation—they've celebrated and honored culture.

These cultural movements are just a few indicators of both the changing demographics in the United States and a shift in what's considered mainstream. Racial minorities, which now account for 30 percent of the U.S. population, are expected to represent more than half of the U.S. population by 2050.[5] These changes have given rise to terms like "total market" to describe public relations strategies. The **total market approach** combines insights and considerations from diverse segments to deliver integrated, culturally nuanced campaigns. It's not designed to be a one-size-fits-all strategy,[6] nor is it meant to pander to or appropriate culture. Instead, the total market approach calls for public relations strategy that is grounded in cultural insights and research from the beginning—not as an afterthought. According to professors Bey-Ling Sha, APR, and Rochelle Ford, APR, "all of us must learn to consider multiple diversities as constituting integral and integrated aspects of the field rather than as 'Others' that are somehow different and separate from 'mainstream' public relations."[7]

Public relations is a global business, and anyone thinking about a public relations career needs to be ready to embrace these cultural movements and globalization, which happens whenever public relations efforts spread across national, geographic or cultural borders. Intercultural and international fluency has become critical in boosting prospects for career success. In this chapter, we approach the topic of global public relations by considering factors that influence communication between people from different cultures and different nations, as well as communication between people from different cultures within the same countries.

Public Relations and Culture

We perceive the world around us from our own personal lenses, and this **ethnocentrism**—the tendency to judge other cultures based on what we may view as our own "superior" culture—can cloud our ability to communicate cross-culturally (with people of different cultures). The Peace Corps, an organization that sends thousands of young people abroad into different global communities every year, defines **culture** as "a system of beliefs, values, and assumptions about life that guide behavior and are shared by a group of people."[8]

The concept of culture applies to any group, not just groups defined by race, ethnicity or nationality. Categorizing people as "White," "Hispanic," "Asian," "African American," and so on is inherently limiting. As families become more multiracial and multicultural, these categorizations will become a less relevant way to understand publics, while shared interests and affinity will become more important.[9]

If we define a *public* as a group of people with shared interests (as we did in Chapter 1), then we see how the concept of *culture* applies to just about any public—residents of a town, students in a school, volunteers of a nonprofit, a company's top management or opponents of a political action. **Intercultural public relations** involves the interaction of an organization and publics across cultures. While we may think we understand different cultures, when we plan and execute public relations campaigns, we have to check our assumptions carefully. Understanding low-context and high-context communication and Hofstede's five cultural dimensions can help us begin to develop our cultural intelligence.

Something as ordinary as food and how it's prepared can be an expression of cultural identity. The Chinese hot pot, for example, is shared by those around the table, creating a collective dining experience.

What might we learn about a culture through food? How could these learnings be applied to public relations?

Culture
A shared system of beliefs, values, customs and so on that guides behavior of a particular group or public.

Intercultural public relations
Management of relationships between organizations and publics of different cultures.

You will likely deal with both high-context tactics like texts and tweets and low-context communication that spells out your organization's goals, policies and positions.

Low-Context Versus High-Context Communication

In his classic book *Beyond Culture*, anthropologist Edward Hall distinguished between **low-context communication**, in which most of the meaning of a message is stated explicitly in the message and words and requires little understanding of context, and **high-context communication**, in which most of the meaning of a message is based on context or something internal to the communicators rather than being directly stated in the message.[10] Restaurant menus, brochures, web pages and even course syllabi include very detailed descriptions and instructions and are tools of low-context communication, while tweeting and text messaging, which may be limited to very few words and characters, illustrate well the concept of high-context communication. Like so many other concepts in social science and public relations, however, high- and low-context communication are best thought of as ends on a spectrum rather than two completely separate ideas.[11]

Think about the shortest text message you have ever sent or received. For many this will be a one-letter message: "K." In the context of a chemistry lab, "K" stands for potassium. In baseball, "K" represents a strikeout. But in text messaging, the single character K—the explicit transmitted message—is often used as an abbreviation for "OK." To understand the actual meaning you have to understand the context. When it works, it may be the most efficient communication tactic ever, bringing a successful communication exchange to a satisfying conclusion with a single keystroke. But according to BuzzFeed's Katie Heaney, "K" is "the one thing you should never text anyone ever." In her eyes it "means you're too lazy to type out just one extra letter," "makes you seem mad," and sends a message that you're on a power trip.[12] The true meaning of "K" totally depends on the context, including the relationship between the sender and receiver.

When organizations develop public relations and branding campaigns, they have to be especially sensitive to high-context communication, too. Branding efforts rely on simple images, icons, logos, words and brief taglines to communicate enormous amounts of meaning about the organization or its products and services. The meaning depends on context. Branding magic happens when communication strategists successfully align an organization's actions, communication and culture with the cultural contexts of key publics.

A major part of the inspiration for Nike's successful "Just Do It" campaign (launched in the late 1980s) was a sensitivity to cultural trends in the United States, where obesity and procrastination were becoming more problematic for a large part of the population. According to Nike's former director of marketing insights and planning Jerome Conlon, the campaign developed by Nike's ad agency Wieden+Kennedy needed to reach people beyond highly motivated athletes. The campaign had to appeal to "the actual role that fitness plays in people's lives, the actual experience of really working out, doing aerobics, going on a bike ride, etc.," wrote Conlon.[13] The power of "Just Do It" lies not in the eight letters of text. It emanates from the contextual meaning assigned to it by millions of Nike fans.

Logos, taglines and advertising copy are essential to marketing, but public relations also entails a great deal of longer-form communication in the management of relationships between organizations and publics. Public relations professionals are often in charge of "spelling out" an organization's goals, policies, position statements, news and responses to inquiries. This type of elaboration requires low-context communication.

Let's consider a critically important moment: crisis (discussed in Chapter 12). The way public relations professionals and organizations react during crises, including if and how they apologize, may be informed by cultural preferences for high- or low-context communication. Imagine an organization you trust is involved in a cybersecurity breach. An Iowa State University study analyzed more than 100 official statements from organizations in the United States and South Korea to compare crisis response strategies and apologies following cybersecurity breaches.[14] The findings showed that statements from organizations in the United States focused on analytical, factual accounts of the crises, while those from South Korea "tended to express their concern for the incidents and show sympathy for the victims," reflecting the publics' cultural expectations. The study underscores that public relations professionals should tailor messages to meet cultural cues.

The distinction between high-context and low-context communication can be useful to people studying and practicing international communication. For example, people from **low-context cultures**—western cultures such as those from America, Switzerland, Germany and Scandinavia—*tend to* use more low-context communication. In low-context cultures, web users are more likely to use search features and links to seek specific information and facts about an organization. On the other hand, people from **high-context cultures**—such as those from Asia, Africa, the Middle East and Latin America—*tend to* rely more on interpersonal exchanges and social recommendations online.[15] One major caution in comparing people using these descriptions (high-context and low-context cultures) is that they are broad generalizations that do not apply to every individual or group within a geographic region. This is why we are careful to emphasize "tend to," as in, "those from Europe *tend to* use more low-context communication than those from Asia."

Low-context culture
A culture that relies on more explicit, direct communication than a high-context culture.

High-context culture
A culture that communicates more implicitly and relies more on nonverbal cues than a low-context culture.

After Cambridge Analytica accessed and weaponized the private information of more than 87 million Facebook users, Mark Zuckerberg posted a 15-paragraph statement of the timeline of events and steps to ensure it wouldn't happen again.

Is this high-context or low-context communication?

Power distance
Cultural dimension describing the difference between cultures that value hierarchy and authority and those that value equal distribution of power.

Individualism-collectivism
Cultural dimension describing the difference between cultures that value loyalty to self and immediate family and those that value loyalty to larger groups and society.

Uncertainty avoidance
Cultural dimension describing the difference between cultures that are uncomfortable with ambiguity (high uncertainty avoidance) and those that are at ease with ambiguity.

Masculinity-femininity
Cultural dimension describing the difference between cultures that value competition, achievement and material success and those that value care, collaboration and modesty.

Cultural Dimensions

To avoid stereotyping, public relations professionals (and anyone else communicating across cultural boundaries) should work to understand the various dimensions of any group's culture. Geert Hofstede is a Dutch social psychologist and professor who worked for years as a management trainer at IBM. In that role, he traveled around the world and systematically studied how IBMers operated and communicated differently in different cultures. Hofstede identified five major cultural dimensions that have been useful to understand and improve how people of different cultures communicate: **power distance**, **individualism-collectivism**, **uncertainty avoidance**, **masculinity-femininity** and **long-term orientation**. (Figure 13.1).[16]

Cultures with high power distance tend to be hierarchical, while those with lower power distance tend to be more egalitarian. In PRSA's *Public Relations Tactics*, global public relations author and professor Kara Alaimo explains how this can impact relationship building:

> *Researchers have found that, in countries with high power distance, governments tend to exert significant control on society and, therefore, it is important for PR practitioners to develop close relationships with government decision-makers. It can also be harder for PR practitioners to influence organizational decision-making if they are not senior enough within their organizations.*[17]

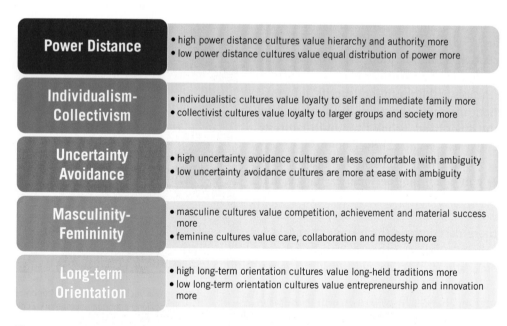

Power Distance
- high power distance cultures value hierarchy and authority more
- low power distance cultures value equal distribution of power more

Individualism-Collectivism
- individualistic cultures value loyalty to self and immediate family more
- collectivist cultures value loyalty to larger groups and society more

Uncertainty Avoidance
- high uncertainty avoidance cultures are less comfortable with ambiguity
- low uncertainty avoidance cultures are more at ease with ambiguity

Masculinity-Femininity
- masculine cultures value competition, achievement and material success more
- feminine cultures value care, collaboration and modesty more

Long-term Orientation
- high long-term orientation cultures value long-held traditions more
- low long-term orientation cultures value entrepreneurship and innovation more

Figure 13.1 Hofstede found these cultural dimensions to be helpful in understanding differences in communication styles.

With which cultural dimensions do you identify most? Which would be the hardest for you to adapt to in practicing intercultural public relations?

Another example is the dimension of individualism-collectivism. Individualistic cultures, like the United States and Australia, value loyalty to the individual, while collectivist cultures, like China and Mexico, value loyalty to society and larger groups. Coca-Cola's famous "Share a Coke" global campaign began in 2012 in Australia, featuring 150 unique names to "strengthen the brand's bond with Australia's young adults"[18] and connecting with the country's individualistic society. The campaign has since expanded to more than 70 countries, like Turkey, China and the United States, taking on new forms to resonate culturally.

Coca-Cola even embraced the diversity *in* the United States when it transformed the "Share a Coke" cans to celebrate Hispanic Heritage Month. Most Latin American cultures are collectivist, taking great pride in family and community. To tap into this pride, Coca-Cola created a special can with common Hispanic last names, like Pérez and Reyes, that would create a cultural connection beyond language.[19] But even genuine attempts can draw ire if consumers feel like public relations pawns. Though celebrated by many, the campaign received pushback from groups like *Latino Rebels*, which deemed it "hispandering" (pandering to Hispanics).[20]

A culture's uncertainty avoidance index can also affect how public relations professionals communicate with publics. Individuals in high uncertainty avoidance cultures are less comfortable with ambiguity. They prefer stricter sets of rules and procedures and seek to define future outcomes as specifically as possible. In low uncertainty avoidance cultures, individuals are more tolerant of not knowing how things will turn out, but it is

Long-term orientation
Cultural dimension describing the difference between cultures that value long-held traditions and cultures that value entrepreneurship and innovation.

Coca-Cola's "Share a Coke" campaign has crossed international and cultural borders, featuring not only individuals' names but also more general terms like cities.

How do "Share a Coke" cans reflect Coca-Cola's understanding of cultural dimensions?

important to still include them in conversations about the future. An organization opening a new plant in a high uncertainty avoidance culture may be required to present a detailed environmental impact statement showing exactly how they expect social, natural and economic environments to be affected.[21] Lower uncertainty avoidance cultures are more likely to seek an open-ended dialogue about the organization's plans for a new plant, and so town hall meetings or online forums for public discussion may be more effective ways to communicate plans and discuss options with low uncertainty avoidance publics.

Case Study

Vicks Redefines "Care" Despite Cultural Prejudice

What happens when a brand challenges a society's traditional notions of family, cultural values and beliefs? Vicks, an American over-the-counter medicine brand, would find out when it launched its "Touch of Care" campaign in India. The campaign highlights the story of Gauri Sawant, a transgender woman who adopts a daughter who has lost both parents.[22]

At the Holmes Report's PRovoke18 Global Public Relations Summit, Rekha Rao, senior vice president of MSL in Mumbai (the PR agency for the campaign), explained that Vicks has always stood for care—especially between a mother and a daughter. But, as Rao pointed out, even with the definition of "family" changing in India, many people don't think about transgender women providing care just like anyone else. Vicks wanted to show that care is what makes a family and that a "touch of care was not limited by social context."[23] But challenging these social and cultural constructs was risky.[24]

On the dimension of masculinity-femininity, India is considered a masculine society driven more heavily by competition and success than caring for others. It's also a high power distance culture that accepts unequal rights between the privileged and those who are not.[25] For years, India's transgender community was criminalized, and despite recent laws that grant transgender people the right to self-identify, discrimination continues.[26] Gauri describes how she and her daughter were ostracized by their community: "People did not want to touch us; they did not want to sit with us." [27]

Given these cultural realities, how would Vicks break through with a successful campaign? Strategy—and a whole lot of courage. The strategic approach centered on creating conversations that showed respect and appreciation for unconventional, caring relationships. Media and influencer outreach focused on showing the many voices that supported Gauri and "Touch of Care."

In India, only 38 percent of adults are internet users. However, those who do go online tend to have a secondary degree or to be younger.[28] To reach its audience, the communications channels had to include a mix of traditional media (like newspapers and TV) and online and social media.

And the results spoke for themselves. Within 24 hours, the campaign video went viral (without paid media support). The video alone garnered 4 million views in two days, and top news and trade publications in India covered Gauri's and Vicks' story positively.[29] Sales jumped an impressive 23 percent. And Vicks was even named "Brand of the Year" in India.[30]

Ed Booty, Chief Strategy Officer of Publicis Communications Asia Pacific, said it best: "Great brands don't just reflect safe and accepted norms, instead they dare to set agendas in culture at large. That is our ambition with this work for Vicks—to give the timeless idea of Family Care a fresh and contemporary meaning."[31]

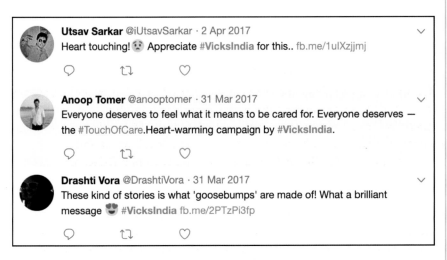

Vicks' "Touch of Care" campaign was met with inspired, congratulatory messages from Twitter users in India.

What do you think made this campaign so successful?

Cultural Intelligence

Unfortunately, merely studying and understanding cultural dimensions is not enough to ensure successful intercultural communication. Successful communication requires **cultural intelligence**. London Business School Professor Christopher Earley and University of Colorado Professor Elaine Mosakowski define cultural intelligence as someone's ability to interpret the cultural nuances of others' communications, even as an outsider. It's someone

Cultural intelligence
Ability to adapt, communicate and interact effectively across cultures by learning and applying cognitive, emotional and behavioral skills.

Build fluency in intercultural public relations with a combination of head (cognition), body (behavior) and heart (emotion/ motivation).

who can identify features of a group of people that are universal and those that are unique to individuals.[32]

Earley and Mosakowski identify three sources of cultural intelligence: head (cognitive), body (physical) and heart (emotional/motivational). Fluency in intercultural public relations comes from a combination of head, body and heart. As professional communicators and managers, public relations professionals succeed with different combinations of the three strengths.

HEAD (COGNITIVE)

Learning about high-context and low-context communication through reading is mostly a cognitive endeavor. You can study foreign languages and learn facts about cultures without ever really interacting with others from those cultures. And, while websites and corporate training programs also offer a wealth of knowledge, this type of knowledge is not sufficient to prepare you for all the situations you might encounter. Before setting up a global webinar, international press conference or site visit to a location where you will be interacting with those from another culture, you'll definitely want to study up. The most valuable learning, however, will come from careful observation and awareness of your surroundings during your actual foray. Earley and Mosakowski recommend developing strategies for this immersive type of cognitive learning:

- Think about what you hope to achieve.

- Learn from your experiences when you encounter something new in a different culture.

- Use those experiences to inform future actions and communication.

- Plan ahead for introductions to new people.

BODY (PHYSICAL)

Physical actions such as body motions, eye contact and gestures are a huge part of intercultural communication. When do you shake someone's hand? How firmly? Do you ever hug someone in a professional setting? Who sits where at a conference table? How much physical space should you give? How should you dress for an in-person press conference? What about a Skype interview? These are all questions of how you present yourself and interact in a physical sense.

Let's look at some examples across countries. A handshake is a common and accepted way to greet others in most business settings, but you'll want to use a lighter grip in China and Japan. In many Latin American countries, a hug or cheek-to-cheek kiss is not uncommon once you've developed a closer friendship, even in a business setting.[33] Be aware of eye contact as you shake hands. While some countries view it as a sign of respect, it can be disrespectful in others. Cultural differences exist when it comes to personal space, too. One study found that Argentinians have the smallest personal space (about 2.5 feet from a stranger), while Romanians have the largest (strangers should stay back more than 4 feet).[34] Someone who doesn't understand these nuances can be mistakenly perceived as rude on the first impression.

HEART (EMOTIONAL/MOTIVATIONAL)

The more experience we have in intercultural interaction, the more confidence we build in our ability to learn and adapt. Social psychologists call this **self-efficacy**, which is our belief that we can perform certain behaviors to achieve certain outcomes. Prior experiences and successes help us build self-efficacy, which motivates us to persist in difficult situations and learn new strategies, which leads to more success, which leads to more self-efficacy, and so on. It's a virtuous cycle if you can maintain it. Stanford psychologist Albert Bandura identified self-efficacy as a key to social learning, and social learning is what cultural intelligence is all about. People with high emotional or motivational cultural intelligence are confident they can work with others from different cultures and find it relatively easy to adapt to different cultures and unfamiliar cultural situations.

International Public Relations

According to the Commission on Public Relations Education, "now as never before, the public relations field is influenced by—and has influence on—evolving global connectedness."[35] **International public relations** involves the interaction of an organization and publics across national boundaries. As discussed in Chapter 3, globalization and global connectivity have facilitated more opportunities for intercultural communication and *cultural convergence*, which is when diverse cultures are imported, exported, exchanged and mixed. *Economic convergence* is also a hallmark of globalization. Economic convergence is evident when multinational advertising, marketing and communication conglomerates like Omnicom, Publicis or Burson Cohn & Wolfe (WPP) conduct their business via subsidiaries operating across the globe. However, you don't have to work for an international company or a global agency to work in international public relations. Even small organizations communicate regularly across national borders.[36]

Global professional associations, like the International Public Relations Association and the Global Alliance for Public Relations and Communications Management, offer guiding principles and provisions of conduct that can be applied by public relations professionals across the globe. These include principles like honesty, transparency, fairness and a commitment to working in the public interest.

For organizations practicing international public relations, the benefits of globalization include increasing the scope of operations, making more money in new markets and opportunities for achieving greater social and environmental impact with more diverse publics. As a global business, public relations can help achieve consistency in messaging that is authentic and credible. But globalization also carries with it greater risks for unintended

Guiding principles such as honesty, transparency and fairness can be applied by public relations professionals across the globe.

Self-efficacy
One's belief that he or she can perform certain behaviors to achieve certain outcomes.

International public relations
Management of relationships between organizations and publics of different nations.

consequences, miscommunication and faux pas. To mitigate these risks, public relations professionals must understand the role of environmental variables and the value of localization in public relations.

Environmental Variables

When was the last time you read a news article? Was it from a print news-paper? Or did you come across it online through a social media feed? Did the article change your opinion about a specific topic? Or did it reinforce the opinion you already had? Answering these questions can help us begin to understand how our environments influence public relations.

There are many different types of environmental variables that affect public relations, but three of the most influential and interconnected are: politics, the economy and media.[37] Public relations professionals must know how to adapt to these environmental variables to be successful in our interconnected world.

POLITICS

Imagine you're a public relations director for Greenpeace, an international organization that seeks to protect the environment. One of your organization's main goals may be to get Congress to create and pass a law that bans single-use plastic. At the same time that you're gathering support and peti-tion signatures, plastic manufacturers and the groups that represent them may be lobbying for just the opposite. Bipartisanship and existing laws may pose roadblocks that hinder your ability to effect change, too. Politics—from the governmental systems to ideology and policy—affect public rela-tions practice, and vice versa.

In December 2018, an animated commercial from Iceland Foods (a British grocery retailer) was banned from airing on TV in the United Kingdom. The commercial, which highlights the impact of palm oil on deforestation and the orangutan population, closed with Iceland Foods' commitment to remove palm oil from its own-label products. The reason for the ban? The Communications Act 2003 is a UK law that prohibits political advertising. Because the commercial from Iceland Foods was originally created by Greenpeace—an organization that could not prove it wasn't a political advertiser—the ad was banned.[38]

Without TV, Iceland Foods turned to public relations to drive results. The campaign video amassed more than 65 million views across social media and Iceland's owned channels. It also resulted in more than 700 pieces of media coverage and endorsements from celebrities like James Corden. One petition on Change.org asking for the ban to be overturned garnered more than 1 million signatures. What's more, sales increased for Iceland Foods.[39] The very ban (and law) that attempted to stop the campaign was what boosted its visibility.

Most research suggests that public relations is most advanced in demo-cratic countries where there are multiple centers of power and groups com-pete to influence policy,[40] like the United States and United Kingdom. Of course, this doesn't mean that there is no role for public relations in countries

James Corden ✓
@JKCorden

Follow ⌄

This commercial was banned from TV for being too political. I think everyone should see it x

🐹 Dan Lewis

0:17 · 19.1M views

Social media and endorsements from celebrities like British comedian James Corden, who is well-known in the United States, stretched this campaign beyond national borders.

How might this campaign be perceived differently in other countries and cultures?

governed by monarchies and authoritarian regimes.[41] However, it does suggest that public relations professionals should candidly consider the role of politics—and how it can inform and affect their efforts—in the countries in which they work.

THE ECONOMY

Believe it or not, a course in macroeconomics or microeconomics can help you better understand and practice public relations, too. That's because economic systems and conditions, including poverty and literacy rates, affect the public relations industry both at home and abroad. Professor Hong Tien Vu, whose research focuses on global and development communication and digital media, describes this simply:

> When you have enough economic resources, you can think about things like the environment or gender equality. When you're living in poverty, it's hard to think about anything other than putting food on the table.[42]

This presents a unique set of challenges for public relations professionals in developing countries. Individuals' literacy, access to media and the

Two-way communication can be particularly challenging when your publics don't have the information or resources to engage in dialogue.

Digital divide
Gap between those people with relatively little access to and use of information and communication technologies and those people with greater access and usage.

number of information sources available can vary drastically. Two-way communication (see Chapter 1) can be particularly challenging when your publics don't have the information or resources to engage in dialogue.[43]

The term **digital divide** refers to a gap in access to digital information and communication technologies. The digital divide concept is a relative one—meaning that it could be used to describe the difference between populations that are completely wired with the latest 5G internet connections and those that have slower access to the internet; or, it could be used to describe the relative difference between parts of the globe with internet access and parts of the globe without any access at all. Pew Research Center surveys of 11 emerging and developing countries in 2018 found that the majority of adults in all but one country, India, are internet users, pointing to the growth of mobile connectivity (Figure 13.2). The center suggests that digital devices can create "swift and encompassing cultural change" in emerging economies, even more dramatic than the effect in developed countries.[44]

Economic downturns, like recessions, can impact the public relations industry, too. According to a study by the USC School of Communication, the Great Recession that occurred between 2007 and 2009 resulted in smaller budgets and employee cuts for many public relations agencies.[45] But not all organizations cut back during these tough times—auto brand Subaru doubled down on public relations instead. A consistent message of "people love Subaru" and proactive storytelling resulted in record sales for Subaru during the recession.[46]

MEDIA

The Economist reported a "global slump in press freedom" in 2018.[47] The First Amendment rights of journalists and media in the United States are not the same across the globe. In China, the government tightly controls and censors the media, including online and social media (Facebook and Twitter are blocked, for example), in what journalist James Griffiths calls "The Great Firewall of China."[48] Recent studies by think tank Freedom House (an independent watchdog organization dedicated to expanding freedom globally)[49] found that freedom of press is worsening in countries like Brazil, Argentina and Colombia, too.[50] Knowing if and how media are controlled can impact the channels you choose to communicate with your publics—and how effective those channels are.

The way individuals perceive and consume media differs internationally, too. The 2019

In most emerging economies surveyed, a majority of adults go online

% of adults who say they use the internet

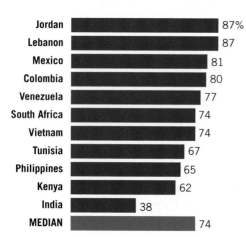

Jordan	87%
Lebanon	87
Mexico	81
Colombia	80
Venezuela	77
South Africa	74
Vietnam	74
Tunisia	67
Philippines	65
Kenya	62
India	38
MEDIAN	74

Note: Internet users include those who say they use the internet, use at least one social media platform or messaging app, or own or share a smartphone or feature phone.
Source: Mobile Technology and its Social Impact Survey 2018. "Mobile Connectivity in Emerging Economies"

PEW RESEARCH CENTER

Figure 13.2 Data from the Pew Research Center show that adults in emerging economies are increasingly accessing the internet.

How might practicing public relations in Jordan be different from practicing public relations in India?

On World Press Freedom Day, protestors in the Philippines march for press freedoms and democratic rights.

How might governmental media control impact public relations efforts?

Edelman Trust Barometer, an annual global study that surveys 26 markets (including the United States, Brazil, Germany, South Korea and the United Arab Emirates), found that although trust in media grew globally, media was still the least trusted institution compared to businesses, nongovernmental organizations (NGOs) and government. But how trust played out in each of the 26 markets varied; people in China and Indonesia were the most trusting of media, while those in Russia and Turkey were the least trusting. Globally, traditional media and search engines were more trusted than social media.[51]

When it comes to media consumption, global trends point to the growth of online TV and news consumption. Still, that's not true of people in all countries. For example, France, Germany and Belgium spend longer times with traditional media (like linear TV, newspapers and magazines) than with digital media.[52]

In the 2000s, social scientists started to pay attention to a second type of digital divide: the usage divide. The **usage divide (or second digital divide)** focuses on differences in how people from different groups (or publics in the case of public relations) actually use the technologies to which they have access. Even if our publics have access to the same communication technologies we use, it doesn't mean they're using that technology to access news or engage with organizations. We have to be careful not to assume that all groups use technology and digital media in the same way we do.

Usage divide (or second digital divide)
Gap between people who use information and communication technologies for education, self-betterment, civic engagement, etc. and those who use the technologies for less constructive reasons.

LOCALIZATION

According to senior global public relations leader Amanda Glasgow, "There is no such thing as global public relations." In a thought leadership essay for the International Public Relations Association, she explains:

> On the most basic level global public relations doesn't work because as most PR practitioners will tell you, the best PR is local. Good PR gets at insights that are specific to a consumer, or has a flavor that is distinctive to her country, her city, her neighborhood.[53]

Importing public relations ideas from other countries may work, but it should be the local markets that make those decisions.

Similarly, global public relations agency Weber Shandwick emphasizes the importance of globalizing strategies and standards, but localizing tactics.[54] A survey of senior corporate communication executives for large multinational companies found that "global integration" called for consistent brand positioning and the quick flow of knowledge across global teams, but that didn't mean replicating tactics in multiple countries. Participants stressed that while introducing ideas from other countries *may* work, it should be the local markets that make those decisions.[55] Some of the most commonly localized tactics are those associated with media relations, such as press releases, media pitching and news conferences. Others include tactics like digital and social media, identifying local spokespeople and influencers, and hosting special events.[56]

Visa's Everywhere Initiative is an example of a program that has supported startups and entrepreneurs across 75 countries in North America, Latin America, Europe, Asia, the Middle East and Africa. Across the globe, the program's core concept of inviting startups to tackle financial tech challenges remains consistent; yet, the challenges are uniquely tailored to each local region. For example, in South Korea, one challenge focused on creating richer experiences for international travelers because the number of travelers had nearly tripled in nine years.[57] Meanwhile in the United States, another challenge focused on making it easier for companies to adopt digital payments[58] because data show that many small business owners still opt for paper checks as a primary payment method.[59]

In 2019, Visa broadened this regional approach with the launch of the "Visa Everywhere Initiative: Women's Global Edition," a worldwide program that invites women entrepreneurs to tackle a financial technology or social impact challenge, showing how their businesses are driving change in areas like financial literacy, environmental sustainability, gender equality and humanitarian relief.[60] The program is rooted in global research: the Global Entrepreneurship Monitor reports that "163 million women were starting businesses across 74 economies worldwide."[61]

Global public relations must achieve a delicate balance between standardization and localization. Making sure your practices and messages are consistent but still reflect local realities takes mindful work and can be tricky. Add to that the global reach of social media, and it can be even more challenging to anticipate how your publics (and even those who are not) will react.

Translations of **car**		
Noun		Frequency ⑦
gli **auto**	car, auto	■■■
la **macchina**	machine, car, machinery, engine, motor	■■■
automobile	car, automobile, auto, motor	■■▫
le **vettura**	car, coach, carriage	■■■
la **carrozza**	carriage, coach, cab, car, chaise, fiacre	■▫▫
il **carro**	wagon, cart, chariot, carriage, car, truck	■▫▫

Localization is not merely translation. A Google Translate search of the word "car" yields six Italian words. While all of these are accurate translations, the proper word choice can vary by region and context. Work with and hire local translators and public relations professionals to avoid mishaps or embarrassing moments.

How might you ensure your word choice is best understood by your publics?

Case Study

Mastercard's World Cup Campaign Gets a Red Card

Some consider soccer's popularity and rise a symbol of globalization. In his book *The World Through Soccer: The Cultural Impact of a Global Sport*, Professor Tarim Bar-On compares soccer to a secular religion with devoted fans and revered deities (e.g., soccer stars).[62]

More than half of the world's population watched the 2018 FIFA World Cup,[63] an international soccer tournament in which 32 teams representing their home countries competed against one another. About 10 percent of those viewers were from South America alone.[64]

You might understand, then, why the World Cup is such an appealing cultural moment for brands. Long-time FIFA World Cup partners include Adidas, Coca-Cola and Visa.[65] But even organizations that are not official partners or sponsors want in on the action—and they often find loopholes to engage their audiences without ever mentioning the actual tournament.

That was Mastercard's plan in 2018 with its "Start Something Priceless" campaign in Latin America and the Caribbean.[66] As part of the broader campaign, the credit card company partnered with soccer stars Lionel Messi (of Argentina) and Neymar Jr. (of Brazil). It planned to donate the equivalent of 10,000 meals to the World Food Programme to fight childhood hunger in Latin America and the Caribbean every time one of the two players scored a goal.[67]

More than 39 million people were living in hunger in Latin America and the Caribbean that year, an increase of nearly half a million from previous years. Of that 39 million, 5.1 million children under five years old suffered from chronic malnutrition.[68]

Neymar Jr. expressed his support of the effort: "Latin Americans know we can do great things when we come together, and this is an example of that. Together we can fight hunger."[69] But even with the backing of two of the biggest names in soccer, backlash on social media was swift. Though many thanked the brand for its efforts, others—especially in the UK and Europe—criticized the campaign, calling it a "publicity stunt" and comparing it to the "hunger games." Some suggested Mastercard donate the funds, instead of gamifying hunger.[70]

This tweet from MasterCard's Twitter account in Latin America prompted a deluge of negative comments.

How might social media prompt unexpected responses to regional public relations efforts?

At first, Mastercard's response was to defend its stance, stating, "This campaign is a small part of our overall global commitment [with WFP] to deliver 100 million meals to those in need of food assistance." But ultimately, in the face of escalating backlash, the brand nixed the campaign altogether, instead donating 1 million meals to the World Food Programme that year.[71]

Though Mastercard's campaign was likely well intended, it distracted from the real economic and social issue: Malnutrition and hunger are increasing in Latin America and the Caribbean—and the world. Even though it was a targeted, regional campaign, social media users let it be heard around the world that they did not want to make a game of feeding the hungry.

Public Diplomacy

Public diplomacy is an important subset of international public relations that deals with communication designed to promote national interests. In most cases, this means that the organization, a key public, or both, are nations, but in certain cases diplomatic actors may include non-state organizations such as NGOs or corporations. If you work in communications for a government organization like the U.S. Department of State or for a U.S. Embassy or Consulate, or if you work for one of these departments' counterparts in another nation, your job will likely entail public diplomacy with the broadest mission of promoting national interests abroad. You may also be involved in public diplomacy working for an NGO or corporation.

Consider the Tech for Good Summit, which was hosted in 2018 by French president Emmanuel Macron, amid growing concern about the role of technology in society.[72] Fifty CEOs and top executives from the world's leading technology companies, like Accenture, Facebook, Microsoft and Uber, attended the summit to discuss how technology can positively contribute to society.[73] And many even made concrete commitments at the summit. Uber, for example, committed to providing free health insurance to its 150,000 drivers in Europe. At the same time, Macron, who has talked about transforming France into a world leader in artificial intelligence (even funding a €1.5 billion plan),[74] made it clear that France's ardent support for innovation is coupled with a call for tougher regulation and working for the common good.[75] To the degree that these corporations and the French government worked to influence one another and effect change, they were practicing public diplomacy as a form of international public relations.

In discussing public diplomacy as a form of public relations, Professor Guy Golan defines two key perspectives. First is **mediated public diplomacy**, which is a nation's strategic use of media to promote its agenda and "impact opinions held by targeted foreign audiences."[76] The second approach is **relational public diplomacy**, which is engagement between a nation and its foreign publics in cultural exchange and two-way communication with the goal

Public diplomacy
Subset of international public relations that focuses on promoting national interests.

Mediated public diplomacy
A nation's strategic use of media to promote its agenda abroad to foreign publics.

Relational public diplomacy
Engagement between a nation and its foreign publics in cultural exchange and two-way communication with the goal of achieving mutual benefits.

Global technology CEOs and French leaders met in Paris for the Tech for Good Summit in 2018.

Why might corporations want to develop close relationships with nations abroad?

Use media to gain favorable exposure that helps set the stage for more interactive relationship building in public diplomacy.

of achieving mutual benefits. Mediated public diplomacy aligns well with the public information and asymmetrical models of public relations that were outlined in Chapter 2. Relational public diplomacy fits better with two-way models and the symmetrical ideal. Golan recommends integrating the two approaches, using media to gain favorable international coverage that helps set the stage for more interactive relationship building.

Voices from the Field

Patrick Ford

PATRICK FORD is an industry leader who has been recognized for his contributions to the practice of public relations by the PR Council, PRWeek, the Institute for Public Relations and the Plank Center for Leadership in Public Relations. Ford is a visiting professional in residence at the University of Florida. Prior to this role, he was most recently Burson-Marstellar's worldwide vice chair and chief client officer. During his 29 years at the firm, he held positions as varied as U.S. CEO, Asia-Pacific chair, global Corporate Practice chair and U.S. Corporate Practice chair. Ford specializes in corporate reputation management, senior executive communications, media strategy, and issues and crisis management.

What's the most challenging intercultural communication situation you've observed in your public relations work?

Running the Asia-Pacific region for a global agency with 18 offices and 11 affiliates was the most exciting experience of my career but also the most challenging with regard to the political, economic and cultural diversity in the region. On one hand, China's economic growth, the expansion of its consumer base and its increasing engagement with other world economies have combined to create robust opportunities for global corporations and agencies. At the same time, multinational companies face daunting regulatory barriers and must adapt their digital and social media engagement systems. Because China blocks or restricts many Western platforms, including Twitter, Facebook, Google and YouTube, companies must deal with other online platforms that operate in their place, including Weibo, WeChat and Baidu. And as they build their local staffing with Chinese nationals, they must be sensitive to the profound differences in their background and understanding of western norms.

What can students do to prepare for international and intercultural public relations assignments in advance?

These are exciting times for new public relations professionals, but you need to be proactive and strategic about how you prepare for those opportunities. Learn a second language, spoken in whatever part of the world you aspire to work in later. In addition, participate in some sort of study-abroad program or secure internships in other countries, and take lots of notes. There are few things more valuable for one's professional development than seizing opportunities to immerse oneself in a foreign business community and culture. If international travel is not an option, then take some sort of international relations course and seek out international public relations and/or business courses that address the challenges involved in transnational business management.

What do you consider to be the greatest opportunity for public relations as a field arising from trends in globalization?

Public relations practitioners should be—and in the best situations are—key players in building and protecting corporate and brand reputation. We help the CEO and other C-suite executives express the companies' values and mission, and we measure the companies' performance on those values and regularly analyze the perceptions of key stakeholders through rigorous qualitative and quantitative research.

Every aspect of this process presents more opportunities than ever for public relations departments, agencies and professionals. This is a significant factor in explaining why chief communications officers are increasingly seen as C-suite level positions. As business globalization creates even greater need for understanding and engaging with stakeholders, the opportunities for public relations will continue to grow.

How do you see public relations practitioners adapting to differences in politics, the economy and media across the globe?

Multinational companies, agencies, and nonprofit organizations have long been accustomed to navigating a host of political, regulatory, cultural, language and economic differences in various countries and regions of the world. For today's and tomorrow's public relations practitioners, who have major responsibility for protecting corporate and product brands, the challenges are magnified because of the speed and ubiquity of digital and social media. Even in societies in which government restricts access to information, public relations practitioners play a major role in their companies' efforts to engage with key stakeholders while complying with and respecting legal, economic and cultural boundaries.

Given changes in demographics and technology, how are new public relations practitioners entering the field more prepared?

They are entering the field with a high degree of digital sophistication and social media fluency, so they are better equipped to source data and recognize productive ways to engage with stakeholders online. They also have access to a wider range of in-depth case studies, which should make them better prepared to anticipate stakeholders' expectations. In addition, they have opportunities to gain highly valuable hands-on experience in a range of intern positions at major companies, agencies and nonprofits. And an increasing number of universities are offering on-campus programs that can also enrich one's professional development, such as PRSSA and student-run agencies, and competitions such as Bateman and the Page Case Study competition. Most importantly, new professionals are emerging from more diverse generations, and thus will be better equipped than any of their predecessors to address some of the most important needs in today's communications world: diversity, equity and inclusivity at all levels of our profession.

Dialogic communication
Exchanges involving people communicating their own views and backgrounds while remaining completely open to seeing the world as others do.

Monologic communication
Communication in which one party attempts to impose its view on others.

Ethics: Dialogic Ethics

In his 1923 book *I and Thou*, Austrian-born philosopher Martin Buber developed the concept of dialogue to explain how people come to understand their own existence through their interactions and relationships with others. **Dialogic communication** happens when people enter into an exchange with an understanding of their own views and backgrounds but also with complete openness to seeing the world as others do.

The opposite of dialogic communication is **monologic communication**, in which communicators strive to impose their views on others. How might this play out in your college classroom? Monologic communication happens when your professors assert their authority and limit opportunities for student collaboration and discourse. Where dialogic communication occurs, professors and students alike openly express and exchange their views. As you might have experienced, this often occurs on a continuum, rather than only one way or the other.[77]

Ethicists hold that the day-to-day practice of public relations leans too much toward monologic and not enough toward dialogic communication. They consider monologic public relations to be less ethical because it treats publics as less important than the powerful organizations conducting public relations. Dialogic public relations facilitates a fairer balance of power, and the growth of the internet and social media as tools for public relations has led a number of public relations scholars to focus on the concept of dialogue as an ethical guidepost.

When this photo of bagels sliced like loaves of bread went viral, Panera posed a question to its followers, admitting that its own team was divided on the #Bagelgate debate.

Why might this be considered an example of dialogic communication?

Asking questions on Twitter (which often start with "Ok Twitter" or "This is crazy, but") has become somewhat of a viral sensation. *The Daily Beast* reported that question tweets are a popular trend: "They're open-ended. They're designed to elicit quick responses. And they're absolutely everywhere."[78] But, think about the last time a brand you follow asked an open-ended question on Twitter. Did it feel like an earnest attempt to openly exchange ideas, or just another way to make a sale?

Studies have found that though a majority of Fortune 500 companies use Twitter in a dialogic way, there are still many that don't. Generally, companies respond to tweets from other users and post newsworthy information about the company. But less than a third of tweets pose questions that promote dialogue with others.[79] There's also typically a lack of transparency—you don't necessarily know who is behind the screen tweeting on behalf of the company.

The decision between monologic and dialogic public relations parallels questions of one-way versus two-way communication (Chapter 1), asymmetrical versus symmetrical public relations (Chapter 2) and advocacy versus accommodation (Chapter 12). Reasonable moral arguments can be made for both sides depending on the circumstances.

In global public relations, reaching across cultural and geographical boundaries to get to know one another better takes extra work, but it is a must. Successful and ethical public relations requires an understanding that not everyone shares your background and culture. It's crucial that you take the time to learn about what matters most to your publics.

Successful and ethical public relations requires an understanding that not everyone shares your background and culture.

In Case You Missed It

Global interconnectedness is influencing public relations, and vice versa. Culture, politics, the economy and media all affect the way we practice public relations globally—both within and across national borders. This means that navigating intercultural challenges is part of everyday public relations work. Here's some advice culled from the chapter:

- Public relations strategy should be grounded in cultural insights and research from the beginning—not as an afterthought.

- You will likely deal with both high-context tactics like texts and tweets and low-context communication that spells out your organization's goals, policies and positions.

- Build fluency in intercultural public relations with a combination of head (cognition), body (behavior) and heart (emotion/motivation).

- Guiding principles such as honesty, transparency and fairness can be applied by public relations professionals across the globe.

- Two-way communication can be particularly challenging when your publics don't have the information or resources to engage in dialogue.

- Introducing public relations ideas from other countries may work, but it should be the local markets that make those decisions.

- Use media to gain favorable exposure that helps set the stage for more interactive relationship building in public diplomacy.

- Successful and ethical public relations requires an understanding that not everyone shares your background and culture.

SUMMARY

13.1 Apply high- and low-context communication and cultural dimensions to public relations strategy and practice.

In high-context communication, most of the meaning conveyed between people lies in the context of the communication or is internal to the communicators. Taglines, tweets, brand logos and text messages are examples of high-context communication because success in this type of messaging depends so heavily on the context and the meaning assigned by the people involved. In low-context communication, most of the meaning lies in the message itself. Low-context communication requires greater elaboration and detail in composing messages.

Understanding cultural dimensions such as power distance, individualism-collectivism, uncertainty avoidance, masculinity-femininity and long-term orientation is an important part of cultural intelligence that involves cognitive skill in designing public relations strategy. Though tailoring communications to meet cultural expectations can be effective, successful public relations campaigns sometimes purposely challenge the status quo.

13.2 Explain how environmental variables, such as politics, the economy and the media can affect international public relations.

Public relations professionals must know how to adapt to environmental variables—like politics, the economy and media—in an increasingly interconnected world. Factors like mobile connectivity and internet access in emerging economies can influence how organizations communicate with their publics internationally. Though a global business, public relations must also count on local perspectives that are relatable and credible.

13.3 Examine the role of nations, corporations and NGOs in public diplomacy.

Public diplomacy is a subset of international public relations that deals with communication intended to promote national interests. In most cases, this means that the organization, a key public, or both, are nations, but in certain cases diplomatic actors may include non-state organizations such as NGOs or corporations. Professionals involved in public diplomacy can use media to gain favorable international coverage that helps set the stage for more interactive relationship building.

13.4 Discuss the ethics of balanced dialogue in global public relations.

Dialogic approaches to public relations are commonly held to be more ethical than monologic approaches. The growth of the internet and social media as tools for public relations has led a number of public relations scholars to focus on the concept of dialogue as an ethical guidepost, because dialogue fosters equality and may lead to an understanding of truth that arises from multiple perspectives. Equality and mutual understanding are particularly noble aspirations for international and intercultural communication.

DISCUSSION QUESTIONS

1. Think about the cultural movements that are shaping the world around you. You can look to pop culture, politics and even fashion. Do you feel you're a part of one of these movements? If so, why? If not, who are those most impacted by these movements?

2. Identify an organization that is really good at high-context communications and compare that organization to one that is really strong in low-context communications. Which would you rather work for and why?

3. How would you describe your own cultural preferences, according to Hofstede's model? (You may want to try this resource: http://geert-hofstede.com/cultural-survey.html.) Which of the dimensions would be hardest for you to adapt to in practicing intercultural public relations?

4. **CASE STUDY** Vicks' "Touch of Care" campaign challenged cultural beliefs and norms in India. Think about one of your favorite brands and examine how it resonates with your culture. Does the brand tailor messages to your cultural expectations or challenge them instead?

5. Select a country outside of your own and jot down everything you know (or think you know) about that country. Then, search the internet to better understand its political system, economy or media. How might what you learned online affect how you communicate with publics in that country?

6. **CASE STUDY** Mastercard's World Cup campaign was criticized by many on social media for gamifying hunger in Latin America and the Caribbean. Most of its critics weren't even from the region. What global campaigns have you seen on social media that weren't directed at you? How did they appear on your newsfeed?

7. Explore the web presence of an international embassy (sites like http://embassy.goabroad.com may be helpful). Explain how the embassy's diplomatic approach is more *mediated* or *relational*, or if it is better described as a mix of the two.

8. Describe an example from your own life when you engaged in dialogic communication. Who was your public? What did you learn from your experience that you could apply to public relations practice?

KEY TERMS

Cultural intelligence 357
Culture 351
Dialogic communication 370
Digital divide 362
Ethnocentrism 350
High-context communication 352
High-context culture 353
Individualism-collectivism 354

Intercultural public relations 351
International public relations 359
Long-term orientation 355
Low-context communication 352
Low-context culture 353
Masculinity-femininity 354
Mediated public diplomacy 367
Monologic communication 370

Power distance 354
Public diplomacy 367
Relational public diplomacy 367
Self-efficacy 359
Total market approach 350
Uncertainty avoidance 354
Usage divide 363

CHAPTER 14

Careers

Curating content on social media is a key skill in public relations and personal brand building. How did posting a picture of high-end bourbon work against a new hire's chances of making a splash right out of college?

KEY LEARNING OUTCOMES

14.1 Apply key attributes of personal branding to help you build your career.

14.2 Identify different types of employers for public relations jobs.

14.3 Assess how different areas of specialization in public relations match your interests.

14.4 Plan for your own continuing education in public relations.

14.5 Discuss ethical dilemmas related to the professional values of competition and loyalty.

RELATED UNIVERSAL ACCREDITATION BOARD COMPETENCY AREAS

2.1 INTEGRITY • **2.2** ETHICAL BEHAVIOR • **3.3** COUNSEL TO MANAGEMENT
5.3 ORGANIZATIONAL STRUCTURE AND RESOURCES • **5.5** LEADERSHIP SKILLS

You're a CEO. You're the world's most valuable asset. You're a Nike swoosh! I can't help but roll my eyes every time I hear a career self-help guru drop this type of bombast on new graduates. But here's the thing—there's some truth to each of these claims. You really are the chief executive of your own career. You are your own most valuable asset in the business you do. And as a metaphor, the Nike swoosh is as good of an image as any to underscore the importance of your own personal brand. Decades of research from marketing, sociology, psychology, organizational behavior and communication affirms the concept of personal branding as a critical career-building activity.[1] What you're learning about managing public relations work can be a tremendous help as you manage your own career too.

So far, we've covered how to build and maintain relationships by communicating on behalf of organizations to publics and communicating to organizations about publics. Now it's time to be a little bit selfish and think about how you represent yourself when it comes to your public relations career. How do you build and maintain mutually beneficial relationships in your professional networks while on the job hunt and when working in your organizations? This chapter starts with some practical information from research and theory on developing a personal brand. In a sense, we're all always on the job market, and our personal brands matter whether we're actively seeking a new employer or building our reputations in school or in a current job. Then the chapter turns attention to the various types of employers and areas of specialization in public relations. We'll reach the finish line (of the chapter and the whole book) with a cautionary tale of someone who pushed the limits of her personal influence in advancement of her career, and we'll close with ethical considerations for climbing the career ladder.

Personal Branding

Researchers in the Netherlands found 100 different scholarly articles from around the world dealing with **personal branding** and boiled them all down to this one definition.

> *Personal branding is the strategic process of creating, positioning, and maintaining a positive impression of oneself, based in a unique combination of individual characteristics, which signal a certain promise to the target audience through a differentiated narrative and imagery.*[2]

Whew! There's a lot going on in that definition. To make sense of how this applies to your career in public relations, consider these key attributes that the researchers found to be core to the idea of personal branding: *strategic, positive, promising, person-centric* and *artifactual.*

Strategic

Effective personal brands—the ones that help people get jobs and promotions—don't happen by accident. Strategic personal brand activities

Personal branding
Strategically creating, positioning and maintaining a positive impression of yourself to signal your professional promise.

are targeted, meaning they are designed for specific audiences/publics, and they are coordinated for consistency across interactions. Think about how you describe yourself on your LinkedIn profile, if your audience is prospective employers, and how you would want that to be coordinated with your resume, and also how you describe yourself in your cover letter and face-to-face interactions.

Sage Quiamno, a 2013 public relations graduate of the University of Hawaii, describes herself on her LinkedIn profile as follows:

> Sage Ke'alohilani Quiamno is the co-founder of Future for Us, a platform dedicated to advancing womxn of color at work through community, culture and career development. She is a passionate pay equity advocate and diversity, equity and inclusion champion.

On a blog outside of LinkedIn, Quiamno introduces herself this way:

> I'm Sage Ke'alohilani Quiamno, a 27 year-old Native Hawaiian woman from Hawai'i, particularly from the island of O'ahu, and the co-founder of Future for Us, a company dedicated to accelerating the advancement of womxn of color at work. I'm a fierce pay equity advocate, diversity, equity and inclusion champion and overall adventure capitalist.[3]

Notice the strategic consistency in her self-presentation and how her profile is targeted to the women she wants to help (her organization's publics). She also is very deliberate in her language. The term *womxn* highlights her attention to issues of sexism and connotes inclusiveness. "Adventure capitalist" adds energy and intention.

Josh Ferrari is a 2016 public relations graduate of the University of Florida. He describes himself on his LinkedIn profile like this:

> Public relations professional based in Washington, D.C. currently leading partnership outreach and strategic communications efforts for federal public health campaigns. Skilled in visual communications and branding, strategy planning and execution, partnership building and stakeholder engagement, metrics reporting and insights generation, and materials development.[4]

Ferrari, too, is strategically consistent across platforms. His brief profile on Twitter describes him as a "Communications consultant on national health campaigns|@UF alumnus "[5] The first part effectively summarizes his professional work in just six words. The second part adds personality and, for a large alumni network audience that may be helpful in Josh's career building, highlights an important affiliation.

Positive

Common sense suggests the importance of staying positive in your personal branding. It's hard to imagine anyone wanting to hire a "negative" person. But research shows that branding yourself as positive means more than just smiling in your profile pic or remaining upbeat in your tone. Positivity means appealing to publics by providing value and making yourself desirable to specific audiences. Sometimes this entails differentiating yourself by showing your willingness to work on difficult issues. Quiamno cites staggering statistics. Women of color[6]:

- Make up only 4 percent of the C-suites in corporations

- Make up 20 percent of the U.S. population

- Hold 40 percent of all the low-wage jobs in the United States

- Make only 66 cents on the dollar, on average, to white males

Then Quiamno clearly states, "My goal is to change this." This sets up the narrative for her personal brand and the mission for her organization.

Ferrari's mission is positive as well. As he describes on joshferrari.com, he is: "using his background in visual and strategic communications to effect positive behavioral health changes across the country."[7] This means tackling issues such as drug use, underage drinking and misuse of opioids as prescription pain medications.

Promising

In marketing, the best brands convey a promise. Ferrari's profile highlights how he has demonstrated higher levels of promise with awards including "Rookie of the Year" at his current employer and working with a team to win a PRSA Award of Excellence. Quiamno conveys promise in the form of results too. In two separate profile pieces, she reinforced performance numbers including more than 75 interviews, panels and conferences with a total audience of more than 4,000 people. "I was able to help negotiate $500K+ in salary increases and positioned 150+ promotions for the women I've met last year in five U.S. cities." Public relations is about mutually beneficial relationships, and conveying promise is a way to indicate how your audiences and publics will benefit from a relationship with you.

Person-Centric

This characteristic reminds us not to get carried away with the product branding metaphor. I am not a tennis shoe and you are not a can of soda. And if we lose sight of the idea that what our publics are looking for is how our personal and professional characteristics can help them, we ignore the fact that the whole idea of personal branding is for other people to get to know us as real humans who are good co-workers, employees, consultants and so on. If you describe yourself as an "energetic self-starter who maximizes potential for game-changing solutions," that doesn't really communicate anything meaningful about you or the work you do. It's just a string of buzzwords.

Quiamno describes herself as a "passionate storyteller, connector and community builder." That is impressive, but it's the following sentence that makes it even more personal and appealing. "I believe because of my Hawaiian culture, this gift is in my blood and a part of my core ethos."

"I must say Jeff, there's something about your personal brand that I find... refreshing."

The self as a product is a metaphor.

How is personal branding different from product branding?

There's a fine line between personality and TMI ... take care to not post anything you think would take you out of consideration for a job someday.

There's a fine line between personality and TMI (too much information). In your professional accounts and social media profiles that are public (and to be safe, you should assume that just about anything shared on social media platforms can be made public), take care to not post anything you think would take you out of consideration for a job someday. This isn't to say you shouldn't show personality in your professional profiles. Everyone, even hiring managers, understands that you have a personal life. Just practice good judgment. For example, on his website, Ferrari briefly mentions his cats Ty and Archie and his proclivity for rearranging furniture. It helps readers relate to him as a real person.

Again, use what you've learned about public relations to make wise decisions based on an understanding of your key publics and the relationships you wish to maintain with them. Good decision-making about what is appropriate for public presentation will be a big part of your appeal as a public relations professional.

Artifactual

All brands need artifacts. Nike's swoosh, Pabst's blue ribbon, and Mercedes' three-pointed star are among the world's iconic logos. Look at your phone for actual icons that are artifacts of brands. I can almost smell coffee when I see the Starbucks icon on my phone, feel my heart rate go up when I see the Garmin Connect fitness icon, and start planning travel when I see the Delta app. Logos on stationery, color schemes on signage, and even "sound logos" such as ESPN's SportsCenter theme that chimes when a new score or update is announced on my phone all also are artifacts that signal brands. What signals your personal brand? Researchers have studied LinkedIn photos, ePortfolios, YouTube videos and even narrated Instagram selfies as brand artifacts.[8]

The Story of Sage Ke'alohilani Quiamno - Co-Founder of Future for Us

MARCH 13, 2019 IN WOMENHISTORYMONTH, INCLUSION

I'm Sage Ke'alohilani Quiamno, a 27 year-old Native Hawaiian woman from Hawai'i, particularly from the island of O'ahu, and the co-founder of Future for Us, a company dedicated to accelerating the advancement of womxn of color at work. I'm fierce pay equity advocate, diversity, equity and inclusion champion and overall adventure capitalist.

I've always been a passionate storyteller, connector and community builder. I believe because of my Hawaiian culture, this gift is in my blood and a part my core ethos. I tap into this skill to fight for gender equity and advocate on behalf of womxn of color, who often marginalized because of our gender, race and beyond. Opening people's eyes to look at feminism with a lens of intersectionality is my recent torch I'd like to continue carrying on.

Last year I've spoken at over 75+ interviews, panels and conferences to over 4,000+ people, coaching salary negotiation strategies and advocating for equal pay. In this effort, I was able to help negotiate $500K+ in salary increases and positioned 150+ promotions for the women I've met last year in 5 U.S. cities. Playing a part in the betterment of women's careers and financial future is what drives me - putting more money into women's pockets.

Online profiles are a key part of personal branding.

How are these two public relations graduates strategic, positive, promising, person-centric and artifactual in their self-presentation?

JOSH FERRARI

HOME   GRAPHIC DESIGN   PHOTO   VIDEO   WRITING   JOSH

Meet Josh

Josh Ferrari is a young public relations professional based in Washington, D.C.

When he isn't using his background in visual and strategic communications to effect positive behavioral health changes across the country, Josh can often be found rearranging his apartment furniture for the dozenth time in a given month or playing with his mischievous—but super cute—cats, Ty and Archie.

Josh's expertise in strategic communications runs the gamut of visual communications and branding to stakeholder engagement, writing/materials development, and creating and executing marketing plans.

His passion for communication has led him to support various national public health campaigns within the U.S. Department of Health and Human Services where he develops and promotes resources for parents, health practitioners, and community leaders to help prevent underage drinking, marijuana use, and the misuse of prescription pain medications (opioids).

He holds a B.S. in Public Relations from the nationally-ranked University of Florida College of Journalism and Communications.

Awards

- 2016 Rookie of the Year, Synergy Enterprises, Inc.
- Josh's work has contributed to a number of campaign awards:
  - PRSA Award of Excellence
  - MarCom Platinum
  - MarCom Gold
  - MarCom Honorable Mention
  - Berreth Silver Medal
  - Videographer Award of Distinction

Most platforms allow us to select and feature a profile picture. That along with our preferred name is the most basic form of artifactual branding. Your account handles and email addresses also matter. An Ohio State master's student once ran a thesis experiment comparing how people rated resumes with unprofessional email addresses (e.g., drunkensquirl@, HtoTHE-hizzy03@) compared to the exact same resumes with more standard email addresses (e.g., mharmon@, jsmith8888@). All else being equal, resume readers in the experiment rated applicants with less professional email addresses lower in effort, personal responsibility, conscientiousness and motivation than those with standard email addresses.[9] In addition to your email address, account names, and profile pictures, remember that your narrative biography, resume items, and any accompanying graphics or images are also personal brand artifacts that represent your writing and design skills.

Internships and Projects

Ferrari and Quiamno were three and six years out of college, respectively, when I checked in on their profiles and personal brand development. If you're still in school, your brand may not be as well developed, but these five attributes (*strategic*, *positive*, *promising*, *person-centric* and *artifactual*) should still be helpful as you maintain your current personal brand and plan for the future. Finding and completing meaningful projects and internships before you enter the world of full-time career work will be especially important. In fact, the push for more attention to personal branding in career building has largely been attributed to trends in the economy that are leading workers to take more ownership of their career paths with less reliance on long-term employers. In a **gig economy**, contract workers really are their own CEOs. In advertising, it's been said that you are only as good as your last ad.[10] In public relations, you may be judged on your latest blog posts, bylined articles, event plans or influencer lists. But before you start picturing yourself as the Lyft driver version of a PR pro, take note that the vast majority of solo public relations professionals have decades of experience before they are sought as independent consultants.[11]

Although you likely don't expect to work for any one organization for your whole career, you also must realize the importance of loyalty to your employers while you work for them, even in internships. "Put your agency first," advises Crispin Porter Bogusky CEO Andrew Keller as he reflects on early jobs in his own career track. That kind of loyalty acknowledges the importance of putting in the time with organizations early in your career as you build your brand and earn new opportunities.

> *Early on, I worked on new biz materials for the agency. It wasn't going to win me an award or go in my book. In the end, I learned so much. That had a huge impact on me and how the agency perceived me. It created a lot of opportunities.*[12]

Of course, agencies are only one place to start and build careers in public relations. The next section describes a range of different types of employers.

Employers

One of your first major considerations in thinking about a career in public relations is what type of employer you want to work for. Discussed throughout this book are cases and examples of public relations conducted by global agencies, for-profit companies, nonprofit organizations, international NGOs and government agencies. During the course of your career, you may work for organizations as big as the U.S. Department of Defense or Wal-Mart, or as small as a two-person business. Or maybe you will eventually start your own firm and become your own boss. As you launch your career, all options are on the table.

Agencies

For many aspiring public relations professionals, an agency job is the first position that comes to mind when they think about starting in the business, and agencies are certainly great places to launch and build careers. Agencies provide corporate clients with specialized services including research, campaign planning and implementation, speechwriting, crisis management, special events and so on, but most large companies also include in-house public relations departments.

Gig economy
A trend in which people increasingly are hired for short periods of time to complete specific tasks or projects, including freelancers, independent contractors and part-time hires.

Top 10 Global PR Agency Ranking 2019

Ranking	Agency	HQ	Fee Income 2018 ($)
1	Edelman	USA	888,405,000
2	Weber Shandwick	USA	840,000,000
3	BCW	USA	723,000,000
4	FleishmanHillard	USA	605,000,000
5	Ketchum	USA	545,000,000
6	MSL	France	450,000,000
7	Hill+Knowlton Strategies	USA	400,000,000
8	Ogilvy	USA	388,000,000
9	BlueFocus	China	336,372,995
10	Brunswick	UK	280,000,000

Figure 14.1 The Holmes Report ranks the world's largest public relations agencies and provides other ranking data each year.

What are the benefits of working in a big agency early in your career?

If you start at an agency, be prepared to move through multiple positions in your first few years.

Agencies range in size from two- to three-person shops to the biggest public relations firms in the world like Edelman, Weber Shandwick, FleishmanHillard and Ketchum (Figure 14.1). The biggest agencies have tens of thousands of employees spread across offices all over the world. Agencies serve multiple clients, very often in different businesses. This means that if you work for an agency, you'll likely have an opportunity to work on multiple projects for multiple organizations.

In mid-size to large agencies, client work is assigned to account teams. Each client has an account with the agency, and agency employees work on multiple accounts simultaneously. From entry level to executive leadership, traditional jobs in agencies include the following:

- Account assistant
- Account coordinator
- Account executive
- Senior account executive
- Account supervisor
- Director
- Vice president

The salary for an entry-level account coordinator in an agency ranges from just over $30,000 to the low $50,000s with a median of about $39,000, according to PayScale.com data in 2019.[13]

Of course, different agencies offer different salaries and different job titles. Convergence and integration have led many firms to rethink how they organize teams and name positions. The work can be nonstop and involve ridiculous amounts of multitasking as employees jump between account projects and urgent client demands, but those who succeed gain experience in a hurry. This combination of jam-packed workdays (and nights), steep learning curves and fast-growing professional networks also means that there is quite a bit of turnover. It's not uncommon for rising stars to move up through two or three positions in their first few years on the job, and often these job changes include lateral moves from one agency to another.

Many young professionals find that agency work just isn't for them. Some will move to other careers altogether. Others will go to work doing public relations for other types of organizations, often finding their new positions with the help of contacts they made in agencies.

Corporations

Working in-house as a full-time employee of one company means that your responsibility in managing organization-public relationships is primarily to a single organization. A corporate job on the client side may look like a posh gig—you have only one "client" to serve, the schedule may be more predictable, and pay is often higher. For example, compared to the median salary of $39,000 for account coordinators, the median salary for communication specialists working in-house at a corporation is $51,000.[14] Keep in mind, however, that the person making $50k working in-house very likely has more years of experience than the entry-level account coordinator at an agency.

In addition, while you may have only one client to serve working in-house, you will still be responsible to many publics. Corporate jobs focus on customers (marketing communications), investors (financial relations), government agencies (public affairs), employees (internal relations) and the publics who live wherever companies operate (community relations). Large corporations may employ separate departments for each of these publics and may also hire public relations agencies for help with various functions, but the departments must still work together.

As discussed in Chapter 4, corporate social responsibility programs (CSR) have become more common in response to negative public sentiment about corporations and their impact on society and the environment. CSR efforts are a prime example of the importance of balancing the interests of various stakeholders, even if you work only for a single organization.

Nonprofits and NGOs

By definition, nonprofit organizations exist to do something other than make money for shareholders. Nonprofit work may appeal to people who work hard to support the missions of those organizations, such as health, education and environmental causes. While nonprofits often benefit from the service of volunteers, as strategic organizations they operate with business models that require full-time paid staff.

Public relations jobs in nonprofits are often just as demanding and require just as much accountability as corporate jobs. In addition, in many ways the stakes are higher at nonprofits because public health, education, social justice and the environment depend on them.

10 Things To Know About Working in an Agency

1. It's a great place to start. Agencies allow you to learn everything about the industry while you work directly with clients. If a next step in life is corporate, an agency background allows you to relate to those from the other side.

2. PR is more than you think. Although a common request from clients is media relations, PR firms offer more than expected. Understanding the core functions and capabilities of your firm will allow you to push the envelope and help your business grow faster than the times.

3. Personal growth is inevitable. In the fast-paced world of an agency, you have no choice but to learn your strengths and weaknesses. You must offer quick and quality work, become accountable and accessible, and push yourself harder than you ever thought was possible, and before you know it, you will have grown as a professional.

4. Passion is essential. In the rollercoaster of an agency, passion is necessary in remaining resilient. Passion engages creativity, ignites progression and allows for business growth.

5. Communication is key. Whether leading account teams, asking questions or exploring new ideas, communication offers opportunities for agencies to surpass the relevant and remain innovative.

6. Managers are like clients. Invest in the relationship to understand how they prefer to work; learn to predict needs and get ahead of asks.

7. Be somebody that others enjoy working with. This can mean being reliable, thoughtful, productive and just being a kind person. Consider your reputation on your teams and with the agency overall.

8. Numbers are part of the job. Research and data matter in making decisions and that means numbers. But it's not calculous so don't run away; train yourself to think about how numbers tell the story or dictate possibilities.

9. Your internal network will grow. Your agency is a gold mine for networking. Find time to meet others with interesting clients or roles you're unfamiliar with to find your passion points and to develop mentors.

10. Become an entrepreneur in your role. Embody a drive to take charge in order to make a difference for clients and internal teams. Seek opportunity to investigate growth and go beyond the requirement. Prove yourself indispensable. Be an eternal learner.

THE PLANK CENTER
FOR LEADERSHIP IN PUBLIC RELATIONS
@PlankCenterPR
plankcenter.ua.edu

Agencies provide great learning experiences.

What appeals to you least and most about working in an agency?

natytamayo • Following
Under Armour World Headquarters

natytamayo Excited to be a part of the #UnderArmour team! I have the opportunity to switch gears from agency life and begin this journey as part of the Consumer Engagement, Digital team working on social! Catch me at our Baltimore headquarters smiling from ear to ear while sporting athletic wear to work. #ProtectThisHouse #IWill #UA

16w

crisypr Congratulations!
16w   1 like   Reply

Liked by sjackson625 and 356 others
FEBRUARY 5

Add a comment...   Post

Moving from working in an agency to working in a corporation is a common career move.

How are corporate public relations jobs different from agency jobs?

Public relations jobs in nonprofits are just as demanding and require just as much accountability as corporate jobs.

In general, public relations management in nonprofits involves similar strategies and skills as for-profits (media relations and publicity, branding, community relations, public affairs, etc.). However, a major difference between nonprofits and corporations is the key publics of donors and volunteers. Fundraising and volunteer management are critical to public relations success at nonprofits.

Similar to agencies, pay at nonprofits can start low—below $30,000 for entry-level jobs, but salaries for communications directors at U.S. nonprofits range from the $30,000s to $125,000 with a median of $60,000, according to one report of 2018 data.[15]

Nongovernment organizations (NGOs) are one type of nonprofit. NGOs are organized at local, national or international levels and advocate fiercely for humanitarian and environmental causes. Many NGOs work closely with the United Nations, and their relationships with corporations and governments range from contentious to cooperative.

Government

According to the World Economic Forum, the U.S. Department of Defense (DOD) is the largest employer in the world. The DOD employs thousands of people—civilian and military—in public relations–related positions, and defense is only one sector of government jobs that include local, state and federal positions. Despite the fact that government public relations jobs are labeled with titles like "public affairs coordinator" and "public information officer," the U.S. government has been said to be the world's largest employer of public relations people. A quick search on USAJOBS.gov for the exact words "public affairs" returned 148 open positions. The results included jobs with the Department of the Army, the Bureau of Land Management in the Department of the Interior, and the Drug Enforcement Administration in the Department of Justice. Two of the jobs are listed as unpaid internships. Four of the jobs pay less than $30,000. The majority pay between $30,000 and $100,000, with the most common job title for positions in the $25,000–$50,000 range being "public affairs specialist."

Historically, government jobs have been known for stability and good benefits. One of the downsides, however, is that large government agencies are often burdened with bureaucratic inefficiencies, which can be frustrating to employees as well as their primary publics—namely, taxpayers. Whereas businesses rely on clients and customers for revenue, and nonprofits rely more on donors, government agencies are funded by taxpayers. As a taxpayer yourself, you've probably been frustrated at times with local, state or federal government operations. That said, these same agencies provide essential public services, and their communication functions are critical to democratic societies.

Careers at Interior ✔
@DOICareers
Following ⌄

⛰Move to Alaska! now #Hiring PUBLIC AFFAIRS SPECIALIST @BLMAlaska #Apply▶go.usa.gov/xUCWj 📷 #prjobs #PRstudents

📷Bob Wick @BLMNational

8:50 AM - 27 Jun 2018 from Alaska, USA

As part of the federal government, the Bureau of Land Management in the Department of the Interior hires often for public relations.

Which government agencies would you consider working for?

As noted throughout this book, open communication and access to information about government operations is a foundation of democracies. The "information age" in many ways has opened government information to easier access than ever before (the USAJOBS.org site is a good example), and public relations jobs play a key role in how our societies continue to evolve.

Self-Employment and Small Business

On the opposite end of the spectrum from jobs with enormous government organizations are small businesses—millions of them worldwide. In the United States, small businesses accounted for 66 percent of new jobs created from 2000 to 2017.[16] These statistics from the Small Business Administration refer to organizations with fewer than 500 employees, but you may plan to work in a business comprised of just a few people. More than 12 million Americans work for companies with fewer than 10 employees.[17] Most of these organizations do not have a full-time position or department labeled "public

Small business owners, startups and self-employed public relations practitioners often work in home offices or co-working spaces such as Camp David in Brooklyn, N.Y.

What do you see as the advantages and disadvantages of this type of work environment?

If you work for a small business, you'll need to be much more of a generalist.

relations," but all of them will require managing relationships with publics.

Whether you are writing code, renting sailboats or wrapping burritos, you'll need to be much more of a generalist in small businesses compared to large companies, nonprofits or government organizations. Instead of specializing in only the communication function, you will likely be involved in core operations in addition to building and maintaining relationships with customers, vendors, regulators, banks and investors and media. If your budget for promotions is small, you may rely more on social media and word of mouth. But good media relations can still lead to big hits in influential channels, if you know how to tell and pitch your stories well (Chapters 4 and 9).

As an owner, operator, partner or employee of a small business you will be directly responsible to your organization for key management decisions. You will also be directly accountable to publics for the outcomes and effects of those decisions. In this sense, working in a small organization can be seen as one of the purest forms of public relations as a management function. Also, many public relations agencies are small businesses themselves and offer opportunities for internships and entry-level jobs that expose you to all facets of client service work from top to bottom.

Areas of Specialization

You'll find as many different areas of specialization in public relations as there are different missions of organizations. That said, some of the major categories are healthcare, sports and entertainment, political and public affairs, financial and entrepreneurial, consumer and international public relations. Within each category are countless types of public relations jobs. This section briefly outlines some major areas of specialization.

Health

The goals of healthcare are as universal as the human race. From family planning to end-of-life hospice care, governments, NGOs, hospitals (for-profit and nonprofit), private physicians, pharmaceutical companies, educational and research institutions, and medical device manufacturers are only some of the organizations that have a stake in fighting disease, caring for the ill and keeping healthy people healthy. Most of these organizations

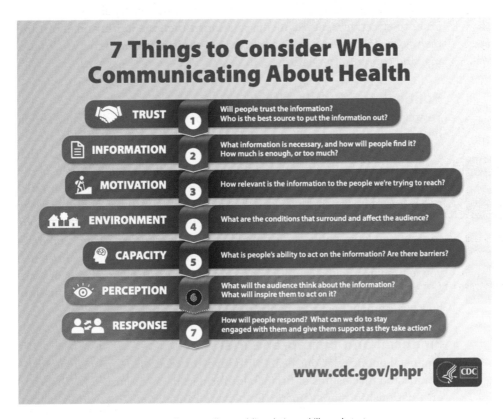

7 Things to Consider When Communicating About Health

1 TRUST — Will people trust the information? Who is the best source to put the information out?

2 INFORMATION — What information is necessary, and how will people find it? How much is enough, or too much?

3 MOTIVATION — How relevant is the information to the people we're trying to reach?

4 ENVIRONMENT — What are the conditions that surround and affect the audience?

5 CAPACITY — What is people's ability to act on the information? Are there barriers?

6 PERCEPTION — What will the audience think about the information? What will inspire them to act on it?

7 RESPONSE — How will people respond? What can we do to stay engaged with them and give them support as they take action?

www.cdc.gov/phpr — CDC

Effective health communication requires excellent public relations skills and strategy.

What have you learned about public relations that would help you in a health communication career?

retain public relations staff, and many hire public relations agencies. The PR Council, a group of more than 100 of America's leading firms, reports that healthcare is one of public relations' biggest growth areas, accounting for more than 15 percent of the revenue of its members.[18]

Sports and Entertainment

Sports and entertainment may be one of the hardest areas to break into right after college because so many people would love to work for the athletes and celebrities they already enjoy following. Most are also willing to work very, very hard to get one of those jobs. Moving from fan to employee can be a rewarding transition, but also humbling and exhausting. It takes a lot more than just pastime levels of enthusiasm to keep up with the business side of the 24/7 ups and downs of sports and entertainment.

Sports information directors, for example, are responsible for documenting and promoting the accomplishments of the athletes, teams and leagues they represent. They provide updated—often real-time—statistics for use by the media. This requires deep knowledge of sports, teams and

It takes more than enthusiasm to keep up with the 24/7 ups and downs of public relations jobs in sports and entertainment.

athletes. Sports information directors must have strong organizational and analytic skills and a solid understanding of how sports media operate in order to effectively serve a media relations function. Sports and entertainment jobs also include issues and crisis management, marketing and branding, and community relations.

Political and Public Affairs

Strategic campaigns are a core function of public relations, and when people hear the word *campaign* many will think of political campaigns. Political campaigning done well is the epitome of a public communication process that builds strategy from research to achieve measurable outcomes. Some jobs in political public relations last only as long as a candidate is running for office or a referendum is being considered on a ballot. Others are tied to politicians and organizations that require continuous public relations efforts from term to term and from political initiative to political initiative. Many candidates and organizations hire agencies that specialize in political communication. If you're fired up about a candidate or a political cause, or if you think of yourself as a policy wonk and want to make a difference in the technical details of how government operates, political public relations may be for you.

Financial and Entrepreneurial

Financial public relations deals with investor relations, financial media relations and disclosures of financial information, as discussed in Chapter 4 on relationship management. Employers range from the world's biggest publicly held companies like JPMorgan Chase, Bank of America, Royal Dutch Shell, Samsung Electronics and Apple to small startup businesses raising capital for entrepreneurial endeavors. Agencies also specialize in serving clients with financial public relations needs. If you've got a good mind for business and finance, you can put your communication skills to work in financial public relations.

Consumer

Consumer public relations is one of the most visible segments of public relations, perhaps because it is so closely tied with the advertising and marketing of brands we all know well and products we consume every day. When the key publics of public relations are consumers, opportunities for convergence and integration abound.

The growth of digital, social and mobile media that reach consumers in so many ways has further blurred the lines between public relations, advertising and marketing. These media afford us more feedback and information from consumer publics than we've ever had before. This convergence has resulted in entirely new career possibilities for those who "get it" when it comes to communicating in these new contexts. If you're into messaging with the right voice, reading feedback well, turning raw data into useful information, and carrying on conversational communication to build relationships with consumers on a large scale, then you might just be perfect for consumer public relations.

Students participating in the Massachusetts Summer Legislative Intern Program learn about career opportunities in politics.

What kinds of political and public affairs jobs appeal to you most and least?

International

All of the previously discussed areas of specialization can involve international work. Healthcare, sports, entertainment, political, financial, and consumer product organizations and publics are spread all over the world, and, as discussed in Chapter 13, the relationships between them cross national borders more than ever before. Many organizations distinctly identify themselves as global or international and specifically seek employees with a strong desire to work and communicate across countries and cultures.

Education and Continued Learning

You're probably reading this text for one of three reasons: (1) you are taking public relations as a required course for your major in college, (2) you are taking a public relations course as an elective for a related degree plan or (3) you are interested in public relations work and educating yourself independently. These three reasons represent three common tracks into the field. Practicing public relations does not necessarily require a specific college major, but public-relations-specific degree programs offer a series of courses designed to prepare students for entry into the field.

A typical course sequence for the public relations major includes a public relations principles course, public relations research, public relations writing, a campaigns course and an experiential course or internship. Other common courses in public relations majors focus on public relations case studies, law, ethics, planning and management.[19]

If you're working on a college degree, however, keep in mind that your broader education is just as important as your public-relations-specific courses. In fact, the Commission on Public Relations Education recommends that 60–75 percent of an appropriate degree plan comprise courses in liberal arts, social sciences, business and language courses.[20] This makes sense, given the importance of relationship building, culture, persuasion, management, law, ethics, societal trends and research to public relations practice.

If you're reading this book independently—or taking advantage of any other professional development resources for that matter—that's a really good sign for your future. Adaptability is a survival strategy for 21st-century learners, according to *Future Shock* author Alvin Toffler.[21] We all must be ready to learn, unlearn and relearn, and that's what will serve us well as the field continues to change. As Ketchum President and CEO Rob Flaherty put it in a keynote presentation to an industry-educator summit, "Half of everything needed now didn't exist ten years ago."[22]

In thinking about your education, it may be useful to identify core competencies and then to identify the other "half" of what you need to continually adapt to and learn—the half that "didn't exist 10 years ago" and that may change drastically in the next 10 years.

Your broader education is just as important as your public relations–specific courses.

Adaptability is a survival strategy for 21st-century learning—be ready to learn, unlearn and relearn.

Build a foundation for lifelong success

Distinguish yourself from other applicants in the job market by adding a professional certificate to your résumé. The Certificate in Principles of Public Relations shows employers that you understand the core elements of strategic communication and real-world application of important concepts such as:

■ Strategic Planning (Research, Planning, Implementation and Evaluation Process)
■ Media Relations
■ Communication Models and Theories
■ Information Technology
■ Ethics and Law

APPLY TO STAND OUT TODAY

| STEP 1 | Review and complete The Certificate in Principles of Public Relations application by visiting www.prcertificate.org. | STEP 2 | Work with your university's faculty coordinator to certify eligibility. |
| STEP 3 | Attend a certificate preparatory course or complete the Certificate in Principles of Public Relations Online Study Course. | STEP 4 | Study for and complete the computer-based Examination for Certificate in Principles of Public Relations. |

" *After graduating, I was interviewed by several hiring managers. Eight out of ten said that the Certificate in Principles of Public Relations stood out to them as they screened my résumé.* "

KIMBERLEY MAXON
CUSTOMER SERVICE COMMUNICATIONS OFFICER

Put yourself on the path to career success—apply for the Certificate today.

www.prcertificate.org

The Universal Accreditation Board offers a Certificate in Principles of Public Relations for public relations students and recent graduates.

What are the benefits of earning a certificate?

The knowledge, skills and abilities tested on the accreditation exam offered by the Universal Accreditation Board (UAB), and which are mapped to each chapter of this text, are lasting foundations for public relations education (see Appendix A for full descriptions). The Accreditation in Public Relations (APR) credential serves to certify professionalism and ethical standards of practitioners who have five or more years of experience in the field. Recent graduates and college seniors enrolled in a public relations or related program who are members of a UAB-affiliated student organization may apply for the Certificate in Principles of Public Relations (see http://www.praccreditation.org/apply/certificate/). The six pillars of the APR exam are:

1. Research, planning, implementation and evaluation (RPIE)
2. Applied ethics and law
3. Issues and crisis management and communications
4. Communication, models, theories and history
5. Leadership in the public relations function
6. Relationship management

Public relations consultant Arik Hanson went out on a limb to suggest "10 Skills the PR Pro of 2022 Must Have."[23] He originally wrote the post in 2012, then he took to his blog to revise the list in 2016.[24] What follows is a condensed list (from 10 items down to five) of what Hanson identified as key skills for the future. Well, the future is here, or almost here, depending on if you are reading this before 2022. And Hanson's list is holding up well.

1. *Ability to write for both internal and external publics*. You must be able to write clearly for internal communication with employees, volunteers and so on as well as for owned, paid, shared and earned media that reach external publics (Chapters 7 and 9). According to Hanson, "PR folks are asked to manage social ad campaigns all the

time," and this requires knowledge of paid media services for platforms like Twitter, LinkedIn, Facebook and Instagram.

2. *Multimedia production skills.* As discussed in Chapter 10, understanding basic multimedia principles is critical in public relations. Online video may be the first format that comes to mind, but audio shouldn't be overlooked, either. An eye for the visual appeal of still photography and logo design also is important. Hanson notes that many firms and brands have creative departments specifically tasked with developing a compelling and consistent visual style, but that practitioners with a good feel for positioning brands visually are in demand to "fill in the gaps," especially in organizations that aren't big enough to employ entire departments for this function.

3. *Ability to manage social media content.* Managing social media content systems means knowing how to tag, organize and sometimes repurpose content for different contexts and platforms. Content should be both "searchable and findable." Managing social media also requires a thorough understanding of analytics (Chapter 8).

4. *Analyzing and presenting data that make sense to management and clients.* Digital and social media can be treasure troves of data on publics and how they engage organizations, but making sense of that data in a way that informs strategy is critical (Chapter 6). Public relations practitioners who can report data with "context, actionable intelligence and clearly articulated next steps" will shine in modern organizations. Hanson acknowledges that analysis and reporting always have been essential in public relations, but the availability of ridiculously large amounts of data elevates the importance of being able to convert raw data into useful knowledge.

5. *Collaborating online.* Be prepared to work with geographically dispersed teams within your organization to complete projects and tasks. If you've ever worked on a challenging group project for an online class, you know that managing workflow, deadlines, communication tools and cultural expectations can be frustrating. Take heart that much of what you learned from the process will be helpful to you when you work with dispersed teams in your career ahead. Digital collaboration also will be key to your communication with external publics, particularly in building online communities and collaborating with influential individuals across social media platforms. Hanson calls it "influencer outreach." Consistent with key points of Chapter 13, he notes that building and maintaining relationships with external publics requires an ability to identify the right people and a sensitivity to the culture of online communities and their leaders—"knowing how to approach them—without offending them."

Case Study

CEO Versus New Hire: Who Wins?

After completing a degree in English literature from Cal State Long Beach, Talia Jane headed north to the San Francisco Bay area to pursue a career in media. Jane's job seemed promising at first. Even though her prior experience was primarily tutoring and freelancing as a writer, Jane landed an interview with Yelp and was hired on the same day that she interviewed.[25]

Although her goal was to work in a media job at Yelp and "be able to make memes and twitter jokes about food," Jane took the entry-level job in customer service to get started. But the pay was low. So low, she wrote in a letter to Yelp CEO Jeremy Stoppelman, that she could afford to eat only free food at work and from a 10-pound bag of rice at home. Her salary, which she calculated to be $8.15 per hour after taxes, was not enough to make ends meet: "Because 80 percent of my income goes to paying my rent. Isn't that ironic? Your employee for your food delivery app that you spent $300 million to buy can't afford to buy food."[26]

Within a few hours of posting her letter on Medium, Jane was fired. Stoppelman later tweeted that Jane's firing was not related to the Medium post, but Jane said in a BuzzFeed News interview that her manager and HR

Yelp entry-level employee Talia Jane went public on Medium to get her CEO's attention about her low pay. It worked. And she was fired.

Do you admire what she did? Why or why not?

representative had told her that her post violated the company's code of conduct.[27]

Meanwhile, Jane's case caught lots of attention on social media. Thousands of people took her side by commenting on her Medium post, supporting her on Twitter, or donating to PayPal and Square Cash accounts that she posted at the end of her letter. One supporter set up a GoFundMe account, "Help A YELP/EAT24 Employee EAT/LIVE," and raised $2,755 in 28 days from 80 donors.[28]

Others were not as sympathetic. Internet users found Jane's Instagram and Tumblr accounts and commented wryly on her ability to make (and post pictures of) prosciutto brie garlic biscuits and margarita-, mint-julep-, and piña-colada-flavored cupcakes. The pictures she posted of a bottle of Bulleit Bourbon that had been delivered to her didn't help her case in the court of public opinion either.

In a blog on the website Ranker titled "Pictures From Talia's Instagram That Aren't Rice," Ranker user Ariel Kana reposted 26 of Jane's photos. "It was a simple dream, really: To work in media, live in her own apartment, and be able to afford to eat a variety of foods," wrote Kana in the sarcastic post. But "armed only with a degree in English literature, a supportive father, and a coveted job in San Francisco at one of the internet's most visited websites, that dream could never become a reality."[29]

Jane defended her position, claiming that her posts on Instagram were designed to make it seem like she was thriving when the reality was otherwise, so people wouldn't worry about her.[30] In weighing the case, tech industry career consultant Gayle Laakmann McDowell wrote for Forbes.com that Jane's post was "Maybe unwise for her future career, but somewhat admirable that she was willing to do it anyway."[31] Do you admire what Jane did? Do you think she should have been fired? What would you do differently if you had been in her position?

Voices from the Field

Krislyn Hashimoto

KRISLYN M. HASHIMOTO is Senior Vice President at Stryker, Weiner & Yokota in Honolulu, where she oversees the agency's travel division. Over the course of her career, Hashimoto has launched several resorts and restaurants, re-branded newly renovated properties, served as an on-property public relations consultant, and assisted with destination marketing campaigns and initiatives. She has worked as an account director with Cinch PR & Branding Group in San Francisco and in the communications department at the Office of the Governor, State of Hawaii. Her clients have included Oahu Visitors Bureau, Four Seasons Hotels and Resorts, Hyatt Hotels and Resorts, Starwood Hotels & Resorts, Hilton Hotels & Resorts, Mystic Hotel by Charlie Palmer, North Block in Napa Valley, Carmel Boutique Inns and Ghirardelli Square.

What was your first job in public relations?
My first paying job was working in the communications department for the Office of the Governor, State of Hawai'i. Prior to that, I interned in the PR department at Starwood Hawai'i.

How is the job for entry-level public relations positions changing?
When I started in PR, we were still faxing news releases both locally here in Hawai'i and to national media, and a ton of my time was spent at the copy machine putting together clip books. In addition, coordinators used to be behind the scenes managing a lot of clerical work—clipping articles, formatting press releases, mailing press invitations, calling all news outlets and looking through Bacon's media books for updated contacts, etc.

The entry level position at an agency has changed quite a bit since then. With most business being handled over email today, coordinators often have direct contact with clients and are often contacted by media directly with inquiries. A successful coordinator in this digital age, in addition to managing traditional clerical needs, is expected to correspond professionally, manage social media accounts, monitor the news for relevant client issues and be a master at multitasking.

In what ways is the job not changing?
From an agency perspective—client service is still key. Also credibility and building strong relationships with everyone from clients to media.

What's the biggest misperception of public relations jobs you've come across from people outside of public relations?
In travel PR, some people think we are party planners and always out-and-about wining and dining with media. I'd say that's about five percent of the job. The other 95 percent is spent writing, researching and strategizing—a lot behind a computer.

What is the best part of your job?
Storytelling. Helping our clients tell their stories in ways that set them apart from their competitors. And seeing the direct impact of our work positively impact our clients' businesses.

Ethics: Competition, Loyalty and Job Changes

As you climb the public relations pyramid from entry level into management, you'll switch jobs and employers. A lot. Most people entering the workforce don't expect to stay in any one job for much longer than three years. Mid-career employees also recognize that switching jobs is often the key to raising earnings and moving up in management.

There was a time when changing jobs every two or three years was seen as suspicious, indicating a flighty work ethic, difficulty getting along with colleagues, or a lack of loyalty. "That stigma is fast becoming antiquated," according to *Fast Company's* Vivian Giang, "especially as millennials rise in the workplace with expectations to continuously learn, develop, and advance in their careers."[32] Some have even argued that frequent job hoppers are *more* loyal because they are willing to work harder for their current colleagues to make a stronger positive impression during the relatively short time that they work with an organization.[33]

All that job hopping, however, creates ethical challenges. While it is healthy and competitive to shift your loyalty to your new organization when you get a new job, what does that mean for your loyalty to your prior employer and coworkers?

Competition is a key provision in the PRSA Code of Ethics, which lists it as a core principle that "preserves an ethical climate while fostering a robust business environment."[34] Ethical dilemmas arise when loyalty (also a key value in the PRSA code) conflicts with competition.

As a legal matter, many employees sign employment contracts that include **non-compete clauses** that prohibit them from working for competitors or sharing competitive information such as trade secrets. However, with so much personnel movement between and among agencies and clients, ethical dilemmas are hard to avoid, even when the legal issues are clear.

For example, suppose you work for an agency and then leave that agency to work for one of the agency's clients. That's a common job change that normally would not raise many ethical issues. But what if a year later your organization—the client—decides to consider bids from other agencies? Do you help your former agency colleagues by giving them a heads-up on what they should do to keep the account? If so, do you give that same information to other agencies bidding for the work? The PRSA code suggests that you should either not offer the information at all or make sure that you give the same information to everyone in order to promote fair competition and respect among professionals.

Competition is also an important principle to honor in recruiting talent for an organization. It may be tempting to hire employees away from other organizations as a way to gain a competitive advantage, but the PRSA code discourages any hiring that could be seen as "deliberately undermining a competitor."[35]

Early in your career your ethical dilemmas may revolve mostly around your own role and personal and professional values as they relate to those with whom you work and compete most closely. As you move into management and become more responsible for others in your organization, your ethical responsibility will expand. When you begin to approach executive levels, you must grow the scope of your ethical attention along with your career responsibilities. This ethical growth includes careful consideration about how your decisions drive your entire organization and affect your publics. Done right, ethical public relations management benefits individuals, groups, organizations and even entire societies. Done right, ethical public relations elevates the practice to a profession.

Non-compete clause
Part of an employment contract that restricts employees from working for competitors or sharing competitive information such as trade secrets even after they no longer work for the organization.

Non-competition or non-compete agreements define expectations in legal terms for employees who change jobs.

Beyond legal obligations, what kinds of ethical dilemmas might you face as you change from one employer to another in public relations?

In Case You Missed It

No two career trajectories will be the same in public relations, but that doesn't mean you can't prepare for the journey. Here are some general tips to consider as you weigh your career options.

- There's a fine line between personality and TMI . . . take care to not post anything you think would take you out of consideration for a job someday.

- If you start at an agency, be prepared to move through multiple positions in your first few years.

- Public relations jobs in nonprofits are just as demanding and require just as much accountability as corporate jobs.

- If you work for a small business, you'll need to be much more of a generalist.

- It takes more than enthusiasm to keep up with the 24/7 ups and downs of public relations jobs in sports and entertainment.

- Your broader education is just as important as your public relations–specific courses.

- Adaptability is a survival strategy for 21st-century learning—be ready to learn, unlearn and relearn.

SUMMARY

14.1 Apply key attributes of personal branding to help you build your career.
Effective personal branding means being strategic, positive, promising, person-centric and artifactual. These five attributes will be helpful as you maintain your current personal brand and plan for the future. Finding and completing meaningful projects and internships before you enter the world of full-time career work will be especially important as you build your online presence. Good decision-making about what is appropriate for public presentation will be a big part of your appeal as a public relations professional.

14.2 Identify different types of employers for public relations jobs.
All types of organizations can benefit from some form of public relations. Most public relations positions are with agencies, large businesses and corporations, nonprofits, NGOs and military and government agencies. Some individuals work in public relations while also performing other core functions in small businesses, startups or self-owned operations.

14.3 Assess how different areas of specialization in public relations match your interests.
Major specialty areas of public relations are health, sports and entertainment, political and public affairs, financial and entrepreneurial, consumer and international. This list is not exhaustive, and within each category are countless types of public relations jobs. Many of the jobs require some of the same skills.

14.4 Plan for your own continuing education in public relations.

Public relations degree programs offer a series of specific public relations courses designed to prepare students for entry into the field. However, given the importance of relationship building, culture, persuasion, management, law, ethics, societal trends and research, a foundation in liberal arts, social sciences, business and language is also important to help you understand your role in society. Willingness to continually learn beyond school is also critical as media and society change rapidly.

14.5 Discuss ethical dilemmas related to the professional values of competition and loyalty.

Competition is a key provision in the PRSA Code of Ethics. Ethical dilemmas may arise when loyalty to colleagues from prior jobs conflicts with responsibility for fair competition in a new job. For example, when working for a company that is accepting bids from agencies, you have to be careful not to give any unfair advantage to an agency for which you used to work. The goal is to promote fair competition and respect among professionals.

DISCUSSION QUESTIONS

1. Complete a report card of your personal brand by reviewing all your publicly available online profiles. Google yourself to make sure you don't miss anything that others might find if they look you up. Give yourself honest grades for being strategic, positive, promising, person-centric and artifactual. What do you need to add, remove or change to bring your grades up?

2. Pick three organizations you would like to work for, and research their job openings. Do any of them list public relations or related jobs? If so, pick the one job that appeals to you most. (If you can't find a public relations–related job opening, keep searching organizations that you like until you find one.) What are the primary duties of the position?

3. Which area of specialization (health, sports, entertainment, political, financial, etc.) appeals most to you, and why? How would a public relations job in that field be similar to and different from other areas of specialization?

4. Find a specific job ad describing a position in public relations that you would like to have three to five years from now. Carefully review the qualifications. Which qualifications do you meet now? Which ones don't you meet? What, specifically, can you do in the next three to five years to make yourself competitive for that type of job?

5. **CASE STUDY** Many people criticized Talia Jane, but many people respect that she voiced her opinion against a powerful corporate employer. Do you admire what she did? Why or why not? Look up what she has done more recently. How did the Yelp incident affect her personal brand?

6. Describe a time that you've been in a position (in games or school or work) where you were responsible for ensuring fair competition despite your loyalty to one of the competitors. Did competition trump loyalty? Why (or why not)? Would you use the same moral reasoning in a professional career in public relations?

KEY TERMS

Personal branding 375	Gig economy 381	Non-compete clause 395

Universal Accreditation Board Competencies

DETAILED KNOWLEDGE, SKILLS AND ABILITIES TESTED ON THE COMPUTER-BASED EXAMINATION FOR ACCREDITATION IN PUBLIC RELATIONS (effective January 2016)		PERCENTAGE TESTED
Objective 1	**Researching, Planning, Implementing and Evaluating Programs**	**33%**
1.1	**Research (Concepts):** Understands and can apply primary and secondary, formal and informal, quantitative and qualitative methods. Decides on the population and sampling techniques. Understands instrument design. Develops a premise and research plan.	
1.2	**Research (Applications):** Uses a variety of research tools to gather information about the employer or client, industry and relevant issues. Investigates stakeholders' understanding of the product, organization and issues. Applies research findings.	
1.3	**Analytical skills:** Continuously analyzes the business environment that includes the client, stakeholders and employer. Objectively interprets data.	
1.4	**Strategic thinking:** Synthesizes relevant information to determine what is needed to position the client, organization, or issue appropriately in its market/environment, especially with regard to changing business, political, or cultural climates.	
1.5	**Planning:** Sets goals and objectives based on research findings. Distinguishes among goals, objectives, strategies and tactics. Distinguishes organizational/operational goals and strategies from communication goals and strategies. Aligns project goals with organizational mission and goals.	
1.6	**Audience identification:** Differentiates among publics, markets, audiences and stakeholders. Identifies appropriate audiences and the opinions, beliefs, attitudes, cultures, and values of each. Assesses interests of influential institutions, groups and individuals. Identifies appropriate communication channels/vehicles for reaching target audiences. Identifies communities formed through technologies. Understands varying needs and priorities of individual constituent groups (e.g., investors, governmental agencies, unions, consumers).	

1.7	**Diversity:** Identifies and respects a range of differences among target audiences. Researches and addresses the cultural preferences and/or needs and barriers to communication of target audiences. Develops culturally and linguistically appropriate strategies and tactics.	
1.8	**Implementation:** Understands sequence of events. Develops timelines and budget. Assigns responsibilities. Executes planned strategies and tactics.	
1.9	**Evaluation of programs:** Determines if goals and objectives of public relations program were met and the extent to which the results or outcomes of public relations programs have been accomplished. Uses evaluation results for future planning.	
Objective 2	**Applying Ethics and Law**	**13%**
2.1	**Integrity:** Conducts professional activities in a lawful and principled manner. Functions as the conscience of the organization.	
2.2	**Ethical behavior:** Understands and adheres to commonly accepted standards for professional behavior. Recognizes ethical dilemmas. Acts to remedy unethical acts.	
2.3	**First Amendment issues:** Understands First Amendment as a foundational principle for public relations. Distinguishes between political and corporate speech. Articulates conditions for libel and defenses thereof. Understands impact of digital record on status as public and private figure.	
2.4	**Privacy issues:** Understands federal law regarding privacy (e.g., HIPAA, FERPA, DPPA), identity protection, ethical implications and digital record. Effectively advises organization on strategic adoption and effective use of technology for listening to, communicating with and engaging priority publics.	
2.5	**Other legal issues:** Upholds applicable federal laws regarding disclosure, copyright, trademarks, fair use.	
Objective 3	**Managing Issues and Crisis Communications**	**13%**
3.1	**Issues and risk management:** Identifies potential or emerging issues that may impact the organization. Identifies potential risks to the organization or client. Analyzes probability and potential impact of risk. Ensures organization develops appropriate response plans. Designs and deploys a strategic public relations response.	
3.2	**Crisis management:** Understands the roles and responsibilities of public relations at the pre-crisis, crisis, and post-crisis phases. Communicates the implications of each of these phases and understands the messaging needs of each. Looks beyond current organizational mindset.	

3.3	**Counsel to management:** Understands the importance of providing counsel to the management team or client regarding issues, risks and crises. Looks beyond the current organizational mindset. Considers and accommodates all views on an issue or crisis. Factors views into communication strategy.	
Objective 4	**Understanding Communication Models, Theories and History of the Profession**	**8%**
4.1	**Communication/public relations models and theories:** Demonstrates familiarity with social science theories and research that guide planning, prioritizing audiences, developing messages, selecting spokespeople, establishing credibility and trust.	
4.2	**Barriers to communication:** Understands how messages and messengers are interpreted by different audiences. Understands barriers that prevent changes to knowledge, attitude and behavior. Understands how semantics, cultural norms, timing, context and related factors impact the practice.	
4.3	**Knowledge of the field:** Defines public relations and differentiates among related concepts (e.g., publicity, advertising, marketing, press agentry, public affairs, lobbying, investor relations, social networking, and branding). Identifies key figures who influenced the field and major trends in the development of public relations as it is practiced today.	
Objective 5	**Leading the Public Relations Function**	**18%**
5.1	**Business literacy:** Understands and explains how employers/clients generate revenue and how their operations are conducted. Identifies relevant business drivers and how they impact the business. Understands how the public relations function contributes to the financial success of the organization.	
5.2	**Resource management:** Takes into account human, financial and organizational resources. Prepares, justifies and controls budgets for departments, programs, clients or agencies. Understands what information needs to be collected, evaluated, disseminated, and retained. Is able to obtain information using innovative methods and appropriately store it, so that it can be retrieved easily for future use.	
5.3	**Organizational structure and resources:** Recognizes chain of command, including boards of directors, senior leadership, middle management, direct line supervision, line positions, and each level's distinctions. Knows how organizations are horizontally and vertically structured. Identifies which divisions within an organization that need to be involved in any communication program. Understands impact of organizational governance. Recognizes the relationships among PR, legal, finance and IT, as essential management functions.	

5.4	**Problem solving and decision-making:** Approaches problems with sound reasoning and logic. Distinguishes between relevant and irrelevant information. Evaluates opportunities for resolution. Devises appropriate courses of action based on context and facts. Makes sound, well-informed and objective decisions in a timely manner. Assesses the impact and implications of these decisions.	
5.5	**Leadership skills:** Influences others to achieve desired goals. Motivates and inspires others, builds coalitions and communicates vision. Influences overall organizational changes in policy, procedures, staffing and structure, as appropriate.	
5.6	**Organizational skills:** Integrates multiple dimensions of a public relations campaign. Integrates internal and external components, so that there is a synergy among the messages.	
Objective 6	**Managing Relationships**	**15%**
6.1	**Relationship building:** Understands consensus-building strategies and techniques to persuade key stakeholders to support a decision. Ensures discussions allow key stakeholders the opportunity to express opinions. Recognizes need for affected parties and stakeholders to find mutually acceptable solutions. Utilizes persuasion, negotiation and coalition building.	
6.2	**Reputation management:** Understands need for maintaining individual and organizational credibility with and among key constituents. Recognizes value of reputation, image, public trust and corporate-social responsibility.	
6.3	**Internal stakeholders:** Understands importance of internal relationships to the public relations function. Understands the importance of organizational culture and communicating key messages through frontline supervisors. Uses mediated and non-mediated channels of communication for effective engagement. Prioritizes internal audiences.	
6.4	**Media relations:** Understands definitions, strengths, weaknesses and needs of different media. Understands the relationships among public relations professionals, journalists and media organizations. Builds effective relationships with media based on mutual respect and trust. Analyzes current events and trends for opportunities and threats. Identifies appropriate controlled and uncontrolled media channels and key influencers.	
6.5	**Networks:** Understands how different tactics can be used to establish and enhance relationships (e.g., electronic communications, special events, face-to-face communication, networking, social networking, word-of-mouth and third-party communication). Recognizes interconnectedness among various stakeholders. Considers broad/global relationships.	

Notes

CHAPTER 1

1. James E. Grunig and Todd Hunt, *Managing Public Relations* (New York: Holt, Rinehart and Winston, 1984), 6.
2. Glen M. Broom and Bey-Ling Sha, *Cutlip and Center's Effective Public Relations*, 11th ed. (Upper Saddle River, NJ: Prentice Hall, 2013), 5.
3. Noah Kirsch, "Papa John's Founder Used N-Word on a Conference Call," *Forbes*, July 11, 2018, accessed May 20, 2019, https://www.forbes.com/sites/noahkirsch/2018/07/11/papa-johns-founder-john-schnatter-allegedly-used-n-word-on-conference-call/#5ef26ca54cfc.
4. Noah Kirsch, "Papa John's Founder Resigns, Gains $50 Million in a Day," *Forbes*, July 13, 2018, accessed May 20, 2019, https://www.forbes.com/sites/noahkirsch/2018/07/13/papa-johns-founder-john-schnatter-resigns-net-worth-rises-50-million-in-a-day/#29f793fd7123.
5. https://www.papajohns.com/doing-better/, accessed May 20, 2019.
6. https://savepapajohns.com, accessed May 20, 2019.
7. Noah Kirsch, "Tensions High at Papa John's, Even with Founder Gone," *Forbes*, August 18, 2018, accessed May 20, 2019, https://www.forbes.com/sites/noahkirsch/2018/08/17/troubled-culture-remains-at-papa-johns-even-with-founder-gone/.
8. "21 Ridiculous Social Media Job Titles," Memeburn, accessed May 20, 2019, https://memeburn.com/2013/05/21-ridiculous-social-media-job-titles/.
9. "Public Relations Defined: A Modern Definition for the New Era of Public Relations," Public Relations Society of America, accessed May 20, 2019, http://prdefinition.prsa.org.
10. Stuart Elliott, "Redefining Public Relations in the Age of Social Media," *The New York Times*, November 20, 2011, accessed May 20, 2019, http://www.nytimes.com/2011/11/21/business/media/redefining-public-relations-in-the-age-of-social-media.html.
11. "Crowdsource," Oxford Dictionaries, accessed May 20, 2019, http://oxforddictionaries.com/us/definition/american_english/crowdsource?q=crowdsourcing.
12. "Snapshot: #PRDefined Word Cloud—Day 12," Public Relations Defined, accessed May 20, 2019, http://prdefinition.prsa.org/index.php/2011/12/02/snapshot-of-the-public-relations-defined-initiative-submission-day12/.
13. Pamela J. Brubaker, "Arthur W. Page: A Man of Vision, Valor, and Values," in *Words from a Page in History* (University Park, PA: Arthur W. Page Center for Integrity in Public Communication, 2011), 5–9.
14. Brad Rawlins, "Give the Emperor a Mirror: Toward Developing a Stakeholder Measurement of Organizational Transparency," *Journal of Public Relations Research* 21, no. 1 (2008): 71–99, 75.
15. Sarosh Waiz, "50 Best Advertising Slogans of Modern Brands," Advergize, December 20, 2018, accessed May 20, 2019, https://advergize.com/advertising/40-best-advertising-slogans-modern-brands/.
16. John Vernon Pavlik and Shawn McIntosh, *Converging Media: A New Introduction to Mass Communication* (New York: Oxford University Press, 2011), 365.
17. Anne Landman, "BP's 'Beyond Petroleum' Campaign Losing Its Sheen," The Center for Media and Democracy's PR Watch, May 3, 2010, accessed May 20, 2019, http://www.prwatch.org/node/9038.
18. Elizabeth Shogren, "BP: A Textbook Example of How Not to Handle PR," NPR.org, April 21, 2011, accessed May20, 2019, https://www.npr.org/2011/04/21/135575238/bp-a-textbook-example-of-how-not-to-handle-pr.
19. Robert Kendall, *Public Relations Campaign Strategies*, 2nd ed. (New York: HarperCollins, 1996), 527.
20. https://twitter.com/DaavidTheRapper/status/1018977376175210497.
21. https://twitter.com/LamarNeagle/status/956773205896654848.
22. Becky Krystal, "Crock-Pot Tells 'This Is Us' Fans: Our Slow Cookers Won't Kill You," *The Washington Post*, January 24, 2018, accessed May 20, 2019, https://www.washingtonpost.com/news/food/wp/2018/01/24/crock-pot-tells-this-is-us-fans-our-slow-cookers-wont-kill-you/?utm_term=.e1c890677ae6.
23. Jessica Wohl, "How Crock-Pot Smoothly Navigated a Potential Brand Disaster," *AdAge*, May 10, 2018, accessed May 20, 2019, http://adage.com/videos/how-crockpot-smoothly-navigated-a-potential-brand-disaster/1511.
24. https://www.facebook.com/CrockPot/videos/1681426968546979/.
25. Jessica Wohl, "How Crock-Pot Smoothly Navigated a Potential Brand Disaster," AdAge, May 10, 2018, accessed May 20, 2019, http://adage.com/videos/how-crockpot-smoothly-navigated-a-potential-brand-disaster/1511.
26. Tom Kelleher, "Conversational Voice, Communicated Commitment, and Public Relations Outcomes in Interactive Online Communication," *Journal of Communication* 59, no. 1 (2009): 172–188.
27. Robert Strohmeyer, "How to Deal with Yelp Disasters," PC World, May 31, 2011, accessed August 21, 2019. http://www.pcworld.com/article/228902/yelp_reviews.html.
28. Arthur W. Page, "Speech Presented at the Bell Telephone System's General Manager Conference—May 1931," The Arthur W. Page Center at Penn State, accessed May 20, 2019, https://bellisario.psu.edu/assets/uploads/sp14_public_relations_bell_telephone_systems_goc_may_1931.pdf.

29. Harold Burson, "Is Public Relations Now Too Important to Be Left to Public Relations Professionals?," lecture delivered to the Institute for Public Relations, London, October 20, 2004.

30. "Ethics and Public Relations," Institute for Public Relations, accessed May 20, 2019, https://instituteforpr.org/ethics-and-public-relations/.

31. Philip M. Seib and Kathy Fitzpatrick, *Public Relations Ethics* (Fort Worth, TX: Harcourt Brace College Publishers, 1995).

32. Kathy R. Fitzpatrick, "Ethical Decision-Making Guide Helps Resolve Ethical Dilemmas," Public Relations Society of America, accessed May 20, 2019, http://www.prsa.org/AboutPRSA/Ethics/documents/decisionguide.pdf.

33. Todd Defren, "Tweeting Under False Circumstances: Social Media Ethical Dilemmas," PR Squared, accessed July 13, 2014, http://www.pr-squared.com/index.php/2010/01/tweeting-under-false-circumstances-social-media-ethical-dilemmas.

34. "About Enforcement," Public Relations Society of America, accessed May 20, 2019, https://www.prsa.org/ethics/malpractice-unethical-improper-behavior/.

35. "PRSA Code of Ethics Preamble," Public Relations Society of America, accessed May 20, 2019, http://www.prsa.org/aboutprsa/ethics/codeenglish.

CHAPTER 2

1. James E. Grunig and Todd Hunt, *Managing Public Relations* (New York: Holt, Rinehart and Winston, 1984), 4.

2. James E. Grunig and Todd Hunt, *Managing Public Relations* (New York: Holt, Rinehart and Winston, 1984), 21.

3. Benjamin Reiss, "PT Barnum, Joice Heth and Antebellum Spectacles of Race," *American Quarterly* 51 (1999): 78–107.

4. Phineas Taylor Barnum, *Life of PT Barnum* (Buffalo, NY: The Courier Company Printers, 1886), 38.

5. http://www.internetlivestats.com/twitter-statistics/.

6. https://www.omnicoreagency.com/facebook-statistics/.

7. https://twitter.com/IHOP/status/1003682801042915328.

8. https://twitter.com/KatieSweat11/status/1005155511447248897.

9. https://www.ihop.com/en/news/2018/ihop-changes-name-to-ihob-and-reveals-the-b-is-for-burgers.

10. Becky Krystal, ""IHOP's name change is what happens when brands exploit the Internet outrage cycle," *The Washington Post*, June 11, 2018, accessed May 20, 2019, https://www.washingtonpost.com/news/voraciously/wp/2018/06/11/ihops-name-change-is-what-happens-when-brands-exploit-the-internet-outrage-cycle/?noredirect=on&utm_term=.a55ecd1d520c.

11. https://twitter.com/Wendys/status/1006198612349673473.

12. Paul R. La Monica, "IHOP president: We're still all about the pancakes," CNN, July 19, 2018, accessed May 20, 2019, https://money.cnn.com/2018/07/19/investing/ihop-president-darren-rebelez-burgers-ihob/.

13. Paul R. La Monica, "IHOP president: We're still all about the pancakes," CNN, July 19, 2018, accessed May 20, 2019, https://money.cnn.com/2018/07/19/investing/ihop-president-darren-rebelez-burgers-ihob/.

14. Zacks Equity Research, "Dine Brands (DIN) Q2 Earnings Surpass Estimates," August 1, 2018, accessed May 20, 2019, https://www.zacks.com/stock/news/314814/dine-brands-din-q2-earnings-surpass-estimates?cid=CS-CNN-HL-314814.

15. Scott M. Cutlip, *The Unseen Power: Public Relations, a History* (Hillsdale, NJ: Lawrence Erlbaum Associates, 1994), 40.

16. Ray Eldon Hiebert, *Courtier to the Crowd: The Story of Ivy Lee and the Development of Public Relations* (Ames: Iowa State University Press, 1966), 45.

17. Scott M. Cutlip, *The Unseen Power: Public Relations, a History* (Hillsdale, NJ: Lawrence Erlbaum Associates, 1994), 41.

18. Scott M. Cutlip, *The Unseen Power: Public Relations, a History* (Hillsdale, NJ: Lawrence Erlbaum Associates, 1994), 44.

19. Ray Eldon Hiebert, *Courtier to the Crowd: The Story of Ivy Lee and the Development of Public Relations* (Ames: Iowa State University Press, 1966), 48.

20. Clive Thompson, "The See-Through CEO," *Wired*, April 1, 2007, accessed May 20, 2019, http://www.wired.com/wired/archive/15.04/wired40_ceo.html.

21. Scott M. Cutlip, *The Unseen Power: Public Relations, a History* (Hillsdale, NJ: Lawrence Erlbaum Associates, 1994), 53.

22. http://emilms.fema.gov/IS29/PIOsummary.htm.

23. Edward Bernays, *Biography of an Idea: Memoirs of Public Relations Counsel Edward L. Bernays* (New York: Simon and Schuster, 1965), 386.

24. Edward Bernays, *Biography of an Idea: Memoirs of Public Relations Counsel Edward L. Bernays* (New York: Simon and Schuster, 1965), 387.

25. Edward Bernays, *Biography of an Idea: Memoirs of Public Relations Counsel Edward L. Bernays* (New York: Simon and Schuster, 1965), 387.

26. Vanessa Murphree, "Edward Bernays's 1929 'Torches of Freedom' March: Myths and Historical Significance." American Journalism 32, no. 3 (2015): 258–281.

27. Edward L. Bernays Beech-Nut Packing Co, accessed May 20, 2019, https://youtu.be/6vFz_FgGvJI.

28. James E. Grunig and Todd Hunt, *Managing Public Relations* (New York: Holt, Rinehart and Winston, 1984), 39.

29. Scott M. Cutlip, *The Unseen Power: Public Relations, a History* (Hillsdale, NJ: Lawrence Erlbaum Associates, 1994).

30. Arthur W. Page, "Speech to the Public Relations Conference of Chesapeake & Ohio Railway Company, October 27, 1939," accessed May 20, 2019, from https://bellisario.psu.edu/page-center/speech/industrial-statesmanship.

31. James E. Grunig, "Two-Way Symmetrical Public Relations: Past, Present, and Future," in *Handbook of Public Relations*, ed. Robert L. Heath (Thousand Oaks, CA: Sage, 2001), 12.

32. Duane Shimogawa, "Robbie Alm leaving Hawaiian Electric Co.," Bizjournals, July 17, 2013, accessed May 20, 2019, http://www.bizjournals.com/pacific/

news/2013/07/17/robbie-alm-leaving-hawaiian-electric.html.

33. Dennis Hollier, "Talk Story with Robbie Alm," HawaiiBusiness, April 8, 2012, accessed May 20, 2019, http://www.hawaiibusiness.com/Hawaii-Business/April-2012/Talk-Story-with-Robbie-Alm/.

34. Marilyn Kern-Foxworth, "Baker, Joseph Varney," in *Encyclopedia of Public Relations*, ed. Robert L. Heath (Thousand Oaks, CA: Sage, 2005), 57–60.

35. Marilyn Kern-Foxworth, "Baker, Joseph Varney," in *Encyclopedia of Public Relations*, ed. Robert L. Heath (Thousand Oaks, CA: Sage, 2005), 57–60.

36. Joseph Lelyveld, "Racial image challenges big business: Business views its racial image pervaded by fervor best for company supervision recommended policies assesses," *The New York Times*, December 19, 1963, p. 59, https://www.nytimes.com/1963/12/19/archives/racial-image-challenges-big-business-business-views-its-racial.html.

37. Robert E. Brown, "St. Paul as a Public Relations Practitioner: A Metatheoretical Speculation on Messianic Communication and Symmetry," *Public Relations Review* 29 (2003): 1–12.

38. Margaret Opdycke Lamme and Karen Miller Russell, "Removing the Spin: Toward a New Theory of Public Relations History," *Journalism & Communication Monographs* 11 (2010): 279–361.

39. Robert E. Brown, "St. Paul as a Public Relations Practitioner: A Metatheoretical Speculation on Messianic Communication and Symmetry," *Public Relations Review* 29 (2003): 232.

40. http://www.religioncommunicators.org/a-brief-history.

41. http://njop.org/resources/social-media-for-synagogues/jewish-treats-top-ten-jewish-influencer-awards/.

42. Margaret Opdycke Lamme and Karen Miller Russell, "Removing the Spin: Toward a New Theory of Public Relations History," *Journalism & Communication Monographs* 11 (2010): 279–361; Scott M. Cutlip, *Public Relations History: From the 17th to the 20th Century: The Antecedents* (Mahwah, NJ: Lawrence Erlbaum Associates, 1995).

43. Scott M. Cutlip, *Public Relations History: From the 17th to the 20th Century: The Antecedents* (Mahwah, NJ: Lawrence Erlbaum Associates, 1995).

44. https://twitter.com/Codeybab/status/979149482268024834.

45. Laura Pappano, "The iGen Shift: Colleges Are Changing to Reach the Next Generation," *The New York Times*, August 2, 2018, accessed May 20, 2019, https://www.nytimes.com/2018/08/02/education/learning/generationz-igen-students-colleges.html.

46. Doug Newsom, J. Vanslyke Turk and D. Kruckeberg, *This Is PR: The Realities of Public Relations*, 8th ed. (Belmont, CA: Wadsworth/Thomson, 2004).

47. Jon Ericson, "Nagle: Howard Dean was the godfather of today's online political campaigns," *The Courier*, February 6, 2012, accessed May 20, 2019, https://wcfcourier.com/news/local/govt-and-politics/nagle-howard-dean-was-the-godfather-of-today-s-online/article_27fe1860-1861-5cd5-8459-e7bfd7be6c71.html.

48. http://www.careerarc.com/blog/2017/04/future-of-recruiting-study-infographic/.

49. Tom Kelleher and Kaye Sweetser, "Social Media Adoption Among University Communicators," *Journal of Public Relations Research* 24 (2012): 113.

50. Günter Bentele and Ivonne Junghänel, "Germany," in *Public Relations and Communication Management in Europe*, ed. Betteke Van Ruler and Dejan Verčič (Berlin: Mouton de Gruyter, 2004). Cited in Lamme and Russell [see note 42], 288.

51. Karl Nessman, "Austria," in *Public Relations and Communication Management in Europe*, ed. Betteke Van Ruler and Dejan Verčič (Berlin: Mouton de Gruyter, 2004). Cited in Lamme and Russell, 288.

52. Paul F. Lazarsfeld and Robert K. Merton, "Mass Communication, Popular Taste and Organized Social Action," in *The Communication of Ideas*, ed. Lyman Bryson (New York: Harper & Bros, 1948). Reprinted in Paul Marris and Sue Thornham, *Media Studies: A Reader*, 2nd ed. (New York: NYU Press, 2000), 20.

53. Emily Harris, "For Palestinians, Google's Small Change is a Big Deal," National Public Radio, May 14, 2013, accessed May 20, 2019, http://www.npr.org/blogs/parallels/2013/05/14/183966785/for-palestinians-googles-small-change-is-a-big-deal.

54. https://www.statista.com/statistics/264810/number-of-monthly-active-facebook-users-worldwide/.

55. Genevieve G. McBride, *On Wisconsin Women: Working for Their Rights from Settlement to Suffrage* (Madison: University of Wisconsin Press, 1993). Cited in Lamme and Russell.

56. Nadia Khomami, "#MeToo: how a hashtag became a rallying cry against sexual harassment," *The Guardian*, October 20, 2017, accessed May 20, 2019, https://www.theguardian.com/world/2017/oct/20/women-worldwide-use-hashtag-metoo-against-sexual-harassment.

57. http://justbeinc.wixsite.com/justbeinc/the-me-too-movement-cmml.

58. http://justbeinc.wixsite.com/justbeinc/the-me-too-movement-cmml.

59. Margaret Opdycke Lamme and Karen Miller Russell, "Removing the Spin: Toward a New Theory of Public Relations History," *Journalism & Communication Monographs* 11 (2010): 340.

60. Patrick Lee Plaisance, "Transparency: An Assessment of the Kantian Roots of a Key Element in Media Ethics Practice," *Journal of Mass Media Ethics* 22 (2007): 187–207.

61. James E. Grunig and Todd Hunt, *Managing Public Relations* (New York: Holt, Rinehart and Winston, 1984), p. 34.

62. http://www.oxforddictionaries.com/us/definition/american_english/objective?q=objective.

63. https://www.people-press.org/1999/03/30/section-i-the-core-principles-of-journalism/.

64. http://www.prsa.org/aboutprsa/ethics/codeenglish/.

65. http://www.spj.org/ethicscode.asp.

66. Genevieve McBride, "Ethical Thought in Public Relations History: Seeking a Relevant Perspective," *Journal of Mass Media Ethics* 4, no. 1 (1989): 5–20, p. 15.

67. *Lewiston Evening Journal*, July 12, 1934, p. 5 (via news.google.com).

CHAPTER 3

1. Henry Jenkins, *Convergence Culture: Where Old and New Media Collide* (New York: New York University Press, 2006), 14.
2. Henry Jenkins, *Convergence Culture: Where Old and New Media Collide* (New York: New York University Press, 2006), 14.
3. Henry Jenkins, "Convergence? I Diverge," *Technology Review* 104, no. 5 (2001): 93.
4. https://www.theglobalist.com/globalization-and-cultural-convergence/.
5. Henry Jenkins, *Convergence Culture: Where Old and New Media Collide* (New York: New York University Press, 2006), 18.
6. https://www.ketchum.com/reach-approach/.
7. https://adage.com/article/news/omnicom-acquires-ketchum/17638.
8. http://www.omnicomgroup.com/home.
9. https://www.holmesreport.com/ranking-and-data/global-pr-agency-rankings/2018-pr-agency-rankings/holding-groups-networks.
10. Marty Swant, "Every Ad Is a Tide Ad: Inside Saatchi and P&G's Clever Super Bowl Takeover Starring David Harbour," *Adweek*, February 4, 2018, accessed May 21, 2019, https://www.adweek.com/brand-marketing/every-ad-is-a-tide-ad-inside-saatchi-and-pgs-clever-super-bowl-takeover-starring-david-harbour.
11. Tim Nudd, "It's Still a Tide Ad: Revisiting Saatchi's Super Bowl Campaign, a Month Later," *Adweek*, March 8, 2018, accessed May 21, 2019, https://www.adweek.com/creativity/its-still-a-tide-ad-revisiting-saatchis-super-bowl-campaign-a-month-later/.
12. Alexandra Bruell, "P&G to Bring Ad Holding Company Rivals Together to Form New Creative Agency," April 9, 2018, accessed May 21, 2019, https://www.wsj.com/articles/p-g-to-bring-ad-holding-company-rivals-to-gether-to-form-new-creative-agency-1523277000.
13. https://www.ama.org/the-definition-of-marketing/.
14. E. Jerome McCarthy, *Basic Marketing: A Managerial Approach* (Homewood, IL: Richard D. Irwin Inc., 1960).
15. https://www.electronichouse.com/about-us/.
16. http://www.wommapedia.org/#section1.
17. http://www.youtube.com/watch?v=Fz22PfPxoXI.
18. https://www.ae.com/aerie/stylegallery/.
19. Bob Lauterborn, "New Marketing Litany; Four P's Passe; C-Words Take Over," *Advertising Age* (1990, October 1): 26.
20. Henry Ford and Samuel Crowther, *My Life and Work* (Sydney: Cornstalk Publishing Company, 1922), 72.
21. *Portlandia*, "Is It Local?" Season 1, Episode 1, http://www.ifc.com/portlandia/videos/portlandia-is-it-local.
22. http://www.cluetrain.com/book/markets.html.
23. http://contentmarketinginstitute.com/what-is-content-marketing/.
24. James O'Brien, "How Red Bull Takes Content Marketing to the Extreme," Mashable, December 19, 2012, accessed May 21, 2019, https://mashable.com/2012/12/19/red-bull-content-marketing/.

25. https://www.shiftcomm.com/blog/2014-will-be-the-year-of-brand-journalism/.
26. http://www.commpro.biz/social-video/views-you-can-use/chrysler-group-vide/.
27. Nitasha Tiku, "Why Your Inbox Is Crammed Full of Privacy Policies," *Wired*, May 24, 2018, accessed May 20, 2019, https://www.wired.com/story/how-a-new-era-of-privacy-took-over-your-email-inbox/.
28. https://myaccount.google.com/privacycheckup/.
29. https://www.prsa.org/ethics/code-of-ethics/.
30. Nitasha Tiku, "Why Your Inbox Is Crammed Full of Privacy Policies," *Wired*, May 24, 2018, accessed May 20,2019,https://www.wired.com/story/how-a-new-era-of-privacy-took-over-your-email-inbox/.
31. Marcia W. DiStaso and James McAvoy, "What PR Pros Need to Know for GDPR Compliance Day," Institute for Public Relations, May 25, 2018, accessed May 21, 2019, https://instituteforpr.org/what-pr-pros-need-to-know-for-gdpr-compliance-day/.

CHAPTER 4

1. John A. Ledingham and Stephen D. Bruning (eds.), *Public Relations as Relationship Management: A Relational Approach to the Study and Practice of Public Relations* (New York: Routledge, 2000), xii–xiii.
2. Linda Childers Hon and James E. Grunig, "Guidelines for Measuring Relationships in Public Relations," The Institute for Public Relations, accessed July 21, 2014, http://www.instituteforpr.org/wp-content/uploads/Guidelines_Measuring_Relationships.pdf.
3. Linda Childers Hon and James E. Grunig, "Guidelines for Measuring Relationships in Public Relations," The Institute for Public Relations, accessed July 21, 2014, http://www.instituteforpr.org/wp-content/uploads/Guidelines_Measuring_Relationships.pdf.
4. Elizabeth L. Toth, "From Personal Influence to Interpersonal Influence: A Model for Relationship Management," in *Public Relations as Relationship Management: A Relational Approach to the Study and Practice of Public Relations* (New York: Routledge, 2000), 205–219.
5. Salary Survey, prnewsonline.com, 2018 edition, accessed May 21, 2019, http://www.prnewsonline.com/wp-content/uploads/2018/03/pr-news-salary-survey-2018.pdf.
6. "Worksheet 1.1: What Is Newsworthy?," PBS News Student Reporting Labs, accessed May 21, 2019, https://studentreportinglabs.org/lesson-plans/lesson-1-1-what-is-newsworthy/.
7. https://www.prnewswire.com/news-releases/moulding-and-trim-in-the-united-states-2018-growth-in-building-construction-spending-to-drive-demand-gains-300712850.html, accessed May 21, 2019.
8. Richard D., Waters, Natalie T.J. Tindall and Timothy S. Morton, "Media Catching and the Journalist–Public Relations Practitioner Relationship: How Social Media Are Changing the Practice of Media Relations," *Journal of Public Relations Research* 22, no. 3 (2010): 241–264.
9. https://www.ibm.com/thought-leadership/wimbledon/uk-en/

10. http://www.greatplacetowork.net/best-companies/about-applying-to-best-companies-lists/how-youre-evaluated

11. Nan S. Russell, "Reality Check: Do You Know the Impact of Trust?" *Psychology Today*, accessed May 21, 2019, https://www.psychologytoday.com/us/blog/trust-the-new-workplace-currency/201210/reality-check-do-you-know-the-impact-trust.

12. Linjuan Rita Men, "Engaging Employees: Effectiveness of Traditional vs. New Media Channels," Institute for Public Relations, accessed May 21, 2019, http://www.instituteforpr.org/2013/10/engaging-employees-effectiveness-traditional-vs-new-media-channels/.

13. David Buss, *Evolutionary Psychology: The New Science of the Mind* (New York: Routledge, 2016), 273.

14. http://www.medtronic.com/us-en/about/mission.html.

15. Frances Robles, *The New York Times*, August 9, 2018, accessed May 21, 2019, https://www.nytimes.com/2018/08/09/us/puerto-rico-death-toll-maria.html.

16. https://finance.yahoo.com/news/medtronic-announces-preliminary-second-quarter-214601883.html, accessed May 21, 2019.

17. https://www.medtronic.com/us-en/about/news/puerto-rico-full-production.html, accessed May 21, 2019.

18. https://www.medtronic.com/us-en/about/news/puerto-rico-full-production.html, accessed May 21, 2019.

19. Medtronic, "Hurricane Can't Bend the Resolve of Medtronic Employees in Puerto Rico," October 9, 2017, accessed May 21, 2019, http://www.medtronic.com/us-en/about/news/puerto-rico-recovery-resolve-of-employees.html.

20. Allison Gatlin, "These Medtech Players Are Flailing on Hurricane-Related Headwinds," October 9, 2017, accessed May 21, 2019, https://www.investors.com/news/technology/medtronic-topples-on-expected-250-million-impact-after-storm/.

21. Medtronic, "Hurricane Can't Bend the Resolve of Medtronic Employees in Puerto Rico," October 9, 2017, accessed May 21, 2019, http://www.medtronic.com/us-en/about/news/puerto-rico-recovery-resolve-of-employees.html.

22. https://www.indeed.com/salaries/Investor-Relations-Manager-Salaries, accessed May 21, 2019.

23. http://www1.salary.com/Investor-Relations-Manager-Salaries.html, accessed May 21, 2019.

24. "About Us," National Investor Relations Institute, accessed May 21, 2019, https://www.niri.org/about-niri.

25. Alexander V. Laskin, "The Value of Investor Relations: A Delphi Panel Investigation," 2007, accessed May 21, 2019, https://instituteforpr.org/wp-content/uploads/2007_Laskin.pdf.

26. Julie O'Neil, "The Link Between Strong Public Relationships and Donor Support," *Public Relations Review* 33, no. 1 (2007): 99.

27. Richard D. Waters, "Measuring Stewardship in Public Relations: A Test Exploring Impact on the Fundraising Relationship," *Public Relations Review* 35, no. 2 (2009): 113–119.

28. Richard D. Waters, "Measuring Stewardship in Public Relations: A Test Exploring Impact on the Fundraising Relationship," *Public Relations Review* 35, no. 2 (2009): 116.

29. Kathleen S. Kelly, *Effective Fund-Raising Management* (Mahwah, NJ: Lawrence Erlbaum Associates, 1998), 441.

30. "Issue," Oxford Dictionaries, accessed May 21, 2019, http://www.oxforddictionaries.com/us/definition/american_english/issue?q=issue.

31. Taylor Telford, "Animal Crackers Have Been Caged for 116 years. Pressure on Nabisco Helped Free Them," *Washington Post*, August 21, 2018, accessed May 21, 2019, https://www.washingtonpost.com/news/food/wp/2018/08/21/animal-crackers-have-been-caged-for-116-years-pressure-on-nabisco-helped-free-them/.

32. https://www.peta.org/about-peta/.

33. Seth Arenstein, "Nabisco Frees Animal Crackers from Their Cages After Push From PETA," August 22, 2018, accessed May 21, 2019, https://www.prnewsonline.com/nabisco-frees-animal-crackers.

34. Larissa Grunig, "Activism: How It Limits the Effectiveness of Organizations and How Excellent Public Relations Departments Respond," in *Excellence in Public Relations and Communication Management*, ed. J. E. Grunig (Hillsdale, NJ: Lawrence Erlbaum, 2009), 504.

35. Mitch McNeil, "The Reality of Surfing in Chicago," The Inertia, accessed May 21, 2019, http://www.theinertia.com/surf/the-reality-of-surfing-in-chicago/.

36. "Surfing Information and Safety Awareness," Chicago Park District, accessed May 21, 2019, http://public.surfrider.org/files/Chicago_Surfing_Info_Safety.pdf.

37. https://www.chicago.surfrider.org/news/2018/7/12/surfrider-opposes-proposed-government-settlement-with-u-s-steel.

38. https://www.opensecrets.org/lobby/clientsum.php?id=D000000632&year=2017

39. https://www.interbrand.com/best-brands/best-global-brands/2017/

40. "Are All Calories Created Equal?," Arthur W. Page Society, accessed May 21, 2019, https://page.org/study_competitions/2014-case-study-competition.

41. "Coca-Cola's Global Commitments to Help Fight Obesity," The Coca-Cola Company, accessed May 21, 2019, https://www.coca-colacompany.com/press-center/press-releases/coca-cola-announces-global-commitments-to-help-fight-obesity.

42. "About CSPI," Center for Science in the Public Interest, accessed May 21, 2019, http://www.cspinet.org/about/index.html.

43. CSPI, May 8, 2013 (12:55 p.m.), commented on Twitter, "Coca-Cola is desperately trying. . . ," https://twitter.com/CSPI/status/332222216836087808.

44. http://www.nielsen.com/us/en/press-room/2015/consumer-goods-brands-that-demonstrate-commitment-to-sustainability-outperform.html.

45. http://www.conecomm.com/research-blog/2017-csr-study

46. "New Study Shows Strong CSR Boosts Profits," Bulldog Reporter, accessed May 21, 2019, http://www.bulldogreporter.com/dailydog/article/pr-biz-update/new-study-shows-strong-csr-boosts-profits-majority-of-companies-incre.

47. "Public Policy Engagement," The Coca-Cola Company, accessed May 21, 2019, http://www.coca-colacompany.com/investors/public-policy-engagement.

48. Michael M. Grynbaum, "New York's Ban on Big Sodas Is Rejected by Final Court," *The New York Times*, June 26, 2014, accessed May 21, 2019, http://www.nytimes.com/2014/06/27/nyregion/city-loses-final-appeal-on-limiting-sales-of-large-sodas.html?_r=0.

CHAPTER 5

1. John E. Marston, *The Nature of Public Relations* (New York: McGraw-Hill, 1963).

2. Jerry Hendrix, Darrell Hayes and Pallavi Kumar, *Public Relations Cases* (Boston: Cengage Learning, 2013).

3. Sheila Clough Crifasi, as cited in Fraser P. Seitel, *The Practice of Public Relations*, 12th ed. (Upper Saddle River, NJ: Pearson, 2014).

4. "Silver Anvil Search," Public Relations Society of America, accessed August 24, 2019, http://apps.prsa.org/awards/silveranvil/Search.

5. Laurie J. Wilson and Joseph D. Ogden, *Strategic Communications Planning for Effective Public Relations & Marketing* (Dubuque, IA: Kendall Hunt, 2008).

6. "Silver Anvil Search," Public Relations Society of America, accessed June 13, 2019, http://www.prsa.org/Awards/SilverAnvil/Search.

7. https://www.chewy.com/app/content/about-us

8. http://www.humanesociety.org/about/overview/

9. https://www.uoregon.edu/our-mission

10. https://www.uoregon.edu/our-mission

11. https://www.jou.ufl.edu/insights/internal-communication/

12. Rita Linjuan Men and Shannon A. Bowen, *Excellence in Internal Communication Management* (New York: Business Expert Press, 2016).

13. Bryan Menegus, "Amazon's Aggressive Anti-Union Tactics Revealed in Leaked 45-Minute Video," Gizmodo, September 26, 2018, accessed June 13, 2019, https://gizmodo.com/amazons-aggressive-anti-union-tactics-revealed-in-leake-1829305201

14. Kurt Lewin, *Field Theory in Social Science* (New York: Harper & Row, 1951), 169.

15. https://www.freepress.net/issues/free-open-internet/net-neutrality

16. https://www.fcc.gov/document/fcc-adopts-strong-sustainable-rules-protect-open-internet

17. Mike Snider, Roger Yu and Emily Brown, "Net Neutrality: The FCC Voted to End It. What That Means for You," *USA Today*, April 26, 2017, accessed June 13, 2019, https://www.usatoday.com/story/tech/news/2017/04/26/what-net-neutrality-and-what-would-its-reversal-mean/100930220/

18. Mieczysław Radochoński and Anna Radochońska, "Attitudes of the Polish University Students Toward Voluntary Blood Donation," *Rzeszow* 4 (2007): 329–334.

19. Lorenz Goette and Alois Stutzer, "Blood Donations and Incentives: Evidence from a Field Experiment," *IZA Discussion Papers*, no. 3580 (2008), accessed June 13, 2019, http://www.econstor.eu/bitstream/10419/35271/1/1/57333479X.pdf.

20. Don W. Stacks, *Primer of Public Relations Research* (New York: Guilford Press, 2010).

21. David Silverman, *Interpreting Qualitative Data: Methods for Analyzing Talk, Text and Interaction* (London: Sage, 2006).

22. David L. Morgan, *Focus Groups as Qualitative Research*, Vol. 16 (Thousand Oaks, CA: Sage, 1997), 11.

23. "About the Survey," National Survey on Drug Use and Health, accessed June 13, 2019, https://nsduhweb.rti.org/respweb/about_nsduh.html.

24. SAMHSA 2018-2022 National Surveys on Drug Use and Health (NSDUH), accessed June 13, 2019, https://www.fbo.gov/?s=opportunity&mode=form&tab=core&id=3903d264e0de6f606b9f9bb6942e7a96&_cview=0.

25. "Underage Binge Alcohol Use Varies Within and Across States," The NSDUH Report, accessed June 13, 2019, https://www.samhsa.gov/data/sites/default/files/NSDUH-SR199-UnderageBinge-2014/NSDUH-SR199-UnderageBinge-2014.htm.

26. Dr. Joseph Sabia, "Minimum Wage and the Business Cycle: Does a Wage Hike Hurt More in a Weak Economy?" Employment Policies Institute, accessed June 13, 2019, https://www.epionline.org/studies/minimum-wages-and-the-business-cycle-does-a-wage-hike-hurt-more-in-a-weak-economy/.

27. Kathleen Maclay, "Low-Wage Fast-Food Jobs Leave Hefty Tax Bill, Report Says," UC Berkeley News Center, accessed June 13, 2019, http://newscenter.berkeley.edu/2013/10/15/low-wage-fast-food-jobs-leave-hefty-tax-bill-report-says/.

28. Shannon A. Bowen and Don W. Stacks, "Understanding the Ethical and Research Implications of Social Media," in *Ethical Practice of Social Media in Public Relations*, ed. Marcia W. DiStaso and Denise Sevick Bortree (New York: Routledge, 2014), 219.

29. "Ethical Standards and Guidelines for Public Relations Research and Measurement 2012," Institute for Public Relations, accessed June 13, 2019, https://instituteforpr.org/wp-content/uploads/Ethical-standards-and-guidelines-for-public-relations-research-ver-1.1.pdf.

CHAPTER 6

1. "Pop up," Lexico.com, accessed August 24, 2009, https://en.oxforddictionaries.com/definition/us/pop_up.

2. Nicole Leinbach-Reyhle, "Pop-Up Retailers: Must Know Details to Make Yours a Success," December 24, 2014, accessed June 13, 2019, https://www.forbes.com/sites/nicoleleinbachreyhle/2014/12/24/pop-up-retailers-must-know-details-to-make-yours-a-success/#615f354827e1.

3. https://www.prnewswire.com/news-releases/timberland-brings-natures-elements-to-life-in-new-pop-up-retail-store-on-fifth-avenue-in-the-heart-of-new-york-city-300722730.html.

4. https://www.prnewswire.com/news-releases/timberland-brings-natures-elements-to-life-in-new-pop-up-retail-store-on-fifth-avenue-in-the-heart-of-new-york-city-300722730.html.

5. Kaitlyn Tiffany, "Every Store Is an Experience and Every Experience Is a Selfie," Vox, October 11, 2018,

accessed June 13, 2019, https://www.vox.com/the-goods/2018/10/11/17955264/timberland-fifth-avenue-rain-room-instagram-experiences-photos.

6. "Use Goal Flow to Perform Funnel Analysis," Google, accessed June 13, 2019, https://support.google.com/analytics/answer/1686005.

7. Wendy Lewis, "Celebrating Women Everywhere on the Journey to Progress," Medium, March 6, 2018, accessed June 13, 2019, https://medium.com/@McDonaldsCorp/celebrating-women-everywhere-on-the-journey-to-progress-791bd17ba287.

8. https://corporate.mcdonalds.com/corpmcd/about-us/our-values.html.

9. "About Us/Vision, Principles & Strategy," Water Supply & Sanitation Collaborative Council, accessed June 13, 2019, https://www.wsscc.org/who-we-are/.

10. Jelena Vujcic and Pavani K. Ram, *Handwashing Promotion: Monitoring and Evaluation Module*, UNICEF, accessed June 13, 2019, https://www.unicef.org/wash/files/M_and_E_Toolkit_.pdf.

11. Jelena Vujcic and Pavani K. Ram, *Handwashing Promotion: Monitoring and Evaluation Module*, UNICEF, accessed June 13, 2019, https://www.unicef.org/wash/files/M_and_E_Toolkit_.pdf.

12. https://www.cdc.gov/handwashing/heroes.html.

13. Jelena Vujcic and Pavani K. Ram, *Handwashing Promotion: Monitoring and Evaluation Module*, UNICEF, accessed June 13, 2019, https://www.unicef.org/wash/files/M_and_E_Toolkit_.pdf.

14. Ronald D. Smith, *Strategic Planning for Public Relations* (Mahwah, NJ: Lawrence Erlbaum Associates, 2006), 240.

15. James Lukaszewski, https://www.e911.com/.

16. Ameet Ranadive, "Demystifying Programmatic Marketing and RTB," Medium, accessed June 13, 2019, https://medium.com/@ameet/demystifying-programmatic-marketing-and-rtb-83edb8c9ba0f.

17. : iDigic, "Buy Real Instagram Followers," accessed August 24, 2009, https://www.idigic.net/buy-instagram-followers/.

18. "Public Relations Society of America (PRSA) Member Code of Ethics," PRSA, accessed June 13, 2019, http://www.prsa.org/aboutprsa/ethics/codeenglish/.

CHAPTER 7

1. https://www.chipotle.com/food-with-integrity.html.

2. https://www.chipotle.com/food-with-integrity.html.

3. Matt Krantz, "How Chipotle Is Eating McDonald's Lunch," *USA Today*, January 22, 2015.

4. Roberto A. Ferdman, "Why Chipotle's Pork Problem Is a Bad Sign for Its Future," *The Washington Post*, January 14, 2015, accessed June 13, 2019, http://www.washingtonpost.com/blogs/wonkblog/wp/2015/01/14/why-chipotles-pork-problem-is-a-bad-sign-for-its-future/.

5. Erin Mosbaugh, "#Carnitasgate: Chipotle Not Serving Pork at One-Third of Its Restaurants," *First We Feast*, accessed June 13, 2019, http://firstwefeast.com/eat/carnitasgate-chipotle-not-serving-pork-at-one-third-of-its-restaurants/.

6. Danny Vena, "Can Chipotle Continue 2018's Strong Gains When It Reports Earnings?" The Motley Fool, January 30, 2019, accessed June 13, 2019, https://www.fool.com/investing/2019/01/30/can-chipotle-continue-strong-gains-2018-earnings.aspx.

7. *APR Study Guide for the Examination for Accreditation in Public Relations*, Universal Accreditation Board, 2017, accessed June 13, 2019, http://www.praccreditation.org/resources/documents/apr-study-guide.pdf.

8. Pramath, "EA Play 2018 Was One of the Worst Press Conferences of All Time," GamingBolt, June 9, 2018, accessed June 13, 2019, https://gamingbolt.com/ea-play-2018-was-one-of-the-worst-press-conferences-of-all-time.

9. "Advertising FAQs," LinkedIn, accessed June 13, 2019, https://business.linkedin.com/marketing-solutions/advertising-faqs.

10. Garett Sloane, "Snapchat Is Asking Brands for $750,000 to Advertise and Won't Budge," *Adweek*, accessed June 13, 2019, https://www.adweek.com/digital/snapchat-asks-brands-750000-advertise-and-wont-budge-162359/.

11. Garett Sloane, "Snapchat Ad Prices Go From Ungodly to Cheap," *AdAge*, June 11, 2018, accessed June 13, 2019, https://adage.com/article/digital/snapchat-prices-ungodly-cheap/313824.

12. Garett Sloane, "Snapchat Ad Prices Go From Ungodly to Cheap," *AdAge*, June 11, 2018, accessed June 13, 2019, https://adage.com/article/digital/snapchat-prices-ungodly-cheap/313824.

13. Christopher Ratcliff, "A Look Inside GoPro's Dazzling YouTube Strategy," *Econsultancy*, accessed June 13, 2019, https://econsultancy.com/blog/64370-a-look-inside-gopro-s-dazzling-youtube-strategy.

14. Carla Herreria, "Lockheed Martin's #WorldPhotoDay Tweet Backfires," Huffpost, August 18, 2018, accessed June 13, 2019, https://www.huffingtonpost.com/entry/lockheed-martin-world-photo-day_us_5b78a2eee4b018b93e948af3.

15. *APR Study Guide for the Examination for Accreditation in Public Relations*, Universal Accreditation Board, 2010, accessed June 13, 2019, http://www.praccreditation.org/resources/documents/apr-study-guide.pdf, 18.

16. "Search Engine Optimization," *Wikipedia, the Free Encyclopedia*, accessed June 13, 2019, https://en.wikipedia.org/wiki/Search_engine_optimization.

17. "Steps to a Google-Friendly Site," Google, accessed June 13, 2019, https://support.google.com/webmasters/answer/40349.

18. https://www.facebook.com/business/success/bark

19. Sami Main, "Why BarkBox Uses Comedians Instead of Marketers to Create Engaging Content," *Adweek*, December 4, 2017, accessed June 13, 2019, https://www.adweek.com/tv-video/why-barkbox-uses-comedians-instead-of-marketers-to-create-engaging-content/2/.

20. Ilyse Liffreing, "BarkBox cuts Facebook spending in favor of traditional channels," Digiday, June 15, 2018, accessed June 13, 2019, https://digiday.com/marketing/barkbox-cuts-facebook-spending-favor-traditional-channels/.

21. Eric Deggans, "Diversity: The Gateway to Accuracy and Fairness in Media," in *Doing Ethics in Media: Theories and Practical Applications*, ed. Jay Black and Chris Roberts (New York: Taylor & Francis, 2011), 155.

22. "PRSA Member Code of Ethics," PRSA, accessed June 13, 2019, http://www.prsa.org/aboutprsa/ethics/codeenglish/.

23. "Agencies Must Find Answers for a Lack of Diversity," *PRWeek*, May 1, 2011, accessed June 13, 2019, http://www.prweek.com/article/1264390/agencies-find-answers-lack-diversity.

24. Rosanna M. Fiske, "PRSA Committed to Increasing Diversity in Public Relations—PRWeek Letter to the Editor," PRSA, June 14, 2011, https://www.prsa.org.

25. Jay Black and Chris Roberts (eds.), *Doing Ethics in Media: Theories and Practical Applications* (New York: Taylor & Francis, 2011), 151.

26. "Kimberly-Clark Names Sue Dodsworth Global Diversity Officer," Kimberly-Clark, November 1, 2010, accessed June 13, 2019, http://investor.kimberly-clark.com/releasedetail.cfm?releaseid=525475.

27. Molly Petrilla, "How Analytics Helped Kimberly-Clark Solve Its Diversity Problem," *Fortune*, December 10, 2014, accessed June 13, 2019, http://fortune.com/2014/12/10/kimberly-clark-dodsworth-diversity/.

28. Molly Petrilla, "How Analytics Helped Kimberly-Clark Solve Its Diversity Problem," *Fortune*, December 10, 2014, accessed June 13, 2019, http://fortune.com/2014/12/10/kimberly-clark-dodsworth-diversity/.

29. "Kimberly-Clark Initiative Wins 2014 Catalyst Award," Kimberly-Clark, accessed June 13, 2019, https://investor.kimberly-clark.com/news-releases/news-release-details/kimberly-clark-initiative-wins-2014-catalyst-award.

CHAPTER 8

1. Lisa Arthur, "What Is Big Data?," *Forbes*, August 15, 2013, accessed June 13, 2019, https://www.forbes.com/sites/lisaarthur/2013/08/15/what-is-big-data/#50260a6f5c85.

2. Seth Duncan, *Using Web Analytics to Measure the Impact of Earned Online Media on Business Outcomes: A Methodological Approach* (Gainesville, FL: Institute for Public Relations), accessed June 13, 2019, http://www.instituteforpr.org/wp-content/uploads/Seth_Duncan_Web_Analytics.pdf.

3. "Summit Agrees [on] Framework of Global Programme Measurement Standard," International Association for Measurement and Evaluation of Communication, June 21, 2010, https://news.cision.com/amec/r/summit-agrees-framework-of-global-programme-measurement-standard,c498817.

4. "Barcelona Principles 2.0 Launched," International Association for Measurement and Evaluation of Communication, accessed June 14, 2019, https://amecorg.com/2015/09/barcelona-principles-2-0-unveiled/.

5. "The Barcelona Declaration of Research Principles," Institute for Public Relations, June 18, 2010, accessed June 13, 2019, https://instituteforpr.org/the-barcelona-declaration-of-research-principles/.

6. "Employee Engagement Survey Final Report," Charlotte-Mecklenburg Schools, October 8–25, 2012, accessed June 13, 2019, http://www.cms.k12.nc.us/mediaroom/Documents/Employee%20Engagement%20Survey%20Final%20Report%202012.pdf.

7. "Google Brand Lift—Measuring Interest in Your Brand," Google, accessed June 13, 2019, https://www.youtube.com/watch?v=gYJQMRSbMlc.

8. "The Barcelona Declaration of Research Principles," Institute for Public Relations, June 18, 2010, accessed June 13, 2019, https://instituteforpr.org/the-barcelona-declaration-of-research-principles/.

9. "We Believe: The Best Men Can Be," Gillette, January 13, 2019, accessed August 25, 2019, https://youtube/koPmuEyP3a0.

10. https://twitter.com/BerniceKing/status/1085027166738440192

11. https://twitter.com/ariannahuff/status/1084970962519494658

12. "We Believe: The Best Men Can Be," Gillette, January 13, 2019, accessed August 25, 2019, https://youtube/koPmuEyP3a0.

13. "We Believe: The Best Men Can Be," Gillette, January 13, 2019, accessed August 25, 2019, https://youtube/koPmuEyP3a0.

14. Justin Joffe, "Gillette's Close Shave: New Ad Debuts a Brand Voice for Modern Times," PR News, January 15, 2019, accessed June 13, 2019, https://www.prnewsonline.com/gillette-close-shave-ad-brand-voice.

15. Marc Pritchard, "Gillette's 'We Believe' Ad Took a Stand. And I'm Proud of the Conversation It Started," CNN Business, February 5, 2019, accessed June 13, 2019, https://www.cnn.com/2019/02/05/perspectives/gillette-we-believe-ad-pg/index.html.

16. Andre Manning and David Rockland, "Understanding the Barcelona Principles," The Public Relations Strategist, March 21, 2011, accessed June 13, 2019, http://www.prsa.org/Intelligence/TheStrategist/Articles/view/9072/1028/Understanding_the_Barcelona_Principles.

17. Daniel Kahneman, *Thinking, Fast and Slow* (New York: Farrar, Straus and Giroux, 2011).

18. Joel Best, *Damned Lies and Statistics: Untangling Numbers from the Media, Politicians, and Activists* (Berkeley: University of California Press, 2012).

19. Joel Best, *Damned Lies and Statistics: Untangling Numbers from the Media, Politicians, and Activists* (Berkeley: University of California Press, 2012), 5.

20. John Stauber and Sheldon Rampton, *Toxic Sludge Is Good for You: Lies, Damn Lies and the Public Relations Industry* (Monroe, ME: Common Courage Press, 1995).

21. "Public Relations Society of America (PRSA) Member Code of Ethics," Public Relations Society of America, accessed June 13, 2019, http://www.prsa.org/about-prsa/ethics/codeenglish.

22. David Michaelson and Don W. Stacks, "Standardization in Public Relations Measurement and Evaluation," *Public Relations Journal* 5, no. 2 (2011): 1–22; Shannon A. Bowen and Don W. Stacks, "Toward the Establishment of Ethical Standardization in Public

Relations Research, Measurement, and Evaluation," *Public Relations Journal* 7, no. 3 (2013): 1–28.

CHAPTER 9

1. Morgan Sung, "10 New Year's Resolutions That Will Make Your Online Life a Little Better," *Mashable*, December 31, 2018, accessed June 13, 2019, https://mashable.com/article/new-year-resolutions-social-media-2019/.

2. Joe Oliveto, "5 Creepy Things A.I. Has Started Doing On Its Own," *Cracked*, February 24, 2019, accessed June 13, 2019, http://www.cracked.com/blog/5-creepy-things-a.i.-has-started-doing-its-own.

3. Wikipedia contributors, "Listicle," *Wikipedia, The Free Encyclopedia*, accessed June 13, 2019, https://en.wikipedia.org/w/index.php?title=Listicle&oldid=859745044.

4. Steve Denning, "Five Reasons Why Millennials Love Listicles," *Forbes*, August 29, 2014, accessed June 13, 2019, https://www.forbes.com/sites/stevedenning/2014/08/29/five-reasons-why-millennials-love-listicles/#656f6a2e63d8.

5. Arika Okrent, "The Listicle as Literary Form," *The University of Chicago Magazine*, Jan/Feb 2014, accessed June 13, 2019, http://mag.uchicago.edu/arts-humanities/listicle-literary-form.

6. Craig E. Carroll, *The Handbook of Communication and Corporate Reputation* (Oxford, UK: Wiley-Blackwell, 2013), 4.

7. Brian Solis and Deirdre K. Breakenridge, *Putting the Public Back in Public Relations: How Social Media Is Reinventing the Aging Business of PR* (Upper Saddle River, NJ: FT Press, 2009), 102.

8. https://worldbicyclerelief.org/en/dairy-farmer-malawi/

9. William Zinsser, *On Writing Well: The Classic Guide to Writing Nonfiction* (New York: HarperPerennial, 1998), 62.

10. Ann Wylie, "One More Phrase to Avoid: Enough Already with the 'At XX, We . . .' Construction," *PR Tactics* 22, no. 3 (March 2015): 7.

11. William Finnegan, "The Best Surfer in History Made a Machine That Creates Perfect Conditions on Demand. Will His Invention Democratize Surfing or Despoil It?" *The New Yorker*, December 10, 2018, accessed June 13, 2019, https://www.newyorker.com/magazine/2018/12/17/kelly-slaters-shock-wave.

12. http://www.nba.com/article/2019/03/06/warriors-draft-first-woman-nba-2k-league

13. https://www.instagram.com/p/Bat1TuYgbvu/

14. Meta G. Carstarphen and Richard H. Wells, *Writing PR: A Multimedia Approach* (Boston: Pearson, 2004).

15. Meta G. Carstarphen and Richard H. Wells, *Writing PR: A Multimedia Approach* (Boston: Pearson, 2004), 192.

16. AP, "BC-NBA 2K League-First Woman,2nd Ld-Write-thru," March 5, 2019, accessed August 25, 2019, https://www.apnews.com/32f435646fff43ea8948298a202fdb7c.

17. Lynn Elber, "'Jeopardy!' Host Alex Trebek Says He Has Pancreatic Cancer," *AP*, March 6, 2019, accessed June 13, 2019, https://www.apnews.com/18c3688aa8b34b63b0d5eacbfc2e5c5e.

18. National Marine Sanctuaries, "NOAA, Partners, Survey 'Amazingly Intact' Historic WWII-Era Aircraft Carrier," April 16, 2015, accessed August 25, 2019, https://sanctuaries.noaa.gov/news/press/2015/independence-survey.html.

19. http://www.publicaffairs.noaa.gov/grounders/noaahistory.html

20. http://sanctuaries.noaa.gov/about/

21. http://sanctuaries.noaa.gov/maritime/contact_us.html

22. Brian Solis and Deirdre K. Breakenridge, *Putting the Public Back in Public Relations: How Social Media Is Reinventing the Aging Business of PR* (Upper Saddle River, NJ: FT Press, 2009), 155.

23. http://www.merriam-webster.com/word-of-the-year/2004-word-of-the-year.htm

24. http://blogs.harvard.edu/whatmakesaweblogaweblog.html

25. Erica Swallow, "10 Tips for Corporate Blogging," *Mashable*, July 20, 2010, accessed on June 13, 2019, http://mashable.com/2010/07/20/corporate-blogging-tips/.

26. Danielle Long, "Weibo Continues to Grow as Users Near 500 Million Mark," *The Drum*, August 13, 2018, accessed June 13, 2019, https://www.thedrum.com/news/2018/08/13/weibo-continues-grow-users-near-500-million-mark.

27. http://www.edelman.com/post/friday5-twitter-vs-sina-weibo/.

28. "Search Engine Optimization," *Wikipedia, the Free Encyclopedia*, accessed June 13, 2019, https://en.wikipedia.org/wiki/Search_engine_optimization.

29. https://support.google.com/webmasters/answer/66358?hl=en

30. https://support.google.com/webmasters/answer/40349?hl=en

31. https://twitter.com/searchliaison/status/973241540486164480

32. "Code of Ethics," PRSA, www.prsa.org/AboutPRSA/Ethics/CodeEnglish

33. Jay Black and Chris Roberts, *Doing Ethics in Media: Theories and Practical Applications* (New York: Taylor & Francis, 2011).

34. Abel Meeropol, "Strange Fruit" (Commodore Records, 1939); Lewis Allan, *Strange Fruit* (New York: Edward B. Marks Music Corporation, 1940).

35. Gary Dinges, "Austin PR Firm Changing Name Some Say Was Racially Insensitive," *Statesman*, December 8, 2014, accessed June 13, 2019, https://www.statesman.com/article/20141208/BUSINESS/312089634.

36. Gary Dinges, "Austin PR Firm Changing Name Some Say Was Racially Insensitive," *Statesman*, December 8, 2014, accessed June 13, 2019, https://www.statesman.com/article/20141208/BUSINESS/312089634.

37. Gary Dinges, "Austin PR Firm Changing Name Some Say Was Racially Insensitive," *Statesman*, December 8, 2014, accessed June 13, 2019, https://www.statesman.com/article/20141208/BUSINESS/312089634.

CHAPTER 10

1. Seth Arenstein, "Back to School: Employers Seek Strategy, Writing, Digital and Global Perspective from PR

Students," *PR News*, August 21, 2018, accessed August 25, 2019, www.prnewsonline.com/skills-for-PR-students.

2. Alex Welch, "Late-Night Ratings, Feb. 25–March 1, 2019: 'Tonight,' 'Late Night' Rise," *TV by the Numbers* by zap2it. com, March 5, 2019, accessed August 25, 2019, tvbythenumbers.zap2it.com/weekly-ratings/late-night-ratings-feb-25-march-1-2019/.

3. "The Jonas Brothers: Year 2019," YouTube video, posted March 5, 2019, by the Late Late Show with James Corden, https://www.youtube.com/watch?v=6ABRsDE9grg.

4. "The Latest YouTube Stats on When, Where, and What People Watch," Google, www.thinkwithgoogle.com/data-collections/youtube-stats-video-consumption-trends/.

5. GSMA, 2018, *The Mobile Economy 2018*, www.gsma.com/mobileeconomy/wp-content/uploads/2018/05/The-Mobile-Economy-2018.pdf.

6. Comscore, 2018, *Global Digital Future in Focus 2018*, https://www.comscore.com/Insights/Presentations-and-Whitepapers/2018/Global-Digital-Future-in-Focus-2018.

7. Nielsen, 2018, *Nielsen Total Audience Report Q2 2018*, https://www.nielsen.com/us/en/insights/report/2018/q2-2018-total-audience-report/.

8. Comscore, 2017, *The 2017 U.S. Mobile App Report*, www.comscore.com/Insights/Presentations-and-Whitepapers/2017/The-2017-US-Mobile-App-Report.

9. Comscore, 2017, *The 2017 U.S. Mobile App Report*, www.comscore.com/Insights/Presentations-and-Whitepapers/2017/The-2017-US-Mobile-App-Report.

10. "Your 2018 Wrapped," Spotify Community, December 6,2018,https://community.spotify.com/t5/Community-Blog/Your-2018-Wrapped/ba-p/4625551.

11. Monica Mercuri, "Spotify Reports First Quarterly Operating Profit, Reaches 96 Million Paid Subscribers," *Forbes*, February 6, 2019, www.forbes.com/sites/monicamercuri/2019/02/06/spotify-reports-first-quarterly-operating-profit-reaches-96-million-paid-subscribers/#4d2b381a5dc9.

12. Giselle Abramovich, "Consumer Demand for Personalized Content Reaches All-Time High," CMO.com, February 8, 2018, www.cmo.com/features/articles/2018/1/31/adobe-2018-consumer-content-survey.html#gs.14ntvo.

13. Paul Hitlin and Lee Rainie, "Facebook Algorithms and Personal Data," Pew Research Center: Internet, Science & Tech, January 16, 2019, www.pewinternet.org/2019/01/16/facebook-algorithms-and-personal-data/.

14. Haley Weiss, "Why People Love Spotify's Annual Wrap-Ups," *The Atlantic*, December 12, 2018, www.theatlantic.com/technology/archive/2018/12/spotify-wrapped-and-data-collection/577930/.

15. "On-Demand Geofilters," Snapchat, https://www.snapchat.com/geofilters.

16. "Order a Whopper® Sandwich for a Penny at McDonald's with the BK® App," Business Wire, December 4, 2018, www.businesswire.com/news/home/20181204005560/en/Order-Whopper®-Sandwich-Penny-McDonald's-BK®-App.

17. "Restaurant Brands International Inc. (QSR) CEO José Cil on Q4 2018 Results—Earnings Call Transcript," Seeking Alpha, February 11, 2019, https://seekingalpha.com/article/4239908-restaurant-brands-international-inc-qsr-ceo-jose-cil-q4-2018-results-earnings-call-transcript.

18. "Report: Mobile Apps Represent Bulk of Digital Orders," *QSR Magazine*, February 4, 2019, www.qsrmagazine.com/news/report-mobile-apps-represent-bulk-digital-orders.

19. "BURGER KING® Restaurants Launches BK® Café Subscription for Only $5 a Month," Business Wire, March 15, 2019, www.businesswire.com/news/home/20190315005025/en.

20. J. G. Blumler, "The Role of Theory in Uses and Gratifications Studies," *Communication Research* 6, no. 1 (1979): 9–36.

21. Ruth Avidar, Yaron Ariel, Vered Malka and Eilat Chen Levy, "Smartphones and Young Publics: A New Challenge for Public Relations Practice and Relationship Building," *Public Relations Review* 39, no. 5 (2013): 603–605.

22. David Shadpour, "How Social Media Can Serve as the New Focus Group for Your Brand," *Forbes*, March 21, 2018, www.forbes.com/sites/forbesagencycouncil/2018/03/21/how-social-media-can-serve-as-the-new-focus-group-for-your-brand/.

23. "Case Study | Pandora: The Power of Data-Driven Marketing," Sysomos, www.sysomos.com/wp-content/uploads/2017/08/CaseStudy_Pandora.pdf.

24. "10 Examples of Social Media Command Centers," Salesforce.com, brandcdn.exacttarget.com/sites/exacttarget/files/10-Examples-of-Social-Media-Command-Centers.pdf.

25. Susan Etlinger, "Image Intelligence: Making Visual Content Predictive," Prophet, Prophet Brand Strategy, July 18, 2016, www.prophet.com/2016/07/image-intelligence-making-visual-content-predictive/.

26. "An Interview with Christophe Folschette—Why Visual Listening Is the Next Big Thing for Marketers," Talkwalker, March 25, 2016, www.talkwalker.com/blog/an-interview-with-christophe-folschette-why-visual-listening-is-the-next-big-thing-for-marketers.

27. Ashley Sefferman, "Most Brands Hear from Less than 1% of Their Customers," Apptentive, January 17, 2019, www.apptentive.com/blog/2019/01/17/most-brands-hear-from-less-than-1-percent-customers/.

28. "Newsjacking," Newsjacking, Freshspot Marketing LLC, www.newsjacking.com/.

29. Patrick J. Lynch and Sarah Horton, Web Style Guide, 3rd ed., http://www.webstyleguide.com/.

30. Robert Wynne, "How to Turbocharge Your Writing for Public Relations," *Forbes*, January 20, 2014, www.forbes.com/sites/robertwynne/2014/01/20/how-to-write-for-public-relations/.

31. Elizabeth Holmes, "In Photo Sharing, Every Picture Tells a Story, When It Has the Right Caption," *The Wall Street Journal*, February 3, 2015, www.wsj.com/articles/in-photo-sharing-every-picture-tells-a-story-when-it-has-the-right-caption-1423007365.

32. "About Text in Ad Images," Facebook Ads Help Center, Facebook Business, www.facebook.com/business/help/980593475366490.

33. "Uncovering Your Brand in Social Media Images: Visual Listening Guide," Sysomos, sysomos.com/wp-content/uploads/2017/03/Visual_Listening_Guide_2017.pdf.

34. Belle Beth Cooper, "10 Big Social Media Changes That You Should Know About," Buffer Social Blog, March 14, 2016, https://buffer.com/resources/10-recent-changes-made-to-twitter-facebook-and-linkedin-that-you-should-know-for-a-better-social-media-strategy.

35. Dara Fontein, "Expert Design Tips for Your Social Media Images," Hootsuite Social Media Management, Hootsuite.com, November 2, 2016, https://blog.hootsuite.com/design-tips-social-media-images/.

36. Joe Wadlington, "3 Ways to Create a Consistent Visual Brand on Twitter," Twitter, Twitter Business, December 20, 2016, https://business.twitter.com/en/blog/3-ways-create-consistent-visual-brand-Twitter.html.

37. Kim Lachance Shandrow, "8 Types of Photos You Should Never Use on Your LinkedIn Profile," Entrepreneur, June 28, 2016, www.entrepreneur.com/article/238624.

38. "Embed Images for Your Non-Commercial Website or Blog in Three Easy Steps," Getty Images, www.gettyimages.com/resources/embed.

39. "YouTube for Press," YouTube, https://www.youtube.com/yt/about/press/.

40. Liz Alton, "How Video Is Reshaping Digital Advertising," Twitter, Twitter Business, March 11, 2019, http://business.twitter.com/en/blog/how-video-is-reshaping-digital-advertising.html.

41. "How to Turn a Horizontal Video into a Vertical Snap Ad | A Snapchat Tutorial | Snapchat for Business." YouTube, https://www.youtube.com/watch?v=d-zjCXI4KYQ.

42. NASA—National Aeronautics and Space Administration. "Spacewalk with NASA Astronauts." Facebook, https://www.facebook.com/NASA/videos/1084151621769803/

43. "In a Mobile-First World, Shorter Video Ads Drive Results," Facebook Business, January 24, 2018, www.facebook.com/business/news/in-a-mobile-first-world-shorter-video-ads-drive-results?ref=fbb-blog_reinventing.

44. "Capture Attention with Updated Features for Video Ads." Facebook Business, February 10, 2016, www.facebook.com/business/news/updated-features-for-video-ads.

45. Jason Bercovici, *Advertising Week*, "Short-Form vs Long-Form Video: The Answer Is Sometimes Both," TheHuffingtonPost.com, July 5, 2017, www.huffingtonpost.com/entry/short-form-vs-long-form-video-the-answer-is-sometimes_us_595d275ae4b0f078efd98de4.

46. "Reinventing Storytelling for the Mobile World," , April 13, 2018, www.facebook.com/business/news/reinventing-storytelling-for-the-mobile-world.

47. Peter Minnium, "The Power of Disruptive Digital Narrative," Marketing Land, October 8, 2018, https://marketingland.com/the-power-of-disruptive-digital-narrative-249533.

48. Instagram, "Introducing Boomerang from Instagram," *Vimeo*, 2016, https://vimeo.com/143161189.

49. Tristan Handy, "New Research Finds the Curation vs Creation Sweet Spot," Convince and Convert, www.convinceandconvert.com/social-media-measurement/new-research-finds-the-curation-vs-creation-sweet-spot/.

50. Christie Barakat, "SXSW: Millennials Trust User-Generated Content 50% More Than Traditional Media." Adweek, March 10, 2014, www.adweek.com/digital/sxsw-millennials-trust-user-generated-content-50-traditional-media/.

51. Jan H. Kietzmann et al., "Social Media? Get Serious! Understanding the Functional Building Blocks of Social Media," *Business Horizons* 54, no. 3 (2011): 241–251., doi:10.1016/j.bushor.2011.01.005.

52. Michel Laroche et al., "The Effects of Social Media Based Brand Communities on Brand Community Markers, Value Creation Practices, Brand Trust and Brand Loyalty," *Computers in Human Behavior* 28, no. 5 (2012): 1755–1767. *Science Direct*, doi:10.1016/j.chb.2012.04.016.

53. Jay Baer, "Why Social Media Customer Service Is the New Marketing," Convince and Convert, www.convinceandconvert.com/podcasts/episodes/why-social-media-customer-service-is-the-new-marketing/.

54. Braveen Kumar, "Community Management: What It Is, Why It's Important, and How to Do It Right," Shopify, June 8, 2017, www.shopify.com/blog/community-management.

55. https://twitter.com/AmazonHelp/with_replies

56. Toby Cox, "How Social Media Is Transforming PR and the Consumer-Business Relationship," Clutch.co, November 1, 2018, clutch.co/pr-firms/resources/how-social-media-transforming-pr-consumer-business-relationship.

57. "Sonic the Hedgehog," Facebook, https://www.facebook.com/Sonic/.

58. "SEGA," Facebook, https://www.facebook.com/SEGA/.

59. "Fitbit," Groups, Facebook, https://www.facebook.com/pg/fitbit/groups/

60. Matt Binder, "YouTube's Pedophilia Problem: More than 400 Channels Deleted as Advertisers Flee over Child Predators," Mashable, February 22, 2019, mashable.com/article/youtube-wakeup-child-exploitation-explained/#2lL_At4z_gqB.

61. Kaitlyn Frey, "Kylie Jenner Overtakes Beyoncé as Most Valuable Instagram Celeb with Posts Worth $1 Million," People.com, May 3, 2018, https://people.com/style/kylie-jenner-highest-paid-kardashian-jenner-social-media-instagram/.

62. Molly St. Louis, "Influencer Marketing Takes an Important Twist in 2018," Inc.com, March 22, 2018, www.inc.com/molly-reynolds/influencer-marketing-takes-an-important-twist-in-2018.html.

63. "Behind Every Seat Is a Story: Southwest Airlines Launches Next Phase of Transfarency Consumer Campaign," Southwest Airlines Newsroom, September 25, 2017, www.swamedia.com/releases/release-9d2f476ff

13ccf13629996404d0d8e60-behind-every-seat-is-a-story-southwest-airlines-launches-next-phase-of-transfarency-consumer-campaign.

64. Kevin Rafferty, "Disney Parks Doubles Make-A-Wish Donation to $2 Million, Thanks All Who Participated in #ShareYourEars," Disney Parks Blog, March 18, 2016, http://disneyparks.disney.go.com/blog/2016/03/disney-parks-doubles-make-a-wish-donation-to-2-million-thanks-all-who-participated-in-shareyourears/.

65. "#ShareYourEars Photos Help Make Wishes Come True: Disney Donates U.S. $3M," Make-A-Wish® America, wish.org/content/disney/share-your-ears-2018-thank-you?cid=WBST-SHAREYOUREARS-MICROSITE.

66. "#Share Your Ears," Disney, dccr.disney.com/share-your-ears.html.

67. "The Walt Disney Company and Make-A-Wish® Invite Fans to 'Share Your Ears' to Help Grant Wishes," The Walt Disney Company, November 5, 2018, www.thewaltdisneycompany.com/the-walt-disney-company-and-make-a-wish-invite-fans-to-share-your-ears-to-help-grant-wishes/.

68. "Cross-Device Trend Roundup," EMarketer, 2014, www.emarketer.com/public_media/docs/eMarketer_Cross_Device_Trends_Roundup.pdf.

69. "Code of Ethics," Public Relations Society of America, www.prsa.org/ethics/code-of-ethics/.

70. Jay Black and Chris Roberts, Doing Ethics in Media: Theories and Practical Applications (New York: Taylor & Francis, 2011), 242.

71. Tim Cook, "Customer Letter," Apple, February 16, 2016, www.apple.com/customer-letter/.

CHAPTER 11

1. https://www.supremecourt.gov/opinions/12pdf/11-697_4g15.pdf.

2. https://www.justice.gov/jm/criminal-resource-manual-1854-copyright-infringement-first-sale-doctrine.

3. Stephen Breyer, The Court and the World: American Law and the New Global Realities (New York: Alfred A. Knopf, 2015), 4.

4. Samuel D. Warren and Louis D. Brandeis, "Right to Privacy," Harvard Law Review 4 (1890): 193.

5. http://www.prsa.org/aboutprsa/ethics/codeenglish/.

6. Jodi Kantor and David Streitfeld, "Inside Amazon: Wrestling Big Ideas in a Bruising Workplace," The New York Times, August 15, 2015, accessed June 18, 2019, http://www.nytimes.com/2015/08/16/technology/inside-amazon-wrestling-big-ideas-in-a-bruising-workplace.html.

7. Jay Carney, "What The New York Times Didn't Tell You," Medium, October 19, 2015, accessed June 18, 2019, https://medium.com/@jaycarney/what-the-new-york-times-didn-t-tell-you-a1128aa78931.

8. Krishnadev Calamur, "A Blistering Response from Amazon," The Atlantic, October 19, 2015, accessed June 18, 2019, https://www.theatlantic.com/business/archive/2015/10/amazon-responds-new-york-times/411232/.

9. Matthew Ingram, "In the Battle of Amazon vs. the New York Times, Who Wins? You Do," Fortune, October 19, 2015, accessed June 18, 2019, http://fortune.com/2015/10/19/amazon-nyt-medium-carney/.

10. Digital Media Law Project, "Simorangkir v. Love," March 30, 2009, http://www.dmlp.org/threats/simorangkir-v-love.

11. http://www.medialaw.org/topics-page/defamation-faqs.

12. https://www.law.cornell.edu/supremecourt/text/418/323.

13. https://www.law.cornell.edu/supremecourt/text/376/254.

14. https://www.law.cornell.edu/wex/patent.

15. https://www.turnitin.com/about/content.

16. https://memeburn.com/2015/09/top-south-african-instagrammer-accused-of-plagiarism/.

17. https://memeburn.com/2015/09/instagrammer-skye-grove-suspended-from-cape-town-partnership-pending-investigation/.

18. https://memeburn.com/2015/09/instagram-plagiarism-scandal-skye-grove-apologises-deletes-herself-off-internet.

19. https://memeburn.com/2015/09/instagrammer-skye-grove-suspended-from-cape-town-partnership-pending-investigation/.

20. https://www.copyright.gov/fair-use/more-info.html.

21. https://www.copyright.gov/fair-use/summaries/fox-news-network-tveyes-02272018.pdf.

22. Alex Johnson, "Twitter Suspends Deadspin, SBNation Accounts over Copyright," NBC News, October 12, 2015, accessed June 18, 2019, http://www.nbcnews.com/news/us-news/twitter-suspends-deadspin-sbnation-accounts-over-copyright-n443306.

23. https://twitter.com/tos.

24. http://khn.org/syndication/.

25. Farhad Manjoo, "Public Protests NPR Link Policy," Wired, June 20, 2002, accessed June 18, 2019, http://archive.wired.com/techbiz/media/news/2002/06/53355.

26. http://cyber.law.harvard.edu/property99/metatags/1998futu.html.

27. https://louisville.edu/law/library/special-collections/the-louis-d.-brandeis-collection/other-peoples-money-chapter-v.

28. https://consumerist.com/2009/04/16/9-legal-drugs-with-extremely-disturbing-side-effects/.

29. https://www.fda.gov/drugs/prescription-drug-advertising/basics-drug-ads#risk_disclosure.

30. https://www.ftc.gov/about-ftc.

31. Aarti Shah, "Fitbit Brings on FleishmanHillard, Burson-Marsteller," The Holmes Report, June 1, 2015, accessed June 18, 2019, http://www.holmesreport.com/latest/article/fitbit-brings-on-fleishmanhillard-burson-marsteller.

32. Ananya Bhattacharya, "Fitbit Stock Surges Nearly 50%," CNN Business, June 18, 2015, accessed June 18, 2019, http://money.cnn.com/2015/06/18/investing/fitbit-ipo-stock-bounce/.

33. https://twitter.com/elonmusk/status/1026872652290379776.

34. Nicholas Jasinski, "Tesla Stock Sank with Elon Musk's Tweet Now Under Criminal Investigation," September

18, 2018, accessed June 18, 2019, https://www.bar-rons.com/articles/tesla-stock-is-sinking-as-elon-musks-tweet-is-reportedly-under-investigation-1537289984.

35. Sissi Cao, "Elon Musk's Surprise Tweet Instantly Made Tesla $900M More Valuable," *Observer*, August 7, 2018, accessed June 18, 2019, https://observer.com/2018/08/elon-musk-take-tesla-private-tweet-add-900m-to-tesla-value/.

36. Benjamin Bain, "Elon Musk Wanted to Impress Girl-friend With $420 Price, SEC Says," *Bloomberg*, September 27, 2018, accessed June 18, 2019, https://www.bloomberg.com/news/articles/2018-09-27/musk-picked-weed-linked-price-to-impress-girlfriend-sec-says.

37. https://www.sec.gov/news/press-release/2018-226.

38. https://twitter.com/elonmusk/status/1098013283372589056.

39. Eric Lutz, "Elon Musk Blasts the S.E.C's Unconstitutional Power Grab," *Vanity Fair*, March 12, 2019, accessed June 18, 2019, https://www.vanityfair.com/news/2019/03/elon-musk-blasts-the-sec-unconstitutional-power-grab.

40. Kirsten Korosec, "Judge to SEC and Elon Musk: Put Your 'Reasonableness Pants on and Work This Out,'" *TechCrunch*, accessed June 18, 2019, https://techcrunch.com/2019/04/04/judge-to-sec-and-elon-musk-put-your-reasonableness-pants-on-and-work-this-out/.

41. https://www.sec.gov/litigation/litreleases/2018/lr24065.htm.

42. https://dockets.justia.com/docket/oregon/ordce/3:2018cv00386/135644.

43. https://www.law.cornell.edu/wex/invasion_of_privacy.

44. http://www.dmlp.org/legal-guide/elements-intrusion-claim.

45. https://www.technologyreview.com/s/613034/the-hipster-effect-why-anti-conformists-always-end-up-looking-the-same/.

46. https://www.cbc.ca/radio/asithappens/as-it-happens-thursday-edition-1.5046925/man-angry-his-photo-was-used-to-prove-all-hipsters-look-alike-then-learns-it-wasn-t-him-1.5046933

47. https://www.law.cornell.edu/wex/false_light.

48. http://www2.bloomberglaw.com/public/desktop/document/JENNIFER_E_PATTERSON_v_NATALIE_D_GRANTHERMS_No_M201300287COAR3CV_/1.

49. http://www2.bloomberglaw.com/public/desktop/document/JENNIFER_E_PATTERSON_v_NATALIE_D_GRANTHERMS_No_M201300287COAR3CV_/1.

50. https://www.prsa.org/AboutPRSA/Ethics/CodeEnglish/.

51. https://www.law.cornell.edu/wex/trade_secret.

52. https://www.wd40.com/faqs.

53. https://instituteforpr.org/social-media-account-really-guidelines-pr-practitioners-organizations-determine-social-media-ownership/.

54. https://bellisario.psu.edu/page-center/about/arthur-w-page/the-page-principles.

CHAPTER 12

1. http://www.davecarrollmusic.com/music/ubg/story/.

2. "'United Breaks Guitars': Did It Really Cost The Airline $180 Million?," Huffpost, http://www.huffingtonpost.com/2009/07/24/united-breaks-guitars-did_n_244357.html.

3. http://www.humansofnewyork.com/post/43997717109/i-am-a-street-photographer-in-new-york-city.

4. Amanda E. Cancel, Michael A. Mitrook and Glen T. Cameron, "Testing the Contingency Theory of Accommodation in Public Relations," *Public Relations Review* 25, no. 2 (1999): 171–197; Sarah Strasburg, Samuel M. Tham and Glen T. Cameron, "Taming Contingency Theory: Creating a Quantitative Decision Tool Using Decision Theory and Game Theory in Conflict Management," *Proceedings of the 18th International Public Relations Research Conference* (2015): 331.

5. Suzanna Caldwell, "Anchorage Restaurant's Facebook Defense of Employee Wins Viral Support," *Anchorage Daily News*, September 28, 2016, accessed June 18, 2019, http://www.adn.com/article/20151112/anchorage-restaurants-facebook-defense-employee-wins-viral-support.

6. https://www.facebook.com/judyberrysinger/posts/10206323203051973.

7. Suzanna Caldwell, "Anchorage Restaurant's Facebook Defense of Employee Wins Viral Support," *Anchorage Daily News*, September 28, 2016, accessed June 18, 2019, http://www.adn.com/article/20151112/anchorage-restaurants-facebook-defense-employee-wins-viral-support.

8. Elizabeth Dougall, "Issues Management," Institute for Public Relations, December 12, 2008, http://www.instituteforpr.org/issues-management/.

9. Elizabeth Dougall, "Issues Management," Institute for Public Relations, December 12, 2008, http://www.instituteforpr.org/issues-management/. Concept for Figure 12.2 comes from Michael Regester and Judy Larkin, *Risk Issues and Crisis Management in Public Relations: A Casebook of Best Practice*, 3rd ed. (London: Kogan Page Publishers, 2005). Regester and Larkin cited research from Brad Hainsworth and Max Meng in developing the model.

10. Paul Lienert and Timothy Gardner, "Volkswagen's 'Clean Diesel' Strategy Unraveled by Outside Emissions Tests," *Reuters*, September 21, 2015, accessed June 18, 2019, http://www.reuters.com/article/2015/09/22/us-usa-volkswagen-emission-idUSKCN0RL2EI20150922#0uoPtue9HzrAyxoo.97.

11. Jack Ewing and Graham Bowley, "The Engineering of Volkswagen's Aggressive Ambition," *The New York Times*, December 13, 2015, accessed June 18, 2019, http://www.nytimes.com/2015/12/14/business/the-engineering-of-volkswagens-aggressive-ambition.html.

12. Michael Regester and Judy Larkin, *Risk Issues and Crisis Management in Public Relations: A Casebook of Best Practice*, 3rd ed. (London: Kogan Page Publishers, 2005), 51.

13. www.nytimes.com/interactive/2015/10/23/business/international/vw-scandal-timeline.html.

14. Russell Hotten, "Volkswagen: The Scandal Explained," *BBC News*, December 10, 2015, accessed June 18, 2019, http://www.bbc.com/news/business-34324772.

15. Alex Davies, "EPA: VW Cheated on Emissions Tests for 10,000 More Cars," *Wired*, November 2, 2015, accessed June 18, 2019, http://www.wired.com/2015/11/vw-epa-3-liter-audi-porsche-emissions/.

16. Jack Ewing, "VW Says Emissions Cheating Was Not a One-Time Error," December 11, 2015, accessed June 18, 2019, http://www.nytimes.com/2015/12/11/business/international/vw-emissions-scandal.html?_r=0.

17. Paul R. La Monica, "Volkswagen Has Plunged 50%. Will It Ever Recover?" *CNN Business*, September 25, 2015, accessed June 18, 2019, http://money.cnn.com/2015/09/24/investing/volkswagen-vw-emissions-scandal-stock/.

18. Doron Levin, "Fallout from the Volkswagen Scandal Is Hitting Consumers and the Courts," October 8, 2015, accessed June 18, 2019, http://fortune.com/2015/10/08/volkswagen-scandal-fallout/.

19. Barry Meier, "Lawyers Jostle for Lead Position in Volkswagen Diesel Suits," *The New York Times*, October 27, 2015, accessed June 18, 2019, http://www.nytimes.com/2015/10/27/business/lawyers-jostle-for-lead-position-in-volkswagen-diesel-suits.html.

20. Jack Ewing, "VW Says Emissions Cheating Was Not a One-Time Error," December 11, 2015, accessed June 18, 2019, http://www.nytimes.com/2015/12/11/business/international/vw-emissions-scandal.html?_r=0.

21. Roger Parloff, "How VW Paid $25 Billion for 'Dieselgate'—and Got Off Easy," *Fortune*, February 6, 2018, accessed June 18, 2019, http://fortune.com/2018/02/06/volkswagen-vw-emissions-scandal-penalties/.

22. Michael Regester and Judy Larkin, *Risk Issues and Crisis Management in Public Relations: A Casebook of Best Practice*, 3rd ed. (London: Kogan Page Publishers, 2005).

23. https://www.reuters.com/article/us-volkswagen-emissions-porsche/volkswagen-unit-porsche-to-pay-535-million-euro-fine-over-diesel-cheating-idUSKCN1SD1BA.

24. https://www.sec.gov/files/complaint-2019-03-14_0.pdf.

25. Taylor Telford, "SEC Sues Volkswagen, Alleging It misled Investors in Emissions Scandal," *The Washington Post*, March 15, 2019, accessed June 18, 2019, https://www.washingtonpost.com/business/2019/03/15/sec-sues-volkswagen-alleging-it-misled-investors-emissions-scandal/.

26. Michael Regester and Judy Larkin, *Risk Issues and Crisis Management in Public Relations: A Casebook of Best Practice*, 3rd ed. (London: Kogan Page Publishers, 2005).

27. Steven Greenhouse, "Anti-Sweatshop Movement Is Achieving Gains Overseas," *The New York Times*, January 26, 2000, accessed June 18, 2019, http://www.nytimes.com/2000/01/26/us/anti-sweatshop-movement-is-achieving-gains-overseas.html.

28. Michael Grimaldi, "RE: Nextdoor," PRSA Open Forum, May 3, 2019, accessed August 26, 2019, https://connect.prsa.org/.

29. http://www.cdc.gov/ecoli/2015/o26-11-15/index.html.

30. Nick Turner and Craig Giammona, "Chipotle Pulls Forecast After E. Coli Scare Crushes Sales," *Bloomberg*, December 4, 2015, accessed June 18, 2019, http://www.bloomberg.com/news/articles/2015-12-04/chipotle-rescinds-16-forecast-after-e-coli-scare-crushes-sales.

31. Nick Turner and Craig Giammona, "Chipotle Pulls Forecast After E. Coli Scare Crushes Sales," *Bloomberg*, December 4, 2015, accessed June 18, 2019, http://www.bloomberg.com/news/articles/2015-12-04/chipotle-rescinds-16-forecast-after-e-coli-scare-crushes-sales.

32. https://www.patagonia.com/working-with-factories.html.

33. http://www.conecomm.com/research-blog/2016-millennial-employee-engagement-study.

34. https://www.doorofclubs.com/z.

35. http://www.instituteforpr.org/state-crisis-communication-evidence-bleeding-edge/.

36. W. Timothy Coombs and Sherry J. Holladay, *PR Strategy and Application: Managing Influence* (Chichester, UK: Wiley-Blackwell, 2010), 248.

37. http://www.foxnews.com/us/2013/09/28/chicago-tylenol-murders-remain-unsolved-after-more-than-30-years.html.

38. Bruce Weber, "Lawrence G. Foster Dies at 88; Helped Lead Tylenol out of Cyanide Crisis," *The New York Times*, October 30, 2013, accessed June 18, 2019, http://www.nytimes.com/2013/10/30/business/lawrence-g-foster-dies-at-88-helped-lead-tylenol-out-of-cyanide-crisis.html.

39. Jerry Knight, "Tylenol's Maker Shows How to Respond to Crisis," *The Washington Post*, October 11, 1982, accessed June 18, 2019, https://www.washingtonpost.com/archive/business/1982/10/11/tylenols-maker-shows-how-to-respond-to-crisis/bc8df898-3fcf-443f-bc2f-e6fbd639a5a3/.

40. Otto Lerbinger, *The Crisis Manager: Facing Disasters, Conflicts, and Failures* (New York: Routledge, 2012), 17.

41. Kevin Duffy, Jonathan Ng, and Joe Dwinell, "Robert Kraft Goes on the Defensive, Denies Soliciting Sex," *Boston Herald*, February 23, 2019, accessed June 18, 2019, https://www.bostonherald.com/2019/02/23/pats-owner-kraft-goes-on-the-defensive-denies-soliciting-sex/.

42. Kevin Draper, "Robert Kraft Apologizes in First Public Comments About Prostitution Case," *The New York Times*, March 23, 2019, accessed June 18, 2019, https://www.nytimes.com/2019/03/23/sports/football/robert-kraft-apology.html.

43. Geoff Colvin, "Chipotle's E.coli Fiasco Teaches Us How Not to Respond to a Crisis," *Fortune*, December 11, 2015, accessed June 18, 2019, http://fortune.com/2015/12/11/chipotle-ecoli-crisis-management/.

44. Jamie Ducharme, "Ethiopian Airlines Denies Reports That Pilot in Boeing 737 MAX Crash Was Not Properly Trained," *Time*, March 21, 2019, accessed June 18, 2019, http://time.com/5555846/ethiopian-airlines-pilot-training/.

45. https://www.facebook.com/EthiopianAirlines/photos/a.243847315699986/2223052747779423/; https://twitter.com/flyethiopian/status/1108687807726399488/photo/1.

46. http://www.reuters.com/article/us-oil-spill-bp-apology-idUSTRE6515NQ20100602.

47. Charles Riley and Jose Pagliery, "Target Will Pay Hack Victims $10 million," *CNN Business*, March 19, 2015, accessed June 18, 2019, http://money.cnn.com/2015/03/19/technology/security/target-data-hack-settlement/.

48. Alex Hern, "Cambridge Analytica: How Did It Turn Clicks into Votes?," *The Guardian*, May 6, 2018, accessed June 18, 2019, https://www.theguardian.com/news/2018/may/06/cambridge-analytica-how-turn-clicks-into-votes-christopher-wylie.

49. Olivia Solon and Oliver Laughland, "Cambridge Analytica Closing after Facebook Data Harvesting Scandal," *The Guardian*, May 2, 2018, accessed June 18, 2019, https://www.theguardian.com/uk-news/2018/may/02/cambridge-analytica-closing-down-after-facebook-row-reports-say.

50. Craig Timberg and Tony Romm, "Facebook CEO Mark Zuckerberg to Capitol Hill: 'It was my mistake, and I'm sorry'," *The Washington Post*, April 9, 2018, https://www.washingtonpost.com/news/the-switch/wp/2018/04/09/facebook-chief-executive-mark-zuckerberg-to-captiol-hill-it-was-my-mistake-and-im-sorry/?utm_term=.7767bec1023a.

51. Craig Timberg and Tony Romm, "Facebook CEO Mark Zuckerberg to Capitol Hill: 'It was my mistake, and I'm sorry'," *The Washington Post*, April 9, 2018, https://www.washingtonpost.com/news/the-switch/wp/2018/04/09/facebook-chief-executive-mark-zuckerberg-to-captiol-hill-it-was-my-mistake-and-im-sorry/?utm_term=.7767bec1023a.

52. https://www.facebook.com/notes/mark-zuckerberg/a-privacy-focused-vision-for-social-networking/10156700570096634/.

53. NEA, School Crisis Guide: Help and Healing in a Time of Crisis, accessed June 19, 2019, http://nvasb.org/assets/handout-nea-school-crisis--guide.pdf.

54. "Code of Ethics," PRSA, https://www.prsa.org/About-PRSA/Ethics/CodeEnglish/.

55. Jay Black and Chris Roberts, *Doing Ethics in Media: Theories and Practical Applications* (New York: Taylor & Francis, 2011).

56. Ralph Barney, "Cases and Commentaries," *Journal of Mass Media Ethics* 1, no. 1 (1985): 80.

57. http://www.instituteforpr.org/crisis-management-communications/.

CHAPTER 13

1. Them. (@Them), "Are You One Of Us? Coming Later This Month, @Them is the Digital Community We Need Now More Than Ever. Go to Them.us for Newsletter Signup!" October 4, 2017, accessed August 26, 2019, https://twitter.com/Them/status/915526289548873728.

2. "Them.", Condé Nast, accessed August 26, 2019, www.them.us/.

3. Tatiana Cirisano, "Bad Bunny Brings Out J Balvin for Fiery Coachella Set," *Billboard*, April 15, 2019, www.billboard.com/articles/news/festivals/8507065/bad-bunny-coachella-2019-performance-recap.

4. Anna Tingley, "BTS Performs on 'SNL' Making History for K-Pop," Chicagotribune.com, April 14, 2019, www.chicagotribune.com/entertainment/tv/ct-ent-bts-snl-history-k-pop-20190414-story.html.

5. Joel Kotkin, "The Changing Demographics of America," *Smithsonian*, August 1, 2010, www.smithsonianmag.com/travel/the-changing-demographics-of-america-538284/.

6. "Addressing Total Market Research Initiative," Culture Marketing Council, 2014, http://www.culturemarketingcouncil.org/Portals/0/Research/Total%20Market/Total%20Market%20Round%20Tables%20Report%20April%202014/AHAA%20Total%20Market-Roundtable%20Reports%20for%20AHAA%20Conf%204-28-14.pdf.

7. Natalie T. J. Tindall, "The Effective, Multicultural Practice of Public Relations," *Public Relations Tactics*, Public Relations Society of America, February 1, 2012, apps.prsa.org/Intelligence/Tactics/Articles/view/9590/1044/The_effective_multicultural_practice_of_public_rel#.XNW31tNKh6-.

8. "Defining Culture," Educator Resources, Peace Corps, www.peacecorps.gov/educators/resources/defining-culture/.

9. Chris Louie, "Uncommon Sense: Back to the Future: Perspectives on 'Thriving in 2020'," Nielsen, July 1, 2015, www.nielsen.com/us/en/insights/news/2015/uncommon-sense-back-to-the-future-perspectives-on-thriving-in-2020.html.

10. Edward Twitchell Hall, *Beyond Culture* (New York: Anchor, 1989), 91.

11. Edward Twitchell Hall, *Beyond Culture* (New York: Anchor, 1989), 91.

12. Katie Heaney, "The One Thing You Should Never Text Anyone Ever," BuzzFeed News, February 28, 2013, www.buzzfeednews.com/article/katieheaney/the-one-thing-you-should-never-text-anyone-ever.

13. Conlon, Jerome, "The Brand Brief Behind Nike's Just Do It Campaign," Branding Strategy Insider, August 6, 2015, www.brandingstrategyinsider.com/2015/08/behind-nikes-campaign.html.

14. Kim Nahyun, "Corporate Apology and Cultural Difference: A Comparison of the United States and South Korea in Cyber-Security Breach Crisis" (master's thesis, Iowa State University, 2017), Graduate Theses and Dissertations 15,336, https://lib.dr.iastate.edu/etd/15336.

15. Marieke De Mooij, *Global Marketing and Advertising: Understanding Cultural Paradoxes* (Thousand Oaks, CA: Sage, 2013).

16. Geert Hofstede, *Culture's Consequences: Comparing Values, Behaviors, Institutions and Organizations Across Nations* (Thousand Oaks, CA: Sage, 2001).

17. Kara Alaimo, "Around the World: 4 Cultural Dimensions That Impact Your Messages." *Public Relations Tactics*, Public Relations Society of America, September 30, 2016, apps.prsa.org/Intelligence/Tactics/Articles/view/11657/1132/Around_the_World_4_Cultural_Dimensions_That_Impact#.XNXAJtNKh69.

18. Jay Moye, "Share a Coke: How the Groundbreaking Campaign Got Its Start 'Down Under'," The Coca-Cola Company, September 25, 2014, www.coca-colacompany.com/

stories/share-a-coke-how-the-groundbreaking-campaign-got-its-start-down-under.

19. "#OrgullosoDeSer: Coke's Hispanic Heritage Month Campaign Embraces Latino Pride," *Coca-Cola Journey*, The Coca-Cola Company, September 16, 2015, www.coca-colacompany.com/stories/orgullosodeser-cokes-hispanic-heritage-month-campaign-embraces-latino-pride.

20. "Hispandering Heritage Month Begins with Coca-Cola's Ridiculous 'Heritage Tattoo Cans'," Latino Rebels, September 5, 2015, www.latinorebels.com/2015/09/05/hispandering-heritage-month-begins-with-coca-colas-ridiculous-heritage-tattoo-cans/.

21. "What Is an Environmental Impact Statement?," Depleted UF6, web.evs.anl.gov/uranium/eis/whatiseis/index.cfm.

22. "Vicks #TouchOfCare," MSL, https://mslgroup.com/work/vicks-touchofcare.

23. Paul Holmes, "PRovoke18: Vicks 'Touch Of Care' Campaign Shows How Courage Can Pay Off," *The Holmes Report*, October 24, 2018, www.holmesreport.com/latest/article/provoke18-vicks-touch-of-care-campaign-shows-how-courage-can-pay-off.

24. "Vicks' New 'Touch of Care' Ad Campaign Is Going Viral for All the Right Reasons." ET BrandEquity, The Economic Times, 31 Mar. 2017, brandequity.economictimes.indiatimes.com/news/advertising/vicks-new-touch-of-care-ad-campaign-is-going-viral-for-all-the-right-reasons/57932443.

25. "Country Comparison—India," Hofstede Insights, www.hofstede-insights.com/country-comparison/india/.

26. Manveena Suri, "India: Transgender Mom Ad Sparks Debate and Tears," CNN, April 20, 2017, www.cnn.com/2017/04/19/health/transgender-india-mom-vicks-advert/index.html.

27. Paul Holmes, "PRovoke18: Vicks 'Touch Of Care' Campaign Shows How Courage Can Pay Off," *The Holmes Report*, October 24, 2018, www.holmesreport.com/latest/article/provoke18-vicks-touch-of-care-campaign-shows-how-courage-can-pay-off.

28. Laura Silver et al., "Mobile Connectivity in Emerging Economies," Internet & Technology, Pew Research Center: Internet, Science & Tech, March 7, 2019, www.pewinternet.org/2019/03/07/mobile-connectivity-in-emerging-economies/.

29. "Vicks #TouchOfCare," MSL, https://mslgroup.com/work/vicks-touchofcare.

30. Paul Holmes, "PRovoke18: Vicks 'Touch Of Care' Campaign Shows How Courage Can Pay Off," *The Holmes Report*, October 24, 2018, www.holmesreport.com/latest/article/provoke18-vicks-touch-of-care-campaign-shows-how-courage-can-pay-off.

31. Vicks' New 'Touch of Care' Ad Campaign Is Going Viral for All the Right Reasons," ET BrandEquity, March 31, 2017, brandequity.economictimes.indiatimes.com/news/advertising/vicks-new-touch-of-care-ad-campaign-is-going-viral-for-all-the-right-reasons/57932443.

32. P. Christopher Early and Elaine Mosakowski, "Cultural Intelligence," *Harvard Business Review*, hbr.org/2004/10/cultural-intelligence.

33. Sue Bryant, "Greetings Around the World: The Do's and Don'ts for Saying Hello," *Country Navigator*, April 5, 2019, countrynavigator.com/blog/global-talent/greetings/.

34. Rachel Hosie, "How Personal Space Boundaries Vary in Different Countries," *The Independent*, May 2, 2017, www.independent.co.uk/life-style/personal-space-boundaries-different-countries-argentina-uk-romania-a7713051.html.

35. "Global Implications," Commission on Public Relations Education, www.commissionpred.org/commission-reports/the-professional-bond/global-implications/.

36. Krishnamurthy Sriramesh and Dejan Verčič (eds.), *The Global Public Relations Handbook: Theory, Research, and Practice* (Mahwah, NJ: Lawrence Erlbaum Associates, 2003), xxv.

37. "Study Shows How Media's Influence on Public Opinion Varies by Country," The University of Kansas, October 1, 2018, today.ku.edu/2018/09/13/study-shows-how-media-influence-public-individual-opinions-varies-country-factors.

38. "Iceland Christmas Ad: Petition to Show It on TV Hits 670k," BBC News, November 13, 2018, www.bbc.com/news/newsbeat-46187070.

39. Arvind Hickman, "Iceland's Rang-Tan Campaign Delivers 65m Views, Sales and Consideration Lift," *PR Week*, December 3, 2018, www.prweek.com/article/1520088/icelands-rang-tan-campaign-delivers-65m-views-sales-consideration-lift.

40. Krishnamurthy Sriramesh, "Globalisation and Public Relations: An Overview Looking into the Future," PRism 6, no. 2 (2009), www.prismjournal.org/fileadmin/Praxis/Files/globalPR/SRIRAMESH.pdf.

41. Krishnamurthy Sriramesh, "Globalisation and Public Relations: An Overview Looking into the Future," *PRism* 6, no. 2 (2009), www.prismjournal.org/fileadmin/Praxis/Files/globalPR/SRIRAMESH.pdf.

42. "Study Shows How Media's Influence on Public Opinion Varies by Country," The University of Kansas, October 1, 2018, today.ku.edu/2018/09/13/study-shows-how-media-influence-public-individual-opinions-varies-country-factors.

43. Graeme Domm, "Public Relations in Emerging Nations: What Do Local Practitioners Themselves Have to Say?," IPRA, 2013, www.ipra.org/news/itle/public-relations-in-emerging-nations-what-do-local-practitioners-themselves-have-to-say/.

44. Laura Silver et al., "Mobile Connectivity in Emerging Economies," Internet & Technology, Pew Research Center: Internet, Science & Tech, March 7, 2019, www.pewinternet.org/2019/03/07/mobile-connectivity-in-emerging-economies/.

45. Evan Goldberg, "PR's Role in a Recession," *O'Dwyer's*, April 2, 2019, www.odwyerpr.com/story/public/12298/2019-04-02/prs-role-recession.html.

46. Tonya Garcia, "Auto Industry Using PR to Boost Sales and Loyalty," *Adweek*, June 13, 2011, www.adweek.com/digital/auto-industry-using-pr-to-boost-sales-and-loyalty/.

47. "The Global Slump in Press Freedom," *The Economist*, July 23, 2018, www.economist.com/graphic-detail/2018/07/23/the-global-slump-in-press-freedom.

48. Yuan Yang, "The Great Firewall of China–Web of Control," *Financial Times*, March 12, 2019, www.ft.com/content/e19b3022-40eb-11e9-9bee-efab61506f44.

49. "About Us," Freedom House, https://freedomhouse.org/about-us.

50. "The Global Slump in Press Freedom," *The Economist*, July 23, 2018, www.economist.com/graphic-detail/2018/07/23/the-global-slump-in-press-freedom.

51. "2019 Edelman Trust Barometer Global Report," Edelman, www.edelman.com/sites/g/files/aatuss191/files/2019-03/2019_Edelman_Trust_Barometer_Global_Report.pdf.

52. "Digital vs. Traditional Media Consumption," GlobalWebIndex, cdn2.hubspot.net/hubfs/304927/Downloads/Digital vs Traditional Summary–Q1 2017.pdf.

53. Amanda Glasgow, "Does Global Public Relations Exist?," International Public Relations Association, 2011, www.ipra.org/news/itle/does-global-public-relations-exist/.

54. Tim Fry, Jennifer Sosin, and Stan Stein, "The New Global World of Public Relations," Weber Shandwick, www.webershandwick.com/uploads/news/files/Global_Comms_Trends.pdf.

55. Tim Fry, Jennifer Sosin, and Stan Stein, "The New Global World of Public Relations," Weber Shandwick, www.webershandwick.com/uploads/news/files/Global_Comms_Trends.pdf.

56. Juan-Carlos Molleda et al., "Tipping the Balance: A Decision-Making Model for Localization in Global Public Relations Agencies," *Public Relations Review* 41, no. 3 (2015): 335–344, doi:10.1016/j.pubrev.2015.05.004.

57. "Visa Everywhere Initiative," Visa Korea, https://www.visakorea.com/visa-everywhere/everywhere-initiative/initiative.html.

58. "Visa Everywhere Initiative," Visa USA, https://usa.visa.com/visa-everywhere/everywhere-initiative/initiative.html.

59. Tanya Roberts, "Why Businesses Are Slow to Adopt Digital Payments," PaymentsJournal, https://www.paymentsjournal.com/why-businesses-are-slow-to-adopt-digital-payments/.

60. "Visa Everywhere Initiative: Women's Global Edition," Visa, https://usa.visa.com/visa-everywhere/everywhere-initiative.html.

61. "Women's Entrepreneurship 2016/2017 Report," Global Entrepreneurship Monitor, 2017, www.gemconsortium.org/report/49860.

62. Tamir Bar-On, *The World Through Soccer: The Cultural Impact of a Global Sport* (Lanham, Maryland: Rowman & Littlefield, 2015).

63. "More than Half the World Watched Record-Breaking 2018 World Cup," Fifa.com, December 21, 2018, www.fifa.com/worldcup/news/more-than-half-the-world-watched-record-breaking-2018-world-cup.

64. "FIFA World Cup Russia 2018 Global Broadcast and Audience Summary," Fifa, img.fifa.com/image/upload/kkiivoviltazeoild16x.pdf.

65. "2018 FIFA World Cup Russia™," Fifa.com, accessed August 27, 2019, www.fifa.com/worldcup/organisation/partners/.

66. "Mastercard Brings Renowned Footballers Messi and Neymar Jr. Together for a Social Movement That Seeks to End Childhood Hunger," MasterCard, April 10, 2018, newsroom.mastercard.com/press-releases/mastercard-brings-renowned-footballers-messi-and-neymar-jr-for-a-social-movement-that-seeks-to-end-childhood-hunger/.

67. Chiara Giordano, "Neymar and Messi Mastercard Campaign to Feed Starving Children Branded 'Disgusting'," *The Independent*, June 3, 2018, www.independent.co.uk/sport/football/world-cup/mastercard-world-cup-campaign-lionel-messi-neymar-starving-children-backlash-a8380516.html.

68. "FAO: Hunger Increases in the World and in Latin America and the Caribbean for the Third Consecutive Year," FAO Regional Office for Latin America and the Caribbean, Food and Agriculture Organization for the United Nations, September 11, 2018, www.fao.org/americas/noticias/ver/en/c/1152157/.

69. Chiara Giordano, "Neymar and Messi Mastercard Campaign to Feed Starving Children Branded 'Disgusting'," *The Independent*, June 3, 2018, www.independent.co.uk/sport/football/world-cup/mastercard-world-cup-campaign-lionel-messi-neymar-starving-children-backlash-a8380516.html.

70. John Harrington, "'The Hunger Games'—Mastercard Slated for 'Goals-for-Meals' Campaign," *PR Week*, June 3,2018,www.prweek.com/article/1466400/the-hunger-games-mastercard-slated-goals-for-meals-campaign.

71. "Mastercard Ends Campaign to Donate Meals for Every Lionel Messi, Neymar Goal at World Cup," ESPN, June 4, 2018, www.espn.com/soccer/fifa-world-cup/story/3517847/mastercard-ends-campaign-to-donate-meals-for-every-lionel-messi-and-neymar-goal-at-world-cup.

72. "Tech for Good Summit: Digital Stakeholders Make Concrete Commitments for the Common Good," Gouvernement.fr, French Republic, May 24, 2018, www.gouvernement.fr/en/tech-for-good-summit-digital-stakeholders-make-concrete-commitments-for-the-common-good.

73. Romain Dillet, "50 Tech CEOs Come to Paris to Talk about Tech for Good—TechCrunch," TechCrunch, May 23, 2018, techcrunch.com/2018/05/23/50-tech-ceos-come-to-paris-to-talk-about-tech-for-good/.

74. Tania Rabesandratana, "Emmanuel Macron Wants France to Become a Leader in AI and Avoid 'Dystopia'," *Science*, March 30, 2018, www.sciencemag.org/news/2018/03/emmanuel-macron-wants-france-become-leader-ai-and-avoid-dystopia.

75. "Macron Hosts CEOs at 'Tech for Good' Summit in Paris," *France 24*, May 23, 2018, www.france24.com/en/20180523-macron-hosts-ceo-tech-good-summit-paris-zuckerberg-facebook-microsoft.

76. Guy J. Golan, Dennis F. Kinsey and Sung-Un Yang (eds.), *International Public Relations and Public Diplomacy: Communication and Engagement* (New York: Peter Lang, 2014), 5.
77. Harsha Kathard et al., "A Study of Teacher–Learner Interactions: A Continuum Between Monologic and Dialogic Interactions," *Language, Speech, and Hearing Services in Schools* 46, no. 3 (2015): 222–241, https://www.researchgate.net/publication/274261504_A_Study_of_Teacher-Learner_Interactions_A_Continuum_Between_Monologic_and_Dialogic_Interactions.
78. Will Sommer, "Whimsical and Annoying Viral Questions Are Taking Over Twitter," *The Daily Beast*, February 19, 2019, www.thedailybeast.com/whimsical-and-annoying-viral-questions-are-taking-over-twitter.
79. Svetlana Rybalko and Trent Seltzer, (2010). "Dialogic Communication in 140 Characters or Less: How Fortune 500 Companies Engage Stakeholders Using Twitter," *Public Relations Review* 36, no. 4 (2010): 336–341.

CHAPTER 14

1. Sergey Gorbatov, Svetlana Khapova, and Evgenia Lysova, "Personal Branding: Interdisciplinary Systematic Review and Research Agenda," *Frontiers in Psychology* 9 (2018).
2. Sergey Gorbatov, Svetlana Khapova, and Evgenia Lysova. "Personal Branding: Interdisciplinary Systematic Review and Research Agenda," *Frontiers in Psychology* 9 (2018): 2238.
3. "The Story of Sage Ke'alohilani Quiamno—Co-Founder of Future for Us," Jasmine Rashae, March 19, 2019, https://www.jasminerashae.com/your-stories/sage-kealohilani-quiamno.
4. https://www.linkedin.com/in/joshferrari/.
5. https://twitter.com/joshferrari.
6. "The Story of Sage Ke'alohilani Quiamno—Co-Founder of Future for Us," Jasmine Rashae, March 19, 2019, https://www.jasminerashae.com/your-stories/sage-kealohilani-quiamno; https://womenintheworkplace.com.
7. http://joshferrari.com/about/.
8. Toni Eagar and Stephen Dann, "Classifying the Narrated# Selfie: Genre Typing Human-Branding Activity," *European Journal of Marketing* 50, no. 9/10 (2016): 1835–1857.
9. Kevin B. Tamanini, "The Perception of Electronic Mail Names and How Those Perceptions Affect a Job-Related Evaluation Process" (PhD dissertation, Ohio University, 2005), https://etd.ohiolink.edu/!etd.send_file?accession=ohiou1129153628&disposition=inline.
10. "'In advertising, you are only as good as your last ad.' —CP+B CEO Andrew Keller," Miami Ad School, https://miamiadschool.com/blog/in-advertising-you-are-only-as-good-as-your-last-ad--cpb-ceo-andrew-keller.
11. Karen Swim, "The Gig Economy and the Solo PR Pro," *CommPro*, September 26, 2018, accessed June 18, 2019, https://www.commpro.biz/the-gig-economy-and-the-solo-pr-pro/.
12. "'In advertising, you are only as good as your last ad.' —CP+B CEO Andrew Keller," Miami Ad School, https://miamiadschool.com/blog/in-advertising-you-are-only-as-good-as-your-last-ad--cpb-ceo-andrew-keller
13. "Average Account Coordinator Salary," Payscale.com, http://www.payscale.com/research/US/Job=Account_Coordinator/Salary .
14. "Average Communications Specialist Salary," Payscale.com, http://www.payscale.com/research/US/Job=Communications_Specialist/Salary .
15. "Median Salaries for Nonprofit Communications Directors," Nonprofit Marketing Guide.com, https://www.nonprofitmarketingguide.com/blog/2019/02/19/median-salaries-for-nonprofit-communications-directors/.
16. "2018 Small Business Profile," U.S. Small Business Administration, https://www.sba.gov/sites/default/files/advocacy/2018-Small-Business-Profiles-US.pdf.
17. "2015-2016 SUSB Employment Change Data Tables," U.S. Census Bureau, https://www.census.gov/data/tables/2016/econ/susb/2016-susb-employment.html.
18. "Healthcare," PR Council, https://prcouncil.net/inside-pr/healthcare/.
19. "Undergraduate Education," Commission on Public Relations Education, http://www.commissionpred.org/commission-reports/the-professional-bond/undergraduate-education/.
20. "Public Relations Education for the 21st Century: A Port of Entry," 1999 Commission on Public Relations Education, October 1999, http://www.commpred.org/_uploads/report1-full.pdf.
21. Alvin Toffler, *Future Shock* (New York: Bantam, 1990).
22. "Summary Report: Commission on Public Relations Education Industry-Educator Summit on Public Relations Education," Commission on Public Relations Education, May 12, 2015, http://www.commpred.org/wp-content/uploads/2015/07/industry-educator-summit-summary-report.pdf.
23. Arik Hanson, "10 Skills the PR Pro of 2022 Must Have," June 12, 2012, ACH Communications, http://www.arikhanson.com/2012/06/12/10-skills-the-pr-pro-of-2022-must-have/.
24. Arik Hanson, "10 Skills the PR Pro of the Future Will Need (Revised)," February 29, 2016, ACH Communications,http://www.arikhanson.com/2016/02/29/10-skills-the-pr-pro-of-the-future-will-need-revised/.
25. Talia Jane, "An Open Letter to My CEO," Medium, February 19, 2016, accessed June 18, 2019, https://medium.com/@taliajane/an-open-letter-to-my-ceo-fb73df021e7a.
26. Talia Jane, "An Open Letter to My CEO," Medium, February 19, 2016, accessed June 18, 2019, https://medium.com/@taliajane/an-open-letter-to-my-ceo-fb73df021e7a.
27. David Mack, "This Woman's Post on Poverty Went Viral and She Lost Her Job," *Buzzfeed News*, February 20, 2016, accessed June 18, 2019, http://www.buzzfeed.com/davidmack/talia-jane-vs-yelp.
28. https://www.gofundme.com/Help-A-%20Yelper-EAT.
29. Ariel Kana, "Pictures on Talia's Instagram That Aren't Rice," Ranker.com, http://www.ranker.com/list/talia-jane-instagram-photos-ariel-kana.

30. Alice Truong, "The Yelp Employee Who Was Fired After Her Incendiary Open Letter to the CEO Speaks Out," *Quartz*, February 22, 2016, accessed June 18, 2019, http://qz.com/622232/ the-yelp-employee-who-was-fired-after-her-incendiary-open-letter-to-the-ceo-speaks-out/.

31. "Does Talia Jane Deserve the Backlash From Her Open Letter to Jeremy Stoppelman, Yelp's CEO?," *Forbes*, www.forbes.com/sites/quora/2016/02/26/ does-talia-jane-deserve-the-backlash-from-her-open-letter-to-jeremy-stoppelman-yelps-ceo/.

32. Vivian Giang, "You Should Plan on Switching Jobs Every Three Years for the Rest of Your Life," *Fast Company*, January 7, 2016, accessed June 18, 2019, https://www.fastcompany.com/3055035/you-should-plan-on-switching-jobs-every-three-years-for-the-rest-of-your-.

33. Penelope Trunk, "Why Job Hoppers Make the Best Employees," CBS News, July 29, 2010, accessed June 18, 2019, http://www.cbsnews.com/news/ why-job-hoppers-make-the-best-employees/.

34. "Code of Ethics," PRSA, https://www.prsa.org/About-PRSA/Ethics/CodeEnglish/.

35. "Code of Ethics," PRSA, https://www.prsa.org/About-PRSA/Ethics/CodeEnglish/.

Glossary

A/B testing Experiment in which one group of participants is randomly assigned to see one version of a message and another group is randomly assigned to see a second version. Results are then compared to test the effectiveness of message variations.

Accredited business communicator (ABC) Credential awarded by IABC to recognize communicators who have reached a globally accepted standard of knowledge and proficiency in their chosen field.

Accredited in public relations (APR) Credential awarded by PRSA and other UAB affiliates to those who have demonstrated competency in the knowledge, skills and abilities required to practice public relations effectively.

Active publics People who behave and communicate actively in response to a problem or issue.

Actual malice When a defamatory statement is made with knowledge of its falsity and reckless disregard for the truth.

Advertising Media space purchased by sponsors to persuade audiences; or the practice of planning and producing this service.

Advertising value equivalency (AVE) A calculation of the value of news or editorial coverage based on the cost of the equivalent amount of advertising space or time.

Advertorial Paid advertising that is presented in the form of editorial content.

Advocacy Public promotion of a cause, idea or policy.

Analytics Researching online data to identify meaningful patterns. In strategic communication, analytics describe, predict and improve how organizations communicate with publics, including tracking website traffic and resulting behavior.

Anchor text Clickable text that provides a hyperlink.

Apology Act of taking responsibility for an issue or crisis and seeking forgiveness or understanding.

Artificial intelligence (AI) A machine's ability to mimic human behavior and intelligence, like learning or solving problems.

Associated Press (AP) style Rules of writing (including grammar, capitalization and punctuation) published by the Associated Press news agency.

Asymmetrical model Model of public relations in which communication is two-way but unbalanced, with the organization using research/feedback in an effort to persuade publics to change attitudes or behaviors.

Attitudinal Having to do with affect, emotion, favor or disfavor toward an organization, brand, product, service, idea or any other attitude object.

Augmented reality Technology that overlays digital information onto media representations of the real world.

Authenticity The degree to which one communicates reliably, accurately and true to his or her own character and the character of the organization that he or she represents.

Automated copy testing Using computer programs to automate the process of testing digital messages such as promotional copy.

Aware publics People who recognize that they are affected by a problem or issue in their environment.

Backgrounder Writing tactic used to give depth and context as background information for news stories.

Backlinks Incoming links that direct web users to a web page from another web page.

Banner ads Advertisements on web pages designed to encourage users to click to reach an advertiser's site.

Behavioral Having to do with observable human action.

Benchmarking Process of setting a point for comparison with eventual program results in order to observe change over time. (Benchmarking can also be used to make performance comparisons with other organizations or industry standards.)

Big data Large amounts of data from traditional and digital sources that can be used for ongoing discovery and analysis of media content and human behavior.

Billable rate Amount that an agency or firm charges clients per hour for an employee's time.

Black box fallacy False notion that predicts that most human communication needs will eventually be satisfied with a single device.

Blog Online post (or web log) with reflections, comments and often links provided by the writer.

Bolstering Attempting to offset reputational damage to an organization during a crisis by emphasizing the good work that the organization has done in the past.

Boomerang effect Unintended consequence of an apology or other attempt to create positive response results instead in a negative response.

Boomerang video Bursts of photos combined into very short videos that play forward and backward.

Bounce rate In online strategy, the percentage of visitors who visit a site but then leave the site instead of continuing toward other goals as defined by the strategist.

Brand advocate A person who is loyal to your brand and speaks favorably about your brand to others.

Brand journalism Application of journalistic skills to produce news content for an organization to communicate directly with its publics without going through a third-party news organization.

Brochureware Web pages that present essentially the same material as printed materials such as brochures.

Business to business (B2B) The relationship between a business and other businesses.

Business to consumer (B2C) The relationship between a business and the end users or consumers of its product or services.

Chatbots An artificial intelligence program designed to mimic human conversation. Chatbots receive and automatically respond to messages.

Clear and present danger Circumstance that may limit rights to free speech in the interest of preventing "substantive evils."

Clickbait Promotional and sensational internet content designed primarily to entice users to visit another website.

Click-through rate Percentage of users who view an ad on the web and click on it to reach an advertiser's site.

Clipping services Businesses that monitor print and electronic media for mentions of clients in local, national or international outlets; see also **media monitoring services**.

Code-switching Alternating between two or more languages or cultural styles.

Cognitive Having to do with mental processes such as thinking, knowing, perceiving, learning and understanding.

Communal relationships Relationships in which each party gives benefits to the other and a primary motivation for each is the other's benefit.

Community management The process of listening to, engaging and moderating online communities and those who make up those communities.

Compensation Crisis response strategy of offering products, services or money to help make amends with publics.

Consequentialism Results-based system of ethics that holds that the best ethical decision is the one leading to the best outcomes or impacts.

Constraint recognition When people detect a problem or situation in their environment but perceive obstacles that limit their behavior to do anything about it.

Content analysis A systematic method for analyzing recorded information such as audio, video or text.

Content curation The process of gathering and sharing content from reputable sources or users.

Content marketing Development and sharing of media content to appeal to consumers as part of an indirect marketing strategy in which consumers are drawn primarily to media content instead of directly to the product being marketed.

Contingency theory A theory that proposes that the best course of action in any situation depends on the specifics of the situation.

Control group A group of subjects or people in an experiment who do not receive or are not exposed to a treatment for the purpose of comparison.

Controlled media Channels of communication that allow public relations practitioners to write, edit, produce and distribute messages as they see fit.

Conversational voice An authentic, engaging and natural style of communication that publics perceive to be personable.

Conversion rate In online strategy, the number of goals reached divided by the number of unique visitors to a site.

Cookie A text file stored on a user's computer that is used to track and remember the user's activity online.

Copyright Claim to intellectual property rights of an original work of authorship including rights to reproduce, distribute, perform, display, license and so on.

Copyright infringement Use of protected works without proper permission from the copyright holder.

Corporate advertising Paid media designed to promote an organization as a whole rather than sell a particular service, product or product category (also sometimes called institutional advertising).

Corporate social responsibility (CSR) Companies' commitment of resources to benefit the welfare of their workforce, local communities, society at large and the environment.

Cost per thousand (CPM) A measure of advertising reach that represents the cost of an advertisement relative to the estimated size of the audience.

Creative Commons Nonprofit organization that encourages fair and legal sharing of content by helping content creators make their work available with clear terms and conditions.

Crowdsource To obtain information or input into a particular task or project by enlisting the services of a number of people, either paid or unpaid, typically via the internet.

Cultural convergence When various forms of culture are exchanged, combined, converted and adapted. On a global scale, this phenomenon has accelerated with the growth of digital media.

Cultural intelligence Ability to adapt, communicate and interact effectively across cultures by learning and applying cognitive, emotional and behavioral skills.

Culture A shared system of beliefs, values, customs and so on that guides behavior of a particular group or public.

Customer relationship management (CRM) Process of tracking and forecasting customers' interactions with an organization, often leveraging data for sales support.

Dateline Text at beginning of a news story that describes when and where the story occurred (e.g., "BEIJING, June 16—").

Deep link Hyperlink that bypasses an organization's home page and takes users directly to resources deeper in an organization's website structure.

Defamation False communication that injures someone's reputation.

Delayed lead A style of beginning a story in a way that entices readers to continue reading without summarizing the story's main points.

Demographics Data describing objective characteristics of a population including age, level of income or highest educational degree obtained.

Deontological ethics System of decision-making that focuses on the moral principles of duty and rules.

Dialogic communication Exchanges involving people communicating their own views and backgrounds while remaining completely open to seeing the world as others do.

Digital divide Gap between those people with relatively little access to and use of information and communication technologies and those people with greater access and usage.

Digital watermarking Information embedded into digital audio and video signals that can be used to track when and where the content is delivered.

Direct lead A style of beginning a news story that summarizes the story's main points (e.g., who, what, where, when, why, how) in the first sentence or two.

Direct-to-consumer Business model in which organizations such as home-delivery and subscription services market products and services directly to consumers and bypass traditional retail channels.

Distributed public relations Intentional practice of sharing public relations responsibilities among a broad cross section of an organization's members or employees, particularly in an online context.

Diversity Inclusion of different types of people and different types of views. The more diverse decision-makers within an organization, the more effective the organization will be in relating to various publics.

Dominant coalition Group of people with the greatest influence in determining how an organization operates and pursues its mission.

Economic convergence When various media organizations and functions are merged under a single ownership structure. This form of media convergence is different from the term economists use to describe trends in world economies.

End-user license agreements (EULA) Legal agreement between a software provider and the person using the software.

Engagement Measure of how (likes, shares, comments, etc.) and how often others interact with your content.

Ephemeral content Images or videos that are available for a limited time and then disappear, like Instagram and Snapchat stories.

Ethics Moral principles that govern a person's or group's behavior.

Ethnocentrism The tendency to judge other cultures based on one's own culture, which one considers superior to others.

Exchange relationships Relationships in which each party gives benefits to the other with the expectation of receiving comparable benefits in return.

External publics Groups of people with shared interests outside of an organization. These groups either have an effect on or are affected by the organization.

Eye tracking Process of measuring eye movements to determine where people are focusing; often used in website testing.

Fact sheet Short (often one-page) document that presents factual information in concise format.

Fair use An exception to copyright laws that allows for the use of otherwise copyrighted material for purposes such as educational use, criticism or commentary.

Feature story A story that explores some angle of an event, a person's life, an organization or a place.

Federal Trade Commission (FTC) U.S. federal agency responsible for regulating all types of consumer products and services, including the promotion of these products and services.

Feed proofing Using text, typography and graphics in a video to communicate a message without the need for audio, making it easy to understand and watch without sound in a user's feed.

Feedback Information returned from the environment in response to an organization's action or communication that can be used for continuous adjustment and improvement of the organization.

First-party data Data on user or consumer behavior that is collected by an organization from the people who use the organization's websites or online services.

Flaming Hostile communication among internet users.

Flash mob When a group of people plans and executes a surprise public event or performance that is usually organized via electronic media and often unanticipated by those who are not participants.

Food and Drug Administration (FDA) U.S. federal agency responsible for regulating food, drugs and health-related products and services including the promotion of these products and services.

Formal research Research designed with clear rules and procedures for collection and analysis of information.

Formative research Research conducted at the beginning of the planning process, or during the implementation of a plan.

Framing When clickable material in a link is actual content from the site to which it links.

Freedom of Information Act (FOIA) U.S. federal law passed to ensure that the government makes its information accessible to citizens.

Freelancers People who work on a project-by-project basis instead of working more permanently for a single employer (e.g., freelance writers, photographers, video producers).

Frequency The average number of times people in an audience are exposed to a particular message in a defined period of time.

Functional magnetic resonance imaging (fMRI) Tests that use magnetic fields to generate images of brain activity, including responses to communication and media stimuli.

Funnel A model for tracking how people move from exposure and awareness to action, particularly in online marketing where the goal is to convert a large number of web page viewers to sales leads or purchases.

General public A nonspecific term referring to everyone in the world, making the concept rather meaningless in strategic communication and relationship building.

Geofencing The use of localization technology, like GPS, to create a virtual geographic boundary for a real-world area. Triggers can be set up to alert when a mobile device enters or leaves that area.

Geofilter Feature of social media (particularly Snapchat) that encourages communication among users within a specified geographic area by allowing users to post images with location-specific overlays.

Geolocation Function of communication devices that identifies the specific geographic location of the device.

Gig economy A trend in which people increasingly are hired for short periods of time to complete specific tasks or projects, including freelancers, independent contractors and part-time hires.

Glass ceiling Metaphor used to describe a present but unseen barrier to promotion for women and minorities.

Goals Statements that indicate a desired result for public relations efforts. In strategic planning, goals are more specific than the organization's mission but more general than objectives.

Golden mean Ethical doctrine holding that the best courses of action are found between extremes.

Golden rule Ethic of reciprocity—treat others as you would like to be treated yourself.

Government relations Management of relationships between an organization and government officials who formulate and execute public policy.

High-context communication Exchanges in which most of the meaning conveyed between people lies in the context of the communication or is internal to the communicators.

High-context culture A culture that communicates more implicitly and relies more on nonverbal cues than a low-context culture.

Human interest A personal or emotional storytelling angle that focuses on the human condition.

Hyperlink A piece of text or an image online that can be clicked on to reach another resource online.

Impacts The broadest and furthest-reaching results of public relations efforts, often stated in terms of societal benefit.

Impression management Process in which people influence perceptions of themselves or their organizations by regulating and controlling information in social interactions.

Impressions A measure of how many people were exposed to a message.

In house When public relations people are employed directly within an organization rather than working for an external agency or contracted as independent consultants.

Inbound marketing Marketing strategy that focuses on tactics for attracting customers with useful, entertaining or valuable information that customers find on blogs, search results and other forms of online and social media.

Independence In public relations ethics, the value of autonomy and accountability in providing objective counsel.

Individualism-collectivism Cultural dimension describing the difference between cultures that value loyalty to self and immediate family and those that value loyalty to larger groups and society.

Influencer Trusted individual who can influence the opinions of established social media audiences.

Informal research Research conducted without clear rules or procedures, which makes the findings difficult to replicate or compare to other research or situations.

Ingratiation A type of reinforcing crisis response strategy in which stakeholders are praised or thanked to win their good favor.

Initial public offering (IPO) Financial event in which a private company offers sale of stocks to public investors for the first time.

Insider trading When a company's employees or executives buy and sell stock in their own organization or share information with others who buy or sell before the information has been made public.

Integrated communication Communicating with publics consistently across organizational functions including public relations, advertising, marketing and customer service.

Integrated marketing communication Strategic coordination of communication functions such as marketing, advertising and publicity to achieve a consistent concept in consumers' minds.

Intellectual property Any product of the human mind that is protected by law from unauthorized use by others.

Intercultural public relations Management of relationships between organizations and publics of different cultures.

Internal publics Groups of people with shared interests within an organization.

International public relations Management of relationships between organizations and publics of different nations.

Internet of things (IoT) Global network of physical objects that are connected to one another in a way that enables them to communicate with one another and the internet at large.

Inverted pyramid A style of newswriting in which the most important information is presented at the broad top of a story and narrower supporting details are written below.

Investor relations Management of relationships between an organization and publics in the financial community—for example, investors, analysts, regulators.

Issue An important topic or problem that is open for debate, discussion or advocacy.

Issues management Systematic process whereby organizations work to identify and resolve issues before they become crises.

Landscape orientation Images or video framed so that width is greater than height, like traditional movies. The aspect ratio is 16:9.

Latent publics People who are affected by a problem or issue but don't realize it.

Legislative relations Management of relationships between an organization and lawmakers, staffers and others who influence legislation.

Level of involvement The degree to which people feel or think that a problem or issue affects them.

Libel Written or otherwise recorded false communication that injures someone's reputation.

Likert-type items Questionnaire items that ask people to respond to statements with a range of defined response options such as the range from "strongly disagree" to "strongly agree."

Linear story arc Storytelling that follows a logical sequence or chronology.

Listening Deliberately paying attention to and processing what others are communicating. In public relations and organizational communication, this means processing feedback.

Listicle An online article presented in the format of a numbered or bulleted list.

Lobbying Working to influence the decisions of government officials on matters of legislation.

Long-term orientation Cultural dimension describing the difference between cultures that value long-held traditions and cultures that value entrepreneurship and innovation.

Looping video Videos that play and repeat multiple times, in a loop.

Low-context communication Exchanges in which most of the meaning of messages is stated explicitly in the messages and requires little understanding of context.

Low-context culture A culture that relies on more explicit, direct communication than a high-context culture.

Loyalty A sense of obligation or support for someone or something, including both organizations and publics.

Management function Part of an organization involved in its overall leadership and decision-making, guiding how the organization operates in its environment, rather than merely following the instructions of others.

Market skimming Marketing strategy that starts with higher prices for early adopters of unique products and services and then lowers prices later to sell to a broader base of consumers when competitors enter the market.

Marketing Business of creating, promoting, delivering and selling products and services.

Marketing mix Combination of product, price, place and promotion strategies in support of profitable exchange.

Masculinity-femininity Cultural dimension describing the difference between cultures that value competition, achievement and material success and those that value care, collaboration and modesty.

Material information Any information that could influence the market value of a company or its products.

Media catching When journalists post queries online inviting public relations people or others with relevant information or expertise to respond. Public relations people "catch" these opportunities rather than "pitching" story ideas to journalists.

Media gatekeepers People or processes that filter information by deciding which content is published, broadcasted, posted, shared or forwarded.

Media kits Packages of information assembled by public relations people for news media. Common contents include news releases, fact sheets, backgrounders, position papers, photos, graphics and so on.

Media monitoring services Vendors that assist public relations practitioners in the collection, analysis and reporting of media data for evaluation; see also **clipping services**.

Media planning Choosing media channels to achieve strategic communication goals and objectives. Media planning drives advertising purchases.

Media relations Management of relationships between an organization and members of the media who write, edit, produce and deliver news.

Mediated public diplomacy A nation's strategic use of media to promote its agenda abroad to foreign publics.

Meta tags Text used to describe a web page to search engines.

Microblog A shorter blog post limited by space or size constraints of the delivery platform.

Mission Overall reason an organization exists.

Mission statement A formal statement of an organization's steady, enduring purpose.

Monologic communication Communication in which one party attempts to impose its view on others.

Morgue Storage space for archived files of old stories, notes and media materials kept by news organizations.

Multimedia The combination of any two or more forms of media such as text, graphics, moving images and sounds.

Multipliers Formulas applied to circulation or other media reach numbers based on assumptions that more than one person will be exposed to each copy of a message or that being covered as part of a news story is more valuable than paid advertising in the same media space.

Multivariate testing A method of message testing to compare how various combinations of message factors (e.g., message selection, message placement, image selection, headline styles, color) lead to various outcomes (e.g., click-through rates, time spent on page, sharing behavior).

Native advertising Paid advertising that is presented in the form of the media content that surrounds it. Advertorials

are a type of native advertising, as are promoted tweets, sponsored posts and so on. Native advertising should be labeled as "advertising," "paid content," "sponsored," etc.

Natural links Hyperlinks to a web page that are provided by other people who see value in the content of the page, as opposed to links that are posted for the primary purpose of manipulating search engines.

Net neutrality When data transmitted on the internet is treated equally by governments and service providers in a way that does not slow down, speed up or manipulate traffic to create a favorable business environment for some organizations or users over others.

News release A statement of news produced and distributed on behalf of an organization to make information public. Traditionally news releases (aka press releases) have been issued to news media with the intent of publicizing the information to the news organization's readers, listeners or viewers.

Newsjacking "The art and science of injecting your ideas into a breaking news story so you and your ideas get noticed," as defined by David Meerman Scott.

Newsworthiness Standard used to determine what is worth covering in news media.

Non-compete clause Part of an employment contract that restricts employees from working for competitors or sharing competitive information such as trade secrets even after they no longer work for the organization.

Nongovernmental organization (NGO) A group of people organized at the local, national or international level, often serving humanitarian functions and encouraging political participation. Many NGOs work closely with the United Nations.

Non-linear story arc Storytelling that portrays the story seemingly out of order.

Nonparticipant observation Research method in which the researcher avoids interaction with the environment or those being observed.

Objectives Statements that indicate specific outputs or outcomes desired. In strategic public relations, objectives are specific steps taken to achieve broader goals.

Objectivity State of being free from the influence of personal feelings or opinions in considering and representing facts.

One-to-many content (1:many) Content from one sender that is designed to reach mass audiences with the same message.

Organic search results Search engine results that are generated because of their relevance to the search terms entered by users and not resulting directly from paid placement as advertising.

Organization A group of people organized in pursuit of a mission, including businesses, nonprofits, NGOs, clubs, churches, unions, schools, teams and government agencies.

Organizational crisis A major threat to an organization's operations or reputation.

Organizational culture The unique character of an organization comprised of beliefs, values, symbols and behaviors.

Outcomes Observable results of public relations work.

Outputs Tasks or work attempted and completed, including communication tactics produced. Outputs can be completed without necessarily leading to meaningful results (i.e., outcomes).

Overhead expenses Costs of running a business that are not directly related to the product or services delivered.

Participant observation Research method in which the researcher deliberately interacts with the environment and those being observed.

Participatory culture A culture in which private citizens and publics are as likely to produce and share as they are to consume; commonly applied in mediated contexts in which consumers produce and publish information online.

Participatory media Media in which publics actively participate in producing and sharing content.

Patent Claim to intellectual property rights of an invention.

Pay per click Model of media sales in which advertisers, marketers or sponsors pay an online publisher or website owner for each time the sponsored message or advertisement is clicked.

Personal branding Strategically creating, positioning and maintaining a positive impression of yourself to signal your professional promise.

Pitching When a public relations person approaches a journalist or editor to suggest a story idea.

Plagiarism Presenting someone else's words or ideas as one's own.

Planning Forethought about goals and objectives and the strategies and tactics needed to achieve them.

Pop-ups Planned events or experiences that are set up quickly in a temporary location for a short time.

Power distance Cultural dimension describing the difference between cultures that value hierarchy and authority and those that value equal distribution of power.

Pre-roll advertising A commercial ad is displayed as online video before the desired video is shown.

Press agentry/publicity model Model of public relations in which communication is mostly one-way, initiated by an organization with little concern for accuracy or completeness in order to gain the attention of publics.

Primary publics Groups of people identified as most important to the success of a public relations campaign or program.

Primary research Systematic design, collection, analysis and application of original data or observation.

Privacy The right to be let alone; or, the right to control access to your personal information.

Pro bono Work conducted as a public service without fee or payment.

Proactive A management style that is anticipatory, change-oriented and self-initiated to improve the organization's environment and its future.

Problem or opportunity statement A concise written summary of the situation that explains the main reason for a public relations program or campaign.

Problem recognition When people detect a problem or situation in their environment and begin to think about it.

Professional convergence When various functions of professional communication such as publicity, advertising, online services and marketing are combined to improve strategy.

Programmatic media buying Automated media buying that is preprogrammed so that advertising purchases are completed when certain criteria set by buyers (marketers) and sellers (media) are met. Programmatic media buying commonly occurs via computer-run, real-time auctions.

Propaganda The spread of information used to promote or support a particular point of view. In modern use, the term usually refers to false, misleading or exaggerated information.

Proselytizing When members of publics advocate or promote to others the goals and objectives of a communication strategy. Proselytizing is a key part of strategic campaigns going viral.

Pseudo-event An event organized primarily for the purpose of generating media coverage.

Psychographics Data describing psychological characteristics of a population including interests, attitudes and behaviors.

Public affairs Management of policy-focused relationships between an organization, public officials and their constituents.

Public diplomacy Subset of international public relations that focuses on promoting national interests.

Public domain Works of intellectual property for which the copyright has expired, the creator has forfeited rights, or copyright laws do not apply, making the works freely available for public use.

Public figures Someone "of general fame or notoriety in the community" who is subject to less protection in libel cases than a private individual.

Public information model Model of public relations in which communication is mostly one-way, initiated by an organization to inform publics with truthful and accurate information.

Public information officer (PIO) A public relations person, commonly working in a government position, whose job focuses on the dissemination of information to appropriate publics in an accurate and timely manner.

Public relations Management of communication between an organization and its publics, or the strategic communication process that builds mutually beneficial relationships between organizations and their publics.

Publicity Unpaid media coverage, or the practice of deliberately planning and producing information and activities to attract this coverage.

Publics Groups of people with shared interests. An organization's publics either have an effect on the organization, are affected by the organization, or both.

Pure accommodation Stance in issues management in which a public relations practitioner fully concedes to a public's demands.

Pure advocacy Stance in issues management in which a public relations practitioner firmly pleads an organization's case without compromise.

Qualitative research Research that results in in-depth description and understanding without relying on the use of numbers or statistics to analyze findings.

Quantitative research Research that results in numerical or statistical data and analysis.

Reach Percentage or number of people exposed to a message at least once via a specific communication channel during a defined period of time.

Reactive A management style that mainly responds to problems as they arise rather than anticipating them and averting them.

Relational maintenance strategies Ways of building and sustaining mutually beneficial relationships between organizations and publics.

Relational public diplomacy Engagement between a nation and its foreign publics in cultural exchange and two-way communication with the goal of achieving mutual benefits.

Reliability Consistency and precision of a particular research technique.

Replicability The ability to perform a research procedure or experiment repeatedly to attain comparable results.

Reputation management Acting and communicating—often in writing—to influence an organization's reputation as part of a process that includes planning, analyzing feedback and evaluating.

Responsible supply chain management Careful monitoring of product production and distribution to ensure that generally high ethical standards of social and environmental responsibility are maintained.

Scapegoating Blaming an outside person or organization for a crisis.

Search advertising Paid placement of advertising on search-engine results pages. Ads are placed to appear in response to certain keyword queries.

Search engine optimization (SEO) Process of improving the position of a specific website in the organic search results of search engines.

Secondary publics Groups of people who are important to a public relations campaign or program because of their relationship with primary publics.

Secondary research Collection, summary, analysis or application of previously reported research.

Securities and Exchange Commission (SEC) U.S. federal agency responsible for regulating financial activities and investing.

Selective attention Process of filtering information by focusing on some stimuli in the environment while ignoring others.

Self-efficacy One's belief that he or she can perform certain behaviors to achieve certain outcomes.

Sentiment A measure of the tone or emotion behind social media mentions or comments, typically categorized as positive, neutral or negative.

Situation analysis A report analyzing the internal and external environment of an organization and its publics as it relates to the start of a campaign or program.

Situational crisis communication theory (SCCT) Theory that proposes that effective crisis communication entails choosing and applying appropriate response strategies depending on how much responsibility for the crisis is attributed to the organization by key publics.

Situational theory of publics Theory that the activity of publics depends on their levels of involvement, problem recognition and constraint recognition.

Slander Oral communication that is false and injures someone's reputation.

Snackable content Easy-to-consume pieces of content that are available on the go.

Social listening The process of tracking, analyzing and responding to conversations about specific topics online.

Social media creators Influential social media users who are among the first to identify and post about crises online.

Social media crisis communication model (SMCC) Model describing the role of social media influencers, followers and inactives in spreading information in crisis situations.

Social media followers Social media users who receive crisis information from social media creators.

Social media inactives People who receive crisis information indirectly from social media via traditional media and offline word of mouth.

Social media influencer Social media user who has earned credibility with specific publics and who can be instrumental in strategic communication programs because of his or her reach and engagement.

Social media release A news release that applies the conventions of social media and includes content designed for social media distribution and sharing.

Social monitoring The process of tracking social media mentions and conversations.

Spambots Computer programs that automatically send unsolicited email or post comments in online forums.

Spin Disingenuous strategic communication involving skewed interpretation or presentation of information.

Status conferral When media pay attention to individuals and groups and therefore enhance their authority or bestow prestige to them.

Stealing thunder Crisis response strategy in which an organization exposes its own problems (and works to address those problems) before opponents have the opportunity to do so.

Stock image Image that is professionally produced for selling or sharing, commonly available in searchable databases.

Story placement The outcome of a successful pitch, when a story involving a public relations practitioner's organization or client is covered in the news media.

Strategic decision-making Daily management and communication decisions made with mindfulness of the objectives, goals and mission of the organization.

Strategy Underlying logic that holds a plan together and offers a rationale for why it will work.

Summative research Research conducted at the end of a campaign or program to determine the extent that objectives and goals were met.

Sunshine law State law that stipulates which documents and records must be open to the public and which meetings and events must be open.

SWOT Analysis Description and discussion of an organization's internal strengths and weaknesses and its external opportunities and threats.

Symmetrical model Model of public relations in which two-way communication is mostly balanced, with the organization as likely to change attitudes or behavior as its publics.

Tactical decision-making Daily management and communication tactics implemented without consideration of the strategic objectives, goals and mission of the organization.

Tactics Specific actions taken and items produced in public relations.

Target audience Group of people strategically identified for their propensity to consume an organization's products, services or ideas.

Technological convergence (aka digital convergence) When information of various forms such as sound, text, images and data are digitized, affording communication across common media.

Tertiary publics Groups of people who indirectly influence or are indirectly affected by a public relations campaign or program.

Third-party credibility Tendency of people to attribute greater trustworthiness or expertise to a source other than the original sender of a persuasive message.

Third-party data Data on user behavior that is collected or aggregated by one organization and sold to another organization.

Total market approach A strategic approach that combines insights and considerations from diverse segments to deliver integrated, culturally nuanced campaigns.

Trade secret Business information that is not generally known to the public and not readily available to others who could profit from its disclosure or use.

Trademark Word, name, phrase, symbol or design used to distinguish a product or service from others in the competitive marketplace.

Transmedia storytelling Telling a story across multiple platforms like games, web pages, apps, social media and traditional media.

Transparency Deliberate attempt to make available all legally reasonable information for the purpose of enhancing the reasoning ability of publics; in research, openness in describing and explaining methods.

Treatment group A group of subjects or people in an experiment who receive or are exposed to a treatment.

Two-way communication When both parties send and receive information in an exchange, as opposed to the one-way dissemination of information from an organization to its publics.

Uncertainty avoidance Cultural dimension describing the difference between cultures that are uncomfortable with ambiguity (high uncertainty avoidance) and those that are at ease with ambiguity.

Unconferences Meetings or conferences organized by their participants for active peer-to-peer exchange of ideas and information. Unconferences are less structured and more participatory (e.g., fewer one-to-many presentations) than traditional conferences.

Uncontrolled media Channels of communication that are outside of the control of public relations practitioners.

Usage divide (or second digital divide) Gap between people who use information and communication technologies for education, self-betterment, civic engagement, etc. and those who use the technologies for less constructive reasons.

User-generated content (UGC) Content voluntarily created by online users.

Uses and gratifications Approach to studying communication that focuses on how people use media and the gratifications they seek from media.

Utilitarianism Principle that the most ethical course of action is the one that maximizes good and minimizes harm for people.

Validity Accuracy of a particular research technique in measuring or observing what the researcher intends to measure or observe.

Vertical video Video framed in an orientation in which height is greater than width. The aspect ratio is 9:16.

Video news release A news release that provides broadcast journalists with pre-produced news packages including audio and video material.

Vision statement A declaration of an organization's desired end-state.

Visual listening The use of image recognition to track and analyze logos or products in online images.

Word-of-mouth promotion Passing of information and recommendations from person to person.

Credits

PHOTOGRAPHS

Page 1 © trailexplorers/Shutterstock; 2 David Albers/Naples Daily News; 5 ©Kathy Hutchins/Shutterstock; 8 Wisconsin Historical Society. WHS-55511.; 9 Agencia Fotograficzna Caro/Alamy; Winner of Greenpeace's Rebrand BP Competition. Designed by Laurent Hunziker; 13 Kevin Wheal/Alamy Stock Photo; 14 Courtesy of Dan Ox via Flickr; 16 Photo by Trust "Tru" Katsande on Unsplash; 22 Courtesy of Kathy Fitzpatrick; 27 © Hong Vo/Shutterstock; 30 New York Historical Society Library; 33 ullstein bild/ullstein bild via Getty Images; 34 Kirn Vintage Stock/Contributor/Getty Images; 35 AP Photo/Bullit Marquez; 37 Marian Weyo/Shutterstock; 38 Bettmann/Contributor/Getty Images; 39 From the Collections of The Henry Ford. Gift of Liberty Mutual Insurance Company.; 40 Courtesy of Tom Kelleher; 41 Stuart A. Rose Manuscript Archives & Rate Book Library; 42 Granger, NYC—All rights reserved.; 43 islamographic.com; Courtesy of Tom Kelleher; 44 The Boston Tea Party, Brauner, Luis Arcas (1934–89)/Private Collection/© Look and Learn/Bridgeman Images; 49 Copyright © Choose Hope, Inc.; 50 Courtesy of Karen M. Russell; 55 © mobil11/Shutterstock; 57 ©Zapp2Photo/Shutterstock; 58 © david pearson/Alamy Stock Photo; 61 Roberto Machado Noa/Contributor/Getty Images; 62 risteski goce/Shutterstock.com; 66 Matthew Stockman/Getty Images Sport; 67 Courtesy of Tom Kelleher; 68 The Washington Post/Getty Images; 72 Popperfoto/Getty Images; 76 Photos courtesy of DefenseImagery.mil. The appearance of U.S. Department of Defense (DoD) visual information does not imply or constitute DoD endorsement.; 79 Courtesy of Bill Imada; 81 Courtesy of Tom Kelleher; 86 © Constantin Iosif/Shutterstock; 88 © Felipe Dávalos/Mexicolore; 89 Courtesy of Tom Kelleher; 95 Charles Trainor Jr./Miami Herald/Tribune News Service via Getty Images; 96 ProfNet; 98 Photo by Emanuele Cremaschi/Getty Images; 104 AP Photo/Richard Drew; 105 Carsten Koall/Stringer/Getty Images; 107 AP Photo/Kiichiro Sato; AP Photo/Charlie Neibergall; 108 Surfrider Foundation; 109 Photo courtesy of Boston Children's Hospital.; 110 Courtesy of Rob Clark; 112 Bychykhin Olexandr/Shutterstock.com; Press Association via AP Images; 114 Cone Communications; 120 Imeh Akpanudosen/Getty Images Entertainment; 126 Photo by LaTerrian McIntosh on Unsplash; 127 Smith Collection/Gado/Getty Images; 132 Brandy Baker/ The Detroit News; 133 Gil C/Shutterstock.com; 134 © ArtBabii/Alamy Stock Photo; 137 Mike Yarish/© AMC/Courtesy: Everett Collection; 139 SAMHSA; 143 ©Stacy Walsh Rosenstock/Alamy; 144 Used with permission of Employment Policies Institute; 150 Diane Bondareff/AP Images for Timberland; 156 Photo by Jay L. Clendenin/Los Angeles Times via Getty Images; 157 Zia Soleil/Iconica/Getty Images; 159 USAID/Indonesia, IUWASH PLUS; 162 © jaime cross/Shutterstock; 163 Yaacov Dagan/Alamy Stock Photo; 169 Photo by Evelyn on Unsplash; 170 © Gene Blevins; 173 Callahan/Shutterstock.com; 177 Sergi Alexander/Stringer/Getty Images; 180 MANDEL NGAN/AFP/Getty Images; 183 ANDREW CULLEN/AFP/Getty Images; 184 PESO Model created by Gini Dietrich; 186 Photo by Jay Clark on Unsplash; 200 © Bborriss.67/Shutterstock; 203 Courtesy of Kristi Camara and Kelly Logan; 204 Courtesy of VWO.com; 211 Courtesy of the Institute for Public Relations; 225 World Bicycle Relief; 226 Silver Screen Collection/Getty Images; 230 World Bicycle Relief; 236 AP Photo/Frank Franklin II; 240 Cision; 245 Casimiro/Alamy Stock Photo; 249 Courtesy of Cornelius Foote; 256 ©stocksolutions/Shutterstock; 259 Spotify, Share Your 2018; 263 Photo by JC Gellidon on Unsplash; 264 Geoff Livingston/Flickr/https://creativecommons.org/licenses/by-sa/2.0/; 273 Isabella Dias/Getty Images; Photo by Sina Katirachi on Unsplash; 284 charnsitr/Shutterstock.com; 288 © medvedsky.kz/Shutterstock; 290 MaxxStudio/Shutterstock.com; 291 JOSH EDELSON/Stringer/Getty Images; Sipa via AP Images; Chris Hondros/Getty Images; 293 AP Photo/Ted Anthony; 295 Pool/Getty Images; 297 Courtesy of Stephen Ball; 299 Photo by Roy Rochlin/Getty Images; 301 Courtesy of Kaiser Health News; 302 Cory Doctorow; 305 Stock Montage/Archive Photos/Getty Images; 308 Natan Dvir/Bloomberg via Getty Images; 311 PeopleImages/Getty Images; 313 Courtesy of Cayce Myers; 315 Bloomberg/Getty Images; 319 © AyselZDesign/Shutterstock; 320 Courtesy of Dave Carroll; 323 AP; 327 AP Photo/Kevin Hagen, File; 328 Courtesy of brandalism.org.uk; 334 Bettmann/Getty Images; 340 Tom Williams/Contributor/Getty Images; 343 Courtesy of Barry Finkelstein; 349 Finnbarr Webster/Alamy Stock Photo; 351 © chuyuss/Shutterstock; 353 © AngieYeoh/Shutterstock; 355 Home Bird/Alamy Stock Photo; 362 Mobile Technology and its Social Impact Survey 2018, Pew Research Center; 363 AP Photo/Bullit Marquez; 368 Jacques Witt/Sipa/Shutterstock; 374 © enricobaringuarise/Shutterstock; 382 The Holmes Report; 386 Photo by Croissant on Unsplash; 390 Public Relations Society of America; 393 Courtesy of Krislyn Hasimoto; 395 © de-focus/Shutterstock.com.

CARTOONS

Page 11 Copyright Grantland Enterprises; www.grantland.net; 57 CARLSON © Milwaukee Journal Sentinel. Reprinted with permission of ANDREWS MCMEEL SYNDICATION. All rights reserved.; 119 Courtesy of Dave Carpenter; 141 Copyright Grantland Enterprises; www.grantland.net; 181 Courtesy of Sean R. Nicholson, www.socmedsean.com; 207 ©Tom Fishburne, marketoonist.com; 221 John Morris/Cartoonstock.com; 228 Lauren Fishman/Cartoonstock.com; 337 © Copyright 2010 Dave Granlund; 338 Courtesy of Tom Kelleher; 378 Brendan Boughen/CartoonStock.

Name Index

Alaimo, Kara, 354
Arenstein, Seth, 108
Arthur, Lisa, 207
Avidar, Ruth, 262

Baer, Jay, 277
Bandura, Albert, 359
Baquet, Dean, 293, 293p
Barney, Ralph, 345
Barnum, P. T., 29–30, 29f, 30, 38, 41, 42
Bar-On, Tarim, 365
Bentham, Jeremy, 143
Bernays, Edward, 29f, 35–38, 38p, 41, 51, 52
Best, Joel, 220
Black, Jay, 195, 251, 284, 344–45
Bowen, Shannon, 17, 145, D–1
Brandeis, Louis, 290, 305
Breakenridge, Deirdre, 229, 243
Breyer, Stephen, 289, 290, 313
Brown, Robert E., 42
Bruning, Stephen, 88
Buber, Martin, 370
Burke, Tarana, 47–48
Buss, David, 102

Calamur, Krishnadev, 293
Cameron, Glen, 322
Canary, Dan, 88
Cao, Sissi, 307
Carroll, Craig, 228
Carstarphen, Meta, 235
Cobain, Dane, 5
Colvin, Geoff, 336
Confessore, Nicholas, 44
Coombs, Timothy, 333, 336
Cutlip, Scott, 38, 45

Defren, Todd, 18–21
Deggans, Eric, 195
Denning, Steph, 226
Dietrich, Gini, 185f
Doctorow, Cory, 302p, 303
Duncan, Seth, 208

Earley, Christopher, 357–58
Elliot, Stuart, 6

Ferdman, Roberto, 180
Finnegan, William, 232–34
Fitzpatrick, Kathy, 17, 18, 19, 20, 22–23, 173
Foote, Cornelius, 249–50
Ford, Rochelle, 350
Fraustino, Daisy, 342
Friedman, Milton, 111

Garsten, Ed, 76
Giang, Vivian, 394
Gilfeather, John, D–1
Golan, Guy, 367–68
Gonzalez, Melissa, 149
Grewal, David Singh, 58
Griffiths, James, 362

Grunig, James, 3, 28, 31, 37–38, 39, 51, 87, 89, 90, 128
Grunig, Larissa, 39, 108

Hall, Edward, 352
Hanson, Arik, 390–91
Harder, Heather, 111, 112
Harris, Emily, 45
Heaney, Katie, 352
Hofstede, Geert, 351, 354, 354f
Holladay, Sherry, 333, 336
Holmes, Elizabeth, 269–70
Holmes, Oliver Wendell, 291
Hon, Linda, 89, 90
Huffington, Arianna, 215
Hunt, Todd, 3, 28, 31, 37–38, 51, 87

Ingram, Matthew, 293

Jenkins, Henry, 56, 58
Jin, Yan, 342
Johnson, Benjamin, 259–60

Kahneman, Daniel, 220
Kant, Immanuel, 51
Kantor, Jodi, 292
Kelly, Kathleen, 106
Kendall, Robert, 11
Kern-Foxworth, Marilyn, 41
Kietzmann, Jan, 276
Kirsch, Noah, 4
Krystal, Becky, 30

Lamme, Margot Opdyke, 42, 43, 44, 45, 48, 50
La Monica, Paul, 30
Larkin, Judy, 326, 328
Laskin, Alexander, 103–4
Lauterborn, Bob, 71, 72, 73
Lazarsfeld, Paul, 45
Ledingham, John, 88
Lee, Ivy Ledbetter, 29f, 32–33, 33p, 35, 38, 41, 51, 52, 74
Lerbinger, Otto, 335–36
Lewin, Kurt, 128
Lichfield, Gideon, 311–12
Liu, Brooke Fisher, 342
Lukaszewski, James, 168

Manning, Andre, 218
McBride, Genevieve, 52
McCarthy, E. Jerome, 66
McGuire, William, 150–55, 162, 172
McIntosh, Shawn, 9
Meeropol, Abel, 252
Men, Rita Linjuan, 101, 127
Merton, Robert, 45
Mill, John Stuart, 143, 144
Morgan, David, 137
Mosakowski, Elaine, 357–58

Nathan, Alison, 309

O'Brien, James, 75
Ogden, Joseph, 120
Okrent, Arika, 226

Page, Arthur W., 7, 8p, 10, 14, 15, 39, 178, 316
Parijat, Pramath, 183
Pavlik, John Vernon, 9
Payne, Katie Delahaye, 218, 218t
Penn, Christopher, 76
Plaisance, Patrick Lee, 51
Pryor, Brooke, 187p

Ranadive, Ameet, 169
Ratcliff, Christopher, 188
Rawlins, Brad, 8, D–1
Regester, Michael, 326, 328
Roberts, Chris, 195, 251, 284, 344–45
Rockland, David, 209, 218
Russell, Karen Miller, 42, 43, 44, 45, 48, 50–51
Russell, Nan, 101

Salcedo, Natalia, 50
Sandrow, Kim Lachance, 271
Scott, David Meerman, 266
Searls, Doc, 73
Seib, Philip, 17, 20
Seiner, Jake, 236
Sha, Bey-Ling, 350
Shadpour, David, 263
Shogren, Elizabeth, 9
Smith, Ronald, 161
Solis, Brian, 229, 243
Stacks, Don, 134, 135, 145
Stafford, Laura, 88
Streitfeld, David, 292
Strohmeyer, Robert, 14
Sun Tzu, 95
Swallow, Erica, 243–45
Sweetser, Kaye, 45

Thiruvengadam, Arvind, 325–26
Thompson, Clive, 33
Tiffany, Kaitlyn, 149
Tiku, Nitasha, 82
Toffler, Alvin, 389
Toth, Elizabeth, 92
Tversky, Amos, 220
Twain, Mark, 220

Van Ruler, Betteke, 31, 63
Vu, Hong Tien, 361

Warren, Samuel, 290
Weinberger, David, 73
Wells, Richard, 235
Wilson, Laurie, 120
Winer, Dave, 243, 244
Wylie, Ann, 231
Wynne, Robert, 269

Yourish, Karen, 44
Yuter, Josh, 42

Zinsser, William, 230, 230p, 235–36, 249

Subject Index

Aarnoutse, Jocelyn, 271
ABC. *See* Accredited Business Communicator credential
ABC Studios, 282
Absolut Vodka, 193
A/B testing, 203, 204f, 206–7, 208, 213, 217
Accenture, 268, 367
Accident crises, 335
Accommodation, 322–23, 324, 371
Accreditation, 24, 390
Accredited Business Communicator (ABC) credential, 24
Accredited in Public Relations (APR) credential, 24, 390
Action/acting
  hierarchy-of-effects model step, 153
  implementation and, 178–81
  loyalty and diversity in, 195
  planning for, 163
  in principled public relations, 9, 178
Active publics, 128, 129, 132
Activists, 108–9, 112
Actual malice, 295
ADCOLOR, 283
Ad Council, 283
Adidas, 365
Administrative costs and supplies, 168–69
Advergize, 9
Advertising, 63–65, 186–87
  corporate, 186
  costs of, 63–65, 68–69, 169–70
  defined, 63
  divergence and, 63–65
  institutional, 77
  native, 186, 187
  PR and marketing integration with (*see* Integrated marketing communication)
  PR compared with, 77–78, 77t, 79
  publicity compared with, 68–69
  safety and accuracy of, 305–6
  search, 65
Advertising Age, 71
Advertising value equivalency (AVE), 216p, 218, 221
  Barcelona Principles on, 216–17
  defined, 64, 216
Advertorials, 80, 186, 187
Advocacy, 109, 221, 323–24, 371, B–2
  brand, 279, 281
  defined, 48
  First Amendment and, 291
  in journalism, discouraged, 51–52
  pure, 322
Adweek, 59, 192
Aerie, 70
Aflac, 121t
African Public Relations Association, 24
Agencies, 381–82, 383p, 384p
"Agencies Must Find Answers for a Lack of Diversity" (*PRWeek* editorial), 195
Agility PR, 206t

Agitation, 46–48
Agreeing (hierarchy-of-effects model step), 153
Agricultural Relations Council, 24
Airbnb, 275, 276
Ajax, 9
Albertsons, 104p
Alexander the Great, 43
Algorithms, 46, 190, 191, 220, 246, 247, 248, 248p
All England Club, 99
Allstate Foundation Purple Purse, 7, 8p
Allstate insurance, 109
Alm, Robbie, 40–41
Amazon.com, 3, 3p, 67, 81p, 82, 97, 98p, 127–28, 127p, 187, 277, 292–93, 310, 339
AMEC. *See* International Association for Measurement and Evaluation of Communication
American Academy of Pediatrics, 218
American Airlines, 79, 193
American Association of Advertising Agencies (4A's), 343
American Cancer Society, 38
American Eagle, 70
American Heart Association, 38, 105
American Humane Society, 124
Americanization, 58
American Marketing Association, 65
American Red Cross, 41, 178, 264
American Time Use Survey, 142
American Tobacco Company, 36
American University School of Communication, 22
Analysis
  content, 134–36, 139, 204, 205
  proactive issues management step, 329t, 330–31
  situation (*see* Situation analysis)
  SWOT, 120–22, 122p
Analytics, 65, 119, 162, 206–9, 245, 391
Ancestry.com, 81
Anchor text, 247
Angie's List, 12
Apologies, 336, 337–38, 340
Apple Computer Inc., 111, 228, 272, 284–85, 388
Appropriation of likeness or identity, 290, 311–12
Apptentive, 265
APR. *See* Accredited in Public Relations credential
APR Study Guide, 182, 189
AP style. *See* Associated Press style
AP Stylebook, The, 187–88, 187p, 249
Aristotle, 43
Arkell, Bartlett, 37
Arnold, Chris, 180
Arthur W. Page Society, 17, 22, 111, 195, 219
Artifactual personal branding, 378–80
Artificial intelligence, 277
Art of War, The (Sun Tzu), 95

Asociación de Relacionistas Profesionales de Puerto Rico, 24
Asociación Mexicana de Profesionales de Relaciones Públicas (PRORP), 24
Asorey, Natalie, 170–71
Associated Press (AP) style, 239, 240, 241p
Assurances, 89
Asymmetrical model, 28, 29f, 35–38, 39, 371
  case study, 35–37
  defined, 38
Atlantic, The, 259, 293
AT&T, 7, 120p, 128
Attainable objectives, 160
Attending (hierarchy-of-effects model step), 151
Attitudinal outcomes, 210, 212
Attribution, 296–98, 302, 303
Attribution-NonCommercial-ShareAlike licenses, 302
Augmented reality (AR), 57–58, 57p
Austin American Statesman, 253
Authenticity, 7, 21, 173, 174
Automated copy testing, 203
Automobile safety improvement, 39, 178
AVE. *See* Advertising value equivalency
Award of Excellence (PRSA), 377
Aware publics, 128, 129, 132
Axe, 283

Babineaux, Codey, 43
Backgrounders, 240–42
Backlinks, 247
Bacon consumption campaign, 37–38, 37p
Bad Bunny, 350
Baidu, 369
Baker, Joseph V., 41–42, 41p
Ball, LaVar, 7
Ball, Stephen (photo by), 297p
Bandwatch, 267
Bank of America, 388
Banner ads, 64p, 65
Barcelona Principles, 209–18, 211f
  AVE limitations (#5), 216–17
  communication outcome measurement (#2), 210–13
  goals and measurement as fundamental (#1), 210
  organizational performance measurement (#3), 213
  qualitative and quantitative methods (#4), 213
  social media measurement, 217 (#6)
  transparent, consistent and valid measurement (#7), 217–18
Bargiel, Andrzej, 75, 75p
BarkBox, 177, 191–92, 193f
Barnum's Animals Cracker box, 107–8, 107p
B2B relationships. *See* Business to business relationships
B2C. *See* Business to consumer relationships
Beats by Dr. Dre, 7

Beech-Nut Packing Company, 37, 52
Behavioral outcomes, 210, 212–13
"Behind Every Seat Is a Story"
    campaign, 281
Benchmarking, 161–62
Bercovici, Jason, 275
Berliner Stadtmission, 105p
Berman, Richard, 144
Berman and Company, 144
Berry, Judy, 323
Beyond Culture (Hall), 352
Bezos, Jeff, 292
Big data, 207, 208–9, 220
Billable rate, 168
Billboard, 350
Bing, 46, 65
Biographical profiles (bios), 242
Biography of an Idea (Bernays), 36
BK® App, 261–62
Black box fallacy, 56–57, 57p, 58
Black Panther (film), 350
Blogs, 133, 243–45
Blood drives, 133–38, 135p
Bloomberg, Michael, 114
Bloomberg.com, 99
Blue Apron, 191
BODEN, 170–71
Boing Boing, 303
Bolstering, 339, 341
Bonaparte, Napoleon, 46
Boomerang effect, 338
Boomerang videos, 275
Booty, Ed, 357
Boston Children's Hospital, 109p
Boston Tea Party, 43, 44, 44p, 50
Bounce rate, 208
BP. *See* British Petroleum
Brand advocates, 279, 281
Branding, 9, 352. *See also* Personal branding
Brand journalism, 76, 80
Brand Lift, 213
Brand reputation management, 265
Bravely, 282, 283
Bridgeport Hospital, 41
Brigham Young University, 120
British Airways, 324
British Petroleum (BP), 9, 9p, 337–38, 337p
Brochureware, 185
BTS, 350
Budgets, 165–70, 167f, 171
Buffalo Bicycles, 230
Buffer, 269
Bureau of Labor Statistics (BLS), U.S., 142
Burger King, 256, 260–62, 261p
BurrellesLuce, 206t
Burson, Harold, 15
Burson Cohn & Wolfe, 359
Burson-Marsteller, 15, 306, 368
Business regulations, 290
Business to business (B2B)
    relationships, 98–99
Business to consumer (B2C)
    relationships, 97–98
BusinessWire.com, 94, 250
Business writing, 249
BuzzFeed, 352, 392
Buzzoid, 172

California Air Resources Board, 326, 327
Cambridge Analytica, 339–41, 353p
Campus crime safety campaigns, 141
Canadian Public Relations Society, 6
Cannes Lions International Festival of
    Creativity, 13
Canva, 272
Cape Town Partnership, 297
Captions, 269–70
Career Arc, 45
Careers, 374–97
    areas of specialization, 386–89
    competition, loyalty and job changes,
        394–95
    education and continued learning for,
        389–91
    employers, 381–86
    largest employer in the world, 384
    personal branding and, 375–81
    salaries in, 382, 383, 384, 385
Carmel Boutique Inns, 394
Carney, Jay, 292–93
#Carnitasgate, 180
Carroll, Dave, 320, 322–23
Case studies
    Amazon v. NYT, 292–93
    BarkBox marks its territory across media,
        191–92
    Bernays' "Torches of Freedom" march,
        35–37
    Burger King uses mobile app, 260–62
    Chipotle's challenge to act on principles,
        179–81
    Coca-Cola and CSR, 111–14
    Crock-Pot keeps cool, 12–13
    Elon Musk *vs.* feds over free speech, 307–9
    Facebook at congressional hearings, 339–41
    Gillette's "We Believe" campaign, 214–15
    GOAT's Surf Ranch helped by feature story,
        231–34
    handwashing campaign, 158–61
    IHOP flips name, 30–31
    Kimberly-Clark's diversity promotion,
        196–97
    Little Italy Restaurante fires customer,
        323–24
    MasterCard's World Cup campaign, 365–67
    Medtronic rebuilds after Hurricane Maria,
        102–3
    Mickey Mouse ears for charity, 281–82
    net neutrality and situational theory of
        publics, 128–30
    Papa John's fiasco, 4–5
    Red Bull's content marketing strategy, 75
    Strange Fruit controversy, 251–53
    tweeting for clients, 18–21
    Vicks redefines "care," 356–57
    VW issue life cycle, 325–28
    World Bicycle Relief storytelling, 229–30
    Yelp CEO *vs.* new hire, 392–93
Catalyst Award, 196–97
Catholic Church, 48
CBS, 38
CDC. *See* Centers for Disease Control and
    Prevention
Celebrities, 279
Censorship, 246, 278, 362

Census data, 132, 133p
Center for Labor Research and Education, 144
Center for Science in the Public Interest
    (CSPI), 112, 113p
Centers for Disease Control and Prevention
    (CDC), 330, 331, 336
Certificate in Principles of Public Relations,
    390, 390p
Change.org, 155p, 360
Channels (communication), 181–82
Characters (unit of analysis), 135
Charity: water (organization), 3, 3p
Charles Schwab, 193
Charlotte-Mecklenburg Schools, 212
Chatbots, 277
Chewy.com, 123–24
China, 362, 369
Chipotle Mexican Grill, 179–81, 180p, 184,
    330–31, 330p, 336
Chrysler Group LLC, 41, 76
Cigarette smoking. *See* Tobacco products
    and companies
Cil, José, 261
Cince PR & Branding Group, 393
Cision, 206t
Clark, Rob, 110
Clear and present danger doctrine, 291, 307
Clickbait, 226
Click-through rate, 65
Clients/customers.
    See also Consumers
    duty to, 17, 20
    "firing," 323–24
    listening to, 10
    management meetings with, 162–63
    tweeting for, 18–21
Clip books, 204
Clipping services, 204–5
Closed captioning, 271
*Cluetrain Manifesto, The: The End of Business as
    Usual* (Searls and Weinberger), 73
CNN, 76
CNN Money, 30
Coca-Cola Company, 79, 86, 111–14, 112p,
    355, 355p, 365
Coco (film), 350
Code of Athens (1965), C–1, 24
Code of Brussels (2007), C–1, 24
Code of Venice (1961), C–1, 24
Codes of ethics, 23–25.
    See also Institute for Public Relations
    Ethical Standards and Guidelines;
    International Public Relations
    Association Code of Conduct; Public
    Relations Society of America Code of
    Ethics; Society of Professional Journalists
    Code of Ethics
Code-switching, 249
Cognitive outcomes, 210, 212
Cognitive sources of cultural intelligence, 358
Collaborative Leaders Network (CLN), 41
Colored ribbon campaigns, 48, 49p
Columbia University, 43
Comcast, 128, 283
"Coming Together" campaign, 112
Comments (social media sites), 244, 278
Commerce-driven relationships, 97–104

Commission on Public Relations Education, 359, 389
Commitment, 90, 91
Communal relationships, 90, 106
Communication
    AVE limitations in, 216–17
    Barcelona Principles on, 210–13
    budgeting for expenses, 169–70
    dialogic, 370–71
    high-context, 352–53
    integrated, 15
    in integrated marketing communication, 73, 98
    low-context, 352–53
    loyalty and diversity in, 195
    monologic, 370, 371
    planning for, 163
    production of materials for, 163
Communications Act 2003 (UK), 360
Community-based problem-solving, 40
Community management, 277–79
Compensation, 338–39
Competence, 90
Competing duties, 17–18, 20
Competition, 394–95, B-3
Comprehending (hierarchy-of-effects model step), 152
Condé Nast, 350
Conductor (typology), 62p, 63
Cone Communications, 113, 114p, 331
Confidences, safeguarding. *See* Safeguarding confidences
Conflict and controversy (in news), 93, 94t
Conflict management, 320–24
Conflicts of interest, 344–45, B-5
Conlon, Jerome, 352–53
Consent fatigue, 82
Consequentialism, 174
Constraint recognition, 129–30
Consumer Expenditure Survey, 142
Consumer-generated media (CGM), 12
Consumers. *See also* Clients/customers
    B2C relationships, 97–98
    corporate social responsibility and, 112–13
    integrated marketing communication and, 71–72, 98
    PR careers in field of, 388
Content
    ephemeral, 275
    latent, 135–36
    for search engines, writing, 248
    for social media, 267–76
    user generated, 276
Content analysis, 134–36, 139, 204, 205
Content curation, 275–76
Content marketing, 74–76, 80
Content Marketing Institute, 74, 268
Contingency theory, 322–24, 322f
Control (of advertising *vs.* publicity), 68, 69
Control group, 134
Controlled media, 182–84, 194
Control mutuality, 90, 91
Controversy. *See* Conflict and controversy
Convenience, 73, 98
Convergence, 56–63, 79
    cultural, 58–59, 80, 359

divergence and, 62–63
    economic, 59–61, 81–82, 81p, 359
    professional, 61–62
    technological (digital), 56–58, 81–82, 81p, 295–96
Converging Media (Pavlik and McIntosh), 9
Conversational voice, 14
Conversion funnel, 155
Conversion rate, 208
Convince & Convert, 277
Cook, Tim, 285
Cookies, 207
Copyright, 272, 289
    defined, 296
    fair use and, 298–301
    linking and, 303
    symbol of, 296
Copyright infringement, 297–98
Copyright Office, U.S., 298
Corden, James, 360, 361p
Cornell-Liberty Safety Car, 39p
Cornell University, 39
Cornell University Law School Legal Information Institute, 310
Corporate advertising, 186
Corporate social responsibility (CSR), 87, 331–32, 383
    case study, 111–14
    defined, 111
Corporations, 382–83, 384p
Cost. *See also* Budgets; Price
    administrative, 168–69
    of advertising by media type, 63–65, 169–70
    of advertising *vs.* publicity, 68–69
    integrated marketing communication and, 72–73, 98
Cost per thousand (CPM), 63–64, 65
Council of Public Relations Firms, 195
Court and the World, The (Breyer), 289
CPM. *See* Cost per thousand
Creative Commons, 272, 302–3
Credibility, 69, 70, 183–84.
    See also Third-party credibility
Crises, 333–43
    accident, 335
    cultural differences in reaction to, 353
    organizational, 333
    preventable, 335
    response strategies to, 335–39
    social media and, 341–44
    victim, 333–35
Crisis Manager, The (Lerbinger), 335–36
Crispin Porter Bogusky, 381
Critical Mention, 267
Crock-Pot, 1, 12–13, 13p
Crowdsourcing, 6–7, 46, 266
CSR. *See* Corporate social responsibility
Cultural convergence, 58–59, 80, 359
Cultural intelligence, 357–59
Culture, 350–59, 368–69
    defined, 351
    dimensions of, 354–56, 354f
    low- *vs.* high-context, 353
    organizational, 125
    participatory, 59

Current/crisis stage (issue life cycle), 324, 325f, 326–28
Customer relationship management (CRM), 310
Customers. *See* Clients/customers
Cutlip and Center's Effective Public Relations (Broom and Sha), 4

Daily Beast, The, 371
Daily Tar Heel, The, 63
Dallas Morning News, The, 249
Damage control, 4, 7, 10, 15, 16
Damico, Joan, 268
Damned Lies and Statistics (Best), 220
Data, 206–9, 290
    analyzing and presenting, 391
    big, 207, 208–9, 220
    Cambridge Analytica scandal, 339–41, 353p
    first-party, 207
    mobile media and, 259–60
    protection of, 80–83
    third-party, 207
Dateline, 239
Dávalos, Felipe (illustration by), 88p
Deadspin, 300–301
Dean, Howard, 43–44
Decision-making, 18, 21, 174
    strategic (*see* Strategic decision-making)
    tactical, 155
"Declaration of Principles" (Lee), 32–33
Deep links, 303
Deepwater Horizon rig explosion, 9
Defamation, 290, 294–95
Delayed lead, 235
Delgado, James, 242
Dell Computer, 264, 264p
Delta Airlines, 378
Delta Airlines Foundation, 190p
Demand-side platforms (DSPs), 169
Demographics, 129, 209, 350
Deny strategies, 336–37, 340
Deontological ethics, 21, 174
Department of Agriculture, U.S. (USDA), 152, 152p
Department of Defense, U.S. (DOD), 384
Department of Education, U.S., 59, 139
Department of Health and Human Services, U.S., 138
Department of Homeland Security, U.S., 34
Department of Justice, U.S., 304, 385
Department of the Army, U.S., 385
Department of the Interior, U.S., 385, 385p
Dependability, 90
Dependent variables, 203
Descriptions, 247
Detroit neighborhood cleanup, 132p
Detroit News, The, 76
Dialogic communication, 370–71
Dieselgate, 325–28
Digital convergence. *See* Technological convergence
Digital divide, 362, 362f, 363
Digital media. *See also* Internet; Social media
    advertising on, 169–70
    collaborating on, 391
    media monitoring services for, 205

Digital media (*continued*)
plagiarism on, 296–98
planning and, 155
Digital watermarking, 202
Digitaslbi, 121*t*
Diminish strategies, 337
Dine Brands, 32, 33
Direct lead, 236–37
Direct observation, 137–38
Direct-to-consumer (DTC) brands, 177,
191–92
Disclosure of information, B-3–B-4
Discovery, 283
Disneyland, 9
Distributed public relations, 15
Divergence, 62–70
advertising and, 63–65
marketing and, 65–70
Diversity, 80, 194, 195, 196–97, 283, 332
DKNY, 321–23, 321*p*
Dodsworth, Sue, 196–97
Doing Ethics in Media (Black and Roberts), 195,
344–45
Dollar Shave Club, 191
Dominant coalition, 17
Donors, 105–6
Doritos, 59
Dormant stage (issue life cycle), 324,
325*f*, 328
#DoUsAFlavor campaign, 266
Dove, 273*p*
Dropbox, 128
Drug use and health study, 138–41
Dumb and Dumber (film), 186
DuPont, 41, 123

Earl Newsom and Company, 38
Early adopters, 66–67
Early On® Michigan and Genesee Intermediate
School District, 121*t*
Early/potential stage (issue life cycle), 324,
325–26, 325*f*
Earned media, 44, 189–92, 205, 208, 239, 331
eBay, 67, 73, 81
Economic convergence, 59–61, 81–82,
81*p*, 359
Economist, The, 362
Economy, 361–62, 369
Econsultancy, 188
Edelman, 12–13, 246, 382
Edelman Trust Barometer, 363
Edison, Thomas, 41
Education
for PR careers, 389–91
PR in, 42–43, 43*p*
Electronic Arts Inc. (EA), 182–83, 183*p*
Electronic House, 66
eMarketer, 284
Emerging stage (issue life cycle), 324, 325*f*,
326, 343
Emotional/motivational sources of cultural
intelligence, 359
Empathy, 95, 195
Employees. *See also* Personnel
corporate character expressed by, 15
corporate social responsibility and, 113
relations with, 100–103

Employment Policies Institute, 143–44
End-user license agreements (EULA), 284
Enearu, Nicole, 156*p*
Engagement, 210–12, 269
Entertainment, PR careers in, 387–88
Entrepreneur.com, 271
Entrepreneurship, 388
Environmental Protection Agency (EPA), 326–27
Environmental variables, 360–63
Ephemeral content, 275
ePortfolios, 379
Esawo (Malawian dairy farmer), 229–30
ESPN, 235, 236, 282, 297, 378
Ethics, 15–25
codes of (*see* Codes of ethics)
competing duties and, 17–18, 20
competition, loyalty and job changes and,
394–95
conflicts of interest and, 344–45
corporate social responsibility and loyalty
and, 111–14
defined, 16
defining specific issues/conflicts in, 18,
19, 173
deontological, 21, 174
dialogic, 370–71
diversity and loyalty and, 195
free flow of information and data protection
and, 80–83
identifying affected parties in, 18, 20, 173
identifying internal/external factors in,
18, 19, 173
identifying key values in, 18, 19, 173
of independence, 220–22
making and justifying a decision in, 18,
21, 174
reasons for studying, 16–17
safeguarding confidences and, 283–85,
314–16
selecting principles for decision-making in,
18, 21, 174
of transparency, objectivity, and advocacy,
51–52
of tweeting for clients, 18–21
utilitarianism and, 143–45, 175
of writing for mutual understanding, 251
of "zombie" followers, 172–74
Ethiopian Airlines, 335, 336–37, 336*p*
Ethnocentrism, 350–51
Etsy, 73, 297
European Summit on Measurement in
Barcelona, 209
European Union (EU), 81, 82, 290
Evaluation, 118, 119*p*, 163, 164–65, 200–224
Barcelona Principles on (*see* Barcelona
Principles)
media monitoring services for, 204–5,
205*f*, 206*t*
message testing in, 202–3
metrics, analytics and data in, 206–9
in proactive issues management, 329*t*,
332–33
Evans, Chiquita, 235–36, 236*p*
Event planning, 163–64
Excel, 142
*Excellence in Internal Communication
Management* (Men), 127

Exchange relationships, 89, 97
Experiments, 133, 134, 139, 203
Expertise, 16, 19, 173, 251, B-2
Exponential, 275
External publics, 100, 125, 126–28, 173,
310, 390–91
Extra-Strength Tylenol, 334, 334*p*
Eye tracking, 202

Facebook, 3, 10, 12, 47, 133, 134, 135, 139,
151, 162, 192, 214, 237, 245, 270, 271,
274, 275, 276, 277–78, 281, 282, 310,
315, 367
advertising on, 65, 170, 186
conflict management and, 321, 322, 323–24
congressional hearings, 319, 339–41, 340*p*
data use by, 81, 82, 209, 290, 339–41, 353*p*
intellectual property issues and, 296
international differences in, 362
libel on, 294
mobile media and, 259–60
net neutrality issue and, 128
number of users, 46
reposting on, 303
Facebook Live, 274
Facebook Messenger, 277
Facial recognition technology, 81
FactCheck.org, 334–35
Fact sheets, 240
Fair Labor Association (FLA), 331
Fairness, B-2
Fair use, 298–301
Falk, Thomas J., 196
False light, portrayal in, 312–13
Fast Company, 394
Fault, 294–95
FCC. *See* Federal Communications
Commission
FDA. *See* Food and Drug Administration
Feature stories, 231–36
Federal Communications Commission (FCC),
128, 130
Federal Emergency Management Agency
(FEMA), 34
Federalist Papers, The, 43
Federal Trade Commission (FTC), 281, 305,
306
FedEx Cup, 99
Feedback, 10
Feed proofing, 270*p*, 271
FEMA. *See* Federal Emergency Management
Agency
Female Moral Reform Society, 46
Fenton, 218, 219*t*
Ferrari, Josh, 376, 377, 378, 380, 380*p*
Fight for the Future, 128, 131*p*
Fight for the Internet, 130
Financial field, PR careers in, 388
Financial information, 306
Finkelstein, Barry, 343–44
First Amendment, 291–94, 295, 298, 308, 362
First-party data, 207
First sale doctrine, 289
Fiske, Rosanna M., 193–94, 195
Fitbit, 277–78, 306
5W's, 269*f*
Flaherty, Rob, 389

Flaming, 14
Flash mobs, 35, 35p
Fleischman, Doris, 38, 38p, 51
FleishmanHillard, 121t, 282, 306, 382
Florida Public Relations Association, 24
Florida State University, 267
Focus groups, 136–37, 137p, 139, 202–3
Focus Groups as Qualitative Research
  (Morgan), 137
Fontes, Kimberly, 108
Food and Drug Administration (FDA), 305–6
Forbes, 197, 207, 226, 263, 269
Forbes.com, 4, 393
Ford, Henry, 72
Ford, Henry, II, 39
Ford, Patrick, 368–69
Ford Motor Company, 38–39, 178
Formal research, 138–41
Formative research, 118–19, 161–62
Fortune, 100, 196, 293, 328, 336
Four C's of integrated marketing
  communication, 71–73, 98.
    See also Communication; Consumers;
    Convenience; Cost
Four P's of marketing, 66–70, 71.
    See also Place; Price; Product; Promotion
Four R's of stewardship, 106
Four Seasons Hotels and Resorts, 394
Fox News, 299, 299p
Framing, 303
Franklin, Nick, 232
Freedom House, 362
Freedom of Information Act (FOIA), 304–5
Free flow of information, 80–83, B-2–B-3
Freelancers, 272
"Free" media, 170
Free Press, 128, 129–30
Free speech, 291–94, 298, 307–9
Frequency, 169
Frito-Lay, 266
Frohnert, Ashley, 108
FTC. *See* Federal Trade Commission
Functional magnetic resonance imaging
  (fMRI), 202
Funnel, 155, 213
Future Shock (Toffler), 389
Future Workplace, 45

GamingBolt, 183
Gantt charts, 164–65, 164f
Gap, 73, 329, 331
Garmin Connect, 378
Gatorade, 264
Gavankar, Janina, 183p
General Data Protction Regulation (GDPR),
  81, 82, 83, 290
General Electric (GE), 71, 193
General Motors, 76
General public, 2
Geofencing, 260, 261
Geofilter, 260, 261
Geolocation technology, 81, 260, 261
George Washington University Graduate
  School of Political Management, 142
Gertz v. Robert Welch, Inc., 295
Getty Images, 273, 273p, 311–12

Ghiradelli Square, 394
Gialopsos, P. J., 320, 320p
Gig economy, 381
Gillette, 41, 59, 200, 214–15, 214p
Girlgaze, 273p
Gizmodo, 127, 128
Glasgow, Amanda, 364
Glass ceiling, 196
Global Alliance for Public Relations and
  Communication Management, 22,
  213, 359
Global Entrepreneurship Monitor, 364
Global Handwashing Day, 158–61, 159p
Globalization, 359–60, 369
Global public relations, 349–73
  intercultural public relations in, 351,
    368–69
  international public relations in
    (*see* International public relations)
  public diplomacy in, 367–68
GMMB, 282
Goals, 158–59, 158f
  Barcelona Principles on, 210
  defined, 157
  social media tracking of, 171
  writing and, 227–28
Goal thermometer, 162p
GOAT's Surf Ranch, 231–33, 233p
Godiva Chcolatiers, 79
Goebbels, Joseph, 52
Golden hours, 341
Golden mean, 113
Golden rule, 15, 251
Google, 46p, 111, 128, 190–91, 193, 204, 213,
  247, 248, 248p, 310
  advertising on, 65
  data use by, 81, 290
  number of searches per day on, 46
Google AdWords, 190, 208
Google alerts, 142, 204, 245
Google Analytics, 65, 155, 213
@GoogleDocs, 278
Google Places, 12
GoPro, 188, 188p, 275, 276
Government
  careers in, 384–85
  PR in, 43–44
  public information dissemination in, 33–34
Government agencies, 109
Government relations, 109
Grant-Herms, Natalie, 312–13
"Great Firewall of China, The," 362
Great Place to Work Institute, 100
Greenpeace, 360
Greenwashing, 22
Grimaldi, Michael, 330
Grissom, Stacie, 192
Grove, Skye, 297
Güd Marketing, 121t

Halpern, Derek, 268
Handwashing campaign, 148, 158–61,
  159p, 162
Harbour, David, 59
HARO (Help a Reporter Out), 97
Harper-Howie, Kerri, 156p
Harpers Weekly, 305

Harris, Neil Patrick, 282
Harvard College, 43
Hashimoto, Krislyn, 393–94
Hawaiian Electric Co. (HECO), 3, 40–41
Hayward, Tony, 337–38, 337p
Headlines, 247
Healthcare, PR careers in, 386–87, 387p
Heaven (neglected girl), 47
Hegemony, 58
Helvey Communications, 121t
Hennessey, Amy, 216
Henry J. Kaiser Family Foundation, 302–3
Heth, Joice, 28–29, 30p
Hewlett-Packard Co., 3
Hierarchy-of-effects model (McGuire),
  150–55, 151f, 172
  for planning, 154–55
  steps in, 151–54
High-context cultures/communication,
  352–53
Hill, George Washington, 36
Hill and Knowlton, 51
Hilton Hotels & Resorts, 394
HiSmile, 186
Hispanic Heritage Month, 355
Hispanic Public Relations Association, 6
Holiday, Billie, 252
Holmes Report, 356, 382f
Honesty/truthfulness, 7–8, 22, 51, B-2
Hootsuite, 206t, 267, 271
Horn, Michael, 327, 327p
H&R Block, 18
HubSpot.com, 167f
Huffington Post, 215, 320
Hulu, 266p
Human interest (in news), 93, 94t, 235
Humans of New York (photography project), 321
Hunt, Bertha, 36
Hurricane Maria, 102–3, 110
Hyatt Hotels and Resorts, 394
Hyperlinks, 303

IABC. *See* International Association of Business Communicators
I and Thou (Buber), 370
IBM, 99, 100p, 354
Iceland Foods, 360, 361p
Identification (proactive issues management
  step), 329–30, 329f
iDigic.net, 172
IG Audit, 174
I.G. Farben, 32
Ikea, 59
Imada, Bill, 79–80
Images (in social media), 271–73
  captions for, 269–70
  consistent look and feel for, 271
  permission for use, 272–73
  quality maintenance, 272
  stock, 273
Impacts, 161
Implementation, 118, 177–99
  choosing channels, 181–82
  by media type, 182–92
  in proactive issues management,
    329t, 331–32
  taking action, 178–81

Impression management, 228–29
Impressions, 154, 217
Inbound marketing, 74
Indeed.com, 103
Independence, 19, 220–22, B-2
Independent variables, 203
India, 356–57
Individualism-collectivism (cultural dimension), 354, 354f, 355
Industrial Revolution, 71, 72p, 73
Influence, 227
Influencer outreach, 391
Influencers, 279–81.
    See also Social media influencers
Informal research, 119, 138–41
Information
    disclosure of, B-3–B-4
    free flow of, 80–83, B-2–B-3
    material, 33, 309
    public (see Public information)
Ingratiation, 339, 341
In house personnel, 123
Initial public offerings (IPOs), 306
Insider trading, 309
Instagram, 7, 47, 133, 149, 162, 165, 169, 170, 172, 192, 214, 245, 270, 271, 275, 276, 281, 282, 297, 379
    advertising on, 186
    blocking users or words from, 279p
    data use by, 80, 209
    @ihavethisthingwithfloors, 272p
    integrated marketing communication on, 70
    libel on, 294
    mobile media and, 259
    #sponsored photos on, 279
Instagram Live, 274
Institute for Public Relations (IPR), 89, 145, 209, 219, 313, 315, 368
Institute for Public Relations (IPR) Ethical Standards and Guidelines, D-1
Institutional advertising, 77
Integrated communication, 15
Integrated marketing communication, 61–62, 62p, 63
    defined, 71
    four C's of (see Four C's of Integrated marketing communication)
    hybrid functions, 73–76
Integrity, 90
Intellectual property, 289–90, 295–303, 313, 322
    copyright (see Copyright)
    defined, 289
    digital age issues, 301–3
    fair use and, 298–301
    patents, 296
    plagiarism, 296–98
    trademarks, 296
Interbrand, 111
Intercultural public relations, 351, 368–69.
    See also Culture
Internal publics, 100, 125–28, 310, 390–91
International Association for Measurement and Evaluation of Communication (AMEC), 209
International Association of Business Communicators (IABC), 24

International Council on Clean Transportation (ICCT), 325
International House of Pancakes (IHOP), 27, 30–31, 31p
International Paper Co., 71
International public relations, 369
    issues in, 359–64
    PR careers in, 389
International Public Relations Association (IPRA), 22, 359, 364
International Public Relations Association (IPRA) Code of Conduct, C-1–C-3, 24–25
International Women's Day, 156–57
Internet, 237.
    See also Digital media; Social media
    advertising on, 64–65
    agitation on, 47–48
    data use on (see Data)
    digital divide and, 362, 362f, 363
    legitimacy conferred by, 46
    marketing on, 67
    net neutrality issue, 117p, 128–30, 130p, 131p
    owned media on, 184–85
Internet of Things (IoT), 283–84
Internships, 380–81
Interpublic Group, 59, 79
Interviews, 136, 139
Intrusion into seclusion, 310
Inverted pyramid writing style, 236–37, 237f, 239
Investor relations, 103–4, 113
Investor's Business Daily, 103
Iowa State University, 353
IPR. See Institute for Public Relations
IPRA. See International Public Relations Association
IRS, 59
Issue, defined, 106
Issue life cycle, 324–28, 325f
Issues-driven relationships, 104–9
Issues management, 324–33, 343–44
    defined, 324
    proactive, 328–33, 329t
"It Can Wait" campaign, 120p
Items (unit of analysis), 135
"It's a Tide Ad" (commercial), 59–60, 60p
iTunes, 67
IW Group, 79

James, Lejuan, 280p
James, Saint, 48
Jane, Talia, 392–93, 392p
Japan National Tourism Organization, 3
Jenner, Kylie, 7, 279
Johnson & Johnson, 334
John Wiley & Sons Inc., 289
Jonas Brothers, 258
Journalism. See also Media relations; News-driven relationships
    advocacy discouraged in, 51–52
    being useful to reporters, 96–97
    brand, 76, 80
    empathizing with reporters, 95
    integrated marketing communication and, 73–74

objectivity and, 51
publicity and, 69
relationship with reporters, 12
Journal of Mass Media Ethics, 52, 345
Journal of Public Relations Research, 50
Joyner, Tom, 249–50
JPMorgan Chase, 388
Judicial awareness, 290, 313
Just Be Inc., 47
"Just Do It" campaign, 352–53

Kaepernick, Colin, 95p
Kaiser Health News, 301p, 302–3
Kam, Nathan, 216
Kana, Ariel, 393
Kardashian, Kim, 279, 335
KC Water, 330
KD/PR Virtual, 121t
Kelleher, Tom, 233p, 249p
Keller, Andrew, 381
"Kelly Slater's Shock Wave" (Finnegan), 231–34
Kelly Slater Wave Company, The, 232–34, 233p, 234p
Ketchum, 59, 121t, 213, 382, 389
Kevo deadbolt, 66, 67, 178
Keywords, 46, 65, 208, 212, 246–47, 267
Keyword stuffing, 247
Kimberly-Clark Corp., 196–97, 197p
Kim Jong Un, 32
Kindelan, Megan, 142
King, Bernice, 215
King, Martin Luther, Jr., 267
King's College, 43
Kirtsaeng, Supap, 289
Kirtsaeng v. John Wiley & Sons, Inc., 289
Kraft, Robert, 336
Kwi, 121t
Kwikset, 66, 67, 179

Landscape orientation (video), 274
Las Vegas Color Run, 163p
Late Late Show with James Corden (television program), 258
Latent content, 135–36
Latent publics, 128, 129, 132
Latino Rebels, 355
Lead
    delayed, 235
    direct, 236–37
Learning (hierarchy-of-effects model step), 152–53
Legal issues, 288–318
    data use, 81, 82
    defamation, 290, 294–95
    free speech, 291–94, 298, 307–9
    intellectual property (see Intellectual property)
    privacy, 310–13
    protecting publics, 305–9
    public information, 304–5
Legislative relations, 109
Legitimacy, 45–46
LEGO, 70
Level of involvement, 129
Levi's, 9
Lewis, Wendy, 156

Li, Tiffany, 82
Libel, 294, 303
Licensure, 23
Likert-type items, 212, 212f
Liking (hierarchy-of-effects model step), 151–52
Linear story arcs, 275
LinkedIn, 186, 271, 315f, 316, 376, 379
Links, 247–48, 303
Lion Air, 337
Listening
    defined, 10
    social, 263–67, 277
    visual, 264–67, 277
Listicles, 226
Little Italy Restaurante, 323–24
Live streaming, 274
Lobbying, 109
Localization, 364, 364p
Lockheed Martin, 188–89, 189p
London Business School, 357
Longer form (writing), 243–45
Long-term orientation, 354, 354f
Looping videos, 275
Love Cobain, Courtney, 294, 295p
#LOVEISON, 61p
Low-context cultures/communication, 352–53
Lowe's, 70
Lowy, Ben, 232
Loyalty, 16, 19, B–2
    corporate social responsibility and, 111–14
    defined, 195
    diversity and, 195
    job changes and, 394–95
Luquire George Andrews, 343

Macron, Emmanuel, 367
Macy's, 186
Maine Public Relations Association, 24
Makalima-Ngewana, Bulelwa, 297
Make-A-Wish® Foundation, 281–82
Management by objectives (MBO), 162
Management function, 11
Managing Public Relations (Grunig and Hunt), 3, 28, 87
Marketing, 65–70
    content, 74–76, 80
    defined, 65–66
    divergence and, 65–70
    four P's of (see Four P's of marketing)
    inbound, 74
    PR and advertising integration with (see Integrated marketing communication)
    PR compared with, 77–78, 77t, 79
Marketing mix, 66–70
Market research reports, 132–33
Market skimming, 66–67
Marriott International, 283
Martin Luther King, Jr. National Historic Park, 190p
Masculinity-femininity (cultural dimension), 354, 354f, 356
Mashable, 75
Massachusetts Summer Legislative Intern Program, 388p
MasterCard, 365–67, 366p
Material information, 33, 309

McCorkindale, Tina, 219–20
McDonald's, 18, 58, 79, 156–57, 156p, 170–71, 186, 260–62
McDonalidization, 58
McDowell, Gayle Laakmann, 393
Measurable objectives, 160
Measurement, D–1, 218–19.
    See also Barcelona Principles; Metrics
Measure What Matters (Payne), 218
Media, 182–92
    budgeting for expenses, 169–70
    consumer-generated, 12
    controlled, 182–84, 194
    duty to, 17, 20
    earned, 44, 189–92, 205, 208, 239, 331
    "free," 170
    global public relations and, 362–63, 369
    mixed, 191
    mobile (see Mobile media)
    multi- (see Multimedia)
    news (see Journalism; News-driven relationships; News media; News stories)
    owned, 184–85, 191–92, 194, 208, 331
    paid, 186–87, 191–92, 208, 331
    participatory, 88
    production of materials for, 163
    shared, 187–89, 191–92, 205, 208, 331
    uncontrolled, 182–84, 194
Media catching, 96, 97
Media gatekeepers, 190, 192, 238–39
Media kits, 241
Media lists, 133
Media monitoring services, 204–5, 205f, 206t, 298–99
Media planning, 169
Media relations, 69, 78, 92–93
Mediated public diplomacy, 367–68
Medium.com, 156, 213, 292–93, 392–93, 392p
Medtronic, 102–3, 110
Memeburn, 5, 297
Mercedes, 378
Mercer University, 313
Merrill Lynch, 38
Message testing, 202–3
Messi, Lionel, 366, 366p
Meta tags, 247
MetLife, 79
#MeToo, 47–48, 47p
Metrics, 206–9. See also Measurement
Mexican Association of Public Relations Professionals, 24
Miami Herald, The, 249
Microblogs, 245–46
Micro-influencers, 280–81
Microsoft, 111, 367
Milano, Alyssa, 47, 47p, 48
Minimum wage issue, 143–44, 143p, 144p
Mission, 157, 158f
Mission statements, 123–24
MIT, 271
MIT Technology Review, 311–12
Mixed media, 191
Mixed-motive model, 39
#MLK2019, 267
Mobile media, 258–63, 263p, 283
    localization and, 260

    personalization in, 259–60
    social networks accessed on, 258–59
    as ubiquitous, 258
    uses and gratifications of, 262–63
Mondelez International, 107–8
Monitoring (proactive issues management step), 328–29, 329f
Monologic communication, 370, 371
Moore, Carissa, 66, 75
Moran, Monty, 336
Morano, Robert M., 309
Morgue (news organization archives), 241
MSL, 356
MTV Networks, 193
Mule Deer Foundation, 281
Multimedia, 268–69, 283, 391.
    See also Images; Text; Video
Multipliers, 216–17, 221
Multivariate testing, 206–7
Musk, Elon, 288, 307–9, 308f
Myers, Cayce, 313–14, 315, 316
Mystic Hotel by Charlie Palmer, 394

NAACP, 41, 51
Nabisco, 107–8
NASA, 274
National Association of Black Journalists, 250
National Association of Minority Media Executives, 250
National Black Public Relations Association, 6
National Black Public Relations Society Inc., 250
National Do Not Call Registry, 306
National Education Association, 342
National Employment Law Project, 144
National Geographic, 218
National Investor Relations Institute, 103
National Jewish Outreach Program, 42
National Kidney Foundation Serving North Texas, 250
National Oceanic and Atmospheric Administration (NOAA), 241–42
National Park Service, 190p
National Public Radio (NPR), 9, 46, 303
National School Public Relations Association, 24
Native advertising, 186, 187
Natural links, 247
Nature Conservancy, 105
Nazis (Lee's work with), 32, 52
NBA, 231, 235, 283
NBA 2K (video game), 235–36, 236p
NBC, 12–13
NBC Nightly News (television program), 30
Netflix, 128, 129, 130p, 266, 310
Net neutrality, 117, 128–30, 130p, 131p
Newell Brands, 12–13
New England Patriots, 336
News-driven relationships, 92–97.
    See also Journalism
Newsjacking, 266–67
News media
    defined, 92
    writing for, 238–42
Newsom, Earl, 38–39, 178
Newspaper advertising, 169
News releases, 30, 189, 239–40, 240p, 250

News stories
    about key publics, 133
    writing, 236–38
Newsworthiness, 74, 93–94, 239, 240
New Yorker, The, 47, 231, 232
New York Times, The, 6, 41, 43, 44, 47, 144, 292–93, 326, 336
New York Times Co. v. Sullivan, 295
New York Times Magazine, The, 111
Nextdoor, 330
Neymar Jr., 366, 366*p*
NFL, 61, 300–301
#NFLBlitz, 274*p*
NGOs. *See* Nongovernmental organizations
Nielsen surveys, 113, 126, 201–2, 258
Nike, 7, 329, 331, 352–53, 378
90-10 rule, 9
Nissan North America, 79
Non-compete clauses, 395, 395*p*
Nongovernmental organizations (NGOs), 2, 108, 383–84
Non-linear story arcs, 275
Nonparticipant observation, 137
Nonprofit organizations, 105–6, 108, 383–84
North Block in Napa Valley, 394
NPR. *See* National Public Radio

Oahu Visitors Bureau, 394
Obama, Barack, 44
Objectives, 158*f*
    defined, 157
    SMART, 159–60, 164, 169, 172, 210
    social media tracking of, 171
    writing and, 227–28
Objectivity, 51–52
Obscene material, 303
Observer, 307
Ocasio-Cortez, Alexandria, 209, 335
Öffentlichkeitsarbeit, 45
Ogilvy Interactive, 282
Ogilvy & Mather, 9
Ogilvy Public Relations Worldwide, 123
Oglethorpe, James, 45
Ohio State University, 380
Olson, Bo, 292
Omar, Ilhan, 335
Omnicom, 59, 359
One Billion Rising movement, 35, 35*p*
#175Stories, 281
One-to-many approach, 277
Openness, 88, 89
OpenSecrets.org, 109
OPI, 275*p*
Opinion elites, 280
Opponents (publics as), 131
Opportunities (SWOT analysis), 120, 121–22
Opportunity statements, 120
Opportunity to see (OTS), 217
Oracle Arena, 99
Organic search results, 46
Organizational crises, 333
Organizational culture, 125
Organizations, 2–3
    Barcelona Principles on performance of, 213
    defined, 2
    beyond offerings, 77

past communication records with key publics, 133
    as publics, 106–9
    research on, 123–25
Outcomes
    attitudinal, 210, 212
    Barcelona Principles on, 210–13
    behavioral, 210, 212–13
    cognitive, 210, 212
    defined, 161
    hierarchy of (*see* Hierarchy-of-effects model)
    measurement models, 218–19, 218*t*, 219*t*
Outputs, 160–61, 210, 212
Overhead expenses, 168
Owned media, 184–85, 191–92, 194, 208, 331

Pabst, 378
Pacific Gas & Electric Company, 79
Page titles, 247
Paid media, 186–87, 191–92, 208, 331
Palestine, UN recognition of, 46
Palm Beach Post, 233
Paluzek, John, 213
Pandora, 263–64
Panera, 266, 370*p*
Papa John's, 4–5, 5*p*, 33
Parker, George, 32
Parker & Lee, 32
Participant observation, 137
Participatory culture, 59
Participatory media, 88
Patagonia, 218, 331, 332*p*
Patent and Trademark Office, U.S. (USPTO), 296
Patents, 296
Patterson, Jennifer, 312–13
Paul, Saint, 42, 42*p*, 44
Pay per click, 186
PayScale.com, 382
PBS, 93
PCWorld, 14
Peace Corps, 351
Pennsylvania Railroad, 32, 33
People for the Ethical Treatment of Animals (PETA), 105, 107–8, 281
Personal branding, 375–81
Person-centric personal branding, 377–78
Personnel. *See also* Employees
    budgeting for, 165–68
    in house, 123
Persuasion, 227
PETA. *See* People for the Ethical Treatment of Animals
Pew Research Center, 51, 259, 362
Physical sources of cultural intelligence, 358–59
Pinterest, 70, 143, 170, 190, 191, 212*p*, 271, 296, 303
Pitching, 93–97
Place (in marketing mix), 67, 73
Plagiarism, 296–98
Plank Center for Leadership in Public Relations, 368, 383*p*
Planning, 118, 148–76
    of budgets, 165–70
    defined, 149

proactive issues management step overlap with, 329*t*
    strategic (*see* Strategic decision-making)
    timelines, 161–65, 166*f*
Policymakers, 114
Politics
    global public relations and, 360–61, 369
    PR careers in, 388
    PR in, 43–44
@Pontifex, 42
Pop-Up Paradigm, The (Gonzalez), 149
Pop-ups, 65, 149
Portlandia (television program), 72–73
Portmanteu words, 226
Portrayal in a false light, 312–13
Positive personal branding, 376–77
Positivity, 88
Postmates, 261
Pötsch, Hans-Dieter, 327
Power distance, 354, 354*f*, 356
PR Council, 368, 387
Pre-roll advertising, 64*p*, 65
Press agentry/publicity model, 29*f*, 34, 37, 38
    defined, 31
    described, 31–32
Press conferences, 182–83
Press releases. *See* News releases
Preventable crises, 335
Price (in marketing mix), 66–67, 72. *See also* Cost
Primary public, 131
Primary research, 138
Princeton University, 43
Principled public relations, 7–15
    action in, 9, 178
    company character expression in, 15
    good-humored attitude in, 12–14
    listening in, 10
    managing for tomorrow in, 10–11
    truthfulness in, 7–9
    whole company approach in, 11
Print media advertising, 63, 169
Prioritization (proactive issues management step), 329*f*, 330
Pritchard, Marc, 60, 215
Privacy, 81, 283–85, 339–41
    defined, 290
    legal issues, 310–13
"Privacy-Focused Vision for Social Networking, A" (Zuckerberg), 341
PRNews, 92, 108, 200, 215
PRNewswire, 94, 97, 250
Proactive issues management, 328–33, 329*t*
Proactive management style, 10–11, 16
Problem recognition, 129, 130
Problem statements, 120
Pro bono work, 165
Procter & Gamble (P&G), 41, 60, 215
Product (in marketing mix), 66, 71
Professional associations, 24–25
Professional convergence, 61–62
Profit, 48–49
ProfNet, 96*p*, 97
Programmatic media buying, 169–70
Projects, 380–81
Promising personal branding, 377
Promotion, 48, 68–70, 73

Propaganda, 48
Proponents (publics as), 131
Proselytizing (hierarchy-of-effects model step), 153–54
PRovoke18 Global Public Relations Summit, 356
Proximity (of news), 93, 94*t*
PRSA. *See* Public Relations Society of America
PR Squared (blog), 18
PRSSA. *See* Public Relations Student Society of America
PR Watch, 9
PRWeek, 195, 368
Pseudo-events, 42, 43, 44*p*, 45
Psychographics, 129
Psychology Today, 101
Public affairs
defined, 109
PR careers in, 388
Public affairs officers (PAOs), 34
Public diplomacy, 367–68
Public disclosure of private facts, 312
Public domain, 272, 304–5
Public figures, 295, 309
Public information, 304–5
Public information model, 28, 29*f*, 38, 41, 51
defined, 32
described, 32–34
Public information officers (PIOs), 33–34
Publicis Communications Asia Pacific, 357
Publicis Groupe, 59, 359
Publicity, 68–70, 78, 87, 88, 183, 189
Public relations
core differences in, 77–78
defining, 2–7
distributed, 15
duty to profession, 17, 20
major motivations for, 44–49
social history of, 41–44
Public Relations as Relationship Management (Ledingham and Bruning), 88
Public Relations Consultants' Association of Malaysia (PRCA Malaysia), 24
Public Relations Ethics (Seib and Fitzpatrick), 17
Public Relations Institute of Ireland (PRII), 24
Public Relations Journal, 142
Public relations models, 28–41.
See also Asymmetrical model; Press agentry/publicity model; Public information model; Symmetrical model
Public Relations Society of America (PRSA), 2, 41, 142, 174, 194, 330, 343, 354
Award of Excellence, 377
PR defined by, 6–7
Silver Anvil awards, 120, 121*t*, 193
Public Relations Society of America (PRSA) Code of Ethics, 22, 23, 24, B–1–B–6
on advocacy, 48, 51–52, 291, B–2
on competition, 395, B–3
on conflicts of interest, 344, B–5
on disclosure of information, B–3–B–4
diversity and, 195
on enhancing the profession, 174, B–5–B–6
on expertise, 251, B–2
on fairness, B–2
on free flow of information, 82, B–2–B–3

on honesty, B–2
on independence, 221, B–2
on loyalty, 112, 195, 395, B–2
member pledge, B–6
member statement of values, B–1–B–2
preamble, B–1
provisions of, B–2–B–6
on safeguarding confidences, 284, 314, B–4–B–5
Public Relations Strategist, The, 218
Public Relations Student Society of America (PRSSA), 3, 6, 111
Public Relations Tactics (PRSA), 354
Publics, 2–3
active, 128, 129, 132
beyond audiences, 77–78
aware, 128, 129, 132
defined, 2, 126, 351
external, 100, 125, 126–28, 173, 310, 390–91
general, 2
internal, 100, 125–28, 310, 390–91
latent, 128, 129, 132
as organizations, 106–9
primary, 131
protecting, 305–9
public utilities and, 40–41
research on, 125–33
secondary, 131
situational theory of, 128–30
tertiary, 131
Public utilities, 40–41
Publix, 2, 2*p*
Pulizzi, Joe, 268
Pure accommodation, 322
Pure advocacy, 322
Putting the Public Back in Public Relations (Solis and Breakenridge), 229

QSR Magazine, 261
Qualitative research, 136–38, 141, 215, 245
Barcelona Principles on, 213
defined, 136
Qualtrics, 339
Quantitative research, 133–36, 141, 215, 245
Barcelona Principles on, 213
defined, 133
Quiamno, Sage, 376, 377, 379*p*, 380
Quintos, Karen, 264

RACE mnemonic, 118, 119
"Racial Image Challenges Big Business" (*Times* article), 41
Radio advertising, 169
Ranker, 393
Rao, Rekha, 356
RCC. *See* Religion Communicators Council
Reach, 169
Reactive management style, 10, 16
Readability tests, 203
Real-time bidding (RTB), 169
"Real You Is Sexy, The" campaign, 70
Rebelez, Darren, 30–31
Rebuild strategies, 337–39, 340
Reciprocity (stewardship step), 106
Recruitment, 44–45
Red Bull, 55, 75, 75*p*

Reddit, 190
Reinforce strategies, 339, 341
Relational maintenance strategies, 88–89
Relational public diplomacy, 367–68
Relationship management, 86–116
commerce-driven, 97–104
issues-driven, 104–9
key outcomes of, 89–92
news-driven, 92–97
strategies for, 88–89
Relationship nurturing (stewardship step), 106
Relationships
communal, 90, 106
exchange, 89, 97
beyond sales, 78
social media for, 88, 276–81
taking care of, 88–89
writing to build, 227
Relevance (of news), 93, 94*t*
Relevant objectives, 160
Reliability, 139–40, 141
Religion, 42, 43*p*, 45, 48
Religion Communicators Council (RCC), 24, 42
Remembering (hierarchy-of-effects model step), 153
Renshae, Mark, 13
Replicability, 218
Reporting (stewardship step), 106
Reposting, 303
Reputation management, 228, 265
Research, 117–47, 163
ethical standards for, D–1
formal, 138–41
formative, 118–19, 161–62
informal, 119, 138–41
primary, 138
proactive issues management step overlap with, 329*t*
qualitative (*see* Qualitative research)
quantitative (*see* Quantitative research)
secondary, 138
situation analysis (*see* Situation analysis)
summative, 119
Research Triangle Institute, 138
Responsibility (stewardship step), 106
Responsible supply chain management, 329
Restaurant Brands International Inc., 261
Reuters, 336
Revlon, 61*p*
Risk Issues and Crisis Management in Public Relations (Regester and Larkin), 326
Ritchie, Steve, 5
Rite Aid, 104*p*
Rockefeller family, 32
Rodriguez, Rafael, 103
ROPE mnemonic, 118, 119
ROSIE mnemonic, 118
Royal Dutch Shell, 388
RPIE Cycle, 118–19, 118*f*, 125, 149*f*, 161, 178, 178*f*, 192, 201, 201*f*, 209, 328, 329*t*. *See also* Evaluation; Implementation; Planning; Research
Rumors, 334–35
Russian government (as a client), 59

Saatchi & Saatchi, 60
Safeguarding confidences, 283–85, 314–16, B–4–B–5
Salaries. *See under* Careers
Salem State University, 42
Salesforce.com, 18
SAMHSA. *See* Substance Abuse and Mental Health Services Administration
Samsung Electronics, 186, 388
San Diego State University, 45, 143
Santiago, Shane, 282–83
Satisfaction, 90, 91
Saturday Night Live (television program), 350
"Save the Internet" campaign, 128
Sawant, Gauri, 356–57
SBNation, 300–301, 300*p*
SBS Studios, 282–83
Scapegoating, 336
SCCT. *See* Situational crisis communication theory
Schnatter, John, 4, 5*p*
Search advertising, 65
Search engine optimization (SEO), 46, 190–91, 246, 248
Search engines, writing for, 246–48
@SearchLiaison, 248
SEC. *See* Securities and Exchange Commission
Secilmis, Argu, 149
Seclusion, intrusion into, 310
Secondary publics, 131
Secondary research, 138
Securities and Exchange Commission (SEC), 3, 33, 305, 306, 307–9, 328
See-say-feel-do model, 218, 219*t*
SEGA, 277
Segmenting referring sources, 208
Selective attention, 257
Self, duty to, 17, 20
Self-efficacy, 359
Self-employment, 385–86, 386*p*
Sentiment, 265
SEO. *See* Search engine optimization
Sexual assault and harassment, 47–48
"Share a Coke" campaign, 355, 355*f*
Shared media, 187–89, 191–92, 205, 208, 331
#ShareYourEars campaign, 281–82, 282*p*
Sharing tasks, 89
SHIFT Communications, 18–21, 76
Shorter form (writing), 245–46
#ShotoniPhone campaign, 272
#ShowUs project, 273*p*
Silver Anvil awards, 120, 121*t*, 193
Silver Lion award, 13
Simorangkir, Dawn, 294
Situational crisis communication theory (SCCT), 333, 336
Situational theory of publics, 128–30
Situation analysis, 120–33
    defined, 120
    examples of, 121*t*
    organization research, 123–25
    publics research, 125–33
    situation research, 120–23
Situation research, 120–23
Slander, 294
Slater, Kelly, 231–34, 236
Small Business Administration, 385

Small businesses, 385–86, 386*p*
SMART objectives, 159–60, 164, 169, 172, 210
SMCC. *See* Social media crisis communication model
Snackable content, 274
Snapchat, 186, 210, 245, 259, 260, 260*p*, 270, 271, 274, 275
Snopes.com, 334–35
Social and Environmental Responsibility (SER) audits, 331
Socialbakers, 174
Social listening, 263–67, 277
Social media, 263–82. *See also* Digital media; Internet
    accounts of key publics' representatives, 133
    analytics, 162
    Barcelona Principles on, 217
    career skills needed for, 391
    comments on, 244, 278
    community management on, 277–79
    conflict management on, 320–24
    content creation for, 267–76
    crises and, 341–44
    duty to, 20
    employee relations and, 101
    ethical communication in, 18, 22
    global public relations and, 362, 363
    images in (*see* Images)
    intellectual property issues, 301–3
    mobile devices and, 258–59
    moderating pages on, 278–79
    organizational control of, 314–16
    politics and, 43–44
    production of materials for, 163
    recruitment via, 45
    relationship management and building on, 88, 276–81
    religions using, 42
    rumors on, 334–35
    sharing on, 187–89
    social listening and, 263–67, 277
    text in, 269–71
    tracking objectives and goals on, 171
    video in, 273–75
    visual listening and, 264–67, 277
    writing for, 243–46, 250
    "zombie" followers on, 172–74
Social media creators, 342
Social media crisis communication model (SMCC), 342–43, 345
Social media followers, 342
Social media inactives, 342
Social media influencers, 7, 70, 227. *See also* Influencers
Social media releases, 239
Social monitoring, 264
Social Native, 263
Social networking, 89
"Social Responsibility of Business Is to Increase Its Profits, The" (Friedman), 111
Social Triggers, 268
Society, duty to, 17, 20
Society of Professional Journalists (SPJ) Code of Ethics, 51, 52
Sonic the Hedgehog, 277
Sons of Liberty, 44
Sons of Maxwell, 320

Sony Pictures, 283
Southwest Airlines, 281, 312–13
Space (unit of analysis), 135
Spam, 278
Spambots, 221
"Special Message from *This Is Us*, A" (video), 13
Specific objectives, 159
Speech, free, 291–94, 298, 307–9
Spin, 4, 7, 10, 15, 16
"Spin Sucks" (blog), 185*f*
Sports, PR careers in, 387–88
Sports Illustrated, 267
Spotify, 259–60, 259*p*
Sprout Social, 269
St. John & Partners, 283
St. Jude Children's Research Hospital, 91*p*
Standard Oil, 38
Stanton, Brandon, 321–23
Starbucks, 262, 264, 378
"Start Something Priceless" campaign, 365–467
Starwood Hotels & Resorts, 394
Statista.com, 46
Status conferral, 45
Stealing thunder, 345
Stefani, Gwen, 282
Stettner, Jon, 282
Stewardship, 106
Stills, Kenny, 95*p*
Stock images, 273
Stoppelman, Jeremy, 392–93
Story arcs, 275
Story placement, 97
Storytelling, 74, 229–38, 257
Strange Fruit Public Relations, 251–53
Strategic Business Insights, 133
Strategic Communications Planning (Wilson and Ogden), 120
Strategic decision-making, 155–61, 171
    defined, 155
    in proactive issues management, 329*t*, 331
Strategic personal branding, 375–76
Strategic Planning for Public Relations (Smith), 161
Strategy, 157
Strengths (SWOT analysis), 120–21, 122
Stryker, Weiner & Yokota, 393
Student Reporting Labs (television program), 93
Subaru, 362
Subject matter experts (SMEs), 280
Substance Abuse and Mental Health Services Administration (SAMHSA), 138–39, 139*p*, 140
Subtitles, 270–71
Summative research, 119
Sunshine laws, 290, 304–5
Super Bowl advertising, 59–61, 63, 215
Supply-side platforms (SSPs), 169
Supreme Court, U.S., 289, 291, 295
Surfrider Foundation, 108*p*, 109
Surveys, 132, 133, 134, 139
Swift, Taylor, 43
Swiss Red Cross, 134
SWOT analysis, 120–22, 122*p*

Symbols (unit of analysis), 135
Symmetrical model, 28, 29f, 371
   defined, 38
   described, 38–41
Sysomos, 264

Tactical decision-making, 155
Tactics, 149, 157, 158f, 171
Talkwalker, 264
Tannehill, Ryan, 300p
Target, 73, 192, 338–39, 338p
Target audience, 78
TechCrunch, 18
Tech for Good Summit, 367, 368p
Technological (digital) convergence, 56–58,
   81–82, 81p, 295–96
Television advertising, 169, 170
Television coverage evaluation, 204
"10 Skills the PR Pro of 2022 Must Have"
   (Hanson), 390–91
Tertiary publics, 131
Tesla, 288, 307–9
Text (in social media), 269–71
Texting, 352
Them, 350
Third-party credibility, 69, 184, 217
Third-party data, 207
This Is Us (television program), 12–13
Threats (SWOT analysis), 120, 121–22
3M, 9
Tide, 59–60
Timberland, 149, 150p
Time (unit of analysis), 135
Time-bound objectives, 160
Timelessness (of stories), 235
Timelines, 161–65, 166f
Timeliness (of news), 93, 94t
T-Mobile, 280p
Tobacco products and companies, 35–37,
   38, 61
Tom Joyner Morning Show
   (television program), 249
Top-tier influencers, 279–80
"Torches of Freedom" march, 35–37
Torts, 310
Total market approach, 350
"Touch of Care" campaign, 356–57, 357p
Town crier (typology), 31, 62p, 63
Toyota, 79, 228
Tracking visitor behavior, 208
Trademarks, 296
Trade secrets, 315–16, 395
Transmedia storytelling, 233
Transparency, 8–9, 17, 19, 21, 33, 51–52, 173,
   174, 221
   Barcelona Principles on, 217–18
   on data use practices, 81, 82
   defined, 8
   in nonprofit organizations, 106
TransWorld Airlines, 38
Treatment group, 134
Trebek, Alex, 237–38, 238p
TripAdvisor, 12
True North, 79
Trump, Donald, 32, 44, 68p, 130, 335
Trust, 78, 90, 91, 100–101, 363
Truthfulness/honesty, 7–8, 22, 51, B–2

Tuning in (hierarchy-of-effects
   model step), 151
Turnitin, 296
TVEyes, 298–99
TweetDeck, 267, 268
Twibel, 294
Twitter, 7, 10, 12, 43, 47, 59, 133, 169, 180,
   187, 188–89, 191, 210, 237, 245–46,
   245f, 248, 263, 271, 276, 281, 342
   advertising on, 65
   asking questions on, 371
   data use by, 81, 209
   integrated marketing communication on, 70
   intellectual property issues and, 296, 301–2
   international differences in, 362
   libel on, 294
   #MLK2019, 267
   number of daily views on, 273
   Pope's page, 42
   reposting on, 303
   @StrangeFruit controversy, 252–53, 252p
   Tesla stock tweet, 307–9
   tweeting for clients, 18–21
Two-way communication, 10, 163, 181, 227,
   276, 362, 371. See also Asymmetrical
   model; Symmetrical model
Tyson Foods, 18

UAB. See Universal Accreditation Board
Uber, 367
Uber Eats, 261
Ultimate Fighting Championship (UFC),
   300–301
Uncertainty avoidance, 354, 354f, 355–56
Uncommitted (publics as), 131
Unconferences, 164
Uncontrolled media, 182–84, 194
UNICEF, 158–59, 160, 161, 162
United Airlines, 320–23, 324
"United Breaks Guitars" (video), 320, 320p
United Nations, 46, 158, 270p
United Nations Foundation, 218
Universal Accreditation Board (UAB), 24, 50,
   390, 390p
Universal Accreditation Board (UAB)
   competencies, 398–401
Universal Pictures, 186
University of Alabama, 42
University of Amsterdam, 31
University of California Berkeley, 144
University of Chicago Magazine, The, 226
University of Colorado, 357
University of Florida, 11, 170, 376
University of Georgia, 42, 50, 313
University of Hawaii, 216, 376
University of Maryland, 39
University of Miami, 134
University of Missouri, 322
University of North Carolina at Chapel Hill, 63
University of Oregon, 124
University of Southern California School of
   Communication, 362
Unnatural links, 247
Unseen Power, The: Public Relations,
   A History (Cutlip), 38
URLs, 247
U.S. Steel, 41, 109

Usage divide (second digital divide), 363
USAJOBS.gov, 384–85
usaspending.gov, 304, 304f
USA Today, 30, 130, 184, 267
Useful Community Development, 131
User generated content (UGC), 276
Uses and gratifications, 262–63
Utilitarian calculus, 144
Utilitarianism, 15, 143–45, 175
UTi Wordwide, Inc., 309

Validity, 140–41, 217–18
VALS™ (values, attitudes and
   lifestyles), 133
Values, 18, 19, 22, 173
Ventimiglia, Milo, 13
Verizon, 128
Vertical videos, 274
Vicks, 349, 356–57, 357p
Victim crises, 333–35
Video, 273–75
Video news releases (VNRs), 239
Vimeo, 128, 212, 273
Vine, 274
Viral posts, 187, 233, 296, 320, 323, 357
Virginia Tech, 313
Virtual reality headsets, 202p
Visa, 365
Visa Everywhere Initiative, 364
Visa Everywhere Initiative: Women's
   Global Edition, 364
Vision statements, 124
Visual listening, 264–67, 277
Voice of Business, The: Hill and Knowlton and
   Postwar Public Relations (Russell), 50
Volkswagen, 325–28, 328p
Volunteers, 105
Vox, 149
Vyond, 274

Wa'ahila ridge, 40p, 41
Wall Street Journal, The, 60, 63, 99,
   154, 169, 269
Walmart, 73, 79
Walt Disney Co., 17, 281–82, 283
Walt Disney Imagineering, 79
Walt Disney Television Studios, 282
Warby Parker blog, 244p
Washington, George, 28
Washington Post, The, 30, 108, 180, 249
Water Supply and Sanitation Collaborative
   Council (WSSCC), 158–59
Watson, Matt, 278
Weaknesses (SWOT analysis), 120, 121, 122
Web 1.0, 185, 303
Web 2.0, 303
"We Believe: The Best a Man Can Be"
   campaign, 200, 214–15, 214p
Weber Shandwick, 364, 382
WeChat, 369
Weibo, 245–46, 245f, 369
Weinstein, Harvey, 47
"Welcome to the Global Collaboratory"
   campaign, 123
Wells Fargo, 193–94
Wendy's, 59
West Virginia University, 325

"What *The New York Times* Didn't Tell You" (Carney), 292–93
Whirlpool, 121*t*
White House home page, 184*p*
White House Office of National Drug Control Policy, 139
Whole Foods, 127–28, 127*p*
"WHOPPER® Detour" stunt, 260–62, 261*p*
Wikipedia, 190, 226
Williams, Patricia, 156*p*
Williams, Serena, 7, 8*p*
Wilson, Albert, 95*p*
Wimbledon tennis championships, 99, 100*p*
Winterkorn, Martin, 327
Wired, 33, 82
Word of Mouth Marketing Association (WOMMA), 6, 69
Word-of-mouth promotion, 69–70
Words (unit of analysis), 135
World Bicycle Relief Organization, 225, 229–30
World Cup (FIFA), 365–67
World Economic Forum, 384
World Food Programme, 366–67
#WorldPhotoDay, 188–89, 189*p*

World Press Freedom Day, 363*p*
World Through Soccer, The (Bar-On), 365
WPP, 59, 359
Wrapped, 259–60, 259*p*
Writing, 225–55
  business, 249
  career skills needed for, 390–91
  ethical, 251
  feature stories, 231–36
  goals and objectives in, 227–28
  impression management and, 228–29
  for influence and persuasion, 227
  for intermediaries, 238–48
  for news media, 238–42
  news stories, 236–38
  relationship building and, 227
  reputation management and, 228
  for search engines, 246–48
  for social media, 243–46, 250
  storytelling and (*see* Storytelling)
Writing PR: A Multimedia Approach (Carstarphen and Wells), 235
Wylie, Christopher, 339

Yahoo, 46, 65
Yahoo News, 30
Yale Law School's Information Society Project, 82
"Year 3000" (song), 258
Yelp, 12, 14, 14*p*, 392–93
YouTube, 9, 10, 129, 188, 188*p*, 212, 213, 214, 215, 228, 237, 258, 379
  average length of videos on, 274–75
  child exploitation scandal, 278–79
  conflict management on, 320
  integrated marketing communication on, 70
  number of monthly users, 273
  "United Breaks Guitars" video, 320, 320*p*
Yue, Cathy, 246

Zappos.com, 67, 73
Zillow, 73
"Zombie" followers, 172–74
Zuckerberg, Mark, 339–41, 340*p*, 353*p*
Zurich Blood Donation Service, 134